Wills

BY STANLEY M. JOHANSON
University of Texas

Eleventh Edition

EDITORIAL OFFICES: 111 W. Jackson Blvd., 7th Floor, Chicago, IL 60604
REGIONAL OFFICES: Chicago, Dallas, Los Angeles, New York, Washington, D.C.

PROJECT EDITOR
Michelle M. Oberts, B.A., J.D.
Attorney At Law

SERIES EDITOR
Elizabeth L. Snyder, B.A., J.D.
Attorney At Law

QUALITY CONTROL EDITOR
Sanetta M. Hister

Summary of Contents

Text Correlation Chart

Gilbert Law Summary WILLS	Clark, Lusky, Murphy, Ascher, McCouch *Gratuitous Transfers* 1999 (4th ed.)	Dobris, Sterk *Estates and Trusts* 1998	Dukeminier, Johanson *Wills, Trusts, and Estates* 2000 (6th ed.)
I. UNIFORM PROBATE CODE			
A. Introduction	Page 11-12	Page 24	Page 40, 72
B. Two Uniform Probate Codes	55-56	24-25	40, 72
II. INTESTATE SUCCESSION			
A. Introduction	11-15, 49-51	43-45, 61-63, 65-71	71-72
B. Patterns of Intestate Distribution	52-73, 151-152	64-91	72-77, 86-96
C. Intestate Distribution in Community Property States	151-159	179-181	471-473, 482, 511, 521-530
D. Attempts to Disinherit— Negative Bequests		69	90
III. INHERITANCE RIGHTS AS AFFECTED BY STATUS OF CHILD OR SIBLING			
A. Adopted Children	73-84	92-98	98-103, 106-113
B. Nonmarital Children	84-91	106-119	108-110, 115-126
C. Posthumous Children	60-61	69	97-98
D. Artificial Insemination and In Vitro Fertilization	61, 91-92	120-125	103-106, 117-128
E. Stepchildren and Foster Children	66, 82-83	98-106	106-114
F. Collateral Kin of the Half Blood	73	91-92	96-97
IV. SUCCESSION PROBLEMS COMMON TO INTESTACY AND WILLS			
A. Simultaneous Death	59-60	125-132	77-86
B. Advancements and Satisfaction of Legacies	106-109, 391	142-144, 265-266	128-131, 469
C. Disclaimer by Heir or Will Beneficiary	109-113, 864-866, 905	132-142	148-157, 236-241, 720-726, 990, 1059
D. Slayer of the Decedent	94-106	15-27	141-147
E. Aliens			
V. RESTRICTIONS ON THE POWER OF TESTATION—PROTECTION OF THE FAMILY			
A. Protection of the Spouse	92-93, 114-116, 120-159	145-175, 177-180, 486-488	148, 471-476, 478-530
B. Protection of the Children	116-117, 159-172	181-192	536-551
C. Protection of the Family	117-120	175-177	476-478
D. Testamentary Gifts to Charity	172-174, 895-897	402, 579-580, 772-787	859-869
E. Provisions Against Public Policy	32-43	1-9	23-34

Gilbert Law Summary WILLS	Clark, Lusky, Murphy, Ascher, McCouch *Gratuitous Transfers* 1999 (4th ed.)	Dobris, Sterk *Estates and Trusts* 1998	Dukeminier, Johanson *Wills, Trusts, and Estates* 2000 (6th ed.)
VI. FORMAL REQUISITES OF WILLS			
A. What Constitutes a Will?	252-258	7, 225-226	35-38, 90, 223-227
B. Governing Law	17-29, 41-43, 297, 614-618	8-16, 193, 899-900	1-13, 242-245
C. Formal Requirements for Wills	178-199, 252-254, 258-279, 297, 318	193-207, 282-309, 367-370	159-175, 213, 223-246
D. Liberalizing Compliance with Will Execution Requirements	279-291	195-196, 207-215	252-262
E. Attestation Clause	291-297	205-207	244-245
F. Self-Proved Wills	291, 294, 297	205-206	245-246, 252-257
G. Attorney Liability for Defective Execution	273, 380	33-43	59-70, 150, 233, 270-271, 535-536, 540-545, 676
H. Holographic Wills	301-315	215-224	262-276, 317-318
I. Oral Wills	315-316		226
J. Conditional Wills	315		271-274
K. Statutory Wills	296	224	269
VII. REVOCATION OF WILLS			
A. Introduction	330, 344-345	315-316	276
B. Revocation by Operation of Law	361-370	177-179, 281, 327-330, 487-488, 891	298-300, 323-329, 343-344, 385-386, 530-536, 545-546
C. Revocation by Subsequent Testamentary Instrument	345-348	316-317, 323-327	277-279, 317-318
D. Revocation by Physical Act	348-354	316-323, 332	276-277, 283-285
E. Proof of Lost Wills	352-353	321	280-284
F. Revival of Revoked Wills	354-357	330-332	296-298
G. Dependent Relative Revocation	357-361	332-337	286-296
VIII. COMPONENTS OF A WILL			
A. Integration	317	226-233	301-302
B. Incorporation by Reference	320-326	227-239	303-318
C. Acts of Independent Significance	319-320	240-241	318-319
D. Pour-Over Gift to Inter Vivos Trust	326-330	241-245	371-386
E. Codicil	317-319, 344-348, 355	326-327, 332, 336	277, 302-303, 317-318, 540-545
IX. CONTRACTS RELATING TO WILLS			
A. Contract to Make a Gift by Will	330-338, 343-344	343, 351-352	320-321
B. Joint Wills	331-343	337-351	323-329
C. Contract Not to Revoke a Will	331-343	337-344	322-329
D. Contract Not to Make a Will	331	343	319-320

Gilbert Law Summary WILLS	Clark, Lusky, Murphy, Ascher, McCouch *Gratuitous Transfers* 1999 (4th ed.)	Dobris, Sterk *Estates and Trusts* 1998	Dukeminier, Johanson *Wills, Trusts, and Estates* 2000 (6th ed.)
X. CHANGES IN BENEFICIARIES AND PROPERTY AFTER EXECUTION OF WILL			
A. Lapsed Gifts	59-61, 393-401, 838	125-132, 266-282	77-86, 438-458, 728-750
B. Class Gifts	780-792, 803	269-271, 675, 680, 706-743	449-458, 713-714, 732, 750-786
C. Classification of Testamentary Gifts	383	251-252, 268	459
D. Ademption	384-391	254-266	459-468
E. Stock Splits and Stock Dividends	387-388, 390-391	264-265	344, 459, 464-465
F. Interest on General Legacies		1010-1011	
G. Exoneration of Liens	392-393	252-253	468-469
XI. WILL CONTESTS AND RELATED MATTERS			
A. Standing to Contest Will	67-72	367, 368-369	41, 647-648
B. Grounds for Will Contest	178-251	216-221, 291-309, 357-409	159-221, 409-437
C. No-Contest Clause	233	413-416	184
D. Tort Liability for Wrongful Interference with Expected Inheritance	245-246		221-222
XII. PROBATE AND ESTATE ADMINISTRATION			
A. Overview of Estate Administration Process	11-15, 614-624	43-45, 896-900, 903-905	34-49, 391
B. Proof of Wills in Probate	250-251, 624-639	193-200, 205-207, 321, 416-417, 903-904	244-246, 280
C. Appointment and Qualification of Personal Representative	11, 639-645	44, 574-575, 827-842, 900-903, 918-942	36, 39-40, 44, 132-134
D. Duties and Liabilities of Personal Representative	645-646, 658-674	916-918, 942-1001, 1011-1015	43-44, 975-976
E. Creditors' Claims	15, 645-658	905-917	41-42
F. Abatement	391-392	246-252	468
G. Source of Payment of Death Taxes	45-48, 616-617, 866, 906-908	253-254, 430-432, 661-668	977-981, 985, 1005-1043
H. Entitlement to Income During Period of Administration	626-630	1005-1011	
I. Informal Administration Procedures	631-636	43, 903	40-41

Capsule Summary

I. UNIFORM PROBATE CODE

A. INTRODUCTION   §1

While 18 states have enacted all or most of the Uniform Probate Code ("UPC"), other states have adopted many of the substantive, but not procedural, provisions. Still other states have made selective adoptions of several UPC provisions. The great variations among the states have resulted in a lack of uniformity as to the impact of the UPC on state laws regarding decedents' estates.

B. TWO UNIFORM PROBATE CODES

1. In General   §3

There are two versions of the UPC: the original UPC and the revised UPC. States have adopted various combinations of provisions from both the original UPC and the revised UPC.

2. Revised Uniform Probate Code   §5

The UPC was substantially modified to include nonprobate transfers, *e.g.*, revocable trusts, life insurance, and employee benefit plans. Additionally, the intestate shares of surviving spouses were greatly increased and significant changes were made to anti-lapse statutes.

II. INTESTATE SUCCESSION

A. INTRODUCTION

1. When Intestate Distribution Rules Apply   §7

Intestacy statutes govern distribution of the property of a person when the person dies **without a valid will**, the will is **denied probate,** or the will does **not completely dispose** of the estate, resulting in a **partial intestacy**.

2. Common Law   §8

At common law, there were separate rules for real property and for personal property.

3. Modern Law   §9

Today, intestate distribution is governed by statutes, and in most states, the rules are the same for real and personal property. "Heirs" (preferred term) and "next of kin" are now synonymous and describe persons who take either real or personal property by intestacy.

the *first $100,000 plus one-half of any balance*; the remaining one-half passes to the decedent's descendants.

  d. Decedent not survived by descendants   **§30**
    The majority rule is that if the decedent is survived by a spouse but not descendants, the *spouse inherits the entire estate*. A substantial minority of states allow the surviving spouse to inherit one-half of the estate with the remaining one-half passing to the decedent's surviving parent(s). If there are no surviving parents, the surviving spouse inherits the entire estate.

    (1) Revised UPC   **§32**
      Under the revised UPC, the spouse inherits the *first $200,000 plus three-fourths of any balance* and the remaining one-fourth passes to the decedent's parent(s). If there are no surviving parents, the surviving spouse inherits the entire estate.

  e. When spouse disqualified from taking as heir   **§33**
    In several states, a surviving spouse is disqualified from taking an intestate share under certain circumstances, *e.g.,* abandonment or failure to support the spouse.

3. Intestate Share of Children and Other Descendants   **§34**
 The remainder of the estate after satisfaction of the spouse's share (or the entire estate if there is no surviving spouse) passes to the decedent's children and descendants of deceased children. Note that, in all states, the decedent's parents and collateral kin *never inherit* if the decedent is survived by children or their descendants.

4. Distributions Among Descendants of Deceased Children

  a. Common law—classic per stirpes   **§36**
    A minority of jurisdictions distribute shares among children and descendants of deceased children by *division of stirpital shares at the child level*, regardless of whether there are any living children.

  b. Majority rule—per capita with representation   **§37**
    Many states and the original UPC use the per capita with representation method under which the shares are *determined at the first generational level at which there are living takers*; *e.g.*, each living child takes one share and the share of a deceased child is divided among her children by representation.

  c. Revised UPC—per capita at each generation   **§38**
    Under the revised UPC and in several non-UPC states, the property is divided into *equal shares* at the first generational level with living takers. Shares of deceased persons at that level are combined and then divided equally among takers at the next generational level so that persons in the *same degree of kinship* to the decedent *always take equal shares.*

5. Decedent Not Survived by Spouse or Descendants   **§47**
 If the decedent is not survived by a spouse or descendants, the decedent's surviving parents inherit the estate (majority rule). Under the revised UPC

and in some states, a parent cannot inherit if he did not openly treat the child as his or refused to support the child.

6. **Decedent Not Survived by Spouse, Descendants, or Parents**   §50

If the decedent is not survived by a spouse, descendants, or parents, in nearly all states the estate passes to the **descendants of the decedent's parents**— *i.e.*, the decedent's brothers and sisters (or their descendants). If there are **no siblings** (or their descendants), the estate passes to the decedent's **grandparents**—one-half to the maternal and one-half to the paternal grandparents **(or their descendants)**.

7. **Intestate Distribution Beyond Grandparent Level**   §52

The majority of states distribute one-half of the estate to the **nearest kin on each side** of the family (*i.e.*, maternal and paternal), no matter how remote the relationship to the decedent.

   a.   **Minority rule—"laughing heir" statutes**   §54

   Some states prevent inheritance by remote relatives, usually those related to the decedent beyond the grandparent (or descendant of grandparent) level.

8. **Escheat**   §55

If the decedent has no surviving relations (or is survived by relations too remote in states having "laughing heir" statutes), the estate escheats to the **state**.

   a.   **Exception**   §56

   In a few states, the estate passes to the heirs of the previously deceased spouse of the decedent before it escheats to the state.

9. **Ancestral Property**   §57

A few states hold that if a decedent leaves no surviving spouse or descendants, property received by gift, will, or inheritance from a parent reverts back to the parent (or to his heirs).

C. **INTESTATE DISTRIBUTION IN COMMUNITY PROPERTY STATES**

1. **Introduction**   §58

The laws of the nine community property states vary considerably, but all use the same basic definitions.

   a.   **Separate property**   §59

   This is property owned by a spouse **before marriage,** and property acquired during marriage by **gift, will, or inheritance.** In three states, the income from separate property is community property. Separate property passes according to the above intestacy rules.

   b.   **Community property**   §60

   This is all property acquired **during marriage** that is **not separate property**. All property on hand on dissolution of marriage (by divorce or death) is **presumed to be community property.**

2. **Decedent Survived by Spouse But Not Descendants**   §61

If the decedent is not survived by descendants, his one-half share of the community estate passes to the surviving spouse. This results in the spouse owning the entire community estate.

3. Survived by Spouse and Descendants
In several states, the surviving spouse takes the entire community estate. Under the revised UPC and other states, the surviving spouse takes the entire community estate **only if** all of the decedent's descendants are also the surviving spouse's descendants; otherwise the decedent's community property interest passes to his descendants.

4. Quasi-Community Property
Quasi-community property is property acquired by one spouse while **domiciled in another state** that would have been classified as community property had it been acquired while domiciled in the community property state. (Real property situated in another state is not quasi-community property.)

a. Quasi-community property statutes
Four states have quasi-community property laws that effectively act as elective share statutes. In these states, the acquiring spouse may dispose of only his one-half interest in quasi-community property by will; the other half passes to the surviving spouse. If there is no will, the surviving spouse inherits all of the quasi-community property.

(1) Distinguish—divorce
Several other community property states apply quasi-community property principles at divorce; then quasi-community property is treated as community property for property divisions. However, upon a spouse's death, the assets are considered separate property of the acquiring spouse.

D. ATTEMPTS TO DISINHERIT—NEGATIVE BEQUESTS

1. Majority Rule
When a testator expressly disinherits an heir but then dies partially intestate, most states permit the heir to take an intestate share in the undisposed of property.

2. Revised UPC—Negative Bequest Rule
Under the revised UPC and in several non-UPC states, a decedent may expressly exclude an individual from taking property passing by intestate succession by a provision in her will.

III. INHERITANCE RIGHTS AS AFFECTED BY STATUS OF CHILD OR SIBLING

A. ADOPTED CHILDREN

1. Early Law
Absent a relevant statute, most courts permitted an adopted child to inherit from the adopting parents but not from their relatives ("stranger to the adoption" rule). Usually, the adopted child continued to have inheritance rights from and through the natural parents.

2. Modern Law

a. Adopting parents §75

Today, all relevant statutes allow an adopted child to have the **same inheritance rights** as a natural child. The adopted child thus can inherit from the adopting parents and their kin.

b. Natural parents §76

An adopted child (and her issue) have **no** inheritance rights from or through the natural parents (and vice versa). An exception is made when a child is adopted by the spouse of a natural parent; the relationship between that parent as well as the adopting parent and the child is not affected. However, in some states adoption by the spouse of a natural parent terminates inheritance rights from the **other** natural parent. The UPC provides that such an adoption has no effect on the relationship between the child and **either** natural parent.

(1) Revised Uniform Probate Code—one-way street rule §81

Under the revised UPC, an adopted child and her kin have inheritance rights from and through **both** natural parents, but the other natural parent (the nonmarrying parent) and his kin have **no** inheritance rights from or through the child.

B. NONMARITAL CHILDREN §82

At common law, a nonmarital child had no inheritance rights from either parent. Today, all states permit the child to inherit from and through his natural **mother.** Also, the child can inherit from and through the natural **father** upon certain proof of paternity (*e.g.*, adjudication or formal acknowledgment).

C. POSTHUMOUS CHILDREN §89

Under both the common law rules and statutory authority, a child born (typically within 280 days) after his father's death is considered the decedent's child for inheritance purposes. The UPC goes further to permit **any relative** of the decedent in gestation at the decedent's death to inherit if the child lives for at least 120 hours after birth.

D. ARTIFICIAL INSEMINATION AND IN VITRO FERTILIZATION §92

Several states provide that a child conceived by the artificial insemination of a married woman is the husband's legitimate child for inheritance purposes **if the husband consented** to the insemination. Statutes are increasingly applying the same rule to children produced by in vitro fertilization or other reproductive technology.

E. STEPCHILDREN AND FOSTER CHILDREN

1. General Rule §93

A stepchild or foster child has **no** inheritance rights from his stepparent or foster parents.

2. Exception—Adoption by Estoppel §94

In many jurisdictions, a stepchild or foster child can inherit from the stepparent or foster parent in cases involving an **unperformed agreement to adopt**. However, the rule applies only to those claiming through the stepparent or foster parent (*e.g.*, child cannot inherit from stepparent's sister) and operates only in favor of the child; *i.e.*, stepparents or foster parents do *not inherit* from the child.

F. COLLATERAL KIN OF THE HALF BLOOD §98
Most states make *no distinction* between siblings of the half blood and whole blood, although some states provide that half bloods take half as much as whole bloods.

IV. SUCCESSION PROBLEMS COMMON TO INTESTACY AND WILLS

A. SIMULTANEOUS DEATH

1. Uniform Simultaneous Death Act §104
All jurisdictions except Louisiana have adopted the Uniform Simultaneous Death Act ("USDA") or the equivalent 120-hour survival rule of the UPC (*see below*). The USDA provides that when there is *no sufficient evidence* that the parties have died otherwise than simultaneously, the property of each person is disposed of *as if he had survived* the other person.

a. Application of USDA §107
In cases of simultaneous deaths, intestate estates, testamentary assets under a will, and life insurance proceeds pass as though the "owner" survived the "heir." In cases involving *joint tenancies, tenancies by the entirety, or community property*, one-half of the property passes as though one party survived and the other half passes as though the other party survived.

b. Evidence of survival—USDA does not apply §110
Remember that if there is sufficient evidence that one party survived the other, even for a brief interval, the USDA does *not apply*. Nor does it apply if the decedent's will (or other instrument) has a contrary survival provision.

2. Uniform Probate Code—120-Hour Rule §115
The UPC addresses the problem of deaths in quick succession by stating that absent a contrary will provision, a person must survive the decedent by *120 hours* in order to take as an heir or will beneficiary. This rule does not apply if it would result in an escheat to the state and it does not apply to survivorship estates (*i.e.*, joint tenancies, tenancies by the entirety), although the *revised UPC* and several states have extended the 120-hour rule to survivorship estates.

B. ADVANCEMENTS AND SATISFACTION OF LEGACIES

1. Advancement of Intestate Share

a. Common law §121
At common law and in a few states today, a lifetime gift to a *child* is *presumed* to be an advance payment of the child's intestate share of the donor's estate.

b. Modern law §122
Most state statutes permit advancements to be made to *any heir* (*e.g.*,

spouse or sister). More importantly, these statutes **reverse the common law presumption** and provide that a lifetime gift to an heir is **not an advancement** unless so proved. In many states, such proof must be shown by an express declaration or acknowledgment in a writing signed by the donor or the donee.

    c. Procedure if advancement found   §129

If an advancement is found, the value of the property given to the advancee is added to the estate ("brought into the hotchpot") in determining the intestate shares. This is done only if the advancee elects to share in the intestate distribution. Note that the advancee never has to return the property.

    d. Date of valuation   §130

The majority view values the advanced property at the **date of gift**; the UPC values it at the date of the advancee's possession or decedent's death, whichever occurs first.

    e. Partial intestacy   §131

In most states, the advancement doctrine does not apply if the decedent left a will that does not make a complete disposition of the estate. However, the revised UPC treats such advancements the same as those under a total intestacy.

    f. Advancee predeceases decedent   §133

If the advancee predeceases the decedent, the advanced property is **not** taken into account in determining the intestate share of the advancee's descendants unless the written declaration or acknowledgment requires the property to be taken into account.

2. Satisfaction of Legacies   §134

At common law and in states without relevant statutes, a gift to a child of the testator is **presumed** to be in partial or total satisfaction of any gifts made to the child in a **previously executed** will. This presumption usually applies also to the child's descendants (*e.g.*, grandchild), but not to other will beneficiaries (*i.e.*, someone other than a child or descendant). The rule applies to general legacies (*i.e.*, legacies payable out of the general assets of the estate and that do not require delivery of a particular item).

    a. Testator's intent controls   §138

Application of the satisfaction doctrine depends on the testator's intent. In determining intent, courts look to the will or to **extrinsic evidence** (*e.g.*, testator's declaration at or near time of gift), and apply certain presumptions (*e.g.*, bequest made for a specific purpose).

    b. Statutory solutions   §140

Most states that have advancement statutes have similar statutes for the satisfaction of legacies (*e.g.*, if state requires signed writing for advancement, it may have a statute requiring proof of satisfaction of legacies in the same manner).

C. DISCLAIMER BY HEIR OR WILL BENEFICIARY

and personal property escheats to the state. The felon is treated as if he predeceased the victim.

E. ALIENS §180

Contrary to common law, most states give aliens an **unrestricted right** to inherit or hold title to real or personal property within the state.

V. RESTRICTIONS ON THE POWER OF TESTATION—PROTECTION OF THE FAMILY

A. PROTECTION OF THE SPOUSE

1. Common Law §187

A surviving spouse's **only** right in a decedent's estate was dower (for a widow) or curtesy (for a widower). A decedent's estate escheated to the Crown if he was survived by a spouse but no kindred.

a. Dower §188

Upon the husband's death, the widow was entitled to a **life estate** in an **undivided one-third** of all real property owned by the husband before marriage or acquired during marriage.

b. Curtesy §190

Upon a wife's death, the husband received a **life estate** in **all** of the real property of which the wife was seized during marriage. However, curtesy rights arose **only if** issue were born of the marriage.

c. Dower and curtesy as limitations on testamentary power §191

Dower and curtesy rights could be asserted regardless of the decedent's will.

d. Dower and curtesy as limitations on lifetime transfers §192

Lifetime transfers (*e.g.*, sale to a bona fide purchaser) were **ineffective** to limit dower or curtesy rights (unless the spouse had joined in the conveyance). The spouse's interest also superseded claims of the decedent's creditors.

e. Modern status §193

Although most states have replaced dower and curtesy with elective share statutes, these common law estates still exist in a few states.

2. Elective Share Statutes

a. In general §195

Most jurisdictions have enacted statutes that allow the surviving spouse to elect a statutory share of the decedent's estate **in lieu of taking under the will.** In most states, this statutory share may be claimed regardless of the will's provisions.

(1) As limitation on lifetime and nonprobate transfers §197

Several elective share statutes apply only to property owned by the decedent at death (**probate** estate); thus, a lifetime transfer **may** cut off a surviving spouse's statutory share with respect to that property. However, some courts have widened the scope of the elective share right to include certain lifetime transfers; *i.e.*, the elective share applies to the *augmented* estate.

(2) Community property states §198
Because the community property system has an inherent protection against disinheritance of spouses, none of the community property states has an elective share statute. However, the quasi-community property statutes found in four states are a form of elective share statute.

b. Amount of elective share §200
In most states and under the original UPC, the elective share amount is *one-third* of the net estate. Under the revised UPC, the amount of the elective share depends on the number of years that the couple was married. Some states provide a different amount if the decedent was survived by descendants.

(1) Revised UPC §202
Under the *original UPC*, the elective share applies to the decedent's *augmented estate,* which comprises the decedent's probate estate plus certain nonprobate transfers made during the decedent's lifetime. The revised UPC approach differs radically from the original UPC. Under the *revised UPC*, the augmented estate also includes the *couple's combined assets*, including those of the surviving spouse. The elective share must be at least *$50,000* (*supplemental elective share*).

c. Property subject to elective share §206
In some states, the elective share applies to the *net probate estate* after payment of administration expenses, creditors' claims, and after satisfaction of the family allowance, homestead right, and any exempt personal property set-aside for the surviving spouse. In other states, the elective share applies to the *augmented estate* (*see supra*).

(1) Situs rule §207
The situs rule limits the elective share of *real property* to that located within the state; a few states include the value of real property located in another state. The elective share applies to *all* of the decedent's *personal property* wherever located.

(2) Settlement agreement with former spouse §210
In some states, a former spouse's right to accrued and unpaid alimony payments or a right secured by a property settlement agreement takes precedence over the surviving spouse's elective share. Other states hold that the surviving spouse's rights are superior.

(3) Property subject to contractual will §213
In most states, property received by the decedent from a former spouse under a contractual will, giving the decedent full use of

the property for life with the remainder on his death to pass to others, is **not** subject to the surviving spouse's elective share.

d. **Who may claim elective share** §216

The elective share can be exercised only **by or on behalf of the surviving spouse**. Thus, a **guardian or conservator** of an incapacitated or minor spouse can make an election (with court approval), but a personal representative cannot.

e. **Considerations affecting surviving spouse's right to elect**

(1) **Decedent's domicile** §220

The decedent must have been a **domiciliary** of the state at death for that state's elective share statute to apply.

(2) **Finality of divorce decree** §222

If a final divorce decree was entered before the decedent's death, there is no right of election. However, a nonfinal decree (*e.g.*, interlocutory or time for appeal unexpired) does not bar a spouse's right to elect.

(3) **Misconduct by surviving spouse** §223

The majority rule **entitles** the surviving spouse to an elective share even in cases of abandonment, failure to support, etc. A few states bar the right of election under these circumstances.

f. **Procedure governing election** §225

The surviving spouse generally must file a **notice of election** to take a statutory share.

(1) **Time period for filing notice of election** §226

Notice must be within the statutory time period. In most states, the time period runs from the date the letters of administration are granted to the personal representative. Election under the UPC must be made **within nine months after the decedent's death** or **within six months after probate**, whichever is later.

(2) **Extension of time period** §228

Some statutes provide that probate court can **extend** the election time period upon a showing of good cause.

g. **Satisfaction of elective share**

(1) **Testamentary gifts to spouse** §229

Under the UPC and in most states, outright testamentary gifts to the surviving spouse are **first applied** in making up the elective share. In several states, the electing spouse takes nothing under the will.

(a) **Life estate** §231

If the surviving spouse received a life estate under the will, in most states and under the revised UPC, it is **not** counted as being in partial satisfaction of the statutory share because the elective share entitles the spouse to outright ownership (although under the original UPC, a life estate *is* counted as being in partial satisfaction of the elective share).

(2) Abatement of gifts §235
In many states, the elective share is paid pursuant to the abatement rules that apply to creditors' claims. Thus, property passing by partial intestacy is first applied; then the residuary estate; then general legacies; demonstrative legacies; and specific bequests.

(a) Uniform Probate Code §236
The elective share is ratably apportioned among recipients of the estate in proportion to the value of their interests therein.

h. Waiver of right of election §237
A spouse may waive the right of election either before or during marriage, but the waiver must be in *writing* and *signed* by the spouse. Generally, there must be *fair disclosure* of the waiver's effect to the spouse.

3. Lifetime and Nonprobate Transfers

a. Case law §240
Although most elective share statutes do not apply to property transferred during the decedent's lifetime or to nontestamentary transfers, courts have developed various doctrines under which a surviving spouse may challenge a particular lifetime transfer.

(1) Illusory transfer §241
If the transferor retained a *significant degree of control* over the property so that the transfer was "illusory," the elective share statute applies.

(2) Motive or intent to defeat share §242
Some courts have held that a lifetime transfer is subject to the surviving spouse's elective share *if* the motive or intent of the transferor was to *defeat the elective share*—especially if the estate has little or no property.

(3) Balancing the equities §243
Other courts favor a balancing approach, considering: (i) the completeness of the transfer; (ii) the transferor's motive; (iii) whether it was a "brink of death" transfer; (iv) participation of the transferee in the alleged fraud; and (v) the degree to which the surviving spouse is stripped of benefits in the decedent's estate by the transfer.

(4) Revocable inter vivos trust §244
The courts are divided as to whether property in a revocable trust is subject to the surviving spouse's elective share.

b. **Original Uniform Probate Code**

(1) **Augmented estate** §245

Under the original UPC, the elective share applies to the decedent's "augmented estate," which consists of the net probate estate **plus** the value of lifetime transfers to persons **other than the decedent's spouse,** for less than full consideration, **if** the transfer falls into one of the following categories: (i) retained life estate; (ii) retained control; (iii) transfers within two years of death; or (iv) survivorship estates.

(2) **Intestacy** §246

The original UPC's elective share statute applies when a decedent dies intestate as well as when a decedent dies testate.

(3) **Transfers to spouse** §247

The augmented estate also includes the value of property **given by the decedent to the spouse** during the marriage. This includes such property owned by the spouse at the decedent's death, such property given by the spouse to third parties, a beneficial interest given to the spouse in a trust created by the decedent during lifetime, property passing to the spouse by the decedent's exercise of a power of appointment, and life insurance proceeds and employee benefits paid to the spouse.

(a) **Burden of proof** §248

The surviving spouse has the burden of establishing that property owned by the spouse at the decedent's death was derived from a source **other than** gifts from the decedent.

(4) **Property not included in augmented estate** §249

The augmented estate does not include any life insurance, joint annuity, or pension benefit payable to a person other than the surviving spouse.

(5) **Waiver by spouse** §250

If a transfer to a person other than the spouse is made with the spouse's **written consent or joinder,** it is not included in the augmented estate.

(6) **Valuation of property** §251

Property included in the augmented estate is valued as of the **decedent's death.** However, property given to a donee during lifetime is valued as of the date the donee came into possession and enjoyment, if that occurred before the decedent's death.

c. **Revised Uniform Probate Code** §252

Under the revised UPC, the augmented estate includes **all of the transfers covered by the original UPC plus the surviving spouse's own property**, including transfers within two years of the decedent's death, transfers with retained life estates, transfers with retained controls, assets received by right of survivorship, and the decedent's retirement benefits paid to the surviving spouse.

(1) Life insurance payable to third parties §253
The augmented estate also includes insurance on the decedent's life paid to *any* beneficiary if the decedent owned the policy, held a general power of appointment over it, or, while married to the surviving spouse, transferred the policy to another person within two years of death.

d. Other statutory solutions

(1) New York §254
The New York elective share statute applies to the decedent's net probate estate *plus testamentary substitutes*, *e.g.,* survivorship estates with third parties, Totten trust bank accounts, and lifetime transfers with retained controls.

(2) Delaware §255
All property includible in the decedent's gross estate under the federal estate tax rules is subject to the elective share.

(3) Other statutes §256
Other states have less complicated statutes, used primarily to prevent the use of revocable trusts to defeat the surviving spouse's right of election.

4. Community Property States

a. No elective share statutes §257
None of the community property states has an elective share statute. Because the surviving spouse automatically owns one-half of the community estate on the first spouse's death, there is no perceived need for a statutory protection against disinheritance.

(1) Exception—quasi-community property §258
Quasi-community property statutes provide a form of elective share that applies to certain assets acquired by the couple before moving to the community property state.

(2) Separate property §259
Each spouse has the *unrestricted power* of testamentary disposition over his separate property.

b. Election wills §260
If the deceased spouse leaves a will that purports to dispose of the *entire interest in community property,* and not just the one-half community interest over which he has the power of testamentary disposition, the surviving spouse is put to an election.

(1) Election against the will §262
The surviving spouse does not have to accept this arrangement and may elect to take the one-half community property to which

she is entitled by law. But if she does so, she ***relinquishes all testamentary gifts*** in her favor made in the will.

(2) Election to take under the will   §263
If the surviving spouse elects to take under the will, the will operates to transfer the surviving spouse's one-half community interest, as well as the decedent's interest, according to the will's terms.

(3) Accidental election wills   §264
An election situation may arise **unintentionally**, *e.g.*, the decedent purports to devise property to one other than his spouse but the property is actually community property. In this case, the surviving spouse is put to an election. An unintentional election may also occur if the testator's will purports to dispose of property which he held in **joint tenancy** with the surviving spouse or with another party.

(4) Common law states   §266
An election will situation can also arise in a common law state.

c. Lifetime gifts of community property

(1) Majority rule   §268
Most community property states allow one spouse to make "reasonable" gifts of community property without the other spouse's consent, as long as such gifts do not violate the other spouse's community rights ("fraud on the spouse" test).

(a) "Fraudulent" transfer   §269
Actual intent to defraud need not be proved; a particular transfer may be constructively fraudulent. The following factors will be considered by the court: (i) **amount of the gift**, (ii) **relationship** of donee, and (iii) **amount of remaining community estate**.

(b) Nontestamentary transfers   §273
In the states following the majority rule, life insurance dispositions and interests passing by right of survivorship are considered lifetime transfers for purposes of these rules.

(2) Minority rule   §274
Except for *de minimis* gifts, the spouse who does not consent to a lifetime transfer of community property can elect to **set aside the transfer** in its entirety during the donor's lifetime or as to her one-half community share after the donor's death.

d. Community property brought to common law state   §275
Under established conflict of laws principles, the ownership of marital assets is determined under the laws of the marital domicile ***at the time the assets are acquired.*** Such ownership interests, once acquired, are not lost upon a move to another jurisdiction.

(1) Uniform Disposition of Community Property Rights at Death Act §277
Several states have adopted the Uniform Disposition of Community Property Rights at Death Act ("UDOCPRADA"), which recognizes both spouses' interests in imported community property regardless of how title is taken in the new state; *i.e.*, only one-half of such property is subject to testamentary disposition or intestate distribution, and the remaining half belongs to the surviving spouse.

B. PROTECTION OF THE CHILDREN

1. Pretermitted Child Statutes §278
Except in Louisiana, a testator may **disinherit** her children. However, many states have pretermitted child statutes to protect children who may have been **accidentally** omitted from the will.

a. Majority rule §279
The statute operates only in favor of children born or adopted **after the execution** of the will.

(1) Exception—child believed to be dead §280
The UPC provides that if the testator fails to provide for a child because she **mistakenly believes the child is dead**, the child receives a share **equal to an intestate share**.

(2) Will written in contemplation of future children §281
In **Georgia**, birth or adoption of a child **revokes** a prior will **in its entirety** unless the will expressly states it was written in contemplation of the birth or adoption of a child.

b. Minority rule §282
The statute applies to children alive when the will was executed, as well as to afterborn and after-adopted children, unless the will names or refers to the children so as to prevent the statute's operation.

c. Grandchildren §283
In most states, the pretermitted child statute does not operate in favor of the grandchildren of the testator. However, in a substantial minority of states, statutes apply to the descendants of a **deceased child** of the testator.

2. When Statute Does Not Apply

a. Intentional omission §285
The child does not take an intestate share of the decedent's estate if the omission was intentional. The majority rule requires that the intent to omit the child appear **on the face of the will. Extrinsic evidence** is **not** admissible in most states.

b. Child provided for by settlement §288
Under many statutes, a child who otherwise would be covered by the pretermitted child statute is not considered pretermitted if provided for by a **lifetime settlement** or **nonprobate transfer**.

children. But these rules have no application if the homestead is held in a tenancy by the entirety. In such a case, title passes to the surviving spouse by right of survivorship.

e.   **Uniform Probate Code** §303

The UPC grants a *lump sum homestead allowance* of $15,000 instead of a right to occupy the homestead. The allowance has priority over all claims against the estate.

f.   **Right of quarantine** §304

Several states give the spouse the *right to occupy the family home rent-free* for a specified time.

2.   **Exempt Personal Property** §305

Some statutes exempt certain items of *tangible* personal property from creditors' claims. This exemption typically applies to household furnishings, appliances, personal effects, farm equipment, and in some states, automobiles up to a certain value. The set-aside may not be permanent and is not automatic—a petition must be filed.

3.   **Family Allowance** §309

In many states, the surviving spouse or minor children may petition for a family allowance, to provide for their maintenance while the decedent's estate is in administration. Under the *revised UPC*, the family allowance may be given in a lump sum up to *$18,000*, or in equal monthly payments up to *$1,500 per month for one year*. The family allowance usually takes precedence over all claims except funeral expenses and estate administration expenses, and it is not chargeable against any benefit or share passing to the surviving spouse (or children) by intestate succession, elective share, or the will.

a.   **Personal right** §313

The death of the person entitled to the allowance terminates the right to any remaining part of the allowance not already paid.

D.   **TESTAMENTARY GIFTS TO CHARITY** §315

At early common law, *mortmain* restrictions were placed on the right to make testamentary gifts to a church. In recent years, all mortmain statutes have either been *repealed* or held *unconstitutional*.

E.   **PROVISIONS AGAINST PUBLIC POLICY** §318

Will provisions that attempt to control a beneficiary's future conduct in a manner contrary to public policy are stricken. Such conditions include *total restraints on marriage*, encouragement of *divorce*, encouragement of the commission of a *crime or tort*, or *destruction of property*.

VI.   FORMAL REQUISITES OF WILLS

A.   WHAT CONSTITUTES A WILL?

1.   **Nature of a Will** §325

A will is an instrument executed with certain formalities that may direct the disposition of a testator's property at death, and is effective *only upon the testator's death.*

    a.   Exception—contractual wills   §327

Generally, a beneficiary has only an *expectancy* unless the testator executed a will *pursuant to a contract,* in which case the beneficiary may have a right under *contract law* to enforce the bargained-for testamentary disposition even though the will was amended or revoked.

    b.   Codicil   §328

A codicil is a *supplement* or an *amendment* to a will.

2. Functions of a Will   §330

A will may be an instrument that does any *one or more* of the following, regardless of whether it disposes of any property: transfers property at death, creates a testamentary trust, amends or revokes an earlier will, appoints a personal representative, exercises a power of appointment, or gives directions concerning disposition of the testator's body or a part thereof.

    a.   Negative bequest statutes—disinheritance of an heir   §332

Under the revised UPC and several state statutes, a will is valid if it does no more than direct how property shall *not* be disposed of, *e.g.,* disinherit an heir. However, this is a *minority* position since, in most states, words of disinheritance are not given effect.

3. Types of Wills

    a.   Attested will   §334

This is a written will, *signed* by the testator, and witnessed by two (and sometimes three) witnesses pursuant to a formal attestation procedure.

    b.   Holographic will   §335

Recognized by about 30 states, a holographic will is one in which the material portions are *entirely in the testator's handwriting, signed* by testator, and is *unattested* (*i.e.,* unwitnessed).

    c.   Oral wills   §336

Oral (nuncupative) wills are valid in some states but in very limited circumstances (*infra*).

B. GOVERNING LAW

1. Legislative Control of Right to Make a Will   §337

Except in Wisconsin, the right to make a will is not a "natural right." Thus, the right to make a will is subject to the legislature's plenary control.

2. Effect of Change in Law After Will's Execution   §339

Generally, a will is admitted to probate if it satisfies either the law in effect when the will was executed *or* the law in effect when the testator died.

3. Conflict of Laws Principles   §341

Disposition of *real property* is determined by the law of the *situs* of the property; disposition of **personal property** is governed by the law of the testator's **domicile** at the time of death.

<table>
<tr><td>a.</td><td>**Uniform Execution of Foreign Wills Act**
Adopted by many states, this Act admits a will to probate if the will was executed in accordance with the law of that jurisdiction, the law of the state where it was executed, the law of the testator's domicile at the time of execution, **or** the law of the testator's domicile at death.</td><td>§343</td></tr>
<tr><td>b.</td><td>**Uniform Probate Code**
The UPC also allows the testator to select the particular state law unless application of that law contravenes public policy of the testator's state of residence.</td><td>§344</td></tr>
</table>

C. FORMAL REQUIREMENTS FOR WILLS

1. **Testamentary Intent**   §346
   A testator must have **subjectively intended** that the document in question **constitute her will** at the time she executed the instrument.

   a. **Legal test**   §347
      Testamentary intent exists if the testator intended to **dispose of property,** the disposition was intended to **occur only upon death,** and the testator intended the **instrument in question to accomplish the disposition**.

   b. **Determining testamentary intent**   §348
      Intent must be ascertained from the **face of the instrument.**

      (1) **Document testamentary on its face**   §349
          An apparent testamentary recital (*e.g.*, "this is my last will and testament") raises a **rebuttable presumption** of testamentary intent, but it can be overcome by clear, convincing, and cogent extrinsic evidence.

      (2) **Ambiguous document**   §350
          If a document lacks any indication that it was intended as a will, extrinsic evidence is **not** admissible to show testamentary intent. However, if the document might reasonably be construed as a will, the overwhelming majority view holds that extrinsic evidence on the issue of testamentary intent is admissible.

      (3) **Character of evidence**   §351
          To show testamentary intent, most courts admit the **testator's statements** made before or after execution of the document, the drafter's testimony, and evidence concerning circumstances attendant to the execution (imminence of death is a relevant circumstance).

   c. **Intent to make future will**   §355
      No testamentary intent is shown if the instrument indicates that it was not meant to be a will, but that a will would be executed in the future.

testator intended by her to signify her signature (*e.g.*, "X"). ***Assistance*** in signing is permissible if the testator so desired; moreover, most states allow ***another person*** to sign the testator's signature ***at her direction and in her presence.***

a. **Location of signature** §388

Generally, the testator's signature can appear ***anywhere*** on the will. A few states require it at the end of the will.

(1) **Minority rule** §389

In states requiring signatures at the ***end*** of the will, provisions appearing ***after the testator's signature*** are ***disregarded***, but provisions ***before*** the signature are valid. Note that any provisions added after the will is executed are ***disregarded***.

b. **Signature (or acknowledgment of signature) in witnesses' presence** §397

Many states require the testator to either ***sign*** the will or ***acknowledge her earlier signature*** in the witnesses' presence. Most states allow the testator to sign the will in one witness's presence and then later acknowledge her signature in the other witness's presence. A few states require the testator to sign or acknowledge her earlier signature in the presence of both witnesses at the same time.

c. **Order of signing** §400

A majority of jurisdictions do not specify the order of signatures as long as the execution ceremony is part of ***one contemporaneous transaction.*** Others require the testator to sign first.

d. **What constitutes signing in someone's "presence"** §403

In many states, each witness must sign in the testator's presence but not necessarily in each other's presence. Other states require the witnesses to sign in the testator's ***and*** each other's presence. Courts differ as to what constitutes presence.

(1) **Majority rule—conscious presence test** §404

The majority of states use the ***conscious presence*** test, wherein a witness has signed in the testator's presence if the testator was ***conscious of where the witness was*** and what he was doing.

(2) **Minority rule—line of sight test** §405

A minority of courts use the ***line of sight*** test. The testator need not see the signing witness, but he must be within the ***uninterrupted range of the testator's vision***.

(3) **Uniform Probate Code** §406

Under the UPC, witnesses do not have to sign in the testator's presence. However, if someone is signing the testator's name by proxy, he must do so in the testator's presence.

6. **Will Need Not Be Dated** §407

Most states do not require a will to bear the date of execution; that can be established by extrinsic evidence.

7. Publication §408

The *majority* rule requires *no* publication; *i.e.*, the witnesses do not need to know they are attesting a will. A few states require a testator to declare to the witnesses that they are attesting to a will.

8. Witnesses

a. Competency of witnesses—in general §411

Competency of witnesses is determined at the *time of the will's execution* and generally means that a witness must be *mature enough and of sufficient mental capacity* to understand the nature of the act so that she could testify in court if necessary.

(1) Signature of notary public §415

The overwhelming *majority view* is that a notary public can be an attesting witness even if he signed a will in his official capacity.

b. Location of signatures §416

There is no requirement that the testator's and witnesses' signatures be on the same page. Note that a *drafting attorney* should *not* be an attesting witness because the attorney and her law firm cannot represent the estate if the will is contested.

c. Interested witnesses—in general §418

At *common law*, an attesting witness who was also a beneficiary was *not a competent witness* and the will was invalid. However, this rule has been *abolished* in all states.

(1) Majority view—purging statutes §419

In most states, a gift to an interested witness is *void* but the will is still admitted to probate. The UPC and several non-UPC states have *abolished* this interested witness rule altogether and so the will is valid and the interested witness may take under it.

(a) What constitutes beneficial interest §421

To be an interested witness, a witness must be a *beneficiary* under a will or trust created by a will; *i.e.*, the interest must be a direct, pecuniary one. Executors, attorneys, relatives of a beneficiary, creditors of beneficiaries, and takers under an anti-lapse statute are not beneficiaries, and a purging statute does not apply.

(b) Exceptions to purging statutes' operation §429

In some states, if a beneficiary is a "supernumerary" witness (*i.e.*, third witness where only two are required), the bequest is *not* purged if the will can be proved without that witness's testimony. Additionally, if the witness-beneficiary would be an intestate heir if there had been no will, many states allow the witness to take the *lesser* of the *intestate share* or the bequest amount.

D. REVOCATION BY PHYSICAL ACT

1. Requirements §537

Acts sufficient to revoke a will are governed by statute. Most statutes provide that the act may be a burning, tearing, cancellation, or obliteration of a *material part* of the will. In any event, the act must have had an *actual effect* on the will and must have been done with a *present intent* to revoke the will.

a. Physical act on testator's signature §542

The testator's crossing or cutting out his signature revokes the will *in its entirety*.

b. Physical act on copy of will §543

The physical act must be *on the will* itself. Destroying a *copy* of the will does not effect a valid revocation.

2. Physical Act of Another §547

In many states, a will can be revoked by a physical act of a third person performed *in the testator's presence and at the testator's direction*. Some states also require two *witnesses* to the act.

3. Partial Revocation by Physical Act §548

Most states permit partial revocation by physical act, although proof of intent may be a problem. However, courts are reluctant to recognize partial revocation where the act results in an *increase* of a *general or specific bequest.*

a. Minority rule—no partial revocation §552

Note that in states that do not recognize partial revocation by physical act, the testator's attempt to revoke a portion of the will is given *no effect*.

4. Effect of Revocation on Another Testamentary Instrument

a. Destruction of codicil §553

Physical destruction of a codicil generally revokes *only* the codicil.

b. Destruction of will—effect on codicil §555

Destruction of a will usually *revokes all codicils* to the will if the testator so intended. If the codicil can stand alone as a *separate testamentary instrument*, the revocation of the will may not automatically revoke the codicil.

c. Duplicate wills §556

If one of two copies of a will, both of which are *executed*, is physically destroyed, both copies are thereby revoked. If an *unexecuted* copy of the will is revoked, the executed copy is still valid. If a duplicate copy of an executed will cannot be found and was last in the testator's possession, it is *presumed that the testator revoked the will*.

5. Presumptions as to Revocation §560

An accidentally destroyed will is *not* revoked since there was no intent to revoke. Thus, if a will cannot be found or is found in a torn or mutilated condition, several presumptions are used in determining the existence or nonexistence of intent.

a. Presumption of continuity	**§561**

If a will is found after the testator's death, absent indications of revocation, it is presumed that the will has had a continuous legal existence since its execution.

b. Will not found or found in mutilated condition	**§562**

Where a will was last seen in the testator's possession and is later found mutilated, it is presumed that the testator mutilated it with an intent to revoke the will. Under the same circumstances, where no will is found, it is presumed that the testator destroyed the will. In the latter case, *extrinsic evidence* is admissible to show the testator's intention.

(1) Adverse party had access to will	**§565**

The presumption of revocation can be overcome if it is shown that a person adversely affected by the will had access to it.

(2) When no presumption of revocation arises	**§566**

There is no presumption of revocation if the will was last in the possession of a *third person.* The presumption is weakened if the will was last in the testator's possession but a person who would be adversely affected by it had access to it.

E. PROOF OF LOST WILLS

1. Admission to Probate	**§567**

If a will has been *inadvertently* or *unintentionally* lost or destroyed, most jurisdictions permit probate of the lost will upon the establishment of the following three elements:

a. Due execution	**§568**

The will proponents must prove that the will was validly executed.

b. Cause of nonproduction	**§569**

Proponents must also show that revocation is not the reason for nonproduction of the will.

c. Contents of will	**§572**

All statutes require proof of the contents of the lost will. The standard of proof is generally quite high (*e.g.*, clearly and distinctly proved). Usually, such proof must come from testimony of persons who had knowledge of the will's contents and may include beneficiaries with an interest in the will.

2. Proof to Show Revocation of Prior Will	**§576**

Evidence of a lost will's due execution plus evidence that it contained revocation language is admissible to show that an earlier will, offered for probate, was revoked. Such proof is *not* an offering of the lost will for probate, but merely shows that the earlier will was revoked.

F. REVIVAL OF REVOKED WILLS

1. Introduction
§577

This problem generally arises where a testator revokes Will #1 by execution of Will #2 (which revokes all earlier wills), and does not destroy the first will. Subsequently, the testator revokes Will #2.

2. Common Law
§578

A few states follow the early rule and hold that no part of a will is effective until the testator's death. Thus, since Will #2 was revoked, Will #1 is still effective.

3. Modern Law

a. Majority rule
§579

A will, once revoked, is *not* revived unless republished by *reexecution* or by *a later codicil.* However, if the earlier will was physically destroyed, a codicil cannot refer to a nonexistent will and thus, cannot revive that will.

b. Uniform Probate Code
§583

The UPC and a substantial minority of states provide that destruction of Will #2 and its language of revocation *may* operate to revive Will #1 *if the testator so intended*. Intent is established by the testator's statements and by reference to all of the surrounding circumstances.

G. DEPENDENT RELATIVE REVOCATION

1. Definition
§584

Dependent relative revocation ("DRR") is a doctrine under which a revocation may be disregarded if it is determined that it was based on a *mistake of law or fact*, and would not have occurred but for the testator's mistaken belief that another disposition of his property was valid.

2. Requirements
§589

Four elements must be established:

a. Ineffective new disposition
§590

DRR will be applied only where it is proved that the testator intended to make a new disposition, which was later shown to be ineffective.

b. Act of revocation
§591

Also, there must have been a valid revocation on which the DRR doctrine may act (*e.g.*, the testator physically destroyed an earlier will and attempted to make a new disposition).

(1) Subsequent testamentary instrument
§593

The majority view permits application of DRR where an earlier will was expressly or impliedly revoked in a later will or codicil that is ineffective. Note that the mistake rendering the instrument ineffective *must appear* (or be inferable) *on the face* of the later testamentary instrument.

as part of that trust so as to provide a single, unified trust management and disposition of (i) assets transferred to the trust inter vivos and (ii) assets owned by the settlor at death.

2. Validity of Pour-Over Gift—Case Law §626

Some early cases invalidated such gifts to a revocable, amendable trust. Other courts upheld the gift on the basis of incorporation by reference. Still other courts upheld the gift and construed it as a gift to the trust under the acts of independent significance doctrine if the trust was funded during the testator's lifetime.

3. Uniform Testamentary Additions to Trusts Act §627

All states have now enacted this Act (or its equivalent), which validates pour-over gifts even if the trust is *revocable or amendable* and even if the trust is *amended subsequent* to the will's execution.

a. Majority rule—trust must be in existence or executed concurrently with will §628

The Act requires that the trust be *sufficiently described* in the testator's will and that the trust must be *in existence before or executed concurrently* with the will.

(1) Exception §629

The Act permits gifts to a trust *not* in existence when the will is executed *if* the trust was created by the will of another person who predeceased the testator.

b. Minority rule §630

Under the revised version of the Act, the gift is valid even if the trust was created *after* the will's execution.

c. Additional requirements in some states §631

In some states, the gift is valid only if trust was executed and acknowledged before a notary public.

d. Pour-over to unfunded trust §632

The size of the trust corpus during the testator's lifetime is immaterial to the validity of the pour-over gift.

E. CODICIL

1. Definition §633

A codicil is a testamentary instrument, executed subsequent to a will, that alters, modifies, or expands the will provisions.

2. Formalities §634

The same formalities necessary for execution of a will are required to execute a codicil. Note that in holographic will jurisdictions, a holographic codicil can alter a typewritten, witnessed will and vice versa.

3. Separate Document Not Required §635

A codicil may be a separate instrument or may be on the will it amends. Remember to determine whether interlineations on a holographic will constitute a valid codicil.

4. Effect of Codicil §636

In addition to modifying, altering, or expanding a prior will, a codicil may: (i) *republish* a prior valid will; (ii) *incorporate by reference* a prior invalid will, thus validating it; or (iii) *revive* a previously revoked, but still existing, will.

a. Republication by codicil §637

When a will is republished by codicil, the will is considered to have been *redated and reexecuted* as of the *date of the codicil*. This may affect issues involving interested witnesses to the will, the pretermitted child or spouse statutes, the incorporation by reference doctrine, etc.

b. Validation of prior invalid will §642

Many courts construe a codicil to a prior invalid will as *impliedly incorporating* the prior defective will by reference, thereby validating the prior instrument.

c. Revival of revoked will §643

Execution of a codicil to a previously revoked will that is still in existence operates to revive the prior will.

IX. CONTRACTS RELATING TO WILLS

A. CONTRACT TO MAKE A GIFT BY WILL

1. Contract Law, Not Wills Law, Controls §644

A promise to make a will is merely a promise to make a will in the future. It is *never* admissible to probate as a will because no *present* testamentary intent was expressed. Contract law controls.

2. Consideration §645

There are no enforceable contract rights unless the promisee gave sufficient consideration for the testator's promise to name her as a will beneficiary.

3. Formalities §646

Although at common law, a contract to make a will or to make a gift by will need *not* be in writing unless real property is involved, today, many states require that such contracts be in *writing*. Some states go even further, requiring that the contract be signed by the testator and two witnesses. Under the UPC, a contract to make a will or testamentary gift must be established by (i) *material provisions* of the contract, (ii) an *express reference in the will* to the contract and extrinsic evidence proving its terms, or (iii) a *writing signed by the testator* evidencing the contract.

4. Remedies

a. During testator's lifetime §651

Generally, a contract to make a testamentary gift cannot be enforced during the testator's lifetime. However, a promisee may file an *anticipatory breach* of contract action if the promisor repudiates the promise *after substantial performance* by the promisee. Some courts will grant specific performance; in any event, the promisee may be entitled to *damages* or to a *quantum meruit* award.

b. **After testator's death** §654

The promisee has a cause of action against the promisor's estate for breach of contract *damages* measured by the value of the promised property. If *specific* property is involved, a constructive trust for the promisee's benefit will be granted.

c. **Enforcement by party other than original promisee** §657

In some circumstances, enforcement by a party other than the original promisee is permitted.

B. JOINT WILLS

1. Terminology

a. **Joint will** §659

A *joint will* is a will of two or more persons executed as a *single testamentary instrument.* It is admissible to probate on the death of *each* of the testators. If the will is revoked by one of the testators, it is no longer admissible as his will, but is still a valid will as to the other testator.

b. **Reciprocal wills** §662

These are *separate* wills of two or more persons that contain reciprocal ("mirror") provisions.

c. **Mutual wills** §663

Some courts interpret "mutual" to mean *"contractual"*; *i.e.,* "joint and mutual will" is a single instrument executed by two (or more) testators with contractual provisions. Other courts construe "mutual" to mean *"reciprocal"*; *i.e.,* mutual wills are separate wills containing reciprocal provisions, and a joint and mutual will is a joint will with reciprocal provisions that *may or may not* be contractual.

2. Survivor's Rights §664

Under a noncontractual joint will, the survivor's rights concern only the decedent's property passing under the will to the survivor. Under a contractual joint will, a survivor's rights *also* concern the survivor's property that is subject to the contractual obligation. Note that if there is a contract not to revoke the will, the survivor's rights generally do *not* include the power to make lifetime gifts of the property subject to the contract.

C. CONTRACT NOT TO REVOKE A WILL

1. Introduction §667

Proof of a contract not to revoke a will is usually based upon the language of the joint will (or reciprocal wills) and extrinsic evidence.

2. Formalities §668

Many states have statutorily mandated that a contract not to revoke a will be in writing and executed with certain formalities.

3. **Presumptions** §669
Jurisdictions without such statutes use various presumptions to determine whether such a contract exists.

   a. **Joint will** §670
   The mere execution of a joint will with reciprocal provisions, without more, does not establish that the will was contractual. However, some courts hold that the will is contractual if the parties *agreed* to execute the joint will.

   b. **Reciprocal wills** §671
   The execution of reciprocal wills with identical provisions does not establish that the wills are contractual, even if they were drafted by the same attorney on the same day. However, some courts hold that the wills are contractual if the parties *agreed* to execute the wills.

4. **Effect of Contract** §672
During both parties' lifetimes, *either party* may revoke a contractual will *if* she gives notice to the other party. If, after one party dies, the *survivor* revokes the contractual will and executes a new will, the contractual will is denied probate but the new will is admissible. Since revocation constitutes breach of contract, the contract beneficiaries should sue to impose a *constructive trust* on the beneficiaries of the new will.

5. **Property Subject to the Contract** §675
Generally, the contract applies to the survivor's own property and to any property received from the decedent. However, the contract is applicable *only* to property owned by the two parties at the time of death of the first decedent; thus, disposition of property *subsequently acquired* by the survivor is *not* controlled by the contract, unless the contrary is *expressly* stated in the contract.

6. **Effect on Elective Share Right** §679
A joint contractual will limits a spouse's elective share right to only property that is *not subject* to the contractual will.

D. **CONTRACT NOT TO MAKE A WILL** §680
A contract not to make a will is enforceable if supported by *consideration.*

1. **Statute of Frauds** §681
Courts are split as to whether the involvement of real property requires the agreement to be written. The *majority* of states hold that the Statute of Frauds is applicable. However, part performance may be sufficient to take it out of the Statute of Frauds.

2. **Remedies** §684
The most common remedy for breach of a contract not to make a will is the imposition of a constructive trust.

X. **CHANGES IN BENEFICIARIES AND PROPERTY AFTER EXECUTION OF WILL**

A. **LAPSED GIFTS**

1. **Definition**   §685
    A gift that was valid when the will was executed but which fails for some
    reason (*e.g.*, subsequent death of beneficiary) is a lapsed gift. A benefi-
    ciary must survive the testator to take under the will.

2. **What Constitutes Surviving the Testator**

    a. **Uniform Simultaneous Death Act**   §687
        Under this Act, if two persons die and there is insufficient evidence
        to show which of them survived the other, each person's property is
        distributed as though he survived the other person.

    b. **Uniform Probate Code's 120-hour survival rule**   §688
        The UPC (and several non-UPC states) provides that a will benefi-
        ciary who does not survive the testator by *120 hours* is considered to
        have predeceased the testator (absent a contrary will provision) and
        the gift lapses.

        (1) **Contrary will provision**   §689
            The 120-hour rule does not apply if the will contains language
            dealing with (i) simultaneous deaths, (ii) deaths in a common
            disaster, (iii) the devisee surviving the testator, or (iv) the devisee
            surviving the testator for a stated period of time. Under the revised
            UPC, the 120-hour rule still applies unless the will made an al-
            ternate gift in the event the devisee predeceases the testator.

3. **Anti-Lapse Statute**   §695
    The majority of jurisdictions have statutorily provided for *substitute takers*
    if the predeceasing beneficiary was within a specified degree of relation-
    ship with the testator *and* left descendents who survive the testator.

    a. **Application in cases of deaths in quick succession—120-hour rule**   §696
        In states that apply the 120-hour rule, the anti-lapse statute applies
        if the beneficiary does not survive the testator by 120 hours.

    b. **Scope of anti-lapse statutes—relationship of beneficiary to testator** §697
        The scope of the anti-lapse statute varies greatly from state to state.
        A few states, taking the narrow approach, provide that the anti-lapse
        statute applies only if the predeceasing beneficiary was a child or *de-
        scendant of the testator*. Other states take an intermediate approach
        and apply the statute if the beneficiary was a *descendant of the
        testator's parents*. Under the UPC, the predeceasing beneficiary must
        have been a grandparent or a *descendant of a grandparent of the
        testator*. Several states take a broad approach and apply the statute
        to *any relative* of the testator, and in a few states, the predeceasing
        beneficiary does not even have to be related to the testator.

    c. **Substitute takers—predeceasing beneficiary's descendants**   §705
        To take under the anti-lapse statute, the predeceasing beneficiary's
        descendants must survive the testator. In states that have enacted
        the 120-hour rule, the descendants must survive by 120 hours to be
        substitute takers.

d. **Contrary will provision—gift contingent on surviving testator** §707

The anti-lapse statute does not apply if the will specifies that the beneficiary must survive the testator in order to take; in that case, the anti-lapse statute will not save the gift for the beneficiary's descendants. Note, however, that under the revised UPC, the anti-lapse statute applies to a bequest contingent on survival by 120 hours unless the will made an alternate gift in the event of the beneficiary's nonsurvival.

e. **Application to nonprobate transfers** §710

The anti-lapse statute does *not apply* to nonprobate transfers or revocable trusts.

4. **Lapse of Specific Gift or General Legacy** §714

Absent a contrary will provision, a lapsed specific, demonstrative, or general bequest that is not saved by an anti-lapse statute falls into the residuary estate.

a. **Residuary clause** §715

If there is no residuary clause or if the clause is not stated broadly enough to encompass the gifts (*e.g.,* "all of my personal property"), lapsed gifts pass by *intestate succession.*

5. **Lapse in Residuary Gift** §717

If one of several residuary beneficiaries predeceases the testator, a minority of states hold that the lapsed share does *not* pass to the surviving residuary beneficiaries unless the will so provides; instead it passes by intestate succession. However, the revised UPC and a majority of states hold that the share passes to the other residuary beneficiaries in proportion to their interests in the residuary gift.

6. **Void Gifts—Beneficiary Deceased When Will Executed** §720

A gift is *void* if the beneficiary is dead when the will is executed. Void gifts lapse unless saved by an applicable anti-lapse statute.

B. **CLASS GIFTS**

1. **Definitional Problems** §723

Absent a controlling will provision, the following rules govern which persons are included in class designations.

a. **"Children"** §724

This includes descendants in the *first degree only* (not grandchildren) and includes children by all marriages of the specified person.

(1) **Adopted children** §726

Most jurisdictions today presume that a gift to someone's children *includes* adopted children. A similar rule applies to *adopted adults* in many states.

(2) **Child placed for adoption** §734

A child adopted by a new family is not included in a class gift made by a natural relative of the child *unless* the adopting parent is also a member of the child's natural family.

(3) Nonmarital children §735

The majority of states hold that nonmarital children are included in a gift to "children." The minority rule **excludes** such children from the "children" designation unless the will shows an intent to include them. Extrinsic evidence is admissible to show the testator's intention.

b. "Issue"; "descendants" §740

These terms are generally held to be synonymous and include lineal descendants of any degree. Modern law includes adopted and nonmarital children if they would be intestate heirs of the decedent. The living issue take **per stirpes** absent a contrary intent.

c. "Heirs" §745

This includes persons who would take the decedent's estate if the decedent had died **intestate.**

d. "Relatives," "next of kin," and other family terms §746

Words such as "relatives," "family," or "next of kin" are usually construed to mean "heirs."

e. "Brothers and sisters" §748

"Brothers and sisters" includes half brothers and half sisters and siblings of the whole blood.

f. "Cousins"; "nieces and nephews" §749

"Cousins" includes first cousins only. "Nieces and nephews" refers to the children of brothers and sisters.

2. Constructional Problems §750

Sometimes problems arise in determining the takers of a class gift.

a. Death of class member after will's execution and during testator's life—class gift rule §751

A testamentary gift to a class of persons, of which one member predeceases the testator, passes to the **surviving** class members absent a contrary will provision. (This is commonly referred to as the class gift rule.)

(1) Anti-lapse statute §752

Many anti-lapse statutes expressly apply to class gifts as long as the other statutory elements are met. The class gift rule gives way to the anti-lapse statute if the predeceasing class member is within the degree of relationship specified by statute and left descendants who survive the testator.

b. Death of class member before will's execution §755

The majority holds that the anti-lapse statute applies whether the class member's death occurred before or after the will's execution. In a minority of states, however, the anti-lapse statute does not apply in favor of descendants of a class member who died before the will's execution.

1. **General Rule** §772

   If specifically devised property is not in the testator's estate at the time of death, the gift is adeemed; *i.e.*, it fails. The doctrine applies only to *specific* gifts and only to property changes occurring *prior* to the testator's death. *Partial ademption* applies where only a portion of the gift has been disposed of.

2. **Role of Testator's Intent—Majority View** §777

   An *objective* test is used to determine whether the specific property is in the testator's estate; his probable intent is disregarded. The only issue is whether the property can be identified as being in the testator's estate at death; if it is not, the gift is adeemed.

3. **Avoiding Ademption—Case Decisions** §784

   Although the testator's intent is held to be irrelevant, various techniques have been developed to avoid ademption: construing a bequest as general rather than specific, construing property as owned at death instead of at time of will's execution, liberal interpretation as to what constitutes a change in form (ademption does not apply if there is a slight change in form), etc.

   a. **Gifts of sale proceeds** §791

      A beneficiary is entitled to the proceeds from the sale of an asset if the will so directs, even if the asset is sold before the testator's death.

   b. **Testator did not have opportunity to change will** §792

      Many states hold that a gift is not adeemed if the testator did not have an opportunity to change the will before his death (*e.g.*, testator's sailboat, which was devised to his wife, was destroyed in a boating accident. If the testator died shortly thereafter from injuries sustained in that accident, his wife is entitled to casualty insurance proceeds on the sailboat).

4. **Statutory Modifications** §793

   The UPC and many states have modified application of the common law rule of ademption in specific situations (*e.g.*, casualty insurance proceeds, condemnation awards, executory contracts, changes in securities, property under guardianship, etc.). In these and other cases, the benefits arising from changes before the testator's death but paid after death generally are directed to the beneficiary.

5. **Satisfaction of Legacies** §802

   If, after executing the will, the testator makes a gift to a person who is a general or residuary legatee under the will, the gift may be in partial or total satisfaction of the legacy *if the testator so intended*—*i.e.*, ademption by satisfaction.

E. **STOCK SPLITS AND STOCK DIVIDENDS**

1. **Stock Splits** §804

   Additional shares of stock produced by a stock split pass to the specific beneficiary regardless of whether the split occurs before or after the testator's death.

2. Stock Dividends §806
In states without statutes that address this issue, additional shares of stock produced by a stock dividend **before** the testator's death are treated the same as cash dividends: They are treated as income on the original capital and do **not pass** to the specific beneficiary.

3. Cash Dividends §809
A specific beneficiary is entitled to any cash dividends if they are declared and paid **after the testator's death**.

4. Statutory Solutions §810
Pursuant to the UPC and several states' statutes, a specific beneficiary of corporate securities is entitled to additional or other securities of that corporation (including stock dividends) owned by the testator by reason of corporate action.

F. INTEREST ON GENERAL LEGACIES §811
Generally, a beneficiary is entitled to interest on a general legacy if it is not paid **within one year after the testator's death**, or, under the UPC, **within one year after the appointment of a personal representative**.

G. EXONERATION OF LIENS

1. Majority Rule §812
If, at the testator's death, specifically devised property is subject to a lien for which the testator was **personally** liable, the beneficiary can demand payment of the lien (exoneration) out of the **residuary estate**.

2. Minority Rule §814
A growing trend is to enact statutes under which such liens are **not** exonerated unless the will directs exoneration. A general instruction in the will to pay all debts is not sufficient to direct exoneration.

XI. WILL CONTESTS AND RELATED MATTERS

A. STANDING TO CONTEST WILL

1. Who May Contest Will §815
Only an **interested** party (*i.e.*, intestate heirs or legatees under an earlier will) can contest a will. Persons without standing to contest a decedent's will are creditors, executors or testamentary trustees named in an earlier will, and legatees who accepted benefits.

a. Necessary parties must receive notice §818
All heirs and legatees named in the will must be given notice of the proceedings.

2. Time for Contest §822
A will may be contested either at the time it is offered for probate or thereafter as governed by statute. Under the UPC, a will contest is made in a

formal testacy proceeding, either three years after the testator's death or, if the will was probated in an informal probate proceeding, 12 months after that proceeding.

3. Burden of Proof §824

Generally, the contestant has the burden of establishing the grounds for contesting the will.

4. Attorney's Fees for Defense of Will §825

The executor has a duty to defend the will and any attorney's fees incurred in doing so may be charged against the estate even if the will is denied probate.

B. GROUNDS FOR WILL CONTEST

1. Testamentary Capacity

a. Legal test §826

A testator must have (i) understood the nature of the act he was doing; (ii) known the natural objects of his bounty; (iii) known the nature and value of his property; and (iv) understood the disposition he was making.

b. Comparison with other legal tests §831

The capacity required to make a will is a lower standard than that required to enter into a contract.

c. Insane delusion §832

A person found to be suffering from an insane delusion lacks testamentary capacity as to the will or a gift therein.

(1) Definition §833

Insane delusion has been held to be a belief in facts that do not exist and which no rational person would believe existed.

(2) Test §834

The test is whether there are *any* facts from which the testator *could* have reached his conclusion.

(3) Effect of insane delusion §835

The delusion must appear to have had some *effect on* the disposition of the property and must *relate to the disposition.*

d. Burden of proof as to testamentary capacity §836

Some states place the burden of proving mental capacity on the *will proponents.* However, many states recognize a *rebuttable* presumption of competency which forces *will contestants* to show a lack of mental competency. *Note:* An adjudication of incapacity is evidence, but not necessarily proof, of testamentary incapacity.

e. Evidentiary matters §839

The fact that the testator was old, physically frail, in poor health, had poor memory, or had a drinking problem does not indicate that he lacked mental capacity. Testamentary capacity is measured *at the time the will was executed.*

(1) Witness cannot testify as to testator's legal capacity §844

A witness can testify as to the testator's *actions and statements* but may not be asked if the testator had legal capacity to make a will or was suffering from an insane delusion. This is because a layperson's understanding of legal capacity may differ from the legal standard. Note that a witness may testify as to the testator's *mental condition.*

f. Lucid and sensible holographic will is evidence of testamentary capacity §846

A rational and sensible holographic will is evidence that the testator wrote the will during a lucid interval.

2. Testamentary Intent §847

To be admitted to probate, it must be shown that the will was written and executed with testamentary intent. However, such intent is generally *presumed,* unless suspicious circumstances surrounding the preparation or execution of the will require proof that the testator knew its contents.

3. Undue Influence §850

Mental coercion that destroys a testator's free will and forces him to substitute the intentions of another in his will renders the will invalid on the basis of undue influence.

a. Legal test §851

This is a subjective test, measured at the time of will execution. The will contestant must show that: (i) undue influence *was exerted*; (ii) the mind and will of the testator had been *overpowered*; and (iii) the influence produced a will that expresses the intent of the one exerting the influence, and that *would not have been made but for the influence*.

b. Circumstantial evidence §852

Since undue influence is difficult to prove, *substantial* circumstantial evidence may be used. Courts consider four factors, no one of which is sufficient by itself: *susceptibility* of the testator; *opportunity* to exert the influence; *some activity* to show undue influence (*e.g.*, isolating the testator from his family); and an *unnatural disposition* in the will (*e.g.,* disinheriting his children in favor of a nonrelative).

c. Undue influence as to part of will §857

If undue influence is shown to have affected only some of the gifts in the will, the remaining parts are valid, unless such construction would contradict the testator's intent. The entire will is set aside if upholding the unchallenged provisions would defeat the testator's intent.

d. Confidential relationship

(1) Effect of confidential relationship §858

The majority rule holds that the mere existence of a confidential relationship between the testator and a will beneficiary does *not,* by itself, raise a presumption of undue influence unless the beneficiary plays an *active part* in procuring the will.

(a) Presumption §859

Many courts recognize a rebuttable presumption where it is shown that a confidential relationship **existed** when the will was executed, the beneficiary actively **participated** in drawing the will, **and** the will makes an **unnatural disposition.** Upon proof of these three factors, the burden of proof then shifts to the will proponent.

(2) Gift to spouse §861

The confidential relationship between a husband and wife does not give rise to a presumption of undue influence.

(3) Illicit relationship §862

The mere existence of an illicit relationship does not give rise to a presumption of undue influence, but it may be considered in determining whether undue influence was exerted.

(4) Gift to testator's attorney §863

Generally, an attorney-client relationship, without more, does not raise a presumption of undue influence. However, many courts recognize a presumption or inference if the attorney prepared a will in his favor and supervised its execution, whereupon the presumption of undue influence can be overcome only by the clearest and most satisfying evidence.

(a) Independent legal advice §865

No presumption of undue influence arises if the will was prepared by independent counsel.

4. Fraud

a. In general §868

If a testator was **willfully deceived** as to the character or content of a will, or as to extrinsic facts that induced the will, the will is invalid. If only a portion of the will is affected by fraud, only that portion is invalid.

(1) Definition §869

Fraud consists of **false statements** of material facts, **known** to be false, made with **intent to deceive** the testator, who is **actually deceived**, that cause the testator to **act in reliance** on the false statements. Usually the fraud must be intended to influence the execution or content of the will, but deceit directed at some other objective (*e.g.*, fraudulently induced marriage) can also prevent probate.

(2) Causation §871

A will is invalid only if the testator was **actually deceived** and **acted in reliance** on the misrepresentations.

(3) Compared to other grounds §872

Mistake does not constitute fraud. Note also that undue influence involves coercion while fraud involves deception. Similarly, fraud is distinguishable from duress (*i.e.*, element of threat).

b.   Fraud in the execution   §875
Situations such as a testator being tricked into signing a writing while
not knowing it was a will involve **no testamentary intent** and constitute fraud in the execution.

c.   Fraud in the inducement   §876
This type of fraud occurs where there is testamentary intent, but the
testator is fraudulently induced into making a will or a gift. The misrepresentation must be the **sole inducement** for making the will or gift and
there is no fraud if the testator knew the true facts.

(1) Fraud perpetrated by someone other than beneficiary   §879
The fact that the fraud was perpetrated on the testator by someone
other than the beneficiary generally is immaterial. The innocent
beneficiary's gift will still be set aside.

d.   Fraudulent prevention of will   §881
Fraudulent prevention occurs when the testator is fraudulently dissuaded from making a will or gift. In such cases, there is **no legal
remedy,** and the estate passes by intestate succession rules. Many
courts will impose a **constructive trust** in favor of the persons who
would have been beneficiaries. Some jurisdictions recognize an action for tort liability for a wrongful interference with an expectancy.

e.   Revocation prevented by fraud   §885
If a testator is tricked into believing her will has been revoked, the
will is still **admitted to probate** because there was no valid revocation. However, upon proof of the fraud, a constructive trust would
probably be imposed.

5. Mistake

a.   In general   §886
Parol evidence is usually admissible in cases involving an alleged mistake in a **will's execution** because it relates to testamentary intent. The
admissibility of parol evidence is less likely if the alleged mistake relates to the **motive** for making the will or the will's **contents.**

(1) Distinguish—mistake as to revocation   §887
Relief is much more freely given if a mistake as to **revocation** is
shown.

b.   Mistake in execution of will

(1) Mistake as to nature of instrument   §888
Extrinsic evidence is **always** admissible to show that the testator was mistaken as to the nature or effect of the writing he
signed. If mistake is proved, probate is denied for lack of testamentary intent.

(2) Wrong will signed   §889
This usually occurs where reciprocal wills are involved. Some
courts deny relief; however, the modern trend is to grant relief
since the existence and nature of the mistake is so obvious.

striking out the inaccurate part if the remaining language is unambiguous or, if ambiguous, the ambiguity can be cured by extrinsic evidence.

c. Patent ambiguity §907
When the uncertainty appears on the *face of the will,* parol evidence is traditionally *inadmissible* for clarification purposes. However, the modern trend is to *admit parol evidence* relating to the testator's intent in *any* case of ambiguity—patent or latent.

d. Type of extrinsic evidence admissible §910
If extrinsic evidence is admissible, any competent extrinsic evidence that may bear on the testator's *actual or probable intent* at the time the will was executed may be used.

(1) Admissibility of testator's declarations §912
The majority rule is that declarations to third parties (other than the drafting attorney) are *not* admissible. The modern and better view admits a testator's statements to cure *latent* ambiguities.

e. Rules of construction where no evidence of testator's intent §916
A will is to be construed *as a whole.* To overcome inconsistencies, courts interpret specific provisions as controlling over general provisions, later provisions take precedence over former provisions, and provisions in the testator's handwriting control over typed or printed provisions. Also, courts will construe the will, if possible, *to avoid intestacy* and generally will choose the interpretation that favors the testator's kin. Also remember that words in the will are given their *ordinary meaning* unless the will was drawn by, *e.g.*, an illiterate testator.

C. NO-CONTEST CLAUSE

1. Effect of No-Contest Clause §924
Sometimes called an in terrorem clause, a no-contest clause provides that if a person contests the will, she forfeits all interests under the will. Under the UPC and in most states, a beneficiary who unsuccessfully contests the will does *not* forfeit her legacy if the challenge was made in *good faith* and with *probable cause*. However, in several states, an unsuccessful will contest triggers a forfeiture even if there was probable cause for the contest.

2. Actions that Do Not Constitute a Contest §930
Suits to construe a will, jurisdictional objections, challenges to the appointment of or an accounting by the executor, offering subsequent wills for probate, and withdrawal of a will contest do *not* trigger a no-contest clause.

D. TORT LIABILITY FOR WRONGFUL INTERFERENCE WITH EXPECTED INHERITANCE

to the probate court's supervision and control. The personal representative is considered a representative of the court. Several states now permit estate administration without court supervision (*i.e.,* independent administration).

a. Uniform Probate Code §960
The UPC provides for two types of administration—unsupervised and supervised. Under the UPC, all administrations are ***unsupervised*** unless a supervised administration is requested by the representative or by any interested party. Under a supervised administration, court approval is necessary before an estate can be distributed, but a personal representative may exercise other administrative powers (*e.g.,* pay claims, sell property) ***without*** court approval.

b. Informal administration procedures §963
In many jurisdictions, no formal administration or court supervision may be necessary for very modest estates.

4. Jurisdiction and Venue §964
The primary probate jurisdiction is the state of the decedent's ***domicile at the time of his death***. A probate proceeding is ***in rem***; *i.e.,* it conclusively determines who takes title to the decedent's property.

a. Venue §967
Usually, venue lies in the ***county*** of the decedent's domicile at the time of death. As to a nonresident, venue is in any county in which the decedent owned real property ***or*** where any debtor of the decedent resides.

b. Real property in another state—ancillary administration §969
Ancillary probate and administration proceedings in another state are required if a decedent owned property in the other state.

c. Choice of law rules §970
Questions as to the validity and construction of a will are settled in the place of primary administration and are binding in any ancillary proceedings.

B. PROOF OF WILLS IN PROBATE

1. Duty to Produce Will §971
A person in possession of a decedent's will must present it to the probate court within a statutorily specified time or face civil, and perhaps criminal, liability.

2. Who May Offer Will for Probate §972
Any person ***interested*** in the estate (*e.g.,* beneficiary, creditor, executor) may offer the will for probate.

3. Time Within Which Will Must Be Probated §973
Most states require that a will be offered for probate within a specified time limit after the decedent's death. The UPC time limit is three years after the decedent's death. If the time limit is not met, the decedent is presumed to have died intestate.

4. Informal vs. Formal Procedure for Admitting Will

a. Common law §977

The procedure for admitting a will could be in either **probate form** (ex parte proceeding and no notice to interested parties) or **solemn form** (notice required for interested parties).

b. Uniform Probate Code §980

The UPC follows the basic common law forms but renames them: An **informal** probate proceeding is ex parte with no notice but is held before a registrar rather than a court. A **formal** testacy proceeding is a formal adjudication brought by any interested party.

c. Majority rule §984

In most states, a formal probate proceeding after **notice** to interested parties is always required.

5. Burden of Proof §985

When the will is offered for probate, the will proponents must show due execution. **After** the will is admitted to probate, the will contestants carry the burden of proof. Proof of proper execution **cannot** be waived even if all interested parties want the will probated.

6. Proof of Due Execution §987

Usually, both attesting witnesses must testify as to the facts surrounding execution. If a witness is dead, incompetent, or cannot be located, the testimony of the remaining witness is usually sufficient. Depositions or interrogatories may be used as a substitute for a nonresident witness. If no attesting witnesses are available, proof of the handwriting of the testator and of at least one witness is usually required.

a. Attestation clause §989

This is **prima facie evidence** of the facts recited therein. However, it is not a substitute for the attesting witnesses' testimony. *But note:* A **self-proving affidavit** does permit a will to be admitted to probate on the strength of the recitals in the affidavit.

7. Whether Will Was Validly Executed Is a Question of Fact §993

Whether a will was validly executed is a question for the fact finder. Thus, a will is **denied probate** if the fact finder determines that it was not validly executed, even if attesting witnesses testify otherwise.

8. Will Written in Foreign Language §994

A will written in a foreign language can be admitted to probate under standard probate procedures if it is accompanied by an English translation.

9. Lost Wills §995

The rules governing proof of lost wills are usually applied in cases involving the issue of revocation (*see supra,* §567).

C. APPOINTMENT AND QUALIFICATION OF PERSONAL REPRESENTATIVE

1. Terminology §997

An **executor** is a person named in the will to serve as personal representative.

An **administrator** is a personal representative appointed by the court to administer an intestate estate. Special situations call for personal representatives with other titles (*e.g.*, administrator c.t.a., temporary administrator, successor personal representative). The UPC uses only the term "personal representative."

a. Guardian §1003

A guardian of the **person** of a minor child has custody and is responsible for the child's care and upbringing.

(1) Guardian of the estate §1005

Since a personal representative usually cannot make a distribution to a minor, a court-appointed guardian is necessary to accept the property. Laws governing such a guardianship are usually cumbersome; thus, several states permit distributions to the child's **custodian** under their version of the **Uniform Transfers to Minors Act.**

(2) Guardian ad litem §1008

This is a court-appointed person who represents the interest of a minor or incompetent heir or beneficiary when no guardian has been appointed and the party's interests are not otherwise represented.

2. Qualification of Personal Representative §1009

A personal representative must have the **capacity to contract** (thus excluding minors and incompetents). Conflicts of interest (*e.g.*, claim against estate) usually do **not** disqualify a person. A few states require a personal representative to be a state resident.

3. Priority for Appointment §1012

Governed by statute in all states, priority relates to who will be appointed personal representative—*e.g.*, named personal representative, spouse, other will beneficiary, etc. The person named as personal representative in the will must be appointed **unless** disqualified by statute or court rule.

4. Bond §1014

Most states require a personal representative to post bond unless the will waives bond.

5. Compensation §1016

The personal representative's rate of compensation is usually set by statutes, absent a contrary will provision. In many cases, a relative named as executor in the will waives compensation.

6. Termination of Appointment §1021

Certain events (*e.g.*, death, misconduct) will terminate a representative's appointment. However, she cannot resign without court permission, which usually is preceded by an accounting. Moreover, a representative can be removed for cause (*e.g.*, incompetency, embezzlement).

D. DUTIES AND LIABILITIES OF PERSONAL REPRESENTATIVE

1. **Qualification**   §1024

    The personal representative must file a statement of acceptance of ap-
    pointment with the court along with giving a fiduciary bond (unless bond is
    waived).

2. **Powers and Duties**   §1025

    A personal representative has the powers and duties required to manage
    and preserve the decedent's assets during administration. These include
    marshalling the probate assets (which she must not commingle with her
    own property), filing an inventory, the making of periodic accountings, us-
    ing reasonable care in preserving the assets (generally prohibits investment
    of assets), etc. Generally, a personal representative has *no* duty or power
    to carry on the decedent's business or to sell, mortgage, or lease property
    unless authorized to do so by the will or court order.

3. **Fiduciary Duties**   §1044

    A personal representative is held to the *general standard of care* that ap-
    plies to trustees: She must act with reasonable care, skill, and prudence
    and owes a duty of *undivided loyalty* to the estate.

4. **Liabilities**   §1049

    A personal representative is liable for any losses resulting from bad faith,
    mismanagement, or breach of a fiduciary duty.

    a. **Torts**   §1050

        A personal representative is *personally* liable for any torts committed
        by her in administering the estate. She may be *reimbursed* by the es-
        tate *if* she was not personally at fault and she breached no duty of
        care.

    b. **Contracts**   §1052

        Similarly, a personal representative is personally liable on any con-
        tracts she entered into on the estate's behalf unless the contract re-
        lieves her from liability. Reimbursement is available if she did not act
        beyond her powers and the contract was entered into as a result of
        proper administration procedures.

E. **CREDITORS' CLAIMS**

1. **Notice to Creditors**   §1055

    Notice by publication must be given to estate creditors.

2. **Unsecured Claims**   §1056

    Generally, creditors' claims must be filed within a certain time or are barred
    by a nonclaim statute. Known and reasonably ascertainable creditors must
    be given *personal notice* before their claims can be barred. The time limits
    do not apply to claims to the extent they are covered by liability insurance.

3. **Secured Claims**   §1063

    Secured creditors must receive *personal notice* of the administration pro-
    ceedings. The creditor has the option to *present the claim for full payment*
    or waive payment from the estate and *rely on its lien* (seeking foreclosure
    if payments are not made).

Approach to Exams

Essay questions on a Wills or Decedents' Estates exam usually follow one of two patterns. The first and most commonly encountered type of question includes several will clauses making various gifts and raises separate issues with respect to each gift. Such a question actually consists of several short answer subquestions because, more often than not, the issues raised by one of the clauses are independent from the issues raised by the other clauses. (*See, e.g.,* Exam Question I.) If, for example, the will in the question includes this gift, "I devise Blackacre to my brother John," you can be sure that something is going to happen either to Blackacre or to John. ***Read the remaining facts carefully,*** because you will be expected to discuss and resolve the proper disposition of the gift to John. While it is possible that a few of the will clauses in the question do not raise any issues calling for discussion (*i.e.,* the clause is a "red herring"), this is the exception rather than the rule. Read (and reread) the facts carefully before you decide that no problems are raised with respect to the particular gift.

The second type of question involves a rolling fact situation, in which a series of facts or events are presented sequentially. (*See, e.g.,* Exam Question IV.) Each sentence or paragraph presents a new fact or event that will call for discussion in your answer. In such a question, if you have read three or four sentences and no issue comes to mind, go back and reread those sentences, because you may have overlooked something.

Sometimes both of these elements (separate will clauses and a chronological sequence of events) are contained in the same exam question.

Set out below are some important issues that you should be prepared to identify and discuss.

1. **Intestate Succession**

    Be thoroughly familiar with the intestate succession rules that the state applies to commonly encountered family situations. The intestate rules most likely to be tested upon are the shares of a surviving spouse, child, or parent, but prudence dictates that you also be familiar with the distribution that would occur if the decedent was not survived by any close relations.

    An exam question may call for application of the intestacy rules to the estate of a decedent who died without a will, but it is more likely that the intestacy rules will be brought into play in a case where the decedent *left a will—e.g.,* there may be a partial intestacy because of a lapse in the residuary clause or the pretermitted spouse or pretermitted child statute may give an intestate share to a new spouse or an afterborn child.

    a. **What is the share of the surviving spouse?**

        Remember that the share of the surviving spouse may be affected by whether the decedent left any surviving descendants and whether those descendants are also the descendants of the surviving spouse.

b. Do grandchildren take per stirpes or per capita?

When no children survive the decedent, be sure to know where the "stirpes" are divided: at the child level (even though there are no living children), or at the first generational level at which there are living takers? (Same for the inheritance by nephews and nieces.)

c. Are there any adopted children?

Adopted children have full inheritance rights from their adoptive families, but the states are split on whether the adopted child continues to have inheritance rights from natural parents and grandparents.

d. Were there any nonmarital children?

A nonmarital child has full inheritance rights from and through his natural mother, but the states apply different tests in determining whether the child has inheritance rights from his natural father.

e. Were any children born after the decedent's death?

A child conceived during the father's lifetime but born within 280 days after his death is presumed to be the child of the decedent.

f. Are stepchildren or foster children involved?

Remember that stepchildren and foster children have no inheritance rights from their stepparent or foster parents unless they were adopted, but watch for facts that might invoke the adoption by estoppel doctrine because of an unperformed agreement to adopt.

g. Does the state have a "laughing heir" statute?

Statutes in several states do not grant inheritance rights to *remote relations* (the UPC draws the line at grandparents and descendants of grandparents). Instead, the property escheats to the state.

h. Did the decedent and an heir die at or near the same time?

Another concern regarding intestate succession includes application of the Uniform Simultaneous Death Act or the UPC's 120-hour rule if parties die simultaneously or in close proximity to one another.

i. Which state's law is used?

If more than one state is involved, remember that the law of the decedent's domicile governs *personal* property wherever located, but that devolution of *real* property is governed by the law of the situs state.

2. Execution of Wills

a. Was the will validly executed?

If the question states that, "Testator left a duly executed will," or other such language, or if the question gives no facts concerning the will's execution, there is no need to discuss the requisites for execution of a will. However, questions may raise an issue as to whether the requirements for due execution were satisfied. If so, you probably should discuss the due execution issue first because, if the will was not validly executed, *none of its provisions are valid.* But if the issue is a close one, do not conclude that there is no need to discuss the issues raised by the will's terms because the will was not validly executed. Unless the will's execution is clearly invalid, continue your discussion by saying, "If the court were to hold that the will was validly executed, the following issues would be raised. . . ." If the facts do raise an issue as to due execution, set out the steps required by the controlling state statute and then discuss whether all the requisites were satisfied. Watch for these issues:

(1) **Did the testator properly sign the will?**
     The test is: Did the testator intend the mark to be his signature? Remember that the will can be signed by another person at the testator's direction and in the testator's presence.

(2) **Did the testator sign the will "at the end thereof"?**
     This is an issue to watch for because some states require the signature to be at the physical end and others require that it be at the logical end of the will. If the facts raise this issue, discuss this point even if the controlling law does not have a "signature at the end" requirement.

(3) **Did the testator acknowledge his earlier signature?**
     In most states it is necessary for the testator to acknowledge his earlier signature to the witnesses if he signed the will at an earlier point in time.

(4) **Did the witnesses know they were witnessing a will?**
     In several states, the testator must publish (*i.e.,* communicate) to the witnesses that they are witnessing a will as distinguished from some other legal document. (The UPC and statutes in many states do not have a publication requirement.)

(5) **Did the witnesses sign in the testator's presence and did the testator sign the will or acknowledge his previous signature in the witnesses' presence?**
     Understand the difference between the liberal "conscious presence" test and the "line of sight" test.

(6) **Did any of the witnesses sign before the testator signed?**
     Most courts hold that the exact order of signing is not critical so long as the execution ceremony is *one contemporaneous transaction.*

b. **Were any of the attesting witnesses also beneficiaries under the will?**
    If so, remember that the interested witness rule *never* results in denial of the will to probate, but the bequest to the witness is usually purged unless the

witness is a supernumerary (*i.e.*, extra) witness or would have been an heir if the decedent had died intestate. Under the UPC and in states that have abolished the interested witness rule, point out that no problem is raised by the fact that a beneficiary is also an attesting witness.

c. Does the will contain an attestation clause or is it self-proved?

Understand the difference: If the will contains an *attestation clause*, that clause is prima facie evidence that the will was duly executed, but the attesting *witnesses must testify* as to the circumstances surrounding its execution. If the will is self-proved by a *sworn affidavit*, the affidavit is evidence of due execution and can *constitute the sworn testimony* of the attesting witnesses.

d. Is a holographic instrument involved?

If the will is handwritten and unattested, consider whether it is valid as a holographic will. In states that recognize holographic wills, remember that the will's *material provisions* must be in the testator's handwriting and the instrument must be signed by the testator. (Remember the signature test above.) Be sure, however, to look for testamentary intent—*i.e.*, whether the particular writing was itself intended to be a will. Casual statements may be included in a letter with no intent that they were to be considered testamentary in effect. Also, if the state does not recognize holographic wills, mention that fact in your answer.

e. Was there an oral will?

Oral wills are valid only in limited circumstances (*e.g.*, during the testator's last sickness) and can dispose of personal property only. There must be at least two witnesses to the uttering of the oral will and some states require that it be reduced to writing within a specified period of time.

f. Is the will a conditional will?

If so, keep in mind that the condition must be stated in the will and the will does not take effect unless the event occurs, although most courts like to find that the condition was merely the *motive* that prompted the testator to write the will, meaning that intestacy is avoided even if the stated event does not occur.

g. Was the attorney guilty of negligence in preparing the will or in supervising its execution?

Discuss this issue in any case in which the attorney has bungled the job. Most states hold that the attorney owes a duty of due care, not just to the client, but also to the beneficiaries under the will.

3. Revocation of Wills

a. Was the will revoked by operation of law?

Think about this if the testator married or divorced after the will was executed. Remember that in some states remarriage to a former spouse revives any provisions that were revoked on divorce.

b. Did the testator attempt to revoke the will by a subsequent testamentary instrument?

Remember that the subsequent instrument of revocation must be executed with the same formalities as are required for a will, and that the testator must meet the test for testamentary capacity. If the subsequent instrument does not expressly revoke the earlier will, then *both instruments* are admitted to probate and the second instrument revokes the first to the extent of any inconsistencies.

c. Did the testator attempt to revoke the will by physical act?

The physical act must deface or otherwise affect the entire will or at least its material provisions (although striking out the testator's signature is usually held to be a revocation of the entire will). Also, the *intent to revoke must accompany the physical act of destruction*. If the will is accidentally destroyed and the testator subsequently decides that he wanted to revoke the will anyhow, there is no effective revocation. The physical act can be by another person provided it is done in the testator's presence and at his direction.

(1) Did the testator attempt to partially revoke the will by physical act?

Changes on the face of a will are a common source of exam issues. In states that do not recognize partial revocations by physical act, the change is disregarded and the will is read as it was originally executed. However, most states do recognize partial revocations by physical act.

(a) Did the testator write in new provisions on the face of the will?

If the will as executed says, "I bequeath $5,000 to Sue," and the testator subsequently strikes the "$5,000" and writes in "$10,000," the attempted increase of the gift is ineffective (unless the will is reexecuted) because it was not part of the duly executed will and therefore is an unattested act. Given that the "$5,000" was stricken from the will with an intent to revoke the gift in that amount, these facts would invoke the doctrine of dependent relative revocation ("DRR") (if the state recognizes partial revocations). But if the testator strikes "Sue" and writes in "Bill," the bequest to Sue is revoked and DRR should *not* be applied because the intent to revoke the gift to Sue was independent of the intent to make the (ineffective) gift to Bill.

(b) Were the changes made on a holographic will?

Unlike attested wills, changes made on the face of a holographic will are valid if they are shown to be in the testator's handwriting, because a holographic will does not have to be written at one sitting.

(2) Do the facts give rise to a presumption of revocation?

For example, if a will was last seen in the testator's possession and control but cannot be found after the testator's death, there is a presumption that the testator destroyed the will with the intent to revoke it. Think about who was in possession of the will to determine whether the presumption arises (*e.g.,* was it a beneficiary?).

d. Was an attempt made to revive an earlier will?

Remember that, in most states, revocation of a second will does not, by itself, revive an earlier will that was revoked by the second will. The first will must be *republished* by reexecution or by a later codicil. But under the UPC and in a few states, the first will might be revived if it can be shown that it was the testator's intent to revive the earlier will.

e. Should DRR be applied?

In the "no revival of revoked wills" situation, be ready to discuss DRR. Under this doctrine, a revocation by physical act can be disregarded if it is shown to have been based on a mistake of law or fact as to the validity of another disposition *and* it is shown that the testator's intent will more nearly be effectuated if the revocation is disregarded.

f. Should the "proof of lost wills" statute be applied to allow probate of the will as a lost will?

Remember that the "proof of lost wills" rules are very stringent. Probate of a lost will requires establishment of the will's (i) valid execution, (ii) cause of its nonproduction, and (iii) contents.

4. Issues Raised If the Testator Was Married

a. Did the testator divorce after the will was executed?

The divorce revokes all gifts and administrative appointments in favor of the former spouse, and the will is read as though the former spouse predeceased the testator. But if the parties later reconcile and remarry, the will is revived.

b. Did the testator marry after the will was executed?

If the testator marries after executing a will and the state has a pretermitted spouse statute, the will is revoked so as to give the spouse an intestate share of the decedent's estate unless (i) the will provides for the new spouse, (ii) the will indicates that the omission was intentional, or (iii) the will was made in contemplation of marriage. In states without pretermitted spouse statutes, it is generally provided that marriage following execution of a will has no effect on the will, but the new spouse has rights under the elective share statute (or, in community property states, under the community property system), homestead laws, exempt personal property set-aside, and family allowance.

c. Should the spouse file for an elective share?

In any question involving a husband and wife, determine whether the surviving spouse should renounce the will and file an election to take a statutory share of the decedent's estate. Discuss this issue even if an election is not warranted, showing that you have considered the issue but found that it would not be advantageous for the spouse to so elect. Remember that only the surviving spouse can filed for an elective share.

(1)   Are any lifetime transfers subject to the elective share?
Some states satisfy the elective share out of the decedent's *probate estate*, which is all probate property owned by the decedent at death less expenses. However, other states satisfy the elective share out of the decedent's *augmented estate*, which is the probate estate plus certain lifetime and nonprobate transfers.

d.   Should the spouse assert a claim to a homestead, family allowance, or exempt personal property set-aside?
While the scope of these rights varies markedly from state to state, remember that they may afford a means of partially reordering the testator's dispositive plan by shifting more assets to the surviving spouse's pile. These rights, along with the elective share, are particularly important if the testator attempted to disinherit her spouse and they take precedence over creditors' claims. The benefits accorded are over and above the amounts passing to the spouse under the elective share, by intestate succession, or under the will. In most states, these rights are also available to minor children.

e.   Are there any community property issues?
Keep in mind that, in a community property state, one spouse can fully dispose all of her *separate* property (unless it was acquired in another state and is subject to a quasi-community property statute), but that she can dispose of only *her one-half* of the couple's community assets. If one spouse purports to dispose of the entire interest in community assets, an election will issue is raised. But note that the courts are reluctant to find that the will put the spouse to an election unless the facts clearly call for an election. Also watch for lifetime gifts of community property made by one spouse. These gifts are subject to challenge by the surviving spouse.

f.   Are there any conflict of laws issues?
Did the testator and her spouse move *from a common law state to a community property state*? In California, Idaho, Washington, and Wisconsin, any imported assets would be classified as quasi-community property, and special rules apply to their disposition at death. Most of the other community property states have a quasi-community property rule that applies to divisions upon divorce, but *not* to dispositions at death. In these states, the imported assets would be the acquiring spouse's separate property. Also consider whether the testator and her spouse moved *from a community property state to a common law jurisdiction*? Know whether the state has enacted the Uniform Disposition of Community Property Rights at Death Act. If so, the statute recognizes the surviving spouse's ownership

rights in any imported community assets. If not, the surviving spouse's rights should be recognized under a resulting or constructive trust theory.

5. Changes in Beneficiaries After Will's Execution

a. Did the testator marry or divorce after the will's execution?
If so, this may have an effect on the will. (*See* discussion in 4., above.)

b. Did the testator have children after the will was executed?
Under most states' pretermitted child statutes, a child born or adopted after the will's *execution* is entitled to an intestate share of the decedent's estate unless the will shows an intent not to make provision for such child. (In a few states, the statute applies to children alive at the time the will was executed as well as to afterborns.) But watch for factors that take the pretermitted child statute out of the question:

(1) Was the child provided for by lifetime settlement?
A lifetime gift, a bank account in the child's favor, and even a life insurance policy naming the child as beneficiary are generally held to be lifetime settlements within the meaning of the statute.

(2) Was the testator's spouse the principal beneficiary under the will?
If so, under the UPC and in many states this factor will prevent the operation of the statute as long as the spouse was the parent of the pretermitted child.

(3) Was the omission intentional?
The pretermitted child statute will not apply if it appears from the terms of the will that the omission was intentional.

(4) Did testator later execute a codicil to her will?
Under the doctrine of republication by codicil, a will is deemed to have been executed on the date of the last codicil thereto, meaning that the child would no longer be considered an afterborn child.

c. Did any beneficiary die during the testator's lifetime?
One or more of the named beneficiaries might die during the testator's lifetime. Probably no other issue is tested upon with greater frequency than the lapsed gift issue. If a beneficiary predeceases the testator, the gift lapses unless the state's anti-lapse statute applies to the gift.

(1) Does the state's anti-lapse statute apply?
The most important facts to look for are the beneficiary's relationship to the testator and the scope of the state's anti-lapse statute. Make sure that the predeceased beneficiary was within the required relationship to the testator or the statute will not apply. Also, be sure that the predeceased

beneficiary left descendants who survived the testator. The anti-lapse statute does *not* save the gift for the beneficiary's estate, but rather, her descendants take by substitution under the anti-lapse statute.

(2) Was the gift contingent on the beneficiary's survival?

If the gift was made to the beneficiary "if she survives me," the anti-lapse statute does not apply. Under the original UPC and in most states, this is true even if no alternate gift was made in the event of the beneficiary's nonsurvival. But under the revised UPC, the anti-lapse statute will apply if the will did not make an alternate gift.

(3) Did the testator and beneficiary die simultaneously, or did the beneficiary die shortly after the testator?

If the Uniform Simultaneous Death Act is applicable, and there is no sufficient evidence that the parties died otherwise than simultaneously, the beneficiary is deemed to have predeceased the testator, invoking the lapsed gift rules. (But watch for evidence of survival, even if for a short period of time.) Likewise, if the UPC's 120-hour rule controls, and if the beneficiary fails to survive the testator by 120 hours, the beneficiary is deemed to have predeceased the testator. But remember that if the gift is conditioned on the beneficiary's surviving the testator, the 120-hour rule does *not* apply and the beneficiary takes the gift even though she survived the testator by only a few hours or minutes.

(4) Was the beneficiary who predeceased the testator a residuary beneficiary?

It is important to know whether the state applies the "no residue of a residue" rule (the lapsed gift falls out of the will and passes by intestacy to the testator's heirs) or has a "surviving residuary beneficiaries" rule (the remaining residuary beneficiaries take). But under either rule, the anti-lapse statute applies if the predeceasing residuary beneficiary was within the scope of the statute *and* left descendants who survived the testator.

d. Was any beneficiary dead at the time the will was executed?

If a beneficiary died before the testator executed his will, the gift to that beneficiary is void. However, the UPC and most states apply their anti-lapse statutes in this situation.

e. Does the will make a class gift?

If the beneficiaries are described as a class (*e.g.*, "Mary Smith's children"), and one of the class members predeceases the testator, under the class gift rule the remaining class members who survive the testator take the gift. *But note:* In most states the anti-lapse statute trumps the class gift rule if the predeceasing class member was within the scope of relationship covered by the anti-lapse statute *and* left descendants who survived the testator.

(1) Was the gift to a class or to individuals?

Make sure that the gift really is to a class. Under the class gift rule, if a class member predeceases the testator his share passes to the surviving class members. But the class gift rule does not apply if the beneficiaries are individually named (*e.g.,* "to Ann, Betty, and Carl, the children of Mary Smith"). Here, if one of the named beneficiaries predeceases the testator, the lapsed gift rules discussed above apply.

(2) When does the class close?

Under the rule of convenience, the class closes when a class member is entitled to a distribution. The class closes on the testator's death if the will makes an outright gift. Only class members alive (or in gestation) at that time share in the gift; later-born class members are excluded. If the class gift is of a future interest (*e.g.,* "to my husband Hank for life, and on his death to the children of Mary Smith"), the class does not close until the termination of the preceding interest (*e.g.,* the life tenant's death).

6. Changes in Property After Will's Execution

a. Does the doctrine of ademption apply to any gifts in the will?

If the will makes a specific bequest of property and the property is not owned by the testator at death (*e.g.,* it was lost, destroyed, stolen, or sold during the testator's lifetime), the gift adeems (*i.e.,* it fails). *But remember:* Ademption applies *only to specific devises and bequests*. It does not apply to general legacies ("$5,000 to Nellie") or to demonstrative legacies ("$10,000, to be paid from the proceeds of sale of my Acme stock").

(1) Is a bequest of securities involved?

The courts apply some unusual rules of construction to bequests of securities. While a gift of "*my* 100 shares of Zircon stock" is a specific bequest, and ademption applies, a gift of "100 shares of Zircon stock" is classified as a general bequest (for purposes of ademption *only*), and ademption does not apply. Also, watch for a change in form: If a corporation is acquired by another corporation and the testator's shares of stock are replaced by the new company's stock, in most states the change is one of form only and the specific beneficiary takes the shares of the acquiring corporation.

(2) Does any statutory exception apply?

The UPC and other statutes carve out exceptions to the ademption rule. These statutes give the specific beneficiary, to the extent unpaid at the testator's death, any casualty insurance proceeds or condemnation awards related to the specific property. Also, if the testator sold the property and the contract is still executory at his death, the beneficiary is entitled to any remaining contract payments. If the testator became incapacitated and specifically devised property was sold by the guardian or conservator, the beneficiary is entitled to an amount equal to the net sale price.

b. Are any stock splits or stock dividends involved?

A specific bequest of stock carries with it any new shares produced by a *stock split* regardless of whether the split occurs before or after the testator's death. But the specific beneficiary is entitled to new shares produced by a *stock dividend* only if the dividend occurs after the testator's death.

c. Is any specifically bequeathed property subject to a lien?

Many states require the lien to be exonerated by payment from the residuary estate. However, the UPC and other states give the beneficiary exactly what the testator owned: title subject to a lien.

7. Components of a Will

a. Do the facts raise an integration issue?

The doctrine of integration is rarely tested upon. Only the sheets that were present when the will was executed comprise the testator's will if the testator intended them to be a part of the will. Watch for cases in which the staple has been removed and one of the sheets has a different typeface than the other sheets.

b. Does the doctrine of incorporation by reference apply?

Do not overlook the possibility of incorporating an extrinsic document, not present at the time the will was executed, into the will. But make sure that all of the required elements for the doctrine's application can be satisfied: the document must have been *in existence when the will was executed*, the will must *identify* the document, and the will must show an *intent to incorporate* the document.

(1) Is a list of tangible personal property involved?

The UPC and statutes in several states carve out an exception to the incorporation by reference doctrine for a list that disposes of *tangible personal property* to named beneficiaries. Such a list, if signed by the testator, is given effect even if it is written *after* the will was executed, and even though it is not witnessed. In states without this special rule, such a list can be given effect only if the incorporation by reference doctrine (above) is satisfied.

c. Does the acts of independent significance doctrine apply?

The testator can designate beneficiaries or the property that is the subject of a gift by referring to specific acts or events that have a nontestamentary motive. For example, courts will give effect to a bequest of "the automobile that I own at my death," or "$5,000 to each of my employees," even if later unattested acts by the testator (*e.g.*, buying a new car or hiring new employees) affect the gift under the will because the testator acted with a nontestamentary motive.

d. Did the testator execute a codicil to an earlier will?

The codicil must be executed with the same formalities that are required for a will. The effect of the codicil may be to: (i) modify or revoke an earlier will; (ii) republish a prior valid will; (iii) validate a prior invalid will (by incorporation by reference); or (iv) revive a previously revoked will.

8. Contractual Wills

a. Did the testator allegedly promise to make a gift by her will?

A promise to make a gift in the future, if not supported by consideration, is unenforceable. But if consideration was given for the promise, the promise may be enforceable under *contract law* and not wills law. Many states require that the contract be in writing and some require that it be referred to in the will. Under the UPC, the material provisions of the contract must be in the will, the will must expressly refer to the contract, or the contract must be in a signed writing.

b. Did the testator allegedly promise not to revoke her will?

This is something you should consider if a *joint will* (the will of two persons in a single instrument) is involved. Many state statutes require that the existence of such a contract be referred to in the will. Absent such a statute, it is generally held that the mere execution of a joint will (or of mutual wills containing reciprocal provisions), without more, is *not* sufficient to prove that such a contract existed. If a contract not to revoke is established, and one party revokes the will and writes a new will, the new will must be admitted to probate even though it was made in breach of the contract. The beneficiaries of the contract must then bring an action outside the probate court, seeking the imposition of a constructive trust.

9. Will Contests

a. Does any party have grounds for contesting the will?

An occasional question will present facts concerning the testator's mental and physical condition and the conduct of others in connection with the will's execution. The question then asks whether there are grounds for contesting the will. Generally, there will be no absolute answer. Fact issues, and not the application of legal doctrines, are involved so keep in mind that a jury would have to decide, on the evidence presented, whether the contestants have met their evidentiary burden. Consider and discuss each of the facts presented in light of the legal tests of testamentary capacity and undue influence.

(1) Does the party have standing to contest the will?

To have standing, the party must have a direct economic interest that would be adversely affected if the will is admitted to probate (generally, only the decedent's heirs or beneficiaries named in an earlier will have standing).

(2) Was the contest filed within the prescribed period of time?

The will must be contested when it is offered for probate or within the statutory time period. Under the UPC, the will contest is made in a formal testacy proceeding which must be initiated within three years after the decedent's death; if the will was probated in an informal probate proceeding then the time period is 12 months after the proceeding is completed.

b. Did the testator have sufficient capacity to make a will?

The contestants must show that the testator lacked the capacity to know and understand: (i) the nature of the act he was doing (*i.e.,* that he was writing a will); (ii) the natural objects of his bounty; (iii) the nature and value of his property; and (iv) the disposition he was making.

c. Was the will the product of an insane delusion?

Even though the testator was otherwise sane (and met the test for capacity), the contestants may be able to show that the will (or a gift therein) was the product of a persistent and irrational belief in supposed facts that have no basis except in the testator's perverted imagination, and which the testator adheres to against all evidence and reason. However, it is not enough that the testator suffered from an insane delusion—the delusion must have had a *direct effect on the will or its provisions*.

d. Did anyone exert undue influence over the testator?

The contestants have the burden of establishing: (i) the existence of the influence, (ii) its effect of overpowering the mind and will of the testator, and (iii) that the product of the influence was a testamentary instrument that expresses the will not of the testator but of the one exerting the influence. The mere opportunity to influence, susceptibility to influence due to age, illness, or physical condition, or the fact that the will makes an unnatural disposition are factors to be considered but are *not individually sufficient* to establish undue influence.

(1) Was the party who procured the will in a confidential relationship with the testator?

Watch out especially for gifts made to the attorney who prepared the will. In most states, a *presumption* of undue influence arises if a beneficiary was in a confidential relationship with the testator and played an active part in procuring the will. In some states, proof of these factors cause the burden of proof to shift to the will *proponent,* who must then show that undue influence was *not* exerted.

e. **Did anyone perpetrate a fraud on the testator?**

To establish fraud, there must have been false statements of material facts, known by the maker to be false and made with the intention of defrauding the testator, who was actually deceived by the false statements and acted in reliance on them. The fraud may consist of signing the wrong instrument (fraud in the execution) or of inducing a testamentary gift (fraud in the inducement).

f. **Did the testator make a mistake in the execution of the will?**

Extrinsic evidence is admissible to show a mistake in the execution of the will because it affects testamentary intent. For example, if evidence shows that the testator was mistaken as to the nature of the instrument she was signing (*e.g.,* she thought it was a deed), the will is denied probate because she lacked the required testamentary intent.

   (1) **Did the testator sign the wrong will?**

   If a husband signs the will prepared for his wife, and the wife signs the will prepared for her husband, be prepared to argue both ways. Some courts have denied relief on the ground that testator lacked testamentary intent with respect to the will she signed, but the better result is to grant relief since both the mistake and what the testator actually intended are so clear.

g. **Was a testamentary gift induced by a mistake?**

Extrinsic evidence is never admissible to show that the testator was mistaken in her motive for making the will. If no fraud was involved, *no relief* will be granted.

h. **Was the testator mistaken as to the contents of the will?**

Extrinsic evidence is never admissible to show a mistake in the contents of the will (an exception exists under the UPC if the testator omitted a child because she mistakenly thought the child was dead). It does not matter whether the allegation is that a gift was mistakenly omitted (or mistakenly included) in the will, or that the testator was mistaken as to the import of the will's terms; no relief will be granted. Absent fraud, it is conclusively presumed that the testator read the will and understood and *intended* its contents.

i. **Are any of the will's provisions ambiguous?**

A *latent* ambiguity arises when the will's terms, although clear on its face, are susceptible to more than one meaning when applied to the facts; *e.g.,* the will names a beneficiary, but two persons (or no person) meet the description. Parol evidence is admissible to cure a latent ambiguity. A *patent* ambiguity arises when the mistake is apparent on the face of the will; *e.g.,* the will refers to a cousin Bill and a cousin Sandy, and then makes a gift "to my cousin." The courts are divided on whether parol evidence is admissible to cure a patent ambiguity, but the better view is that it is admissible.

j. **Does the will contain a no-contest (*"in terrorem"*) clause?**

Most states enforce no-contest clauses, but such a clause does not result in a forfeiture if the court finds that the contesting party acted in *good faith* and had *probable cause* for bringing the contest, even if the contest was unsuccessful. Be sure the action is a "contest"—*e.g.,* a suit to construe the terms of a will is generally held *not* to be a contest that triggers a no-contest clause because it does not challenge the validity of the will.

10. Other Important Issues

a. **Are any nonprobate assets involved in the question?**

Nonprobate (or nontestamentary) assets are interests that pass at death *other than by will or intestacy*, and which are not subject to the personal representative's possession for purposes of administering the estate. However, the elective share statutes found in some states do apply to certain nonprobate assets. Be familiar with the scope of the state's statute with respect to such assets. The nonprobate assets you are most likely to encounter are:

(1) *Life insurance and employee benefits;*

(2) *Survivorship estates* (joint tenancies, tenancies by the entirety, and joint bank accounts with survivorship provisions); and

(3) *Interests in a revocable inter vivos trust* drafted so as to continue in operation after the testator's death.

b. **Did the decedent make a lifetime gift to any heir or will beneficiary?**

Under modern law, if the decedent died intestate and made a lifetime gift to an heir, the gift is an advancement only if there is proof that an advancement was intended. Most states require either a contemporaneous writing by the testator stating that the gift is an advancement or a written acknowledgment of the advancement by the donee. If an advancement is proven, the value of the advanced property is taken into account in making distribution of the intestate shares. If the lifetime gift is to a beneficiary named in the testator's will, the gift is presumed to be in partial or total satisfaction of the legacy. However, under the UPC and in some states satisfaction of a legacy can be shown only by a writing signed by either the donor or the donee of the lifetime gift.

c. **Has any heir or beneficiary attempted to disclaim an interest in the decedent's estate?**

To be valid for gift tax purposes, a disclaimer must be in writing, irrevocable, and filed within nine months after the decedent's death or the beneficiary's 21st birthday. Partial disclaimers are also permitted. Remember that a disclaimer cannot be made if the beneficiary has accepted the property or any of its benefits.

d. Did an heir or beneficiary murder the decedent?

Generally, a party who wrongfully brought about the death of the decedent cannot take under the decedent's will or by intestate succession, and cannot take as beneficiary under insurance policies on the life of the decedent (if he does take the gift, a constructive trust is usually imposed). Watch out for cases in which the alleged slayer is tried and found not guilty in criminal proceedings. In most states, this does not preclude a finding in a *civil proceeding* (where the evidentiary standard is "preponderance of the evidence," not "beyond a reasonable doubt") that the party did wrongfully bring about the death of the decedent.

11. Estate Administration

How much you need to know about the rules governing estate administration will depend on the scope of your course. Coverage of this area varies widely. Some professors make only passing references to the probate process, while others go into considerable detail. At the very least, be familiar with these issues:

a. What proof is required to probate a will?

Look for a valid self-proving affidavit executed by the testator and the witnesses at (or after) the will execution ceremony, which will allow the will to be admitted to probate on the strength of the affidavit. If the will was not self-proved, most states require that both attesting witnesses testify as to the circumstances surrounding the execution of the will. Be sure to know the test that must be satisfied (usually, proof of signatures) if the attesting witnesses are dead or cannot be located.

(1) When must the will be probated?

Most states require that a will must be probated within a specified time after the decedent's death (*e.g.*, three years under the UPC); otherwise, it is conclusively presumed that the decedent died intestate.

b. Are any alternatives to court-supervised administration available?

If you are in a UPC state, know the difference between an unsupervised and a supervised administration. In any state, be familiar with the jurisdiction's small estate administration rules and any other procedures that may be available for small or uncomplicated estates.

c. What powers can a personal representative exercise without court approval?

How much you are expected to know about this issue will turn on the attention given to probate procedures in your course. At the very least, know that most states have detailed rules governing a personal representative's power to sell or mortgage real property unless an unsupervised (or independent) administration is involved. Also, a personal representative usually does not have the power to continue operation of the decedent's business (*e.g.*, a sole proprietorship) without court approval.

d. **When must creditors' claims be filed?**

Most states have a special statute of limitations ("nonclaim statute") applicable to creditors' claims against the estate. Such claims must be filed within a specified period of time or the claims are barred. (A few states do not have nonclaim statutes. In these states, failure to file within the time specified in the statute simply means that the creditor will not be paid until after all timely filed claims are paid.) But remember that known and reasonably ascertainable creditors must be given *personal notice* of the estate administration before their claims can be barred under the nonclaim statute. Also, nonclaim statutes do not defeat valid security interests held by a creditor and they do not apply to the extent that the claim (*e.g.,* a tort claim) is covered by liability insurance.

e. **Is the estate partially insolvent?**

Abatement rules apply when the residuary estate is insufficient to satisfy creditors' claims. Under the UPC and in most states, gifts abate in the following order to satisfy all creditors' claims: (i) any property passing by intestacy; (ii) the residuary estate; (iii) general legacies (which abate pro rata); (iv) specific devises and bequests. As to each category, know whether personal property abates before real property.

Chapter One:
Uniform Probate Code

CONTENTS

Chapter Approach

Your Wills or Decedents' Estates casebook probably gives a lot of attention to the Uniform Probate Code ("UPC"), and your professor is likely to make quite a few references to the UPC during the semester. This probably will be true even if the course focuses on the laws of a particular jurisdiction, for the professor is likely to contrast your state's statutes and rules with the UPC provisions dealing with the same issues. This chapter briefly introduces you to the original and revised versions of the UPC and explains the history of the UPC and its current status with regard to adoption by the states. The UPC is important to know not only because it represents the modern view with respect to Wills law, and thus is often the focus of law school Wills courses, but also because most states have enacted at least a few provisions of the UPC.

A. Introduction

1. State Adoptions [§1]

The Uniform Probate Code ("UPC") has had a major impact on the laws governing decedents' estates. Eighteen states have enacted all or most of the UPC (either the original UPC promulgated in 1969 or the revised UPC promulgated in 1990): Alaska, Arizona, Colorado, Hawaii, Idaho, Maine, Michigan, Minnesota, Montana, Nebraska, New Jersey, New Mexico, North Dakota, Pennsylvania, South Carolina, South Dakota, Utah, and Wisconsin. [8 Uniform Laws Annotated Master Edition 1 (West Supp. 2002)] (Florida, although officially listed as a UPC jurisdiction, has enacted only a few UPC provisions.) Other states (*e.g.*, Alabama, California) have adopted many of the substantive UPC provisions governing wills and intestate succession, but have not adopted the UPC's procedural rules governing the administration of estates. Finally, many states have made selective adoptions of several of the UPC provisions governing wills and intestate succession. As a result, the laws of nearly all American jurisdictions have been affected by the UPC. [Roger W. Anderson, *The Influence of the Uniform Probate Code in Nonadopting States*, 8 U. Puget Sound L. Rev. 599 (1985)]

2. "Uniformity" of Adoption [§2]

Do not be misled by the caption, "*Uniform* Probate Code." The UPC has not had the same reception as, *e.g.*, the Uniform Commercial Code ("U.C.C."). As you probably know from your Sales or Commercial Transactions course, nearly all of the Articles of the UCC have been enacted virtually without change in almost all states. By contrast, as noted above, only 18 states have enacted all or nearly all of the UPC provisions, and even in these states there sometimes are variations in the provisions that have been enacted. For example, nine UPC states have enacted all or virtually all of the 1990 UPC's intestate distribution provisions; three of the UPC states have enacted (and have retained) the intestacy provisions of the original UPC; and three states listed as UPC states have borrowed some of the intestate succession rules from the UPC, but the distribution schemes are their own.

B. Two Uniform Probate Codes

1. In General [§3]

There are two Uniform Probate Codes: the original UPC (promulgated in 1969) and the revised UPC (promulgated in 1990 and amended in 1993). Several of the original UPC states have decided not to adopt all or even any of the provisions of the revised UPC, some of which have proven to be controversial. As a result, if a particular jurisdiction is described as a "UPC state," it is necessary to determine whether that state has enacted all (or most) of the revised UPC or whether, instead, that state has decided to adhere to the original UPC.

2. Original Uniform Probate Code [§4]

The original UPC, promulgated in 1969, had three objectives: First, the original UPC sought to modernize and clarify a number of substantive rules of Wills and Intestacy law that were deemed unsuitable under modern conditions. Second, the procedural rules governing the probate of wills and the administration of estates were modernized to provide a simpler and less costly alternative to court-supervised administrations. Third, the original UPC sought to bring greater uniformity to the laws governing wills and estates. (As noted above, this objective has not been realized.) The UPC was amended frequently, a number of amendments having been made in 1975, with amendments of lesser scope between 1977 and 1988.

3. Revised Uniform Probate Code [§5]

Article II, named "Intestate Succession and Wills" in the original UPC, was substantially modified in the revised UPC to reflect the increased use of nonprobate transfers (*e.g.*, revocable trusts, life insurance, and employee benefit plans) in passing wealth from generation to generation. (The Article was renamed "Intestacy, Wills and Donative Transfers.") Many of the rules formerly applicable only to wills (*e.g.*, the effect of divorce on a previously executed will) were extended to nonprobate transfers. Also, the intestate shares of surviving spouses were greatly increased. Conversely, the rules governing the effect of marriage on a previously executed will were modified to reflect the increased number of remarriages by parties with children from an earlier marriage. The rules governing a surviving spouse's elective share were radically altered to reflect a partnership theory of marriage. Significant changes, some of them controversial, also were made to the anti-lapse statute (which applies when certain will beneficiaries predecease the testator) and to other rules governing the substantive law of Wills.

4. **Terminology and Coverage in this Book [§6]**

This Summary includes citations to both the original UPC ("original UPC") and the revised UPC ("UPC") because a number of states that enacted the original UPC have not yet adopted (and may not adopt) the revised version.

Chapter Two:
Intestate Succession

CONTENTS

Chapter Approach

Chapter Approach

The typical Wills exam will contain at least one question raising intestate succession issues. Even when the particular question involves a will, intestate succession laws may be involved in distributing the estate. Also, the intestacy rules may come into play if the question involves a pretermitted child (born or adopted after the will was executed) or a pretermitted spouse (marriage after the will was executed). Therefore, for virtually every question, you should at least consider whether the laws of intestate succession apply. Ask yourself:

1. **Is There a Valid Will Disposing of All the Property?**

    If the will is valid, then it governs. If, however, the decedent in the question has left no will, the will is invalid for some reason (*e.g.*, not witnessed), or the will does not make a complete disposition of the decedent's property, then the intestate succession statute applies.

2. **Which State's Intestate Succession Statute Applies?**

    For *personal* property, the law of the *decedent's domicile* governs, regardless of where the property is located. For *real* property, under the situs rule, the law of the state in which the *property is located* governs.

3. **What Property Passes by Intestate Succession?**

    Only the "probate estate" can pass by intestacy, *i.e.*, cash, real estate, and personal property owned by the decedent at death. Nonprobate assets (*e.g.*, life insurance proceeds or property passing by right of survivorship) are not subject to the intestate distribution rules.

4. **How Should the Property Be Distributed?**

    Your question may require application of the intestacy statute of a particular jurisdiction. If your question does not provide the statute, follow the general rules:

    a. *The spouse* always takes a share, the size of which depends upon whether the decedent's descendants survive. In many states, the spouse takes one-half or one-third if there are descendants; the spouse takes all if there are no surviving descendants.

    b. *Children* inherit the entire estate if there is no surviving spouse, or a smaller share if the spouse survives the decedent.

    c. *Grandchildren and other descendants* take if their parent predeceased the decedent. In making a distribution among grandchildren, it is important that you understand how the distribution may differ depending on whether the controlling distribution rule is classic per stirpes, per capita with representation, or per capita at each generation.

> d. *Parents* (or the surviving parent) *or the descendants of parents* take if the decedent left no spouse or descendants.
>
> e. *Other relatives* ("next of kin") take before the state.
>
> f. *If there are no other takers*, the property escheats to the state.

5. **Is the Domicile a Community Property State?**

   If the decedent was domiciled in a community property state, remember that the above rules apply only to separate property. Different rules apply to community property. Keep in mind that the surviving spouse already owns half of all community property; only the deceased spouse's one-half community interest passes by intestacy.

A. Introduction

---

1. **When Intestate Distribution Rules Apply [§7]**

   The rules governing intestate succession apply when: (i) the decedent *left no will*; (ii) the decedent's *will is denied probate*, either because the will was not properly executed (*see infra*, §§345 *et seq.*) or because the will is successfully contested by the decedent's heirs (*see infra*, §§815 *et seq.*); or (iii) the decedent left a valid will but the *will does not make a complete disposition of the estate*, resulting in a partial intestacy. The intestate distribution rules also may be involved in a question involving a pretermitted spouse (*see infra*, §§195 *et seq.*) or a pretermitted child (*see infra*, §§278 *et seq.*).

2. **Common Law [§8]**

   At common law, separate rules applied to the inheritance of real property and personal property: Real property *descended* to the decedent's *heirs,* while personal property was *distributed* to the decedent's *next of kin.*

3. **Modern Law [§9]**

   Today, every jurisdiction has supplanted the common law rules by enacting statutes that regulate the distribution of property by intestate succession. In nearly all states, the rules governing intestate succession are the *same* for real and personal property. However, in determining the intestate share of a surviving spouse, a few states have separate schemes for the descent of land and the distribution of personal property. [*See, e.g.,* Del. Code tit. 12, §502; Tex. Prob. Code §38(b); Va. Code §§64.1-1, 64.1-11] In modern usage, the terms "heirs" and "next of kin" are synonymous, although "heirs" is the preferred term for describing persons who take either real or personal property by intestacy.

4. **What Law Governs [§10]**

   In general, the law of the state where the decedent was *domiciled at death* governs the disposition of *personal property*, and the law of the state where *real property is located* governs the disposition of real property. (*See* Conflict of Laws Summary.)

Example: Rochester, a New York domiciliary, dies intestate. Rochester owned real property and tangible personal property situated in New York. He also owned real property located in North Carolina and had several stock certificates and two items of valuable jewelry in a safe deposit box in a Boston bank. Devolution of the New York land and *all personal property* (including the contents of the safe deposit box in Boston) is governed by the New York intestacy statutes. Devolution of the North Carolina land is governed by the North Carolina intestacy statutes.

---

5. Property Subject to Intestate Distribution [§11]

The intestacy statutes (or for that matter a will, if the decedent left one) apply only to the decedent's *probate* or *testamentary* estate.

a. Probate estate [§12]

The probate estate consists of those assets owned at death that pass by will or inheritance and that are subject to administration by the decedent's personal representative (*e.g.*, real estate owned solely by the decedent or any share he owned as tenant in common, cash, stocks and bonds in the decedent's name, etc.).

b. Nonprobate assets [§13]

The intestate succession rules do not apply to nonprobate assets, and those assets are not subject to administration by the decedent's personal representative. Also, nonprobate assets (sometimes called nontestamentary assets) are not subject to disposition by the decedent's will. There are four categories of nonprobate assets:

(1) Contract [§14]

Property that passes at death pursuant to a contract or agreement is a nonprobate asset. The two most commonly encountered examples are life insurance proceeds, which are payable to the beneficiary designated by the insured in his contract with the insurance company, and death benefits paid to designated beneficiaries under an individual retirement account or an employee pension or profit-sharing plan.

Example: Mary has a $100,000 Prudential life insurance policy that names her daughter Susan as beneficiary. Mary dies leaving a will that provides: "I direct that the proceeds of my Prudential life insurance policy be paid to my son John." The will provision is ineffective, and Susan takes the insurance proceeds as a valid nonprobate transfer. Naming and changing a life insurance beneficiary is governed by the terms of the

---

contract between the insured and the insurance company, and the contract does not permit naming a new beneficiary by will.

(2) Right of survivorship [§15]

Property held in a valid joint tenancy with the right of survivorship, property owned by spouses as tenants by the entireties, and funds on deposit in a valid survivorship bank account pass by right of survivorship to the surviving party. These interests do not pass under the decedent's will, and are not subject to estate administration or to the intestacy laws.

(3) Trust [§16]

Interests owned by the decedent merely as a trustee or trust beneficiary are nonprobate assets.

Example: Olivia places assets in a revocable or irrevocable *inter vivos* trust that names Ted as trustee. Under the terms of the trust, the trustee is to pay the income to Olivia for life, and on Olivia's death is to distribute the trust principal to Olivia's descendants. Legal title to the trust assets is in Ted; Olivia and her descendants have equitable interests. On Olivia's death, disposition of the trust principal is governed by the terms of the trust, and not by Olivia's will or the intestacy statutes. (*See* Trusts Summary.)

Example: Similarly, Ted in the example above cannot pass title to the trust property to his descendants, even though he has legal title to the trust property. Ted has a fiduciary duty to hold the trust property for the benefit of the beneficiaries (Olivia and her descendants) and cannot control disposition of the property by his will.

(4) Power of appointment [§17]

If the decedent held a power of appointment over an asset, that asset is not subject to the intestacy laws. (*See* Future Interests & Perpetuities Summary.)

Example: Testator's will devises property in trust, to pay the income to Beneficiary for life, and on Beneficiary's death to distribute the trust principal to such one or more of Beneficiary's descendants as Beneficiary appoints by will. If Beneficiary does not exercise the power by will, the property is to pass to Beneficiary's children. **If Beneficiary dies intestate,** the appointive assets pass to the "takers in default of appointment" specified in Testator's will (Beneficiary's children). The intestacy statutes have no application to the property. **If Beneficiary leaves a will that exercises the power** in favor of her child, Daughter, by the appointment Beneficiary is regarded as having "filled in the blanks" in

Testator's will. Although Beneficiary's will is the instrument by which the taker of the property is identified, *the property is deemed to have passed from Testator to Daughter.* The appointive assets are not part of Beneficiary's probate estate and are not subject to administration by Beneficiary's personal representative.

EXAM TIP	**gilbert**

You will sometimes encounter an exam question where the decedent attempts to dispose of a nonprobate asset by will (*e.g.,* give away property held in joint tenancy with the right of survivorship or change the beneficiary of his life insurance policy). Don't be fooled by the will provision. Such nonprobate assets are not affected by the will. The *will provision is disregarded*, and the property passes to the survivor or original beneficiary despite the will provision.

PROBATE ESTATE VS. NONPROBATE ASSETS — gilbert

	PROBATE ESTATE ASSETS	NONPROBATE ASSETS
TYPE OF ASSETS	Assets owned by decedent at death that pass by will or inheritance and that are subject to administration by personal representative	Assets that do not pass by will or inheritance and that are not subject to administration by personal representative
EXAMPLES	Real property held solely by decedent or his share of tenancy in common property	Real property held in joint tenancy *with right of survivorship* or *by the entireties*
	Cash or bank account solely in decedent's name	Joint bank account with *right of survivorship*
	Stocks, bonds in decedent's name	Trust assets or life insurance or pension plan proceeds
	Personal property	Power of appointment property

B. Patterns of Intestate Distribution

1. Rules Vary from Jurisdiction to Jurisdiction [§18]

Except for states that have enacted the UPC, there are no two states whose intestacy laws are identical. There are even variations among the UPC states. The revised UPC made significant changes to the intestate distribution rules in the original UPC. To date, about one-half of the UPC states have chosen to stay with the intestacy rules of the original UPC (sometimes with variations).

a. Common law jurisdictions and community property states compared [§19]

In classifying states with respect to marital property, jurisdictions can be divided into two categories. In *common law states* (sometimes called "separate property" states), a husband's earnings belong to the husband, and a wife's earnings belong to the wife. In *community property states*, the salary and wages of either spouse (and the acquisitions therefrom) are community property, owned one-half by each spouse. In those states, separate property consists of property owned by either spouse before marriage, and property acquired during the marriage by gift, will, or inheritance. Community property states have two sets of intestacy statutes: one governing community property and the other governing separate property. In most of the community property states, separate property passes under the inheritance rules described below. The intestate succession rules applicable to community property are discussed *infra, §§58 et seq.*

b. Representative intestacy statutes [§20]

The following discussion summarizes the general patterns of intestate distribution found in many states. For the intestacy rules of a particular state, it is essential to consult that state's statutes. The Appendix to this Summary contains the intestate succession rules of the original UPC and the revised UPC, and also examines representative intestacy statutes of both common law jurisdictions and community property states. For common law jurisdictions, the Florida, Illinois, and New York statutes are summarized. For community property states, the California and Texas statutes are outlined.

2. Intestate Share of Surviving Spouse

a. Spouse takes as heir in all states

(1) Common law [§21]

At common law, a spouse was not an heir. The decedent's property passed by intestacy to his descendants or (if no descendants) to collateral kin. If the decedent left no blood relations, the estate escheated to the Crown. The surviving spouse took only a dower interest (if a widow) or a curtesy estate (if a widower) in the decedent's property. (*See infra, §§188-194.*)

(2) Modern law [§22]

Under modern law, the surviving spouse takes an intestate share of the decedent's estate *in all jurisdictions*.

b. Decedent survived by descendants—non-UPC states [§23]

If the decedent is survived by a spouse and by descendants (children, grandchildren, etc.), in most states the spouse inherits a fractional share of the decedent's estate (typically, *one-third or one-half*), whether the descendants are from the decedent's marriage to the surviving spouse or from an earlier marriage. [*See, e.g.,* Kan. Stat. §59-504—one-half; Tenn. Code §31-2-104] In a few states, the spouse inherits the entire estate if all of the decedent's surviving descendants are also descendants of the surviving spouse, but inherits only one-half if the decedent was survived by descendants from an earlier marriage. [*See, e.g.,* Iowa Code §633.212; Wis. Stat. §852.01(a)]

(1) Terminology—"descendants" and "issue" [§24]

Some intestacy statutes use the term *descendants* when referring to children and more remote offspring, while other statutes refer to them as *issue*. The terms "descendants" and "issue" are synonymous. This Summary uses the term "descendants" in referring to the children and more remote offspring of a person.

c. Decedent survived by descendants—original UPC [§25]

Under the original UPC, the surviving spouse inherits *one-half* of the decedent's estate if the decedent was survived by one or more descendants who are not descendants of the surviving spouse. The remaining one-half passes to the decedent's descendants, whether from this marriage or an earlier marriage. If all of the decedent's surviving descendants are also descendants of the surviving spouse (*e.g.,* a one-marriage situation), the surviving spouse takes the *first $50,000 plus one-half of any balance* of the estate. The descendants take the remaining one-half. [Original UPC §2-102]

(1) Rationale

The surviving spouse is given a larger share than in most statutes on descent and distribution in existence when the UPC was promulgated. The UPC section reflects the desires of most married persons, who almost always leave all of a moderate estate or at least one-half of a larger estate to the surviving spouse when a will is executed. For a small estate (less than $50,000 after homestead allowance, exempt property, and family allowance) the UPC goes even further by giving the surviving spouse the entire estate if there are only children who are issue of both the decedent and the surviving spouse. This avoids protective proceedings as to property otherwise passing to their minor children. [Original UPC §2-102 Comment]

d. Decedent survived by descendants—revised UPC [§26]

The revised UPC, in addition to increasing the intestate share of the surviving spouse, recognizes that, in today's society, one or both spouses may have descendants from an earlier marriage as well as descendants from their marriage to each other. [UPC §2-102] The revised UPC provides for the following distribution:

(1) Neither has descendants from earlier marriage [§27]

If all of the decedent's surviving descendants are also descendants of the surviving spouse and the spouse does not have other descendants who survived the decedent, the surviving spouse inherits the *entire estate*.

(2) Surviving spouse has descendants from earlier marriage [§28]

If all of the decedent's surviving descendants are also descendants of the surviving spouse, but the spouse has other descendants who survived the decedent, the surviving spouse inherits the *first $150,000 plus one-half of any balance* of the decedent's estate. The remaining one-half of the balance (if any) passes to the decedent's descendants.

(3) Decedent has descendants from earlier marriage [§29]

If one or more of the decedent's descendants are not descendants of the surviving spouse, the spouse takes the *first $100,000 plus one-half of any balance* of the decedent's estate. The remaining one-half of the balance (if any) passes to the decedent's descendants.

EXAM TIP	gilbert

Always look for any *surviving descendants* in an exam fact pattern *before* computing the surviving spouse's share of the decedent's estate. If there are surviving descendants, depending on the intestacy statute involved, you may have to determine whether they are descendants of the decedent, surviving spouse, or both. At that point, you can decide how much of the decedent's estate is given to the surviving spouse, and how much, if any, is given to the descendants.

SURVIVING SPOUSE'S SHARE WHEN THERE ARE DESCENDANTS			gilbert
SHARE OF SPOUSE	NON-UPC STATE	ORIGINAL UPC STATE	REVISED UPC STATE
WHEN SOME DESCENDANTS NOT SPOUSE'S	Typically 1/3 or 1/2 of estate	1/2 of estate	First $100,000 plus 1/2 of any balance of estate
WHEN DESCENDANTS ARE ALSO SPOUSE'S	Typically 1/3 or 1/2 of estate	First $50,000 plus 1/2 of any balance of estate	Entire estate if no descendants from earlier marriage, *or* First $150,000 plus 1/2 of any balance of estate if spouse has descendants from earlier marriage

e. Decedent not survived by descendants

(1) Majority rule—spouse inherits entire estate [§30]

In most states, if the decedent is survived by a spouse but not by any descendants, the surviving spouse inherits the *entire estate*—even if the decedent was survived by one or both of his parents. [*See, e.g.,* Ga. Code

§53-2-1(b)(1); Ill. Comp. Stat. ch. 755, §5/2-1; Miss. Code §91-1-7; Tenn. Code §31-2-104]

(2) Minority rule—parents also inherit [§31]

In a substantial minority of jurisdictions, if the decedent is survived by a spouse and one or both of his parents, the spouse inherits *one-half* of the estate, and the other one-half passes to the *parents or surviving parent*. In these states, the surviving spouse inherits the entire estate only if the decedent was not survived by either parent. [*See, e.g.,* D.C. Code §19-302; Wash. Rev. Code §11.04.015] Under the original UPC, the spouse inherits the *first $50,000, plus one-half of any balance* of the estate. The remaining one-half passes to the parents or surviving parent. [Original UPC §2-102]

(3) Revised UPC [§32]

Under the revised UPC, the spouse inherits the *first $200,000, plus three-fourths of any balance* of the estate, and the remaining one-fourth of the balance (if any) passes to the decedent's parents or surviving parent. [UPC §2-102(2)] The spouse inherits the entire estate only if the decedent was not survived by descendants or either parent.

f. When spouse disqualified from taking as heir [§33]

In several states, the surviving spouse is disqualified from taking an intestate share under certain circumstances. [13 A.L.R.3d 446] While the list of disqualifying circumstances varies from state to state, the New York statute is fairly typical. A spouse is disqualified if he: (i) obtained a divorce in another jurisdiction, not recognized as valid in New York; (ii) abandoned the deceased spouse and the abandonment continued until the spouse's death; or (iii) failed or refused to support the deceased spouse. [N.Y. Est. Powers & Trusts Law §5-1.2] Under most of these statutes, the same conduct disqualifies the spouse from taking an elective share (*see infra*, §§222-224), a family allowance, exempt personal property, and homestead rights (*see infra*, §§295-314). [*See, e.g.,* Va. Code §64.1-16.3]

3. Intestate Share of Children and Other Descendants [§34]

The remaining estate that does not pass to the surviving spouse, or the entire estate if the decedent is not survived by a spouse (or if the spouse is disqualified from taking), passes to the decedent's children and descendants of deceased children. In all states, *parents and collateral kin never inherit if the decedent was survived by children* or more remote descendants. Also, a decedent's grandchildren inherit only if the parent through whom they claim did not survive the decedent.

---

e.g. **Example:** Widower dies intestate survived by his daughter, Delilah, and his grandchild (Delilah's child), Gregory, as his nearest kin. Delilah inherits the entire estate.

---

4. **Distributions Among Descendants of Deceased Children [§35]**

In making distributions among children and the descendants of deceased children, three different patterns of distribution are used by the states: (i) *classic per stirpes*, under which the shares are divided at the child level even if no children survived the decedent; (ii) *per capita with representation* ("modern per stirpes"), under which the shares are first divided at the first generational level at which there are living takers; and (iii) *per capita at each generation*, under which takers at each generational level always take equal shares.

a. **Common law—classic per stirpes [§36]**

At common law and in a minority of jurisdictions today, the distributions among children and the descendants of deceased children is per stirpes, whose literal translation is "by the roots." Each child is a root, and one share passes to each child or, if the child is deceased, to her descendants by representation. *The division of stirpital shares is always made at the child level, regardless of whether there are any living takers at that level.* This method of distribution is sometimes called "classic" or "strict" per stirpes, to distinguish it from "modern" per stirpes. (*See infra*, §37.) [*See, e.g.*, Fla. Prob. Code §732.104; Ill. Comp. Stat. ch. 755, §5/2-1; Restatement (Second) of Property §28.2]

b. **Majority rule—per capita with representation [§37]**

The method of distribution applied in most jurisdictions, which is also called "per stirpes," is sometimes referred to as "modern" per stirpes, to distinguish it from "classic" or "strict" per stirpes (*see supra*). A more accurate label is "per capita with representation." Under this method of distribution, *the shares are determined at the first generational level at which there are living takers.* Each living person at that generational level takes one share, and the share of each deceased person is divided among her descendants by representation. This form of distribution is adopted by the original UPC and a number of states. [*See, e.g.*, Original UPC §2-106; Mass. Gen. Laws ch. 190, §§3, 8; Mo. Rev. Stat. §474.020; Tex. Prob. Code §43; Va. Code §64.1-3; Wash. Rev. Code §11.04.015(2)(c)]

c. **Revised UPC—per capita at each generation [§38]**

Under the revised UPC and in several non-UPC states, descendants take per capita at each generation. Under this pattern of distribution, the property is divided into equal shares at the first generational level at which there are living takers. Each living person at that level takes an equal share, but the shares of deceased persons at that level are combined and then divided equally among the takers at the next generational level. Thus, *persons in the same degree of kinship to the decedent always take equal shares.* [UPC §2-106; N.Y. Est. Powers & Trusts Law §1-2.16; N.C. Gen. Stat. §29-16]

d. **Illustration [§39]**

W, who was single, died intestate, survived by the family members indicated in the diagram, below. She was survived by one child (A) and six grandchildren.

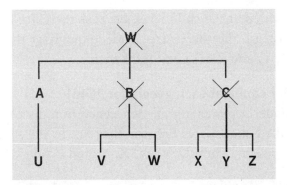

(1) Classic per stirpes [§40]

Under a classic per stirpes distribution, the shares are always divided at the child level. Thus, A takes one-third; V and W take B's one-third share or one-sixth each; and X, Y, and Z take C's one-third share or one-ninth each. U does not inherit because A is alive to take as heir.

(2) Per capita with representation [§41]

Under a per capita with representation distribution, the shares are divided at the child level because there is a living taker at that level. A takes one-third; V and W again split B's share and take one-sixth each; and X, Y, and Z split C's share and take one-ninth each. V, W, X, Y, and Z take by representation the shares their parents would have inherited had they survived to be heirs.

(a) Comment

Note that if there is at least one living taker at the first generational level, there is *no difference* between a per capita with representation distribution and a classic per stirpes distribution.

(3) Per capita at each generation [§42]

Under a per capita at each generation distribution, the shares are initially divided at the child level, and A takes one-third. The other two one-third shares are combined into a single share (amounting to two-thirds of the estate) and distributed in equal shares at the next generational level. V, W, X, Y, and Z take two-fifteenths each.

e. Distinguish—all children deceased [§43]

Consider the same facts, except that A also predeceased W. W was survived by her six grandchildren as her nearest kin.

(1) Classic per stirpes [§44]

Under a classic per stirpes distribution, the shares are always divided at the child level. U takes one-third, V and W take one-sixth each, and X, Y, and Z take one-ninth each.

(2) Per capita with representation [§45]

Under a per capita with representation distribution, the shares are *not* divided at the child level, because there are no living takers at that level. Instead, the shares are divided equally at the grandchild level. U, V, W, X, Y, and Z take one-sixth each.

(3) Per capita at each generation [§46]

Under a per capita at each generation distribution, all six grandchildren take equal shares because they are in the same degree of kinship to the decedent. Thus, U, V, W, X, Y, and Z take one-sixth each.

DIVISION OF DECEDENT'S INTESTATE ESTATE AMONG DESCENDANTS—A COMPARISON	**gilbert**
PER STIRPES	Division made at child level even if there are no surviving takers at that level. Shares of deceased members descend to that member's descendants.
PER CAPITA WITH REPRESENTATION	Division made at first generational level with living takers. Shares of deceased members descend to that member's descendants.
PER CAPITA AT EACH GENERATION	Division made at first generational level with living takers. Shares of deceased members are combined and divided equally among all takers at the next generational level.

5. Decedent Not Survived by Spouse or Descendants

a. Majority rule—to parents or surviving parent [§47]

If the decedent is not survived by a spouse or descendants, in most jurisdictions the estate is inherited by the decedent's parents (one-half to each) or the surviving parent (who takes all). [See UPC §2-103; Ala Code §43-8-42; Iowa Code §633.219(2); Tenn. Code §31-2-104(b)(2)]

b. Minority rule [§48]

In several states, the decedent's parents, brothers, and sisters take equal portions. [See, e.g., Ill. Comp. Stat. ch. 755, §5/2-1; Miss. Code §§91-1-3, 91-1-11] In a few states, if only one parent survives, that parent takes one-half of the estate, and the other one-half passes to the decedent's brothers and sisters (and the descendants of deceased brothers and sisters). [See, e.g., Tex. Prob. Code §38]

EXAM TIP	gilbert
Remember that in most states, parents, descendants of parents (brothers and sisters), and collateral kin (e.g., cousins, aunts, uncles) never inherit if the decedent is survived by a *spouse, children, or more remote descendants*. So always check for a spouse and descendants (including grandchildren, etc.) before considering the shares of other family members.	

c. When parent disqualified from inheritance [§49]

Under the revised UPC and by statute in several states, a parent or his kin cannot inherit from or through a child unless the parent has openly treated the child as his and has not refused to support the child. [UPC §2-114(c); *and see* N.Y. Est. Powers & Trusts Law §4-1.4; Va. Code §64.1-16.3]

6. Decedent Not Survived by Spouse, Descendants, or Parents [§50]

In nearly all states, if the decedent is not survived by a spouse, descendants, or parents, the estate passes to the *descendants of the decedent's parents*. In making a distribution among brothers and sisters and the descendants of deceased siblings, a particular state will apply the same rule (classic per stirpes, per capita with representation, or per capita at each generation) that is applied to distributions among the decedent's descendants. (*See supra,* §§35-46.)

7. Decedent Not Survived by Spouse, Descendants, Parents, or Descendants of Parents [§51]

In nearly all states, if the decedent left no parents or descendants of parents, one-half of the estate passes to *maternal grandparents* (or their descendants), and the other half passes to *paternal grandparents* (or their descendants). [*See, e.g.,* Tenn. Code §31-2-104(a)(4); Wash. Rev. Code §11.04.015]

8. Intestate Distribution Beyond Grandparent Level [§52]

With respect to inheritance beyond grandparents and their descendants, the rules vary from state to state.

a. Majority rule [§53]

If the decedent is not survived by a spouse, grandparents, or descendants of grandparents, in many states the estate is divided into maternal and paternal shares. One-half of the estate goes to the nearest kin on each side of the family, regardless of how remotely they are related to the decedent. [*See, e.g.,* Tex. Prob. Code §38; Va. Code §64.1-1]

b. Minority rule—"laughing heir" statutes [§54]

A substantial minority of states cut off inheritance by "laughing heirs"—*i.e.,* persons so remotely related to the decedent that they suffer no sense of loss, but only gain, at the news of his death. Typically, these statutes prevent inheritance by persons related to the decedent beyond the level of grandparent or descendant of a grandparent. [*See* UPC §§2-103, 2-105; Fla. Prob. Code §732.103] The estate instead *escheats to the state* (*see* below). Other states limit inheritance to relatives within a specified degree of kinship to the decedent. [*See, e.g.,* Kan. Stat. §59-509—sixth degree of kinship] In these states, a person with no close relatives must write a will to avoid an escheat. [*See **In re Estate of Jurek,*** 428 N.W.2d 774 (Mich. 1988)]

9. Escheat [§55]

If the decedent is not survived by any living relations (in states that do not limit the degree of relationship required for inheritance) or is not survived by grandparents

gilbert

THE DECEDENT'S INTESTATE ESTATE PASSES IN THE FOLLOWING ORDER:

Surviving Spouse
Share may vary based on whether decedent was survived by descendants.

↓

Descendants of Decedent
Adopted children take same share as natural children; stepchildren and foster children do not inherit. (*See infra*, §§75, 93.)

↓

Parents of Decedent
Parents share estate equally or if only one parent survives, he takes entire estate.

↓

Descendants of Parents
Take in the same manner as descendants of decedent would have taken (*i.e.*, per stirpes, etc.).

↓

Grandparents and Their Descendants
One-half of estate passes to maternal side and the other half passes to paternal side.

↓

Nearest Kin
One-half of estate passes to nearest maternal kin and the other half passes to nearest paternal kin.

↓

The State
Called "escheat."

or descendants of grandparents (in states that have a "laughing heir" statute), the estate passes ("escheats") to the state.

a. Exception [§56]
In a few states, if the decedent left no living relations to take as heirs, the estate passes to the heirs of the decedent's previously deceased spouse (if any) before it escheats to the state. [*See* Va. Code §64.1-1]

10. Ancestral Property [§57]
A few states apply a special rule to property that the decedent received by gift, will, or inheritance *from a parent*. If the decedent is not survived by a spouse or descendants, this "ancestral property" reverts back to the parent or (if the parent is deceased) to his heirs. [*See, e.g.,* Ky. Rev. Stat. §391.020] *Rationale:* This rule is consistent with the parent's probable intent that the property return and be distributed to the donor's other children or grandchildren, rather than pass to the decedent's collateral heirs. [**Francis v. Justice,** 687 S.W.2d 868 (Ky. 1985)]

C. Intestate Distribution in Community Property States

1. Introduction [§58]
Eight states have been community property jurisdictions since their inception: Louisiana, Texas, New Mexico, Arizona, California, Washington, Idaho, and Nevada. In 1987, Wisconsin became the ninth community property jurisdiction by enacting the Uniform Marital Property Act ("UMPA"). [Wis. Stat. §766.001] (The Wisconsin terminology is different—community property is called "marital property," and separate property is called "individual property"—but the UMPA's basic features essentially make Wisconsin a community property state.) Although the community property laws of the nine states vary markedly in detail, there is agreement on certain basic definitions:

a. Separate property [§59]
Separate property is defined as property owned by a spouse *before marriage* and property acquired during marriage *by donation* (*i.e.,* gift, will, or inheritance). In most of the states, the income from separate property is separate property; however, in Idaho, Louisiana, and Texas, the income from separate property is community property. In all nine states, separate property passes by intestacy in accordance with the rules described above.

b. Community property [§60]
Community property is negatively defined as *all property acquired during marriage* that is *not separate property*. The primary sources of community

property are the salary and wages of either spouse and the acquisitions therefrom. Under the "community presumption," all property on hand on dissolution of the marriage (whether by divorce or death) is presumptively community property. The burden of establishing that a particular asset is separate property (*i.e.,* owned before marriage, acquired during marriage by donation, or purchased with separate funds) is on the party so contending.

2. Decedent Survived by Spouse But Not Descendants [§61]

In all community property states, if the decedent is not survived by descendants, his one-half share of the community estate passes to the surviving spouse. The other one-half of the community estate does *not* pass to the spouse by inheritance; it already belongs to her. [**Jones v. State,** 5 S.W.2d 973 (Tex. 1928)] As a result, the surviving spouse succeeds to the *entire community estate.*

3. Decedent Survived by Spouse and Descendants [§62]

There are two basic patterns for distribution of community property if the decedent is survived by descendants.

a. All to surviving spouse [§63]

In several states, the surviving spouse takes the entire community estate even if the decedent is survived by descendants from an earlier marriage. [*See* Original UPC §2-102A; Cal. Prob. Code §6401(a)]

b. Descendants from earlier marriage [§64]

Under the revised UPC and in other states, the surviving spouse takes the entire community estate *only if* all of the decedent's descendants are also the surviving spouse's descendants. If the decedent was survived by descendants some of whom are not descendants of the surviving spouse, the decedent's one-half community property interest passes to his descendants, and the surviving spouse takes only her one-half community property share. [*See* UPC §2-102A; Ariz. Rev. Code §14-2102; Tex. Prob. Code §45]

4. Quasi-Community Property [§65]

Quasi-community property is property acquired by one spouse while *domiciled in another state* that would have been characterized as community property had it been acquired while domiciled in the community property state.

a. Quasi-community property statutes [§66]

Four community property states have quasi-community property statutes that apply to decedents' estates. [*See* Cal. Prob. Code §6401(b); Idaho Code §15-2-201; Wash. Rev. Code §26.16.220; Wis. Stat. §§851.055, 861.02] (The Wisconsin statute calls this property "deferred marital property.") These statutes are, in effect, elective share statutes (*see infra,* §§195 *et seq.*) that restrict the "acquiring spouse's" power of lifetime and testamentary disposition over these imported assets. The acquiring spouse may dispose of only his one-half interest in quasi-community property by will; the other one-half passes to the surviving spouse, who cannot be deprived of this amount by will. If the acquiring spouse leaves no will, all of the quasi-community property is inherited by the surviving spouse.

(1) Distinguish—divorce [§67]

Several of the other community property states apply the quasi-community property principle to divisions upon *divorce,* but not to distributions upon the acquiring spouse's death. In these states, quasi-community property is treated the same as "true" community property for purposes of property divisions upon divorce [*see* Ariz. Rev. Stat. §25-318; Tex. Fam. Code §7.001; **Rau v. Rau,** 432 P.2d 910 (Ariz. 1967)]; but if the marriage is dissolved by the death of one spouse, these imported assets are considered the *separate* property of the acquiring spouse (*see* below).

b. Conflict of laws—separate property [§68]

In the states that do not have quasi-community property statutes applicable to distributions at death, there is a source of separate property, not covered by the statutory definitions, that is the product of conflict of laws principles.

Example: Harry and Wendy were married in Minnesota in 1998, and lived there until they moved to Texas in 2002. At the time of the move, Harry owned securities worth $100,000, acquired from his earnings in Minnesota. Two years after the move, Harry died intestate. Intestate succession of Harry's estate is governed by Texas law because he was domiciled in Texas at his death. The securities brought from Minnesota pass by intestacy under the rules applicable to separate property. [*See* **Hanau v. Hanau,** 730 S.W.2d 663 (Tex. 1987)] *Rationale:* Although the securities were acquired during marriage, they were acquired while the couple was domiciled in a common law state, where a husband's salary is his property and a wife's salary is her property. The ownership character of an asset is governed by the laws of the marital domicile at the time the asset was acquired, and that ownership is not altered when the couple moves to another state. Stated another way: Under the Constitution, property rights are not lost by moving to another state. (*See* Conflict of Laws Summary.) Since the securities were Harry's property in Minnesota, they were his separate property in Texas.

Compare: In California, Idaho, Washington, and Wisconsin, the $100,000 in securities brought from Minnesota would be classified as quasi-community property.

D. Attempt to Disinherit—Negative Bequests

1. **Introduction [§69]**

   Suppose that a testator's will expressly disinherits an heir, but then the testator dies partially intestate. Does the heir take an intestate share when she has been expressly disinherited by the will?

2. **Majority Rule [§70]**

   At common law and in most states today, the heir takes an intestate share notwithstanding the words of disinheritance in the will. *Rationale:* If the decedent does not make a complete disposition of his estate, the undisposed of property passes by force of statute to the heirs, and the testator's intent is irrelevant as to any property passing under the intestacy statutes. [*In re* **Estate of Cansik,** 476 N.E.2d 738 (Ill. 1985); *In re* **Smith's Estate,** 353 S.W.2d 721 (Mo. 1962)]

3. **Revised UPC—Negative Bequest Rule [§71]**

   The revised UPC and statutes in several non-UPC states have overturned this formalistic and intent-defeating result. Under these statutes, a decedent by will may expressly exclude the right of an individual to succeed to property passing by intestate succession. These are sometimes called "negative bequest" statutes because they specify how property shall *not* be disposed of. [UPC §2-101(b); N.Y. Est. Powers & Trusts Law §1-2.18; Tex. Prob. Code §§3(ff), 58(b)]

   EXAM TIP   gilbert

   If you encounter a fact pattern on your exam in which the testator wants to disinherit an heir, the best approach is to have him *dispose of all of his property by a valid will or lifetime transfer* (e.g., a gift) to ensure that there are no assets remaining in the estate that can pass through intestacy. This is the only sure way to disinherit an heir. If the state in question has a negative bequest statute, the testator can also, just to be safe, include a provision in the will specifying that the heir is disinherited. *But note:* If the state does *not* have a negative bequest statute, the will provision is irrelevant, and if the testator does not effectively dispose of all of his property by will or lifetime transfer, the heir will take.

Chapter Three: Inheritance Rights as Affected by Status of Child or Sibling

---

CONTENTS

Chapter Approach

Inheritance rights may be affected by the "status" of the heirs (*e.g.*, an adopted child may inherit from the adopting parent but not from the natural parent). Exam questions covering these issues sometimes appear as part of an intestate distribution problem. Therefore, keep a watchful eye out for the following:

1. **Adopted Children**

    Adopted children become the children of the adopting parents for purposes of intestate succession, and in most cases they lose the right to inherit from the natural parent.

2. **Nonmarital Children**

    Nonmarital children inherit from the mother and her kin, but generally need some additional proof (*e.g.*, an adjudication or formal acknowledgment of paternity) to inherit from and through the father.

3. **Posthumous Children**

    Children conceived during the father's life but born after his death generally may inherit from the decedent.

4. **Stepchildren and Foster Children**

    Stepchildren and foster children may *not* inherit from a stepparent or foster parent absent certain circumstances giving rise to "adoption by estoppel."

5. **Half Bloods**

    Half brothers and half sisters (who share only one common parent with the decedent) take the same shares as whole bloods in most states; however, in some states they take only half as much as siblings of the whole blood.

A. Adopted Children

1. **Early Law [§72]**

    Although the adoptive relationship was recognized in Roman and Hebrew law, adoption was unknown to the English common law. Beginning with legislation in Massachusetts in 1851, all of the states now permit adoptions. However, in many states the statutes governing inheritance by adopted children were not enacted until well into the 20th century. As a result, early cases had to deal with the inheritance rights of adopted children without the aid of a statute.

    a. **Stranger to the adoption rule [§73]**

        Absent a statute, most courts held that an adopted child could inherit from the adopting parents, but not from the adopting parents' kin. The rationale was that an adoption should not make an adopted child the heir of a "stranger to the adoption" (*i.e.,* anyone other than the adopting parent). [*See* **Welch v. Funchess,** 71 So. 2d 783 (Miss. 1954); **Hockaday v. Lynn,** 98 S.W. 585 (Mo. 1906)]

b. Natural parents [§74]

It was generally held that an adopted child continued to have inheritance rights from and through his natural parents, even though adopted into a new family. [80 A.L.R. 1398]

2. Modern Law

a. Adopting parents [§75]

In all states that have enacted statutes governing inheritance rights of adopted children, an adopted child has the *same inheritance rights as a natural child.* Thus, the adopted child and her issue can inherit from the adopting parents *and* from the adopting parents' kin. Also, the adopting parents and their kin can inherit from and through the adopted child. [*See* UPC §2-114; Kan. Stat. §59-501(a); Wash. Rev. Code §11.04.085]

b. Natural parents [§76]

The right of an adopted child to inherit from and through her natural parents (and the right of natural parents and their kin to inherit from and through the child) depends on whether the child has been adopted by a new family or by the spouse of a natural parent.

(1) Adoption by new family [§77]

In nearly all states, adoption of the child by a new family *severs the parent-child relationship* between the child and the natural parents. As a result, the adopted child and her descendants have no inheritance rights from or through the natural parents, and the natural parents and their kin have no inheritance rights from or through the child. *Rationale:* Allowing the child to inherit from her biological family interferes with the establishment and development of the relationship with the adoptive family. [*See* Tenn. Code §31-2-105(a)(1); Wash. Rev. Code §11.04.085]

Example: Teenager gives birth to Child out of wedlock. Child is placed for adoption and is adopted by a new family. Nearly all states require, as a predicate to the adoption, a judicial termination of the parent-child relationship between Teenager and Child. After the adoption, Child and her kin have no inheritance rights from or through Teenager, and Teenager and her kin have no inheritance rights from or through Child.

(2) Adoption by natural parent's spouse [§78]

When a child is adopted by the spouse of a natural parent, the child has inheritance rights from that natural parent as well as the adopting parent (and vice versa), but the statutes take different positions as to inheritance rights vis-a-vis the other natural parent.

(a) Inheritance rights from other natural parent terminated [§79]

In several states, adoption of a child by the spouse of a natural parent terminates inheritance rights from and through the *other* natural parent. [*See* Del. Code tit. 12, §508; Md. Est. & Trust Code §1-207(a); Mo. Rev. Stat. §474.060]

> **e.g. Example:** H and W have a child, C. H dies and W marries H2, who adopts C. Then H's mother, Grandmother, dies intestate. Under this type of statute, C has no inheritance rights from Grandmother because the adoption terminated the relationship between C and H. [**Hall v. Vallandingham,** 540 A.2d 1162 (Md. 1988)] Likewise, if C had died intestate, H's kin could not inherit from C.

(b) Inheritance rights from other natural parent preserved [§80]

In other states, adoption of a child by the spouse of a natural parent has no effect on the relationship between the child and *either* natural parent. [*See* Original UPC §2-109; Ill. Comp. Stat. ch. 755, §5/2-4; N.Y. Dom. Rel. Law §117(1)(e)]

> **e.g. Example:** Under the facts of the example above, C can inherit from Grandmother. Also, if C had died intestate, H's kin could inherit from C.

(c) Revised Uniform Probate Code—one-way street rule [§81]

Under the revised UPC, the adopted child and her kin have inheritance rights from and through the natural parent who married the adopting parent (and vice versa), and the child and her kin have inheritance rights from and through the other natural parent, but the other natural parent and his kin have *no inheritance rights* from or through the child. [UPC §2-114(b)]

> **e.g. Example:** Under the revised UPC view, C in the example above can inherit from Grandmother, but if C had died intestate, H's kin could *not inherit* from C.

B. Nonmarital Children

1. Common Law [§82]

At common law, a nonmarital child was *filius nullius* (*i.e.,* a child of no one) and had no inheritance rights from either parent. Only the child's spouse and issue could inherit from the child.

2. Modern Law—Inheritance from Mother [§83]

In all states today, a nonmarital child inherits from his natural mother and her kin, and they can inherit from and through the child.

3. Inheritance from Father [§84]

Until recently, many statutes provided that a nonmarital child had inheritance rights from and through the father (and vice versa) *only if* the child was legitimated by the marriage of the father and mother after the child's birth. [*See, e.g.,* Ill. Prob. Act §12—before amendment in 1975]

a. Constitutional problem [§85]

The above Illinois statute was held unconstitutional on equal protection grounds. The Supreme Court held that a statute fixing the inheritance rights of a nonmarital child can exact a higher standard of proof of fatherhood than of motherhood because of the evidentiary problems involved. However, a statute that allows for *no* means of proving fatherhood for inheritance purposes denies equal protection. [**Trimble v. Gordon,** 430 U.S. 762 (1977)]

b. Modern law [§86]

Nearly all states have amended their intestacy statutes to eliminate the constitutional problem. Generally, these statutes provide that the inheritance rights may be established by one of several means, including (i) the father's marriage (or attempted marriage) to the mother; (ii) a formal acknowledgement of paternity; (iii) a judgment in a paternity suit; or (iv) (after the man's death) proof of paternity by clear and convincing evidence. [*See* Ala. Code §43-8-48(2); Miss. Code §91-1-15; Tex. Prob. Code §42] Other states look to the existence of a family relationship or the existence of paternal support to establish inheritance rights. [*See* Cal. Prob. Code §6453]

c. Original Uniform Probate Code [§87]

The original UPC treats the child as an heir of the father if: (i) the father and mother participated in a void marriage ceremony before or after the child's birth, (ii) paternity is established by adjudication during the man's lifetime, or (iii) paternity is established by clear and convincing evidence after the man's death. *But note*: The father and his kin cannot inherit from or through the child **unless** the father openly treated the child as his own and did not refuse to support the child. [Original UPC §2-109]

d. Revised Uniform Probate Code [§88]

The revised UPC expands the inheritance rights of nonmarital children by providing that a child is the child of his natural parents regardless of their marital status. Establishment of a parent-child relationship for purposes of inheritance is governed by the Uniform Parentage Act or (in states that have not enacted it) applicable state law. Also, *either* parent's refusal to support the child or treat the child as his or her own precludes inheritance by that parent. [UPC §2-114]

C. Posthumous Children

1. In General [§89]

Under common law principles and by statute in many states, a child conceived during the father's lifetime but born after the father's death is considered the decedent's child for inheritance purposes. [*See* Ill. Comp. Stat. ch. 755, §5/2-3; Tex. Prob. Code §41(a)]

2. Presumption [§90]

The courts have developed a **rebuttable** presumption that the normal period of gestation is 10 lunar months (280 days). Thus, a child born more than 280 days after the decedent's death presumptively was sired by someone else. However, the presumption is rebuttable, and whether the child is the decedent's child even though born more than 280 days after the "father's" death is a jury question. [**Byerly v. Tolbert,** 108 S.E.2d 29 (N.C. 1959)]

3. Uniform Probate Code [§91]

The UPC extends the above rule: Any relative (and not just the decedent's child) in gestation at the decedent's death inherits as if she had been born in the lifetime of the decedent if the child lives for at least 120 hours after birth. [UPC §2-108]

D. Artificial Insemination and In Vitro Fertilization

1. In General [§92]

In several states, it is provided by statute that a child conceived by the artificial insemination of a married woman is the husband's legitimate child for inheritance purposes *if the husband consented* to the insemination. Some of these statutes raise a presumption that the husband gave consent [Mich. Comp. Laws §333.2824], while other statutes require written evidence of consent. Increasingly encountered are statutes that apply the same rule to children produced by in vitro fertilization or other reproductive technology.

E. Stepchildren and Foster Children

1. General Rule [§93]

In general, a *stepchild or foster child* has *no* inheritance rights from his stepparent or foster parent. For example, if a woman with a child marries, and her husband does not adopt the child, there is no legal relationship between the stepchild and the stepfather. There may be a *familial* relationship (*i.e.*, the child may have lived in the man's home and may have called him "daddy"), but inheritance requires a *legal* relationship. [**Bank of Maryville v. Topping**, 393 S.W.2d 280 (Tenn. 1965)] However, a few states permit inheritance by stepchildren (but not by foster children) if the decedent left no kin within a prescribed degree of kinship. [*See, e.g.,* Md. Est. & Trust Code §3-104(e); Wash. Rev. Code §11.04.095]

2. Exception—Adoption by Estoppel [§94]

A number of jurisdictions apply the doctrine of adoption by estoppel (sometimes called equitable adoption) in cases involving an *unperformed agreement to adopt*. This doctrine, based on estoppel principles, allows a stepchild or a foster child to inherit from the stepparent or foster parent just as though the child had been adopted. *Rationale:* It would be inequitable to allow the stepparent or foster parent to avoid performing the agreement because, *e.g.*, the child's relationship with her natural parents may have been terminated in reliance on the agreement.

Example: Foster parents obtain custody of a child based on an agreement with the natural parent that they will adopt the child and "give him our name." After obtaining custody, the foster parents do not perform their agreement. One of the foster parents dies intestate. The child may inherit from the decedent. Because in equity the foster parent would be estopped to deny performance of the agreement, so also are the foster parent's natural kin estopped to deny that an adoption took place. [**Barlow v. Barlow,** 463 P.2d 305 (Colo. 1969); **Perry v. Boyce,** 34 N.W.2d 570 (Mich. 1948)]

a. **Minority rule [§95]**

Some jurisdictions do not recognize the adoption by estoppel doctrine, and thus the child has no right to inherit even if the stepparent or foster parent had promised to adopt the child. [**Bank of Maryville v. Topping,** *supra,* §93; **Clarkson v. Briley,** 38 S.E.2d 22 (Va. 1946)]

b. **Applies only to estate of stepparent or foster parent [§96]**

Because the basis of the estoppel is the stepparent's or foster parent's conduct in failing to perform the agreement to adopt, only those claiming through the stepparent or foster parent are estopped. Thus, if the sister of one of the foster parents dies intestate, the child has no interest in his "aunt's" estate. [**Sheaffer v. Sheaffer,** 292 N.W. 789 (Iowa 1970)]

c. **One-way street [§97]**

The doctrine operates only in favor of the child. Suppose there is an unperformed agreement to adopt, but it is the stepchild or foster child who dies intestate, single, and wealthy. The stepparent or foster parents do *not inherit* from the child. Application of the doctrine of adoption by estoppel does not result in the creation of an adoptive parent-adoptive child relationship; rather, it operates to estop the stepparent or foster parents from denying that an adoption took place. The child did not do anything to give rise to an estoppel. [**Heien v. Crabtree,** 369 S.W.2d 28 (Tex. 1963)]

F. Collateral Kin of the Half Blood

1. **Half Bloods Defined [§98]**

Persons are related by the half blood if they have only one common ancestor, whereas they are related by the whole blood if they have two common ancestors. Most inheritance cases dealing with half bloods and whole bloods involve brothers and sisters (and their descendants), but the same rules apply to inheritance by other collateral relatives.

2. **Common Law Rule [§99]**

The common law rule wholly excluded relatives of the half blood from inheritance of real property. This rule has been abolished by statute in all states.

3. **Majority Rule [§100]**

Most states now ignore the common law rule and make *no distinction* between siblings of the whole blood and half blood. [UPC §2-107; Ala. Code §43-8-46; Wis. Rev. Stat. §854.21(4); **Gradwohl v. Campagna,** 46 A.2d 850 (Del. 1946)] e.g. **Example:** Consider the following family tree:

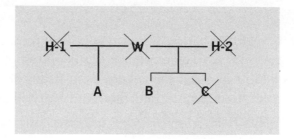

Suppose that C dies intestate, survived by her half brother A and her whole sister B as her nearest relations. What distribution should be made? In most states, A and B take equal shares of C's estate.

a. Exception for ancestral property [§101]

Several states that have adopted the majority position make an exception for "ancestral property." Kindred of the half blood inherit equally with those of the whole blood in the same degree, unless the decedent acquired the property by devise or gift from one of her ancestors, in which case only those kin who are related to that ancestor by the whole blood can participate in the inheritance. [*See* Okla. Stat. tit. 84, §222; Wash. Rev. Code §11.04.035]

4. Other Solutions

a. Whole bloods preferred [§102]

In some states, siblings of the same ancestral blood are preferred over siblings of the half blood. (Thus, in the above example, C's entire estate would pass by intestacy to B.) *But note:* Half bloods are not entirely excluded from inheritance; they take if the decedent was not survived by siblings of the whole blood (or descendants of those siblings). [*See* Miss. Code §91-1-5]

b. Half bloods take half as much as whole bloods [§103]

In several states, siblings of the half blood may inherit, but they take only half as much as siblings of the whole blood. Under this rule, in the above example, B would inherit two-thirds of C's estate, and A would inherit one-third. [*See* Fla. Prob. Code §732.105; Tex. Prob. Code §41(b); Va. Code §64.1-2]

EXAM TIP   **gilbert**

Remember that the rules in this chapter apply only if the decedent died *intestate*. If the decedent executed a valid will, the terms of the will control. For example, if the decedent left his entire estate to his natural child who was placed for adoption, that child will inherit the entire estate, even if the child would not have inherited *any* part of the estate if the decedent had died intestate.

INHERITANCE RIGHTS OF CHILDREN—A REVIEW

gilbert

ADOPTED CHILDREN	Generally, adopted children inherit *from the adoptive parents* in the same manner *as any natural child*. Inheritance rights from *natural parents* are usually severed, except in a few limited circumstances (*e.g.,* child adopted by natural parent's spouse).
NONMARITAL CHILDREN	The majority of states allow nonmarital children to inherit from the father if the father *married* the mother after the child's birth *or if paternity can be established* (*e.g.,* father's acknowledgment, judgment in paternity suit).
POSTHUMOUS CHILDREN	Children born after their father's death are entitled to inherit from the father if born within *280 days after the father's death*.
STEPCHILDREN AND FOSTER CHILDREN	Stepchildren and foster children generally *cannot inherit* from stepparents or foster parents unless they are adopted. Some states allow them to inherit if adoption by estoppel can be proved (*i.e.,* there was an unperformed agreement to adopt).
HALF BLOODS	In the majority of states, children of the half blood *take the same* as children of the whole blood.

Chapter Four: Succession Problems Common to Intestacy and Wills

CONTENTS

Chapter Approach

This chapter covers certain problem areas common to intestacy and wills. Some topics are more likely than others to be tested, but all deserve careful consideration. Consider especially the following:

1. When the decedent and an heir or will beneficiary *die together or in quick succession*, you need to know whether the question is governed by the *Uniform Simultaneous Death Act* or the UPC's *120-hour rule*. The applicable statute will affect distribution of the estate. Also, look for a will provision making survival a condition of the gift, because this may keep the Uniform Act and the 120-hour rule from applying.

2. When the decedent makes a *lifetime gift to an heir or will beneficiary*, consider whether the gift should be treated as an *advancement* or *partial satisfaction of a legacy*. If so, it may affect the donee's share of the estate.

3. Always remember that an heir or will beneficiary can *disclaim* all or part of her share of the estate, but the disclaimer must meet specific statutory requirements to be valid and tax-free.

4. Occasionally, an heir or will beneficiary *causes the death of the decedent*. By statute in some states, and under a constructive trust theory in other states, a slayer forfeits his interest in the estate, but only if the killing is intentional and unlawful.

5. This chapter also covers a *nonresident alien's right to take property*. This right may be limited by statute, but the statute cannot violate any United States treaty or constitutional provision.

A. Simultaneous Death

1. In General [§104]
A person cannot take as an heir or will beneficiary unless she survives the decedent for at least an instant of time. However, it is often difficult to determine whether the person survived the decedent (*e.g.*, when the person and the decedent are both fatally injured in the same accident). To address this problem, all jurisdictions except Louisiana [La. Civ. Code art. 936] have enacted either the Uniform Simultaneous Death Act ("USDA") or the UPC's 120-hour survival rule.

2. Uniform Simultaneous Death Act [§105]
Under the USDA, if the title to property or the devolution thereof depends upon

priority of death, and if there is *no sufficient evidence* that the parties have died otherwise than simultaneously, the *property of each person is disposed of as if he had survived the other person*. [*See* Ga. Code §53-10-2; Mass. Gen. Laws ch. 190A, §1; N.Y. Est. Powers & Trusts Law §2-1.6]

a. Purposes of the USDA [§106]

The USDA prevents property from passing to the estate of an heir or beneficiary who died simultaneously with the decedent and therefore did not live long enough to enjoy ownership of the property. Instead, the *property passes to the decedent's surviving heirs or beneficiaries*. The USDA also tends to avoid administration of the same assets in two estates in quick succession (*i.e.*, the decedent's and heir's estates), and may avoid double estate taxation of the same assets in two estates.

Example: Carol and her son Shawn are both killed instantly in an automobile accident; neither left a will. For purposes of distributing Carol's intestate estate, she is deemed to have survived Shawn and her estate is distributed to her surviving heirs as though Shawn predeceased her. Conversely, Shawn's intestate estate descends to his surviving heirs and Carol is deemed to have predeceased him.

EXAM TIP   **gilbert**

Whenever you see an exam question that has people *die at or about the same time*, you should discuss the Uniform Simultaneous Death Act (and probably the UPC 120-hour rule—*see infra*). To understand the **USDA**, keep in mind its purpose and its limitations. Its main purpose is to avoid having property pass to someone who basically takes it only technically—*i.e.*, doesn't live long enough to enjoy it, and so the property *just passes through his estate*. The USDA prevents this from happening by providing that each person's property passes to his heirs or beneficiaries as if the other person had predeceased him. *But note:* This happens *only in the limited situation where it seems the people died simultaneously*—if there is evidence that one person outlived the other even by just a short period of time, the USDA does not apply and the property passes from the first decedent to the second and then through the second decedent's estate to his heirs or will beneficiaries.

b. Application of USDA

(1) Intestate succession, wills, life insurance policies [§107]

Under the USDA, in the case of simultaneous deaths, an intestate estate is distributed as though the owner of property survived the heir, testamentary assets are distributed as though the testator survived the will beneficiary, and life insurance proceeds are paid as though the insured survived the beneficiary (absent a contrary provision in the will or insurance policy). Application of the USDA to wills is discussed more fully in Chapter X. (*See infra*, §§687, 691-694.)

> **e.g.** **Example:** George is the insured under a $100,000 life insurance policy that names his wife, Barb, as the primary beneficiary "if she survives the insured," and his son, Junior, as the alternate beneficiary. George's will devises his residuary estate "to Barb if she survives me; otherwise to his other son, Jeb." Barb has no will. George and Barb die simultaneously in the crash of a private plane. The life insurance proceeds are payable to Junior, and George's residuary estate passes to Jeb because George is deemed to have survived Barb. For purposes of distributing Barb's intestate estate, she is deemed to have survived George.

(2) Joint tenancies; tenancies by the entirety [§108]

If joint tenants or tenants by the entirety die simultaneously, *one-half* of the property passes through one party's estate as though he survived and the other half passes through the other party's estate as though she survived, regardless of which party furnished the consideration for the joint property's acquisition. *Rationale:* There is no evidence of survival to trigger the right of survivorship.

(3) Community property [§109]

If a husband and wife die simultaneously, *one-half* of the community property passes through the husband's estate as though he survived his wife, and the other half passes through the wife's estate as though she survived her husband.

c. Evidence of survival—USDA does not apply [§110]

The USDA applies only when there is *no sufficient evidence* that the parties died other than simultaneously. If there is sufficient evidence that *one party survived the other*, even for a brief period of time, the USDA does not apply.

> **e.g.** **Example:** Edna and her daughter are fatally injured in an automobile accident. Edna is pronounced dead at the scene of the accident; her daughter dies at a local hospital 71 minutes later. Since there is clear evidence of survival, for purposes of distributing Edna's estate, her daughter is deemed to have survived Edna. [**White v. Taylor,** 286 S.W.2d 925 (Tex. 1956)]

> **e.g.** **Example:** Husband and Wife are killed instantly in the crash of a private plane. An autopsy reveals that Husband's brain was smashed and there was no carbon monoxide in his blood stream. Wife's brain was intact, and carbon monoxide in her blood stream indicated that she was breathing when fire broke out after the crash. According to one court, this constituted sufficient evidence that Wife survived Husband. [*In re* **Bucci's Will,** 57 Misc. 2d 1001 (1968)]

(1) Comment

Finding sufficient evidence of survival based on an autopsy, as in the above example, undermines the policy of the USDA. However, the problem does not lie with the court's accepting the evidence, but with the USDA itself. The USDA covers only simultaneous deaths and not deaths in quick succession (such as the 71-minute example), even though these cases raise the same concerns about double administration and possibly double taxation of the same assets.

(2) Standard of proof—no sufficient evidence [§111]

"Sufficient evidence" is a very low standard of proof. It can be met with expert testimony in almost all cases. Thus, some states have increased the standard of proof of survival to "clear and convincing evidence." [*See, e.g.*, Cal. Prob. Code §220]

EXAM TIP **gilbert**

In real life, the USDA is of rather limited use. With modern medical/forensic technology, often one can find evidence that *one person survived the other for at least a short time*. However, the USDA continues to come up on law school exams, and quite often it resolves the "simultaneous" death issue because your professor wants to see if you know how to apply the Act. (Of course, if the question has facts showing one party's survival, then after stating the rule, you should discuss why it does not apply.)

---

d. Contrary provision—USDA does not apply [§112]

The presumption raised by the USDA does not apply if the decedent's will or other instrument makes some other provision regarding survival. (*See infra*, §113.)

(1) Planning recommendation [§113]

When drafting wills, it is advisable to make a beneficiary's taking contingent on surviving the testator by a specific period of time (*e.g.*, 30 days). Such a provision would produce a satisfactory result in the 71-minute case and the plane crash case discussed in the above examples.

(2) Marital deduction [§114]

In making a federal estate tax marital deduction gift by will, it may be advisable to *reverse* the USDA presumption in order to take advantage of the deduction. Such a *reverse presumption clause* in a will is given effect for federal tax purposes. (*See* Estate & Gift Tax Summary.)

Example: Wendy's will makes a marital deduction gift to her husband "if he survives me." The will further provides: "For purposes of the marital deduction gift, if my husband and I die under such circumstances that there is no sufficient evidence as to which of us survived, my husband shall be considered to have survived me." This clause would secure the marital deduction for Wendy's estate if she and her husband died simultaneously.

3. Uniform Probate Code—120-Hour Rule [§115]

The UPC deals with the problem of deaths in quick succession by providing that absent a contrary will provision, a person must survive the decedent by *120 hours* in order to take as heir or will beneficiary. Several states that have not adopted the UPC have nevertheless adopted the 120-hour survival rule. [*See, e.g.,* Tex. Prob. Code §47]

a. Intestate heir must survive by 120 hours [§116]

Under the UPC, a person who fails to survive the decedent by 120 hours is deemed to have predeceased the decedent for purposes of intestate succession, homestead allowance, and exempt personal property set-aside. [UPC §2-104]

(1) But note—rule does not apply if result is escheat [§117]

The 120-hour survival rule does *not* apply if the result of its application would be an escheat to the state. In such a case, the person takes as an heir even if he survives the decedent by less than 120 hours.

b. Will beneficiary must survive by 120 hours [§118]

Absent a contrary provision in the will, a will beneficiary who does not survive the testator by 120 hours is deemed to have predeceased the testator. [UPC §2-601] Application of the 120-hour rule to wills is discussed more fully in Chapter X. (*See infra,* §§688-690.)

c. Joint tenancies [§119]

The original UPC's 120-hour rule does *not apply* to joint tenancies with right of survivorship or tenancies by the entirety. *But note:* The revised UPC and several states that have adopted the 120-hour rule have *extended* its application to survivorship estates. Thus, if neither owner survives the other by 120 hours, the property passes one-half as though one party had survived and one-half as though the other party had survived. [UPC §2-702(c); *and see* Tex. Prob. Code §47]

Example: Andy and Brian own 1,000 shares of Acme Corporation common stock as joint tenants with right of survivorship. Andy dies; Brian dies 36 hours later. Under the original UPC, the 120-hour rule does not apply and title to the Acme stock passes to Brian by right of survivorship since Brian survived Andy. Under the revised UPC rule, a one-half interest in the stock passes under Andy's will as though he survived Brian, and the other one-half interest passes under Brian's will as though Brian survived Andy.

EXAM TIP   **gilbert**

Note that the UPC attempts to solve the simultaneous death problem by *requiring an heir or will beneficiary to outlive the decedent by at least 120 hours* (five days). Basically, the rule just avoids evidence problems like checking blood for carbon monoxide, etc., to see who lived a few minutes longer. The 120-hour rule still has its *limitations*: If the heir or will beneficiary lives, *e.g.,* a mere six days, the property passes through his estate even though he may not have had much time to enjoy it. Also, the rule doesn't apply if it would result in escheat to the state. And finally, the rule does not apply to joint tenancies with right of survivorship or tenancies by the entirety, although the revised UPC rule would divide such property as if each joint tenant survived the other.

---

d. Standard of proof [§120]

Under the original UPC, if the time of death of the decedent and the other person cannot be determined, and it cannot be established that the person survived the decedent by 120 hours, it is *presumed* that the person *failed to survive* for the required period. However, the UPC did not specify what standard of proof had to be established to overcome the presumption. [Original UPC §2-104] Under the revised UPC, proof that the person survived the decedent by 120 hours must be established by *clear and convincing evidence*. [UPC §2-702]

COMPARISON OF UNIFORM SIMULTANEOUS DEATH ACT AND UPC 120-HOUR RULE   **gilbert**

	USDA	UPC 120-HOUR RULE
RULE	Each party is treated as having survived the other unless there is sufficient evidence that the parties did not die simultaneously.	Heir or will beneficiary must have survived the decedent by 120 hours to share in the estate. The rule does not apply if the result would be escheat.
STANDARD OF PROOF	Evidence of survival must be by sufficient evidence in some states and clear and convincing evidence in other states.	Evidence of survival must be by clear and convincing evidence.

B. Advancements and Satisfaction of Legacies

1. Advancement of Intestate Share

a. Common law [§121]

At common law, any lifetime gift to a *child* was presumed to be an advancement (*i.e.,* an advance payment) of the child's intestate share, to be taken into account in distributing the decedent's property at death. The common law rule is based on the assumption that a parent would want to treat all his children equally and would want lifetime gifts to be considered in making a distribution of his estate. [*See* **Clement v. Blythe,** 248 S.W.2d 883 (Ark. 1952)] The burden of establishing that a lifetime gift is *not* an advancement is on the party so contending. Note that the common law presumption of advancement applies only to gifts to *children*—not to collateral kin (*e.g.,* a sister).

b. Modern law [§122]

Although a few states continue to apply the common law rule that a lifetime gift to an heir is presumptively an advancement (and in Kentucky the presumption is irrebuttable [**Remmele v. Kinstler,** 298 S.W.2d 680 (Ky. 1957)]), nearly all states have enacted statutes governing advancements. Most state statutes now apply the advancements doctrine to gifts to *any heir* (*e.g.,* a nephew), and not just to a child or other descendant, and have *reversed the common law presumption* entirely. Under these statutes, a gift to an heir is *not* presumed to be an advancement absent proof that an advancement was intended. These statutes follow several patterns:

(1) Minority view—oral or written proof of advancement [§123]

A few statutes merely provide that a lifetime gift to an heir is not an advancement unless proved to be an advancement. Proof of intent to make an advancement can be based on *oral testimony* or *written evidence.* [*See* Iowa Code §633.224; Wash. Rev. Code §11.04.041]

(2) Majority view—written evidence of advancement [§124]

In many states, a lifetime gift to an heir can be treated as an advancement *only if* (i) expressly declared as such in a writing signed by the donor, *or* (ii) acknowledged as such in a writing signed by the donee. A finding of an advancement in these states cannot be based on oral testimony or other evidence.

(a) Timing of written evidence [§125]

Under statutes requiring written evidence of an advancement, the timing of the writing may be important.

1) UPC and majority view [§126]

A majority of states follow the revised UPC pattern: A writing signed by the *donor* must be *contemporaneous* with the gift, but a written acknowledgment of the advancement by the *donee* can be made *at any time.* [UPC §2-109; Fla. Prob. Code §733.806]

2) Contemporaneous writing [§127]

In other states, the writing signed by the donor *or* the acknowledgment signed by the donee must be *contemporaneous* with the gift in order to be admissible as establishing an advancement. [*See* N.Y. Est. Powers & Trusts Law §2-1.5]

3) Writing made at any time [§128]

In yet another group of states, the written evidence of an advancement (whether a statement by the donor or an acknowledgment by the donee) can be made *at any time*. [*See* Ill. Comp. Stat. ch. 755, §5/2-5; Or. Rev. Stat. §112.135]

(b) Comment

The requirement of a writing has effectively abolished the advancement doctrine in these jurisdictions. A person sophisticated enough to see the need for a writing is probably also sophisticated enough to write a will so as to avoid the intestacy rules altogether. There has been a sharp decline in litigation raising advancement issues in these states. [Mary Louise Fellows, *Concealing Legislative Reform in the Common-Law Tradition: The Advancements Doctrine and the Uniform Probate Code*, 37 Vand. L. Rev. 671 (1984)]

EXAM TIP   **gilbert**

Although cases dealing with advancements are not a widely litigated area of probate law, they are a likely source of Wills exam questions. Remember to discuss the advancements doctrine anytime you see a *lifetime gift to an heir*.

---

c. Procedure if advancement found [§129]

If an advancement is established, the advancee must allow the value of the advanced property to be "brought into hotchpot" in order to share in the intestate estate. ("Hotchpot" is the common law term still used by many courts to describe the advancement computation.) This does not mean that the advancee must give the property back (even in cases where the advancement exceeds the intestate share). It simply means that the value of the property is added to the estate, in an accounting sense only, to determine the intestate shares of each heir.

Example: Wilma, a widow, gives land to her daughter Andrea. Thereafter, Wilma dies intestate survived by three children: Andrea, Brian, and Charles. Wilma's estate is worth $90,000. The gift to Andrea is determined to be an advancement, and the property's value for advancement purposes is $30,000. This figure is added to Wilma's estate:

$$\begin{array}{ll} \$90,000 & \text{Wilma's intestate estate} \\ +30,000 & \text{value of advancement to Andrea} \\ \hline \$120,000 & \end{array}$$

The total amount ($120,000) is then divided into three shares of $40,000, and Andrea is deemed already to have received $30,000 of her share. Thus Wilma's intestate estate is distributed as follows: $10,000 to Andrea, $40,000 to Brian, and $40,000 to Charles.

Compare: Suppose instead that the value of the property given to Andrea was $60,000 and not $30,000. The value of the advanced property would exceed Andrea's one-third share of the estate as augmented by the advancement—($90,000 + $60,000) ÷ 3 = $50,000. Would Andrea have to give any portion of the property back? No. Andrea must allow the advanced property to be brought into hotchpot *only if* she wishes to share in the intestate distribution. Here Andrea would not come into hotchpot. She would keep the land, and Brian and Charles would inherit equal shares of $45,000 each.

EXAM TIP	gilbert

For advancement questions, remember that the advancee doesn't have to give the property back—in fact she may not even have it anymore. She must only bring the *value of the gift* into hotchpot, and she does this *only if she wants to share* in the decedent's intestate estate. If she chooses not to share in the estate, she keeps the gift and the decedent's estate is distributed among the remaining heirs.

d. When valuation of advancement is made [§130]

In most states, the advanced property is brought into hotchpot at its *date-of-gift* value, not its value at the time of decedent's death. [*See* D.C. Code 19-319; Ill. Comp. Stat. ch. 755, §5/2-5] Under the revised UPC, the property is valued at the time the heir came into *possession or enjoyment* of the property or at the *decedent's death*, whichever occurs first. (In most cases, of course, this would be the date of the gift.) [UPC §2-109] In a few states, the property is valued as of the decedent's death. [*See, e.g.*, N.Y. Est. Powers & Trusts Law §2-1.5]

Example: Juanita leases Blackacre for a five-year period and executes a deed to transfer Blackacre to her son Pedro after the lease expires. The properly executed deed is delivered to Pedro but Juanita dies before the termination of the lease. In most states, the value of Blackacre will be determined as of the date of delivery of the deed (*i.e.*, date of gift). In a few states, Blackacre is valued as of the date of Juanita's death. Under the UPC, Blackacre is valued as of the date of Juanita's death, because she died before Pedro came into possession of Blackacre.

DETERMINING THE VALUE OF AN ADVANCEMENT	gilbert
MAJORITY VIEW	Value of advancement determined as of the *date of the gift*.
MINORITY VIEW	Value of advancement determined as of the date of the *decedent's death*.
UPC VIEW	Value of advancement determined as of date of the *advancee's possession* or the date of the *decedent's death*, whichever occurs first.

e. **Partial intestacy [§131]**

In most states, the advancement doctrine does *not* apply if the decedent left a will that does not make a complete disposition of the estate. *Rationale*: It is presumed that the testator was mindful of the lifetime gifts he had made at the time he executed the will. (However, the doctrine of satisfaction of legacies (*see infra,* §§134-142) might be applicable to any gifts made after the will's execution.)

(1) **Revised Uniform Probate Code [§132]**

The revised UPC treats advancements under partial intestacy the same as those under a total intestacy. Thus, an advancement is deducted from a partially intestate estate if the statutory requirements are satisfied (*i.e.,* contemporaneous writing by the donor or written acknowledgment by the donee). [UPC §2-109]

f. **Advancee predeceases decedent [§133]**

If the party who received the advancement predeceases the decedent, in most states with statutes requiring that advancements must be evidenced by a writing, the advanced property is not taken into account in determining the intestate share of the advancee's descendants *unless* the written declaration or acknowledgment so provides. [UPC §2-109]

2. **Satisfaction of Legacies [§134]**

Suppose that a person writes a will, and thereafter makes a lifetime gift to a beneficiary named in the will. Is the gift treated as being in partial or total satisfaction of the legacy?

a. **Common law [§135]**

At common law, and in states that have not enacted statutes dealing with the question, a gift to a *child or other descendant* of the testator is *presumptively* in partial or total satisfaction of any gifts made to the child in a previously executed will. [*See* **Selby v. Fidelity Trust Co.,** 51 A.2d 822 (Md. 1947)] But in the case of a gift to *any other will beneficiary,* no presumption as to satisfaction of the legacy arises. The gift is treated as being in satisfaction of the legacy *only* if it is shown to have been so intended by the testator. [*See* **Lake v. Harrington,** 48 So. 2d 845 (Miss. 1950)]

(1) **General legacy [§136]**

The above rule applies to *general* legacies (*i.e.,* legacies payable out of the general assets of the estate and that do not require delivery of a particular item of property). [26 A.L.R.2d 9]

---

e.g. **Example:** Theresa's will includes legacies of $20,000 to her daughter Dana and $10,000 to her niece Nora. Thereafter, Theresa gives Dana $5,000, and gives Nora $3,000. Under the common law rule, the gift to Dana is presumptively in partial satisfaction of the $20,000 legacy, but the presumption is rebuttable. The gift to Nora is treated as being in partial satisfaction of the $10,000 legacy only if it is shown that Theresa intended this result (*e.g.*, she told a friend that the gift to Nora was in satisfaction of her legacy).

EXAM TIP · **gilbert**

The doctrine of satisfaction of legacies applies *only to general legacies* (*i.e.*, those payable out of general assets of estate). It does *not* apply to *specific bequests* (*i.e.*, a gift that can be satisfied only by delivery of the particular item of property). If a decedent makes a lifetime gift of a specific item of property devised in her will, the doctrine of *ademption by extinction* applies (*see infra*, §§772-802). For example, if in the above example Theresa had devised her gold watch to Nora by her will and subsequently gave the watch to Nora, the gift adeems (*i.e.*, it fails because it is no longer in Theresa's estate).

---

(2) Gifts prior to will's execution [§137]

The satisfaction of legacies doctrine does *not* apply to gifts made by the testator *before* the will's execution. *Rationale:* The testator was no doubt conscious of the earlier gift when she made the legacy in her will. [*See* **Lake v. Harrington**, *supra*, §135] However, the doctrine of republication by codicil (*see infra*, §637) does not operate to revive a legacy that already has been satisfied by an earlier gift. [*See* **Colley v. Britton**, 123 A.2d 296 (Md. 1956)]

b. Testator's intent controls [§138]

Under the common law rule, application of the satisfaction doctrine depends on the testator's intent. In ascertaining intent, courts look to statements made in the will itself or to *extrinsic evidence*, particularly declarations made by the testator at or near the time of the gift.

(1) Specific purpose presumption [§139]

If a bequest was made for a specific purpose, and a lifetime gift is made for the same purpose, it is presumed that the gift was in partial or total satisfaction of the bequest. [*See* **Austin v. Austin**, 22 N.W.2d 560 (Neb. 1946)

Example: Tammy executes a valid will that includes a clause that states, "I give $100,000 to my brother, Brad, so that he can buy a house." One year later, Tammy gives Brad $75,000 and tells him that she wants him to buy a house with the money. The lifetime gift is presumed to be in partial satisfaction of the legacy in the will because Tammy made it clear that it was for the same purpose—so that Brad could buy a house.

---

c. **Statutory solutions [§140]**

In contrast to the doctrine of advancements, only about one-half of the states have statutes dealing with satisfaction of legacies. However, most states with statutes requiring that an advancement must be proved by a writing impose the same requirements for proof of satisfaction of legacies.

(1) **Timing of written evidence [§141]**

As with advancements, some statutes require that the donor-testator's statement that the gift is intended as being in satisfaction of the legacy must be written *contemporaneously* with the gift, but the *donee's* acknowledgment of the gift as a satisfaction may be written *at any time*. [*See* UPC §2-609; Fla. Prob. Code §732.609] In other states, *both* the donor's written statement and the donee's acknowledgment must be made *contemporaneously* with the gift. [*See* N.Y. Est. Powers & Trusts Law §2-1.5] In still other states, the written statement by the testator or acknowledgment by the donee can be made *at any time*.

(2) **Will provides for deduction of lifetime gifts [§142]**

By statute in several states, a lifetime gift to a will beneficiary is also treated as in partial or total satisfaction of a legacy if the will expressly states that legacies are to be reduced by lifetime gifts. [*See* Mass. Gen. Laws ch. 197, §25A]

C. Disclaimer by Heir or Will Beneficiary

1. **Introduction [§143]**

No one can be compelled to be a donee of a gift against her will. It has always been held that a will beneficiary can disclaim any gift. If a beneficiary makes a valid disclaimer, the disclaimed interest passes *as though the disclaimant predeceased the testator*.

a. **Reason for making disclaimer—tax advantage [§144]**

Although there may be many reasons to disclaim a gift, the vast majority of disclaimers are made for tax purposes.

e.g. **Example:** Ted dies leaving a will that bequeaths his $500,000 estate to his daughter Debbie if she survives Ted, otherwise to Debbie's children. Debbie, a successful attorney, already has a substantial estate and enjoys a substantial income. If she accepts the bequest, it will aggravate her own estate tax and estate planning problems and will give her more income to be taxed in the highest tax bracket. Debbie could accept the bequest and then give the property to her children, but this would result in a taxable gift for federal gift tax purposes. Thus, the better solution is for her to disclaim the bequest in whole or in part. The disclaimed interest will pass from Ted to Debbie's children as though she predeceased Ted. The effect of the disclaimer is to cause the property to pass to the next generation free of any gift tax.

b. Statutory requirements for disclaimer

(1) Federal disclaimer statute [§145]

To be effective for gift tax purposes, a disclaimer must satisfy the federal gift tax statute governing disclaimers. The most important requirements are that the disclaimer must be: (i) *in writing*, (ii) *irrevocable*, and (iii) *filed within nine months* after the decedent's death or the beneficiary's 21st birthday. [I.R.C. §2518; *and see* Estate and Gift Tax Summary] *Note:* A minor beneficiary is given until the age of 21 to file a disclaimer because she may not be competent to decide whether it is in her best interest to disclaim the gift.

(2) State disclaimer statutes [§146]

Most states have enacted statutes that set forth the procedures to be followed in making a valid disclaimer. Most of the statutes have been drafted so as to conform to the federal statute. [*See* UPC §2-801; Cal. Prob. Code §260-295; Tex. Prob. Code §37A] However, some statutes impose additional procedural requirements that are not required under the federal statute—*e.g.*, that the instrument of disclaimer be acknowledged before a notary public. [*See* Fla. Prob. Code §732.801(4); N.Y. Est. Powers & Trusts Law §2-1.11]

c. Terminology [§147]

At common law, an inter vivos donee or a will beneficiary *disclaimed* the gift; an heir *renounced* her intestate share. Today, the terms "disclaimer" and "renunciation" are synonymous and are used interchangeably. The term used by the federal statute and by most state statutes is "disclaimer." This terminology is also more convenient because it permits one to refer to the "disclaimant," rather than to a "renunciator."

2. Interests that May Be Disclaimed

a. Testamentary gifts [§148]

Even before statutes governing disclaimers were enacted, it was held that a will beneficiary could disclaim a testamentary gift without making a taxable gift. [*See* **Brown v. Routzahn**, 63 F.2d 914 (6th Cir. 1933)] The disclaimer must be made within nine months of the decedent's death or the beneficiary's 21st birthday. [I.R.C. §2518]

b. Intestate shares

(1) Common law [§149]

At common law, an intestate heir could not make a tax-free disclaimer of her intestate share because it was held that title to the decedent's property passed to the heirs by force of law at the moment of the decedent's death.

Example: Hank dies intestate, survived by his wife Lisa and by his two children: Sam and Diane. Lisa and Diane, generous as well as rich in their own right, wish to disclaim their intestate shares. However, under the common law principle that title to the decedent's property passes to Lisa and Diane at the moment of his death, their subsequent "renunciation" constitutes an assignment of *their* property to Sam, and thus, each made a taxable gift of their property.

---

(2) Modern law [§150]

Federal law now recognizes that a disclaimer of an intestate share is valid for federal gift tax purposes (*i.e.*, no gift tax will be assessed) *if* the disclaimer is made within nine months after the decedent's death or the beneficiary's 21st birthday. [I.R.C. §2518] States that have disclaimer statutes all expressly authorize disclaimers of an intestate share.

Example: Under modern law, Lisa and Diane in the example above can disclaim their intestate shares under the state's disclaimer statute and the entire estate passes to Sam with no tax consequences to Lisa and Diane.

---

c. Life insurance and employee benefit proceeds [§151]

Most state statutes permit a beneficiary to disclaim the proceeds of a life insurance policy or an employee death benefit plan if the disclaimer is made within nine months after the decedent's death. The disclaimer of such an interest is valid for federal gift tax purposes. [I.R.C. §2518]

d. Joint tenancies; tenancies by the entirety [§152]

Statutes in a number of states permit the surviving joint tenant (or surviving tenant by the entirety) to disclaim within nine months after the first tenant's death. Such a disclaimer is also recognized for federal gift tax purposes. [I.R.C. §2518]

e. Present life estates [§153]

A present life estate must be disclaimed within nine months after the decedent's death. If a life tenant disclaims the life estate, future interests following the life estate are accelerated (*i.e.,* they vest in possession) unless the testator has made an alternative provision for what is to happen if the life tenant disclaims. [*See* N.Y. Est. Powers & Trusts Law §2-1.11(d)]

f. Future interests [§154]

Many *state* disclaimer statutes permit the holder of a future interest to disclaim that interest within nine months after the future interest *vests in possession. But note:* Under current *federal* gift tax law, such a disclaimer would have *gift tax consequences* (*see* below).

(1) Former law—*Keinath* case [§155]

John died in 1944, leaving a will that devised property in trust: Income to wife Edna for life, and on Edna's death, to her descendants then living. On John's death in 1944, his son Cargill (then in his 20's) gave no thought to disclaiming his share of the remainder interest. When Edna died in 1963, Cargill (who had become wealthy in the meantime) disclaimed his share of the remainder, which passed to his children as a result of the disclaimer. The disclaimer was held valid for gift tax purposes because the disclaimer had been made within a reasonable time after the future interest vested in possession. [**Keinath v. Commissioner,** 480 F.2d 57 (8th Cir. 1973)]

(2) Current law [§156]

The result in the *Keinath* case was legislatively overturned when section 2518 of the Internal Revenue Code was enacted in 1976, and was judicially overturned by the United States Supreme Court in **Jewett v. Commissioner,** 455 U.S. 305 (1982). To be tax-free for gift tax purposes, a future interest must be disclaimed *within nine months after the interest is created* (on the *Keinath* facts, when John died in 1944), even though the interest is a contingent remainder.

g. Partial disclaimers [§157]

Under most disclaimer statutes, an heir or beneficiary can make a partial as well as a total disclaimer (*e.g.,* by disclaiming one-half or two-thirds of the interest that otherwise would pass to her). Partial disclaimers are recognized as valid for federal gift tax purposes.

3. Disclaimer by Personal Representative or Guardian

a. Common law [§158]

Most states have a statute covering this situation. In the handful of cases that have considered the question without the aid of a statute, it is generally held that a decedent's personal representative or an incapacitated person's guardian or conservator can, *with court approval,* make a disclaimer on behalf of a decedent or incapacitated beneficiary. [*See* **Estate of Hoenig v. Commissioner,** 66 T.C. 471 (1976); 3 A.L.R.3d 6]

b. Statutes [§159]

Nearly all state disclaimer statutes permit a personal representative or guardian to disclaim on behalf of a minor, incapacitated, or deceased beneficiary, upon a court finding that it is in the *best interest of the decedent's estate or the ward* to do so. [*See, e.g.,* UPC §2-801; N.Y. Est. Powers & Trusts Law §2-1.11; Tex. Prob. Code §37A]

Example: Jack dies leaving a $1.5 million estate, and a will that devises "all my property to my wife Sherry if she survives me; otherwise to my children." Sherry survives Jack, but only by three months. Because of the unlimited federal estate tax marital deduction, there is no estate tax on Jack's estate. But Sherry is left with an estate of $1.5 million and no marital deduction available to reduce taxes in her estate. Sherry's executor could disclaim one-half of the gift from Jack's will; the disclaimed one-half would bypass Sherry and go directly to the children. Jack and Sherry each would have taxable estates of $750,000. Because of the federal estate tax unified credit, no estate tax would be due from either estate. (*See* Estate and Gift Tax Summary.)

DISCLAIMERS—A REVIEW — gilbert

PROPERTY DISCLAIMED	TIME FOR MAKING DISCLAIMER	EFFECT OF DISCLAIMER
TESTAMENTARY GIFTS AND INTESTATE SHARES	Nine months after the decedent's death or the beneficiary's 21st birthday.	Gift lapses. Consider application of the anti-lapse statute (*see infra,* §§695 *et seq.*).
LIFE INSURANCE AND EMPLOYEE DEATH BENEFITS	Nine months after the decedent's death.	Proceeds pass to alternate or contingent beneficiary, if any.
JOINT TENANCIES AND TENANCIES BY THE ENTIRETY	Nine months after the decedent's death.	Property reverts to estate of decedent as if he had survived disclaiming joint tenant.
PRESENT LIFE ESTATES	Nine months after the decedent's death.	Future interests following life estate are accelerated.
FUTURE INTERESTS	Nine months *after the interest is created*.	Property passes as if disclaimant predeceased decedent.

4. Estoppel [§160]

A beneficiary or heir cannot disclaim an interest after having accepted the property or any of its benefits. Thus, a person will be estopped from disclaiming if he has *exercised any dominion or control* over the property, as by receiving a partial distribution of the property, transferring or encumbering the property, or entering into a contract for the sale of the property. In these situations, a "disclaimer" will be treated as an assignment or transfer, and will be subject to gift tax.

5. Creditors' Claims

a. Majority rule [§161]

In most states, a disclaimer *can* be used to defeat creditors' claims. If an heir or beneficiary disclaims an interest in the decedent's estate, the property passes as though the heir or beneficiary predeceased the decedent, and thus the disclaimant has no interest that can be reached by creditors. [*See* Cal. Prob. Code §283; 39 A.L.R.4th 633] A debtor "is not under any legal obligation, however strong the moral obligation may be, to acquire property as a gift that would benefit his creditors." [**Lynch v. Lynch**, 21 S.E.2d 569 (S.C. 1942)] A disclaimer is not a fraudulent transfer under creditors' rights law because, by disclaiming, the party never owned the property, and "one cannot dispose of something one does not have." [**Dyer v. Eckols**, 808 S.W.2d 531 (Tex. 1991)]

b. Minority rule [§162]

In a substantial minority of jurisdictions, a disclaimer is *not* effective as against the creditors of the disclaimant. The creditors can reach the property as though the disclaimer had not been made. [*See* Fla. Prob. Code §732.801; Mass. Gen. Laws ch. 191A, §8(2); **Stein v. Brown**, 480 N.E.2d 1121 (Ohio 1985)]

6. Disclaimer Cannot Defeat Federal Tax Lien [§163]

A disclaimer cannot be used to avoid the imposition of a federal tax lien. When a decedent dies, her heir acquires a right of considerable value—the right either to inherit his share of the estate or to channel the inheritance to another family member by disclaiming that share. The heir's power to determine who will receive the property—himself if he does not disclaim it or a known other if he does—constitutes "property" or a "right to property" within the meaning of the statute that imposes a federal tax lien. [**Drye v. United States**, 528 U.S. 49 (1999)]

D. Slayer of the Decedent

1. Common Law [§164]

Suppose that an heir or will beneficiary wrongfully brings about the death of the decedent. Should that person be entitled to inherit from the estate? Working without the aid of statutes, the courts have developed various solutions to this problem.

a. Majority rule [§165]

Under the equitable principle that a person should not be allowed to profit from his wrongful conduct, most courts hold that one who wrongfully brings about the death of a decedent should not be allowed to inherit from the victim's estate. A constructive trust is imposed on the inheritance, and the property passes as though the *slayer predeceased the victim*. [*See, e.g.,* **Dutill v. Dana**, 113 A.2d 499 (Me. 1952); **Kelley v. State**, 196 A.2d 68 (N.H. 1963); **Pritchett v. Henry**, 287 S.W.2d 546 (Tex. 1955); 39 A.L.R.2d 477]

(1) Note

A constructive trust *is not a trust*. Imposition of a constructive trust does not give rise to a true trust relationship under which the trustee holds legal title for the benefit of others. "Constructive trust" is, instead, the name given to a flexible equitable remedy designed to disgorge unjust enrichment. In the same decree that imposes a constructive trust, the court compels a conveyance to the persons who would have taken had the slayer predeceased the victim. (*See* Trusts Summary.)

EXAM TIP — gilbert

Remember that the slayer is precluded from taking **any** interest in the decedent's estate. This includes benefits under **life insurance policies, intestate succession, and devises in a will** (see infra, §§175 et seq.). Since the property passes as though the beneficiary predeceased the victim, be sure to consider application of the anti-lapse statute if a will is involved (see infra, §§695 et seq.).

---

b. Minority rule overturned [§166]

A few courts once held that the legal title passes to the slayer and can be retained by him in spite of the crime; however, these decisions have been overturned by statute. [*See, e.g.,* **Bird v. Plunkett**, 95 A.2d 71 (Conn. 1953)—overturned by Conn. Gen. Stat. tit. 45a, §447]

c. Nature of homicide [§167]

For the slayer to lose his interest in the estate, he must have *wrongfully brought about the victim's death*. Thus, murder would certainly trigger a constructive trust. If the slayer is found guilty of manslaughter and not murder, some courts have held that a constructive trust should not be imposed. [Restatement of Restitution §187, comment e] However, most courts draw a distinction between *voluntary* and *involuntary* manslaughter, and refuse to impose a constructive trust only in the involuntary manslaughter situation. [*See In re* **Mahoney's Estate**, 220 A.2d 475 (Vt. 1966)] Also, a slayer who is found not guilty by reason of insanity does *not forfeit* his rights. [*See* **Blair v. Travelers Insurance Co.**, 174 N.E.2d 209 (Ill. 1961)]

2. Statutory Solutions [§168]

Many states now have "slayer statutes" that govern the right of a killer to receive property from the victim's estate. [*See* **Ford v. Ford**, 512 A.2d 389 (Md. 1986); 125 A.L.R.4th 787]

a. Scope of statutes [§169]

The statutes vary in their scope:

(1) Conviction required [§170]

In some states, the statute applies only if the heir or will beneficiary is *convicted* of intentionally and unlawfully killing the decedent. [*See* Vt. Stat. tit. 14, §551(6)]

(2) Conviction not required [§171]

In other states, a final judgment of conviction of murder is conclusive, but even in the absence of conviction, the court may determine by a *preponderance of the evidence* that the killing was unlawful and intentional. [*See* Fla. Prob. Code §732.802]

b. Uniform Probate Code [§172]

The original UPC provision applies if the slayer *feloniously and intentionally* kills the decedent, and provides that the property passes as though the slayer predeceased the victim. [Original UPC §2-803] The revised UPC provides that the property passes as though the slayer *disclaimed* the interest passing from the victim, which amounts to the same result. [UPC §2-803] Both statutes apply to cases of intestacy, wills, life insurance policies, and any other acquisition of property by reason of the victim's death.

(1) Conviction not required [§173]

Under both versions of the UPC, conviction of a felonious and intentional killing is conclusive, but in the absence of a conviction the court may determine that the killing was felonious and intentional by a *preponderance of the evidence*.

EXAM TIP   **gilbert**

In an exam question about an heir or will beneficiary killing the decedent, it is likely that the killer will not be convicted of murder—that would be too easy. The more common question in this area will present someone who has **not been tried for the crime**, possibly even because there isn't enough evidence to convict him. Recall that a lesser standard of proof is needed for a civil action such as probate (preponderance) than for criminal proceedings (beyond a reasonable doubt). Thus, check the facts of your question to see whether there is some evidence that the killing was **unlawful and intentional**. If so, discuss whether the killer will lose his inheritance or gift.

---

c. Effect of statute [§174]

Where a statute governs the effect of slaying the decedent, there is no occasion for applying the two-step reasoning involved in the imposition of a constructive trust (*i.e.,* that title passes to the slayer, who holds as constructive trustee). Under the statute, *title* to the decedent's property *passes directly* to the persons who would take if the slayer had predeceased the victim.

3. Forms of Disposition Affected [§175]

Case decisions and statutes dealing with this problem do not limit application of the rule to cases involving intestate succession.

a. Wills and life insurance policies [§176]

Forfeiture is applied where the slayer is a legatee under the decedent's will [36 A.L.R.2d 960], or a beneficiary under an insurance policy on the life of the victim [**Beck v. West Coast Life Insurance Co.,** 38 Cal. 2d 643 (1952); **Dill v. Southern Farm Bureau Life Insurance Co.,** 797 So. 2d 858 (Miss. 2001); 26 A.L.R.2d 979 (1952)].

b. Joint tenancy or tenancy by the entirety [§177]

If the slayer and the victim owned property as joint tenants or as tenants by the entirety, in most states and under the UPC the tenancy is *severed*. The slayer takes one-half of the property, and the other one-half passes as though the slayer disclaimed the property. [UPC §2-803; *and see* **Bradley v. Fox,** 129 N.E.2d 699 (Ill. 1955); *In re* **Shields's Estate,** 584 P.2d 139 (Kan. 1978); 32 A.L.R.2d 1099]

(1) Rationale

While the slayer should not profit from his wrongful conduct, neither should he forfeit his one-half interest in the property based on speculation as to who might have survived. [*See In re* **Matye's Estate,** 645 P.2d 955 (Mont. 1982)]

(2) But note

Some courts award everything but the actuarial value of the slayer's life income interest in one-half of the property to the victim's estate, on the ground that the slayer deprived the victim of the chance to be the surviving tenant. [*See, e.g.,* **Neiman v. Hurff,** 93 A.2d 345 (N.J. 1952); **Hargrove v. Taylor,** 389 P.2d 36 (Or. 1964)] In a few states, the slayer loses the entire interest in the property. [*See, e.g., In re* **King's Estate,** 52 N.W.2d 885 (Wis. 1952)]

4. Conviction of Felony—"Corruption of Blood"

a. Common law [§178]

At common law, a convicted felon forfeited his real and personal property, which passed by *escheat* to the crown and not to his heirs or distributees.

b. Modern law [§179]

Nearly all states have eliminated the common law rule by constitutional or statutory provision. Conviction of a felony does not result in corruption of the blood, forfeiture, or escheat. However, when the felony involves killing the person whose property is being distributed, the above rules apply, and the felon is treated as having predeceased the person. Thus, if the decedent died intestate, the property will descend to her surviving heirs (excluding the felon) according to the jurisdiction's intestacy statutes. If the decedent left a will making a gift to the felon, the property will pass to the felon's heirs pursuant to the anti-lapse statute, if applicable. If the anti-lapse statute does not apply, the property will pass under the will's residuary clause, or, if none, under the intestacy statutes. [*See, e.g.,* Tex. Prob. Code §41(d)]

---

e.g. Example: Corinna executes her will and leaves a $1 million legacy to her beloved son Joseph and the residue of her estate to the American Red Cross. Years later, their relationship has turned sour and Corinna mentions to a family friend that she intends to change her will to disinherit Joseph and to leave her entire estate to Joseph's daughter, Lydia. Joseph learns of Corinna's plans and during a confrontation loses his temper and kills Corinna. Joseph is treated as having predeceased Corinna and the $1 million legacy to Joseph passes to Lydia under the jurisdiction's anti-lapse statute. (Note that the residue passes to the American Red Cross regardless of Corinna's stated intentions because she never executed a new will.)

E. Aliens

1. **Common Law [§180]**

   At common law, aliens were *denied* the right to inherit *real property* either by will or intestate succession.

2. **Modern Law [§181]**

   In most states, there are *no restrictions* on the right of an alien to inherit or hold title to real or personal property within the state. [*See* Fla. Prob. Code §732.1101; Ill. Comp. Stat. ch. 765, §60/7; Comment, *Rights and Restrictions on Interests in Aliens in U.S. Estates: Federal and State Laws,* 15 Real Prop. Prob. & Trust J. 659 (1980)]

   a. **Minority view [§182]**

      In several states, aliens can inherit land but must sell it within a specified time. [*See* Neb. Rev. Stat. §76-402—five years; Okla. Stat. Ann. tit. 60, §123—five years] *But note:* If the United States government has extended inheritance rights to nonresident aliens by treaty, the *treaty prevails* over any statute to the contrary. [**De Tenorio v. McGowan,** 364 F. Supp. 1051 (S.D. Miss. 1973)]

   b. **"Iron curtain" statutes [§183]**

      Some states have enacted *reciprocity statutes* that bar inheritance by a nonresident alien unless the alien's country grants reciprocal rights to American citizens. [*See, e.g.,* N.C. Gen. Stat. §64-3] Other states have enacted *impounding statutes* under which the inheritance will be impounded if the court determines that the alien would not have the benefit of use and enjoyment of the property. [*See* N.Y. Surr. Ct. Proc. Act §2218]

(1) Constitutional problem [§184]

Some of these statutes have met with constitutional objections. For example, an Oregon reciprocity statute was held unconstitutional on the facts presented, on the ground that a state court's inquiry into whether a foreign government is communist or nondemocratic constitutes an invasion into the field of foreign affairs reserved exclusively to the federal government. [**Zschernig v. Miller,** 389 U.S. 429 (1968)]

(2) Testamentary gifts [§185]

A gift in a will conditioned on an alien's ability to freely and fully enjoy the benefits of the property in his homeland is valid and requires a court determination that the condition has been satisfied. [*See **In re** **Kosek's Estate,*** 31 N.Y.2d 475 (1973)]

c. Uniform Probate Code [§186]

Under the UPC, *no person is disqualified* to take as an heir because he or a person through whom he claims is or has been an alien. [UPC §2-111]

Chapter Five: Restrictions on the Power of Testation— Protection of the Family

---

CONTENTS

Chapter Approach

Although a testator must comply with the formalities required for will execution in order to make an effective disposition, the law imposes few limitations on how, or to whom, a testator may bequeath his estate. This chapter outlines those restrictions on the power of disposition that are designed to protect the testator's family against disinheritance. Whenever you encounter an exam question in which a testator is survived by a spouse or child, you must consider whether any of these limitations on testation designed to protect the family apply.

1. **Protection of Spouse**

   a. **Common law states**

   The *elective share statute* is a likely source of exam questions and will be at the forefront of your answer if the will makes a small bequest (or no bequest at all) to the surviving spouse. However, in *any* question involving a surviving spouse, you will strengthen your answer if you mention the elective share statute even if only to dismiss it. For example, an answer might state, "Since Husband's will bequeathed one-half of his estate to Wife, she would have no reason to file for an elective share, which would entitle her to only one-third of Husband's net estate." Remember that the amount of the elective share and the procedure to be followed are set by statute, and thus statutory terms must be followed. Remember, too, that the UPC's elective share statute applies to the *augmented estate*, which encompasses most nonprobate transfers, and that several non-UPC states have similar rules.

   b. **Community property states**

   None of the community property states has an elective share statute, although several of the states have quasi-community property statutes that apply to property acquired in another state. Remember that one spouse can dispose of *all of his separate property* by will, but can dispose of only *one-half of his community interest*. If the decedent's will purports to devise the entire interest in community property, including his spouse's one-half share, the spouse can elect to take against the will, but she will then lose all gifts under the will.

2. **Protection of Children**

   Pretermitted child questions frequently turn up on Wills exams. Read the statute carefully, as most apply only to children born or adopted *after* execution of the will (although a few apply to children who were born or adopted before the will was executed). Remember that the statute may *not* apply if: (i) the child was *intentionally omitted*; (ii) the child was provided for by a *lifetime settlement or nonprobate transfer*; or (iii) the surviving spouse (parent of the child) is the *principal beneficiary under the will*.

3. Protection of Family

Statutes in many states provide for *homestead* rights, *exempt personal property*, and *family allowance* to protect the decedent's family. These rights are *in addition to* the spouse's elective share and gifts under the will, and they are generally not subject to creditors' claims.

4. Provisions Against Public Policy

The courts will not enforce will provisions that are against public policy (even if not barred by statute). For example, look for provisions that impose a total restraint on marriage, encourage divorce, or encourage the commission of a crime or the destruction of property.

A. Protection of the Spouse

1. Common Law [§187]

A surviving spouse never took as an heir under the common law. A decedent's estate passed by intestacy to his descendants or, if he was not survived by descendants, to his parents or collateral kin. If a decedent was survived by his spouse but no kindred, his estate escheated to the Crown. A surviving spouse's only rights in a decedent's estate were *dower* (if a widow) or *curtesy* (if a widower).

a. Dower [§188]

Dower was the provision the law made for a *widow* out of the husband's property. Upon the husband's death, the widow was entitled to a *life estate* in an *undivided one-third* of the *real property* owned by the husband before marriage or acquired during the marriage.

(1) Inchoate dower [§189]

The wife's dower interest was "inchoate" until her husband died, *i.e.,* she had no rights in the property (*e.g.,* possession) while her husband was alive. If the wife predeceased her husband, her inchoate dower was extinguished.

b. Curtesy [§190]

A husband had an interest comparable to dower in his wife's real property. Upon a wife's death, her husband's curtesy right gave him a *life estate* in *all* (and not just one-third of) *real property* owned by the wife during marriage. However, a husband's curtesy estate arose *only if issue were born* to the marriage.

c. Dower and curtesy as limitations on testamentary power [§191]

Dower and curtesy rights could be asserted regardless of provisions in the decedent's will involving the property. For example, a wife's dower interest in her husband's real property was not affected by the fact that the husband had devised the real property to another. To this extent, each spouse's power of testamentary disposition was limited by the other spouse's dower or curtesy right.

d. Dower and curtesy as limitations on lifetime transfers [§192]

The rights of the surviving spouse also could not be defeated by lifetime conveyance. Even a sale to a bona fide purchaser was ineffective to cut off the spouse's dower or curtesy right *unless the spouse joined in the conveyance.* Similarly, a spouse's dower or curtesy interest was superior to the claims of the deceased spouse's creditors.

DOWER AND CURTESY—A COMPARISON			gilbert
	WHO HAS RIGHT	**COVERAGE**	**STATUS**
DOWER	Widow only	Life estate in *1/3* of husband's real property acquired before or during marriage	Abolished in most states
CURTESY	Widower only and only if issue born to marriage	Life estate in *all* of wife's real property acquired during marriage	Abolished in most states
STATUTORY DOWER	*Either* widow or widower	Life estate in *1/3* of spouse's real property acquired during marriage	Available in only a few jurisdictions

e. Modern status [§193]

Dower and curtesy may have served adequate protective functions in a society where land was the principal form of wealth, but they provide virtually no protection or support in today's society, where the most significant forms of wealth are intangibles (*e.g.,* stocks, bonds, business interests). For this reason, most jurisdictions have *abolished* dower and curtesy by statute, and have enacted elective share statutes in their stead. [*See, e.g.,* Ala. Code §43-8-57; Mo. Rev. Stat. §474.110; Pa. Cons. Stat. tit. 20, §2105; W. Va. Code §43-1-1] Dower and curtesy were never a part of the laws of the community property states (*see supra,* §58). Today, only a handful of states continue to recognize dower and curtesy. [*See* Mich. Comp. Laws §558.1—dower for widows only; Ohio Rev. Code §3103.04]

(1) Statutory dower [§194]

The rules governing dower and curtesy have been assimilated by statute in a few jurisdictions. The estate is called "dower" or "statutory dower," and the surviving spouse (whether wife or husband) takes a *life estate in one-third* of all the decedent's real property. In most of these states, the spouse must elect whether to take dower, an elective share, or under the decedent's will. [*See, e.g.,* Mass. Gen. Laws ch. 189, §1; N.C. Gen. Stat. §29.30]

2. Elective Share Statutes

a. In general [§195]

All of the common law jurisdictions except Georgia have enacted elective share statutes designed to give surviving spouses some protection against disinheritance. Under these statutes, a surviving spouse can elect to take a statutory share (typically one-third) of the decedent's estate. Some states call the elective share entitlement a "right of renunciation" to take a "forced share" of the decedent's estate, the theory being that the spouse must renounce the decedent's will in order to take an elective share. Although the spouse who elects is sometimes said to be taking *in lieu of* the gifts devised to the spouse in the decedent's will, this is not exactly true. To avoid disrupting the decedent's testamentary plan as far as possible, under many of the statutes testamentary gifts to the spouse are first applied in making up the elective share entitlement. (*See infra,* §229.)

(1) As limitation on testamentary power [§196]

As with dower or curtesy, elective share statutes operate as a restriction on the decedent's power of testation. The surviving spouse has a right to claim a designated share of the decedent's estate regardless of the decedent's will.

---

e.g. **Example:** Jack's will leaves $100,000 to his wife, Diane, and the remainder of his multimillion dollar estate to his friend, Johnny. Diane can exercise her right to an elective share and receive a larger share of Jack's estate, thus indirectly limiting his testamentary power.

(a) Comment

Cases in which the surviving spouse actually elects to take a statutory share are relatively infrequent. In large part, this is because most decedents leave the bulk of their estates to the surviving spouse. (Such a disposition is encouraged by the federal estate tax, which grants a marital deduction for qualifying dispositions to a spouse.) Moreover, if a testator is inclined to disinherit his spouse, the existence of the elective share statute has the salutary effect of inducing the testator to bequeath at least the elective share amount to his spouse.

(2) As limitation on lifetime and nonprobate transfers [§197]

Historically, the elective share applied only to the decedent's "estate," meaning the decedent's *probate* estate. Thus, the elective share applied only to property owned by the decedent at death. As a result, a lifetime or nonprobate transfer of property—including a transfer to a revocable trust in which the grantor retained the right to income and other benefits—could be used to effectively cut off the surviving spouse's statutory share. While this is still the law in several states, by statute or case decision in the majority of states the scope of the elective share has been extended to encompass certain lifetime and nonprobate transfers (*i.e.,* the elective share applies to the decedent's *augmented* estate). (*See infra,* §§202, 245-253.)

(3) Community property states [§198]

None of the community property states has an elective share statute because of the inherent protection given to spouses by the community property system (*see supra,* §§58 *et seq.*).

(a) Qualification [§199]

The quasi-community property statutes found in California, Idaho, Washington, and Wisconsin are a form of elective share statute that applies to certain assets brought to one of those states from a common law jurisdiction. (*See supra,* §§65 *et seq.*)

EXAM TIP **gilbert**

Whenever you encounter a surviving spouse in an exam question, check to see if the decedent *adequately provided for her* in his will. If not, discuss whether she should exercise her option to renounce the will and take her elective share of the decedent's estate. Keep in mind that the amount of the elective share and the property subject to the elective share will differ depending on the law of the particular jurisdiction.

---

b. Amount of elective share [§200]

The amount of the elective share entitlement varies from state to state. Under the original UPC and in many states, the amount is *one-third* of the estate regardless of whether the decedent was survived by descendants. [*See* Original UPC §2-201; N.Y. Est. Powers & Trusts Law §5-1.1-A; Pa. Cons. Stat. tit. 20, §2203] In several states, the amount is *one-third* of the decedent's net estate if the decedent was survived by descendants, and *one-half* if the decedent was not survived by descendants. [*See* Ill. Comp. Stat. ch. 755, §5/2-8; Md. Est. & Trusts Code §3-203; Ohio Rev. Code §2106.01(C)] In other states, the statutory share ranges from 30% [Fla. Prob. Code §732.2065] to one-fourth [Or. Rev. Stat. §114.105] to one-half of the amount the spouse would have inherited if the decedent had died intestate [Mich. Comp. Laws §700.2202]. In Massachusetts, the elective share amount is a *life estate* in one-third *or* one-half of the net probate estate. [Mass. Gen. Laws ch. 191, §15]

DETERMINE THE *AMOUNT* OF THE ELECTIVE SHARE.

- The amount varies from state to state and may be affected by whether or not the decedent was **survived by any descendants**.

- If the jurisdiction has adopted the revised UPC, the amount of the elective share is determined according to a sliding scale but must be at least **$50,000**.

WHAT PROPERTY IS INCLUDED IN THE ELECTIVE ESTATE?

- Check to see whether the elective share applies to the decedent's **net probate estate** or his **augmented estate**.

- Include all of the decedent's **personal property** and any **real property located within the state**.

- Under the revised UPC, the couple's **combined assets** are included in the elective estate.

- If the decedent left any property subject to a **settlement agreement** or **contractual will**, consider whether the jurisdiction includes that property in the elective estate.

WHO HAS THE RIGHT TO FILE FOR AN ELECTIVE SHARE?

- Only a **surviving spouse** or someone acting on her behalf (*e.g.*, guardian or conservator) can claim an elective share.

- The right of election is **terminated if the surviving spouse dies** before it is filed.

- A divorce decree that is **finalized before the decedent's death** terminates the spouse's right to elect.

- In a minority of states, a spouse who is guilty of **misconduct** (*e.g.*, abandonment) has no right to file for an elective share.

- The decedent must have been a **domiciliary of the state** where the election is filed.

- A waiver of the elective share is **binding**.

DID THE SURVIVING SPOUSE PROPERLY *FILE A NOTICE OF ELECTION*?

- Notice must be filed within statutory **time period**.

- Time period begins to run upon **opening of administration** or when **will is admitted to probate**.

HOW IS THE ELECTIVE SHARE *SATISFIED*?

- First apply any **outright testamentary gifts** to the surviving spouse.

- Then **abate** other gifts to make up the outstanding amount of elective share.

(1) Revised UPC [§201]

The revised UPC takes a radically different approach in determining the amount of the surviving spouse's elective share.

(a) Augmented estate—spouse's own property included [§202]

Under the original UPC, the elective share applies to the decedent's *augmented estate*, which includes the decedent's probate estate *and* certain nonprobate transfers made during the decedent's lifetime (*see infra*, §§245-253). [Original UPC §2-201] Under the revised UPC, the augmented estate against which the elective share is computed is redefined to include *the couple's combined assets*, including assets titled in or owned by the surviving spouse (*see infra*, §252). [UPC §2-203]

(b) Accrual approach [§203]

The spouse's elective share amount is computed pursuant to a formula along the lines of the "vesting" rules applicable to many employee pension plans. The share varies according to the *length of the marriage*, with the spouse receiving a greater elective share percentage in a marriage of longer duration. The elective share amount is determined according to the table set out below. Several non-UPC states have adopted this accrual schedule. [*See, e.g.,* Kan. Stat. §59-6a202; W. Va. Code §42-3-1]

Length of Marriage	Elective Share Percentage
Less than 1 year	$50,000
1 year but less than 2 years	3% of augmented estate
2 years but less than 3 years	6% of augmented estate
3 years but less than 4 years	9% of augmented estate
4 years but less than 5 years	12% of augmented estate
5 years but less than 6 years	15% of augmented estate
6 years but less than 7 years	18% of augmented estate
7 years but less than 8 years	21% of augmented estate
8 years but less than 9 years	24% of augmented estate
9 years but less than 10 years	27% of augmented estate
10 years but less than 11 years	30% of augmented estate
11 years but less than 12 years	34% of augmented estate
12 years but less than 13 years	38% of augmented estate
13 years but less than 14 years	42% of augmented estate
14 years but less than 15 years	46% of augmented estate
15 years or more	50% of augmented estate

(c) Supplemental elective share—$50,000 [§204]

Under the revised UPC, the surviving spouse is entitled to a *minimum* elective share (called in the statute a "supplemental elective share"), which assures the spouse's total entitlement to *at least $50,000*, regardless of the number of years of marriage and regardless of the size of the decedent's augmented estate. [UPC §2-202(b)]

EXAM TIP   gilbert

Remember that when determining the surviving spouse's elective share under the table above, the *minimum amount must be at least $50,000*. For example, if the surviving spouse was married to the decedent for eight years, she is entitled to 24% of his augmented estate. If the decedent's augmented estate is so small that 24% of it is less than $50,000, other gifts in the will are *abated* until the spouse's share reaches $50,000. (See *supra*, §§203-204.)

(d) Incapacitated spouse [§205]

If the surviving spouse is incapacitated, the elective share amount, to the extent payable from probate assets, is placed in a *custodial or support trust* for the spouse's benefit. Enacting statutes are given a choice as to whether the trustee of such a trust is authorized to take governmental benefits such as Medicaid into account in making distributions for the spouse's benefit. [UPC §2-212(b)]

(e) Rationale

The theory underlying the revised UPC is that marriage is an economic partnership. This marital-sharing theory is recognized in the equitable distribution system that is applied when a marriage ends in divorce and, according to the revised UPC, also should be recognized when a marriage ends on the death of a spouse. A fixed-fraction share tends to give the surviving spouse a windfall if the marriage was of short duration, or if assets acquired during marriage were disproportionately titled in the deceased spouse's name. By contrast, a fixed-fraction elective share tends to undercompensate the surviving spouse in a long-term marriage, or if the marital assets were disproportionately titled in the surviving spouse's name. [UPC §2-201]

c. Property subject to elective share [§206]

In some states, the elective share applies to the decedent's *net probate estate* (*see supra*, §200) after payment of expenses of administration and creditors' claims. In an increasing number of states, however, the elective share fraction is applied to the decedent's "*augmented estate*," a concept that is designed to encompass certain lifetime and nonprobate transfers (*see infra*, §§245-253).

(1) Real property—situs rule [§207]

The estate to which the elective share statute applies includes all of the decedent's *personal property* wherever located. However, because of the "situs rule" and the lack of jurisdiction over *real property* in another state, most elective share statutes apply only to real property located within the state. [Ind. Code §29-1-3-1]

(a) Minority rule—value of real property awarded [§208]

A few states have expanded the situs rule by providing that the net estate against which the elective share fraction applies includes the *value of real property located in another state*, even though the property itself cannot be awarded in making up the elective share entitlement. [*See* N.Y. Est. Powers & Trusts Law §5-1.1A(c)(7)]

(2) Family allowance and exempt property set-aside [§209]

The elective share statute applies to the decedent's net estate *after* satisfaction of the family allowance, homestead right, and any exempt personal property set-aside for the surviving spouse (*see infra*, §§295-314). [UPC §2-202(c); Fla. Prob. Code §732.2105] Thus, a spouse who files for an elective share is entitled to a family allowance *and* the statutory elective share.

EXAM TIP   **gilbert**

In the outside world, the amount of the family allowance and the value of exempt personal property would be subtracted **when computing the net (or augmented) estate,** and before applying the elective share fraction. However, this is not possible when writing your answer to an exam question because the professor is not likely to give you any values for the family allowance and exempt personal property. First, providing you with a value for these items gives a too obvious reminder that you are expected to mention these items in your answer. Second, if you are expected to compute the elective share, the professor is likely to give you nice, round numbers that are easily divisible by, *e.g.*, one-third—the value produced by taking into account the family allowance or exempt property would undercut those round numbers. To strengthen your answer, mention these items **at the end of your answer** to show that you are aware of them even though you have not included them in your computation. For example, after determining the amounts of the, *e.g.*, net estate and elective share entitlement, you can conclude your answer by stating, "In computing the net estate, the first step should be to deduct the amount of any family allowance and the value of an exempt personal property set-aside, because the spouse is entitled to these items over and above her elective share. Thus, the net estate would actually be less than the above amount. Since, however, no values were given for these items, I have not included them in my computation."

---

(3) Settlement agreement with former spouse [§210]

Suppose that in a property settlement agreement attendant to a divorce, the husband promises to make a will that devises certain property to his ex-wife (or to the couple's children). The husband remarries, and later dies survived by his second wife, who files for an elective share. Does the elective share apply to property that is subject to the settlement agreement? The courts are divided on this issue. [85 A.L.R.4th 418]

(a) View that surviving spouse prevails [§211]

Some courts have held that the surviving spouse's rights are superior to the rights of the beneficiaries under the settlement agreement, on the ground that the beneficiaries of the agreement are legatees and not creditors of the decedent's estate [*In re* **Donner's Estate**, 364 So. 2d 753 (Fla. 1978)], and that the policy of protecting the surviving spouse against disinheritance overrides a husband's ability to contract away the spouse's statutory rights [*See, e.g., In re* **Dunham's Estate**, 36 A.D.2d 467 (1971); **Budde v. Pierce**, 375 A.2d 984 (Vt. 1977)].

(b) View that settlement beneficiaries prevail [§212]

Other courts have held that the rights under the settlement agreement are superior, on the ground that the settlement agreement gave the former spouse equitable title to the property subject to the agreement, and that the elective share applies only to property in which the decedent held a beneficial interest. [*See, e.g., In re* **Davis's Estate**, 237 P.2d 396 (Kan. 1951); **Harris v. Harris**, 43 S.E.2d 225 (W. Va. 1947)]

(4) Property subject to contractual will [§213]

Most courts hold that the elective share applies only to property equitably as well as legally owned by the decedent. Thus, the elective share does not apply to property subject to a contractual will because the beneficiaries, and not the decedent, hold equitable title to the property. [*See, e.g.,* **Keats v. Cates**, 241 N.E.2d 645 (Ill. 1968); **Luthy v. Seaburn**, 46 N.W.2d 44 (Iowa 1951); 85 A.L.R.4th 418]

(a) Illustration [§214]

Conrad and Bertha execute a joint and contractual will under which the survivor inherits the other's estate. Upon the death of the survivor, the estate is to go to certain named beneficiaries. Bertha dies and Conrad subsequently marries Martha. Upon Conrad's death, Martha files for an elective share of Conrad's estate. The elective share does *not apply to the property subject to the contractual will*. Under the contractual will, Conrad takes only "an interest during his life with a power to use or otherwise dispose of principal"; the beneficiaries of the contractual will take the interest that remains on Conrad's death. Conrad had no interest against which the elective share could operate. [**Rubenstein v. Mueller**, 19 N.Y.2d 228 (1967)]

(b) Minority view [§215]

Some courts have ruled in favor of the surviving spouse on the ground that the power to make a will, including a contractual will, is subordinate to the elective share statute and its policy of protecting the surviving spouse against disinheritance. [*See* **Shimp v. Huff**, 556

A.2d 252 (Md. 1989)] In reaching this result, some courts have emphasized that the spouse was unaware of the contractual will arrangement. [*See, e.g.,* **Tod v. Fuller,** 78 So. 2d 713 (Fla. 1955); **Patecky v. Friend,** 350 P.2d 170 (Or. 1960)]

WHAT PROPERTY IS SUBJECT TO THE ELECTIVE SHARE?	gilbert
PERSONAL PROPERTY	Elective share applies to **all** of the decedent's personal property wherever located.
REAL PROPERTY	Elective share applies only to the decedent's real property **located in the state of the decedent's domicile**.
FAMILY ALLOWANCE, HOMESTEAD, AND EXEMPT PROPERTY	Elective share does **not apply** to the amount of the family allowance, homestead, or exempt property set-aside; it is **in addition** to these rights.
PROPERTY SETTLEMENT AGREEMENT	The **courts are divided**. Some hold that the elective share applies to the property under the settlement agreement, while others hold that it does not.
PROPERTY UNDER A CONTRACTUAL WILL	The majority of courts hold that the elective share **does not apply** to property subject to a contractual will.
NONPROBATE ASSET	Under the UPC's augmented estate concept, certain nonprobate transfers are subject to the elective share (*e.g.,* life insurance proceeds). (*See infra,* §§245-253.)

d. Who may claim elective share [§216]

The purpose of the elective share is to *protect the surviving spouse against disinheritance*. Thus, it can be exercised only *by or on behalf of the surviving spouse*. If the surviving spouse dies before the election is made, the right of election dies with her; her personal representative cannot make an election on behalf of her estate. *Rationale:* The purpose of the elective share is to protect the surviving spouse, not to provide an inheritance for her heirs. [UPC §2-212; *and see* Md. Est. & Trusts Code §3-204; 83 A.L.R.2d 1077]

(1) Incapacitated or minor spouse [§217]

It is generally provided that the *guardian or conservator* of an incapacitated or minor spouse may make an election on behalf of the spouse, but only upon a finding by the court that the election is in the spouse's *best interest*. [*See* Pa. Cons. Stat. tit. 20, §2206; 3 A.L.R.3d 6; 21 A.L.R.3d 320]

(a) Original Uniform Probate Code [§218]

Under the original UPC, the right of election on behalf of a protected person may be exercised only by order of the court in which protective proceedings are pending, after a finding that exercise is necessary to provide adequate support for the spouse during her probable life expectancy. [Original UPC §2-203]

(b) Revised Uniform Probate Code [§219]

The revised UPC eliminates the requirement of a court order. It permits the election to be made by the spouse's guardian, conservator, or an agent acting under a *durable power of attorney*. [UPC §2-212(a)]

EXAM TIP	gilbert

You will sometimes see an exam question where someone is trying to claim the elective share on behalf of a spouse. Keep in mind that the elective share protects a *surviving spouse* against disinheritance. Thus, a *guardian or conservator* of a surviving spouse can make an election for her, but a *personal representative* (executor or administrator) cannot make an election for a spouse who has died before making the election.

---

e. Considerations affecting surviving spouse's right to elect

(1) Decedent's domicile [§220]

A particular state's elective share statute is available to a surviving spouse only if the *decedent was a domiciliary* of that state at the time of death. [*See* Ala. Code §43-8-70; Or. Rev. Stat. §114.105] The surviving spouse has a right of election even if she is *not* a domiciliary of that state; it is the decedent's domicile that controls.

(a) New York [§221]

In New York, the surviving spouse has a right of election even if the decedent was not a New York domiciliary, if the decedent's will provided that the disposition of his property situated in New York is to be governed by New York law. [N.Y. Est. Powers & Trusts Law §5-1.1-A(c)(6)] Such a provision is sometimes found in the will of a person who moved to another state (*e.g.*, Florida) after retirement.

(2) Finality of divorce decree [§222]

The party filing for an elective share must be a surviving *spouse.* If the marriage was terminated before the decedent's death by a *final* decree of divorce or annulment, there is no right of election. If, however, an *interlocutory* decree of divorce had been entered but was not final on the decedent's death, or if a decree of divorce had been entered but the decree was not final because the time for appeal had not expired, the surviving spouse has a right of election. [*See In re* **Lueke's Estate,** 78 Misc. 2d 904 (1974)]

EXAM TIP   **gilbert**

Watch out for an exam question in which one spouse dies while the couple is in process of divorce. Even if the facts try to steer you into thinking that the marriage is over (*e.g.,* all the paperwork has been filed, or the parties have signed a settlement agreement or are dating other people, etc.), always check to see if the ***divorce was final*** before determining whether the "surviving spouse" can take an elective share. If there is some requirement (*e.g.,* a time period) before the divorce is final, the surviving spouse can take, as unfair as it may seem.

---

(3) Misconduct by surviving spouse

(a) Majority rule [§223]

In most states, the surviving spouse is *entitled to an elective share* even if he abandoned the deceased spouse, refused to support her, has committed adultery, or is guilty of some other misconduct. [13 A.L.R.3d 446]

1) Rationale

The right of election is granted by statute. If the legislature has not conditioned the surviving spouse's taking upon his good conduct, the courts should not read such a condition into the statute. [**Fogo v. Griffin**, 551 S.W.2d 677 (Tenn. 1977)]

(b) Minority rule [§224]

In several states, the surviving spouse has *no right of election* (or right to take an intestate share, family allowance, or exempt personal property set-aside) if: (i) he abandoned the deceased spouse (*e.g.,* openly and notoriously cohabitated with another woman); (ii) he failed or refused to support the deceased spouse; (iii) he procured a divorce or annulment in another jurisdiction that is not recognized as valid in the domiciliary state; or (iv) a final decree of separation was rendered against him. [*See* N.Y. Est. Powers & Trusts Law §5-1.2] *But note:* In these states, neither cruelty nor adultery, by itself, bars the right of election.

f. Procedure governing election [§225]

To take an elective share, the surviving spouse must file a *notice of election* (and under many statutes must deliver a copy of the notice to the decedent's personal representative) within the time period fixed by statute.

(1) Time period for filing notice of election [§226]

The time periods for filing notice of the election range from four months [S.D. Laws §29A-2-211] to six months [N.Y. Est. Powers & Trusts Law §5-1.1-A(d)(1)] to seven months [Ill. Comp. Stat. ch. 755, §5/2-8(a); Md. Est. & Trusts Code §3-206]. The time period begins to run from the date the administration is opened by the granting of letters testamentary to the personal representative. In some states, the time period is measured from the date the will is admitted to probate. [*See* Pa. Cons. Stat. tit. 20, §2210(b)]

(a) Uniform Probate Code [§227]

Under the UPC, the election must be made within *nine months after the decedent's death* or within *six months after probate* of the decedent's will, whichever is later. [UPC §2-211]

(2) Extension of time period [§228]

Several statutes expressly provide that the probate court can extend the time period for filing the notice of election upon a showing of good cause. [*See, e.g.,* Fla. Prob. Code §732.2135; N.Y. Est. Powers & Trusts Law §5-1.1]

g. Satisfaction of elective share

(1) Testamentary gifts to spouse [§229]

Under the UPC and in most states, outright testamentary gifts to the surviving spouse are *first applied* in making up the elective share entitlement. [*See, e.g.,* UPC §2-207; Fla. Prob. Code §732.2075; S.C. Code §62-2-207] The purpose of this rule is to prevent disruption of the decedent's testamentary plan insofar as possible.

(a) Minority rule [§230]

In several states, the *electing spouse takes nothing under the will*. The will is read as though the spouse predeceased the testator. [*See* Md. Est. & Trusts Code §3-208]

(b) Life estate [§231]

If the decedent's will gave the surviving spouse a life estate (*e.g.,* a trust income interest), in most states and under the revised UPC, the life estate is not counted as being in partial satisfaction of the statutory share because the elective share is designed to give the spouse outright ownership of assets. Instead, the spouse who elects to take a statutory share is deemed to have *renounced the life estate*, and the remainder interest following the life estate is accelerated.

1) Minority rule [§232]

In South Carolina, the decedent can satisfy the elective share of one-third by transferring that amount of his property in a trust that qualifies for the federal estate tax marital deduction. For example, if the spouse is entitled to an elective estate worth $250,000, the elective share can be satisfied by a marital deduction trust funded with $250,000 that gives the spouse an income interest only. [S.C. Code §62-2-207]

2) Original Uniform Probate Code [§233]

Under the original UPC, a life estate is counted as being in partial satisfaction of the elective share. The value of the life estate is computed as if it is worth one-half of the total value of the property subject to the life estate, unless a higher or lower value is established by proof. [Original UPC §2-207(a)] Thus, the spouse's entitlement to an elective share could be partially (or perhaps totally) satisfied by giving the spouse a life estate rather than outright ownership of property.

3) Revised Uniform Probate Code [§234]

The original UPC rule, which was carried over into the revised UPC as promulgated in 1990, was criticized as being sexist, inasmuch as most surviving spouses are female. [Ira Mark Bloom, *The Treatment of Trusts and Other Partial Interests of the Surviving Spouse Under the Redesigned Elective Share System*, 55 Alb. L. Rev. 941 (1992)] Thus, in 1993, the UPC was amended to eliminate the rule that a life estate can be used to satisfy the elective share. Under the revised UPC, only outright dispositions count toward the spouse's entitlement. As a result, a widely used mechanism for securing the federal estate tax marital deduction, the qualified terminable interest property ("QTIP") trust, cannot be used to satisfy the elective share. (*See* Estate & Gift Tax Summary.)

(2) Abatement of gifts [§235]

In many states the elective share is satisfied pursuant to the abatement rules that apply to creditors' claims. (*See infra*, §§1070-1078.) Property passing by partial intestacy is first applied; then the residuary estate; then general legacies, demonstrative legacies, and specific bequests are abated (in that order). [*See, e.g.,* Ill. Comp. Stat. ch. 755, §5/24-3] Thus, in the ordinary case, the burden of the elective share falls entirely on the decedent's residuary estate. [36 A.L.R.2d 291]

(a) Uniform Probate Code [§236]

Under the UPC and in several non-UPC states, the elective share is ratably apportioned among recipients of the estate in proportion to the value of their interests therein. [*See, e.g.,* UPC §2-209(b); N.Y. Est. Powers & Trusts Law §5-1.1-A]

h. Waiver of right of election [§237]

By statute in most states and by case law in other states, a spouse may waive the right of election (and also the right to an intestate share, homestead allowance, exempt personal property set-aside, and family allowance) either before or during the marriage. [*See, e.g.,* UPC §2-213; Kan. Stat. §59-6a213]

(1) Writing required [§238]

To be valid, a waiver must be in *writing* and *signed* by the spouse. In some states, the waiver also must be acknowledged before a notary public. [*See* N.Y. Est. Powers & Trusts Law §5-1.1-A(e)]

(2) No consideration but fair disclosure required [§239]

In most states, a waiver is valid even if there is no consideration for the waiver, but there must be fair disclosure as to the effect of the waiver. [*See, e.g.,* S.C. Code §62-2-204; **Geddings v. Geddings,** 460 S.E.2d 376 (S.C. 1995)] "Fair disclosure contemplates that each spouse should be given information, of a general and approximate nature, concerning the net worth of the other." [*In re* **Lopata's Estate,** 641 P.2d 952 (Colo. 1982)] In a few states, fair disclosure is required for waivers made during the marriage, but not for waivers that are part of an antenuptial agreement. [*See* Fla. Prob. Code §732.702]

EXAM TIP   **gilbert**

Filing a waiver of an elective share entitlement is theoretically similar to filing a disclaimer against the decedent's estate. (*See supra,* §§143-163.) Once a valid waiver has been filed, it is *binding*. As long as there was fair disclosure, the surviving spouse will not be able to withdraw the waiver and file for an elective share.

---

3. Lifetime and Nonprobate Transfers

a. Case law [§240]

Historically, elective share statutes applied to the decedent's "estate," which was construed to mean the testamentary or probate estate. Thus, the statutes did not apply to nontestamentary transfers or to property transferred during the decedent's lifetime. As a consequence, absent judicial intervention, a spouse might make substantial lifetime or nonprobate transfers, perhaps retaining the right to income and other economic benefits, then die leaving a modest probate estate, and thereby defeat the surviving spouse's elective share right. With the increased use of testamentary substitutes (such as revocable trusts), the courts developed various doctrines under which the surviving spouse may be able to challenge a particular transfer.

(1) Illusory transfer doctrine [§241]

Following the lead of **Newman v. Dore,** 250 A.D. 708 (1937), a number of courts adopted the "illusory transfer" doctrine, under which the transferred property was subject to the elective share statute if the transferor retained so many controls over the property that the transfer was "illusory." This test does not depend on the motive that may have prompted the transfer, but rather looks to the *degree of control* retained by the transferor.

Example: Ricky executes a will that devises one-third of his estate (the elective share amount) to his estranged wife Lucy. However, shortly before his death, Ricky transfers the bulk of his estate to the trustee of a revocable trust, retaining trust income for life, the power to revoke or amend the trust, and the power to control the trustee in its administration of the trust. The trustee cannot take any significant actions in administering the trust without Ricky's prior approval. The trust is to terminate on Ricky's death, and the trust principal is to be distributed to his sister. Because the majority of Ricky's estate is settled in the trust (and not in the probate estate), on Ricky's death the elective share statute gives Lucy one-third of zero. On these and similar facts, and particularly because of the controls over the trustee, some courts held that such a transfer was illusory; *i.e.,* the transfer was "colorable" and not "real." Thus, the trust assets were subject to the surviving spouse's elective share. [*See* **Newman v. Dore,** *supra*]

(a) Criticism

The illusory transfer doctrine has been criticized because of its vagueness and imprecision. Concepts such as "illusory" and "colorable" have no inherent meaning and do not provide a basis for analysis or predicting the outcome of decisions. In states that have adopted the illusory transfer doctrine, there has been considerable litigation over whether particular forms of transfer (*e.g.,* revocable trusts with no retained power to control the trustee, Totten trust bank accounts) are illusory. After numerous cases dealing with the issue, New York, the "home" of the illusory transfer doctrine, rejected it in favor of a bright line test for determining which transfers are subject to the elective share. (*See infra,* §242.)

EXAM TIP   **gilbert**

Remember that the illusory transfer doctrine takes into consideration only the decedent's **retained degree of control** over the property. The motive for the transfer is **irrelevant**. For example, assume the decedent transfers property into a nonrevocable trust for the specific purpose of defeating his surviving spouse's elective share; he does not retain any control over the trust assets. The trust assets will not be subject to the elective share **even though the motive to create the trust was to defeat the elective share**.

---

(2) Motive or intent to defeat share [§242]

A number of courts rejected the "illusory transfer" doctrine and hold that a lifetime transfer is subject to the surviving spouse's elective share if the motive or intent of the transferor was to **defeat the elective share right**. [*See* Mo. Rev. Stat. §474.150.1; **Hanke v. Hanke,** 459 A.2d 246 (N.H. 1983); **Patch v. Squires,** 165 A. 919 (Vt. 1933)] In these states, various factors have been recognized by the courts as indicative of an intent to defraud the spouse such as whether: (i) there was **consideration** for the transfer, (ii) the decedent **retained control** over the transferred asset, (iii) the **amount** of the transfer was **disproportionate** compared to the value of the decedent's total estate, and (iv) the transfer was made **openly** and with frank disclosure. [*See* **Nelson v. Nelson,** 512 S.W.2d

455 (Mo. 1974)] In some states, the intent to deprive a surviving spouse of the elective share is deemed material only when the estate contains little or no other property to which the election might attach. [*See* **Conner v. Nationwide Maintenance Service,** 44 So. 2d 684 (Fla. 1950)]

(3) Balancing the equities [§243]

Some courts adopt a "balancing" approach that considers the equities on a case-by-case basis. Under this approach, in deciding whether a particular transfer is subject to the elective share, the court considers such factors as the completeness of the transfer (revocable or irrevocable), the transferor's motive, whether it was a "brink of death" transfer, participation of the transferee in the alleged fraud, and the degree to which the transfer deprived the surviving spouse of benefits in the decedent's estate. [*See, e.g.,* **Whittington v. Whittington,** 106 A.2d 72 (Md. 1954); **Windsor v. Leonard,** 475 F.2d 932 (D.C. Cir. 1973)]

(4) Revocable inter vivos trusts [§244]

Absent a statute on the question, the courts are divided as to whether property in a revocable trust, in which the settlor has retained the income for life and the right to revoke or amend the trust, is subject to the surviving spouse's elective share right. A number of courts have subjected such assets to the right of election on the ground that the powers and benefits retained by the settlor are tantamount to ownership. [*See, e.g.,* **Sullivan v. Burkin,** 460 N.E.2d 572 (Mass. 1984); 39 A.L.R.3d 14] Other courts have ruled that since revocable trusts constitute valid transfers under state law, they are not subject to the elective share statute. [*See, e.g.,* **Cherniack v. Home National Bank & Trust Co.,** 198 A.2d 58 (Conn. 1964); **Johnson v. La Grange State Bank,** 383 N.E.2d 185 (Ill. 1978)]

TESTS TO DETERMINE WHETHER LIFETIME AND NON-PROBATE ASSETS ARE SUBJECT TO THE ELECTIVE SHARE **gilbert**	
ILLUSORY TRANSFER DOCTRINE	Transferred property is subject to the elective share if the transferor *retained enough control over the property* to make the transfer illusory. Does not consider the motive of the transferor.
MOTIVE OR INTENT TO DEFEAT ELECTIVE SHARE	A transfer is subject to the elective share if the motive or intent of the transferor was to *defeat the surviving spouse's elective share right*.
BALANCING THE EQUITIES	The court *balances the equities* in the particular case and weighs factors such as the transferor's motive, whether the transfer is irrevocable, and the degree to which the spouse is deprived of benefits in estate to determine whether the property is subject to the elective share.
REVOCABLE INTER VIVOS TRUSTS	The courts are *divided*. Some courts hold that assets in a revocable trust are subject to the elective share, while others hold that they are not.

b. Original Uniform Probate Code

(1) Augmented estate [§245]

Under the original UPC, the elective share statute applies to the decedent's "augmented estate." The augmented estate consists of the net probate estate *plus* the value of property transferred *to persons other than the decedent's spouse* during his lifetime for less than adequate and full consideration, if the transfer falls into one of the following categories:

(i) *Retained life estate*—transfers in which the decedent retained the right to possession or enjoyment of, or the income from, property;

(ii) *Retained controls*—transfers in which the decedent retained the right to revoke, or to invade, consume, or dispose of the principal for his own benefit;

(iii) *Transfers within two years of death*—gifts made within two years of death, to the extent that such gifts to any one donee in any year exceeded $3,000; or

(iv) *Survivorship estates*—transfers whereby property is held at the time of the decedent's death by the decedent and another with right of survivorship (joint tenancies, joint bank accounts, etc.).

[Original UPC §2-202]

(2) Intestacy [§246]

The original UPC's elective share statute applies when the decedent died intestate as well as when the decedent left a will. The purpose of this provision is to prevent avoidance of the augmented estate rules. Otherwise, a spouse could make massive gifts shortly before death, or gifts with the retained power to revoke, etc., and then die intestate, leaving the surviving spouse with a right of election in an estate of zero.

(3) Transfers to spouse [§247]

Under the original UPC, the augmented estate also includes the value of property *given to the spouse by the decedent* during the marriage. Under this rule, the augmented estate includes: any property owned by the spouse at the decedent's death and also such property given by the spouse to third parties; a beneficial interest given to the spouse in a trust created by the decedent during lifetime; property passing to the spouse by the decedent's exercise of a power of appointment; and life insurance proceeds and employee benefits (other than Social Security benefits) paid to the spouse.

(a) Rationale

If the decedent provided for the spouse by gifts during the marriage, these gifts should be taken into account in determining the amount to which the spouse is entitled at death. Including such gifts in the augmented estate reduces the amount passing to the spouse under the elective share. While the inclusion has the effect of increasing the amount against which the one-third elective share fraction applies, such gifts count dollar for dollar as in partial satisfaction of the elective share amount.

(b) Burden of proof [§248]

The surviving spouse has the burden of establishing that property owned by the spouse at the decedent's death (and property given by the spouse to others during the decedent's lifetime) was derived from a source *other than* gifts from the decedent.

1) Comment

A troublesome feature of this rule is the tracing required to show how the surviving spouse acquired the property that she owned at the decedent's death (*i.e.*, whether by gift from the decedent or from an independent source). As noted below, the revised UPC eliminates this tracing problem by redefining the augmented estate to include *all* property owned by the surviving spouse at the decedent's death.

(4) Property not included in augmented estate [§249]

Under the original UPC, the augmented estate does not include any *life insurance*, joint annuity, or pension benefit payable to a person *other than* the surviving spouse.

(5) Waiver by spouse [§250]

A transfer to a person other than the spouse is *excluded* from the augmented estate if made with the spouse's *written* consent or joinder.

(6) Valuation of property [§251]

Property included in the augmented estate is valued *as of the decedent's death*, except that property given irrevocably to a donee during lifetime is valued as of the date the donee came into possession and enjoyment, if that occurred before the decedent's death.

c. Revised Uniform Probate Code [§252]

The augmented estate under the revised UPC includes *all of the transfers covered by the original UPC*. However, as noted earlier, to implement the marital partnership theory the augmented estate has been expanded to include the *surviving spouse's own property*, including assets transferred by the spouse within two years of the decedent's death, transfers with retained life estates, and transfers with retained controls. The augmented estate also includes assets passing from the decedent to the surviving spouse by right of survivorship, and benefits paid to the spouse under a retirement plan in which the decedent was a participant (except for Social Security). [UPC §2-206] Including the surviving spouse's own property in the augmented estate produces a result more closely attuned to the division of marital property that occurs in a community property state.

(1) Life insurance payable to third parties [§253]

In another major expansion, the augmented estate under the revised UPC includes insurance on the decedent's life paid to *any* beneficiary if the decedent owned the policy, held a general power of appointment over it (*i.e.*, had the power to name new beneficiaries), or, while married to the surviving spouse, transferred the policy to another person within two years of death. [UPC §2-205] As noted above, the original UPC included insurance proceeds in the augmented estate only if paid to the surviving spouse. (*See supra*, §247.)

EXAM TIP | **gilbert**

Notice that the original and revised UPCs are essentially the same in their treatment of what is included in the decedent's augmented estate with two important distinctions: (i) the revised UPC includes *all of the surviving spouse's property* and not just property transferred to her by the decedent, and (ii) the revised UPC includes *life insurance payable to third parties* under certain limited circumstances.

---

d. Other statutory solutions

(1) New York [§254]

The New York elective share statute takes an approach similar to the UPC by applying the elective share statute to the decedent's net probate estate *plus testamentary substitutes.* [N.Y. Est. Powers & Trusts Law §5-1.1-A] The list of testamentary substitutes includes interests passing to the surviving spouse by right of survivorship (but only one-half thereof); survivorship estates with third parties (to the extent that the decedent furnished the consideration); Totten trust bank accounts and other pay on death ("P.O.D.") arrangements; lifetime transfers with the retained power to revoke or to consume, invade, or dispose of the principal; gifts exceeding federal gift tax annual exclusions made within one year of death; and one-half of qualified pension plan benefits.

(2) Delaware [§255]

In Delaware, the property subject to the elective share is defined as all property includible in the decedent's gross estate under the federal estate tax, regardless of whether the decedent's estate must file an estate tax return. [Del. Code tit. 12, §902] This approach has the advantage of incorporating into elective share law the well-defined rules governing the federal estate tax with which estate practitioners are used to dealing.

(3) Other statutes [§256]

Several states have statutes that are less comprehensive (and considerably less complicated) than the UPC and New York models. These statutes reach lifetime transfers in which the decedent retained a testamentary power of appointment, a power to revoke, or a power to consume the property. [*See, e.g.,* Pa. Stat. Ann. tit. 20, §2203] One major consequence of these statutes is to prevent the use of revocable trusts to defeat the surviving spouse's right of election.

4. Community Property States

a. No elective share statutes [§257]

None of the community property states has an elective share statute. Each spouse has the power of testamentary disposition over only his one-half community interest. Because the surviving spouse automatically owns one-half of the community estate on the first spouse's death, there is no perceived need for a statutory scheme to protect against disinheritance.

(1) Exception—quasi-community property [§258]

Four of the community property states have enacted "quasi-community property" statutes, a form of elective share statute that applies to certain assets acquired by the couple before they moved to the community property state. (*See supra,* §199.)

(2) Separate property [§259]

Each spouse has the *unrestricted* power of testamentary disposition over his separate property.

b. Election wills [§260]

In a community property state, the surviving spouse is put to an election if the deceased spouse leaves a will that purports to dispose of the *entire interest* in community property and not just the one-half community interest over which he has the power of testamentary disposition. In this type of situation, the surviving spouse can elect to take under or against the will.

(1) Illustration—language giving rise to an election will [§261]

Language that puts the surviving spouse to an election might read as follows: "It is my intention by this will to dispose of the entire interest in the community property of my wife and myself, and not just the one-half share over which I have the power of disposition . . . ." A typical dispositive plan under such a will is to devise the family residence and tangible personal property outright to the spouse (free of any election), and then leave the remaining community estate in trust: income to the surviving spouse for life, remainder to the decedent's descendants.

(a) Election against the will [§262]

Since the decedent does not have testamentary power over the surviving spouse's one-half community interest, the surviving spouse does not have to accept the terms of the will. She can *elect to take the one-half community to which she is entitled* by law, rejecting the will's terms. If she does so, however, she *relinquishes all testamentary gifts* in her favor made in the will. [**Estate of Murphy**, 15 Cal. 3d 907 (1976)]

(b) Election to take under will [§263]

If the surviving spouse elects to take under the will, the decedent's will operates to transfer the surviving spouse's one-half community interest, as well as his own, according to the terms of the will.

(c) Comment

Election wills were occasionally used in the 1960s and 1970s because of perceived advantages under the federal estate tax. Election wills are rarely employed today largely because of changes in the tax laws.

(2) Accidental election wills [§264]

The illustration above involved a deliberate attempt to dispose of the surviving spouse's one-half community property interest. However, the election situation may arise **unintentionally**.

---

e.g. **Example:** Hal's will includes this provision: "I own Blackacre, my farm in Hunt County, as my separate property. I devise the fee simple title thereto to my brother Bill. I devise all the rest of my property to my wife, Wanda." However, Blackacre is actually the community property of Hal and Wanda. Since the will purports to dispose of the entire fee simple title in Blackacre, Wanda is put to an election. If Wanda elects against the will, she takes her one-half interest in Blackacre (and will be a tenant in common with Bill); *but* she must give up all gifts made to her by Hal's will. If Wanda wants to take the interests given to her by the will, she must allow the will to operate to transfer her one-half interest in Blackacre to Bill. [*See, e.g., In re* **Johnson's Estate**, 178 Cal. App. 2d 826 (1960)]

---

cf. **Compare:** However, a gift of "all of my property, of all kinds and wherever located, in which I have an interest at the time of my death" does *not* put the surviving spouse to an election. Such a will disposes of only the interests over which the decedent had the power of disposition—*i.e.*, his separate property and his one-half community interest. There is a presumption that the decedent by his will did not intend to dispose of property that he did not own (*i.e.*, his spouse's one-half community interest). [*See, e.g., In re* **Wolfe's Estate**, 48 Cal. 2d 570 (1957); 60 A.L.R.2d 736]

(a) Joint tenancy property [§265]

An election may be required where a testator's will purports to dispose of property that he held in joint tenancy with the surviving spouse or with another party.

---

e.g. **Example:** Henry's will purports to devise the entire interest in property that he holds in joint tenancy with his wife Georgia, "one-half to my daughter Virginia, and the other half to Georgia," and bequeaths his residuary estate to Georgia. Georgia is put to an election to assert her right to the whole of the joint tenancy property (*i.e.,* by right of survivorship), or to accept the gifts provided in the will (half of the joint tenancy property plus the residue). [**Estate of Waters,** 24 Cal. App. 3d 81 (1972)]

---

(3) Common law states [§266]

An election will also can be encountered in a common law jurisdiction if a will that makes a gift to a beneficiary also purports to dispose of property that is owned by that beneficiary [*See, e.g.,* Ga. Code §53-4-70; **Holliday v. Pope,** 53 S.E.2d 350 (Ga. 1949)], or if the testator purports to devise her interest in property held in joint tenancy with right of survivorship [60 A.L.R.2d 736].

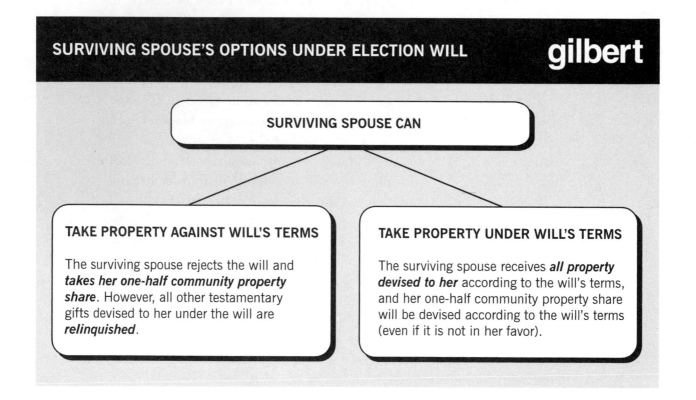

SURVIVING SPOUSE'S OPTIONS UNDER ELECTION WILL **gilbert**

SURVIVING SPOUSE CAN

TAKE PROPERTY AGAINST WILL'S TERMS

The surviving spouse rejects the will and *takes her one-half community property share*. However, all other testamentary gifts devised to her under the will are *relinquished*.

TAKE PROPERTY UNDER WILL'S TERMS

The surviving spouse receives *all property devised to her* according to the will's terms, and her one-half community property share will be devised according to the will's terms (even if it is not in her favor).

c. Lifetime gifts of community property [§267]

Suppose that one spouse gives community property to a third party without the other spouse's joinder or consent. Can the other spouse set aside the transfer?

(1) Majority rule [§268]

Most of the community property states take the position that one spouse can make "reasonable" gifts of community property, so long as those gifts are not "in fraud of the other spouse's community rights." [**Howard v. Howard,** 96 So. 2d 345 (La. 1957)] This is often referred to by courts as the "fraud on the wife" doctrine since the husband was, until recently, the sole "manager" of the community estate, and most of the litigated cases involved gifts by the husband. However, a lifetime gift of community property by a wife may be found to be in fraud of the husband's community rights. [*See* **Cockerham v. Cockerham,** 527 S.W.2d 162 (Tex. 1975)]

(a) Criticism

The "fraud on the spouse" doctrine has the advantage of flexibility, but the concomitant disadvantage of not providing clear guidelines for predicting the outcome of cases. Also, while the rule has a historical basis (*i.e.,* it is applied under the Spanish and French community property systems), it is difficult to justify a *gift* of community property as being within the power to *manage* such assets.

(b) "Fraudulent" transfer [§269]

An actual intent to defraud need not be proved; a particular transfer may be "constructively" fraudulent. [**Davis v. Prudential Insurance Co.,** 331 F.2d 346 (5th Cir. 1964)] The courts consider various factors in determining whether a particular transfer is in fraud of the other spouse's community rights. [**Barnett v. Barnett,** 985 S.W.2d 520 (Tex. 1998)]

1) Amount of gift [§270]

One factor is the amount of the gift in relation to the size of the community estate. Thus, a husband's gift of $30,000 to his children by a former marriage might seem excessive when considered by itself, but in the context of a $250,000 community estate the gift might be considered reasonable. [*See* **Brown v. Brown,** 282 S.W.2d 90 (Tex. 1955)]

2) Relationship of donee [§271]

The donee's close relationship to the donor (*e.g.,* child, parent, sibling) is a factor that tends to support upholding the gift. [*See* **Kemp v. Metropolitan Life Insurance Co.,** 220 F.2d 952 (5th Cir. 1955)] On the other hand, if the donee is not related to the donor, there is a strong *presumption* that the gift is constructively fraudulent. [**Givens v. Girard Life Insurance Co.,** 480 S.W.2d 421 (Tex. 1972)]

3) Amount of remaining community estate [§272]

If the remaining community estate is sufficient to make ample provision for the surviving spouse, this factor tends to support the gift. [*See* **Krueger v. Williams,** 359 S.W.2d 48 (Tex. 1962)]

(c) Nontestamentary transfers [§273]

In the states following the majority rule, life insurance dispositions and interests passing by right of survivorship are considered lifetime transfers for purposes of these rules; *i.e.,* they are subject to the "fraud on the spouse" doctrine, and not the surviving spouse's right of election. Thus, if they are not "reasonable" gifts of community property, they may be set aside.

Example: Colin is the insured under a $100,000 life insurance policy that names his mother as the primary beneficiary. On Colin's death, his wife, Sheila, cannot set aside the beneficiary designation as to her one-half community interest in the policy proceeds unless she establishes that naming Colin's mother as beneficiary was in fraud of Sheila's community rights.

---

(2) Minority rule [§274]

In several states, lifetime transfers of community property are treated the same as testamentary transfers under an election will: Except for *de minimis* gifts, the spouse who does not join in or consent to such a transfer can *elect* to set the transfer aside (or receive reimbursement from other community assets) as to her one-half community share. [*See, e.g.,* Cal. Fam. Code §1100; Wash. Rev. Code §26.16.030; **United States v. Stewart,** 270 F.2d 894 (9th Cir. 1959)—California law, life insurance proceeds; **Bryant v. Bryant,** 882 P.2d 169 (Wash. 1994)]

CAN A LIFETIME GIFT OF COMMUNITY PROPERTY BY ONE SPOUSE BE SET ASIDE BY THE OTHER SPOUSE?	**gilbert**
MAJORITY RULE ("FRAUD ON THE SPOUSE" DOCTRINE)	The gift will not be set aside unless it is *unreasonable* or *fraudulent on the other spouse's community property rights*. To determine if the gift is fraudulent, consider: (i) The *amount* of the gift, (ii) The *relationship* of the donee to the donor, and (iii) The *size* of the community estate after the gift is deducted. Nonprobate transfers are also subject to this analysis.
MINORITY RULE	The spouse can elect to *set aside the lifetime gift* or receive *reimbursement* from other community assets (except for *de minimls* gifts).

d. Community property brought to common law state [§275]

Suppose that a husband and wife live in a community property jurisdiction for a number of years and then move to a common law state, bringing community property assets with them. Suppose further that the community funds are invested in new assets, title to which is taken in the husband's name. What is the ownership status of the assets acquired with "imported community property"? It should be clear that since the wife owned an undivided one-half interest in the community property before the move, those property rights should not be lost even though title is taken in the husband's name. Under established conflict of laws principles, the ownership of marital assets is determined under the laws of the marital domicile *at the time the assets are acquired.* Such ownership interests, once acquired, are not lost upon a move to another jurisdiction.

(1) Case decisions [§276]

Surprisingly, there are relatively few cases dealing with imported community property. This may be because the possible significance of the community history of such assets has been overlooked, as the general rule in common law jurisdictions is that ownership is determined by the manner in which title is held or registered. In the handful of reported cases in which the surviving spouse has asserted an ownership interest, she has been successful under either a constructive trust theory [**Edwards v. Edwards,** 233 P. 477 (Okla. 1924)] or a resulting trust theory [**Quintana v. Ordono,** 195 So. 2d 577 (Fla. 1967)].

(2) Uniform Disposition of Community Property Rights at Death Act [§277]

Several jurisdictions have enacted the Uniform Disposition of Community Property Rights at Death Act ("UDOCPRADA"), which recognizes both spouses' interests in the imported community property regardless of how title is taken in the new state. [*See, e.g.,* Ky. Rev. Stat. §391.210; N.Y. Est. Powers & Trusts Law §6-6.1; Or. Rev. Stat. §112.705] The UDOCPRADA applies to all property that was acquired as community property under the laws of another jurisdiction or was acquired with the income from or the proceeds of sale of such community property. Under the UDOCPRADA, upon the death of one spouse, only one-half of such property is subject to testamentary disposition or intestate distribution. The remaining one-half of the property belongs to the surviving spouse and does not pass through the decedent's estate.

B. Protection of the Children

1. Pretermitted Child Statutes [§278]

Except in Louisiana, which has forced heirship rules [La. Civ. Code art. 1493], it is possible for a testator to *disinherit* her children. A parent need not bequeath anything

gilbert

Was a child who is omitted from his parent's will **born or adopted after the will's execution**? (Check for codicils.)

— NO →

Was the child **intentionally omitted** from the will? (Check the facts for clues to the testator's intent; generally intent must appear on face of will.)

— YES →

Was the child **provided for by a lifetime settlement or nonprobate transfer**? (Look for trusts, life insurance policies, etc.)

— YES →

Child is **not covered by the pretermitted child statute** and will not receive a share of the estate.

Did the testator have another child alive at the time the will was executed and did the testator devise substantially all of his estate **to the other parent of the omitted child**? (Under the UPC and in a minority of states.)

— YES →

↓ NO

Child is **covered by the pretermitted child statute** and receives a share of the estate.

to the children—not even the proverbial one dollar. [*See* **Brown v. Drake,** 270 S.E.2d 130 (S.C. 1980)] However, many states have statutes called "pretermitted child" statutes which are designed to protect children who may have been *accidentally* omitted from the will.

a. Majority rule [§279]

In most states, the statute operates only in favor of children born or adopted *after the will's execution*. [*See* UPC §2-302(a); Tex. Prob. Code §67; Va. Code §64.1-70]

---

e.g. Example: Elizabeth has a child, Charles, at the time she executes a will that bequeaths her estate one-third to her husband, Philip, and two-thirds to her sister Margaret. The will makes no mention of Charles or of any future children that Elizabeth might have. There is nothing to indicate that Charles's omission was intentional. Thereafter, Elizabeth and Philip have another child, Anne. Elizabeth then dies without having revoked or modified her will. Anne takes a share of Elizabeth's estate as a pretermitted child, but Charles takes nothing because he was alive at the time the will was executed.

EXAM TIP   **gilbert**

The pretermitted child issue comes up fairly often on exams, sometimes as one issue in a question of many issues. So, whenever you see a child born or adopted *after a will has been executed*, don't overlook the possibility that the pretermitted child statute may apply.

---

(1) Exception—child believed to be dead [§280]

Under the UPC, if a testator fails to provide for a child solely because she mistakenly believes that the child is dead, the child receives a share of the estate *equal to an intestate share*. [UPC §2-302(c)]

(2) Georgia rule [§281]

In Georgia, birth or adoption of a child revokes an earlier will *in its entirety* [Ga. Code §53-4-48] unless the will states in unmistakable terms that it was written in contemplation of the future birth or adoption of a child [**McParland v. McParland,** 211 S.E.2d 748 (Ga. 1975)].

b. Minority rule [§282]

In several states, the pretermitted child statute applies to children *alive when the will was executed*, as well as to afterborn and after-adopted children. [*See, e.g.,* Okla. Stat. tit. 84, §132] This is a very different type of statute, as it requires a testator to name or at least refer to her children in order to prevent the statute's operation.

---

e.g. Example: In these states, *Charles and Anne* in the above example would both take a share of Elizabeth's estate.

---

c. Grandchildren [§283]

In most states, the pretermitted child statute *operates only in favor of children*, and not grandchildren, of the testator. [UPC §2-302(a)] However, in a substantial minority of states, the statute also applies to the descendants of a *deceased* child of the testator. [*See, e.g.,* Ohio Rev. Code §2107.34; Okla. Stat. tit. 84, §132]

2. When Statute Does Not Apply [§284]

Under the typical pretermitted child statute, the child takes an intestate share of the decedent's estate *unless* an exception written into the statute applies.

a. Intentional omission [§285]

A number of statutes provide that a child who is born or adopted after the will is executed is *not protected* if it appears that the omission was *intentional*. (*See supra,* §282.)

(1) Majority rule [§286]

A majority of these states require that the decedent's intention to omit the child must appear *on the face of the will*. If the will does not speak to the situation, extrinsic evidence is *not admissible* to show that the omission was intentional. [*See, e.g.,* **Armstrong v. Butler,** 553 S.W.2d 453 (Ark. 1977); *In re* **Glomset's Estate,** 547 P.2d 951 (Okla. 1976)] Such statutes raise the issue of what language is required in the will to evidence such intent.

(2) Minority rule [§287]

Some courts admit *extrinsic evidence* on the issue of whether the testator intended to disinherit her children. [*See, e.g.,* Wis. Stat. §853.25(1); 88 A.L.R.2d 616]

b. Child provided for by settlement [§288]

Under a number of statutes, the child who otherwise would be protected by the statute is not pretermitted if provision is made for the child by a *lifetime settlement* or *nonprobate transfer*.

---

e.g. **Example:** Yuri executes a will that bequeaths his estate one-third to his wife Lara and two-thirds to his son Nicolai. Thereafter, Yuri and Lara have another child, Boris. Two years after Boris's birth, Yuri creates a trust for Boris's benefit. Yuri then dies survived by Lara, Nicolai, and Boris. Boris is not a pretermitted child within the meaning of the statute because he was provided for by a lifetime settlement.

---

(1) Comment

It is the *existence* of the settlement, not its amount, that controls. If, in the above example, the trust was funded with assets worth $10,000 and Yuri left a $3 million estate, Boris would take considerably less than Nicolai (who would take $2 million under the will). The purpose of pretermitted child statutes is to cover *accidental omission* of a child who is not provided for by settlement, *not* to provide equality of treatment among siblings.

c. **Uniform Probate Code [§289]**

Under the UPC and in a minority of states, there is no pretermission of an afterborn or after-adopted child if:

(i) It appears *from the will* that the omission was *intentional;*

(ii) The testator had one or more children when the will was executed and devised substantially all of his estate to the other *parent* of the omitted child; *or*

(iii) The testator provided for the omitted child by *transfer outside the will* and the *intent* that the transfer be in lieu of a testamentary bequest is shown by the testator's statements, the amount of the transfer, or other evidence.

[UPC §2-302]

3. **Amount of Pretermitted Child's Share**

a. **Majority rule [§290]**

Under most statutes, the pretermitted child takes an amount equal to an *intestate share* of the deceased parent's estate—*i.e.*, the share the child would have taken if the parent had died intestate. [*See* Iowa Code §633.267; Wash. Rev. Code §11.12.091] The will controls the disposition of the remaining assets.

(1) **Abatement [§291]**

In most jurisdictions, the ordinary rules of abatement apply when making up the pretermitted child's share (*see infra*, §§1070-1078). The child's share comes first out of intestate property (if any), then the residuary estate, etc. [*See* Original UPC §§2-302(c), 3-902; Wash. Rev. Code §11.12.091]

(2) **Pro rata abatement [§292]**

In some states, the residuary estate is not burdened with the entire cost of the pretermitted child's share. All testamentary gifts abate proportionately unless this would defeat the testator's obvious intent with respect to some specific gift. [*See, e.g.*, Tenn. Code §32-3-103]

EXAM TIP   **gilbert**

To determine what the pretermitted child's share of the estate is, you will have to refer to the state's intestate succession statutes. Recall that the child's intestate share may vary depending on whether the testator was survived by a spouse and whether that *spouse was the child's other parent*.

b. Revised Uniform Probate Code [§293]

Under the revised UPC, the pretermitted child who is not provided for by lifetime settlement does not take an intestate share (unless the testator had no other living children when the will was executed) and the will is not void. Instead, to the extent feasible, the pretermitted child takes the *same share of the parent's estate as the testator's other children*, and the other children's testamentary gifts are *reduced ratably* in making up the pretermitted child's share. [UPC §2-302(a)] Several non-UPC states have enacted similar statutes. [*See, e.g.,* N.Y. Est. Powers & Trusts Law §5-3.2; Tex. Prob. Code §67(a)]

Example: Giulio bequeaths $60,000 to each of his children, Gina and Frank, and devises his residuary estate to his sister Laura. Thereafter, he adopts a child, Marina, who is not provided for by lifetime settlement. Under the revised UPC, the gifts to Gina and Frank are reduced in Marina's favor; each takes $40,000. Laura takes the residuary estate.

---

(1) Comment

Unlike most statutes, the revised UPC *does* attempt to provide equality of treatment among all of the testator's children—those given gifts in the will and those born or adopted thereafter. Only the gifts to the testator's other children are reduced; no other beneficiary is affected by the pretermission.

4. Republication by Codicil [§294]

The doctrine of republication by codicil (*see infra*, §640) can operate to eliminate the rights of a child born to, or adopted by, the testator after the will's execution.

Example: In 1998, Tony executes a will that devises one-half of his estate to his wife Silvana and the remaining one-half to his daughter, Rose. In 2001, a son Bob is born to Tony. In 2002, Tony executes a codicil that changes the alternate executor. Under the doctrine of republication by codicil, the will is deemed to have been executed in 2002; therefore, Bob is not entitled to any protection under the pretermitted child statute. [*See, e.g.,* **Azcunce v. Estate of Azcunce,** 586 So. 2d 1216 (Fla. 1991); **Laborde v. First State Bank & Trust Co.,** 101 S.W.2d 389 (Tex. 1936)]

EXAM TIP	gilbert

Questions about republication of a will by codicil are another possible way for a professor to test your knowledge of the pretermitted child statutes. You may see facts indicating a potential pretermitted child issue—*e.g.,* Testator executes his will and then has a child—but watch out for a codicil. If Testator executes a *codicil after the child was born*, under most statutes, the child is no longer "pretermitted" (but is "out of luck"): Because the child was alive when the codicil was executed, he no longer falls under the protection of the statute and does not receive a share of the estate.

C. Protection of the Family

1. **Homestead [§295]**

   Several states have homestead laws designed to give the family residence or farm limited protection (or in several states very substantial protection) from creditors' claims. Homestead laws differ so markedly from jurisdiction to jurisdiction that easy generalizations are not possible. Representative features of several states' homestead laws are summarized below.

   a. **Protection from creditors' claims [§296]**

      The most common feature of the homestead laws is that property that qualifies as a homestead cannot be reached to satisfy creditors' claims *except for valid liens on the homestead* itself (*e.g.,* purchase money or other mortgage lien, real property taxes). In most jurisdictions, this homestead protection applies to claims asserted by creditors of an insolvent decedent's estate *if* the decedent was survived by a spouse or minor children.

   b. **What property qualifies as a homestead [§297]**

      In general, to qualify as a homestead the property must have been acquired for *actual or intended use as a primary residence*. In most jurisdictions, there is either an acreage limit or a dollar limit on the amount of property that can qualify for homestead protection.

      (1) **Acreage limit [§298]**

          The Texas and Florida laws are very generous in determining what constitutes a homestead. In Texas, homestead protection is given to up to 10 acres of land if urban, and up to 200 acres if rural—in both cases, without regard to the value of improvements on the land. [Tex. Prop. Code §41.002] In Florida, the acreage limits are one-half acre for land located within a municipality, and 160 acres for rural lands, without regard to the value of improvements. [Fla. Const. art. 10, §4(a)(1)]

      (2) **Dollar limit [§299]**

          In many states, property qualifying for homestead protection is limited to a dollar amount. In several states, the dollar amount is so small that it does not cover the full value of the homestead. As a result, the homestead law in these states merely gives the surviving spouse a cash allowance that is free from creditors' claims. [*See, e.g.,* Utah Code §75-2-402—$15,000]

   c. **Texas—probate homestead [§300]**

      In Texas, the surviving spouse (or, if there is no surviving spouse, the decedent's minor or dependent children) is entitled to *occupy the homestead* as a residence for as long as she chooses to occupy it. [Tex. Const. art. 16, §52] This right of occupancy is personal to the spouse (or children) and cannot be assigned. If the spouse or children cease to occupy the homestead as a residence, the homestead is said to be "abandoned," and the property is free of any homestead occupancy claim. The homestead right in favor of minor children terminates when the children reach the age of majority.

---

e.g. **Example:** Carlos owns the family residence, which qualifies as a homestead, in fee simple. Carlos dies leaving a will that devises "all my property," including his interest in the residence, to his sister Janet. Legal title to the residence passes to Janet. Under the Texas homestead law, however, Carlos's wife has the exclusive right to occupy the residence as a homestead for as long as she chooses to do so. [*See* Tex. Prob. Code §284]

---

d. Florida—restrictions on devise of homestead [§301]

In Florida, the homestead laws operate to *restrict the owner's power of testamentary disposition*. A Florida homestead cannot be devised if the decedent is survived by a spouse or by minor children. The following rules apply:

(i) If the decedent is survived by his *spouse and a minor child*, the spouse takes a life estate with a vested remainder in the decedent's *lineal descendants* (not just minor children).

(ii) If the decedent is survived by his *spouse and adult children* (but no minor children), the homestead can be devised to the spouse only. If the homestead is devised to anyone else, the devise is ineffective; the spouse takes a life estate, with a vested remainder in lineal descendants.

(iii) If the decedent is survived by his *spouse but not by lineal descendants*, the homestead cannot be devised. Instead it passes to the spouse in fee simple.

(iv) If the decedent is *not survived by his spouse* but is survived by *minor* children, the homestead cannot be devised; it passes to the lineal descendants (and not just the minor children).

(v) If the decedent is *not survived by a spouse or by minor children*, then and only then does the decedent have the power of testation.

[Fla. Const. art. 10, §4(c)]

(1) Distinguish—tenancy by entirety [§302]

The Florida rules restricting the power of disposition do not apply if the homestead is held in a *tenancy by the entirety*. In such a case, title passes to the surviving spouse by right of survivorship.

e. Uniform Probate Code [§303]

The UPC grants a lump sum *homestead allowance* of $15,000 rather than a right to occupy the homestead. The allowance has priority over all claims against the estate, and is over and above the amount passing to the surviving spouse, minor children, or dependent adult children by intestate succession, elective share, or will (unless the will provides otherwise). [UPC §2-402]

f. Right of quarantine [§304]

Several states, mostly on the east coast, grant the surviving spouse a right of quarantine adapted from the common law. This gives the spouse the *right to occupy the family home rent-free* for a specified period after the decedent's death. [*See, e.g.,* Mass. Gen. Laws ch. 196, §1—six months] A Virginia statute provides that if the decedent died intestate survived by descendants from an earlier marriage, or if the surviving spouse files for an elective share, the spouse has the right to occupy the principal residence until her rights are determined and satisfied. [*See* Va. Code §64.1-16.4]

2. Exempt Personal Property [§305]

As with the homestead laws, in many states exempt personal property statutes give added protection to the surviving spouse and minor children of a deceased owner. Items of *tangible* personal property that are exempt from creditors' claims during the owner's lifetime are "set aside" for the spouse or children. Typically, the exemption applies to household furnishings, furniture, appliances, personal effects, farm equipment, and (in a number of states) automobiles up to a stated value. [*See, e.g.,* Cal. Prob. Code §6510; Fla. Prob. Code §732.402] In most states, there is a dollar limit on the items within each category that are eligible for a set-aside. [*See* UPC §2-403—$10,000] The exempt property is over and above the amounts passing to the surviving spouse or minor or dependent children by intestate succession, elective share, or will (unless the will provides otherwise).

a. Illustration—New York [§306]

The New York statute is quite generous. Eligible for set-aside are furniture, appliances, computers, etc., up to $10,000 in value; books, videotapes, software, etc., up to $1,000 in value; domestic animals, farm machinery, lawn equipment, etc., up to $15,000 in value; an automobile (up to $15,000 in value); and a $15,000 cash allowance. Thus, property up to $56,000 in value can be claimed as exempt property. [N.Y. Est. Powers & Trusts Law §5-3.1]

b. Set-aside may not be permanent [§307]

In a few states, the exempt property set-aside may be temporary. For example, in Texas, the exempt property set-aside is not permanent unless the decedent's estate is insolvent. On completion of the estate administration, the property must be returned to the estate for distribution pursuant to the decedent's will or by intestate succession, if the estate is solvent. [Tex. Prob. Code §278]

c. Set-aside not automatic [§308]

The specified items of personal property are awarded to the spouse (or, if there is no spouse, to the minor children) only if petition is made for a set-aside. In most estates, the right to an exempt property set-aside is not asserted.

> **Example:** Faith dies leaving a will that bequeaths "all of my real and personal property" to her husband Tim, who survives her. Because all of Faith's personal property passes to Tim under the will, Tim has no reason to petition for a set-aside—unless Faith's estate is insolvent; in that case, the set-aside will secure protection of the assets from creditors' claims.

3. Family Allowance [§309]

In many states, the surviving spouse or minor children are entitled to petition for a family allowance, to provide for their maintenance during the period in which the decedent's estate is tied up in the probate administration. In some states, the allowance is limited to a stated dollar amount. [*See, e.g.,* Fla. Prob. Code §732.403—$18,000] In other states, the allowance is the amount needed to maintain the spouse or children for nine months [Ill. Comp. Stat. ch. 755, §5/15-1] or one year [Ga. Code §53-3-1; Tex. Prob. Code §287], or is specified as a "reasonable" amount to be fixed by the court [Cal. Prob. Code §§6540-6542; D.C. Code §19-101.104].

a. Revised Uniform Probate Code [§310]

Under the revised UPC, the decedent's personal representative may determine the family allowance in a *lump sum not exceeding $18,000*, or in *periodic installments not exceeding $1,500 per month for one year*. Amounts in excess of these amounts may be ordered by the court. [UPC §2-405]

b. Allowance takes precedence over other claims [§311]

Typically, the allowance takes precedence over all claims *except funeral expenses* (up to a stated dollar amount) and *expenses of estate administration*. However, the UPC's family allowance has priority over *all* claims except the homestead allowance. [UPC §2-404]

c. Allowance in addition to other benefit or share [§312]

The family allowance is not chargeable against any benefit or share passing to the surviving spouse (or children) by intestate succession, elective share, or the will of the decedent. However, the testator by his will may make provision for his spouse in lieu of an allowance, in which case the spouse must elect whether to take the allowance or the testamentary gift. [*See* **Studstill v. Studstill,** 204 S.E.2d 496 (Ga. 1974)]

d. Personal right [§313]

Typically, the death of the person entitled to the allowance terminates the right to any remaining part of the allowance not already paid. [*See, e.g.,* Fla. Prob. Code §732.403]

e. Family maintenance [§314]

Two states have enacted statutes that do not set a time limit on the period over which a family allowance may be paid. Maine has enacted UPC section 2-404, (*see supra*, §311) but deleted the limitation on the family allowance to the period of estate administration. [Me. Rev. Stat. tit. 18A, §2-403] Wisconsin provides for the support of a surviving spouse for life, if necessary, and for minor children until age 18. [Wis. Stat. §861.35]

PROTECTIONS AVAILABLE TO THE DECEDENT'S FAMILY	gilbert
HOMESTEAD	Protects family's *primary residence or farm* from creditors' claims. Most jurisdictions impose an *acreage or dollar limit* on the amount that can be protected. Under the UPC, the surviving spouse or children receive a *homestead allowance of $15,000*.
EXEMPT PERSONAL PROPERTY	Items of *tangible personal property* up to a stated value are set aside for the surviving spouse and children. The set-aside is *not automatic*; a petition must be filed.
FAMILY ALLOWANCE	*Specified dollar amount* to assist the spouse or minor children after the decedent's death. Some jurisdictions limit the amount to that needed to support the family for the period during which the estate is being administered, while others extend the period to, *e.g.,* one year. The revised UPC provides for a lump sum payment not exceeding $18,000 *or* monthly payments in an amount not exceeding $1,500 for one year.

D. Testamentary Gifts to Charity

1. Common Law [§315]

At early common law, "*mortmain*" restrictions were placed on the right to make testamentary gifts to a *church*. The reasons were twofold: (i) testators otherwise might be inclined to favor the church over their heirs in wills made shortly before death, out of a concern for increasing their chances in the hereafter, and (ii) the sovereign was concerned about great accumulations of wealth (at common law, land) by the church.

2. Modern Law [§316]

At one time, a number of states imposed restrictions on a person's ability to make testamentary gifts to charity. The restrictions took the form of either voiding all charitable bequests in wills executed within a short time before death or limiting testamentary gifts made within the specified period to a fixed percentage of the estate. [6 A.L.R.4th 603] In recent years, every one of these statutes has either been *repealed* or held *unconstitutional*.

3. **Constitutionality [§317]**

Several statutes voiding gifts in wills made within 30 days of death were held to violate the Equal Protection Clause. The courts reasoned that a statute voiding gifts in a will made 29 days before death but upholding such gifts in a will made 31 days before death was arbitrary, and was not fairly or substantially related to the legislative purpose of protecting the testator's family members from excessive charitable gifts. [*See, e.g., In re* **Kinyon's Estate,** 615 P.2d 174 (Mont. 1980); *In re* **Cavill's Estate,** 329 A.2d 503 (Pa. 1974)] One of the statutes, which applied only to religious gifts, was held unconstitutional on the further ground that there was no rational basis for voiding religious gifts but not gifts to other charities. [*See* **Estate of French,** 365 A.2d 621 (D.C. 1976)]

E. Provisions Against Public Policy

1. **Attempts to Control Beneficiary's Conduct [§318]**

"A testator . . . may choose the objects of his bounty. He may exclude a child or other descendant . . . for sound reason, or because of whim or prejudice which might seem unreasonable to others. He may prefer a prodigal son or even an unrepentant sinner to a son who has been an exemplar and pattern of virtue. . . . The courts do, nevertheless, at times deny validity to a condition annexed to a testamentary gift where the condition is calculated to influence the future conduct of the beneficiary in a manner contrary to the established policy of the State." [*In re* **Liberman,** 279 N.Y. 458 (1939)]

a. **Total restraint on marriage [§319]**

A condition calculated to induce a beneficiary to remain single is against public policy and *void*. [*See, e.g., In re* **Seaman's Will,** 218 N.Y. 77 (1916); **Goffe v. Goffe,** 94 A. 2 (R.I. 1915)] The condition is stricken, and the beneficiary takes the gift free of the restriction. Also, a gift conditioned on marriage with the approval and consent of another beneficiary, whose own interest would be reduced if he gave such consent, is void. [*See In re* **Liberman,** *supra*]

(1) **Distinguish**

However, a trust provision that terminates the interest of a surviving spouse if she remarries is valid. The primary purpose of such a provision is not to restrain remarriage but to provide support to the beneficiary while single, a lawful motive. [*See, e.g., In re* **Lewis Trust,** 652 P.2d 1106 (Colo. 1982); **United States National Bank v. Duling,** 592 P.2d 257 (Or. 1979)]

b. **Partial restraint on marriage [§320]**

A condition in partial restraint on marriage, which merely narrows the beneficiary's range of choices as to who he can marry, is not against public policy. A number of cases have upheld gifts conditioned on the beneficiary marrying within a particular religious faith. [*See, e.g.,* **Gordon v. Gordon,** 124 N.E.2d 228 (Mass. 1955); **Shapira v. Union National Bank,** 315 N.E.2d 825 (Ohio 1974); **United States National Bank v. Snodgrass,** 275 P.2d 860 (Or. 1954)] A condition tied to a daughter's not marrying a particular person (named in the will) is valid. [*See, e.g.,* ***In re* Seaman's Will,** *supra,* §319]

c. Encourage divorce [§321]

A condition whose purpose is to induce a beneficiary to divorce her spouse is against public policy and ***void.*** The beneficiary takes the property free of the condition. [*See, e.g.,* ***In re* Gerbing's Estate,** 337 N.E.2d 29 (Ill. 1975); ***In re* Keffalas's Estate,** 233 A.2d 248 (Pa. 1967)] However, the condition is not against public policy if the court finds that its purpose was not to induce a beneficiary to divorce her spouse but rather to provide for her support *in the event of a divorce.* [**Hunt v. Carroll,** 157 S.W.2d 429 (Tex. 1941)]

d. Other restrictions [§322]

A gift in trust to named relatives on condition that they have no communication or social relations with a disinherited brother has been held invalid as disruptive of family relations. [*See* **Girard Trust Co. v. Schmitz,** 20 A.2d 21 (N.J. 1941)]

2. Encouraging Commission of Crime or Tort [§323]

A provision attached to a gift is ***unenforceable*** if it tends to encourage the commission of a crime or a tortious act by either the trustee or a beneficiary. [*See, e.g.,* Ind. Code §30-4-2-12—trustee; **Myerson v. Myerson,** 357 P.2d 133 (Ariz. 1960); **Stout v. Stout,** 233 S.W. 1057 (Ky. 1921)]

3. Destruction of Property [§324]

Provisions that call for the destruction of property or some other capricious act are ***not enforceable*** because it is against public policy to give effect to them. [*See, e.g.,* **Eyerman v. Mercantile Trust Co.,** 524 S.W.2d 210 (Mo. 1975); ***In re* Scott's Will,** 93 N.W. 109 (Minn. 1903)—direction that executor destroy money belonging to estate] "Although a person may wish to deal capriciously with his property, while he is alive, his self-interest will usually prevent him from doing so. After his death there is no such restraint. . . ." [**Will of Pace,** 93 Misc. 2d 969 (1977)]

Chapter Six: Formal Requisites of Wills

CONTENTS

Chapter Approach

The formal requirements of a will are a rich source of exam questions, and you are likely to see some of the topics covered in this chapter on your exam. In particular, watch for the following issues:

1. **Is the Writing a Will?**

    Although some states allow oral wills in limited circumstances, oral wills are not likely to be tested on your exam. Invariably, you will be dealing with a question that involves a written instrument. But is the writing a will? Other writings (*e.g.*, a list of property to be distributed, a letter expressing a desire to give the property to someone, a deed, etc.) may appear to be wills but are not written with testamentary intent. Remember that a document that has operative effect *during the maker's lifetime* cannot be a will, and that a writing may be a will even if it does *not dispose of property* (*e.g.*, merely revokes an earlier will).

2. **Did the Testator Intend the Writing as a Will?**

    If the writing was not drafted with *testamentary intent*, it is not a will. This is an issue that you should discuss if the facts of the exam question do not indicate that the instrument is a will, or the document does not state "This is my last will" or words of like effect. To establish testamentary intent, look for an intent (i) to accomplish some *testamentary act* (*e.g.*, dispose of property, appoint an executor, etc.); (ii) that the act *does not take effect until the testator's death*; and (iii) that *this writing* accomplish the specified testamentary act. If a document is ambiguous as to whether it was intended as a will, extrinsic evidence may be used to show testamentary intent.

3. **Did the Testator Have Capacity to Make a Will?**

    The key time for judging capacity is *at the time the will is executed*. Don't be fooled by questions where the testator becomes incapacitated *after* the will is executed; if the testator has capacity at the time of execution, the will is valid. Also keep in mind that *the test for capacity is an easy one to meet*. The testator can be mentally retarded, suffering from the afflictions of extreme old age, or even intoxicated. But if the testator has sufficient capacity to (i) know he is *making a will*; (ii) know the *relationship between himself and the "natural objects of his bounty"*; (iii) know the *nature, extent, and approximate value of his property*; and (iv) understand the *disposition he is making*, the will is valid.

4. **Were the Statutory Requirements for Execution of a Will Met?**

    This topic is a fertile source of exam questions. For example, did the witnesses sign the will in the testator's presence? The statutory requirements for valid execution vary from state to state, so be sure to read your question carefully to determine what the particular state requires, then follow those requirements. If the requirements are not met, the will cannot be admitted to probate even if the maker clearly intended it to be a valid will.

5. Was an Attesting Witness also a Beneficiary Under the Will?

Besides the general competency requirements (maturity, mental capacity, etc.), watch out for the "interested witness"—a witness who is also a *beneficiary under the will*. If the witness is "interested," the bequest may be *void* (due to a purging statute), but *the will itself is valid.* Be aware, too, that some statutes allow the interested witness to take in certain circumstances (*e.g.,* if the beneficiary would take as an heir if there were no will), and that the UPC and several states have *abolished* the interested witness rule.

6. If There Are No Attesting Witnesses, Is the Will Valid as a Holographic Will—(*i.e.,* One Entirely in the Testator's Handwriting)?

Be sure the will meets the state's specific requirements for holographic wills. If the state does not recognize holographic wills, it is important to mention that a handwritten, signed instrument cannot be a valid will unless it was properly witnessed.

Finally, note that the above issues should be considered for a *codicil* as well as a will.

A. What Constitutes a Will?

1. Nature of a Will [§325]

A will (other than an oral will, *see infra,* §§474 *et seq.*) is a written instrument executed in accordance with certain formalities that directs the disposition of a person's (the "testator's") property at his death.

a. Effective only on death [§326]

The principal distinction between a will and any other type of conveyance (*e.g.,* a deed) is that a will takes effect only upon the death of the maker. A will is an ambulatory document that has *no operative effect during the testator's lifetime* (other than to revoke or modify an earlier will). It is generally held that an instrument that has any operative effect during the maker's lifetime cannot be a will. [*See* **Palmer v. Riggs,** 46 So. 2d 86 (Miss. 1950); **Spinks v. Rice,** 47 S.E.2d 424 (Va. 1948)] A will is fully revocable or amendable *at any time,* and the beneficiaries named therein have no rights or benefits under the will until the testator dies; until that time, they have only an *expectancy.* (*See infra,* §493.)

EXAM TIP	gilbert

Always keep in mind that the will is *effective only at the testator's death*. Exam questions sometimes try to trick you into thinking that a beneficiary named in the will of a living person has some rights, but unless there is a contractual will (see below), the testator can change his will as he pleases and the beneficiary can do nothing about it.

(1) Exception—contractual wills [§327]

A beneficiary may have rights under a will prior to the testator's death if the testator has *executed his will pursuant to a contract* with the beneficiary or some other person. In such a case, the beneficiary may have rights and remedies *under contract law, not wills law,* to compel the bargained-for testamentary disposition even though the testator subsequently amends or revokes his will. (*See infra,* §§644 *et seq.*)

EXAM TIP   **gilbert**

Even though the will has no legal effect until the testator's death, for purposes of *construing the will*, the circumstances that existed at the time the will was *executed* (and not at the testator's death) are considered to determine, *e.g.*, the testator's intent. Likewise, whether the testator had *testamentary capacity* is determined according to the circumstances surrounding the execution of the will. (*See infra,* §358.)

---

b. Codicil [§328]

A *supplement or amendment* to a will is called a *codicil*. A codicil may add to, partially revoke, or alter a previously executed will, or it may confirm the will in whole or in part. [*See* N.Y. Est. Powers & Trusts Law §1-2.1] In states that have a statutory definition of a will, it is generally provided that the term "will" includes codicil unless a particular statute provides otherwise. [*See, e.g.,* Tex. Prob. Code §3(ff); N.Y. Est. Powers & Trusts Law §1-2.19] A codicil must be executed with the same formalities that are required for a will. [*See* Ga. Code §53-4-20; *see infra,* §634]

c. Terminology—testator or testatrix [§329]

At common law, a male will-maker was referred to as a "testator," while a female will-maker was called a "testatrix." Although some lawyers and courts continue to follow this practice, using gender-based terminology to refer to persons who execute wills is as inappropriate as referring to a female doctor as "doctress." Following the modern and better practice, this Summary uses the term "testator" when referring to either a male or a female will-maker.

2. Functions of a Will [§330]

Although many people believe that an instrument is a will only if it disposes of a person's property at death, this is not the case. By statute in many states and by case decision in other states, a will is defined as an instrument that does any *one or more* of the following things: transfers property at death, creates a testamentary trust, amends or revokes an earlier will [*See In re* **Parker's Estate,** 356 N.E.2d 967 (Ill. 1976)], appoints a personal representative, exercises a testamentary power of appointment, or disposes of the testator's body or a part thereof.

a. Minority rule—will must dispose of property [§331]

In Georgia, an instrument that does not dispose of property cannot be a will and is not admissible to probate. [**Lawson v. Hurt,** 125 S.E.2d 480 (Ga. 1962)]

b. Negative bequest statutes—disinheritance of an heir [§332]

Under the revised UPC and by statute in several states, a will (or a provision therein) is valid if it does nothing more than direct how property shall *not* be disposed of. This is called a *negative bequest* statute. [UPC §2-101(b); N.Y. Est. Powers & Trusts Law §1-2.19; Tex. Prob. Code §58(b)]

Example: Toby dies leaving a will that devises all of his real property to his brother Bob and further provides: "I hereby direct that my son John shall not take any part of my estate." The will contains no residuary clause, meaning that because Toby did not provide for disposition of his personal property in his will, there is a partial intestacy as to that property. Under a "negative bequest" statute, the provision regarding John is given effect. Toby's personal property passes to Toby's heirs under the intestacy statutes as though John predeceased him.

---

(1) But note

This is decidedly a *minority* position. At common law and in most states, words of disinheritance in a will are *not* given effect. The theory underlying the common law rule is that when a person dies partially intestate, the affected property passes "by force of law" under the intestacy statutes. The statute, not the testator's will, controls devolution of the property. [*See* **Cook v. Estate of Seeman**, 858 S.W.2d 114 (Ark. 1993); *In re* **Estate of Cancik**, *supra*, §70; *In re* **Smith's Estate**, *supra*, §70; *In re* **Estate of Baxter**, 827 P.2d 184 (Okla. 1992); 100 A.L.R.2d 325] Thus, in the example above, John would take an intestate share of Toby's personal property.

FUNCTIONS OF A WILL   **gilbert**

A TESTATOR CAN EXECUTE A WILL FOR ANY OF THE FOLLOWING PURPOSES:

- ☑ *Dispose of the testator's property* at death;
- ☑ *Disinherit an heir* (in some states);
- ☑ Create a *testamentary trust*;
- ☑ *Amend or revoke* an earlier will;
- ☑ Appoint a *personal representative*;
- ☑ Exercise a *testamentary power of appointment*; or
- ☑ Make an *anatomical gift* of the testator's body.

3. Types of Wills [§333]

A valid will may be in one of three forms:

a. Attested will [§334]

The standard form of will is one that is *written, signed* by the testator, and *witnessed* by two (and in Vermont, three) witnesses pursuant to a formal attestation procedure. (*See infra*, §§367 *et seq.*)

b. Holographic will [§335]

About 30 states recognize holographic wills. A holographic will is an *unattested* (*i.e.*, unwitnessed) will that is *entirely* in the *testator's handwriting* and *signed* by the testator. A few states also require that the will be dated. (*See infra*, §§457 *et seq.*)

EXAM TIP   **gilbert**

Be aware that an attested will may also be handwritten. There is no requirement that an attested will be typed, but it must be signed by the testator and witnesses pursuant to the prescribed formalities. "Holograph," however, is a term of art that refers to handwritten, *unattested* wills that are recognized as valid in some, but not all, states.

---

c. Oral wills [§336]

A number of states give effect to oral ("nuncupative") wills in very limited circumstances. (*See infra*, §474.)

B. Governing Law

1. Legislative Control of Right to Make a Will [§337]

The right to make a testamentary disposition of one's property has never been regarded as a natural right. A property owner's right to dispose of property by will is subject to the legislature's plenary control; the legislature can withhold or condition the right as it chooses. [*See* **Irving Trust Co. v. Day,** 314 U.S. 556 (1942); **Hotarek v. Benson,** 557 A.2d 1259 (Conn. 1989); *In re* **Moore's Estate,** 223 P.2d 393 (Or. 1950)] However, the complete abolition of both the descent and devise of particular property is unconstitutional. [*See* **Hodel v. Irving,** 481 U.S. 704 (1987)]

a. Minority view [§338]

The Wisconsin courts have taken the position that the right to dispose of property by will is a natural right that cannot be taken away or substantially impaired by legislative action. [**Tyler v. Dane County,** 289 F. 843 (W.D. Wis. 1923); **Nunnemacher v. State,** 108 N.W. 627 (Wis. 1906)]

2. Effect of Change in Law After Will's Execution

a. **Common law [§339]**

While some cases declare that the validity of a will's execution is determined under the laws in effect when the will was executed, and others apply the laws in effect at the testator's death, the decisions are in fact harmonious. If the requirements of due execution were increased by the later statute, the courts apply the statute in existence when the will was executed. If the requirements were liberalized by the later statute, the courts apply the laws in effect at the testator's death. The effect is to admit the will to probate if it satisfies either the laws in effect when the will was executed or the laws in effect when the testator died. [111 A.L.R. 910]

b. **Statutory solutions [§340]**

The UPC and statutes in several states expressly provide that a will is valid if it satisfies the law in effect either at the time of the testator's death or at the time of the will's execution. [UPC §2-506; Cal. Prob. Code §6113]

3. **Conflict of Laws Principles**

a. **Real property—law of situs [§341]**

The validity and effect of a will, insofar as it disposes of real property, are determined by reference to *the law of the situs* of the real property. [Restatement (Second) of Conflicts ("Rest. 2d Conflicts") §240] Thus, if a testator who died domiciled in State A owned real property in State B, it will be necessary for the testator's will to be probated in State B in *ancillary administration* proceedings. (*See infra,* §969.) Under the situs rule, the courts of one state cannot adjudicate ownership and transfer of title to real property located in another state.

b. **Personal property—law of testator's domicile [§342]**

With respect to dispositions of personal property, *the law of the testator's domicile* at the time of her death generally governs the validity and effect of the will, regardless of where the personal property is located. [Rest. 2d Conflicts §263]

c. **Uniform Execution of Foreign Wills Act [§343]**

Many states have enacted the Uniform Execution of Foreign Wills Act or its equivalent. Under the Act, a will is admissible to probate in the jurisdiction if it has been executed in accordance with:

(i) The law of the *jurisdiction* where will is sought to be probated;

(ii) The law of the *state in which the will was executed*;

(iii) The law of the testator's *domicile at the time the will was executed*; or

(iv) The law of the testator's *domicile at death*.

[UPC §2-506]

d. Uniform Probate Code [§344]

The UPC also allows the testator to select the particular state law to be applied to dispositions under the will, unless application of that law would be contrary to the public policy of the testator's state of residence. [UPC §2-703]

C. Formal Requirements for Wills

1. Introduction [§345]

There are four main requirements to the formation of a valid will:

a. The will must have been executed with *testamentary intent*;

b. The testator must have had *testamentary capacity*;

c. The will must have been executed *free of fraud, duress, undue influence, or mistake*; and

d. The will must have been *duly executed*.

2. Testamentary Intent [§346]

A will must be executed with testamentary intent. The testator must have *subjectively intended that the document in question constitute her will* at the time she executed it. In the ordinary case, testamentary intent is established on the face of the will (*e.g.*, "I, Martha Green, do hereby declare this instrument to be my Last Will and Testament . . ."). Most of the cases dealing with the issue of testamentary intent have involved instruments that contain no such recital but, instead, are ambiguous as to whether they were intended to be a will. However, testamentary intent may be put in issue even if the instrument contains a recital to the effect that "this is my will." [21 A.L.R.2d 319]

EXAM TIP **gilbert**

Remember that the testator's intent must be a *present* intent (*i.e.*, the testator intends that the document operate as her will at the time of its execution). Promises to make a will in the future and wills that are executed without a present testamentary intent *do not meet the requirement for testamentary intent*.

---

a. Legal test [§347]

A person is held to have testamentary intent only if she in fact intended the words executed to operate as her will. Testamentary intent consists of three elements:

(1) The testator must have intended to, *e.g.*, *dispose of property* or accomplish some other testamentary act;

(2) The testator must have intended the disposition to *occur only upon death*; and

(3) The testator must have intended *the instrument in question to accomplish the disposition.*

b. Determining testamentary intent [§348]

Testamentary intent must be ascertained from the *face of the instrument.* [*See* **Wolfe v. Wolfe,** 448 S.E.2d 408 (Va. 1994)]

(1) Document testamentary on its face [§349]

A document containing a recital that it is intended to be testamentary (*e.g.,* "This is my last will and testament") raises a strong (but not irrebuttable) presumption that it was written with testamentary intent. [*See, e.g., In re* **Sargavak's Estate,** 35 Cal. 2d 93 (1950); *In re* **Cosgrove's Estate,** 287 N.W. 456 (Mich. 1939)] The presumption can be overcome by extrinsic evidence, provided that the evidence is clear, convincing, and cogent. [*See* **Madden v. Madden,** 118 S.E.2d 443 (S.C. 1961)]

---

e.g. **Examples:** To show that a particular will was a "sham," extrinsic evidence has been admitted to show that a person made out a will naming his girlfriend as beneficiary to induce her to sleep with him [**Fleming v. Morrison,** 72 N.E. 499 (Mass. 1904)]; that the maker intended the instrument as a deed [**Belgarde v. Carter,** 146 S.W. 964 (Tex. 1912)]; that the instrument was executed as part of a ceremonial initiation into a secret order [**Vickery v. Vickery,** 170 So. 745 (Fla. 1936)]; or that the maker was merely showing how brief a will could be [**Nichols v. Nichols,** 161 Eng. Rep. 1113 (1814)].

(a) Rationale

"If the fact is plainly and conclusively made out, that the paper which appears to be the record of a testamentary act, was in reality the offspring of a jest, or the result of a contrivance to effect some collateral object, and never seriously intended as a disposition of property, it is not reasonable that the court should turn it into an effective instrument." [**Lister v. Smith,** 164 Eng. Rep. 1282 (1863)]

(2) Ambiguous document [§350]

A purported will is likely to either contain testamentary language, making it testamentary on its face, or it will be ambiguous on the issue of testamentary intent. If a document lacks any indication that it may have been intended as a will, extrinsic evidence is *not admissible* to show that the document was written with testamentary intent. If, however, a document might reasonably be construed as either a will or some other type of instrument, the overwhelming majority view is that extrinsic evidence is admissible on the issue of whether the document was written with testamentary intent. [*See* **Bailey v. Kerns,** 431 S.E.2d 312 (Va. 1993); 21 A.L.R.2d 319]

Examples: The many cases on this issue have involved letters containing testamentary language [***In re* Briggs's Estate,** 134 S.E.2d 737 (W. Va. 1964)]; informal memoranda containing the names of persons and lists of property, but nothing else [**Hopson v. Ewing,** 353 S.W.2d 203 (Ky. 1961)]; documents that appear to be partial drafts of a will [***In re* Stickney's Estate,** 101 Cal. App. 2d 572 (1951)]; instruments having characteristics both of wills and of deeds of gift [**Estes v. Estes,** 27 So. 2d 854 (Miss. 1946)]; and powers of attorney [***In re* Sargavak's Estate,** *supra,* §349].

---

(3) Character of evidence

(a) Testator's statements [§351]

Most courts admit statements made by the testator before or after execution of the instrument on the issue of whether she regarded the instrument as her will. [*See **In re* Sargavak's Estate,** *supra*] This parol evidence may be used to disprove or contradict statements of intent made in the will itself. Thus, even though the will recites, "this is my last will and testament," parol evidence is admissible to show that the maker did not intend the instrument as her will (*e.g.,* that it was a sham will). [*See* **Fleming v. Morrison,** *supra,* §349]

(b) Drafter's testimony [§352]

The testimony of the drafter of the document is admissible to show the testator's intent. [*See **In re* Estate of Schultheis,** 747 A.2d 918 (Pa. 2000)]

(c) Surrounding circumstances [§353]

Evidence may be admitted to show the circumstances attendant to the document's execution [*See, e.g., **In re* Sharp's Estate,** 183 So. 470 (Fla. 1938)—lodge initiation] and the maker's attitudes and family relationships at the time [*See, e.g.,* **Connecticut National Bank & Trust Co. v. Chadwick,** 585 A.2d 1189 (Conn. 1991)].

(d) Imminence of death [§354]

The fact that the maker was near death, or was about to undergo a serious operation, is admissible as a relevant circumstance bearing on testamentary intent. [*See, e.g.,* **Chambers v. Younes,** 399 S.W.2d 655 (Ark. 1966)]

EXAM TIP   **gilbert**

When analyzing whether a will was drafted with testamentary intent, ask yourself if the will is testamentary *on its face*—does it contain *testamentary language* or is the document *ambiguous*? If the will contains testamentary language, note that a *presumption* of testamentary intent arises. You then need to consider whether that presumption can be *rebutted by extrinsic evidence*. For example, did the testator make any statements indicating that she did not actually intend the document to serve as her will? What were the circumstances surrounding the will's execution? On the other hand, if the document is *not testamentary on its face*, think about whether the ambiguity can be cured by extrinsic evidence, but this would only be in cases where the document can be reasonably construed to be a will.

---

c.   **Intent to make future will [§355]**

If the instrument indicates that the maker did not intend this particular document to be her will, but rather that her will would be executed in the future, there is *no testamentary intent*.

---

e.g.   **Example:** In a jurisdiction that recognizes *holographic wills*, Sarah writes and signs a handwritten letter to her attorney: "Dear Mr. Smith: Please prepare a will for me. I want all of my property to go to my husband, John, if he survives me; otherwise to my daughter Agnes. I also want John to be my executor, to serve without bond. After you prepare the will, I will come into town to sign it. /s/ Sarah Jones." Although the letter sets forth a complete dispositive plan and meets all of the formal requirements of a holographic will, it is not admissible to probate. It is clear from the letter that Sarah did not intend this instrument to be her will, but instead looked to the preparation of another document that was to be executed by her with testamentary intent. [*See* **In re Moore's Estate**, 277 A.2d 825 (Pa. 1971); **Price v. Huntsman**, 430 S.W.2d 831 (Tex. 1968)]

---

cf.   **Compare:** If it is shown that Sarah *intended* her instructions to be given effect as her will until a more formal document embodying those instructions could be prepared, the document will be given effect as her will (assuming the document otherwise satisfies the required formalities). [*In re* **Crick's Estate**, 230 Cal. App. 2d 513 (1964)]

---

d.   **Conditional will [§356]**

A will may be expressly made contingent on the happening of a specified event (*e.g.*, the testator's returning from a trip). If the event does not occur, the will is denied probate. If, however, the court interprets the conditional language as merely expressing the testator's *motive* for executing the will, probate will be granted. (*See infra*, §§481 *et seq.*)

e.   **Ineffective deeds as wills [§357]**

If a deed is validly executed but fails as an inter vivos conveyance because it is not delivered, it cannot be admitted to probate as a will because it was not executed with testamentary intent. To be effective as a will, the testator must have intended the instrument to be effective *at her death*, not during her lifetime. [*See* **First National Bank v. Bloom,** 264 N.W.2d 208 (N.D. 1978)]

EXAM TIP   **gilbert**

Don't be fooled if the above scenario (where someone tries to call a deed a will) arises on your exam. The intended *beneficiary is not entitled to the property* because the deed was an ineffective conveyance, regardless of the testator's intent that the beneficiary receive that property. And the deed cannot be construed as a will because there was no *testamentary* intent.

---

3. **Testamentary Capacity [§358]**

    In addition to testamentary intent, the testator must have had testamentary capacity, as defined in the rules set out below, *at the time the will was executed.* Similarly, the testator must have testamentary capacity when he executes a *codicil* to the will or attempts to *revoke* a will. The testator's capacity at some time before or after execution of the will is not controlling. [*See* **Fields v. Fields,** 499 S.E.2d 826 (Va. 1998); *In re* **Reardon's Will,** 36 Misc. 2d 307 (1962)] However, evidence of the testator's *mental condition* a reasonable time before or after making the will is relevant to show his mental condition when the will was signed, especially where the condition was of a continuous nature. [*See* **Peters v. Peters,** 33 N.E.2d 425 (Ill. 1941)]

    a. **Testamentary capacity compared to capacity for other acts [§359]**

        Mental capacity for testamentary purposes is a totally different concept from mental capacity for other purposes (*e.g.*, criminal capacity, ability to contract, etc.). In general, it takes *less capacity* to make a will than to do any other legal act—perfect sanity is not required. Even an *adjudication of incapacity* does not conclusively establish that a person lacks mental capacity for testamentary purposes, although such an adjudication is *evidence* of lack of testamentary capacity [*See* **Gibbs v. Gibbs,** 387 S.E.2d 499 (Va. 1990)], and in some states raises a *presumption* of incapacity [*See* **Hugenel v. Estate of Keller,** 867 S.W.2d 298 (Mo. 1993)].

    b. **Requirements—four-point test [§360]**

        To establish that the testator had the requisite capacity to make a will, it must be shown that he had sufficient capacity to:

        (i) *Know the nature of the act:* The testator must have had the ability to understand the nature of the act that he is doing, *i.e., executing a will* and not some other legal document.

        (ii) *Know the natural objects of his bounty:* The testator must have had the capacity to *understand the relationship* between himself and those persons he ought to have in mind at the time of making his will.

(iii) *Know the nature and extent of his property:* The testator must have had the ability to understand the *nature and approximate value of the estate* that will be affected by the will.

(iv) *Understand the disposition:* The testator must have had the capacity to relate the previous factors and formulate an *orderly scheme of disposition.*

[**Estate of Bullock,** 140 Cal. App. 2d 944 (1956); **Pace v. Richmond,** 343 S.E.2d 59 (Va. 1986)]

(1) Statutory modifications [§361]

A few jurisdictions have modified the above test for testamentary capacity. In some states, the testator must be "of sound and disposing mind and capable of executing a valid deed or contract." [D.C. Code §18-102]

(2) Relation to will contests [§362]

The issue of testamentary capacity is invariably raised in the context of a will contest. Therefore, more extended discussion of this topic is given *infra,* §§826 *et seq.*

c. Testator's status as affecting capacity

(1) Age [§363]

The age at which a person can write a valid will is fixed by statute. In nearly all states, a person must be at least 18 years old to make a will. [*See* Cal. Prob. Code §6100; Idaho Code §15-2-501; Utah Code §75-2-501] Some states set a different minimum age for devises of land than for bequests of personal property, and a few states impose no age requirement for married persons and persons serving in the armed forces. [*See, e.g.,* Tex. Prob. Code §59]

EXAM TIP **gilbert**

On your exam, watch out for a fact pattern where a person who is not yet 18 years of age writes a will, is satisfied with it, never executes another will, and dies at a ripe old age. That will will **not be admitted to probate** because the testator did not have capacity **when he executed it**. It is irrelevant that when he reached the age of majority he adopted it as his will. To make that will valid he would have had to reexecute it (with the appropriate formalities) or he could have validated it by **incorporating** it into a subsequent and properly executed codicil. (See *infra,* §§603 *et seq.*)

---

(2) Aliens [§364]

At common law, an alien could devise real or personal property, but the sovereign was given powers of confiscation within a year and a day. This restriction has been eliminated in all states.

(3) Felons [§365]

At common law, a person convicted of a serious crime was deprived of testamentary capacity. Again, this is no longer true in most states. [*See, e.g.,* Ga. Code §53-4-10—felons are not deprived of testamentary capacity]

4. Absence of Fraud, Duress, Undue Influence, and Mistake [§366]

A will or testamentary gift that is the product of fraud, duress, undue influence, or mistake is *invalid*. For a complete discussion of these elements, *see infra*, §§850 *et seq.*

5. Due Execution of Attested Wills—In General [§367]

For a will to be valid and admissible to probate, the testator must meet the formal requirements of due execution imposed by the statutes of the appropriate state. These statutes are sometimes referred to as the Statute(s) of Wills. Under these statutes, except for holographic wills and oral wills, a will must be:

(i) In *writing*,

(ii) *Signed* by the testator, and

(iii) *Witnessed* by a specified number of witnesses in compliance with specified procedures.

It is generally held that failure to satisfy each and every one of the requirements of due execution makes the will *void*—not merely voidable. Thus, if the will is signed by the testator but witnessed by less than the required number of witnesses, the will is not admissible to probate even though all of the beneficiaries thereunder and all of testator's heirs join in the petition for probate and fervently desire to have the instrument probated. [*See* **Hopkins v. Hopkins**, 708 S.W.2d 31 (Tex. 1986)] *Rationale*: Since the prescribed formalities have not been satisfied, the instrument *is not a will*.

a. Functions of required formalities

(1) Ritual [§368]

One function of the statutory formalities is to impress upon the testator the seriousness of the act; *i.e.,* that she is performing a legally binding act, the effect of which will be to dispose of all of her property at death. If the statutory requirements are met in a formal will-signing ceremony, the courts will be justified in concluding that the decedent deliberately intended the document to be her will.

(2) Evidentiary [§369]

By meeting the requirements of the Statute of Wills, the testator provides the proof that the instrument expresses her intent. A written instrument signed by the testator and by attesting witnesses avoids the problems inherent in oral evidence and tends to reduce the chances of mistake and perjury. These are particularly important considerations given that the testator will not be alive to testify or explain herself when the will takes effect.

(3) Protective [§370]

The formalities tend to protect the testator against undue influence and other forms of imposition by requiring competent, disinterested witnesses.

(4) Channeling [§371]

Compliance with the Statute of Wills tends to produce uniformity in the organization, form, and content of wills, increasing the likelihood that the testator's wishes will be effectively communicated and given effect by the courts. [John H. Langbein, *Substantial Compliance with the Wills Act*, 88 Harv. L. Rev. 489 (1975)]

b. Requirements—in general [§372]

The formal requirements for execution of a will vary from state to state. The variations are largely due to the fact that England had two statutes governing the execution of wills, each with different requirements: the Statute of Frauds (1677) and the Wills Act (1837). American jurisdictions tended to borrow from one or the other of the English statutes—and sometimes a little from each—or added new wrinkles of their own.

(1) Formalities that may be required [§373]

The following is a list of the various formalities that *may* be required in a particular state. No one state requires all of these formalities, and there is a trend toward simplifying the requirements for execution of a will.

(a) Signed by testator [§374]

The will must be *signed by the testator* or signed for the testator by another person at the testator's direction and in her presence.

(b) Signed at the end [§375]

Several states have adopted the requirement of the English Wills Act that the testator's *signature be "at the foot or end"* of the will.

(c) Signed in presence of attesting witnesses [§376]

The testator may be required to sign the will (or acknowledge her earlier signature) in the *presence of all attesting witnesses* all of whom must be present at the same time.

(d) Will "published" [§377]

In several states, the testator must "publish" the will, *i.e.*, *declare or otherwise communicate to the witnesses that they are witnessing a will*, as distinguished from some other legal document.

(e) Number of attesting witnesses [§378]

Most states require only *two attesting witnesses*. However, three witnesses are required in Vermont. [Vt. Stat. Ann. tit. 14, §5]

(f) Witnesses signed in testator's and each others' presence [§379]

Under many statutes, the witnesses must *sign in the testator's presence*. Some statutes require that the witnesses also must sign in each other's presence.

(g) Witnesses signed within required time period [§380]

New York requires that the two attesting witnesses each must sign within 30 days of each other. [N.Y. Est. Powers & Trusts Law §3-2.1(a)(4)] However, most states impose *no such time requirement*.

(2) Variations among states [§381]

No jurisdiction requires all of the above formalities. Thus, it is necessary to consult the statutes of a particular state to determine which particular formalities are required. Some jurisdictions have much more liberal will execution statutes than others.

(a) Illustration—strict statutes [§382]

The Florida statute is fairly strict. The testator must sign the will (or have it signed for her by another person at her direction and in her presence) *at the end* of the will, and the testator's signing (or acknowledgment of her previous signature) must be *in the presence of two attesting witnesses*, both *present at the same time*. The two attesting witnesses must sign the will in the testator's presence *and in the presence of each other*. [Fla. Prob. Code §732.502] Thus, the only requirements found in some states but not required in Florida are that the testator "publish" the will and that there be three attesting witnesses.

(b) Illustration—liberal statutes [§383]

Under the UPC, all that is required for due execution of an attested will is that the testator sign the will (or have it signed for her by another person at her direction and in her presence), that there be two attesting witnesses, and that the witnesses witness *either* the testator's signing *or* the testator's acknowledgment of her previous signature *or* the testator's acknowledgment of the will. [UPC §2-502] *Note:* The UPC does *not* require that the testator sign (or acknowledge her previous signature) in the presence of both attesting witnesses present at the same time, that the testator's signature be at the end of the will, that the testator publish the will, that the witnesses sign in the testator's presence or in each other's presence, or that the execution ceremony be completed by any particular time.

1) Revised Uniform Probate Code [§384]

The revised UPC adds the requirement that the witnesses must sign the will within a reasonable time after the testator signs or acknowledges the will. [UPC §2-502] However, the Official Comment indicates that this requirement was added to liberalize the statute, and would even permit the witnesses to sign the will after the testator's death. (*See infra*, §406.)

(c) Practice tip

Even though a will is executed in a state that has a liberal will execution statute, the better practice is to have the will executed in a manner that satisfies the seven-point maximum formalities listed above (*supra*, §§374-380). *Rationale:* The testator may move and then die in a state with a more stringent will execution statute. Or the testator may own real property in another state, meaning that ancillary probate may be required (*see infra*, §969). Although most states have enacted the Uniform Execution of Foreign Wills Act or its equivalent (*see supra*, §343), not all states have done so. Also, unless the will is *executed* in Vermont, it is *not* necessary to have three attesting witnesses. However, it may be a good idea to have three witnesses. If witnesses are needed to prove the will, having three witnesses may make it easier to find a witness to testify. Also the extra witness may avoid "interested witness" problems (*see infra*, §§418-420, 430-431).

6. Testator's Signature

a. What constitutes a signature [§385]

Most courts take a liberal position on what constitutes the testator's signature. The signature requirement is satisfied by the testator's signing her first name or nickname, her initials, "Love, Mother" [**Will of Kenneally,** 139 Misc. 2d 198 (1988)], or by the "X" of an illiterate person [**Ferguson v. Ferguson,** 47 S.E.2d 346 (Va. 1948)]—provided that the mark was intended to be the testator's signature or mark and it was made by the testator's volitional act. [98 A.L.R.2d 841] The testator's fingerprints constitute a valid signature. [28 A.L.R.2d 1157] A few courts have even held that the signature requirement is satisfied by a rubber-stamped or typewritten name, but this is decidedly the minority position. [98 A.L.R.2d 893]

(1) Assistance in signing [§386]

The signature requirement is satisfied even if the testator's hand was guided or steadied by another because the testator was blind, illiterate, or palsied, as long as the testator *desired and intended* to sign the instrument. [*See In re* **Will of Bernatowicz,** 233 A.D.2d 838 (1996); 98 A.L.R.2d 824] But if the testator was "coma-like" and the party had to grab and then drag the testator's hand across the paper, the signing was not the testator's volitional act. [*See, e.g.,* **In re Sheehan's Will,** 51 A.D.2d 645 (1976)]

(2) Proxy signature [§387]

Nearly all statutes provide that the testator's signature may be made by another person, as long as the signing is *at the testator's direction and in her presence.* [*See* Cal. Prob. Code §6110(b)] A few states require that, where this procedure is followed, the person signing the testator's name (i) must also sign his own name, and (ii) cannot serve as one of the required attesting witnesses. [*See* N.Y. Est. Powers & Trusts Law §3-2.1] In most states, however, if the person signs his own name, his signature can be counted as one of the two needed witnesses' signatures. [*See* **In re Will of Jarvis,** 430 S.E.2d 922 (N.C. 1933)]

DETERMINING WHAT CONSTITUTES A VALID SIGNATURE — **gilbert**

TO DETERMINE IF A SIGNATURE OR MARK ON THE WILL IS THE VALID SIGNATURE OF THE TESTATOR, ASK YOURSELF THE FOLLOWING QUESTIONS:

☑ Did the testator *sign her own name* (including a nickname)?

☑ Is there a *mark on the will* indicating the testator's signature (*e.g.,* the "X" of an illiterate person or the testator's initials)?

☑ Was the signature created by the *testator's hand being guided* by the help of another person (the testator must intend to sign the will)?

☑ Did *another person sign for the testator* at the testator's *direction* and in her *presence*?

---

b. Location of signature

(1) Majority rule [§388]

In most states, there is no requirement that the testator *subscribe* his signature (*i.e.,* sign at the foot or end of the will). The signature can appear *anywhere* on the will, provided it was intended by the testator to be his signature. [*See* **Potter v. Richardson,** 230 S.W.2d 672 (Mo. 1950); **In re Estate of Carroll,** 548 N.E.2d 650 (Ill. 1989)]

EXAM TIP — **gilbert**

If you encounter an exam question where the testator didn't sign his will at the end of the document, before deciding that the will has not been properly executed, check to see if the testator *signed anywhere in document*. Often, especially with do-it-yourself or form wills, the testator will have signed his name at the beginning of the document (*e.g.,* where the form says "Last Will and Testament of . . ."), and in most states this could pass as a signature.

---

(2) Minority rule [§389]

A few states require "subscription" for formal wills, *i.e.*, a signing *"at the end thereof."* [*See, e.g.*, Ark. Code §28-25-103; Fla. Prob. Code §732.502; Kan. Stat. 59-606; Ohio Rev. Code §2107.03] In these jurisdictions, two main questions arise: (i) where is "the end" of the will; and (ii) what is the effect of provisions appearing after the testator's signature?

(a) What constitutes "the end" of will [§390]

In states that require the testator to sign at the end of the will, two tests have been applied to determine "the end" of the will:

1) Physical end [§391]

A few courts apply a purely *objective test* and require the testator's signature to be on the *last line of the document* in a physical or sequential sense (except for the attestation clause and signatures of the attesting witnesses).

e.g. Example: Proley writes her will by filling in the blanks on a printed form. The form calls for the testator's signature at the bottom of the first page. The two witnesses sign there, but Proley does not. Instead, pursuant to the form's instructions, Proley folds the sheet in thirds so that the middle third of the back side becomes the document's spine, which says "Will of _____." Proley signs on that line. The will is denied probate because it was not signed at its *sequential* end. [*In re* **Proley's Estate,** 422 A.2d 136 (Pa. 1980)—rejecting dissenting opinion's "misguided effort to effect what they perceive to be decedent's intent."]

2) Logical or literary end [§392]

Other courts apply a *subjective test* and hold that even if a portion of the will (other than the attestation clause) follows the testator's signature, it will not invalidate the will as long as that portion can be read *as a logical or literary part of the will itself.* Under this test, the question is whether the testator subjectively thought that she was signing at the end of the will.

e.g. Example: On the above facts, Proley will have signed the will at the end because this is what she thought she was doing.

(b) Effect of provisions appearing after testator's signature [§393]

In states that require the testator's signature to be at the end of the will, what is the effect of provisions following the testator's signature? Early cases held that if any material provision appeared after the testator's signature (other than the attestation clause), the *entire will was void.* [*In re* **Winter's Will,** 302 N.Y. 845 (1951)—overturned by N.Y. Est. Powers & Trusts Law §3-2.1(a)(1)(A)]

1) Modern view—provisions before signature are valid [§394]
The modern view is that everything appearing *before* the signature is given effect; only the provisions that follow the signature are void.

a) Exception [§395]
If the matter following the signature is so material that deletion of it, and giving effect only to the matter preceding the signature, would subvert the general testamentary plan, the *entire will is void.* [N.Y. Est. Powers & Trusts Law §3-2.1(a)(1)(A)]

2) Distinguish—provisions added *after* will's execution [§396]
The previous discussion assumes that the provisions in question were part of the will when the testator signed it. Provisions added after the will is executed are *disregarded* in all states (unless they can be given effect as a codicil), since they were not part of the duly executed will.

a) Note
Some courts adopt a *rebuttable presumption* that any provisions appearing below the testator's signature were added after the will was executed. [*See In re* **Bogart's Estate,** 96 Pa. Super. 26 (1929)]

c. Signature (or acknowledgment of earlier signature) in witnesses' presence [§397]
Many states require that the testator either sign the will or acknowledge her earlier signature in the witnesses' presence. In some states, this requirement is met by the testator signing in one witness's presence and then later acknowledging that signature in the presence of the other witness. A few states require that the signature (or acknowledgment of the earlier signature) be in the presence of both witnesses *present at the same time.*

(1) Acknowledgment of earlier signature [§398]
It is generally held that a proffering of the will with the testator's signature clearly visible constitutes a sufficient acknowledgment of the signature; the testator does not have to make verbal reference to her signature. [*See In re* **Levine's Will,** 2 N.Y.2d 757 (1956)] If, however, the testator proffers the will folded over so that the fold-over covers her signature and only the witnesses' signature lines are visible, there has been no acknowledgment of the signature, and the will has not been validly executed. [*See In re* **Weinstock's Will,** 78 Misc. 2d 182 (1974); 7 A.L.R.3d 317]

(2) Uniform Probate Code—acknowledgment of will [§399]
The UPC requires only that each witness must witness either the testator's

signing, the testator's acknowledgment *of her earlier signature*, or the testator's acknowledgment *of the will*. [UPC §2-502] Thus, in a UPC state, the will would be validly executed even in the "fold-over situation" (*i.e.*, where the witness could not see the testator's signature) if the testator acknowledged the instrument as her will.

(a) Comment

In this latter situation, how can a court be sure that the testator's signature was actually on the will when the witnesses signed? *Answer*: There is a *rebuttable presumption* that the testator's signature was affixed prior to the attestation; the burden of persuasion is on the contestants to prove otherwise. [**Betts v. Lonas**, 172 F.2d 759 (D.C. Cir. 1949)]

d. Order of signing [§400]

The witnesses are attesting witnesses, and what they attest to is the testator's signature. What is the result if one of the attesting witnesses signs the will immediately *before* the testator signs?

(1) Majority rule [§401]

Most courts have held that it makes no difference whether the testator or an attesting witness signs first, as long as the execution ceremony is part of *a single, continuous transaction*. [*See* **Waldrep v. Goodwin**, 195 S.E.2d 432 (Ga. 1973); **Hopson v. Ewing**, *supra*, §350; 91 A.L.R.2d 737] This is sometimes called the *contemporaneous transaction* doctrine. Nor is it material that the signatures of the attesting witnesses are located above the testator's signature. This is true even in states that require the testator to sign "at the end" of the will (*see supra*, §389). The requirement to sign at the end usually refers to the dispositive provisions of the will, and hence it is immaterial that the witnesses' signatures appear before the testator's.

(2) Minority rule [§402]

A few states follow the English rule, which requires that the testator sign first even though the signings occur in a single transaction. [*See* **Marshall v. Mason**, 57 N.E. 340 (Mass. 1900)] *Rationale*: The witnesses cannot attest to the testator's signature unless the testator signs first.

e. What constitutes signing in someone's "presence" [§403]

Signing the will in another's "presence" is a requirement under many statutes, although the requirement takes various forms. In many states, each witness must sign in the testator's presence, but not necessarily in each other's presence. [*See* Ill. Comp. Stat. ch. 755, §5/4-3] In other states, the attesting witnesses must sign in the testator's presence *and* in the presence of each other. [*See* Fla. Prob. Code §732.502(1)] In still other states, the witnesses do not have to sign in the testator's presence, but the testator must sign the will or acknowledge her previous signature in the presence of each witness. [*See* N.Y. Est. Powers & Trusts Law §3-2.1] Under such statutes, there may be a question as to what constitutes "presence."

(1) Majority rule—conscious presence test [§404]

The majority of states adopt the liberal view that a witness has signed in the "presence" of the testator (and vice versa) if the testator was *conscious of where the witness was* and what he was doing when he signed. [*See In re* **Demaris's Estate,** 110 P.2d 571 (Or. 1941)] However, telephonic presence is not sufficient—the witness's talking to the testator over the phone when he signs does not satisfy the "presence" requirement. [*See In re* **Heaney's Will,** 75 Misc. 2d 732 (1973)]

e.g. **Example:** Bruce signs his will while lying in a hospital bed. A vinyl screen separates him from the doorway where the witnesses are standing, which is 12 feet away. A nurse takes the will around the screen to the witnesses where they sign. Since Bruce was conscious of where the witnesses were and of what they were doing, the witnesses signed in his presence even though they were not in his line of sight. [*See* **Nichols v. Rowan,** 422 S.W.2d 21 (Tex. 1967)]

(2) Minority rule—line of sight test [§405]

A minority of courts hold that a witness has signed in the testator's presence only if he was in the testator's *line of sight* when he signed. Under this test, the testator does not have to see the witness when he signs, but the witness must be within the uninterrupted *range of the testator's vision*. This test is met if the witness signs the will on a table behind the testator, because the testator could have seen the witness had she turned around in her chair. [*See* **Newton v. Palmour,** 266 S.E.2d 208 (Ga. 1980)] An exception to the "line of sight" test is made for blind persons. [*See* **Morris v. West's Estate,** 643 S.W.2d 204 (Tex. 1982)]

e.g. **Example:** Tess signs her will in a hospital bed, and then lays down on her back. The two witnesses take the will into the hallway, where they sign. If Tess could have seen the witnesses through the doorway had she looked, they signed in her presence. [**Newton v. Palmour,** *supra*] But if Tess's line of sight was interrupted by the wall or a divider, the witnesses did not sign in her presence and probate will be denied.

(3) Uniform Probate Code [§406]

The UPC dispenses with the "presence" requirement (except where someone signs for the testator at her request and in her presence). Under

UPC section 2-502, the witnesses must witness the testator's act of signing the will or her acknowledgment of either her earlier signature or the will, but they do not have to sign in the testator's presence. The revised UPC permits the witnesses to sign the will within a reasonable time after witnessing one of the required acts—which presumably could be after the testator's death. [UPC §2-502]

(a) But note

Without the aid of such a statute, the courts have held that the witnesses must sign *during the testator's lifetime*. [*See In re* **Estate of McGurrin,** 743 P.2d 994 (Idaho 1987)]

DID THE WITNESSES SIGN IN THE TESTATOR'S PRESENCE?	**gilbert**
MAJORITY VIEW	*Conscious presence test*—The testator must be *conscious of where the witness is* and *what he is doing* when the witness signs the will.
MINORITY VIEW	*Line of sight test*—Witness must sign the will within the *testator's uninterrupted range of vision*.
UPC VIEW	Witnesses do *not* have to sign the will in the testator's presence. They must sign within a *reasonable time* of witnessing the testator's *signature* or *acknowledgment* of an earlier signature.

7. Will Need Not Be Dated [§407]

In most states, it is not necessary that a will bear the date of its execution. The time of execution can be established by extrinsic evidence. [*See, e.g., In re* **Swan's Estate,** 284 N.W. 599 (Mich. 1939); *In re* **Will of Dujenski,** 147 A.D.2d 958 (1989)] *Note:* A few states require that a holographic will be dated. (*See infra,* §469.)

8. Publication

a. Majority rule [§408]

Under the UPC and in most states, there is *no* "will publication" requirement; *i.e.*, there is no requirement that the witnesses know they are attesting witnesses to a *will*. All that is required is that the witnesses sign and satisfy the other requirements imposed by the particular state. In these states, the witnesses have validly attested even if they thought they were witnessing, *e.g.*, a power of attorney. [*See, e.g., In re* **Beakes's Estate,** 306 So. 2d 99 (Fla. 1974); **Genovese v. Genovese,** 153 N.E.2d 662 (Mass. 1958); *In re* **Brantlinger's Estate,** 210 A.2d 246 (Pa. 1965); 71 A.L.R.3d 877]

b. **Minority rule [§409]**

Publication of a will is required by statute in several states. [*See, e.g.*, Cal. Prob. Code §6110; N.Y. Est. Powers & Trusts Law §3-2.1(a)(3)] Where required, the testator must publish (*i.e.*, declare) to the attesting witnesses that the instrument that they are requested to attest is a will, so that they know that they are serving as witnesses to a *will* rather than some other legal document. [60 A.L.R.2d 165] The attesting witnesses need not know the contents of the will; all that is required is that they know they are serving as witnesses to a testamentary instrument. [*See* **Strahl v. Turner**, 310 S.W.2d 839 (Mo. 1958)]

Example: Bob asks two bank employees: "Please witness my signature. I am going away on a trip. I have some instructions that I want carried out if anything happens. With all the accidents you have these days, you never know what may happen." The employees watched Bob sign the document; then they added their signatures. However, the instrument contained no attestation clause, and the witnesses testified that they did not know whether they were signing a will, a power of attorney, or some other document. The will was not validly executed. [*In re* **Pulvermacher's Will**, 305 N.Y. 378 (1953)]

MUST A WILL BE "PUBLISHED"?	gilbert
MAJORITY AND UPC VIEW	There is *no publication requirement*. Witnesses do not need to know that they are witnessing a will but must meet other requirements (*e.g.*, must sign in the testator's presence).
MINORITY VIEW	Will *must be published* (*i.e.*, witnesses must know it is a will) before the witnesses sign.

(1) **Publication on behalf of testator [§410]**

Publication may be made by someone on the testator's behalf. For example, suppose that the testator is in the hospital and in critical condition. In the presence of the testator and the witnesses, a nurse says, "This is *his* last will and testament, and he wants you to witness his signature." This would constitute a valid publication since the nurse's statement was made in the testator's presence and with his acquiescence. [**Estate of Eckert**, 93 Misc. 2d 677 (1978)]

9. **Witnesses**

a. **Competency of witnesses—in general [§411]**

Witnesses must possess certain minimal qualifications or their attestation may be legally insufficient, and the will may fail for lack of due execution.

(1) Competency [§412]

All jurisdictions require that a witness be competent. [*See* UPC §2-505] This generally means that *at the time the will is executed* the witness must be *mature enough and of sufficient mental capacity* to understand and appreciate the nature of the act she is witnessing and her attestation, so that, if need be, she could testify in court on these matters. [*See* **In re Estate of Edwards,** 520 So. 2d 1370 (Miss. 1988)]

(2) When determined [§413]

As in the case of the testator, competency of an attesting witness is determined *at the time the will is executed.* The fact that a competent witness subsequently becomes incapacitated does not render her attestation invalid. [*See, e.g.,* **Howard v. Fields,** 156 P.2d 139 (Okla. 1945)] Conversely, if the witness was incapacitated at the time the will was executed, the attestation is invalid regardless of subsequent events by which competency is restored. [*See, e.g.,* **Vrooman v. Powers,** 24 N.E. 267 (Ohio 1890)]

(3) Age [§414]

In a few states, statutes provide that a person must be a certain minimum age in order to serve as an attesting witness. [*See, e.g.,* Conn. Gen. Stat. §45a-250—age 18; Tex. Prob. Code §59—age 14] However, most states do not impose a minimum age requirement. [*See* Ala. Code §43-8-134]

(4) Signature of notary public [§415]

Suppose that a will is signed by the testator and one attesting witness before a notary public, who then signs ("Subscribed and sworn to before me," etc.) and affixes his notarial seal. A few courts have held that if the notary intended to sign the will *as a witness* and added his notarial seal merely to add solemnity to the will, his signature is valid. If, however, he did not intend to sign as a witness but signed in his *official capacity as a notary,* the signature cannot be counted. [*See* **Osborn v. Sinnett,** 503 S.W.2d 30 (Mo. 1973)] However, the overwhelming *majority view* is that a person can be an attesting witness even if he signed the will in his capacity as a notary public and affixed his notarial seal. [*See* **Reagan v. Bailey,** 626 S.W.2d 141 (Tex. 1981)]

EXAM TIP   **gilbert**

If your exam question raises the issue of a witness's competency to attest a will, remember that the witness must have sufficient *mental capacity* and, in some states, must be of the required *age*, at the time of the *will's execution*. For example, if the witness does not meet the competency requirements when the will is executed but does when the will is offered for probate, the court will deny probate because the will was *invalidly executed*.

b. Location of signatures [§416]

There is no requirement that the signatures of the testator and the witnesses be on the same page. [*See, e.g., In re* **Estate of Brannon**, 441 S.E.2d 248 (Ga. 1994)]

EXAM TIP   **gilbert**

Be sure to remember that under majority law the will is valid even if the witnesses sign *above* the testator's signature. (See *supra*, §401.)

---

c. Drafting attorney as attesting witness [§417]

The attorney who drafts a will should not serve as an attesting witness. If after the client's death the attorney or her law firm is retained to represent the estate, and if the will is contested, the attorney would have to testify as to the will's execution, and would have to withdraw as attorney for the personal representative. [A.B.A. Model Rules of Professional Conduct 1.7, 3.7; A.B.A. Model Code of Professional Responsibility DR5-102A]

d. Interested witnesses—in general

(1) Common law view [§418]

At common law, if one of two attesting witnesses was also a beneficiary under the will, the witness-beneficiary was *not a competent witness* and the will was *denied probate* because it was not signed by two competent witnesses. The harsh common law rule has been *abolished* in all states. In all jurisdictions today, the fact that a will makes a gift to an attesting witness *never affects the validity of the will*. [*See, e.g., In re* **Watts's Estate**, 384 N.E.2d 589 (Ill. 1979)]

(2) Majority view—purging statutes [§419]

Most jurisdictions have "interested witness" statutes, which provide that if an attesting witness is also a will beneficiary, the *gift to the witness is void* (with certain exceptions, discussed below), but she is a competent witness and the will may be probated. [*See, e.g.,* D.C. Code §18-104; Ohio Rev. Code §2107.15; Tenn. Code §32-1-103] These laws are called *"purging" statutes* because they eliminate the problem of interest by purging the bequest to the witness.

(3) Minority view—interested witness rule abolished [§420]

The UPC and several non-UPC states have *abolished* the interested witness rule—neither the will nor any of its provisions is affected by the fact that an attesting witness is also a beneficiary under the will. [*See, e.g.,* UPC §2-505; Del. Code tit. 12, §203; Fla. Prob. Code §732.504; Or. Rev. Stat. §112.245; Va. Code §64.1-51]

(a) Rationale

A person who uses improper means to write himself into a will is probably shrewd enough to have disinterested persons serve as witnesses to the will. Thus, purging statutes are not likely to reach cases of improper overreaching. Instead, they tend to void gifts to family members, innocently made, in wills whose execution is not supervised by an attorney.

VALIDITY OF WILL ATTESTED TO BY INTERESTED WITNESS	**gilbert**
COMMON LAW VIEW	The will is *denied probate*.
MAJORITY VIEW	The will is *admitted to probate* but the *purging statutes* operate to make the gift to the interested witness *void*.
MINORITY (AND UPC) VIEW	The will is *admitted to probate* and the *interested witness is entitled to any devises* made to him in the will.

e. Purging statutes

(1) What constitutes beneficial interest [§421]

Under the purging statutes, it is generally held that, for a person to be "beneficially interested" in the will, the interest must be a direct, pecuniary one; *i.e.*, the witness must be a *beneficiary* under the will or under a trust created by the will.

(a) Executor or trustee [§422]

A person designated in the will as executor or testamentary trustee is *not a beneficiary* within the meaning of the statute unless he is also given a bequest in the will. While executors and trustees receive money from the estate, this is *compensation for services rendered*; it is not a gift. [*See, e.g.*, Mo. Rev. Stat. §474.330.3; *In re* **Giacomini's Estate**, 603 P.2d 218 (Kan. 1979); 74 A.L.R.2d 297]

1) Minority rule [§423]

In a small number of states, a person named in the will as executor or trustee who signs as an attesting witness is not entitled to compensation for serving as fiduciary. [*See* Ill. Comp. Stat. ch. 755, §5/4-6(b)]

(b) Spouse or other family member of beneficiary [§424]

If a spouse, parent, or other relative of a will beneficiary is an attesting witness, the purging statute does *not* apply, and the beneficiary is entitled to the gift. [*See In re* **Estate of Harrison**, 738 P.2d 964 (Okla. 1987)] *Rationale:* The interests of family members are only *indirect*—as prospective heirs or donees of the one who is the named beneficiary.

1) Minority rule [§425]

In a few states, a beneficial gift to the *spouse* of an attesting witness is invalid. [*See, e.g.*, Ill. Comp. Stat. ch. 755, §5/4-6(a); Ky. Rev. Stat. §394.210; Wis. Stat. §853.07; **Dorfman v. Allen,** 434 N.E.2d 1012 (Mass. 1982)—upholding statute against constitutional challenge]

(c) Creditors [§426]

A will beneficiary does not lose his gift merely because one of his creditors is an attesting witness. [*See* D.C. Code §18-106] Similarly, creditors of the *testator* are deemed competent witnesses. Even though they may be paid from the testator's estate, they do not take under the will and have no "beneficial" interest in it.

(d) Indirect benefits [§427]

A witness is not disqualified by indirect benefits that he may receive as an officer or member of a church, fraternal society, or other charitable corporation named as a beneficiary in a will. [*See, e.g.*, **Estate of Tkachuk,** 73 Cal. App. 3d 14 (1977); *In re* **Jordan's Estate,** 519 S.W.2d 902 (Tex. 1975)]

e.g. **Example:** Liza and Antonio met during their church's summer retreat and regularly attend Bible study together. Liza recently contracted a life-threatening illness and executes a will witnessed by her mother and Antonio. The will devises her substantial estate to her church. The will is *valid* despite the fact that Antonio will indirectly benefit from the gift to the church.

(e) Taker under anti-lapse statute [§428]

If a witness takes under the will only because of an anti-lapse statute, the purging statute does not apply.

e.g. **Example:** Suppose that a will makes a bequest to the testator's daughter, Betty, and Betty's son Sam is one of the two attesting witnesses. Betty predeceases the testator. On the testator's death, Sam takes the bequest to Betty under the state's anti-lapse statute (*see infra*, §§695 *et seq.*). The purging statute does not apply because Sam is not a beneficiary *under the will*. Thus, Sam may take the bequest. [*In re* **Ackerina's Estate,** 195 Misc. 383 (1949)]

(2) Exceptions to purging statutes' operation [§429]

The interested witness statutes do not always purge legacies to attesting witnesses. Several exceptions to the purging rule have been written into the statutes or have been engrafted by case decision.

(a) Supernumerary witness [§430]

If a beneficiary is one of *three* attesting witnesses, *and if the will can be proved* without that witness-beneficiary's testimony, the bequest is not purged. The beneficiary is a "supernumerary" witness; *i.e.*, she was not needed to have a validly executed will. [*See, e.g.*, Ga. Code §53-4-23; Iowa Code §633.281; Tenn. Code §32-1-103; *In re* **Pye's Estate**, 325 F. Supp. 321 (D.D.C. 1971); **Rogers v. Helmes**, 432 N.E.2d 186 (Ohio 1982)]

(b) Beneficiary would be heir—"whichever is least" exception [§431]

Many of the purging statutes provide that if the witness-beneficiary would be an heir if there were no will, the witness-beneficiary takes the *lesser* of (i) her *intestate share* or (ii) the amount of the *bequest*. [*See, e.g.*, D.C. Code §18-104(b); Tex. Prob. Code §61] *Rationale:* To the extent that the beneficiary would take if there were no will, she is not interested. If the amount of the bequest is less than her intestate share, the will actually operates against the beneficiary's interest. *But note:* Statutes in a few states do not recognize this exception. [*See, e.g.*, Mass. Gen. Laws ch. 191, §2; N.C. Gen. Stat. §31-10; **Rosenbloom v. Kokofsky**, 369 N.E.2d 1142 (Mass. 1977)—court refused to adopt exception judicially]

---

e.g. Example: Turner, who is single, dies leaving a typewritten will that devises $100,000 to his sister Sue and his residuary estate to his mother. Turner leaves an estate worth $400,000. Sue is one of the two attesting witnesses to the will. Under the state's intestacy statutes, if Turner had died intestate, his estate would have passed one-half to his mother and one-half to his sister. Since Sue would take more by intestacy than under the will, the interested witness statute does not apply, and Sue takes the $100,000 legacy under the will.

DID THE WITNESS VALIDLY ATTEST THE WILL?   **gilbert**

TO DETERMINE IF THE WITNESS PROPERLY ATTESTED THE TESTATOR'S WILL, ASK YOURSELF THE FOLLOWING:

☑ Was the witness *mentally competent* at the time of the will's execution?

☑ Did the witness meet the statutory *age* requirement (if any) at the time of the will's execution?

☑ Did the witness sign in the *testator's presence*?

☑ Was the witness *"interested"* in the will? If so, was the interest a *direct pecuniary interest* and does the *purging statute* apply?

(3) Subsequent testamentary instrument; effect on purging statute [§432]

The operation of a purging statute may be affected by a subsequently executed will or codicil. This is illustrated by the following situations:

(a) Codicil that makes gift to will's witness [§433]

If the codicil makes a gift to a witness who witnesses the *will* but not the codicil, the purging statute does *not* apply because the codicil making the gift was attested to by two disinterested witnesses.

> **Example:** Tad executes a will that makes various gifts (but none to Bonnie); Bonnie is one of two attesting witnesses. Thereafter, Tad executes a codicil that gives $5,000 to Bonnie. Bonnie is not a witness to the codicil. The purging statute does not apply. Bonnie may take the $5,000 because she was not an attesting witness to the codicil that made the beneficial gift.

(b) Codicil that reduces gift under will [§434]

If the codicil *reduces* a gift to a beneficiary under the will who *witnesses the codicil but not the will*, the purging statute *does not* apply.

> **Example:** Testator's will devises real property outright to her husband. The will is witnessed by two neighbors. Thereafter, Testator executes a codicil devising the same real property to her husband for life, with the remainder on his death to pass to Clyde. Testator's husband is one of the two attesting witnesses to the codicil. The purging statute does not apply to the codicil because the husband did not receive a beneficial devise under the codicil. The codicil *reduced* the gift to him under the will. [*In re* **Moore's Will**, 32 Misc. 2d 429 (1961)]

(c) Codicil that increases gift under will [§435]

If the codicil *increases* the gift to a beneficiary under the will who *witnesses the codicil but not the will*, the purging statute *applies*.

> **Example:** Testator executes a will that makes a legacy to Eugene and bequeaths the residue of the estate to Ruth. Later, Testator executes a codicil that *revokes* the legacy to Eugene, with Ruth acting as one of the two attesting witnesses to the codicil. Ruth cannot take the accretion to the residuary estate caused by the codicil because the purging statute applies: By revoking the gift to Eugene, in effect the codicil made a new gift to Ruth. [*In re* **Hunt's Estate**, 122 N.Y.S.2d 765 (1953)]

(d) Effect of republication by codicil [§436]

An interested witness may nonetheless receive the gift in a will if a later testamentary document *republishes the will* that made the gift.

---

e.g. Example: Tad's will leaves his entire estate to Bonnie, who is one of the two attesting witnesses. At this point, the gift to Bonnie is void. However, Tad later duly executes a codicil that is witnessed by two disinterested persons; the codicil makes a minor change in the will (*e.g.*, names a new executor). Execution of the codicil has the effect of republishing the earlier will under the doctrine of "republication by codicil" (*see infra*, §§637-642), thus validating the otherwise void gift to Bonnie.

EXAM TIP	gilbert

Interested witnesses often appear in law school exam questions. The important things to remember are:

1. *The will is valid* although the *interested witness may lose her gift* under a purging statute.

2. There are a lot of ways *around the purging statutes*, the most common being:

   - *Is the state in question a UPC state?* If so, the will *and the gift* to the interested witness are valid.

   - *Is the "interested witness" a will beneficiary?* Recall that executors, trustees, and creditors of the testator are *not will beneficiaries* and thus are not interested witnesses.

   - *Are there more than the required number of witnesses to the will?* If so, the interested witness is "supernumerary" and may take her gift under the will.

   - *Is the interested witness an heir of the testator?* If so, she will take the *lesser* of her gift in the will or what she would receive in intestacy if there were no will.

   - *Is there a subsequent will or codicil?* If a validly executed later will or codicil republishes the will, the interested witness is no longer "interested" (because she did not sign the new instrument) and may take her gift under the original will.

D. Liberalizing Compliance with Will Execution Requirements

1. **In General [§437]**

   In recent years, the courts' strict application of the formal requirements for will execution, in cases where it is clear that the testator intended the particular document to be her will, has come under increased criticism. [*See, e.g.*, John H. Langbein, *Substantial Compliance with the Wills Act*, 88 Harv. L. Rev. 489 (1975)] The original UPC's approach to this concern was to simplify the procedures for executing a will. (*See supra*, §383.) While this has been seen as a step in the right direction, two much bolder approaches have been proposed.

   a. **Substantial compliance doctrine [§438]**

      The Restatement (Second) of Property urges the adoption of a "harmless error" principle in resolving cases where the will was defectively executed. If the will was executed in substantial (although not total) compliance with the statutory formalities, the will should be *admitted to probate* if the proponent establishes by clear and convincing evidence that the decedent intended the document to constitute his will. [Rest. 2d Property: Donative Transfers §33.1, Comment g (1992)] To date, only one court has applied the substantial compliance doctrine to admit a defectively executed will to probate. [*See In re* **Will of Ranney**, 589 A.2d 1339 (N.J. 1991)]

      Example: The following events take place in a state that requires the attesting witnesses to sign the will in the testator's presence. Tony's will is signed in a hospital room, with two nurses, Mike and Nancy, serving as witnesses. After announcing that "this is my will and I want you to witness it," Tony signs the will. At that moment, Mike is called out of the room to tend to another patient. Nancy signs the will as a witness. Mike returns to the room three minutes later and signs the will, but in the meantime Tony has been wheeled down to the X-ray room at the end of the hall. In most states, Tony's will would be denied probate because both witnesses did not sign in Tony's presence. But under the substantial compliance doctrine, the court would likely rule that the will was executed in substantial compliance with the Statute of Wills and would admit Tony's will to probate.

      ---

   b. **Revised Uniform Probate Code—dispensing power [§439]**

      The revised UPC has added a *dispensing power* that allows the probate court to excuse literal compliance with the formal requirements for executing a will. [UPC §2-503] Unlike the substantial compliance doctrine, which requires that the testator must have come close to satisfying the statutory requirements (a near-miss standard), under the UPC a will can be admitted to probate without regard to the statutory requirements, if there is *clear and convincing evidence* that the testator intended the document to be her will.

      Example: The following events take place in a state that requires two attesting witnesses to a will. Tommy's will is prepared by a notary public and is signed in the notary's office. Although two of Tommy's friends are present in the room, after Tommy signs the will only the notary signs as witness and then affixes her notarial seal. Even in a state that applies the substantial compliance doctrine, probate is likely to be denied because the will-signing was not in substantial compliance with the statute. In a state that has enacted revised UPC section 2-503, however, the court would likely admit the will to probate, as there is clear and convincing evidence that Tommy intended the document to be his will.

LIBERALIZING COMPLIANCE—A REVIEW	**gilbert**
SUBSTANTIAL COMPLIANCE (MINORITY VIEW)	The will is admitted to probate if it is executed in *substantial compliance with statutory formalities*. Clear and convincing evidence must establish that the testator intended the document to serve as his will.
DISPENSING POWER (REVISED UPC VIEW)	The will is admitted to probate *without regard to statutory formalities* if clear and convincing evidence shows that the testator intended the document to serve as his will.

EXAM TIP	gilbert

Do not confuse the two theories. Under the substantial compliance doctrine, the execution must come *very close* to satisfying the statutory requirements. However, under the dispensing power, the court *dispenses with the formal requirements* altogether and focuses on evidence of the testator's intent.

E. Attestation Clause

1. Recites Facts of Due Execution [§440]

An attestation clause is a provision, placed immediately below the testator's signature line and immediately above the signature lines for the witnesses, that recites all of the elements of a duly executed will. An attestation clause is not a requirement for a valid will. [*See* **Estate of Bochner**, 119 Misc. 2d 937 (1983)] However, such a clause can serve a useful function and should always be included in a well-drafted will.

Example: An attestation clause might read as follows: "On the above date, Bob Jones, the testator, declared to us, the undersigned, that this instrument was his last will, and he asked us to sign as attesting witnesses to it. He then signed the will in our presence, we being present at the same time. Each of us then signed the will in the testator's presence and in the presence of each other, we and each of us believing that the testator was of sound mind."

---

2. **Presumption of Due Execution [§441]**

An attestation clause in proper form raises a rebuttable presumption that the *facts recited therein actually occurred,* and establishes a prima facie case that the *will was duly executed.* [*See, e.g.,* **Estate of Smith,** 668 N.E.2d 102 (Ill. 1996); **Goff v. Knight,** 206 P.2d 992 (Okla. 1949)] As a result, the burden of proving the contrary is on those contesting probate of the will. The prima facie case of proper execution is not abandoned by contradicting evidence of one of the witnesses; it is then for the jury to decide who is telling the truth. [*See* **Whitlow v. Weaver,** 478 S.W.2d 57 (Tenn. 1970)] In some states, clear and convincing evidence is required to rebut the presumption of valid execution raised by an attestation clause. [*See* **In re Politowicz's Estate,** 304 A.2d 569 (N.J. 1973)] Attestation clauses are particularly useful in two situations:

a. **Witness with bad memory [§442]**

Suppose that both attesting witnesses testify that they recognize their signatures but have no recollection of signing; they do not even recall meeting the testator. If the will contains an attestation clause, it can be admitted to probate on the strength of the presumption of due execution. [*See* **In re Estate of Collins,** 60 N.Y.2d 466 (1983)] "The probate of a will cannot be made to depend upon the recollection or veracity of subscribing witnesses, for if it were necessary for them to remember and testify to the fact that all of the prescribed formalities were in fact complied with, very few wills could be upheld." [**Collins v. Collins,** 151 N.E.2d 813 (Ill. 1958)]

b. **Hostile witness [§443]**

The probate court may admit a will to probate even if one attesting witness testifies that (i) she had not signed in the testator's presence, and (ii) the signature on the will was not the testator's signature, if the trier of fact finds that the evidence given by the attestation clause, and not the witness's testimony, is to be believed. [*See* **In re Koss's Estate,** 228 N.E.2d 510 (Ill. 1967)— witness's testimony contradicting recitals in attestation clause "is to be viewed with suspicion and received with caution"]

3. **Distinguish—Presumption of Due Execution Based on Witnesses' Signatures [§444]**

Some states recognize a *rebuttable presumption* of due execution simply upon proof of the genuineness of the signatures of the attesting witnesses. [40 A.L.R.2d 1223] In those states, it is not necessary to rely on an attestation clause for the presumption of due execution. Still, the inclusion of an attestation clause is good practice. Its presence lends added weight to the presumption of due execution, and it may be used to impeach a hostile witness.

F. Self-Proved Wills

1. In General [§445]

Nearly every state has enacted self-proving affidavit statutes. Under such a statute, the testator and the witnesses sign the will in the usual manner, and then the testator and the witnesses sign a *sworn affidavit,* usually on a separate sheet of paper, before a notary public. The affidavit recites all the elements of due execution and serves as a *substitute for live testimony* of the attesting witnesses in open court. This makes the will self-proved; *i.e.,* the will is admitted to probate on the strength of the recitals in the affidavit. [*See, e.g.,* Mo. Rev. Stat. §474.337; Tex. Prob. Code §59]

a. Attestation clause and self-proving affidavit compared [§446]

An attestation clause, which is not sworn to, is *evidentiary and corroborative only.* A will *cannot be admitted* to probate simply because it contains an attestation clause. The attesting witnesses must testify in the probate proceeding or, if the witnesses cannot be located, the other requirements of the statute governing probate of wills (*e.g.,* proof of signatures) must be satisfied. Once such testimony is presented, the recitals in the attestation clause can be relied upon—even in the face of hostile testimony. [*See, e.g.,* **Slack v. Truitt**, 791 A.2d 129 (Md. 2002)] In contrast, *a self-proving affidavit is sworn testimony,* and serves the same function as a witness's deposition or interrogatory.

b. Uniform Probate Code [§447]

As noted above, in most states the testator and the witnesses sign the will (which contains an attestation clause), *and then* they sign the self-proving affidavit, which is notarized. The UPC and several non-UPC states recognize this two-step procedure, but also permit the *attestation clause* itself to be *in affidavit form.* Under this procedure, the testator and the witnesses sign only once. The testator signs the will; then the attesting witnesses sign beneath the attestation clause, which is in affidavit form; then the notary public signs and affixes the notarial seal. [*See, e.g.,* Fla. Prob. Code §732.503; UPC §2-504]

2. Purpose of Self-Proving Affidavit [§448]

If a will is not self-proved, practical difficulties and minor irritants are often encountered in proving up a will—even though, in most cases, no one challenges the will's due execution. The attesting witnesses must be located and made to appear in probate court, where they sit around waiting for the docket call. If a witness resides outside the county or state, her testimony must be obtained by deposition or interrogatory. The self-proving affidavit procedure recognizes that most probates are harmonious, nonlitigious proceedings in which no one is questioning whether the will was duly executed. Even when wills are contested on grounds of lack of capacity or undue influence, valid execution of the will is seldom challenged. Thus, use of the affidavit as evidence of due execution eliminates the need to locate the witnesses and secure their testimony.

a. **Challenges to affidavit [§449]**

Of course, it would be possible for a will opponent to establish that "the affidavit lies" (*e.g.*, the witnesses did not sign in the testator's presence). [*See, e.g., **In re** **Mackaben's Estate**,* 617 P.2d 765 (Ariz. 1980)] However, the burden of proof is on the opponent to overcome the recitals in the affidavit.

3. **Improper Execution of Affidavit [§450]**

Suppose that the testator signs the will, but the witnesses do not; the signature lines below the attestation clause are left blank. However, the self-proving affidavit, on a separate piece of paper, is duly signed by the testator and the witnesses, and is sworn to before a notary public. Can the signatures on the affidavit be used to validate the will?

a. **Majority rule [§451]**

Most courts have *admitted the will to probate* by counting the witnesses' signatures on the affidavit as the signatures needed for a duly executed will, since the *affidavit recites that the execution formalities were complied with.* [*See, e.g., **In re** **Will of Carter**,* 565 A.2d 933 (Del. 1989); *In re* **Charry's Estate**, 359 So. 2d 544 (Fla. 1978); *In re* **Petty's Estate**, 608 P.2d 987 (Kan. 1980); 1 A.L.R.5th 965]

b. **Minority rule [§452]**

A few courts have *denied probate* on the ground that the self-proving provisions attached to the will are *not a part of the will* but concern the matter of its proof only; *i.e.*, the affidavit is not part of the instrument that must be executed with testamentary intent. "A testamentary document[,] to be self-proved, must first be a will." [**Boren v. Boren**, 402 S.W.2d 728 (Tex. 1966)—*overturned* by Tex. Prob. Code §59; *and see **In re** **Sample's Estate**,* 572 P.2d 1232 (Mont. 1977)]

COMPARISON OF ATTESTATION CLAUSES AND SELF-PROVED WILLS	gilbert
ATTESTATION CLAUSES	**SELF-PROVED WILLS**
• A *provision* at end of will	• *Sworn affidavit* (usually on separate sheet of paper)
• *Recites all elements of a duly executed will*	• *Recites all elements of a duly executed will*
• Raises a *rebuttable presumption* that the recited facts occurred and establishes prima facie case that the will was duly executed	• Makes will *"self-proved"*—can be admitted to probate on strength of recitals in affidavit alone
• *Witness's live testimony* (or other form of proof) *required*	• *Substitute for witnesses' testimony*; no additional proof required.
• *Helpful where the witness does not remember* the surrounding circumstances *or is hostile*	• *Avoids need for locating witnesses*, bringing them to testify, or deposing them, etc.

G. Attorney Liability for Defective Execution

1. In General [§453]

Suppose that although an attorney supervises the execution of a will, the Statute of Wills is not complied with (*e.g.*, the will has only one witness, or the witnesses do not sign in the testator's presence as required by the statute). As a result, the will is denied probate and the testator's estate passes by intestacy to his heirs. Can the intended will beneficiaries sue the attorney for negligence, with the amount of their recovery being the amount they would have received if the will had been validly executed?

2. Majority View—Privity of Contract Not a Defense [§454]

In an increasing number of states, privity of contract has been rejected as a defense. In a will preparation setting, an attorney's duty not to be negligent extends to the *extended beneficiaries of her legal work*, and they can sue the attorney for negligence. [*See, e.g.,* **Licata v. Spector**, 225 A.2d 28 (Conn. 1966); **Ogle v. Fuiten**, 466 N.E.2d 224 (Ill. 1984); **Guy v. Liederbach**, 459 A.2d 744 (Pa. 1983); **Auric v. Continental Casualty Co.**, 331 N.W.2d 325 (Wis. 1983)]

a. Rationale

Privity of contract unjustifiably insulates an entire class of negligent attorneys from the consequences of their wrongdoing since, as a practical matter, no one has the right to sue for the attorney's frustration of the testator's intent. Allowing beneficiaries to sue would provide accountability and thus an incentive for attorneys to use greater care in will preparation. Recognizing an action by the intended beneficiaries will not extend an attorney's duty to the general public, but only to a limited, foreseeable class—the beneficiaries named in the will. The attorney's duty to the testator is not conflicted, because her duty is to see that the testator's intentions are carried out by the very documents the testator has hired the attorney to draft. [*See* **Barcelo v. Elliott**, 923 S.W.2d 575 (Tex. 1996)—dissenting opinion]

b. Statute of limitations [§455]

In states that have rejected the privity of contract defense, the statute of limitations on an action against the attorney for negligence commences on the *date of the testator's death*, and not the date the will was executed. Because a will can be revoked or amended by the testator during his lifetime, no injury occurs until the testator's death.

3. Minority View—Privity of Contract Is a Defense [§456]

At common law and in a substantial minority of states today, privity of contract is a defense to such a negligence action. [*See, e.g.,* **Viscardi v. Lerner,** 125 A.D.2d 662 (1986); **Simon v. Zipperstein,** 512 N.E.2d 636 (Ohio 1987); **Barcelo v. Elliott,** *supra*—citing numerous cases on both sides of the issue; **Copenhaver v. Rogers,** 384 S.E.2d 593 (Va. 1989)] Under this view, the attorney's duty runs only to the ***client who contracted for the attorney's services***, and only the client can sue for negligence. (This is a rather convenient theory when applied to wills, since the mistake is not discovered until after the client's death!) Privity of contract is a defense even if the beneficiary harmed by the alleged mistake hired the attorney and paid the attorney's fee. Even in this circumstance, the client to whom the attorney owed a duty not to be negligent was the testator, not the beneficiary. [*See* **Conti v. Polizzotto,** 169 Misc. 2d 354 (1996)]

a. Rationale

An attorney owes a duty of undivided loyalty to her client. A strict privity standard protects the attorney's obligation to devote her full attention to the needs of the client. A determination that the attorney also owes a duty to the will beneficiaries might raise conflicting duties. Also, absent privity there would be virtually no limit on the persons to whom the attorney might be obligated. Imposing potential liability to nonclients would be unduly burdensome on the legal profession. [*See* **Noble v. Bruce,** 709 A.2d 1264 (Md. 1997)]

ATTORNEY'S LIABILITY FOR NEGLIGENT PREPARATION OF WILL	**gilbert**
MAJORITY VIEW	Will *beneficiaries can sue* the attorney for negligence. The statute of limitations begins to run on the date of the testator's death.
MINORITY VIEW	Will *beneficiaries cannot sue* the attorney for negligence; under privity of contract, the attorney's duties extend only to the testator.

H. Holographic Wills

1. In General [§457]

About 30 states recognize holographic wills, *i.e.,* wills in the *testator's handwriting and signed by the testator* but which have *no attesting witnesses.* [*See, e.g.,* UPC §2-503; Cal. Prob. Code §6111; Tenn. Code §32-1-105; Tex. Prob. Code §60] Where holographic wills are recognized, they may generally be made by any testator who has capacity, although two states limit the making of holographic wills to soldiers, sailors, and mariners at sea. [*See* Md. Est. & Trusts Code §4-103; N.Y. Est. Powers & Trusts Law §3-2.2] North Carolina imposes the additional requirement that the holographic will must be found among the testator's valuable papers. [*See* N.C. Gen. Stat. §31-3.4(3); *In re* **Gilkey's Will,** 124 S.E.2d 155 (N.C. 1962)]

2. **Testator's Handwriting [§458]**

To be a valid holographic will, the instrument or at least its material provisions must be ***written entirely in the testator's handwriting*** (or block printing). To be admissible to probate, witnesses who know the testator's writing must testify in probate court or by deposition that the instrument was written by the testator's hand. [*See* Tex. Prob. Code §84]

a. **General rule—entirely handwritten [§459]**

The general rule is that the will must be *entirely* in the testator's handwriting. Suppose that a testator begins to type his will, and then for some reason takes the sheet out of the typewriter and completes the will in his handwriting. The instrument is signed by the testator but it is not witnessed. This instrument is generally ***not admissible*** to probate because it is not entirely in the testator's handwriting. [*See, e.g.,* **Hinson v. Hinson,** 280 S.W.2d 731 (Tex. 1955)]

b. **Distinguish—surplusage rule [§460]**

If, however, the typewritten or mechanically reproduced words are not necessary to complete the meaning of the will—*i.e.,* if the handwritten provisions make sense and *form a complete will* without them—the typewritten or printed words will be disregarded as "surplusage" and the instrument may be probated. [*See, e.g.,* ***In re* Will of Allen,** 559 S.E.2d 556 (N.C. 2002); **Maul v. Williams,** 69 S.W.2d 1107 (Tex. 1934)]

Example: Testator used a partially preprinted stationer's will form and filled in blanks in the form's introduction, executor, and attestation clauses. Since none of the printed matter was material to the substance of the will or essential to its validity, the "will" was valid as a holographic will. [*See, e.g.,* **Estate of Black,** 30 Cal. 3d 880 (1982); **Fairweather v. Nord,** 388 S.W.2d 122 (Ky. 1965)]

---

c. **Original Uniform Probate Code [§461]**

Under the original UPC and in several non-UPC states, a holographic will is valid if its *material provisions* are in the testator's handwriting. [Original UPC §2-503; Cal. Prob. Code §6111; Tenn. Code §32-1-105]

d. **Revised Uniform Probate Code [§462]**

Under the revised UPC, a holographic will is valid if *material portions* of the document are in the testator's handwriting. [UPC §2-502]

e. **Tape recording [§463]**

A tape recording is not a writing and thus cannot be admitted to probate as a holographic will. [*See, e.g.,* **Muka v. Estate of Muka,** 517 N.E.2d 673 (Ill. 1987); ***In re* Reed's Estate,** 672 P.2d 829 (Wyo. 1983)]

3. **Testator's Signature [§464]**

All states require that a holographic will must be *signed by the testator*.

a. **What constitutes signature [§465]**

As with attested wills, the courts take a liberal position on what constitutes a valid signature (*see supra*, §385). A testator's initials, first name, and nickname have been held to be valid signatures. However, an engraved monogram is not sufficient, because it is not in the testator's handwriting. [*See* **Pounds v. Litaker**, 71 S.E.2d 39 (N.C. 1952)]

b. **Where signed [§466]**

By majority rule, there is no requirement that a holographic will be signed at the end of the will. The testator's signature may appear *anywhere*: in the margin or in the opening caption ("I, Joan Smith, do hereby declare . . ."). [**Ward v. First-Wichita National Bank**, 387 S.W.2d 913 (Tex. 1965)] If, however, the signature does not appear at the end of the holographic will, some courts require a showing that, in writing her name, the testator intended it as her signature, and that the instrument was the *complete* will intended by the testator. [*See* **Slate v. Titmus**, 385 S.E.2d 590 (Va. 1989)]

(1) **Minority rule [§467]**

A few states require that a holographic will must be signed *at the end* thereof.

4. **Date of Execution**

a. **Majority rule [§468]**

In all but a handful of states, there is no requirement that a holographic will be dated in order to be valid. [*See, e.g.,* UPC §2-502; N.J. Stat. §3B:3-3; Va. Code §64.1-49]

b. **Minority rule [§469]**

In a few states, a holographic will must be dated in the testator's handwriting in order to be valid. [La. Civ. Code art. 2883; Okla. Stat. tit. 84, §54]

EXAM TIP   **gilbert**

Remember that a holographic will does *not need to be witnessed*. The only requirements are that the material provisions (or portions) of the will are in the *testator's handwriting* and *signed by the testator* (and in a few states, the will must be *dated*).

---

5. **Testamentary Intent [§470]**

Because a holographic will is still a will, it must be made with testamentary intent —*i.e.*, the maker must have *intended to write a will*. Suppose, for example, that the testator writes a three-page letter to a friend in which he says, among many other things, "After my death, Blackacre will be yours." Is this a valid holographic will?

a. Was writing intended as will? [§471]

The crux of the problem is whether the testator intended the writing to serve *in and of itself* as his will. If it appears that some future writing was contemplated, then the letter clearly will not suffice. (*See supra*, §§346, 355.) Vagueness, an informal or abbreviated signature, discussion of other matters, etc., may all support the conclusion that testamentary intent was lacking, although no one of these factors is conclusive.

 Example: A memorandum, entirely in J. B. Curtis's handwriting, is found among papers on Curtis's desk after his death. The memo reads:

> Jewel and mother get ½ of stock sales.
> Jewel and mother get Greenville property.
> Little brick house.
> ½ of oil property.
> ½ of bank account.

This instrument might have been intended by Curtis to be his will. However, "it is more reasonable to conclude therefrom that it was intended as a memorandum from which a will might be drawn, or of the manner in which he planned to dispose of his property in his life time." [**Curtis v. Curtis**, 373 S.W.2d 367 (Tex. 1963)] Thus, the instrument does not show on its face that it was written with testatmentary intent.

b. Extrinsic evidence [§472]

Extrinsic evidence is admissible to establish that an otherwise ambivalent document was written with testamentary intent.

Example: A handwritten note, written while William Kuhlmann was in the hospital, was handed to a nurse with this declaration, "Take care of this; it's my will." The note read:

> Dec. 17, To Mrs. Eugenia Poss auto and $5,000 Dollars.
>
> Wm. Kuhlmann 1918

The circumstances of the note's writing, plus the statement to a witness, show that this brief note was intended to serve as a will. [**Poss v. Kuhlmann**, 222 S.W. 638 (Tex. 1920)] Thus, in *Curtis, supra*, if there was any evidence, even parol evidence, that J. B. Curtis intended the memo to be his will, that evidence would be admissible and would support a finding of testamentary intent.

6. Interlineations [§473]

Suppose that a testator writes and signs a valid holographic will that leaves a particular piece of property to Byron and the residue of her estate to Candace. Later, the testator scratches out Candace's name and writes in the name of another person. What is the effect of the interlineation? Nearly all states that recognize holographic wills give effect to such interlineations, as long as the evidentiary test for probating holographic wills is met—*i.e.*, the will, *including the interlineations*, is entirely in the testator's handwriting and signed by her. Put another way, a testator can write a holographic will in spurts.

I. Oral Wills

1. In General—Limited Use [§474]

Borrowing from the Statute of Frauds and the English Wills Act of 1837, statutes in about 20 jurisdictions permit oral ("nuncupative") wills in very limited circumstances. The statutes vary greatly in detail as to the circumstances under which an oral will is permitted, and also as to the formalities required. In some states, persons who can make oral wills are limited to *soldiers, sailors, and mariners at sea*, with the further limitation, in some states, that the will must be made *during a time of declared or undeclared war* or other armed conflict. [*See* N.Y. Est. Powers & Trusts Law §3-2.2] In other states, oral wills can be made by any person, but only during the person's *last sickness* or in *contemplation of immediate death*. [*See, e.g.,* Miss. Code §91-5-15; Tex. Prob. Code §65] In yet another group of jurisdictions, oral wills can be made by soldiers and sailors, but *only* during their last illness. [*See* D.C. Code §18-107]

2. Uniform Probate Code [§475]

The UPC makes *no provision* for oral wills.

3. Personal Property Only [§476]

In nearly all states that allow oral wills, such wills can *dispose of personal property only*. However, in a few states allowing "soldier and sailor" oral wills, the statute does not limit oral wills to personal property dispositions. [*See* N.Y. Est. Powers & Trusts Law §3-2.2]

4. Dollar Limit [§477]

In most states that allow oral wills, there is *no limit* on the amount of personal property that can pass under an oral will. However, a few states impose a dollar limit [*See, e.g.*, Mo. Rev. Stat. §§474.340—$500], and in other states additional formalities must be satisfied if the value of the property passing thereunder exceeds a specified amount [*See, e.g.*, N.H. Rev. Stat. §555:16—three witnesses required if amount exceeds $100].

5. Formalities Required [§478]

It is usually provided that there must be *two* (and in some states three) *witnesses* to the uttering of the oral will. Some states impose additional requirements, *e.g.*, that the oral will be reduced to writing by the witnesses within a specified period [D.C. Code §18-107—10 days], and that it be offered for probate within a specified time.

6. Automatic Revocation [§479]

Under some statutes, an oral will automatically *expires after a stipulated time*. For example, in New York a mariner's will becomes invalid three years after its making, and a soldier's or sailor's will expires one year after discharge from military service. [N.Y. Est. Powers & Trusts Law §3-2.2]

7. Oral Codicil [§480]

Judicial hostility toward oral wills is reflected in cases holding that an oral will cannot be made by a testator who has previously executed a written, attested will. [*See In re* **Carlton's Estate**, 221 So. 2d 184 (Fla. 1969)] *Rationale:* To give the oral will effect would result in a partial revocation of the attested will, and oral revocations are invalid. [*See In re* **Grattan's Estate**, 138 P.2d 497 (Kan. 1943)] *But note:* A number of states permit oral wills (in effect, oral codicils) even though the effect is to alter the dispositions made by an earlier attested will. [*See, e.g.*, **Connor v. Purcell**, 360 S.W.2d 438 (Tex. 1962)]

SATISFYING REQUIREMENTS FOR ORAL WILLS	**gilbert**

REMEMBER TO ADDRESS THE FOLLOWING WHEN DETERMINING THE VALIDITY OF AN ORAL WILL:

☑ Is there a statutory limitation on who can make an oral will (*e.g.*, *soldiers, sailors, and mariners at sea* or persons during their *last sickness*)?

☑ Can the will dispose of *real and personal* property (most states permit only the disposal of personal property by oral will)?

☑ Is there a *dollar limit* on the value of property that can be disposed?

☑ Was the will *witnessed* by the appropriate number of witnesses and, in some states, *reduced to writing*?

J. Conditional Wills

1. In General [§481]

A conditional will is one that expressly provides that it shall be operative only if some *condition stated in the will is satisfied* (*e.g.*, "This will shall be effective only in the event my wife survives me."). In such a case, testamentary intent exists only if the condition occurs; if it does not (*e.g.*, if the wife predeceases the testator), the will *fails* for lack of testamentary intent. [*See* Cal. Prob. Code §6105]

2. Condition Must Appear on Face of Will [§482]

A will that is absolute on its face cannot be shown to have been executed conditionally. Parol evidence is *not admissible* to prove a condition that does not appear on the face of the will. [*See In re* **Trager's Estate**, 108 N.E.2d 908 (Ill. 1952)] *Rationale:* Courts are reluctant to allow extrinsic testimony that would overturn a written, attested will that is unconditional on its face.

3. Condition vs. Motive [§483]

The most commonly litigated question concerning conditional wills is whether the language in the will imposed a condition or, instead, merely expressed the *motive or inducement for making the will*. The litigation occurs when the testator dies some years later, having survived the apprehended peril referred to in the will.

Example: Testator's will provides: "I am going on a mountain-climbing trip to the Himalayas, and I may not ever return. If anything happens to me on the trip, here is how I want my property disposed of. . . ." On these and similar facts, many courts have held that Testator's language merely expressed what was on her mind as the occasion and inducement for making a will. "She was thinking of the possibility of death or she would not have made a will. But the possibility at that moment took the specific shape of not returning from her journey, and so she wrote 'if I do not return' before giving her last commands." Thus the will is admissible to probate even though Testator died some years after returning from the journey. [*See* **Eaton v. Brown,** 193 U.S. 411 (1904); *In re* **Taylor's Estate,** 119 Cal. App. 2d 574 (1953)]

---

cf. **Compare:** On very similar facts, a number of courts have found the will to be conditional, and have denied probate if the condition did not occur. [*See, e.g., In re* **Pascal's Estate,** 2 Misc. 2d 337 (1956)]

---

a. **Factors supporting finding of absolute will [§484]**

The tendency of the more recent decisions is to find that the will was not intended to be conditional unless a *contrary intent* clearly appears. [1 A.L.R.3d 1048] Various factors have been cited in support of a finding that the will was intended to be absolute and not conditional.

(1) **Intestacy avoided [§485]**

The fact that a will was executed by the testator is an indication that she did not intend to die intestate, which would be the result if the will were found to be conditional. [*See* **Ferguson v. Ferguson,** 45 S.W.2d 1096 (Tex. 1931)]

(2) **Preservation of will [§486]**

The fact that the testator preserved the document after returning from the journey or surviving the operation is an indication that the will's operation was not intended to be limited. [*See In re* **Desmond's Estate,** 223 Cal. App. 2d 211 (1963)]

b. **Extrinsic evidence [§487]**

By majority rule, extrinsic evidence *is admissible* to show whether the testator intended by conditional language to make an absolute or conditional will. [*See, e.g., In re* **Taylor's Estate,** *supra;* **Barber v. Barber,** 13 N.E.2d 257 (Ill. 1938)]

EXAM TIP **gilbert**

Don't get confused here. Extrinsic evidence can be used to determine the testator's intent if the language in the will is *conditional*. However, if the language in the will is *absolute*, extrinsic evidence is inadmissible. (*See supra,* §482.)

---

4. **Conditional Codicils [§488]**

A codicil also may be executed subject to a condition. If the condition does not occur, the codicil is not given effect.

a. **Republication of will [§489]**

However, even if the condition has failed, a conditional codicil may be admissible to probate for the sole purpose of *republishing* the will. (On republication by codicil, *see infra*, §§637 *et seq*.)

---

e.g. **Example**: Tomas executes a will that leaves all his property to Jose, but unbeknownst to anyone, the will is invalid because it was not properly executed. Later, Tomas duly executes a codicil providing that in the event Dino returns home from China before Tomas's death, Jose and Dino are to share the estate equally. Dino does not return home from China. The terms of the codicil are not effective because the condition never occurred (Dino did not return home), but the codicil is admissible to probate to republish and thus validate the earlier will under the incorporation by reference doctrine.

K. Statutory Wills

1. California Statutory Will [§490]
The California statutory will is a state-sponsored and distributed will form. [Cal. Prob. Code §§6200-6243] Several other states have enacted statutes patterned after the California statutory will. [*See, e.g.*, Me. Rev. Stat. tit. 18A, §2-514]

2. Uniform Statutory Will Act [§491]
In lieu of offering state-sponsored will forms, the Uniform Statutory Will Act permits a testator to incorporate by reference a plan of distribution set out in the statute, by stating in his will that all or a specified portion of his estate is to be disposed of in accordance with the Act. Only two states have adopted the Act. [Mass. Gen. Laws ch. 191B, §§1 *et seq*.; N.M. Stat. Ann. §§45-2A-1 *et seq*.]

3. Execution [§492]
Both the California statutory will and the Uniform Statutory Will Act require that the will be executed in accordance with the state's statute governing due execution of wills.

Chapter Seven:
Revocation of Wills

CONTENTS

Chapter Approach

This chapter covers revocation of wills, lost wills, revival of revoked wills, and the doctrine of dependent relative revocation ("DRR").

1. **Revocation of Wills**

    The issue of whether a will has been partially or totally revoked comes up frequently on Wills exams. You need to keep in mind two important principles:

    a. A testator may *always revoke* her will. Even when she has signed a contract not to revoke, the testator is free to do so, although the contract may be enforced by the imposition of a constructive trust.

    b. A will may be revoked by one of *three methods:*

        (i)   *By operation of law:* If the testator is married or divorced after executing a will, the change in her status *may revoke all or part of the will*, or may have no effect whatsoever, *depending on the law of the jurisdiction.*

        (ii) *By a subsequent will or codicil*: Be sure that the subsequent instrument is a valid will or codicil (*i.e.,* it has been validly executed; *see* Chapter VI). If the subsequent instrument does not contain language that *expressly revokes* the will (in whole or part), look for *inconsistent provisions* that *impliedly revoke it.*

        (iii) *By physical act*: Most (but not all) states recognize partial revocations by physical act—generally *burning, tearing, or obliterating* a material part of the will, or *canceling* by writing across the face of the will. Questions about this method of revocation can be tricky. Recall, too, that another person can do the physical act for the testator, but it must be in the testator's presence and at her direction.

        Note: For all of these methods, the testator must *intend to revoke* the will; however, for the first method (*by operation of law*), the court will *presume* the testator's intent to revoke.

2. **Lost Wills**

    Remember that under certain circumstances, a lost or destroyed will may be probated by *witnesses' testimony* and/or a *copy of the lost will.*

3. **Revival of Revoked Wills**

    In many states, merely revoking a later will does *not* automatically revive an earlier will; there must be reexecution of the will or republication by codicil, both requiring *full testamentary formalities* (signature, witnesses, etc.; *see* Chapter VI).

4. **Dependent Relative Revocation**

    Discuss dependent relative revocation ("DRR") when you see a situation where the testator has revoked a will based on a *mistake of law* that another disposition of her property is valid; if the requirements for DRR are met, the court will *disregard the revocation* and probate the will as if it had not been revoked. In this situation it also may be necessary to apply the rules regarding proof of lost wills.

5. **Interlineations**

    Watch for questions in which the testator makes changes on the will after it has been executed. Remember that in most states, these interlineations are *ineffective* unless the will is a holograph. Under the revised UPC, however, the interlineations will be given effect if there is clear and convincing evidence that this is what the testator intended. If the testator crossed out an existing gift in making the changes, the strikeout may or may not be an effective partial revocation, depending on the state's laws. If the state recognizes partial revocations, think about whether the revocation can be disregarded under DRR.

A. Introduction

1. **All Wills Are Revocable by Testator [§493]**

    A testator always has the power to revoke his will *at any time*. Even a testator who has validly contracted not to revoke his will may do so, although the revocation may give rise to a constructive trust or some other remedy in favor of the beneficiaries of the contract. (*See infra*, §674.)

2. **Methods of Revocation [§494]**

    Revocation of a will may occur in one of three ways.

    a. **By operation of law [§495]**

        Revocation of a will or a portion thereof may result from a *change in the family circumstances* of the testator, *e.g.*, marriage, birth or adoption of children, or divorce. (*See* below.)

    b. **By subsequent testamentary instrument [§496]**

        A *subsequent will or codicil* may expressly or impliedly revoke an earlier will. (*See infra*, §§526 *et seq.*)

    c. **By physical act [§497]**

        A will may be revoked by an *act of destruction* performed on the will by the testator or by another acting at the testator's direction and in his presence. (*See infra*, §§536 *et seq.*) In most jurisdictions, a will may be partially revoked by physical act. (*See infra*, §§548 *et seq.*)

APPROACH TO WHETHER A WILL HAS BEEN REVOKED

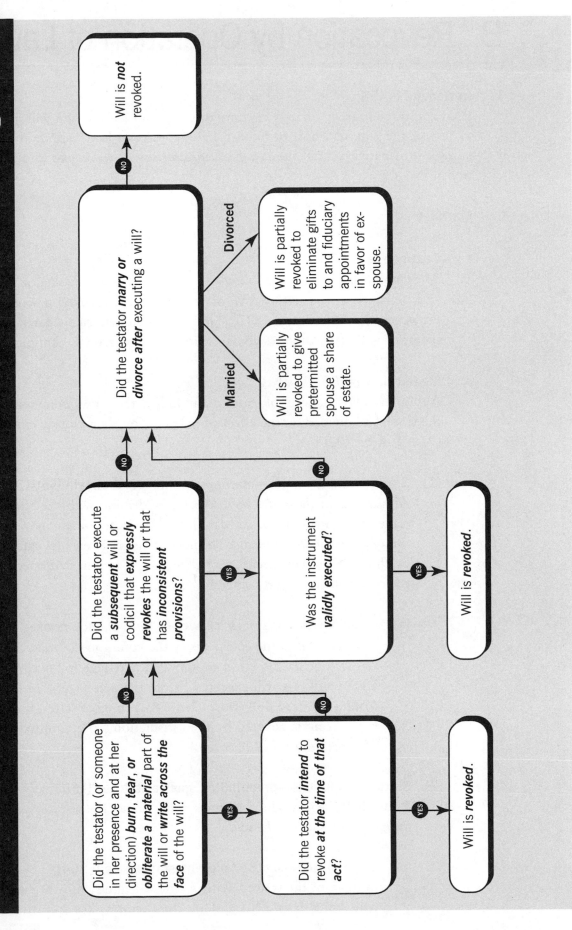

Did the testator (or someone in her presence and at her direction) **burn, tear, or obliterate a material** part of the will or **write across the face** of the will?

→ YES →

Did the testator **intend** to revoke **at the time of that act?**

→ YES → Will is **revoked.**

→ NO →

Did the testator execute a **subsequent** will or codicil that **expressly revokes** the will or that has **inconsistent provisions?**

→ YES →

Was the instrument **validly executed?**

→ YES → Will is **revoked.**

→ NO →

Did the testator **marry or divorce after** executing a will?

→ NO → Will is **not** revoked.

Married → Will is partially revoked to give pretermitted spouse a share of estate.

Divorced → Will is partially revoked to eliminate gifts to and fiduciary appointments in favor of ex-spouse.

B. Revocation by Operation of Law

1. In General [§498]

Changes in the testator's family circumstances after execution of a will may operate to revoke the will, in whole or in part, by operation of law. Despite the testator's lack of affirmative action, the law *presumes an intent to revoke* in certain situations.

2. Marriage

a. Common law [§499]

At common law, *marriage followed by birth of issue* revoked a man's will, and marriage alone, irrespective of birth of issue, revoked a woman's will. However, the Wills Act of 1837 established a uniform rule: Marriage revoked the prior will of a man or a woman, with certain narrow exceptions.

b. Modern law [§500]

Although only a handful of states today follow the above common law rules, the states are divided on the effect of marriage on a previously executed will. [97 A.L.R.2d 1026]

(1) States without statute—marriage has no effect on will [§501]

About half of the states have no statute dealing with the effect of marriage on a previously executed will. In these states, *marriage has no effect on an earlier will*. *Rationale*: The new spouse is given adequate protection by the state's elective share statute (or, in a community property state, by the community property system).

(a) Minority view—marriage followed by birth of issue revokes will [§502]

In a few states, the courts apply the common law rule: While marriage alone has no effect on the will, marriage followed by birth of issue revokes a will executed before the marriage. [*See* **Pascucci v. Alsop,** 147 F.2d 880 (D.C. Cir. 1945)] In most states, however, this fact setting is covered by the jurisdiction's pretermitted child statute. (*See supra,* §§278 *et seq.*)

(2) Statutory solutions—pretermitted spouse statutes [§503]

About half the states have statutes under which the *testator's subsequent marriage does affect the will.*

(a) Majority rule—spouse takes intestate share [§504]

In most of the states having statutes dealing with the situation, the will is only *partially revoked*. Marriage revokes an earlier will only to the extent of providing the new spouse with an amount equal to an intestate share. After distribution of the spouse's intestate share, the will operates to dispose of the remaining assets. [*See* UPC §2-301(a); Cal. Prob. Code §6560] These are sometimes referred to as *pretermitted spouse* statutes. [*See* Fla. Prob. Code §732.507(1)]

1) Exception [§505]

The above statutes often provide that the will is *not* partially or totally revoked if: (i) the will makes *provision for the new spouse;* (ii) it appears from the will that the spouse's *omission was intentional*; *or* (iii) it appears that the *will was made in contemplation of marriage.* [Original UPC §2-301(a); Mass. Gen. Laws ch. 191, §9; **Evans v. Palmour**, 553 S.E.2d 585 (Ga. 2001)]

(b) Revised Uniform Probate Code [§506]

The revised UPC also partially revokes the will, but *limits* the new spouse's intestate share to the portion of the estate that is *not devised to the testator's children* (or descendants of deceased children) by a prior marriage. Thus, if the testator devised his entire estate to his children by his first marriage, the omitted spouse takes nothing. [UPC §2-301]

1) Rationale

The pretermitted spouse statute serves a useful function in the case of a first marriage, where the decedent may have left a premarital will that benefits his parents or siblings. But in a society in which remarriages are common, with the dramatically increased intestate share given to surviving spouses by the revised UPC (*see supra*, §§26-29), in the case of a remarriage the *omitted spouse might unduly benefit to the detriment of the decedent's descendants.*

Example: Husband and Wife have reciprocal wills under which, after making modest bequests to siblings, each leaves his or her estate to the other, with an alternate gift to the couple's children in the event of the spouse's nonsurvival. Husband dies; several years later, Wife remarries. It does not occur to Wife that she should revise her will, as it now makes provision for her children. If Wife dies without changing her will, under the revised UPC her second husband's intestate share as a pretermitted spouse will apply only to property bequeathed to Wife's siblings, not to the property she bequeathed to her children.

---

2) Nonprobate transfers to spouse [§507]

Under the revised UPC and in several non-UPC states, the new spouse *does not take a share of the estate* if the testator made transfers to the spouse outside the will (*e.g.*, life insurance proceeds), and the intent that the transfers were *in lieu of testamentary gifts* is shown by declarations of the testator, by the amount of the transfers, or by other evidence. [*See, e.g.,* UPC §2-301(a); Mo. Rev. Stat. §474.235]

(c) Minority rule—entire will revoked [§508]

In several states, marriage following execution of a will *revokes the will in its entirety*. [*See, e.g.,* Mass. Gen. Laws ch. 191, §§8, 9; R.I. Gen. Laws §33-5-9] However, several of the statutes operate to revoke the will only if the spouse survives the testator. [*See, e.g.,* Or. Rev. Stat. §112.305]

EFFECT OF TESTATOR'S MARRIAGE ON PREVIOUSLY EXECUTED WILL	**gilbert**
STATES WITHOUT STATUTES	The testator's subsequent marriage has **no effect** on the will.
STATES WITH STATUTES	
• **MAJORITY VIEW**	Will is **partially revoked** to give spouse an amount equal to her **intestate share**; remaining assets are disposed of pursuant to will's provisions. *Note:* The spouse will **not** receive an intestate share if she is provided for in the will, her omission was intentional, or the will was made in contemplation of marriage.
• **MINORITY VIEW**	Will is revoked in its **entirety**.
• **UPC VIEW**	Will is **partially revoked** to give spouse an amount equal to her **intestate share** but only to the extent that it **does not reduce the gifts to the testator's children** (or their descendants) from a previous marriage. *Note:* The spouse will not receive any share of the estate if the testator provided for her by **nonprobate transfers** in lieu of testamentary gifts.

(d) Republication by codicil [§509]

The doctrine of republication by codicil (*see infra*, §§637 *et seq.*) can operate to eliminate the rights of a spouse who married the testator after the will's execution.

 Example: In 1998, Testator, who is single, executes a will that devises his entire estate to his mother. In 2000, Testator marries

Wife. In 2001, Testator executes a codicil to his original will that names a new executor. Testator dies in 2002. Under the doctrine of republication by codicil, Testator's will is deemed to have been executed in 2001; therefore, Wife is not entitled to a share of Testator's estate as a pretermitted spouse. [*See, e.g.,* **In re Estate of Ivancovich,** 728 P.2d 661 (Ariz. 1986); **In re Will of Marinus,** 493 A.2d 44 (N.J. 1985)]

EXAM TIP	gilbert

Depending on the circumstances of your question, an omitted surviving spouse may have two options for getting a share of the testator's estate: (i) under a **pretermitted spouse statute** or (ii) through the **elective share** (*see supra,* §§197 *et seq.*). Note, however, that a spouse is entitled to a share of the estate as a pretermitted spouse only if the testator **married after writing his will**, whereas **any surviving spouse** can claim an elective share. Also note that although the end result will sometimes be the same—e.g., the spouse may get a one-third share under either option—this is not always the case. For example, under the revised UPC, the pretermitted spouse's share is limited to property not devised to the testator's children. Thus, if the testator left everything to his children, the surviving spouse would receive nothing under the pretermission statute, but if she elected against the estate she would get her elective share. Also, if the testator republishes his will by codicil (*see infra,* §§637 *et seq.*) a surviving spouse would lose her pretermitted status (and her share) but still might be able to take an elective share.

c. Attorney liability for negligence [§510]

An attorney who fails to take into account a statute dealing with subsequent marriage may be held liable for negligent will drafting. If the attorney is aware of the impending marriage at the time the will is executed but fails to specify (per the testator's instructions) that the new spouse is to take nothing, the attorney may be held liable to the intended will beneficiaries for the amount passing to the spouse under the pretermitted spouse statute. [*See, e.g.,* **Heyer v. Flaig,** 70 Cal. 2d 223 (1969); **McAbee v. Edwards,** 340 So. 2d 1167 (Fla. 1976)]

3. Divorce

a. Common law [§511]

The common law and early American law had no rule dealing with the effect of divorce on a previously executed will. This is not surprising, because divorces rarely occurred in that era.

b. Modern law [§512]

Before the enactment of statutes expressly dealing with the effect of the testator's divorce on a will, it was generally held that divorce accompanied by a property settlement revoked all provisions in favor of the former spouse. [*See* **Luff v. Luff,** 359 F.2d 235 (D.C. Cir. 1966); 71 A.L.R.3d 1297] The will was read as though the former spouse had predeceased the testator. [74 A.L.R.3d 1108]

Today, however, virtually every state has a statute addressing the effect of the testator's divorce on a previously executed will.

(1) Provisions in favor of former spouse are revoked [§513]

Under these statutes, a divorce or annulment of the marriage *automatically revokes* all dispositive provisions of a will, including gifts made by the exercise of a power of appointment, and all fiduciary appointments in favor of the former spouse. The will is read *as though the former spouse predeceased the testator.* [UPC §2-804; Fla. Prob. Code §732.507(2); Ill. Comp. Stat. ch. 755, §5/4-7(b)]

(a) Rationale

"We can be sure that in almost every instance a divorced person does not desire a bequest to the former spouse to remain in effect. The legislature realized this, too, and wrote the statute to accomplish what was perceived to be the desired outcome in most divorces." [*In re* **Bloomer's Estate**, 620 S.W.2d 365 (Mo. 1981)]

EXAM TIP   **gilbert**

Remember that *all* will provisions in favor of a former spouse are automatically revoked, even appointments as *executor, guardian, or trustee*. However, in most states any *nonprobate transfers* in favor of the former spouse (*e.g.,* life insurance policies, trusts) are *not revoked*—the testator will have to change the beneficiary (see *infra,* §§518-522).

---

(2) Provisions in favor of former spouse's kin are not affected [§514]

The "divorce revokes" statutes apply only to provisions in favor of the former spouse; they *do not apply to provisions in favor of the former spouse's kin*. Suppose, *e.g.,* that the testator's will makes a gift "to my wife if she survives me, but if not, to my stepson Wayne." Thereafter, the testator is divorced by his wife (Wayne's mother), and the gift to her is revoked. The alternate gift to Wayne is not affected by the divorce. [*See, e.g.,* **Clymer v. Mayo**, 473 N.E.2d 1084 (Mass. 1985); *In re* **Coffed's Estate**, 46 N.Y.2d 514 (1979); **Bloom v. Selfon**, 555 A.2d 75 (Pa. 1989); *In re* **Estate of Graef**, 368 N.W.2d 633 (Wis. 1985)]

(a) Distinquish—Revised Uniform Probate Code [§515]

Under the revised UPC, provisions in favor of relatives of the former spouse are also revoked unless, after the divorce or annulment, such persons are related to the testator by blood, adoption, or affinity. The will is read as though the former spouse *and her relatives* predeceased the testator. [UPC §2-804] *Rationale:* In most cases, relationships with the former spouse's relatives are likely to weaken after a divorce. Giving effect to gifts to the former spouse's relatives is likely to be inconsistent with the testator's probable intent.

(3) Remarriage [§516]

Several of the statutes expressly provide that if the couple remarries, the revoked provisions are revived. [UPC §2-804(e); Tex. Prob. Code §69]

(4) Statutes apply only to testator's divorce [§517]

If a will makes a gift "to my brother-in-law, Bob Benson," and Bob later divorces the testator's sister, the gift to the brother-in-law is *not revoked*. The "divorce revokes" statutes apply only to gifts to the *testator's* former spouse. The reference to "brother-in-law" is merely descriptive, and is not a condition of the gift. [*See In re* **North's Will,** 32 A.D.2d 862 (1969)]

c. Effect on nonprobate transfers [§518]

Despite the increased use of will substitutes in recent years, most of the "divorce revokes" statutes apply only to wills, and not to life insurance policies, revocable trusts, or other nonprobate transfers. For example, if a life insurance policy names the insured's spouse as beneficiary and this beneficiary designation is not changed after the divorce, on the insured's death the proceeds are payable to the former spouse *pursuant to the terms of the contract* between the insured and the insurance carrier. [*See, e.g.,* **Allen v. Allen,** 589 N.E.2d 1133 (Ill. 1992); **Pepper v. Peacher,** 742 P.2d 21 (Okla. 1987)—retirement plan; *In re* **Adams's Estate,** 288 A.2d 514 (Pa. 1972)—retirement plan]

EXAM TIP   gilbert

Again note that under the majority view these statutes do *not affect nonprobate transfers*. Thus, the remarriage of the testator and former spouse will *never* revive any change in the beneficiary designation. For example, if the insured changes the beneficiary designation on his insurance policy after his divorce from the former spouse, but later remarries the former spouse, she will not automatically become the beneficiary on the policy *unless* the insured changes the beneficiary designation again. Contrast this with the statutes in some states that remarriage may automatically revive provisions in the testator's *will* in favor of the former spouse (*see supra*, §516).

---

(1) Minority view [§519]

Several states have recently enacted statutes extending the "divorce revokes" rule to certain nonprobate transfers, including revocable trusts [*See, e.g.,* Ohio Rev. Code §1339.62; Okla. Stat. tit. 60, §175], life insurance policies, and employee death benefits [*See, e.g.,* Ohio Rev. Code §1339.63; Tex. Fam. Code §§9.301, 9.302]. Under these statutes, the trust or insurance policy is read as though the former spouse predeceased the grantor or insured. A few courts have reached this result without the aid of a statute. [*See, e.g.,* **Clymer v. Mayo,** *supra,* §514—unfunded revocable trust funded by pour-over gift from will; **Vasconi v. Guardian Life Insurance Co.,** 590 A.2d 1161 (N.J. 1991)] Statutes in several states convert a joint tenancy between spouses into a tenancy in common upon divorce. [Ohio Rev. Code §5302.20(C)(5)]

(2) Revised Uniform Probate Code [§520]

Under the revised UPC, any revocable disposition in favor of the former spouse is revoked upon dissolution of the marriage. This includes life insurance policies, where the decedent had the power to name new beneficiaries, and revocable trusts. Also, dissolution of the marriage severs any survivorship estate between the spouses, and transforms it into a tenancy in common. [UPC §2-804]

(3) Qualified plans governed by ERISA—federal preemption [§521]

Under federal preemption, a state statute that extends the "divorce revokes" rule to nonprobate transfers does not apply to a beneficiary designation under a "qualified" employee retirement plan that is governed by the Employee Retirement Income Security Act of 1974 ("ERISA").

(a) State statute cannot alter beneficiary designation [§522]

Under ERISA, to be a qualified plan (*i.e.*, to be qualified for certain federal tax benefits), the beneficiary must be designated either by the plan participant or by the terms of the plan itself. A state statute that has the effect of naming a beneficiary other than the one named by the participant or the plan violates the federal standard. [**Egelhoff v. Egelhoff** *ex rel.* **Breiner**, 532 U.S. 141 (2001)]

Example: Paul is a participant under the General Electric qualified pension plan, which is governed by ERISA. Paul names his wife Nancy as primary beneficiary and his daughter Donna as contingent beneficiary of the plan proceeds in the event of Paul's death before retirement. Nancy divorces Paul, who dies a year later without having changed the beneficiary designation under his pension plan. Although a *state* statute applies the "divorce revokes" rule to retirement plan benefits and other nonprobate transfers, Nancy takes the plan proceeds as beneficiary because there is no *federal* rule that revokes a beneficiary designation upon divorce.

Compare: Same facts, except that Paul, upon reaching retirement age, rolled his pension plan benefits into an individual retirement account ("IRA"), naming Nancy as primary beneficiary and Donna as contingent beneficiary. Nancy divorces Paul, who dies a year later without having changed the beneficiary under the IRA. The state statute revokes the designation of Nancy as beneficiary and the IRA proceeds are payable to Donna. There is no federal preemption because ERISA does not apply to IRAs.

d. Legal separation [§523]

In states that recognize legal separation as an alternative to a divorce, a decree of separation that does not effect a dissolution of the marriage has *no effect* on an earlier will.

EFFECT OF TESTATOR'S DIVORCE ON GIFTS TO FORMER SPOUSE	**gilbert**
TESTAMENTARY GIFTS	Divorce or annulment **automatically revokes** all provisions in favor of the former spouse **only**—it does not affect any provisions in favor of the former spouse's kin (except in states that have adopted the revised UPC). In some states, the couple's **remarriage revives** any provisions in favor of the former spouse. *Note:* A legal separation does not affect provisions in favor of a spouse in an earlier will unless the separation effects a **dissolution of the marriage**.
NONPROBATE TRANSFERS	Divorce or annulment does **not** affect any beneficiary designations in favor of the former spouse—the insured must **change the beneficiary designation**. *Minority view:* Under the revised UPC and in some states, the designation is **revoked** and the former spouse is treated as having predeceased the, *e.g.,* insured. *Exception:* Beneficiary designations under employee retirement plans governed by ERISA are **not revoked** upon divorce.

4. Other Changed Circumstances Have No Effect [§524]

No change in the testator's circumstances besides marriage, divorce, or birth of issue operates to revoke a will or any portion thereof. [UPC §2-508] Thus, a testamentary gift is not revoked by proof of the testator's changed feelings toward the beneficiary, or by a huge and unexpected increase in the value of property devised to a beneficiary. [*See* **Ater v. McClure**, 161 N.E. 129 (Ill. 1928)]

C. Revocation by Subsequent Testamentary Instrument

1. In General [§525]

All states have statutes providing that a **will may be revoked in whole or in part** by a subsequent will or codicil. [*See, e.g.,* UPC §2-507; Okla. Stat. tit. 84, §105; Wis. Stat. §853.11(1)] The revocation may be **express or implied**. In either case, however, the subsequent instrument must be **testamentary**; *i.e.*, it must be validly executed with the necessary formalities by a testator having testamentary capacity. [**Maddox v. Mock**, 220 N.E.2d 773 (Ind. 1966)]

EXAM TIP	**gilbert**

When you see a later will or codicil in a question, check to see that it meets **all formalities for a will** (*i.e.*, it must be witnessed, signed by the testator with testamentary intent, etc.). If the original will was properly executed but the subsequent instrument is not properly executed (*e.g.*, it is signed by one witness instead of two), it is **not a valid revocation** of the will. Also keep in mind that a **nontestamentary instrument** (*e.g.*, a deed) cannot revoke a will.

2. **Express Revocation [§526]**

Typically, a subsequent testamentary instrument will explicitly state that it revokes an earlier will in whole or in part.

a. **Need not be dispositive [§527]**

The revoking instrument does *not* have to contain dispositive provisions. Most jurisdictions recognize a duly executed testamentary instrument that does nothing more than revoke an earlier will. [*See, e.g.,* **Grotts v. Casburn**, 129 N.E. 137 (Ill. 1920); 22 A.L.R.3d 1346]

b. **Revoking language must be explicit [§528]**

The words used by the testator must indicate an *intent to revoke* the earlier will. Well-drafted wills invariably contain an express revocation clause ("I hereby revoke all prior wills and codicils made by me"). However, a subsequent instrument that merely states that "this is my last will" does not revoke an earlier will in its entirety; it is revoked only to the extent of inconsistent provisions. [59 A.L.R.2d 11]

c. **Present intent to revoke [§529]**

The testator's words must show a present intent to revoke. An instruction to another (*e.g.,* "Please destroy my will") is insufficient, even if executed with testamentary formalities. The words in the testamentary instrument must themselves accomplish the revocation. [*See, e.g.,* *In re* **McGill's Will**, 229 N.Y. 405 (1920); *In re* **Estate of Langan**, 668 P.2d 481 (Or. 1983)]

d. **Holographic instrument [§530]**

In states that recognize holographic wills, it is generally held that a holographic instrument may revoke a typewritten, attested will. [*See, e.g.,* *In re* **Morris's Estate**, 488 P.2d 1015 (Ariz. 1971); 49 A.L.R.3d 1223]

e. **Oral will [§531]**

Jurisdictions that recognize oral (nuncupative) wills are divided on whether such a will may alter an earlier written will. Some courts give effect to such an oral "codicil." [*See* **Connor v. Purcell**, *supra,* §480] Other courts refuse to do so, on the ground that to hold otherwise would be to permit a partial revocation by oral statement rather than by a writing executed with due formalities. [*See* *In re* **Carlton's Estate**, *supra,* §480; *In re* **Estate of Mantalis**, 671 N.E.2d 1062 (Ohio 1996)]

3. **Implied Revocation by Inconsistency [§532]**

If a subsequent testamentary instrument does not expressly revoke an earlier will, both instruments are admitted to probate, and to the extent possible, the second instrument is treated as a codicil. The second instrument revokes the first will only to the extent that *its provisions are inconsistent* with the first will. [*See, e.g.,* Cal. Prob. Code §6120; Ga. Code §53-4-47; Va. Code §64.1-58.1; **Gilbert v. Gilbert,**

652 S.W.2d 663 (Ky. 1983); **Currier Gallery of Art v. Packard,** 504 N.E.2d 368 (Mass. 1987); 59 A.L.R.2d 11]

a.   **Partial inconsistency [§533]**

When the subsequent instrument is only partially inconsistent with the first will, the court reads both documents together to determine the testator's intent. Where the provisions of the two documents are wholly inconsistent with each other, the *subsequent instrument controls* because it is a later expression of the testator's intent. Note that a residuary bequest in the first will is not revoked by specific bequests in the subsequent will, although the size of the residue is reduced by those specific bequests. Likewise, a change in the residuary bequest in the subsequent will does not revoke specific bequests in the first will.

Example: Tyra's first will leaves all her property to Ron. Her second will makes no mention of the first will; it leaves her house to Harry and her car to Carol. When Tyra dies, both wills are read together; *i.e.,* the second will is treated as a codicil to the first will, and Harry takes the house, Carol takes the car, and Ron takes the residuary estate.

Example: Tyra's first will leaves her house to Harry and the remainder of her estate to Ron. Her second will does not expressly revoke the first will, but it leaves her antique desk to Pat and the remainder of the estate to Fred. The change in the residuary devise does not revoke Harry's gift. Harry takes the house, Pat takes the desk, and *Fred* takes the remainder of Tyra's estate. Absent evidence of contrary intent, the residuary clause in the second will is not deemed inconsistent with the first will's specific bequest to Harry, but it does operate to revoke the residuary gift to Ron.

b.   **Second instrument totally inconsistent [§534]**

If the subsequent testamentary instrument is wholly inconsistent with the first will, the first will is revoked *in its entirety*. To be entirely inconsistent, none of the dispositive provisions may be the same, and the provisions of the second will must purport to make a *complete* disposition of the testator's estate. [*See, e.g.,* **Maddox v. Mock,** *supra,* §525; *In re* **Estate of Thompson,** 407 N.W.2d 738 (Neb. 1987); 59 A.L.R.2d 11]

EXAM TIP	gilbert

If you see multiple wills (or codicils) in an exam question, first check to see if the subsequent instrument has **expressly revoked** the earlier ones (language such as "I hereby revoke all prior wills and codicils"). If so, you need only consider the last instrument. If not, recall that **all** validly executed instruments **are admitted** to probate, and where there are inconsistent provisions, the most recent expression of the testator's intent (*i.e., the last* will or codicil) controls.

REVOKING A WILL BY A SUBSEQUENT TESTAMENTARY INSTRUMENT

KEEP IN MIND THE FOLLOWING WHEN DETERMINING WHETHER THE SUBSEQUENT INSTRUMENT IS A VALID REVOCATION:

EXPRESS REVOCATION

☑ The subsequent instrument must have been executed with *all the required will formalities*.

☑ The instrument does *not have to dispose of the testator's property*.

☑ The instrument must contain language that *expressly revokes* the will.

☑ The intent to revoke the will must be a *present intent*—any intent or instruction to revoke the will in the future will not suffice.

☑ Holographic wills *may expressly revoke an earlier written will* in most states that recognize holographic wills.

IMPLIED REVOCATION

☑ The subsequent instrument must have been executed with *all the required will formalities.*

☑ The subsequent instrument is treated as a *codicil* because it *does not expressly revoke the will*.

☑ The will is revoked only to the extent that it is *inconsistent with the subsequent instrument* (the will may be revoked *in its entirety* if it is *wholly inconsistent* with the subsequent instrument).

c. **Neither will dated [§535]**

If the testator leaves two wills containing inconsistent provisions, each of which declares that it is "my last will and testament," the determination of which instrument is the testator's last will is a fact question to be determined by the trier of fact. If it cannot be determined when the wills were executed, both instruments are *denied probate*. [*See In re* **Westfeldt's Will**, 125 S.E. 531 (N.C. 1924)]

D. Revocation by Physical Act

1. **General Rule [§536]**

Nearly all statutes provide that a will may be revoked by some unattested physical act, either by the testator or by a third person acting at the testator's direction and in his presence. The physical act must be accompanied by a present intent to revoke. [*See, e.g.,* Cal. Prob. Code §6120; 24 A.L.R.2d 514]

2. **Requirements**

a. **Physical act [§537]**

The will must be physically acted upon. The statutes prescribe the acts sufficient to revoke a will. [*See, e.g.,* UPC §2-507—"burning, tearing, canceling, obliterating, or destroying"]

(1) Types of acts

(a) Burning [§538]

The will is revoked if a *material portion of the will's language* is burned by the testator. Merely singeing the will's corners and edges is insufficient. [**Payne v. Payne,** 100 S.E.2d 450 (Ga. 1957)]

(b) Tearing [§539]

A tearing or cutting of the will is generally sufficient to revoke it if a *material part* (*e.g.,* a dispositive provision or the testator's signature) is torn. [*In re* **Estate of Deskins,** 471 N.E.2d 1018 (Ill. 1984); **Crampton v. Osborn,** 201 S.W.2d 336 (Mo. 1947)] But if only one of the will's several pages is torn, this indicates that the testator did not intend to revoke the will in its entirety. [*In re* **Becklund's Estate,** 497 P.2d 1327 (Wash. 1972)]

(c) Obliterating or canceling [§540]

A revocation by obliteration, *e.g.,* by inking out or erasing, generally requires damage to a *material part* of the will. [*See, e.g.,* **Lovell v. Anderson,** 533 S.E.2d 64 (Ga. 2000); **Estate of DeWald v. Whittenburg,** 925 P.2d 903 (Okla. 1996)] Lining out or writing "void" across the face of the will operates as a cancellation, and revokes the will if the line-out at least *touches the words of the will.* [*See In re* **Davies's Estate,** 282 N.E.2d 528 (Ill. 1972); *In re* **Estate of Shaw,** 202 A.D.2d 433 (1994)]

Example: Testator has words of cancellation written on the *back* of the will by her attorney. This is not an effective revocation by cancellation because the attorney's writing, although done in Testator's presence and at her direction, did not cancel or deface the will. [**Thompson v. Royall,** 175 S.E. 748 (Va. 1934)]

Example: Testator writes in the *margin* of the will, "I hereby revoke this will." This cannot be considered an effective revocation by cancellation because the writing *does not touch the words of the will.* [*See, e.g., In re* **Mulligan's Will,** 40 A.D.2d 136 (1972); **Kronauge v. Stoecklein,** 293 N.E.2d 320 (Ohio 1972)]

(d) Distinguish—revised Uniform Probate Code [§541]

Under the revised UPC, burning, tearing, or canceling is a valid revocatory act "whether or not the burn, tear, or cancellation touched any of the words on the will." [UPC §2-507]

EXAM TIP **gilbert**

Revocation by physical act issues tend to focus on the technicalities of the act, especially whether the *act of revocation affected a material part of the will*. If not, the revocation usually is *not effective*. Thus, singeing or tearing the corners of the will, or writing on the back of it or in the margin, will not be enough to revoke the will by physical act (although the revised UPC is much more lenient and probably would find these acts sufficient if the intent to revoke is present). *But note:* If the state allows *holographic wills*, keep in mind that although a particular writing might not be an effective cancellation or obliteration, it could possibly be a valid revocation *by subsequent instrument* if it is in the testator's handwriting and signed by her.

(e) Physical act on testator's signature [§542]

It is generally held that the testator's crossing or cutting out his signature operates to revoke the will *in its entirety*. [*See In re* **McCaffrey's Estate,** 174 Misc. 162 (1940); *In re* **Estate of Funk,** 654 N.E.2d 1174 (Ind. 1995)] "The signature is the most important part of the will and if one not familiar with the statute were to revoke a will, the cutting of the signature from the will would be an ordinary mode to adopt, since the cutting of signatures from documents is frequently used to indicate their cancellation." [*In re* **Bakhaus's Estate,** 102 N.E.2d 818 (Ill. 1951); *but see* **Livelar v. Arnold,** 233 So. 2d 760 (Miss. 1970)—*contra*]

(2) Physical act on copy of will [§543]

The physical act of revocation must be performed *on the will* itself. Destruction of a copy of the will, even a xerographic copy that shows the testator's and witnesses' signatures, is insufficient. [*See In re* **Estate of Tolin,** 622 So. 2d 988 (Fla. 1993)]

(a) Constructive trust [§544]

If the act was performed on the wrong document due to a party's wrongful conduct, a constructive trust may be imposed on the will beneficiaries in favor of the parties who would have taken if the will had been revoked. [*See, e.g.,* **White v. Mulvania,** 575 S.W.2d 184 (Mo. 1978); **Morris v. Morris,** 642 S.W.2d 448 (Tex. 1982)]

(b) Revised Uniform Probate Code [§545]

Under the revised UPC, if the testator performs a revocatory act on a copy of the will that she *mistakenly thought was the will*, and the intent to revoke is proved by clear and convincing evidence, the revocation is *valid*. [UPC §2-507] A few courts have imposed a constructive trust in this situation. [*See, e.g., In re* **Estate of Tolin,** *supra*]

b. Intent [§546]

The act must be accompanied by a *present intent* to revoke the instrument. If a will is accidentally destroyed, a subsequent expression that the testator intended to revoke the will is ineffective. [*In re* **McCaffrey's Estate**, 309 A.2d 539 (Pa. 1973); *but see* **Cutler v. Cutler**, 40 S.E. 689 (N.C. 1902)—*contra*]

EXAM TIP   **gilbert**

The issue of intent to revoke often arises in a question presenting a testator whose will is ***destroyed without intent***—*e.g.*, the house burns down with the will in it or the testator tears up the will thinking it is her paid off mortgage papers—and ***then*** she says, "That's okay; I was going to revoke it anyway." Don't be fooled by her after-the-fact statement of intent. If she didn't have intent to revoke ***at the time the will was destroyed***, it has not been revoked.

---

3. **Physical Act of Another [§547]**

Many statutes permit revocation of a will by a physical act performed by a third person *in the testator's presence and at the testator's direction*. [UPC §2-507] Some states also require that the third person's act be *witnessed* by two persons besides the testator. [*See, e.g.,* N.Y. Est. Powers & Trusts Law §3-4.1(a)(2); Wash. Rev. Code §11.12.040] *Note:* There is no such requirement when the physical act is performed by the testator.

---

e.g. **Example:** Husband accidentally tears Wife's will while pulling out a desk drawer. When Wife is later told of the accident, she says it is unimportant because she was planning to revoke the will anyway. There has been *no revocation* because the physical act was not done in Wife's presence nor at her direction. Also, she did not have the present intent to revoke it.

---

e.g. **Example:** Margaret writes a letter to her friend, who has possession of Margaret's will, with instructions to destroy the will. If the will is destroyed, there is no effective revocation because the physical act was not done in Margaret's presence. Moreover, the letter, although entirely in Margaret's handwriting, was not written with a present intent to revoke and hence is not a holographic revocation by subsequent instrument. [*In re* **McGill's Will**, *supra*, §529]

---

4. **Partial Revocation by Physical Act**

a. **Majority rule [§548]**

Most revocation statutes expressly authorize partial as well as total revocation of a will by physical act. [*See, e.g.,* UPC §2-507; Ky. Rev. Stat. §394.080; Pa. Cons. Stat. tit. 20, §2505; *In re* **Palmer's Will**, 359 So. 2d 752 (Miss. 1978); **Goriczynski v. Poston**, 448 S.E.2d 423 (Va. 1994)]

(1) **Intent [§549]**

With respect to partial revocations, determining the testator's intent may be a problem. Did the testator intend only a partial revocation, or did he intend to revoke the entire will, but happened to touch only the part that he crossed out? [*See, e.g.,* **Watson v. Landvatter,** 517 S.W.2d 117 (Mo. 1974); *In re* **Estate of Lavigne,** 52 N.Y.2d 1008 (1981)] Extrinsic evidence is generally admissible to show what the testator intended.

(2) Limitation [§550]

Even where partial revocation by physical act is permitted, courts are reluctant to give effect to nontestamentary actions that operate to *increase* the size of a gift to the beneficiary of a *general or specific bequest*. However, the testator can always increase the *residuary* gift by canceling or destroying a general or specific bequest. [24 A.L.R.2d 514; *but see* **In re Estate of Malloy,** 925 P.2d 224 (Wash. 1996)—*contra*] *Rationale:* This is the logical consequence of recognizing partial revocations by physical act.

Example: Testator's will provides: "I devise Blackacre to Mary for life, remainder to Marsha." If Testator subsequently strikes the words "for life, remainder to Marsha," the action will *not* be given effect. *Rationale:* Giving effect to such an act operates to make a new gift of property, by increasing the gift to Mary from a life estate to a fee simple, without complying with testamentary formalities. [*See, e.g.,* **Patrick v. Patrick,** 649 A.2d 1204 (Md. 1994)]

Compare: In the example above, if Testator struck the entire devise of Blackacre (*i.e.,* neither Mary nor Marsha takes the property), the residuary gift would increase because Blackacre would become part of the residue. The revocation will be given effect.

(a) UPC view [§551]

Under the UPC, partial revocations are permitted even if the revocation operates to increase any gifts in the will. [UPC §2-507]

b. Minority rule—no partial revocation [§552]

In the absence of clear statutory language authorizing partial revocations, several states do not recognize partial revocation by physical act. In these jurisdictions, if the testator attempts to revoke a portion of the will, the *act is given no effect*. For example, if the testator crosses out a bequest, the beneficiary takes the bequest despite the attempted cancellation. [*See, e.g.,* Ill. Comp. Stat. ch. 755, §5/4-9; Ind. Code §29-1-5-6; **Leatherwood v. Stephens,** 24 S.W.2d 819 (Tex. 1930); 34 A.L.R.2d 619] If the destroyed portion cannot be recreated by extrinsic evidence (*e.g.,* a copy of the will), only the destroyed portion fails; the rest of the will is given effect. [*In re* **Lyons's Will,** 75 N.Y.S.2d 237 (1947); *but see* **In re Johannes's Estate,** 227 P.2d 148 (Kan. 1951)—will denied probate]

<table>
<tr><td colspan="2">PARTIAL REVOCATION BY PHYSICAL ACT   gilbert</td></tr>
<tr><td>MAJORITY VIEW</td><td>Partial revocation by physical act is permitted provided it does not increase the size of a general or specific bequest. Extrinsic evidence can be used to determine the testator's intent.</td></tr>
<tr><td>MINORITY VIEW</td><td>An attempted partial revocation by physical act is not given effect. The destroyed portion will fail if it cannot be proved by extrinsic evidence.</td></tr>
<tr><td>UPC VIEW</td><td>Partial revocations are permitted regardless of the effect on the remaining will provisions.</td></tr>
</table>

5. Effect of Revocation on Another Testamentary Instrument

a. Destruction of codicil [§553]

A physical act of destroying a codicil is generally held to *revoke only the codicil* and not the prior will. The will is read as though the codicil had never been executed. [*See, e.g., **In re** Estate of Ivancovich, supra,* §509; 7 A.L.R.3d 1153]

(1) Minority rule [§554]

New York applies a "no revival" rule to gifts that are revoked by a codicil. If the testator executes a codicil that revokes a gift in the will, and then revokes the codicil, the testamentary gift is *not* revived. [***In re** Moffat's Estate,* 5 Misc. 2d 991 (1956)]

b. Destruction of will—effect on codicil [§555]

A physical act of destruction performed on a will is generally held to *revoke all codicils* to the will if the testator so intended. It is presumed that the will and codicils were interdependent, and that the testator would want the codicils to be revoked along with the will. [*See, e.g.,* Va. Code §64.1-58.1; ***In re** Halpern's Estate,* 32 Misc. 2d 808 (1962); **Bowles's Estate v. Bowles's Heirs,** 114 N.E.2d 229 (Ohio 1953); 7 A.L.R.3d 1143] However, if the codicil is so complete that it can stand alone as a *separate testamentary instrument*, revocation of the will may not automatically revoke the codicil. [*See **In re** Cuneo's Estate,* 60 Cal. 2d 196 (1963)]

c. Duplicate wills [§556]

The execution of duplicate wills (*i.e.,* two **signed and witnessed** copies of the will) is a very bad practice because of the problems that are raised if only one of the duplicate originals can be located after the testator's death. It is generally held that **both wills must be accounted for**. The failure to produce one of the duplicate originals *may* raise a presumption of revocation, depending on the circumstances.

(1) Practice tip [§557]

The client should have a copy of the will to enable him to review the will without having to retrieve it from, *e.g.*, his safe deposit box. The attorney also should have a copy of the will for her files. However, only one will should be executed and then xerographic copies can be made showing the testator's and witnesses' signatures.

(2) Destruction of duplicate will [§558]

If two copies of a will are executed, destruction by the testator of an *executed* duplicate will in his possession and control revokes the will, including the untouched duplicate. [Cal. Prob. Code §6121] For this purpose, it is the copy of the executed will in the testator's possession and control that counts. [*See, e.g.,* **Roberts v. Fisher,** 105 N.E.2d 595 (Ind. 1952); **Olsson v. Waite,** 368 N.E.2d 1194 (Mass. 1977)] However, destruction of an *unexecuted* copy of the will does not have the effect of revoking the executed will. The physical act of destruction must be *on the will itself*. [*See, e.g., In re* **Krieger,** 191 A.D.2d 994 (1993); *In re* **Wehr's Will,** 18 N.W.2d 709 (Wis. 1945)]

(3) Only one duplicate copy located [§559]

If the testator retains possession of one executed copy of the will and the other executed copy is in the possession of the testator's attorney or another person, and the copy retained by the testator cannot be located, it is *presumed that the testator revoked the will* by physical act. [*See, e.g.,* **Horton v. Burch,** 471 S.E.2d 879 (Ga. 1996); 17 A.L.R.2d 805; *but see* **Stiles v. Brown,** 380 So. 2d 792 (Ala. 1980)—*contra*] If, however, the will in the testator's possession is found, but the duplicate original left in the possession of the attorney or another person cannot be located, no presumption of revocation arises. If the testator retains possession of both duplicate originals but only one can be located after the testator's death, most courts hold that a presumption of revocation arises. [*See, e.g.,* **Phinizee v. Alexander,** 49 So. 2d 250 (Miss. 1950); *In re* **Mittelstaedt's Will,** 280 A.D. 163 (1952); 17 A.L.R. 805, 817 (1951); *but see* **Etgen v. Corboy,** 337 S.E.2d 286 (Va. 1985)—*contra*]

EXAM TIP	gilbert

An easy way to remember this is that whenever an executed duplicate copy of the testator's will cannot be found, and that copy was in the *testator's possession and control*, a presumption of revocation arises. The presumption of revocation *never* arises if the executed duplicate will was in the possession of anyone other than the testator.

REVOCATION OF TESTAMENTARY INSTRUMENTS   gilbert

INSTRUMENT REVOKED	EFFECT
CODICIL	There is *no effect* on the prior will; it is read as if the codicil had never been executed. *Minority view:* If the codicil revoked a gift in the will, that gift is *not revived* when the codicil is revoked.
WILL	Any codicils to the will are also *revoked* unless the codicil can be read as an *independent testamentary instrument*.
DUPLICATE WILL	If duplicate copies are *executed*, then revocation of one duplicate *automatically revokes* the other duplicate. If one of the duplicates is *unexecuted*, then a revocation of the *unexecuted* duplicate has *no effect* on the executed duplicate.

6. Presumptions as to Revocation [§560]

A testator can destroy a will and thereby revoke it without any witnesses to the act. On the other hand, the accidental destruction of a will does not revoke it because there was no intent to revoke. When the will cannot be found after testator's death, or if it is found but it has been torn or mutilated, problems of proof arise as to the *testator's actions or intentions*. As an aid in resolving these problems, the courts have developed various presumptions.

a. Presumption of continuity [§561]

In most jurisdictions, the party offering a will for probate has the burden of establishing that the will was *not revoked*. However, if the will is found after the testator's death and there is nothing to indicate that it might have been revoked (*i.e.*, it is not cancelled or mutilated), the will is presumed to have had a *continuous legal existence* from the time of its execution. This is sometimes called the "presumption of continuity."

b. Will not found or found in mutilated condition [§562]

When the will cannot be found at the testator's death, or if it is found in a mutilated condition, the courts have developed another presumption.

(1) Presumption of revocation [§563]

If the will was last seen in the testator's possession or under his control, and is found after the testator's death in a mutilated condition, the presumption is that the testator was the one who mutilated or destroyed it, and that he did so with the intent to revoke the will. [*See, e.g.,* **Jessup v. Jessup,** 267 S.E.2d 115 (Va. 1980); 70 A.L.R.4th 323] Similarly, if a will last known to be in the testator's possession or control is not found after his death, the presumption is that the testator destroyed the will with the intent to revoke it. [*See, e.g., In re* **Estate of Perry,** 33 P.3d 1235 (Colo. 2001); *In re* **Donigian's Will,** 60 N.W.2d 732 (Wis. 1953); 24 A.L.R.2d 514, 522] The strength of the presumption may turn on the relative control the testator had over the instrument and the access that others had to it. [*See* **First Interstate Bank v. Henson-Hammer,** 779 P.2d 167 (Or. 1989)]

(2) Evidence to overcome presumption [§564]

Where a presumption of revocation arises from the will's nonproduction, extrinsic evidence is admissible to rebut the presumption. In several jurisdictions, clear and convincing evidence is needed to rebut the presumption of revocation. [*See, e.g., In re* **Crozier's Estate,** 232 N.W.2d 554 (Iowa 1975); *In re* **Estate of Mitchell,** 623 So. 2d 274 (Miss. 1993)] In other states, the presumption is rebuttable by a preponderance of the evidence. [*See, e.g., In re* **Estate of Glover,** 744 S.W.2d 939 (Tex. 1988)] Most jurisdictions admit declarations by the testator as to his intent; thus, the testator's references to the will and its provisions shortly before his death tend to support a finding that the will was not revoked. [*See, e.g.,* **Mimms v. Hunt,** 458 S.W.2d 759 (Ky. 1970); 28 A.L.R.3d 994] However, some courts limit the testator's declarations concerning the will to statements that are part of the res gestae; *i.e.,* to statements made at the time the physical act is made on the will. [*See In re* **Bonner's Will,** 17 N.Y.2d 9 (1966)]

(3) Adverse party had access to will [§565]

Evidence that a party adversely affected by the will had access to it has been held sufficient to overcome the presumption of revocation. [*See, e.g.,* **Barksdale v. Pendergrass,** 319 So. 2d 267 (Ala. 1975); **Garrett v. Butler,** 317 S.W.2d 283 (Ark. 1958); **Barngrover v. Barngrover's Estate,** 618 P.2d 386 (N.M. 1980); *but see In re* **Travers's Estate,** 589 P.2d 1314 (Ariz. 1978)—*contra*]

(4) When no presumption of revocation arises [§566]

If the will was last known to be in the possession of a *third person* (*e.g.,* the testator's attorney), most courts hold that the will's loss or damage does *not* give rise to a presumption of revocation. If the will was in the testator's possession but a person who would be adversely affected by the will had access to it, the presumption of revocation is weakened. [*See* **First Interstate Bank v. Henson-Hammer,** *supra*]

EXAM TIP gilbert

Just as with duplicate wills (*supra*), only if the missing or mutilated will was in the **testator's possession or control** will a presumption of revocation arise. If someone else has the will, there is no such presumption.

E. Proof of Lost Wills

1. Admission to Probate [§567]

To avoid frustration of a testator's intentions when the will has been *inadvertently* or *unintentionally* lost or destroyed, most states have enacted statutes authorizing probate of a lost will. In states without "lost will" statutes, essentially the same rules are applied by the courts. Because the actual will is not before the court, a stringent test must be satisfied before the allegedly lost will can be admitted to probate. Generally, probate of a lost will requires the establishment of three elements: (i) valid *execution*; (ii) the *cause* of nonproduction; and (iii) the *contents* of the will.

2. Due Execution [§568]

The proponents of the will must prove that the will was *validly executed*. The means of proof are the same as in any other case involving probate of a will. (*See infra*, §§987-993.) *Rationale:* To hold otherwise would make it easier to probate a lost will than an existing one. The case would "derive its strength from its intrinsic weakness." [**Tynan v. Paschal**, 27 Tex. 286 (1863); 41 A.L.R.2d 393] *Note:* This requirement cannot be satisfied if, given that the will is lost, the attesting witnesses cannot be identified.

3. Cause of Nonproduction [§569]

The will proponents must establish that revocation of the will is not the reason for its nonproduction. In this, the proponents may be aided—or hurt—by the presumptions as to revocation discussed *supra* in §§560-566. [86 A.L.R.3d 980; 70 A.L.R.4th 323]

a. Presumption [§570]

In some states, the fact that the will was last known to be in the possession of someone adversely affected by its contents raises a presumption of nonrevocation.

b. Fraudulent destruction [§571]

A few statutes require proof that the lost will either was in existence at the time of the testator's death, or was fraudulently destroyed during her lifetime. Generally, these statutes are liberally construed to allow proof of no revocation, thus avoiding intestacy. Some courts have held that the word "existence" in the statute means "legal existence," and that if a will was not lawfully revoked, it continues in legal existence until the testator's death. Other courts have ruled that a will destroyed without the testator's consent was "fraudulently destroyed," even if no actual fraud was involved. [*In re* **Fox's Will**, 214 N.Y.S.2d 405 (1961)]

4. Contents of Will [§572]

All statutes require proof of the contents of the lost will.

a. Standard of proof [§573]

The standard of proof is generally quite high and requires contents to be fully and precisely proved [Fla. Prob. Code §733.207], or that *all* the will's provisions be "clearly and distinctly proved" [N.Y. Surr. Ct. Proc. Act §1407].

b. Means of proof [§574]

Most statutes require proof by testimony of persons who had knowledge of the contents of the will, as by having read the will or having heard it read. [*See* Tex. Prob. Code §85] Generally, since these witnesses are proving content and not execution, they are *not* disqualified by beneficial interest. (*See supra*, §§418 *et seq.*) [*In re* **Reynolds's Estate,** 94 Cal. App. 2d 851 (1949); *and see* Fla. Prob. Code §733.207] Typically, the statutes require proof by two witnesses, but often allow a true copy of the will to substitute for the testimony of one witness.

ADMISSION OF A LOST WILL TO PROBATE

REMEMBER THE FOLLOWING WHEN DETERMINING WHETHER A LOST WILL CAN BE ADMITTED TO PROBATE:

☑ Was the will *validly executed*? (Proof required is the same as for any will.)

☑ What is the *cause of the will's nonproduction*? (Presumptions may come into play.)

- Was the will *revoked* by the testator?

- Was the will last in the *possession of someone adversely affected* by its contents?

☑ What are the *contents* of the will? (Standard of proof is high; "interested" witness can testify as to content.)

---

5. Uniform Probate Code [§575]

The UPC does not have a provision expressly dealing with proof of lost wills. If a state repealed a statute relating to lost wills when it enacted the UPC, it is not an indication that lost wills can no longer be proved and probated in that state. [*See In re* **Hartman's Estate,** 563 P.2d 569 (Mont. 1977)]

6. Proof to Show Revocation of Prior Will [§576]

Even if a lost will is not admissible to probate (*e.g.*, because all of its contents cannot be substantially proved), evidence of the will's due execution *plus* evidence that it contained language of revocation is admissible to show that an *earlier* will, now being offered for probate, was revoked. Proof of execution of the lost will is *not* an attempt to offer it for probate, but simply to show that the earlier will was revoked. [*See, e.g., In re* **Martin's Estate,** 554 S.W.2d 646 (Tenn. 1977); 31 A.L.R.4th 306]

Example: When Testator's first will is offered for probate, evidence is presented showing that a later will that cannot be found, which revoked the first will, was properly signed and witnessed. The witnesses do not recall the contents of the later will, except that it contained language revoking the first will. The evidence is admissible to show that the will being offered for probate was revoked by a subsequent testamentary instrument. [*See, e.g.,* **May v. Brown**, 190 S.W.2d 715 (Tex. 1945)]

F. Revival of Revoked Wills

1. Introduction [§577]

The issue of revival of revoked wills typically involves the following situation: Testator executes Will #2, which includes a clause that expressly revokes Will #1. However, Testator does not destroy Will #1. Later, Testator revokes Will #2. Testator's intention with respect to Will #1 may or may not be known. She may have forgotten entirely about Will #1 and intended to die intestate. Or she may have intended that, by revoking Will #2, Will #1 would again become effective. What should the court do?

2. Common Law [§578]

The early common law rule, still adhered to in a few states, is that no part of a will is effective until the death of the testator. Therefore, if the revoking instrument (Will #2) is itself revoked before the testator's death, Will #1 *remains in effect and is operative* upon the death of the testator. Destruction of Will #2 operates to "revive" Will #1. [59 A.L.R.2d 11]

3. Modern Law

a. Majority rule [§579]

The common law rule has been rejected in most jurisdictions. In most states, a will, once revoked, is *not revived unless* republished by (i) *reexecution* or (ii) *a later codicil* under the doctrine of republication by codicil. (*See infra,* §§637-643.) Hence, revocation of a later will that contained language revoking an earlier will does not, by itself, revive the earlier will or any of its provisions. [*See, e.g.,* Md. Est. & Trusts Code §4-106; N.Y. Est. Powers & Trusts Law §3-4.6; Va. Code §64.1-60]

(1) Rationale

The theory behind the "no revival of revoked wills" rule is that Will #2 operated *immediately* to revoke Will #1, despite the fact that its dispositive provisions would not take effect until the testator's death. Will #1, once revoked, had no further legal existence and could not be resurrected or revived simply by revoking Will #2.

(2) Revival by testamentary act [§580]

In these states, if the testator wishes to reestablish Will #1 as her will, she must do so in one of two manners:

(a) Reexecution [§581]

The will may be *reexecuted* with full testamentary formalities or *reacknowledged* before the same attesting witnesses.

(b) Republication by codicil [§582]

The first will may be revived by the valid execution of a codicil that expressly refers to it. [*See* **Wade v. Sherrod,** 342 S.W.2d 17 (Tex. 1960)] If, however, the first will has been *physically destroyed,* such a reference cannot be effective to revive the will.

b. Uniform Probate Code [§583]

Under the UPC and in a substantial minority of states, destruction of Will #2 and its language of revocation *may* operate to revive Will #1, *depending upon the testator's intent.* Such intent is established by the testator's contemporary or subsequent statements and by reference to all of the circumstances of the case. [*See, e.g.,* UPC §2-509; Cal. Prob. Code §6123]

REVIVAL OF REVOKED WILLS	gilbert
MAJORITY VIEW	The *earlier will is not revived* when the subsequent revoking instrument is revoked. To be effective, it must be *reexecuted* with full formalities or *republished* by a later codicil.
MINORITY AND UPC VIEW	The *earlier will may be revived* upon the revocation of the subsequent revoking instrument *if it was the testator's intent* to revive it.

G. Dependent Relative Revocation

1. Definition [§584]

Dependent relative revocation ("DRR") is an equity-type doctrine under which a court may *disregard an act of revocation* if it determines that the act of revocation was premised on a *mistake of law or fact* as to the validity of another disposition, and that the revocation would not have occurred but for the testator's mistaken belief that another disposition of his property was valid. Thus, if the other disposition is for some reason ineffective, the revocation accompanying the attempted disposition also fails and the original will remains in force. [*See, e.g.,* **Onions v. Tyrer,** 2 Vern. 742 (Ch. 1716)— leading common law case; **Carter v. First United Methodist Church,** 271 S.E.2d 493 (Ga. 1980); **Chambers v. Chambers,** 542 S.W.2d 901 (Tex. 1976)]

2. Rationale

Revocation of a will requires two things: the revocatory act (by an instrument or by physical act) *and* the intent to revoke. If the court finds that the testator's intent to revoke was premised, conditioned, or dependent on a mistake as to the validity of another disposition, the court can find that the testator's intent to revoke was flawed, and can *disregard the revocation.*

a. Illustration—attempted revival of revoked will [§585]

In a state that applies the "no revival of revoked wills" doctrine (*see supra*, §§579-583), Truman executes Will #1, which gives the residue of his estate to his nephew Andy. Truman later executes Will #2, which expressly revokes Will #1 and gives the residue of his estate in trust: Income to Andy for life with the remainder to Andy's children. However, Truman does not destroy Will #1. Some time later, Truman again changes his mind and destroys Will #2 with the intent to revoke it and to revive Will #1. Will #1 cannot be probated because it was revoked by Will #2 and was not revived. In this situation, Will #2 can be probated under DRR *if* the court finds that its revocation was conditioned and dependent upon Truman's mistaken belief that Will #1 would be revived, and further finds that probating Will #2 more closely effectuates Truman's intent than would an intestate distribution.

b. Illustration—later will not validly executed [§586]

Ted (whose nearest kin are a brother and his sister Ann) executes a will that devises his entire estate to Ann. A year later, Ted executes a second "will" that bequeaths $10,000 to his friend Fred and devises the rest of his estate to Ann. The second "will" contains a revocation clause, but it is signed by only one witness. Believing he has a valid new will, Ted destroys the first will. On Ted's death, the second instrument is denied probate. On these facts, DRR should be applied so as to disregard the revocation of the first will. *Rationale:* Although Ted revoked the first will by physical act, his act of revocation was based on his mistaken assumption that the second instrument was a valid will. Had Ted known that the second instrument was invalid, he would not have revoked the first will. (Of course, if he had known the true situation, he would have properly executed the second will! However, it's too late for that now.) As Ann was the principal beneficiary under both instruments, disregarding the revocation of the first will comes closer to what Ted tried but failed to do than would an intestate distribution. [*See, e.g.,* **Putnam v. Neubrand**, 109 N.E.2d 123 (Mass. 1952); *In re* **Rice**, 390 A.2d 1146 (N.H. 1978)]

EXAM TIP   **gilbert**

Note that in both of the above illustrations, persuading the court to apply DRR does not end the matter. Because the wills whose revocation is to be disregarded were physically destroyed, it will be necessary to establish the wills under the rules governing **proof of lost wills**. (*See supra,* §§567 *et seq.*) So when you answer a question about DRR, consider whether you also need to discuss the proof of lost wills rules.

c. **Illustration—partial revocation [§587]**

In a jurisdiction that recognizes partial revocations by physical act, George executes Will #1 which makes a bequest to Barbara of $10,000. Later, George strikes through the bequest and writes in the margin, "see codicil." At George's death, Will #1 and the codicil are found. The typewritten "codicil" leaves Barbara $15,000 and is signed by George, but it is not witnessed. The codicil cannot be given effect because it was not validly executed. Barbara should take the bequest of $10,000 under DRR. The partial revocation by physical act was premised on the mistaken belief that the codicil was validly executed. Giving effect to the original bequest more closely accomplishes George's intent than does eliminating the bequest. [*See, e.g.,* **Woodson v. Woodson,** 255 S.W.2d 771 (Mo. 1953); 24 A.L.R.2d 514]

d. **Distinguish—DRR not used if result contrary to testator's probable intent [§588]**

Suppose, in the illustration immediately above, the attempted codicil purported to give Barbara $2,000. Here, DRR should *not* be applied because to do so would defeat George's intent to substantially reduce Barbara's bequest. (*See infra,* §597.)

3. **Requirements [§589]**

Before the doctrine of DRR will be applied, four elements must be established:

a. **Ineffective new disposition [§590]**

DRR applies only where it is shown that the testator, at the time of revocation, intended to make a new testamentary disposition which for some reason was *ineffective*. The doctrine will *not* apply if the new disposition is valid, or if no such disposition accompanies the revocation. [*See, e.g.,* **Larrick v. Larrick,** 607 S.W.2d 92 (Ark. 1980); **Estate of McKeever,** 361 A.2d 166 (D.C. 1976)]

b. **Act of revocation [§591]**

There must have been a *valid revocation* on which the doctrine may act.

(1) **Physical act [§592]**

The doctrine may apply if the testator destroyed an earlier will and the destruction was accompanied by an attempt to make a new disposition, or where the testator simply attempted to change some *portion* of her will (*e.g.,* by lining out a bequest and writing in a new amount). [24 A.L.R.2d 514]

(2) **Subsequent testamentary instrument**

(a) **Majority view [§593]**

Most jurisdictions apply DRR if the earlier will was expressly or impliedly revoked in a subsequent will or codicil that is ineffective. [*See* **Carter v. First United Methodist Church,** *supra,* §584]

(b) Minority view [§594]

Some jurisdictions are reluctant to apply DRR if the revocation is by instrument and not by physical act. *Rationale:* Revocation by physical act is inherently ambiguous. Extrinsic evidence must be used to show the testator's intent; proof that such intent was conditional is, in that case, proper. No such ambiguity exists when the revocation is by a subsequent testamentary instrument. [*See* **Crosby v. Alton Ochsner Medical Foundation,** 276 So. 2d 661 (Miss. 1973)]

(c) Mistake must appear on face of will [§595]

Courts applying DRR in cases involving revocation by subsequent testamentary instrument require that the mistake appear *on the face of the subsequent instrument* or at least be inferable from it. For example, if the testator makes a will revoking an earlier bequest to John and the later will leaves the property to Marsha "because John is dead," when John is in fact alive, DRR may operate to nullify the revocation.

c. Mistake of law [§596]

The testator's intent to revoke must have been premised or conditioned on a *mistaken belief as to the validity of another disposition.* As discussed above, DRR has been applied where a testator mistakenly believes that a new will was validly executed, or mistakenly believes that the revocation of a subsequent will revived an earlier one. [24 A.L.R.2d 514]

d. Probable intent of testator [§597]

The last and most important element in the application of DRR is that the *invalidation of the revocation must be consistent with the testator's probable intent.* DRR should be applied only when the court concludes that the testator would have preferred a distribution under the "revoked" disposition rather than an intestate distribution. Some commentators refer to DRR as the *second best solution* doctrine. The best solution—giving effect to the disposition that the testator intended to make—is not available because the attempted disposition was ineffective for some reason. DRR should be applied if, but only if, disregarding the revocation *is* the second best solution—*i.e.,* if the testator would probably prefer that the revoked disposition be given effect.

Example: Suppose, in the illustration in §585, *supra,* Andy would not be an heir, or would be one of several heirs, if Truman were held to have died intestate. DRR should apply and the revocation of Will #2 should be disregarded. Since Truman tried (but failed) to give his estate outright to Andy, it can be assumed that he would prefer a gift in trust for Andy over an intestate distribution among his heirs.

Example: Tomas's typewritten, witnessed will makes a bequest of $5,000 to his niece Maria. Some years later, Tomas decides to increase the gift to Maria. He crosses out the "$5,000," writes in "$10,000" above it, carefully initials the margin, and dies two years later. The change to $10,000 cannot be given effect because it was not part of the duly executed will. (*See supra*, §396.) If the jurisdiction recognizes partial revocations by physical act (*see supra*, §§548 *et seq.*), the cross-out was a valid partial revocation. If the story stopped here, Maria would take nothing. However, this is a classic case for applying DRR. Tomas revoked the $5,000 bequest on the mistaken belief (a mistake of law) that he could change his will in this manner. Because it can easily be concluded that Tomas would rather Maria take $5,000 than nothing, the partial revocation is disregarded.

Compare: In a jurisdiction that recognizes partial revocation by physical act, Bill's typewritten will includes a devise of Blackacre "to my wife, Hillary." Thereafter, Bill strikes "wife Hillary" and writes "daughter Chelsea" over the strikeout, thereby attempting to make the devise of Blackacre to Chelsea. The interlineation cannot be given effect because it was not part of Bill's duly executed will. However, Bill's revocation of the gift to Hillary should *not* be disregarded under DRR. Bill's intent to revoke the gift to Hillary was *independent* of his attempt to make a new gift to Chelsea. To disregard the partial revocation would be contrary to Bill's clearly manifested intent that he did not want Hillary to take Blackacre under the will. [*See, e.g., In re* **Houghten's Estate,** 17 N.W.2d 774 (Mich. 1945)]

CHECKLIST OF REQUIREMENTS FOR DRR · gilbert

TO DISREGARD A REVOCATION, THE FOLLOWING MUST BE SATISFIED:

- ☑ The testator intended to make a *new testamentary disposition* and that disposition is *invalid*.

- ☑ The new testamentary disposition is pursuant to a *valid revocation* of an earlier instrument.

- ☑ The testator's act of revocation is based on a *mistaken belief* that another disposition is *valid*.

- ☑ Distributing the testator's estate under the revoked instrument *comes closer to what the testator tried but failed to do* than would an intestate distribution.

Chapter Eight:
Components of a Will

CONTENTS

Chapter Approach

Chapter Approach

In most cases, a will is a complete, formally executed document that needs no other document or fact to administer and distribute the decedent's estate. However, sometimes you will see a will that makes a reference to another document or fact. Whether the court will recognize the other document or fact usually depends on whether it falls within one of the following categories:

1. **Integration**

   Integration problems rarely arise on Wills exams, but you may see one where heirs are contesting the will or where there are suspicious circumstances (*e.g.*, pages that are typed with different typefaces). It is important to remember that *all* of the pages being offered for probate must have been *present* when the testator signed the will and that the testator must have *intended* them to be part of the will.

2. **Incorporation by Reference**

   If you cannot "integrate" the particular paper into the will but you believe that the testator intended it to be given effect at his death, try applying the incorporation by reference doctrine. Be sure that the paper was *in existence at the time the will was executed*; that the *will identifies* and refers to the paper; and that the testator's *intent* was to incorporate this paper.

3. **Acts of Independent Significance**

   Sometimes a testator's will requires the court to look outside the document to determine what a gift shall be or who shall receive it (*e.g.*, "I give $10,000 to each full-time employee of my company at the date of my death."). The critical issue is whether the fact or event has independent significance; *i.e.*, whether the fact or event is based on a *nontestamentary act*. For instance, the determination of whether an employee should be hired or fired serves a valid function *other than* affecting the will.

4. **Pour-Over Gift to Inter Vivos Trust**

   If you see a gift in a will to a revocable trust set up during the testator's lifetime, remember that some states require that the trust be in existence *before* or executed *concurrently* with the will, while other states permit the recipient trust to be established *after* the will is executed.

5. **Codicil**

   Your Wills question may involve one or more codicils. Besides altering, modifying, or expanding the will, the other important functions of a codicil are:

   (i) *Republishing a prior will*, *i.e.*, redating and reexecuting it so that the execution date of the prior will is moved up to the date of the codicil. (This may be important for interpreting the will or for applying the pretermitted child statute.)

   (ii) *Validating a prior will that was invalid* (*e.g.*, because it was not properly executed); and

(iii) *Reviving a will* that has been revoked but not physically destroyed.

Remember that although a codicil must be executed with all the formalities of a will, in states that recognize holographic instruments it is possible to have a holographic (handwritten, signed, and unwitnessed) codicil to a typewritten, witnessed will (and vice versa).

A. Integration

1. Introduction [§598]

All of the pages or other writings that were intended to be part of a will must be present at the time the will is executed. "Integration" of a will is the process of embodying several sheets of paper or documents into a *single, entire will*, validated by a *single action of execution*. [*See* **Appeal of Sleeper,** 151 A. 150 (Me. 1930)] The doctrine of "integration of wills" concerns this question: What sheets were present at the will's execution so as to constitute the decedent's last will that should be admitted to probate?

Example: Integration problems arise when, for example, the will being executed is casually spread in loose sheets on a coffee table at a cocktail party [*In re* **Beale's Estate,** 113 N.W.2d 380 (Wis. 1962)]; or where pages 1-3 and 5-6 are typed in an elite typeface and page 4 is in pica, and there is a clear indication that the original staple was removed and the pages were restapled. In these fact settings, the question arises: Were *all* of those pages present when the will was signed by the testator and witnessed by the attesting witnesses? [**Estate of Hall,** 118 Misc. 2d 1052 (1983)]

a. Comment

The doctrine of integration is rarely the subject of litigation, because in the ordinary case the will is physically connected by a staple, and there is an internal coherence as well—*i.e.,* consecutively numbered clauses on consecutively numbered pages.

2. Requirements for Integration [§599]

To show that the will being offered for probate was integrated, all the various pages involved must have been *actually present* at the time of execution, and the testator must have *intended* the several pages to constitute his will. [*In re* **Beale's Estate,** *supra*]

3. Proving Integration [§600]

The issue of whether the will being offered for probate is an integrated document does not arise unless there are suspicious circumstances or the issue is pleaded by someone who is contesting the will.

a. Presumption of integration [§601]

There is a strong presumption of integration if the will's attestation clause recites the total number of pages of the will and if the testator has initialed each page. [30 A.L.R. 427] A presumption of integration also arises if the pages are found *physically connected* to each other by staple or paper clip. Even if the pages are not physically attached, there is a presumption of integration if there is a sequence in numbering of consecutive pages [**Appeal of Sleeper,** *supra*, §598]; if the sentences carry over from page to page [*In re* **Puckett's Estate,** 38 N.W.2d 593 (Iowa 1949)]; if there is a grammatical sequence [*In re* **Callahan's Estate,** 237 Cal. App. 2d 818 (1965)]; or if there is logical continuity in thought of the provisions running from one page to another [**deGraaf v. Owen,** 598 So. 2d 892 (Ala 1992); 38 A.L.R.2d 477].

b. Extrinsic evidence [§602]

In the absence of any presumption, integration can be proved by the *testimony of witnesses* or by *reference to surrounding circumstances*. [*See* **Murphy v. Clancy,** 163 S.W. 915 (Mo. 1914)]

Example: The doctrine of integration was held to have been satisfied where two sheets of paper, not physically connected, were found in Grace's safe deposit box in an envelope in which she had written, "November 20, 1933, Last Will and Testament of Grace Caldwell," and an examination of the two sheets showed that they were written with the same ink and the same pen in a continuous operation.

PROVING WILL IS AN INTEGRATED DOCUMENT — **gilbert**

PRESUMPTION OF INTEGRATION ARISES IF:

☑ *Identification by Testator*—Will recites total number of pages and testator initialed each page,

☑ *Physical Connection*—All pages physically connected by staple, clip, etc., or

☑ *Internal Coherence*—Sequence in numbering or sentences carry over from page to page; or logical continuity in thought of provisions from page to page.

IF NO PRESUMPTION, USE EXTRINSIC EVIDENCE:

☑ *Testimony of Witnesses*, or

☑ *Reference to Surrounding Circumstances.*

B. Incorporation by Reference

1. Introduction [§603]

The doctrine of incorporation by reference recognizes that a duly executed will may, by appropriate reference, incorporate the terms of an *extrinsic document or writing*, even though the other document was not properly executed and is not otherwise of testamentary character. Statutes in over one-half of the states have codified the common law incorporation by reference doctrine. [*See, e.g.,* UPC §2-510; Ala. Code §43-8-139; Cal. Prob. Code §6130; N.J. Stat. §3B:3-10; Ohio Rev. Code §2107.05] Only the states of Connecticut, Louisiana, and New York do not recognize the doctrine of incorporation by reference. [**Waterbury National Bank v. Waterbury National Bank,** 291 A.2d 737 (Conn. 1972); **Hessmer v. Edenborn,** 199 So. 647 (La. 1940); *In re* **Whyte's Will,** 283 A.D. 947 (1954)]

2. Requirements for Incorporation by Reference [§604]

The doctrine of incorporation by reference enables the court to read into the will nontestamentary writings that were not part of the duly executed will and that were not executed with statutory formalities. To limit the danger of fraud or substitution, the following requirements must be satisfied:

a. Document must be in existence [§605]

The document to be incorporated must have been in existence *at the time the will was executed.* [*See* **Phelps v. La Moille Lodge,** 201 N.E.2d 634 (Ill. 1964); **Lawless v. Lawless,** 47 S.E.2d 431 (Va. 1948); 3 A.L.R.2d 682] As discussed below, however, if the testator subsequently executes a codicil to the will, it may be sufficient for the document to be in existence at the time the codicil was executed. (*See infra,* §639.)

(1) Additional requirement in some states [§606]

The courts in some states additionally require that the will refer to the document as an existing document. Thus, a reference to "a sealed letter which *will be found* with this will," or to "an inventory *to be prepared by me* and deposited herewith" is *insufficient*—even if the document was in existence when the will was executed. [**Phelps v. La Moille Lodge,** *supra;* **Kellom v. Beverstock,** 126 A.2d 127 (N.H. 1956); 152 A.L.R. 1238] However, most courts do not insist on this, as long as the document is proved to have been in actual existence at the time the will was executed.

This requirement was deliberately omitted from the UPC's codification of the incorporation by reference doctrine. [UPC §2-510]

b. Will must identify and describe document [§607]

The will must identify and describe the document to be incorporated so clearly that there can be *no mistake as to the identity of the document* referred to. [**Estate of McGahee,** 550 So. 2d 83 (Fla. 1989); **Baarslag v. Hawkins,** 531 P.2d 1283 (Wash. 1975)] A mere reference to "the attached document" is *not* a sufficient identification, even if a document is found stapled to the will, since the reference does not unequivocally refer to one and only one document. [**Taylor v. Republic National Bank,** 452 S.W.2d 560 (Tex. 1970)]

c. Will must show intent to incorporate [§608]

The will must manifest an intent to *incorporate the terms of the extrinsic document* as part of the will. [**Lewis v. SunTrust Bank,** 698 So. 2d 1276 (Fla. 1997); **Estate of Sneed,** 953 P.2d 1111 (Okla. 1998)]

CHECKLIST OF REQUIREMENTS FOR INCORPORATION BY REFERENCE

TO INCORPORATE THE TERMS OF AN EXTRINSIC DOCUMENT INTO A WILL, THE FOLLOWING MUST BE SATISFIED:

☑ The document must have been *in existence at the time the will was executed,*

☑ The document must be *clearly identified and described,* and

☑ The *will must show the testator's intent* to incorporate the terms of the document.

---

d. Incorporation of printed material into holographic will [§609]

The courts are divided on the question of whether a holographic will (*see supra,* §§457 *et seq.*) can incorporate the terms of an extrinsic document that is typewritten or printed. Courts holding that incorporation by reference does not apply have concluded that giving effect to the printed material is inconsistent with the requirement that the material provisions of a holographic instrument must be in the testator's handwriting. [**Scott v. Gastright,** 204 S.W.2d 367 (Ky. 1947); *In re* **Watts's Estate,** 160 P.2d 492 (Mont. 1945); **Hinson v. Hinson,** 280 S.W.2d 731 (Tex. 1955)] Other courts have taken the position that such an incorporation is permitted, on the ground that the nonholographic materials are read into the holographic instrument but do not become part of it. [**Estate of Nielson,** 105 Cal. App. 3d 796 (1980); **Johnson v. Johnson,** 279 P.2d 928 (Okla. 1954)]

3. Validation of Earlier, Invalid Will [§610]

The doctrine of incorporation by reference can be used to give effect to an earlier instrument that otherwise would be ineffective because not validly executed. [21 A.L.R.2d 821]

---

e.g. **Example:** On January 1 of this year, Tessa signed her will and had it witnessed. She did not know that under applicable state law it had to be witnessed by two competent witnesses; she had just one person witness the will. Later in the year she decided to make a few changes to her will, and this time she properly executed a codicil that stated that she "hereby republish[es] all terms of the will I signed on January 1 of this year that are not inconsistent with the terms of this codicil." The codicil incorporates by reference the terms of the earlier, invalid "will."

EXAM TIP	gilbert

Do not confuse validation of an earlier invalid will with republication by codicil. Incorporation by reference allows the testator to validate an earlier instrument that is ineffective because it was **not** validly executed by incorporating it into a subsequently executed codicil. However, republication by codicil (see *infra*, §§637-641) applies only if the earlier instrument **was validly executed** in the first place (*e.g.*, if the testator revoked the previously executed will and wants to revive it with the codicil).

4. Ineffective Deed as Will [§611]

Occasionally, courts are confronted with the situation where a decedent executed a deed purporting to convey property during his lifetime but the conveyance failed for some reason (*e.g.*, lack of delivery). The deed is then offered as the decedent's will (*i.e.*, a testamentary disposition) as to that property.

a. Majority rule [§612]

Most courts *deny probate* to such an instrument on the ground that it was not executed with testamentary intent. That is, because the instrument was intended to be effective during the grantor's lifetime, the grantor did not intend the instrument to operate at his death as his will.

b. Exception [§613]

If the decedent left a valid will that *refers to the inter vivos deed* (*e.g.*, "I make no provision for my brother Lenny because I have already deeded my farm to him"), the will may be held to have *incorporated the ineffective deed by reference.* Thus, even though the deed was otherwise invalid, and even though the testator thought the property was no longer in his estate, the reference in the will to the deed is enough to carry out the transfer. [*In re* **Dimmitt's Estate**, 3 N.W.2d 752 (Neb. 1942)]

5. Disposition of Items of Tangible Personal Property [§614]

Some clients, especially older clients, appear to be more concerned about the disposition of items of great sentimental value but little economic value (*e.g.*, china cups from Montreal, needlepoint chairs, hunting rifles, etc.) than about the disposition of, *e.g.,* their 5,000 shares of Microsoft stock. It is important that the client's testamentary wishes be satisfied, and yet the recital of a detailed list of such items presents some practical problems, including ademption by extinction. (*See infra*, §§772-801.) The situation is particularly troublesome if (as often happens) the client wants to add to the list or change the beneficiaries for some of the objects. The economics of the law practice require that an attorney charge an appropriate professional fee for preparation of a will and supervision of the will's execution, yet the client may be reluctant to pay an appropriate fee for such a "small" task.

a. Holographic will [§615]

In states that recognize holographic wills (*see supra*, §§457 *et seq.*), one solution might be to encourage the client to write a holographic codicil disposing of such items, which the client can revoke or amend as the spirit moves him. However, the UPC offers a more practical solution (*see* below).

b. Original Uniform Probate Code [§616]

The original UPC carves out an exception to the requirements for incorporation by reference where a list of *tangible personal property* is involved. A will may refer to a written statement or list to dispose of items of *tangible personal property*—not money, intangibles such as shares of stock, and property used in trade or business—not otherwise specifically disposed of by the will. It is not necessary that the writing have any significance apart from its effect on the dispositions made in the will. The writing must be either in the testator's handwriting *or* signed by the testator, and must describe the items and the devisees with reasonable certainty. It may be referred to as one in existence at the time of the testator's death. The writing may be prepared *before or after* the execution of the will, and it *may be altered* by the testator after its initial preparation. [Original UPC §2-513] Several non-UPC states have enacted similar statutes [Ark. Code §28-25-107; Del. Code tit. 12, §212; Fla. Prob. Code §732.515; Wash. Rev. Code §11.12.260], and courts in a few states have recognized this exception by judicial decision. [**Clark v. Greenhalge,** 582 N.E.2d 949 (Mass. 1991)]

c. Revised Uniform Probate Code [§617]

Although the original UPC provides that the list of items must be in the testator's handwriting *or* signed by him [Original UPC §2-513], the revised UPC requires that the list be *signed* by the testator *in all cases*. Also, the original UPC provision does not permit the disposition of trade or business personal property by such a list, but the revised UPC eliminates this restriction and permits the disposition of *any* tangible personal property by such a list. [UPC §2-513]

d. Limited to tangible personal property [§618]

Note that neither the original UPC nor the revised UPC permits the disposition of *intangible* personal property (*e.g.,* stocks and bonds), cash, or real property by such a list.

6. Oral Statements Not Incorporated by Reference [§619]

Oral instructions *cannot* be incorporated into a will by reference, and in such cases extrinsic evidence is *not* admissible to show the testator's intent. In the absence of fraud, the person designated to take under the will is entitled to the property, and is not bound by the restrictions contained in the testator's instructions.

Example: Testator's will states: "I devise Blackacre to my good friend Ben." Testator told his brother that he was going to leave Blackacre to Ben "for the purposes I have already communicated to him," but there was nothing in the will about these purposes. The oral statement cannot be incorporated into the will by reference and Ben takes the property free of any such purposes.

a. Distinguish—beneficiary agrees to instructions [§620]

If the testator makes such a provision only after the designated beneficiary has assured testator that he will dispose of the property as the testator has instructed, extrinsic evidence is admissible to show fraud, and a constructive trust may be imposed in favor of the intended beneficiary. (*See* Trusts Summary.) Thus, if, in the example above, Testator devises Blackacre to Ben in reliance on Ben's agreement to take care of Testator's aged mother for the rest of her life, a constructive trust would be imposed on Ben's gift if he fails to comply with the agreement.

C. Acts of Independent Significance

1. Nontestamentary Acts [§621]

A testator may refer in the will to extrinsic acts or events that have some *independent significance* (*i.e.*, that ordinarily are not testamentary in nature), for the purpose of either designating the beneficiaries (*e.g.*, "I bequeath $1,000 to each of my servants in my employ at my death") or designating the property that is the subject of the gift (*e.g.*, "I bequeath the furniture and furnishings in my living room to my sister Sue"). Under the "acts of independent significance" doctrine (sometimes called the doctrine of "nontestamentary acts"), these gifts are given effect even though the identity of the beneficiaries or the property will be determined by resorting to unattested acts. *Rationale:* The testator's act of, *e.g.*, hiring or firing servants or decorating his living room has a lifetime purpose or motive that is *independent from its effect on the testator's will*. [21 A.L.R.4th 383] This common law doctrine has been codified by the UPC and by statute in several non-UPC states. [UPC §2-512; Cal. Prob. Code §6131; Minn. Stat. §524.2-512]

a. Acts of testator [§622]

The acts referred to may be those of the testator: "I bequeath the contents of my hope chest to my sister Sue." [**Jeffreys v. Glover,** 50 S.E.2d 328 (Ga. 1948); *In re* **Evans's Estate,** 133 N.E.2d 128 (Ohio 1956)]

b. Acts of another person [§623]

The acts referred to may be the acts of a third person: "I devise Blackacre to the persons named as beneficiaries in my brother's will." [**First National Bank v. Klein,** 234 So. 2d 42 (Ala. 1970)]

EXAM TIP   **gilbert**

The most important thing to remember when analyzing the validity of nontestamentary acts is that they must have *significance apart from their effect on the testator's will*. Although the resulting effect of the nontestamentary act or event designates a beneficiary or disposes of certain property, the effect must be merely incidental and independent of the act. For example, assume John bequeathes $100 to "each member of my health club at my death" and subsequently joins a new health club. Although John's act of changing health clubs designated new beneficiaries, that effect was merely incidental to his changing health clubs. It is unlikely that John went through the trouble of joining a new health club merely to change the beneficiaries to his will.

---

2. Test [§624]

The critical issue in any question involving the acts of independent significance doctrine is whether the extrinsic act or event in question has a legal significance apart from and independent of its impact on the will. The act or event must be one that ordinarily has some *nontestamentary motive* or function.

Example: A bequest of "$1,000 to each person employed in my business at the time of my death" is a valid designation. [**Shoup v. American Trust Co.,** 97 S.E.2d 111 (N.C. 1957); **Welch v. Trustees of Robert A. Welch Foundation,** 465 S.W.2d 195 (Tex. 1971)] The act of hiring or firing employees is normally done to enhance the business of the testator, not to designate the beneficiaries in a will. The event of employment, therefore, has "independent significance"—something apart from its effect on the testamentary disposition.

Example: Lisa's will devises "the automobile that I own at my death" to her nephew Ned. At the time the will was executed, Lisa owned a 10-year-old Chevrolet. Shortly before her death, Lisa traded the Chevrolet for a new Cadillac, with the result that she died owning a $40,000 car instead of a $4,000 car. The disposition is valid. While Lisa's purchase of the Cadillac had the practical effect of greatly increasing the value of the gift to Ned, it is unlikely that this motivated her purchase. More probably, she bought the new car because she wanted to own and drive a Cadillac—a lifetime motive for a lifetime act that also had an effect on her will.

Compare: A bequest of "$1,000 to the person bearing a letter from me identifying him as my beneficiary" is clearly invalid, since the giving of such a letter has *no significance* apart from its effect on the will. Allowing such a gift would enable the testator to change her will by an unattested act.

D. Pour-Over Gift to Inter Vivos Trust

1. Introduction [§625]

A "pour-over" gift is a testamentary gift to a trust created during the decedent's lifetime, with the testamentary assets to be administered and distributed as part of that trust. Suppose, for example, that Carol creates a revocable inter vivos trust, and later executes a will devising her residuary estate "to the First National Bank, trustee of the trust that I executed on January 11, 2002." The objective of such a pour-over gift is to provide a *single, unified trust management and disposition* of (i) assets transferred to the trust during lifetime, and (ii) assets owned by the testator at death. (*See* Trusts Summary.)

2. Validity of Pour-Over Gift—Case Law [§626]

A number of early cases invalidated such gifts to a revocable, amendable trust on the ground that the settlor could amend the trust after the will's execution, and thus could indirectly change her will without complying with testamentary formalities. [*See* **Atwood v. Rhode Island Hospital Trust Co.**, 275 F. 513 (1st Cir. 1921)] Other jurisdictions upheld the gift under the theory that the inter vivos trust was incorporated by reference into the will. [21 A.L.R.2d 220] This had the result of giving effect to the bequest to the trust as it existed when the will was executed, without regard to subsequent amendments of the trust. Still other courts upheld the testamentary gift and construed it as a gift to the trust, *including subsequent amendments,* under the acts of independent significance doctrine, provided the trust had been funded with substantial assets during the testator's lifetime. [*See* **Canal National Bank v. Chapman**, 171 A.2d 919 (Me. 1961); **Second Bank-State Street Trust Co. v. Pinion**, 170 N.E.2d 350 (Mass. 1960)]

3. Uniform Testamentary Additions to Trusts Act [§627]

The validity and effect of a pour-over gift to a revocable inter vivos trust is no longer in doubt in any jurisdiction. All states have enacted the Uniform Testamentary Additions to Trusts Act (1960), the Revised Uniform Testamentary Additions to Trusts Act (1991), or similar legislation. [UPC §2-511; Cal. Prob. Code §6300] The Uniform Testamentary Additions to Trusts Act ("Act") validates a testamentary gift to an inter vivos trust created by the testator or by another person, even if the trust is revocable or amendable, and even if the trust is *amended after the will's execution.* The testamentary assets are added to the assets placed in the trust during the testator's lifetime, and the combined assets are administered as one trust under the trust terms as they exist at the testator's death, including any amendments made after the will's execution.

a. Majority rule—trust must be in existence or executed concurrently with will [§628]

Under the 1960 version of the Act, the only substantive requirements for a valid pour-over gift are that (i) the trust must be *sufficiently described* in the testator's will, and (ii) the trust must be *in existence before* or *executed concurrently* with the will.

(1) Exception [§629]

The Act validates testamentary gifts to a trust *not* in existence when the testator executed the will, if the trust was created by the will of *another person who predeceased* the testator.

b. Minority rule [§630]

Under the 1991 revised Act and by statute in several non-UPC states, a pour-over gift is valid if the trust was created before, with, *or after* the will's execution. [UPC §2-511; Tex. Prob. Code §58a]

c. Additional requirement in some states [§631]

In some jurisdictions, a revocable, amendable trust must be *executed and acknowledged before a notary public* in order to receive testamentary pour-over gifts. [*See* N.Y. Est. Powers & Trusts Law §3-3.7]

d. Pour-over to unfunded trust [§632]

The size and character of the trust corpus during the testator's lifetime is immaterial. This means that a testator can, during her lifetime, create a trust funded with only a few dollars, and by subsequent amendments of this token trust control the disposition of assets that will pass under the will. [*See* **Trosch v. Maryland National Bank**, 359 A.2d 564 (Md. 1976)] The fact that the amendments are made without testamentary formalities is irrelevant. Both versions of the Act specifically validate testamentary gifts to an unfunded life insurance trust, even though the trust will not be funded until the insured dies and the trustee collects the insurance proceeds.

EXAM TIP   **gilbert**

Be careful that you do not confuse testamentary gifts to existing trusts (*i.e.*, pour-over gifts) with testamentary trusts. A testamentary trust is a trust that is **created by the decedent's will** (*i.e.*, the trust was not in existence during the decedent's lifetime). A pour-over gift is a gift made by the decedent's will to an **existing trust**—the decedent is adding assets from his estate to the trust. (*See* Trusts Summary.)

E. Codicil

1. Definition [§633]

A codicil is a testamentary instrument, executed *after* the execution of a will, that *alters, modifies, or expands* the provisions of the will in some manner.

2. Formalities [§634]

A codicil must be executed with the *same formalities required for execution of a will*. [**Leggett v. Rose**, 776 F. Supp. 229 (E.D.N.C. 1991); *In re* **Robert's Estate**, 437 N.E.2d 1205 (Ohio 1980)] However, the codicil does not have to be in the same form as the will it amends. In states that recognize holographic instruments (*see supra,* §§457 *et seq.*), it is possible to have a *holographic codicil* to a typewritten, witnessed will, and vice versa. [40 A.L.R.2d 698]

EXAM TIP   **gilbert**

Codicils crop up often in exam questions. When you see one, the first thing to do is to check that the codicil has been **executed with all the formalities of a will** (testator signed, proper witnesses, etc.). Look for all the things you would look for if the document were a will. Don't forget that if the state allows holographic wills, you need to check that the codicil meets those requirements.

---

3. **Separate Document Not Required [§635]**

The codicil may appear as a separate document, or it may appear on the same piece of paper as the will it amends.

Example: The third paragraph of Tomas's typewritten, witnessed will makes a $2,000 bequest to his niece Nell. Some time later, Tomas writes at the bottom of the page: "I have changed my mind about the gift in paragraph 3. I want Nell to have $5,000 rather than $2,000." Tomas signs and dates this addition. In jurisdictions that recognize holographic testamentary instruments, this is a valid holographic codicil to the will. In jurisdictions that do not recognize holographs, his attempted change of the will would not be effective because it was not witnessed.

Compare: Consider the same will except that, instead of writing a new provision at the bottom of the page, Tomas strikes "$2,000" and writes above it "$5,000." He initials and dates the margin alongside this change. The interlineation is not given effect because "$5,000" has no meaning without its context, and the context consists of the typewritten provisions making the gift to Nell. Thus as to the interlineation, the requirements of a valid holographic instrument are not satisfied. (*See supra,* §§458-460.)

EXAM TIP   **gilbert**

If you encounter a question involving alterations on the face of the will, remember that any addition, alteration, interlineation, or deletion made **after** the will has been signed and attested is **ineffective** to change the will, unless the will is **reexecuted** with proper formalities or the changes qualify as a valid holographic codicil in a jurisdiction that recognizes them.

---

4. **Effect of Codicil [§636]**

In addition to modifying the prior will, a codicil may have one of the following legal effects: (i) it may *republish* a prior valid will; (ii) it may *incorporate by reference* and thus validate a prior invalid will (*see supra,* §610); or (iii) it may *revive* a previously revoked will that is still in existence.

a. **Republication by codicil [§637]**

The doctrine of "republication by codicil" concerns this question: When does a will "speak"—*i.e.,* when is a will deemed to have been executed? Under this doctrine, the execution of a codicil has the effect of "republishing" the will it-self, so that the will is deemed to have been *redated and reexecuted as of the date of the codicil.* [Va. Code §64.1-72]

(1) Illustration—interested witness statute [§638]

If the original will contains a gift to one of the attesting witnesses, that gift will be held invalid in many states (*see supra,* §419). A subsequent codicil, however, republishes the prior will and (assuming there are dif-ferent attesting witnesses) operates to validate the gift to the beneficiary-witness under the original will. The earlier attestation is disregarded.

(2) Illustration—incorporation by reference doctrine [§639]

Thetis's will, dated March 25, 1999, devises her estate "to the persons named in a letter I have written to Jane Jones, my executor." A week later, Thetis writes a letter to Jane Jones, telling her that this is the letter referred to in her will and naming those to whom she wants her estate distributed. On January 15, 2002, Thetis executes a codicil to her will. Ordinarily, Thetis's letter to her executor would not be given effect un-der the theory of incorporation by reference because it was not in exist-ence when her will was executed (*see supra,* §605). However, her 2002 codicil republished the will as of that date, and since the letter was in ex-istence *then*, it is incorporated by reference. [*See* **Simon v. Grayson**, 15 Cal. 2d 531 (1940)]

(3) Illustration—pretermitted child or pretermitted spouse statute [§640]

Ty executes a will that devises one-half of his estate to his wife Wilma and the remaining one-half to his daughter Debbie. A year later, a son Sam is born to Ty. A few months later, Ty executes a codicil that changes the alter-nate executor. The will is deemed to have been executed when the codicil was executed; therefore, Sam is not entitled to any protection under the state's pretermitted child statute because it only protects children born after the will's execution (*see supra,* §279). The republication by codicil doctrine also can eliminate a surviving spouse's rights under a pretermitted spouse statute (*e.g.,* when the testator executes a will, then marries, and then executes a codicil to the premarital will). (*See supra,* §509.)

(4) Limitation [§641]

The republication doctrine is not applied mechanically, or if the result would be patently inconsistent with the testator's apparent intention. The purpose of the doctrine is to effectuate, not frustrate, the testator's plan. [*See* **Massachusetts Audubon Society v. Ormand Village Improvement Asso-ciation**, 10 So. 2d 494 (Fla. 1942)]

---

e.g. **Example:** Ordinarily a will speaks as of the date of its execution for purposes of identifying beneficiaries. Thus, a bequest "to my first cousin" would generally be interpreted as meaning the one first cousin the testator had at the time the will was executed. If the testator subsequently executes a codicil, and in the meantime his uncle has had another child, the gift to "my first cousin" could be interpreted as creating a latent ambiguity. (*See infra,* §905.) However, this is not very likely if the codicil had nothing to do with the gift in question (*e.g.,* where the codicil merely names a new executor).

b. **Validation of prior invalid will [§642]**

The doctrine of republication by codicil technically applies only to valid testamentary instruments. Thus, wills or intervening codicils that were never valid to begin with (*e.g.,* because they were not properly executed) cannot be "republished" by a later codicil. However, many courts are willing to construe a codicil as impliedly *incorporating* the prior defective will *by reference,* thereby validating the prior testamentary instrument. (*See supra,* §610.)

Example: Theo signs a will on January 15, 2002, but it is not properly attested. Later, he executes an instrument with proper testamentary formalities which provides simply: "This is a codicil to my will dated January 15, 2002. I hereby nominate my wife to serve as my executor." Theo then dies. The later instrument is not, in fact, a "codicil" because there is no preexisting valid will. Rather, the later instrument (being properly executed) is Theo's *will,* and it incorporates by reference the dispositive provisions in the earlier, defective instrument.

c. **Revival of revoked will [§643]**

Execution of a codicil to a will that previously had been revoked but not physically destroyed is generally held to "revive" the prior will. [*See* **Kimbark v. Satas,** 231 N.E.2d 699 (Ill. 1967); **Jarvis v. Ernhart,** 823 S.W.2d 155 (Mo. 1992)] (*See supra,* §§577-583, for revival of revoked wills.)

EXAM TIP   **gilbert**

After you have checked to see that the codicil has been validly executed, consider the effects of the codicil:

• If the previous will was *not validly executed*, recall that the codicil may *incorporate it by reference* and in effect validate it.

• If the will was validly executed but there is an *interested witness problem*, the codicil may clear up that problem, assuming different people witnessed the codicil.

• If the will had been *revoked but not physically destroyed*, the codicil may revive it.

• The trickiest issue involves a *pretermitted child or spouse*. Remember that republication of a will by codicil *redates the will* to the *date of the codicil*. If the pretermitted person was in existence when the republished will (*i.e.,* the codicil) was executed, she will lose the protection of the pretermission statute and not take any share of the estate. (*Note:* Of course a spouse in such a situation has the option to take an elective share against the will; *see supra,* §§195 *et seq.*)

COMPONENTS OF A WILL—A SUMMARY	**gilbert**
INTEGRATION	The process of combining more than one sheet of paper into a single will. Requires *presence* of papers at execution of will and testator's *intent*.
INCORPORATION BY REFERENCE	If *intended* by testator, incorporates into the will extrinsic writings that were *in existence* when will was executed and that are *clearly identifed* by the will. Can also be used to validate earlier wills that were ineffective.
ACTS OF INDEPENDENT SIGNIFICANCE	The testator can designate a beneficiary or dispose of property by a *nontestamentary act* only if it has significance *independent from its effect on the will*.
POUR-OVER GIFT TO INTER VIVOS TRUST	Majority rule is that the trust must be described in the testator's will and be in existence *before or executed concurrently with the will*.
CODICIL	Alters, modifies, or expands a previously executed valid will, revives a previously revoked will, or may incorporate by reference an invalidly executed will. *Must be executed with the same formalities* required for execution of a will.

Chapter Nine: Contracts Relating to Wills

CONTENTS

Chapter Approach

Although the topics in this chapter relate to wills, they actually involve contracts. Specifically:

(i) A *contract to make a gift* by will;

(ii) *Joint wills* that may or may not be contractual (if they are, they are subject to a contract not to revoke);

(iii) A *contract not to revoke* a will or a provision therein; and

(iv) A *contract not to make a will* at all.

For questions on these topics, keep in mind that *contract law* rather than wills law governs. However, a number of states have statutes dealing explicitly with contracts relating to wills. If a will is found to be contractual, remember that the will itself is *valid* and may be probated even though its execution was in *breach of contract*. If the contract is valid, contract remedies are available, the most common being the imposition of a *constructive trust* for the benefit of the promisee.

A. Contract to Make a Gift by Will

1. Contract Law, Not Wills Law, Controls [§644]

A promise to make a will, even if in writing and witnessed, is *never* admissible to probate *as a will*, because there is no expression of *present* testamentary intent (*see supra*, §355) but merely a promise to make a will in the future. In any case involving an alleged promise to make a testamentary gift, contract law rather than the law of wills controls. Thus, there must be an offer, acceptance, and consideration, and the parties must have the capacity to contract. Whatever rights the promisee acquires are contract rights and are enforceable only as such.

> **e.g.** **Example:** Thurston promises to make a will that devises Blackacre to his niece Betty if she will move in with him and take care of him. Betty performs her part of the bargain, but Thurston dies without having made such a will. This commonly litigated fact situation is a contracts problem controlled by contract law, not by the law of wills. [69 A.L.R. 14] Betty cannot simply claim the land in probate court, but she may pursue a remedy for breach of the contract.

2. Consideration [§645]

As a general proposition, the promisee has no enforceable contract rights unless there was consideration for the testator's promise to name her as a will beneficiary. Without consideration, the testator's promise is simply a promise to make a gift in the future, and therefore is unenforceable.

---

e.g. **Example:** In the previous example, if Thurston's promise to devise Blackacre to Betty was not based on her taking care of him but simply because she is his favorite niece, Betty will have no right to the property when Thurston dies unless he makes an appropriate will. There is no consideration for the promise to give her Blackacre.

EXAM TIP	gilbert

Even though you may be taking a Wills exam, don't forget basic contract law. If a contract to make a gift by will is involved, look for the *basic elements of a contract* (offer, acceptance, consideration, and capacity) because without these there is no contract to enforce. If there is a valid contract that has been breached, recall that *contract remedies*—damages and equitable remedies such as constructive trust—are available.

3. Formalities

a. Common law [§646]

At common law and in states without statutes dealing with the question, a contract to make a will or to make a gift by will need *not be in writing* unless real property is involved. (If land is involved, the Statute of Frauds applies because the promise is treated as a contract for the sale of land. [*See* **Rape v. Lyerly,** 215 S.E.2d 737 (N.C. 1975)]) However, the Dead Man's Statute may be applicable to prohibit testimony offered to establish the alleged contract. (The Dead Man's Statute operates to disqualify an interested witness from testifying to a personal transaction or communication with a deceased person in a case against the representative or successors of the deceased. *See* Evidence Summary.) Also, several states require clear and convincing evidence that such a contract was entered into. [*See, e.g.,* **Greenwood v. Commercial National Bank,** 130 N.E.2d 753 (Ill. 1955); **Super v. Abdelazim,** 139 A.D.2d 863 (1988)]

b. Statutory solutions [§647]

Concerns about spurious claims, and the inability of the now-deceased alleged promisor to refute the promisee's testimony, have prompted many states to enact statutes requiring that a contract to make a gift by will (or a contract not to revoke a will) must be *in writing*. In general, the statutes take one of three forms:

(1) Promise in writing and signed [§648]

In several states, the statutes require that an agreement to make a testamentary provision of any kind or an agreement not to revoke a will must be *in writing and signed by the promisor*. [N.Y. Est. Powers & Trusts Law §13-2.1] Additionally, some states require that the writing be signed by *two witnesses*. [Fla. Prob. Code §732.701]

(2) Reference to contract in will [§649]

Some statutes go considerably further and provide that a contract relating to a will can be established *only* by provisions of a will (i) stating that a *contract does exist*, *and* (ii) stating the *material provisions* of the contract. [Tex. Prob. Code §59A]

(3) Uniform Probate Code [§650]

The UPC requires that a contract to make a will or testamentary gift (or not to revoke a will or testamentary gift) can be established only by (i) provisions in a will stating the *material provisions* of the contract, (ii) an *express reference* in a will to the contract and extrinsic evidence proving the terms of the contract, *or* (iii) a *writing signed by the decedent* evidencing the contract. [UPC §2-514]

FORMALITIES REQUIRED FOR CONTRACTS TO MAKE A GIFT BY WILL—A COMPARISON	**gilbert**
COMMON LAW	A writing is *not* required unless land is involved.
STATE STATUTES	Split of authority: (i) Agreement must be in a *writing signed by the promisor* (and, in some states, witnessed); (ii) Will must state the existence of the contract *and* its material terms; and (iii) UPC—Will must set forth the *material terms of the contract*, the will must expressly *refer to the contract* and extrinsic evidence must be available to prove the terms, *or a signed writing by the decedent* that evidences the contract must be produced.

4. Remedies

a. During testator's lifetime

(1) General rule [§651]

A contract to make a testamentary gift ordinarily is not enforceable during the testator's lifetime. *Rationale:* There is no way to determine whether the testator will perform the contract until after his death. [*See, e.g.,* **Clark v. Clark,** 288 N.W.2d 1 (Minn. 1979); **Galloway v. Eichells,** 62 A.2d 499 (N.J. 1948)]

(2) Exception—anticipatory breach [§652]

If, however, the promisor repudiates the promise *after substantial performance by the promisee*, this may be construed as an anticipatory breach of contract, entitling the promisee to maintain an immediate action against the promisor. [*See* **Story v. Hargrave,** 369 S.E.2d 669 (Va. 1988)]

---

e.g. **Example:** Jesse agrees to leave his home in Texas and relocate to Virginia to live with Theresa and take care of her in her last years. Theresa agrees to execute a will devising her entire estate to him. Theresa executes a valid will naming Jesse the sole beneficiary and Jesse moves to Virginia and takes care of Theresa and her farm for several years. Theresa subsequently revokes her will and drafts a new one in favor of her neighbor, Dixie, following an argument with Jesse. Jesse can bring an action for breach based on Theresa's repudiation of the contract and his performance until the point of repudiation.

(a) Remedies [§653]

If the promisor repudiates the contract, the promisee is entitled to *damages* for breach of contract [**Spinks v. Jenkins,** 43 S.E.2d 586 (Ga. 1947)], or to a *quantum meruit* recovery for the value of the consideration paid or services rendered [**Cramer v. McKinney,** 49 A.2d 374 (Pa. 1946)]. Also, the promisee may be entitled to *equitable relief,* requiring the promisor (or any non-bona fide purchaser to whom he has deeded the property) to hold the property for the promisor's benefit during his lifetime and convey the property to the promisee upon the promisor's death. [*See* **Matheson v. Gullickson,** 24 N.W.2d 704 (Minn. 1946)]

b. After testator's death [§654]

If the testator fails to make the promised testamentary gift, the promisee has a cause of action against the promisor's estate for breach of contract. [*See* **In re Soles's Will,** 253 N.W. 801 (Wis. 1934)]

(1) Remedies [§655]

Generally the remedy for breach of contract to make a gift by will is *damages*. The measure of damages is the *value of the property* promised to be devised or bequeathed. [*See* 65 A.L.R.3d 632] If, however, the case involves a promise to make a devise or bequest of *specific* property, the usual remedy is to grant a *constructive trust* for the promisee's benefit, the effect of which is to give the promisee the very property contracted for. [*See* 106 A.L.R. 742] (On the constructive trust remedy, *see* Trusts Summary.)

(2) Statute of limitations [§656]

The courts are divided as to what statute of limitations applies to a suit seeking to enforce the contract: Some cases hold that the claim must be presented within the "nonclaim" period required for filing creditors' claims against the estate; others hold that the applicable period is the time within which a will contest must be filed; others hold that the statutes governing actions for the recovery of land are applicable; and still others hold that the statute of limitations applicable to equitable claims is controlling. [*See* 94 A.L.R.2d 810]

REMEDIES FOR BREACH OF CONTRACT TO MAKE A GIFT BY WILL—A REVIEW	**gilbert**	
	REMEDY	EXAMPLE
BEFORE TESTATOR'S DEATH	***General rule:*** No remedy is available before the testator's death. If the testator repudiates the contract ***after the promisee substantially performed*** on the contract, available remedies include damages, a suit in quantum meruit, or imposition of a constructive trust.	Larry promises to leave Blackacre to Judy if she keeps up with the maintenance of the property. Judy subsequently discovers that Larry's will bequeaths Blackacre to Jack. Judy has no cause of action against Larry until his death. However, if she began maintaining the property while Larry was still alive and expended a large sum of money in doing so, she substantially performed on the contract and may bring an action for anticipatory breach.
AFTER TESTATOR'S DEATH	Available remedy is ***damages*** for the value of the property promised or if the promise involved ***specific*** property, imposition of a constructive trust.	Larry promises to leave "100 shares of Pepsi stock" to Judy if she takes care of him during his illness. When Larry dies, his will is probated and Judy discovers that he did not leave her any shares of Pepsi stock. Judy is entitled to the value of 100 shares of Pepsi stock. However, if Larry promised to leave his 1980 red Corvette to Judy, the car can be held on constructive trust for Judy's benefit.

c. **Enforcement by party other than original promisee [§657]**

In certain cases, someone other than the original promisee may enforce the contract.

Example: Suppose that Lyerly promises to devise real property to his daughter Mildred if she will move in with and take care of him. Mildred and her family move in with Lyerly and take care of him for several years. Mildred dies, but her husband and children continue to live with and care for Lyerly. Lyerly dies several years later; his will makes no devise to Mildred or her family. The contract is enforceable by Mildred's husband and children. While Lyerly could have rescinded the agreement on the ground that it was a personal service contract, his failure to do so and his continued acceptance of benefits from Mildred's successors bound him to perform as promised. [**Rape v. Lyerly,** *supra,* §646; 84 A.L.R.3d 908]

B. Joint Wills

1. Introduction [§658]

In states that have not enacted statutes relating to contractual wills, a frequently litigated question concerning joint wills is whether the particular joint will was executed *pursuant to a contract*—namely, whether the surviving party to the joint will agreed not to revoke the will or alter its dispositive provisions. However, other issues concerning joint wills, discussed below, can arise even if it is determined that the particular joint will was not contractual.

2. Terminology

a. Joint will [§659]

A "joint will" is the will of *two or more persons* executed as a *single testamentary instrument* (*e.g.,* "This is *our* last will and testament . . . .").

(1) Admissibility to probate [§660]

A joint will is admissible to probate on the death of *each* of the testators, just as if it had been written on separate pieces of paper. The fact that the document is the will of more than one testator does not affect its admission to probate in each testator's estate. [*See* **Olive v. Biggs,** 173 S.E.2d 301 (N.C. 1970)]

(2) Revocation by one testator [§661]

If one of the joint testators has revoked the will, it is no longer admissible to probate as *his* will, but the document still would be admissible to probate as the will of the other testator.

b. Reciprocal wills [§662]

In contrast to joint wills, "reciprocal" wills, sometimes called "mirror" wills, are *separate wills of two or more persons* that contain reciprocal provisions.

EXAM TIP   **gilbert**

Be sure to keep these two terms straight. A "joint" will is not the same as "reciprocal" wills. A joint will is **one instrument** executed by at least two testators; reciprocal wills are **separate instruments** executed by separate testators that contain mirror dispositive provisions.

c. Mutual wills [§663]

The courts are not uniform in their use of the word "mutual" in connection with joint wills and reciprocal wills. Some courts use the term "mutual" as synonymous with "contractual." Under this usage, a "joint and mutual will" is a single instrument executed jointly by two or more testators, the provisions of which are contractual. [*See* **Buettner v. Rintoul**, 553 N.E.2d 6 (Ill. 1990)] However, many courts use the term "mutual" as a synonym for "reciprocal." Under this parlance, "mutual wills" are separate wills containing reciprocal provisions; and a "joint and mutual will" is a joint will containing reciprocal provisions that may or may not be contractual. In reading cases involving joint wills or reciprocal wills, exercise care in determining which meaning the court intended when it refers to mutual wills.

3. Survivor's Rights [§664]

What are the surviving party's rights in the property subject to a joint will? This issue can arise even if the joint will is held *not* to be contractual, in which case the issue concerns only the decedent's property that passes under the will to the survivor. The issue also can arise if the will *is* held to be contractual, in which case the question of the survivor's rights concerns not only the decedent's property but *also* the survivor's property that is subject to the contractual obligation. In either case, the issue is this: Does the surviving party have only a life estate, a life estate with powers of invasion, or a fee simple subject to defeasance on her death? If the will is subject to a contract not to revoke, there is a greater tendency to find that the surviving party's rights do *not* include the power to make lifetime gifts, since the effect of such gifts would be to defeat the rights of the beneficiaries of the contract. [*See* 85 A.L.R.3d 8]

a. Life estate with invasion powers [§665]

A life estate with invasion powers may give the survivor a right to *invade the principal*.

(1) Illustration

"We and each of us give all of our property, real and personal, to the survivor of us, to be used, possessed, and enjoyed by the survivor during his or her lifetime, and on the death of the survivor all of the property shall pass as follows . . . ."

(2) Effect

A joint will drafted along the above lines gives the survivor a *life estate* ("during his or her lifetime"). However, the survivor may not be limited to the income from, or the right to possess, the property. The survivor's right of use will depend upon the language employed, and infinite variations in the words used by different testators make generalization difficult. However, the very broad language frequently employed in such wills (*e.g.,* "to be used, possessed, and enjoyed") is often found to give the survivor a right to *consume the principal* for her own support and benefit, but does *not* permit lifetime gifts with the purpose or effect of defeating the remainder interests. [*See* **Thomas v. Thomas**, 446 S.W.2d 590 (Tex. 1969)]

b. Defeasible fee simple [§666]

A grant of a defeasible fee may allow the survivor to *defeat the rights* of the beneficiaries under the contract.

(1) Illustration

"We give and bequeath to the survivor of us, absolutely, all our property, real, personal, and mixed, to use as he or she may see fit. After the death of both of us, the remainder of our property, of which the survivor shall die seised and possessed, shall go to . . . ." [*See* **Harrell v. Hickman**, 215 S.W.2d 876 (Tex. 1948)]

(2) Effect

Under a joint will drafted along the above lines ("to the survivor of us, *absolutely*"), it is generally held that the survivor has all the powers of a fee simple owner during her lifetime. This includes the power to make inter vivos gifts, even though such gifts have the intent and effect of defeating the interest of the takers at death. The beneficiaries take only what remains on the survivor's death. [*See* **Brack v. Brodbeck**, 466 S.W.2d 600 (Tex. 1971)]

C. Contract Not to Revoke a Will

1. Introduction [§667]

A frequently litigated situation involves an alleged promise by the testator not to revoke the will. Nearly all of the cases involve a joint will or reciprocal wills executed by a husband and wife; but the issue also can arise with respect to wills executed by siblings or unrelated parties. Of course, the parties could expressly provide that the joint will or reciprocal wills were not to be revoked by either party. However, this is decidedly the exception; and proof of the contract usually is based upon the language of the joint will (or reciprocal wills) and upon extrinsic evidence.

a. Illustration

Hector and Wilma are married, and each has a child by a former marriage. On the same day, they execute identical wills. Hector's will leaves his entire estate to Wilma if she survives him, otherwise one-half to Hector's son Saul and one-half to Wilma's daughter Davida. Wilma's will contains reciprocal terms: to Hector if he survives her, otherwise one-half to Saul and one-half to Davida. Hector dies, and his entire estate passes to Wilma. Thereafter, Wilma writes a new will that revokes her earlier will, makes a bequest of five dollars to Saul, and devises "all the remainder of my property to my beloved daughter, Davida." Saul now contends that Hector and Wilma executed their wills pursuant to an agreement under which the survivor would not revoke her will.

b. Comment

The case is a difficult and troublesome one. Given the similarity of the wills, it is very likely that Hector and Wilma discussed the wills before they were prepared and executed; and it may be shown that, after such discussion, they orally "agreed" to write reciprocal wills under which their estates ultimately would pass to their respective children. But should this discussion and "agreement" to write similar wills lead to a finding that they entered into an irrevocable commitment and enforceable obligation, the effect of which would be to prevent the survivor from ever changing her will regardless of changed circumstances? If that was their intent, it certainly would have been more appropriate to put their agreement in writing, or to use some formal arrangement (such as a trust) whereby their estates would be divided between the two children on the survivor's death.

2. Formalities [§668]

As noted earlier, a number of states have enacted statutes requiring that any agreement relating to a will, including a contract not to revoke a will, be in a writing executed with certain formalities (*see supra,* §647). In these states, the statutes have accomplished their avowed objective of eliminating litigation over claims, based on oral testimony or other extrinsic evidence, that a will was executed pursuant to a contract.

3. Presumptions [§669]

Because these cases continue to arise in jurisdictions that do not have statutes requiring that contracts relating to wills be in writing, the courts have developed various presumptions as to whether such a contract exists.

a. Joint will [§670]

It is invariably *stated* (as distinguished from *held*) by the courts that the mere execution of a joint will containing reciprocal provisions, without more, is *insufficient* to support a finding that the joint will was contractual.

(1) Rationale

Many husbands and wives execute joint wills without intending to irrevocably bind the survivor. "Contracts of this nature are viewed by the courts with caution; they can be established only by full and satisfactory proof; and no presumptions or inferences will be indulged in favor of them." [**Magids v. American Title Insurance Co.,** 473 S.W.2d 460 (Tex. 1971)]

(2) Comment

However, more than a few cases, after solemnly stating the above rule, nonetheless uphold findings that a joint will with reciprocal provisions, coupled with evidence that the parties "agreed" to execute the joint will, *does establish the existence of a contract*, especially when the testators use plural possessive pronouns to make a joint disposition of all of their collective properties. "A will like that could not have been made without agreement between the testators that it should be so made. Its very terms are evidence that an agreement was made." [**Nye v. Bradford,** 193 S.W.2d 165 (Tex. 1946)] However, the cases, even if from the same jurisdiction, are not at all predictable. [*See, e.g.,* 169 A.L.R. 9; 17 A.L.R.4th 167]

b. Reciprocal wills [§671]

By the overwhelming weight of authority, the execution of reciprocal wills containing identical provisions, drafted by the same attorney and executed on the same day, does *not constitute evidence* that the wills were *intended to be contractual.* [*See, e.g.,* **Proctor v. Handke,** 452 N.E.2d 742 (Ill. 1983); **Plemmons v. Pemberton,** 139 S.W.2d 910 (Mo. 1940)]

---

e.g. **Example:** Charles has two children by his first marriage and two children by his second marriage to Grace. Charles and Grace execute reciprocal wills: Charles's will provides that his estate is to go to Grace if she survives him; otherwise to the four children. Grace's will provides that her estate is to go to Charles if he survives her; otherwise to the four children. Charles dies; some years later Grace executes a new will that revokes her earlier will and leaves her entire estate (including the property received from Charles) to her two children and omits Charles's other two children. On these and similar facts, it is usually held that the reciprocal wills, by themselves, do not support a finding that the wills were contractual. "The power to dispose of one's property by will is not lightly to be denied . . . . No express promise or representation was proved in writing or orally to have been made by [Grace] that she would not change her testamentary intent as expressed in the will which she executed contemporaneously with the will of her husband . . . . The law requires clear evidence of the existence of a promise of this nature." [**Oursler v. Armstrong,** 10 Misc. 2d 654 (1961)]

---

(1) Comment

Nonetheless, an occasional court has found reciprocal wills to be contractual based on evidence that the parties "agreed" to write such wills. Here, too, the cases are not altogether predictable. [*See* 17 A.L.R.4th 167]

4. Effect of Contract

a. During both parties' lifetimes [§672]

It is generally held that either party may revoke a contractual will provided she gives notice to the other party to the contract. [*See, e.g.,* **Peck v. Drennan,** 103 N.E.2d 63 (Ill. 1951); **Ankeny v. Lieuallen,** 113 P.2d 1113 (Or. 1941); 169 A.L.R. 50] If one party secretly revokes a contractual will but predeceases the other party, the survivor has *no remedy* because he has not suffered any loss in reliance on the contract because he can freely change his own will. [*See* **Canada v. Ihmsen,** 240 P. 927 (Wyo. 1925)] "The only object of notice is to enable the other party to the bargain to alter his or her will also, but the survivor in the present case is not in any way prejudiced. He has notice as from the death." [**Stone v. Hoskins,** (1905) L.R. Prob. 194]

b. **Revocation of will by survivor [§673]**

By the overwhelming weight of authority, if the surviving party to the contract revokes her will and executes a new one, the *new will is admissible to probate* notwithstanding the breach of contract. [*See* **Moats v. Schoch,** 332 A.2d 43 (Md. 1975)] Moreover, the contractual will cannot be probated because it was revoked. [*See, e.g., In re* **Shepherd's Estate,** 130 So. 2d 888 (Fla. 1961); **Salvation Army v. Pryor's Estate,** 570 P.2d 1380 (Kan. 1977)]

(1) **Note**

This does not mean that the beneficiaries of the contract are without a remedy; it simply means that wills law, and not contract law, determines which will should be probated. The issue of whether a will is contractual cannot be determined in a probate proceeding, as that proceeding concerns only whether the proffered will is the duly executed last will of the decedent. The contractual issue and any resulting remedy must be pursued in a subsequent proceeding. [*See, e.g., In re* **Marcucci's Estate,** 296 N.E.2d 849 (Ill. 1973); **Rogers v. Russell,** 733 S.W.2d 79 (Tenn. 1986); 17 A.L.R.4th 167]

(2) **Remedies [§674]**

Since revocation of the contractual will and execution of a new will constitute a breach of contract, the contract beneficiaries have a remedy for the breach. The proper remedy is not damages but a *constructive trust* [169 A.L.R. 9], although the remedy is described by some courts as "in the nature of specific performance" or "quasi-specific performance." [*See* **O'Connor v. Immele,** 43 N.W.2d 649 (N.D. 1950)] The beneficiaries under the new will, which was executed in breach of contract, hold on a constructive trust for the benefit of the contract beneficiaries.

EXAM TIP — gilbert

It is important to remember that a person can *always change her will*—even if she made a contract not to do so. And, assuming the new will is properly executed, recall that it is *valid and will be probated*. That doesn't mean that the original beneficiaries are out of luck. Although they cannot challenge the will in the probate proceeding, they can bring a suit for *breach of contract*, and a constructive trust will allow them to receive the property they were to get under the original will.

EFFECT OF CONTRACT NOT TO REVOKE WILL				**gilbert**
A AND B ENTER INTO A CONTRACT NOT TO REVOKE THEIR WILLS. BOTH WILLS PROVIDE FOR THE DISPOSITION OF A PARTICULAR ITEM OF PROPERTY				
STATUS OF PARTIES		**ACTION**	**RESULT**	**RATIONALE**
A	B	A revokes will; notifies B. B sues.	No relief granted.	B has not been damaged; B still has an opportunity to change his will.
̶A̶	B	A revokes will without notifying B, and then dies. B sues.	No relief granted.	B has not been damaged; B still has an opportunity to change his will.
̶A̶	̶B̶	A dies in compliance (no revocation); B then revokes, makes a new will, and dies.	New will probated, but a constructive trust imposed in favor of the beneficiary of the contractual will.	A died with an estate plan made in reliance on B's promise, and unjust enrichment would result from allowing B to make an alternate disposition of his estate.

5.   **Property Subject to the Contract**

a.   **In general [§675]**

Since the purpose of a contractual will is to make a unified disposition of both parties' estates regardless of which party dies first, it is generally held that the contract applies to the survivor's *own property* as well as to the property that passed to her from the decedent.

b.   **After-acquired property [§676]**

Does the contract not to revoke apply only to property on hand when the first party died, or does it also apply to property *subsequently acquired* by the survivor?

(1)   **General rule [§677]**

The contract presumptively applies only to property owned by the two parties *at the time of death* of the first decedent. Thus, property thereafter acquired by the survivor could be devised by a later will. If, for example, the will contained language to the effect that "upon the death of the survivor of us, all of our said property" shall be distributed in a particular way, this would lead to a finding that "our *said* property" referred only to property on hand at the death of the first party. A will should not be construed to apply to after-acquired property "unless the intention to do so is set forth in the will by very plain, specific, and unambiguous language." [**Murphy v. Slaton,** 273 S.W.2d 588 (Tex. 1954)]

(2) Exception [§678]

However, the particular language used may lead to a finding that the contract also applies to property acquired by the survivor after the first party's death. Thus, if the contractual will provides that "upon the death of the survivor, *all of our property* shall be distributed . . . ," this has been held to connote an intent that the contract was to apply to after-acquired property. [*See* **Weidner v. Crowther,** 301 S.W.2d 621 (Tex. 1957)]

6. Effect on Elective Share Right [§679]

Suppose that Husband and Wife execute contractual wills under which the parties agree that the survivor will not revoke the agreed upon disposition of their property. Husband dies and Wife remarries. On Wife's death, her second husband files for an elective share. As is discussed more extensively *supra* (§213) most courts hold that the surviving spouse's elective share does not apply to property that is subject to the contractual will.

D. Contract Not to Make a Will

1. Introduction [§680]

Less frequently litigated are cases involving an alleged promise to die intestate (*i.e.,* to not make a will). Such agreements are not against public policy, and thus they are enforceable *if supported by consideration.* [*See, e.g.,* **Roberts v. Conley,** 626 S.W.2d 634 (Ky. 1981); 32 A.L.R.2d 370]

2. Statute of Frauds [§681]

If the property affected by a promise not to make a will includes real property, the courts are divided on whether the agreement must be evidenced by a memorandum that satisfies the Statute of Frauds.

a. Majority rule [§682]

Most courts hold that the Statute of Frauds applies, since the agreement constitutes a contract for the sale of land. [*See, e.g.,* **Griffin v. Driver,** 42 S.E.2d 368 (Ga. 1947); *In re* **Hayer's Estate,** 12 N.W.2d 520 (Iowa 1944)] Moreover, if the contract is invalid as to real property because of the Statute of Frauds, it is also invalid as to personal property in the estate; *i.e.,* the contract is *indivisible.* [*See* **Wolf v. Rich,** 121 P.2d 270 (Kan. 1942)] However, part performance by the promisee may be sufficient to take the case out of the Statute of Frauds. [*See* **Smith v. Nyburg,** 16 P.2d 493 (Kan. 1932)—daughter fully performed oral agreement with parents to postpone impending marriage for three years to stay home and assist parents with household duties in exchange for substantial share in parents' estate]

b. Minority rule [§683]

Several courts have held that the Statute of Frauds does not apply to such a contract, as the agreement has no necessary connection to any specific real property owned by the promisor. [*See* **Braden v. Neal,** 295 P. 678 (Kan. 1931)] Also, it has been held that a statute requiring that an agreement to make a will must be in writing does not apply to an agreement to *not* make a will. [*See, e.g.,* **Foman v. Davis,** 316 F.2d 254 (1st Cir. 1963)—Massachusetts law; **Frantz v. Maher,** 155 N.E.2d 471 (Ohio 1957)]

3. Remedies [§684]

As with cases involving a promise to make a will or not to revoke a will, the remedy most commonly granted for breach of a contract not to make a will is to impose a *constructive trust* against the beneficiaries under the will. [*See* **Ashbauth v. Davis,** 227 P.2d 954 (Idaho 1951)]

Chapter Ten:
Changes in Beneficiaries and Property After Execution of Will

CONTENTS

Chapter Approach

From the time a will is executed until the testator's death, a number of things can happen that may have an effect on the will's terms. A well-drafted will should cover all reasonably foreseeable contingencies that could affect the will, and should specify what is to happen if the indicated events occur. However, because well-drafted wills are no challenge to students, you are not likely to see one on your exam. Rather, the will you are likely to encounter may require you to consider the rules and statutes discussed in this chapter. Indeed, the odds are very high that one, and perhaps several, of the topics in this chapter will be tested on your exam. If, for example, the will in your question says "I devise Blackacre to my brother Bob," you can be pretty certain that something is going to happen to either Blackacre or Bob.

1. **Lapsed Gifts**

   A frequently encountered feature of Wills questions is to have one or more beneficiaries predecease the testator. In that situation, you will need to determine whether an *anti-lapse statute* saves the gift for the beneficiary's descendants. (If the anti-lapse statute does not apply, the gift will usually pass to the residuary beneficiaries.) You also may need to know the rules that apply if the predeceasing beneficiary was named in the will's residuary clause. If the testator and the beneficiary die simultaneously or within a short time of each other, you may be called upon to apply either the *Uniform Simultaneous Death Act* or the UPC's *120-hour rule*.

2. **Class Gifts**

   If the will leaves property to a class (*e.g.*, to someone's "children"), keep in mind that additional class members may be born or existing members may die. Your task will be to identify *who is part of the class* and *when class members are determined*. Here, either the *class gift rule* or the *rule of convenience*, or perhaps both rules of construction, may be tested, so you need to be familiar with both of these rules. If a class member predeceases the testator, it is important to determine whether an anti-lapse statute applies to the gift.

3. **Ademption**

   The will may make a *specific bequest* of property, but the particular asset may not be in the testator's estate at death—either because of the testator's voluntary act (*e.g.*, sale or gift) or due to events beyond the testator's control (*e.g.*, destruction). The general rule is that if property described in a specific bequest is not in the testator's estate at death, ademption applies and the beneficiary is out of luck. But be ready to discuss the ways that courts sometimes try to avoid application of ademption (as by construing the gift as a general legacy) and the statutes that modify the common law rule.

4. **Stock Splits and Stock Dividends**

   The testator's ownership of specifically bequeathed corporate securities may be affected by the corporation's declaration of a stock split or stock dividend. Although the common law gives the beneficiary the additional shares due to a split, the beneficiary does *not* get the stock dividends. (Be careful here! The UPC and other statutes give the additional stock to the beneficiary in both situations.)

5. **Exoneration of Liens**

    The testator may leave to a beneficiary a particular piece of property that is subject to a mortgage lien at the testator's death. If so, you will need to determine whether the beneficiary is entitled to demand that the lien be "exonerated" from the residuary estate (the common law rule) or, instead, he takes the property subject to the lien (the UPC rule).

Remember that all of the above rules apply *only if the will does not make provisions* for these contingencies. If the will in your question states the testator's intent in such cases, be sure to follow the will.

A. Lapsed Gifts

1. **Definition [§685]**

    If a beneficiary named in a will dies during the testator's lifetime, the gift to the beneficiary lapses; *i.e.*, *the gift fails*. This result is based on a fundamental principle: A will cannot make a gift to a dead person because a dead person cannot hold title to property.

EXAM TIP	**gilbert**

    The death of the beneficiary during the testator's lifetime is the most common scenario that causes a gift to lapse. However, look for fact patterns on your exam where the beneficiary *disclaims* a testamentary gift—the testamentary gift will lapse in this scenario as well. (*See supra*, §§143 *et seq.*)

2. **What Constitutes Surviving the Testator [§686]**

    If a will beneficiary and the testator die in quick succession, whether the gift to the beneficiary lapses is contingent on whether the beneficiary survived the testator. This depends on what rule or presumption applies to the situation.

    a. **Uniform Simultaneous Death Act [§687]**

        Many jurisdictions have enacted the Uniform Simultaneous Death Act ("USDA") (*see supra*, §§104-114). Under the USDA, if two persons die under such circumstances that there is *no sufficient evidence* as to which of them survived, the property of each is distributed as though he survived the other person (absent a contrary provision in the will). Thus, if a testator and a will beneficiary die simultaneously, the testator's estate is distributed as though the beneficiary predeceased the testator (*i.e.*, the gift lapses). [*See, e.g.*, Cal. Prob. Code §220; N.C. Gen. Stat. §28A-24-1; Tenn. Code §31-3-101]

b. Uniform Probate Code's 120-hour survival rule [§688]

Under the original UPC and also in several non-UPC states, a will beneficiary who fails to survive the testator by 120 hours is deemed to have *predeceased the testator* (absent a contrary will provision) and the *gift lapses*. [Original UPC §2-601; *and see* Tex. Prob. Code §47] The revised UPC and several non-UPC states have added the requirement that there must be clear and convincing evidence that the beneficiary survived the testator by 120 hours. [UPC §2-702; Kan. Stat. §58-709] (For a complete discussion of the 120-hour rule, *see supra*, §§115-120.)

(1) Contrary will provision [§689]

Under the original UPC, the 120-hour rule does not apply (and the gift is valid) if the will contains language explicitly dealing with (i) simultaneous deaths, (ii) deaths in a common disaster, (iii) the devisee surviving the testator, or (iv) the devisee surviving the testator for a stated period in order to take under the will. [Original UPC §2-601]

Example: Fritz's will devises Blackacre "to Beate if she survives me." Fritz dies; Beate dies 48 hours later. Under the original UPC, the 120-hour rule does not apply because the will contains a provision dealing with survival. Since Beate met the condition attached to the testamentary gift (she survived Fritz), the gift does not lapse. Instead, Blackacre passes to Beate (and then through her estate to her successors).

(a) Revised Uniform Probate Code [§690]

Under the revised UPC, a provision requiring that the beneficiary survive the testator does *not* override the 120-hour rule unless the will made an *alternate gift* in the event of the beneficiary's nonsurvival (*see infra*, §708). [UPC §2-702]

Example: In the example above, the gift to Beate *lapses* even though she survived Fritz, because she did not do so by 120 hours and the will did not provide for an alternate beneficiary in the event of her nonsurvival.

EXAM TIP	gilbert

Do not overlook the connection between the USDA or the UPC's 120-hour rule and the lapse of a gift to a beneficiary. If the will fails to make a provision for survival, application of the USDA or 120-hour rule may be necessary to determine whether the gift to the beneficiary lapses by determining whether or not she survived the testator. If under the USDA or 120-hour rule, the beneficiary is deemed to have predeceased the testator, the gift lapses, but an *anti-lapse statute may save the gift for her descendants* (*see infra*, §§695 *et seq.*).

c. Drafting recommendation [§691]

As noted above, both the USDA and the 120-hour rule apply absent any contrary will provision. In drafting wills, it is not advisable to rely on either of these "default" rules to cover the contingency of deaths in quick succession. Instead, a beneficiary's taking should be made contingent on surviving the testator by a specified period of time (*e.g.*, 30 or 60 days). If the testator and a beneficiary die in close proximity, such a provision is more likely to prevent the same assets from being administered in two estates in quick succession. Also, the provision tends to insure that disposition of the property will be governed by the testator's will, rather than passing to the kin of a beneficiary who did not live long enough to enjoy the property. While the UPC's 120-hour rule provides a better solution than the USDA, in most cases it is preferable to require a longer period of survival than 120 hours.

(1) Simultaneous death clause—not recommended [§692]

Making a bequest to a beneficiary with an alternate gift "if we die simultaneously" is not recommended because the USDA itself is not a satisfactory solution to the problem of deaths in quick succession. (*See supra*, §113.)

(2) Common disaster clause—not recommended [§693]

Making an alternate gift "if we die as a result of a common disaster" is not recommended because the parties may die from *independent* causes within a few days or hours of each other. [*In re* **Davis's Estate**, 186 Misc. 955 (1946)]

(3) Marital deduction [§694]

In making a federal estate tax marital deduction gift by will, it may be advisable to reverse the USDA presumption to preserve the deduction. Such a *reverse presumption clause* is given effect for federal tax purposes. (*See* Estate & Gift Tax Summary.)

Example: Christina's will makes a marital deduction gift to her husband "if he survives me." The will further provides: "for purposes of the marital deduction gift, if my husband and I die under such circumstances that there is no sufficient evidence as to which of us survived, my husband shall be considered to have survived me." This clause would secure the marital deduction for Christina's estate if she and her husband die simultaneously.

---

3. Anti-Lapse Statute [§695]

All jurisdictions have enacted anti-lapse statutes, which provide *substitute takers* if the predeceasing will beneficiary (i) was within a *specified degree of relationship* to the testator, *and* (ii) *left descendants* ("issue") who survived the testator. Such

DID THE GIFT LAPSE?

- If the beneficiary is dead, determine whether he *predeceased the testator*.

- If the testator and beneficiary died in *quick succession*, apply the USDA or 120-hour rule to determine whether the beneficiary predeceased the testator.

- If the beneficiary is alive, ask yourself whether he did an *act that results in his being treated as having predeceased* the testator (*e.g.,* he disclaimed the gift).

IS THE GIFT SAVED BY AN ANTI-LAPSE STATUTE?

- Check to see if the beneficiary was *related to the testator within the degree of relationship* specified by the applicable anti-lapse statute.

- Make sure the beneficiary left *descendants* who survived the testator.

descendants are substituted as takers of the gift. While these statutes are sometimes called "lapse" statutes, "anti-lapse" is a more descriptive title, since the purpose of the statutes is to *prevent* gifts from lapsing by designating a substitute taker.

EXAM TIP   **gilbert**

Be careful in your application of the anti-lapse statute. Most statutes require that the beneficiary be *related to the testator* within a specified degree (*e.g.*, child or grandchild) for the gift to be saved for his descendants. When applying that type of anti-lapse statute, don't be fooled by a fact pattern where a *friend* of the testator predeceases the testator but leaves descendants who survive the testator. The anti-lapse statute will *not* save that beneficiary's gift; it will lapse.

---

a. **Application in cases of deaths in quick succession—120-hour rule [§696]**

In jurisdictions that have enacted the UPC's 120-hour survival rule, the anti-lapse statute applies if a beneficiary is deemed to have predeceased the testator by failing to survive the testator by 120 hours. In these states, the beneficiary's descendants also must survive the testator by 120 hours in order to be substituted as takers of the gift.

b. **Scope of anti-lapse statutes—relationship of beneficiary to testator [§697]**

Not all cases in which a beneficiary dies during the testator's lifetime are covered by the anti-lapse statute. The states' statutes vary widely as to their scope.

(1) **Narrow statutes—descendants of testator [§698]**

In a few states, the anti-lapse statute applies *only* if the predeceasing beneficiary was a child or other *descendant of the testator*. [*See, e.g.*, Ark. Code §28-26-104; Ill. Comp. Stat. ch. 755, §5/4-11] In all other cases, the gift lapses.

Example: Patrick's will devises Blackacre "to my niece Maureen," and his residuary estate to his wife. Maureen (a child of Patrick's sister) predeceases Patrick, leaving a son, Neal, who survives Patrick. The anti-lapse statute does not operate to save the gift for Neal because Maureen is not Patrick's *descendant*.

---

(2) **Intermediate statutes—collateral kin [§699]**

In several states, the anti-lapse statute applies if the predeceasing beneficiary was a *descendant of the testator's parent*, and thus applies to brothers and sisters and their descendants as well as to the testator's own descendants. [*See, e.g.*, La. Civ. Code art. 1593; Pa. Cons. Stat. tit. 20, §2514(9); Tex. Prob. Code §68] *But note:* The Connecticut and New York statutes apply if the predeceasing beneficiary was a descendant, brother, or sister of the testator (but *not* if the beneficiary was the testator's niece or nephew). [*See* Conn. Gen. Stat. §45a-441; N.Y. Est. Powers & Trusts Law §3-3.3]

> **Example:** On the above facts, the anti-lapse statute does apply because Maureen is a descendant of Patrick's parents and Neal takes Blackacre by substitution. Note, however, that the anti-lapse statute will not apply on these facts in New York or Connecticut because Maureen is Patrick's niece.

(3) Uniform Probate Code—grandparent or descendant of grandparent [§700]

Under the UPC and in several non-UPC states, the statute applies if the predeceasing beneficiary was a *grandparent* or a *descendant of a grandparent* of the testator. [*See, e.g.,* UPC §2-603; Ala. Code §43-8-224; Del. Code tit. 12, §2313; Va. Code §64.1-64.1; Wash. Rev. Code §11.12.110] Note that the scope of the UPC anti-lapse statute coincides with the degree of relationship required for inheritance under the UPC. (*See supra,* §§18 *et seq.*)

> **Example:** On the above facts, the anti-lapse statute saves the gift for Neal because Maureen is a descendant of Patrick's grandparents.

(a) Revised Uniform Probate Code—stepchildren included [§701]

The revised UPC has expanded the scope of the anti-lapse statute to include *stepchildren of the testator.* [UPC §2-603] The anti-lapse statutes in a small number of non-UPC states also apply to stepchildren. [*See, e.g.,* Conn. Gen. Stat. §45a-441]

(4) Broad statutes—all relatives [§702]

In a number of states, the anti-lapse statute applies if the predeceasing beneficiary was a *child or other relative* of the testator. [*See, e.g.,* Mass. Gen. Laws ch. 191, §22; Mo. Rev. Stat. §474.460; Neb. Rev. Stat. §30-2343] The only situation not covered by this type of statute is one in which the predeceasing beneficiary was not related to the testator.

(a) Relatives by blood or adoption only [§703]

In states whose anti-lapse statutes apply to relatives of the testator, it is generally held that this means relatives by blood or adoption, and not relatives by affinity. Thus, the anti-lapse statute does not apply to a spouse or a relative of the spouse who predeceases the testator. [*See, e.g.,* **Estate of McReynolds,** 800 S.W.2d 798 (Mo. 1990); **In re Dodge's Estate,** 84 N.W.2d 66 (Wis. 1957)]

> **Example:** Testator makes a gift to Stepchild, whom Testator did not adopt. Stepchild predeceases Testator leaving descendants who survive Testator. The anti-lapse statute does *not* apply because Stepchild was not related to Testator by blood or adoption.

(b) Distinguish—all beneficiaries [§704]

In several jurisdictions, the anti-lapse statute applies when *any beneficiary, whether related or unrelated* to the testator, dies during the testator's lifetime. [*See, e.g.,* D.C. Code §18-308; Ga. Code §53-4-64; Iowa Code §633.273; Ky. Rev. Stat. §394.400; Tenn. Code §32-3-105]

> **Example:** In the example above, the gift to Stepchild will be saved for her descendants because this type of anti-lapse statute applies even if the beneficiary is not related to the testator.

EXAM TIP   gilbert

Because the anti-lapse statutes vary so much from state to state, an exam question will usually tell you what the state's anti-lapse statute says. If so, you obviously must apply the provisions of that statute. If the question does **not provide the particulars** of the statute, discuss the **purpose** of the anti-lapse statutes (to prevent gifts from lapsing by designating a substitute taker) and the two basic provisions of an anti-lapse statute: (i) the beneficiary must be **within a statutorily defined degree of relationship** to the testator, and (ii) the beneficiary must have **left descendants** who survive the testator.

---

c. Substitute takers—predeceasing beneficiary's descendants [§705]

In virtually every state, the anti-lapse statute operates *only* if the predeceasing beneficiary left descendants who survived the testator. Under the UPC and in non-UPC states that have enacted the 120-hour rule, the descendants must survive the testator by 120 hours. [UPC §2-702] *Note:* The statute *does not save the gift for the deceased beneficiary's estate*. Instead, the statute names the substitute takers—the beneficiary's *descendants* who survived the testator.

> **Example:** Tom's will bequeaths 1,000 shares of Acme stock "to my daughter Mary," and devises his residuary estate to his wife. Mary dies in Tom's lifetime, leaving a will that devises "all my property, including all of my interest in my father's estate, to my husband Jack." Mary is survived by Jack and by her only child, Sam, both of whom survive Tom. Sam takes the bequest of the Acme stock under the anti-lapse statute. Mary's will cannot bequeath any interest in her father's estate to Jack because Mary had only an *expectancy*. (*See supra*, §326.) The anti-lapse statute does not save the gift for Mary's estate but rather designates Mary's descendants (Sam) as substitute takers.

> **Compare:** Consider the same facts as above, except that Sam also predeceases Tom. Thus, none of Mary's descendants survived the testator. The bequest of 1,000 shares of Acme stock lapses. The Acme stock falls into Tom's residuary estate as undisposed-of property, and passes under the residuary gift to Tom's wife.

(1) Minority rule [§706]

In Maryland, the property passes "to those persons who would have taken the property if the legatee had died, *testate or intestate,* owning the property." [Md. Est. & Trusts Code §4-403(b)] Thus, in the above example, the 1,000 shares of Acme stock would pass under Mary's will to her husband Jack.

d. Contrary will provision—gift contingent on surviving testator [§707]

An anti-lapse statute is a default rule that applies absent contrary provision in the testator's will. In nearly all states, the statute does *not* apply if the gift is contingent on the beneficiary's surviving the testator. For example, if the will makes a gift "to such of my children as are living at my death," this is a clear indication that only those children are to take; thus, the anti-lapse statute does not operate in favor of the descendants of a child who predeceases the testator. [*See, e.g.,* Tex. Prob. Code §68(e); Wis. Stat. §854.06; *In re* **Stroble's Estate,** 636 P.2d 236 (Kan. 1981); **Roysten v. Watts,** 842 S.W.2d 876 (Mo. 1992); *In re* **Estate of Rehwinkel,** 862 P.2d 639 (Wash. 1993); 63 A.L.R.2d 1172]

(1) Revised UPC and minority view [§708]

The revised UPC and a handful of non-UPC states apply the above rule only if the will makes an alternate gift (*e.g.,* "to my son John if he survives me; but if he does not survive me, to my sister Sue"). If no alternate gift is made in the event of the beneficiary's nonsurvival, the beneficiary's descendants take under the anti-lapse statute. The theory underlying this minority view is that anti-lapse statutes are remedial and should receive a liberal construction in favor of the deceased beneficiary's descendants unless the testator has explicitly directed a different disposition. [*See* **Detzel v. Nieberding,** 219 N.E.2d 327 (Ohio 1966—criticized as "clearly and completely erroneous" in **Cowgill v. Faulconer,** 385 N.E.2d 327 (Ohio 1978); UPC §2-603(b)]

(a) Criticism [§709]

The revised UPC's position, which has been enacted in only a few of the UPC states, has been criticized as arrogant: "Apparently, the revisers believe their own anti-lapse provisions are likely to reflect any particular testator's intent more faithfully that the testator's own will. This conclusion is not only pretentious, it disputes what should be obvious—that most testators expect their wills to dispose of the property completely—without interference from a statute of which they have never heard." [Mark L. Ascher, *The 1990 Uniform Probate Code: Older and Better, or More Like the Internal Revenue Code?* 77 Minn. L. Rev. 639 (1993)]

> **e.g.** **Example:** Tillie's will devises Blackacre "to my son John if he survives me," and her residuary estate to her daughter Mary. John predeceases Tillie, leaving two children who survive her. In nearly all states, the anti-lapse statute does not operate in John's children's favor, and Blackare passes to Mary under the residuary clause. The gift to John was conditioned upon his surviving Tillie. Since this condition was not satisfied, the *gift failed according to its terms.* [*See, e.g.,* Ariz. Rev. Stat. §14-2603(A)(3); **Rossi v. Rossi,** 448 S.W.2d 162 (Tex. 1969); 63 A.L.R.2d 1172] Under the revised UPC, however, John's children would be substituted as takers of Blackacre because the will did not provide an alternate gift in the event of John's nonsurvival.

e. **Application to nonprobate transfers [§710]**

In nearly all states, the anti-lapse statutes apply only to wills, and do not apply to nonprobate transfers. However, the revised UPC provides an anti-lapse statute (with the same scope as the statute applicable to wills) to beneficiaries of life insurance policies, bank accounts in "pay on death" ("P.O.D.") form, securities in "transfer on death" ("T.O.D.") form, pension plans, and the like. [UPC §2-706]

(1) **Exercise of power of appointment [§711]**

The revised UPC expands the anti-lapse statute's scope to cover beneficiaries ("appointees") named by the exercise of a testamentary power of appointment. If an appointee predeceases the testator, the anti-lapse statute applies if the appointee (i) was a grandparent, descendant of a grandparent, or stepchild of either the testator or the "donor" (creator) of the power of appointment, *and* (ii) left descendants who survive the testator by 120 hours. [UPC §2-603(a)(3), (4)]

(2) **Revocable trusts [§712]**

Anti-lapse statutes, which typically by their terms apply to "wills" or "devises," do not apply to inter vivos trusts, including revocable trusts. Such trusts typically create vested remainders and remainders contingent on survivorship, which are governed by the law of future interests. [*See, e.g.,* **First National Bank v. Anthony,** 557 A.2d 957 (Me. 1989); *In re* **Capocy's Estate,** 430 N.E.2d 1131 (Ill. 1981); **Detroit Bank & Trust Co. v. Grout,** 289 N.W.2d 898 (Mich. 1980)]

(a) **Minority view [§713]**

A few courts have applied an anti-lapse statute to a revocable trust if the remainder beneficiary died during the settlor's lifetime. [*See, e.g.,* **Dollar Savings & Trust Co. v. Turner,** 529 N.E.2d 1261 (Ohio 1988)—overturned by Ohio Rev. Code §§2107.01; *In re* **Button's Estate,** 490 P.2d 731 (Wash. 1971)]

4. **Lapse of Specific Gift or General Legacy [§714]**

Absent a contrary will provision, a specific, demonstrative, or general bequest that lapses (and is not saved by the jurisdiction's anti-lapse statute) falls into the residuary estate and passes to the residuary beneficiaries. [*See* UPC §2-604(a); Mo. Rev. Stat. §474.465; Tex. Prob. Code §68]

a. Exception—narrow residuary clause [§715]

A lapsed gift passes under the residuary clause *only if the clause is broad enough to encompass it*. If, for example, the residuary clause makes a gift of "all of my remaining property, *other than the property I have referred to above*," a lapsed gift in a preceding will provision would not be caught by the residuary clause. However, the courts try to avoid reading residuary clauses narrowly, on the ground that the testator presumptively intended that her will would dispose of her entire estate, including any lapsed gifts.

b. No residuary clause [§716]

If the will does not contain a residuary clause, or if the gifts fall outside the clause (as above), lapsed gifts pass by *intestate succession*.

EXAM TIP   **gilbert**

Note that even when there is a will, you will occasionally have to resort to the intestate succession statutes to answer an exam question. One way partial intestacy results is when the will has *no residuary clause*—*i.e.,* the testator made only specific gifts and did not provide for the rest of her property. On an exam, this may happen where the testator has limited property (*e.g.,* only a house and a car) and gives each away specifically by will. This plan will work only if that is all that is in her estate, but often in an exam question there are other items that aren't accounted for; *e.g.,* the day before she dies, the testator wins the lottery or her great uncle leaves her something in his will, or the testator forgot about the money she had socked away for a rainy day. Without a residuary clause in her will, these items *pass by intestate succession to her heirs, even if that would be contrary to her intent*.

---

5. Lapse in Residuary Gift [§717]

Suppose that the testator's residuary estate is devised to two or more beneficiaries, one of the residuary beneficiaries predeceases the testator, and neither the will nor the state's anti-lapse statute covers the situation. Does the share of the deceased beneficiary go to the remaining residuary beneficiaries, or does it "fall out of the will" and pass by intestate succession?

a. Common law and minority rule—no residue of a residue [§718]

At common law and in a handful of states today, the share of the deceased residuary beneficiary does *not* pass to the remaining residuary beneficiaries unless the will so provides. Instead, that share "falls out of will" and passes by *intestacy* to the testator's heirs. [*See, e.g., In re* **Levy's Estate**, 415 P.2d 1006 (Okla. 1966); 36 A.L.R.2d 1117] This is commonly referred to as the "no residue of a residue" rule, the theory being that the residuary clause cannot "catch" property that is itself a part of the residuary estate. The rule is also said to rest on the testator's intent that the residuary beneficiaries were to receive the indicated shares and no more.

b. **Majority and revised UPC rule—surviving residuary beneficiaries take [§719]**
The "no residue of a residue" rule has been criticized as being merely a play on words and inconsistent with the testator's probable intent in most cases. The very fact that the testator wrote a will is an indication that she probably would want her estate to go to the named beneficiaries who survived her rather than to her heirs. The "no residue of a residue" rule has been overturned by statute in a substantial number of states. Under these statutes, if the residue is devised to two or more beneficiaries and the share of one of the residuary beneficiaries fails for any reason, then absent application of an antilapse statute his share *passes to the other residuary beneficiaries* in proportion to their interests in the residue. [*See, e.g.*, UPC §2-604(b); Mass. Gen. Laws ch. 191, §1A(5)] Also, several courts have discarded the "no residue of a residue" rule by judicial decision. [*See, e.g.*, **Corbett v. Skaggs**, 207 P. 819 (Kan. 1922); *In re* **Frolich's Estate**, 295 A.2d 448 (N.H. 1972)]

---

e.g. **Example:** Tanya's will devises her residuary estate "in equal shares to my daughter Ann, my brother Bill, and my cousin Charlie." Ann predeceases Tanya, leaving a child (Arnie) who survives Tanya. Bill also predeceases Tanya, leaving no descendants. When Tanya dies, she is survived by Arnie and by Charlie.

- *In a jurisdiction that applies the "no residue of a residue" rule*, Charlie takes one-third of the residuary estate under the will, Arnie takes one-third under the anti-lapse statute, and the one-third share devised to Bill passes by intestacy. (If Tanya was a widow and Arnie was her only surviving descendant, Arnie would take another one-third share by intestate succession.)

- *In a jurisdiction that applies the "surviving residuary beneficiaries" rule*, Arnie (substituted for Ann under the anti-lapse statute) would take one-half of the residuary estate, and Charlie would take the remaining one-half.

- *But the best solution* would have been careful drafting of Tanya's will to explicitly address what is to happen if a residuary beneficiary predeceases the testator.

EXAM TIP	gilbert

Another way partial intestacy issues can arise is when a gift in a will to the *residuary beneficiary lapses*. Note that in these cases the property is distributed according to the will as much as possible, and that property "falling out of the will" is distributed according to the intestate succession statutes. Because this result is usually not what the testator intended (or she wouldn't have written a will), courts try to avoid partial intestacy if possible. Therefore, check the *terms of the will for a contingent gift* in the event a residuary beneficiary predeceases the testator. Also consider whether the state's *anti-lapse statute applies*—was the predeceasing residuary beneficiary within the specified degree of relationship to the testator and did he leave descendants who survive the testator? If so, those descendants will take his share of the residuary estate. Finally, note that many state *statutes* provide that the share of a predeceasing residuary beneficiary will *pass to surviving residuary beneficiaries* rather than fail.

6. Void Gifts—Beneficiary Deceased When Will Executed [§720]

A testamentary gift is *void* if the beneficiary was dead at the time the will was executed, because the gift could not be given effect even if the testator had died the moment after the will was signed. [*See, e.g.,* 3 A.L.R. 1673]

EXAM TIP **gilbert**

Note that this scenario is different from a *lapsed* gift, which occurs when the beneficiary dies *after* the will is executed. However, the rationale underlying void and lapsed gifts is the same: A gift cannot be made to a dead person.

---

a. Effect [§721]

In general, a void gift is treated the same as a lapsed gift. In the absence of statute or a controlling will provision, void specific gifts and general legacies fall into the residuary estate, while void residuary gifts either pass to the remaining residuary legatees or pass by intestate succession. (*See supra,* §§18 *et seq.*)

b. Application of anti-lapse statute [§722]

It is generally held that anti-lapse statutes apply to void gifts in the same manner that they apply to lapsed gifts, if the other requisites to the statutes' operation are met. [UPC §2-603; N.Y. Est. Powers & Trusts Law §3-3.3] (The result may be different, however, if a *class* gift, rather than a gift to an individually named beneficiary, is involved. *See infra* §§752-754.)

B. Class Gifts

1. Definitional Problems [§723]

When a gift is made to a group or class of persons, such as the "children," "brothers and sisters," "descendants," or "heirs" of a named individual, questions sometimes arise as to *what persons were intended to be included in the class designation.* This section outlines the rules of construction applied by the courts *in the absence of a controlling will provision.*

a. "Children"

(1) Grandchildren not included [§724]

A gift to someone's "children" includes *descendants in the first degree only.* Such a gift does not include grandchildren unless the will as a whole shows an "unmistakable intent" that the term "children" has been used in other than its dictionary meaning, *i.e.,* that it has been used synonymously with "issue" or "descendants." [*See, e.g., In re* **Gustafson,** 74 N.Y.2d 448 (1989)]

(2) Children by all marriages included [§725]

Absent a contrary indication, a gift to a person's "children" includes children from *all* of that person's marriages, and not just the children from that person's present marriage.

(3) Adopted children

(a) Former law—"stranger to the adoption" rule [§726]

Adoption, which derives from Roman law, was unknown to the common law. The first state to recognize the adoptive status was Massachusetts (by statute in 1851). Even after the adoptive relationship came to be widely recognized, for many years judicial decisions favored relations by blood over relations by adoption. Thus, until the 1960s, in nearly all states a gift to someone's "children," "descendants," "issue," etc., presumptively included adopted children *only if* the will, deed, or trust being construed was that of the *adopting parent*—the idea being that the adopting parent would intend to include his adopted children along with natural children. But if, *e.g.*, the will being construed were that of a "stranger to the adoption" (*i.e.*, anyone other than the adopting parent), a gift to someone's children, etc., presumptively did *not* include adopted offspring. [*See* 36 A.L.R.5th 395]

(b) Modern and UPC view [§727]

In nearly all states today, either by statute or by case decision, a gift to someone's "children," "issue," "descendants," and the like, presumptively *includes* adopted children. [*See, e.g.*, UPC §2-705(a); N.Y. Est. Powers & Trusts Law §2-1.3(a)(1); *In re* **Coe's Estate**, 201 A.2d 571 (N.J. 1964); **Bowles v. Bradley,** 461 S.E.2d 811 (S.C. 1995); **Vaughn v. Gunter,** 461 S.W.2d 599 (Tex. 1970)]

1) Distinguish—"born to" language [§728]

If a will creates various gifts for someone's *existing* children and provides for additional trusts for children *"born to* my son after my death," the reference "born to" has been held to *preclude* adopted children from sharing in the trusts. [*See, e.g.*, **Vaughn v. Vaughn,** 337 S.W.2d 793 (Tex. 1960); **Schroeder v. Danielson,** 640 N.E.2d 495 (Mass. 1994)—"children of the body"]

(c) Adoption of adult [§729]

What if a person adopts an adult for the purpose of allowing him to inherit? For example, suppose that a will creates a trust: "Income to my son John for life, and on John's death, principal to his children" (or "issue"). After the testator's death, John, who is childless, adopts his adult nephew for the purpose of making the nephew a remainderman. Should the adopted person be allowed to take the remainder interest? The *courts are divided* on this question.

1) Adult adoptee is included [§730]

Many courts have allowed the adopted adult to take, as long as the *controlling law allows the adoption of adults*. [*See, e.g.,* **In re Fortney's Estate,** 611 P.2d 599 (Kan. 1980); **Evans v. McCoy,** 436 A.2d 436 (Md. 1981)] Thus, in the example above, John's nephew will take the gift if state law permits the adoption of adults.

2) Adult adoptee is *not* included [§731]

Other courts have ruled otherwise, reasoning that the adoption of an adult for the sole purpose of enabling the person to take under the will was not within the testator's intent or contemplation. [*See, e.g.,* **Cross v. Cross,** 532 N.E.2d 486 (Ill. 1988); **Davis v. Neilson,** 871 S.W.2d 35 (Mo. 1993); *In re* **Tafel's Estate,** 296 A.2d 797 (Pa. 1972)—rule codified in Pa. Cons. Stat. tit. 20, §2514(7)] In some states, an adopted adult is included within a class gift only if he was raised as a member of the adopting parent's household.

3) Revised Uniform Probate Code [§732]

Under the revised UPC, a gift to someone's "children," "issue," etc., includes an adopted individual only if the individual, while a minor, lived as a regular member of the adopting parent's household either before or after the adoption. [UPC §2-705(c)]

EXAM TIP   **gilbert**

Be careful here. Although the individual was not adopted until he was an adult, he can still be classified as a person's child if he was a member of that person's household **when he was a minor**. For example, Mike and Carol are married and each has three young children from previous marriages. Mike and Carol never adopt their stepchildren. Mike subsequently dies and his sons continue to live with Carol until they go to college. When Mike's youngest son reaches the age of 21, Carol adopts all three stepsons. Although they were adopted when they were adults, they will still be treated as Carol's children because they lived with her when they were minors.

---

4) Drafting note [§733]

To prevent adult adoptees from being included in a gift, it is advisable to define a gift to descendants and the like as including adopted persons only if adopted before attaining, *e.g.*, age 18.

(d) Child placed for adoption [§734]

If a child is adopted by a new family, is the child included in a class gift made by a *natural relative* of the child? Most courts have said no (absent a contrary expression of intent) *unless* the adopting parent is also a member of the child's natural family. (*See supra*, §§76-81.)

---

e.g. **Example:** As a teenager, Amy has a child, Pat, born out of wedlock. Pat is placed for adoption and is adopted by a new family. Later, Amy marries and has a child by that marriage. In the meantime, Amy's grandparent has established a trust: Income to Amy for life, remainder to her "issue." Although the adoption records are sealed, on Amy's death the trustee somehow learns of the existence and identity of Pat as Amy's natural child. Pat does *not* take a share of the remainder. To hold otherwise would put an undue burden on executors and trustees to determine, in every case, whether there were any such adopted-out children to share in a class gift. [*See, e.g.,* **Newman v. Wells Fargo Bank**, 14 Cal. 4th 126 (1996); *In re* **Estate of Best**, 66 N.Y.2d 151 (1985)—rule codified in N.Y. Dom. Rel. Law §117(2)(a)]

---

cf. **Compare:** If, instead, Pat were adopted by a natural relative (*e.g.,* an aunt), she takes a share of the remainder. The adopted child is presumptively included in a class gift made by another natural relative. [N.Y. Dom. Rel. Law §117(2)(b)]

---

(4) Nonmarital children

(a) Common law [§735]
At common law and in a handful of states today, a gift to someone's "children," "issue," and the like does *not* include nonmarital children *unless* the will shows an intent that they were to be included. [34 A.L.R.2d 4]

1) Extrinsic evidence admissible [§736]
In these states, the testator's intention to include nonmarital children can be shown by express statements or by necessary implication from words in the will. In some states, such an intent also can be shown by surrounding facts and circumstances. For example, if the child was raised as a member of a person's family, a gift to the person's "children" may be construed as including the nonmarital child. [*See, e.g.,* **In re** **Parsons's Trust**, 203 N.W.2d 40 (Wis. 1973)]

(b) Majority rule [§737]
Reflecting changing societal attitudes toward nonmarital children, by case decision or statute in most states a gift to a person's "children"

presumptively *includes* a nonmarital child. [*See, e.g.*, **Powers v. Wilkinson**, 506 N.E.2d 842 (Mass. 1987); **Will of Hoffman**, 53 A.D.2d 55 (1976)] In some states, this is the result if the child would be an heir if the person died intestate. However, a gift to a person's "lawful issue" includes legitimate offspring only, and does not include nonmarital children or descendants. [*See, e.g.*, **Traders Bank v. Goulding**, 711 S.W.2d 872 (Mo. 1986)]

(c) Original Uniform Probate Code [§738]

The original UPC adopts a rule of construction that a gift to someone's "children" presumptively *includes* the mother's nonmarital child, but the father's nonmarital child is *not* treated as the child of the *father* unless openly and notoriously so treated by the father. [Original UPC §2-611]

(d) Revised Uniform Probate Code [§739]

Under the revised UPC, a nonmarital child is treated as a child of ***both the mother and the father***, but only if the child, while a minor, lived as a regular member of the household of that parent or the parent's parent, sibling, or spouse. [UPC §2-705(b)]

CLASS GIFTS TO "CHILDREN"

IF YOU ENCOUNTER A FACT PATTERN WHERE THE TESTATOR MAKES A CLASS GIFT TO "CHILDREN," REMEMBER THE FOLLOWING:

- ☑ Grandchildren are *not included*.

- ☑ Children from *all marriages* are included.

- ☑ Adopted *children* are included (under the revised UPC, the child must have lived with the adopting parent while he was a minor).

- ☑ Adopted *adults* may or may not be included, depending on the jurisdiction.

- ☑ A child placed for adoption generally is *not included* in a class gift to the children of a member of the child's *natural* family *unless* the adoptive parent is also a member of the natural family.

- ☑ Generally, nonmarital children *are included*. (The UPC imposes limitations on whether nonmarital children are included.)

---

b. "Issue"; "descendants" [§740]

A gift to someone's issue presumptively includes lineal descendants of *any degree* (children, grandchildren, etc.). The terms "issue" and "descendants" are generally held to be synonymous.

(1) Adopted and nonmarital issue [§741]

Under the traditional view, "issue" and "descendants" were interpreted as meaning natural, legitimate issue only, thereby excluding adopted or nonmarital offspring. [*See* 86 A.L.R.2d 12] But as indicated above, by majority rule today a gift to the "issue" or "descendants" of a person presumptively includes adopted descendants [UPC §2-705; N.Y. Est. Powers & Trusts Law §1-2.10(a)], and includes nonmarital descendants if they would be intestate heirs of the person. (*See supra*, §737.)

EXAM TIP   **gilbert**

Remember that under the *majority rule*, adopted and nonmarital descendants are included as "issue" or "descendants" but that under the revised UPC they are included only if they lived as a *member of the adoptive parent's household* while they were minors.

---

(2) Per stirpes distribution [§742]

Whenever a gift is made to someone's "issue" or "descendants," in most states, the issue or descendants who are alive when the distribution is to be made (the testator's death, if an outright gift by will; death of life tenant, if a remainder interest) take per stirpes; *i.e.*, by representation (absent a contrary expression of intent). [*See, e.g.*, **First Illini Bank v. Pritchard**, 595 N.E.2d 728 (Ill. 1992); **Clarke v. Clarke**, 159 A.2d 362 (Md. 1960); **Wilkes v. Wilkes**, 488 S.W.2d 398 (Tex. 1972)] In determining whether the distribution is to be "classic per stirpes" or per capita with representation ("modern per stirpes"), the courts apply the same rule that applies under the state's intestacy statutes. (*See supra*, §§35-46.) In a *majority* of states, a *per capita with representation* distribution is made. [Original UPC §2-106]

(3) Per capita at each generation [§743]

Under the revised UPC and in a few states, a distribution to "issue" or "descendants" is made per capita at each generation. (*See supra*, §38.) [N.Y. Est. Powers & Trusts Law §2-1.2(b); UPC §2-708]

(4) Drafting suggestion [§744]

In drafting a will or trust that provides that the remainder shall pass to descendants (or issue), the instrument should provide, in *unambiguous language*, whether the distribution among descendants is to be on a classic per stirpes basis or on a per capita with representation basis.

c. "Heirs" [§745]

A gift to someone's "heirs" is interpreted as meaning those persons who would take the person's estate *if she had died intestate.* As a general rule, the courts refer to the laws of intestate succession in effect at the time of the testator's death. [*See* 65 A.L.R.2d 1408] Under this rule, a gift to a person's "heirs" presumptively includes the person's spouse. [*See, e.g.*, **Gustafson v. Svenson**, 366 N.E.2d 761 (Mass. 1977)] However, a gift to a person's "next of kin" presumptively includes only relatives by blood or adoption, and not the person's spouse. [*See, e.g.,* **First Safety Deposit National Bank v. Westgate,** 193 N.E.2d 683 (Mass. 1963)]

d. "Relatives," "next of kin," and other family terms [§746]

Other terms such as "relatives," "family," or "next of kin" are generally interpreted as being *synonymous with "heirs"*—*i.e.,* those who would take the named person's estate according to the laws of descent and distribution—unless, of course, there is a showing of contrary intent by the testator. [*See, e.g.,* Ind. Code §29-1-6-1(c); N.Y. Est. Powers & Trusts Law §2-1.1]

(1) Distinguish—"friends" [§747]

Terms such as "relatives" and the like represent the outer limit on how far a court will go in giving meaning to "class gift" terms used by a testator in a will. A gift to a person's *"friends"* is beyond the pale. It is *void* for vagueness, and the gift fails for want of clearly identified beneficiaries. Extrinsic evidence is *not* admissible to show whom the testator intended to include within the term "friends."

e. "Brothers and sisters" [§748]

By majority rule, a gift to someone's "brothers and sisters" is construed to include half brothers and half sisters as well as siblings of the whole blood, absent a contrary expression of intent.

f. "Cousins"; "nieces and nephews" [§749]

A gift to someone's "cousins" includes *first cousins only* (*i.e.,* children of aunts and uncles), absent a contrary expression of intent. The words "nieces and nephews" presumptively refer to the children of brothers and sisters. A gift to "my nieces and nephews" includes the testator's nieces and nephews, but not the nieces and nephews of his spouse.

DETERMINING WHO IS INCLUDED IN A GIFT TO A CLASS	gilbert
"CHILDREN"	Includes children from *all marriages*, *adopted children*, and *nonmarital children*. May or may not include adopted adults. Does not include grandchildren.
"ISSUE," "DESCENDANTS"	Includes descendants of *any degree*, *adopted descendants*, and *nonmarital descendants* who would be intestate heirs.
"HEIRS"	Includes all those persons who would take under *intestacy*.
"BROTHERS AND SISTERS"	Includes siblings of the *half blood*.
"COUSINS," "NIECES AND NEPHEWS"	"Cousins" includes only *first cousins*. "Nieces and nephews" includes only the *children of siblings*.
"FRIENDS"	Gift to "friends" is *void* for vagueness.

Remember that the above rules apply only if the testator's will does not provide any contrary intent. The testator can limit or expand any of the above rules by his will. For example, the testator can make a class gift to his brothers and sisters and exclude those of the half blood or he can make a class gift to his cousins and include all seconds cousins, *but the terms of the will must be specific*.

2. Constructional Problems [§750]

In addition to deciding what is meant by the terms "issue," "children," etc., the courts sometimes face problems in determining what members of the group are to be included in the class. For example, suppose Testator executes a will that devises Blackacre "to the children of my friend John." At the time the will is executed, John has two children (Ann and Bill). Between that time and Testator's death, Ann dies, and John has another child (Carol). Two years after Testator's death, John has another child (Donna). Who takes Blackacre? If the will had made a disposition "to the children of my friend John *who are living at my death*," there would be no problem in identifying the takers of the gift: Bill and Carol would take. But all too often, the will does not specify the time at which the takers of the class gift are to be determined. This section outlines the rules of construction applied by the courts *absent a contrary will provision*.

a. Death of class member after will's execution and in testator's lifetime—class gift rule [§751]

If a testamentary gift is made to a class of persons and a class member dies during the testator's lifetime, and if the will does not cover the contingency, *the class members who survive the testator* take the gift. [*See, e.g.*, **Jennings v. Newman**, 221 S.W.2d 487 (Mo. 1949); Ill. Comp. Stat. ch. 755, §5/4-11] The gift is interpreted as applying to the members of the class alive at the testator's death. [*See* 33 A.L.R.2d 242] Although this is commonly referred to as the "class gift *rule*," in most states this result is not based on any statute or rule, but instead is a rule of construction based on presumed intent.

(1) Rationale

Perhaps the best way to understand the class gift rule is to contrast it with the courts' treatment of a gift to individually named beneficiaries. Suppose, in the example above, that Testator's will devised Blackacre "to John's children, Ann, Bill, and Carol, in equal shares," and devised his residuary estate to the American Cancer Society. Each beneficiary has been given a one-third share of Blackacre. Ann predeceases Testator, and the case is not covered by the state's anti-lapse statute. The gift of Ann's one-third share lapses and falls into the residuary estate (*see supra*, §685). The American Cancer Society becomes a tenant in common with Bill and Carol. [*See, e.g.*, **Dawson v. Yucus**, 239 N.E.2d 305 (Ill. 1968)] By contrast, under the class gift rule it is presumed that the testator did not want that result to occur. Instead, Testator probably wanted *only* John's children, as a class constituted at Testator's death, *and only that group,* to share in the ownership of Blackacre.

(2) Anti-lapse statute [§752]

If the class member who predeceases the testator is within the degree of relationship covered by the state's anti-lapse statute, and if he left descendants who survived the testator, do the descendants take by substitution under the statute?

(a) Majority rule—anti-lapse statute applies [§753]

Many anti-lapse statutes expressly apply to class gifts, as long as the other elements of the statute are met. [*See, e.g.,* UPC §2-603(b)(2); Cal. Prob. Code §21110; Tex. Prob. Code §68] In states in which the anti-lapse statute does not expressly refer to class gifts, the majority of cases have held that the statute does apply to such gifts. In these states, the class gift rule ("surviving class members take") gives way to the anti-lapse statute if the predeceasing class member is within the degree of relationship covered by the statute *and* left descendants who survive the testator. [*See, e.g.,* **Stolle v. Stolle,** 66 S.W.2d 912 (Mo. 1933); **Gianoli v. Gabaccia,** 412 P.2d 439 (Nev. 1966); **Hoverstad v. First National Bank & Trust Co.,** 74 N.W.2d 48 (S.D. 1955); 56 A.L.R.2d 948]

(e.g.) Example: Jessie's will devises Blackacre "to the children of my daughter Mary." At the time the will is executed, Mary has three children: Ann, Bill, and Carl. Carl predeceases Jessie, leaving two children: Celia and Cedric. On Jessie's death, Celia and Cedric take one-sixth shares under the anti-lapse statute and are tenants in common with Ann and Bill, who take one-third each.

(cf.) Compare: If Carl did not leave any descendants who survived Jessie, the anti-lapse statute would not apply. Ann and Bill would take Blackacre under the class gift rule since they are the class members alive at Jessie's death.

(b) Minority rule [§754]

A few states take the position that the anti-lapse statute does not apply to class gifts. *Rationale:* Since under the class gift rule the surviving class members take the bequest, *there is no lapse* on which the statute can operate. [*See, e.g.,* **Campbell v. Clark,** 10 A. 702 (N.H. 1887)]

b. Death of class member before will's execution [§755]

What happens if a testator bequeaths property to a class and one of the class members is already deceased when the will is executed? For example, suppose Louis executes a will that bequeaths property "to my brothers and sisters." Louis has two living brothers and two sisters at the time the will is executed, but another brother has already died, leaving two children. If "brothers and sisters" are within the scope of the jurisdiction's anti-lapse statute, does the anti-lapse statute operate in favor of the predeceased brother's two children? Only about one-half of the states' anti-lapse statutes explicitly address this issue.

(1) Majority and Uniform Probate Code rule [§756]

In the majority of states that address the issue, the anti-lapse statute *applies* to a class member whether his death occurred before or after execution of the will. [*See, e.g.,* UPC §2-603(a)(4); Del. Code tit. 12, §2313(a)(2)] "[T]hough contrary to some decisions, [it] seems likely that the testator would want the issue of a person included, [for example,] in a class term but dead when the will is made to be treated like the issue of another member of the class who was alive at the time the will was executed but who died before the testator." [Originial UPC §2-605, Comment; *and see* Mass. Gen. Laws ch. 191]

(2) Minority rule [§757]

In a minority of states, the anti-lapse statute does *not* apply in this situation. [*See, e.g.,* Md. Est. & Trusts Code §4-403; N.Y. Est. Powers & Trusts Law §3-3.3; Or. Rev. Stat. §112.395; Tex. Prob. Code §68] *Rationale:* It is more logical to assume that the testator intended to benefit only his living brothers and sisters, and did not intend to confer a benefit on a deceased brother *or the brother's descendants*. [*See, e.g.,* **Drafts v. Drafts,** 114 So. 2d 473 (Fla. 1959)]

c. Closing the class—the rule of convenience [§758]

In determining the "membership" of the class (*i.e.,* the maximum number of takers to share in the class gift), the common law courts devised the "rule of convenience," a rule of construction that applies absent contrary provision in the will. Under the rule, the class closes (which simply means that later-born class members are excluded from sharing the gift) *when a class member is entitled to a distribution* of his share of the gift. [*See* 6 A.L.R.2d 1342] The class closes at that time so that the minimum size of each class member's share can be determined, permitting a distribution that will not be subject to recall in the future.

(1) Outright gift by will [§759]

If a will makes an outright gift to a class, *the class closes on the testator's death* if any member of the class is alive at that time.

(a) Rationale

This result is based on the presumed intent of the ordinary testator.

Since this was a gift to a class and not to named individuals, the testator probably intended to include all members who fit the description, whenever born, *as long as this would not cause any undue inconvenience.* The rule of convenience closes the class at the testator's death because the testator would probably want as early a distribution as possible, so that the beneficiaries can begin enjoying the property. Any alternative solutions (*e.g.,* leaving the estate administration open to provide for future members of the class; making a full distribution but requiring the distributees to return a portion if more class members come into existence) are deemed to be *inconvenient,* and disruptive of property ownership and enjoyment. Unless the class is closed at the testator's death, final determination of ownership will be delayed, possibly for a very long time.

---

e.g. Example: Demi executes a will that devises her farm "to the children of my friend Alex." At the time the will is executed, Alex has two children (Marie and Josh). Between the time of the will's execution and Demi's death, Marie dies, and Alex has another child (Sasha). Five years after Demi's death, Alex has another child (Dimitri). Who is included in the class? Josh and Sasha are included because they fit the description ("the children of my friend Alex"), and *no inconvenience results* from including Sasha even though she was born after the will's execution. However, Dimitri was born *after* Demi's death and he loses out. The class closes on Demi's death so that Josh and Sasha can begin enjoying the property. It would be inconvenient to hold the class open (or make a partial distribution, etc.) to cover the possibility that Alex may have more children in the future. The courts apply the rule of convenience to close the class to avoid this problem of waiting to distribute the property until the class is biologically closed at Alex's death—the only time one can be sure that he will not have any more children. (Note what happens to Marie's share of the class gift. Since she died *after the will's execution,* the class gift rule applies, and her share goes to Josh and Sasha. The anti-lapse statute *will not save the gift for her descendants* because she was not related to Demi.)

(b) **Children in gestation included [§760]**

If children who are in gestation *at the time for closing the class* are later born alive, they are treated as being alive at the time the class closed. (*See supra,* §§89-91.) Thus, in the example above, if Dimitri had been born within 280 days after Demi's death, he presumptively would have been included in the class.

(c) Exception—no class members when will executed or testator died [§761]

If there are no class members in existence when the will is executed or on the testator's death, all class members, *whenever born,* are included in the class regardless of any inconvenience that may arise. *Rationale:* The testator knew that there was the possibility that no class members would be alive at her death and must have contemplated that distribution and enjoyment might be postponed beyond her death.

(2) Postponed gifts [§762]

The rule of convenience applies to postponed gifts—*i.e.,* gifts that take effect some time after the testator's death. The class closes at the time *some member is entitled to a distribution.*

---

e.g. **Example:** Scarlett's will creates a trust, to pay income for life to her husband, Rhett, and on his death to distribute the corpus of the trust "to the children of my sister Suellen." At the time Scarlett executes her will, Suellen has two children, Ashley and Belle. After Scarlett's death but during Rhett's lifetime, Suellen has another child, Charles. Two years after Rhett's death, Suellen has a fourth child, Gerald. Under the rule of convenience, the class closes at Rhett's death, when his life estate comes to an end and at least one class member is entitled to a distribution. At that time the class membership is determined: Ashley, Belle, and Charles are each entitled to a one-third share of the trust corpus. Gerald, who was born after the time set for distribution (Rhett's death), is not entitled to a share. *Note:* There is no need to close the class at Scarlett's death because the class gift is not to be distributed at that time. There is no inconvenience in leaving the class open until Rhett's life estate ends. But when it ends, it is time to make a distribution and the class closes at that time.

---

(3) Per capita gifts [§763]

The rule of convenience may apply to per capita gifts. For example, suppose that Scarlett's will makes legacies of $10,000 "to each of my sister Suellen's children," and devises her residuary estate to her husband. This is *not a class gift,* because the size of each beneficiary's gift will not fluctuate and is not determined by the number of children that Suellen has. However, *the identity of the beneficiaries is determined by reference to a class.* The problem is a different one: How many gifts of $10,000 are to be made? The size of the residuary estate cannot be determined, and the residuary gift cannot be distributed, until the number of legacies is known. If the class were to remain open after Scarlett's death, distribution of the residuary estate would be postponed until Suellen died, for

RULES OF CONSTRUCTION FOR CLASS GIFTS		gilbert
RULE	**PURPOSE**	**PROVISIONS**
CLASS GIFT RULE	Who takes?	If gift is to a class and a member *dies during testator's lifetime*, the surviving class members take the gift. *Exceptions:* When *will provides otherwise* or the *anti-lapse statute* applies to save gift for deceased class member's descendants.
RULE OF CONVENIENCE	When does class close and what is each member's share?	Class closes when *a member is entitled to a distribution*: • At testator's death if an outright gift and class member(s) alive or in gestation. (If no member alive when will executed or at testator's death, class remains open until *all members* born.) • At the time the gift is to take effect if a postponed gift (*e.g.,* after a life estate). *Exception:* When *will provides otherwise*.

she could have or adopt children until her death. Hence, courts prefer a rule of construction that immediately determines the number of class members.

EXAM TIP　　　　　　　　　　　　　　　　　　　　　**gilbert**

Don't be confused. Class gifts and per capita gifts are *not* synonymous. A *class gift* is a gift to be shared by a class of individuals; *the size* of each class member's gift *is contingent on the number of members in the class*. However, a *per capita gift* is a specified gift to each member of a group; *i.e.*, each individual receives that particular gift *regardless of the number of members in the group*. The rules of construction for class gifts are useful in this instance to determine *when distribution should be made*, though it does not affect the size of each individual's gift.

(a) Living beneficiaries [§764]

If any beneficiaries are *alive* (or in gestation) at the time of the testator's death, the class closes at that time. Those beneficiaries take the legacies. After-born beneficiaries are *excluded*.

(b) No living beneficiaries [§765]

If there are no beneficiaries alive or in gestation at the testator's death, the *gift fails* (only one case has considered this question). This is again based on the supposed inconvenience of postponing determination of the class membership. The principle of prompt distribution controls, and the per capita gift fails, in order to facilitate the administration and distribution of the testator's estate. [*See* **Rogers v. Mutch**, 10 Ch. Div. 25 (1878)]

(c) Distinguish—contrary intent in will [§766]

If the testator's will indicates that all beneficiaries, "whether alive at my death or born thereafter," shall have $10,000 legacies, then the executor must set aside enough money to meet such legacies; the gift does not fail.

EXAM TIP　　　　　　　　　　　　　　　　　　　　　**gilbert**

Keep in mind that these rules—the "class gift rule" and the "rule of convenience"—are rules of construction based on presumed intent, *not rules of law*. The constructional rules *apply only in the absence of a clear expression of intent*.

C. Classification of Testamentary Gifts

1. Importance of Classification [§767]

There are four categories of testamentary gifts: *specific, demonstrative, general,* and *residuary*. How a particular gift is classified is sometimes important because classification *establishes the order of distribution and abatement* if the estate's assets are insufficient to satisfy all of the testamentary gifts after payment of administration expenses and creditors' claims. (*See infra*, §§1070-1078.) Classification also determines whether or not a testamentary gift is *satisfied* by a lifetime gift (*see supra*, §§134-142), or *adeemed* if it is no longer in the testator's estate at her death (*see infra*, §§772-802).

2. Specific Devise or Bequest [§768]

A specific devise or bequest is a gift of a *particular item* of property that is capable of being *identified and distinguished* from all other property in the testator's estate. A specific devise or bequest can be satisfied only by distribution of the specific asset. [*See, e.g.*, **Moffatt v. Heon**, 136 N.E. 123 (Mass. 1922)]

Examples: A gift of "Blackacre," "my Rolex watch," "my household furnishings," and "all of my land in Tarrant County" are all specific gifts because they describe particular property. [*See, e.g.*, **Haslam v. Alvarez**, 38 A.2d 158 (R.I. 1944)] A gift of "the balance in my bank account at First Federal Bank" is specific because, although the amount is unspecified, the gift is nevertheless identifiable and definite, apart from all other funds or property in the testator's estate. [*See, e.g.*, **Willis v. Barrow**, 119 So. 786 (Ala. 1929)]

---

a. Comment

Traditionally, the term "devise" has been used to describe testamentary gifts of real property, and "bequest" has been used in making gifts of personal property. However, there has never been a requirement that these terms be so limited. "I give," "I devise," and "I bequeath" all mean the same thing and can be used for testamentary gifts of either real or personal property.

3. Demonstrative Legacy [§769]

A demonstrative legacy is a gift of a *general amount* to be paid *from a specific source or a particular fund*—*e.g.,* "I bequeath $10,000 to my niece Nellie, to be paid out of proceeds from the sale of my Acme stock." [*See, e.g.*, **Shamberger v. Dessel**, 215 A.2d 177 (Md. 1965)]

a. Comment

A demonstrative legacy is, in a sense, a hybrid. It is treated the same as a specific bequest to the extent that the fund or property from which it is to be satisfied is on hand at the testator's death. And yet it is treated the same as a general legacy (*see* below) to the extent that it must be satisfied from the general assets of the estate. A demonstrative legacy has the advantage of a specific bequest for purposes of determining its priority in the order of abatement, but receives the benefit of being treated as a general bequest for purposes of ademption (*see* below).

4. **General Legacy [§770]**

A general legacy is a gift that is *payable out of the general assets* of the estate and does not require delivery of any specific asset or satisfaction from any designated portion of the testator's property—*e.g.*, "I bequeath the sum of $10,000 to my nephew Norbert."

5. **Residuary Estate [§771]**

The residuary estate consists of the **balance** of the testator's property on hand *after* payment of administration expenses, taxes, and claims against the estate, *and after* satisfaction of all specific, general, and demonstrative bequests—*e.g.*, "I give, devise, and bequeath all of the rest, residue, and remainder of my estate to my brother Bob."

CLASSIFYING TESTAMENTARY GIFTS		gilbert
TYPE OF GIFT	**DEFINITION**	**EXAMPLE**
SPECIFIC	A gift of a *particular and identifiable item* in the testator's estate.	"I give my car . . ." "I give my lot at 13 Mulberry Lane"
DEMONSTRATIVE	A *monetary gift* to be paid *from a specific source*.	"I give $5,000 from the sale of my home . . ."
GENERAL	A *monetary gift* to be paid *from the general assets* of the testator's estate. (Compare this to a demonstrative gift, above, where the gift is satisfied not from the general estate assets but from a particular source.)	"I give $5,000 to . . ."
RESIDUARY	A gift of the *remainder* of the testator's estate that has not been devised to others and that is not needed to satisfy claims and expenses.	"I give the rest, residue, and remainder of my estate . . ."

D. Ademption

1. **General Rule [§772]**

If specifically devised property is not in the testator's estate at the time of her death, the gift is *adeemed; i.e.,* it fails. [*See* 61 A.L.R.2d 449] Ademption applies because the property that was to have satisfied the bequest is not in the estate, and a testator cannot make a gift of property she does not own. This is sometimes

gilbert

Is **specific bequest** property in the estate **at the testator's death**?

YES →

↓ **NO**

Can the specific bequest be **construed as**:

- A **general** legacy (especially stock);

- Property **owned at death** rather than property owned at time will was made;

- A **slight change in form** of property; or

- A gift of **sale proceeds**?

YES →

↓ **NO**

Did the testator have an **opportunity to change her will** in light of the property's loss or sale?

NO → **No ademption**

↓ **YES**

Does any **statutory exception** to ademption apply? Check for:

- **Casualty insurance proceeds** paid **after** testator's death;

- **Condemnation award** paid **after** testator's death;

- Property subject to an **executory or installment contract**;

- **Change in stocks and bonds** as a result of merger, consolidation, etc.; or

- Property under **guardianship**.

YES →

↓ **NO**

Property is **adeemed**.

referred to as the doctrine of *ademption by extinction,* to distinguish it from ademption by satisfaction (*see supra,* §§134 *et seq.*).

a. Gifts affected [§773]

The doctrine of ademption applies *only* to *specific devises and bequests.* Ademption does *not* apply to demonstrative or general legacies.

---

e.g. **Example:** Carly's will bequeaths "my two-carat diamond ring to Alan," and "$5,000, to be paid out of the proceeds of sale of my Acme stock, to Betty." Thereafter, Carly's diamond ring is stolen; and she sells all of her Acme stock to finance a vacation trip. Neither of these assets is in Carly's estate at her death. The gift of the diamond ring is a specific bequest. Ademption applies and Alan takes nothing. However, the gift of "$5,000, to be paid out of the proceeds of the sale of my Acme stock" is a demonstrative legacy. Ademption does not apply to demonstrative legacies. [*See, e.g., In re* **Estate of Lung,** 692 A.2d 1349 (D.C. 1997); *In re* **Will of Young,** 137 Misc. 2d 744 (1987)] Betty is entitled to $5,000. Other assets must be sold, if necessary, to raise the $5,000 to be distributed to Betty.

EXAM TIP **gilbert**

Many ademption questions present specific and demonstrative gifts. Because specific gifts adeem but demonstrative gifts do not, you must be able to distinguish between the two types of gifts. How do you keep the gifts straight? Remember that a *"specific"* devise or bequest is a gift of a **specific item of property**, and once that item is gone there is nothing for the beneficiary to take. A demonstrative legacy is a **monetary gift** (rather than an item of property) but the testator **demonstrates (shows) where she wants the money to come from**. However, she isn't insisting on that source of funds and so if it is gone, the gift does not adeem, but rather it can be paid from the general assets of the estate. (See *also infra,* §§784 *et seq.*)

b. Partial ademption [§774]

Ademption need not be of the entire gift; it applies pro tanto where only a *portion* of the gift has been disposed of. [*See, e.g.,* N.Y. Est. Powers & Trusts Law §3-4.3] If, for example, the testator executes a will that devises a large tract of land and then sells a portion of the tract, ademption applies to the portion of property not in the estate at her death. The remaining portion passes to the specific beneficiary.

c. Distinguish—post-death changes [§775]

The doctrine of ademption applies only to changes in specifically devised property occurring *before* the testator's death. Hence, acts done by an executor that affect specifically bequeathed property after the testator's death are not subject to the ademption doctrine; the devisee is entitled to compensation for the loss or sale of the property.

Sometimes in an exam question, property subject to a specific bequest is sold or destroyed and the person who was to receive the property under the will claims that he is entitled to the sale proceeds or insurance money. To decide this issue, you need to determine **when** the sale or destruction of the property occurred. If it occurred before death, so that the property was **not in the estate at the testator's death**, ademption applies and the will beneficiary is out of luck. (The testator can't give what she doesn't have and she had no obligation to keep the property for the beneficiary's benefit.) However, if the property **was in the estate at her death** and was sold **by the executor** or lost or destroyed **while the estate was being administered**, the will beneficiary will be entitled to the value of the property.

d. Will substitutes [§776]

The ademption doctrine has been applied to will substitutes, such as trusts.

Example: The settlor creates a revocable trust under which, on the settlor's death, a parcel of real estate is to be distributed to a beneficiary. If the settlor sells the property during her lifetime, the gift adeems. [*See, e.g.,* **Wasserman v. Cohen,** 606 N.E.2d 901 (Mass. 1993)]

Remember these basic points when answering an ademption question:

- Only **specific** gifts can be adeemed.

- Ademption can be **partial**.

- Ademption applies only to property that is not in the estate **at** the testator's death.

- Ademption applies to **will substitutes**—such as trusts.

2. Role of Testator's Intent—Majority View [§777]

At common law and in many states today, application of the ademption doctrine involves an **objective test**; the doctrine applies without regard to the testator's probable intent. This is sometimes referred to as the "**identity**" (or "in specie") **theory**: The only issue is whether the specifically bequeathed property can be identified as being in the testator's estate at his death. [*See, e.g.,* **Ashburner v. McGuire,** 29 Eng. Rep. 62 (1786)—oft-cited case; **BayBank Harvard Trust Co. v. Grant,** 504 N.E.2d 1072 (Mass. 1987)] Thus, it does not matter whether the property is not in the estate due to an act of the testator (*e.g.,* sale of the property), an act of God (*e.g.,* tornado), or an act of a third person (*e.g.,* withdrawal of funds in a bank account pursuant to a power of attorney). [*See* **McGee v. McGee,** 413 A.2d 72 (R.I. 1980)] If the specifically bequeathed asset is not in the estate *for any reason,* the gift is adeemed. [*See* **In re Kamba's Estate,** 282 N.W. 570 (Wis. 1938)]

a. Illustrations

(1) Similar asset [§778]

Chauncey's will bequeaths "my Rolex watch to my friend Nigel." After the will's execution, Chauncey sells the Rolex watch and uses the exact amount of the sale proceeds to purchase a Cartier watch. Ademption applies because the testamentary gift was of a Rolex watch, *not some other watch*. If the subject matter of a specific bequest or devise is sold by the testator, the gift is adeemed, and neither the proceeds nor similar items purchased with the proceeds go to the beneficiary.

(2) Executory contract [§779]

Wallace's will devises Blackacre to Edna. Thereafter, Wallace enters into a specifically enforceable contract to sell Blackacre to Roy. The contract is still executory at Wallace's death. Under the doctrine of *equitable conversion* (*see* Property Summary), the purchaser (Roy) is deemed to own Blackacre from the moment the contract becomes specifically enforceable, and the vendor (Wallace) is deemed to own only personal property (a "chose in action")—a right to compel payment of the remaining sale proceeds. Thus, Wallace no longer owned Blackacre at his death, and the gift to Edna is adeemed. Edna is not entitled to Blackacre nor the remaining proceeds of sale under the contract. [*See In re* **Hills's Estate**, 564 P.2d 462 (Kan. 1977)]

(a) Distinguish—gift of an "interest" [§780]

If, in the above example, Wallace's will did not devise "Blackacre," but instead devised "*all of my interest* in Blackacre," ademption would *not apply*. Notwithstanding the doctrine of equitable conversion, Wallace did have at death an *interest* in Blackacre—*i.e.*, the right to the remaining contract payments secured by a vendor's lien. Edna would be entitled to the remaining contract payments and the security interest. [*See, e.g.*, **Robinson v. Lee**, 136 S.E.2d 860 (Va. 1964)]

(b) Comment

Moreover, if specific performance would not be available at Wallace's death because some material condition to the contract's performance had not been satisfied (*see* Property Summary), equitable conversion would not apply. Wallace's interest in Blackacre (the right to the remaining contract payments and any security interest) would pass to Edna.

(3) Casualty insurance proceeds [§781]

Claire's will bequeaths her diamond ring to Helen. The ring is stolen shortly before Claire's death, and $4,920 is paid to Claire's executor under an insurance policy that covered the theft. Helen is not entitled to the ring because it was not owned by Claire at her death. Helen is not entitled to the insurance proceeds because the will did not give her insurance proceeds. The gift to Helen is adeemed. [*See In re* **Barry's Estate**, 252 P.2d 437 (Okla. 1952); 35 A.L.R.2d 1056]

(4) Condemnation proceedings [§782]

Margaret's will devises her Oliver Strect property to Lizzie. Before Margaret's death, the property is taken by the state in eminent domain proceedings, but the condemnation award is paid to Margaret's executor after her death. The gift is *adeemed,* even though it is arguable that because Margaret's loss of ownership was from an act beyond her control, she would have wanted Lizzie to take the condemnation award. [*See* **Ametrano v. Downs**, 170 N.Y. 388 (1902)]

b. Comment on majority view [§783]

The identity theory has been criticized for failing to take into account the probable intent of the testator, especially in cases in which the property is not in the estate because of something other than a volitional act of the testator. However, the objective approach has the advantage of simplicity of application and predictability of result, and it eliminates speculation as to what the testator's actual intent may have been. To permit extrinsic evidence as to the testator's probable intent would result in property passing on the basis of oral testimony rather than pursuant to the writing contained in the testator's duly executed will. [*See* **McGee v. McGee**, *supra,* §777]

3. Avoiding Ademption—Case Decisions [§784]

Although the courts in many states declare that the testator's intention is immaterial, various techniques have been developed by the courts to avoid the ademption doctrine's application.

a. Construction as general legacy [§785]

Some courts will classify a bequest as general rather than specific wherever possible to avoid ademption. This constructional approach is encountered most frequently with respect to bequests of *shares of stock*, where use of the word "my" in a gift may make the gift specific and the absence of the word "my" makes it general.

Example: Maury's will bequeaths "my 200 shares of Baker stock" to Billie and "100 shares of Centex stock" to Cindy. Thereafter, Maury sells all of his Baker and Centex stock. Because the gift of Baker stock was a specific bequest ("*my* 200 shares"), ademption applies, and Billie takes nothing. However, most courts reach a different result with respect to the Centex stock. The courts seize on the absence of the possessive pronoun "my," and hold that this was not a specific gift of stock for ademption purposes. Rather, it was a general legacy of the *value* of 100 shares of Centex stock. This result is reached even if Maury owned exactly 100 shares of Centex stock at the time he wrote the will. Because ademption does not apply to general legacies, Cindy is entitled to the date-of-death value of 100 shares of Centex stock. [*See, e.g., In re* **McFerren's Estate,** *76 A.2d 759 (Pa. 1950); In re* **Blomdahl's Will,** 258 N.W. 168 (Wis. 1935)] The only way to explain this result is that courts are looking for a way to avoid ademption in cases such as this.

cf. **Compare:** Suppose, however, that Maury did not sell the Centex stock and, thereafter, the Centex stock *split* two-for-one. The gift of "100 shares of Centex stock" would be treated as a specific bequest for purposes of determining whether the beneficiary is entitled to the stock split (*see infra,* §§803 *et seq.*).

EXAM TIP | **gilbert**

In an *ademption* question, when you see a bequest of stock, always look closely at the wording of the bequest because the presence or absence of the little word "my" can make a big difference. Remember:

"My" → *specific* bequest → ademption → beneficiary doesn't get the stock or its value

No "my" → *general* bequest → no ademption → beneficiary gets value of stock

---

(1) Minority rule [§786]

Some courts draw a distinction between publicly traded stock and stock in a closely held corporation. A bequest of stock in a company whose securities are regularly traded ("I bequeath 200 shares of Kodak stock") is classified as a general legacy and is not subject to ademption. [*See In re* **Fitch's Will,** 281 A.D. 65 (1952)] However, a bequest of closely held stock ("I bequeath 200 shares of FamilyCo stock") is a specific bequest that is subject to ademption. [*See In re* **Security Trust Co.,** 221 N.Y. 213 (1917)]

b. **Construction as referring to property owned at death [§787]**

Even if the language of the gift cannot be classified as general, it may be construed as referring to an asset in the estate at death rather than an asset owned at the time the will was executed.

---

e.g. **Example:** Juanita's will devises "my residence in Seattle" to Carlos. Normally, such a gift would be construed to refer to the residence owned by Juanita at the time of the will's execution. Under this construction, if Juanita later replaced that residence with another house in Seattle, Carlos would take nothing. However, to prevent ademption, the court may construe the gift as applicable to the residence owned by Juanita *at death*. [*See, e.g.,* **Milton v. Milton,** 10 So. 2d 175 (Miss. 1942); *In re* **Lusk's Estate,** 9 A.2d 363 (Pa. 1939)]

Example: Some courts have gone so far as to hold that a gift of "that certain Buick automobile *now owned by me*" is not adeemed if the testator thereafter trades that car for a new Buick which she owned at death.

Example: Helen's will bequeaths "my shares of XYZ Mutual Fund" to Beverly. Beverly takes all 1,500 shares of the mutual fund Helen owned at death, even though she owned only 900 shares when she wrote her will and purchased 600 additional shares thereafter. [*See* **Estate of Russell,** 521 A.2d 677 (Me. 1987)]

c. Construction as change in form [§788]

Ademption does not apply if there is only a *slight* change in the form or name of the asset. Of course, there may be a problem in determining what constitutes a change in form, as distinguished from a change of substance. Changes in the name of a corporation or partnership are ordinarily considered purely formal changes, which do *not* result in ademption. Similarly, most courts have held that a gift of "my bank account at Travis Bank" is not adeemed by transfer of the account to another bank—the gift is of the *funds*, wherever located. [*See, e.g.,* **Willis v. Barrow,** *supra*, §768; *In re* **Hall's Estate,** 160 A.2d 49 (N.J. 1960); *but see In re* **Rubinstein's Estate,** 169 Misc. 273 (1938)—*contra*]

(1) Incorporation of business [§789]

If a will bequeaths the testator's interest in a partnership and thereafter the business is incorporated, *no ademption* occurs because the change is one of form and not of substance. Thus, the beneficiary takes all of the testator's interest (now shares of stock) in the business. [**Will of Block,** 91 Misc. 2d 92 (1977)]

(2) Merger; takeover [§790]

A merger, takeover, or consolidation may result in only a slight change in form and no ademption occurs.

Example: Oliver's will bequeaths "my 18 shares of Farmers' Bank stock" to Selma. Farmers' Bank later merges with Deposit Bank to form Farmers' Deposit Bank, leaving Oliver with 18 shares of Farmers' Deposit Bank stock at death. Most courts hold that Selma takes the 18 shares of stock since the change is purely formal. [*See, e.g., In re* **Will of Strauss,** 137 Misc. 2d 686 (1987); **Stenkamp v. Stenkamp,** 723 P.2d 336 (Or. 1986); UPC §2-606(a)(5)] "The likeness of the new shares to the old is more important than their differences." [**Goode v. Reynolds,** 271 S.W. 600 (Ky. 1925)]

d. Gifts of sale proceeds [§791]

If the will directs that an item of property be sold and the *proceeds* given to a specific beneficiary, the beneficiary may be entitled to the proceeds even if the testator sells the property *before* his death.

---

e.g. **Example:** Marlene's will directs the executor to sell Blackacre and distribute the sale proceeds to Brian. Thereafter Marlene enters into an installment contract for the sale of Blackacre. The gift is adeemed as to the installments received by Marlene during her lifetime. However, Brian is entitled to the *balance remaining payable after Marlene's death*. Rationale: Since the testamentary gift was not of Blackacre but of the sale proceeds, Brian should receive the sale proceeds whether the sale was made by Marlene during her lifetime or by the executor after Marlene's death. [*See* 45 A.L.R.3d 10]

---

e. Testator did not have opportunity to change will [§792]

The courts in an increasing number of states have tempered the ademption doctrine by requiring some act of the testator from which it can be *inferred that she wanted the gift to be adeemed*. In these states, ademption is not applied if the testator did not have the opportunity to change her will.

---

e.g. **Example:** Tisha's will bequeaths her car to Lionel. Tisha later dies in an accident in which the car is demolished. Lionel takes the casualty insurance proceeds resulting from the car's destruction. [*See, e.g., In re* **Wolfe's Estate**, 208 N.W.2d 923 (Iowa 1973)] The same result has been reached in cases where a specifically devised house was destroyed by fire. [*See, e.g., In re* **Estate of Kolbinger**, 529 N.E.2d 823 (Ill. 1988); **White v. White**, 251 A.2d 470 (N.J. 1969)]

---

4. Statutory Modifications [§793]

The UPC and statutes in a number of states have ameliorated operation of the common law rule of ademption in certain well-defined situations.

a. Casualty insurance proceeds [§794]

By statute in several states, if casualty insurance proceeds for the loss, theft, or destruction of specifically bequeathed property are paid *after* the testator's death, the beneficiary is entitled to the insurance proceeds. [*See, e.g.,* UPC §2-606(a)(3); Fla. Prob. Code §732.606; N.Y. Est. Powers & Trusts Law §3-4.5]

b. Condemnation award [§795]

In several states, statutes provide that if specifically devised property is taken by eminent domain before the testator's death and the condemnation award is paid *after* his death, the specific beneficiary is entitled to the condemnation award. [*See* UPC §2-606(a)(2)]

c. **Executory contract [§796]**

Several states have statutes that overturn the common law ademption rule where specifically devised property is subject to an executory contract or installment contract at the testator's death. (*See supra*, §779.) Under these statutes, the beneficiary is entitled to all of the testator's rights under the contract—the *remaining* contract payments and any security interest retained by the testator-vendor. [UPC §2-606(a)(1); N.Y. Est. Powers & Trusts Law §3-4.4]

d. **Distinguish—payments *before* death [§797]**

The statutory rules above relating to the payment of sale proceeds, condemnation awards, and insurance proceeds on specifically devised property operate *only* to the extent that the proceeds are paid *after* the testator's death. If the contract is fully performed during the testator's lifetime, or if the insurance proceeds or condemnation award are paid to the testator *during his lifetime*, the statutes have no application. Ademption applies and the specific beneficiary takes nothing. [*See, e.g.*, N.Y. Est. Powers & Trusts Law §3-4.3] *Rationale:* The testator presumably had the opportunity to amend or revise his will to reflect the loss, sale, or taking of the property, but did not do so.

e. **Distinguish—property destroyed or damaged *after* testator's death [§798]**

If specifically bequeathed property is destroyed or damaged *after* the testator's death, all courts hold that the beneficiary is entitled to any insurance proceeds on the property. The specific beneficiary is deemed to own the property from the moment of the testator's death, subject to probate of the will and subject to the executor's right of possession during the estate administration period. [*See In re* **Gehring's Will**, 202 N.Y.S.2d 922 (1960)]

f. **Changes in securities [§799]**

Under the UPC and by statute in a number of states, if a will makes a specific bequest of securities (*i.e.*, stocks and bonds), the beneficiary is entitled to any additional securities owned by the testator as the result of (i) an *action by the organization*; (ii) *merger, consolidation, reorganization, or other distribution*; and (iii) plan of *reinvestment*. [UPC §2-605(a)(2)]

g. **Property under guardianship [§800]**

Under the UPC and in several non-UPC states, if a person executes a will and later becomes incapacitated, and if specifically devised property is sold by the guardian or conservator, or a condemnation award or insurance proceeds are paid to the guardian or conservator, the devisee is entitled to a *general pecuniary legacy* equal to the net sale price, condemnation award, or insurance proceeds. [*See* Fla. Prob. Code §732.606] Several states have extended this rule to include sales by an agent acting under a durable power of attorney. [*See, e.g.*, UPC §2-606(b); Va. Code §64.1-62.3(B)]

(1) **Rationale**

To hold otherwise would allow the guardian or conservator to effectively change the testator's will by deciding which assets to sell. Also, the testator did not have the capacity to change his will in light of the fact that the property had been sold. [*See, e.g.,* **Lewis v. Hill**, 56 N.E.2d 619 (Ill. 1944)]

(2) Partial ademption of proceeds [§801]

Other statutes give a narrower remedy in this situation. The specific beneficiary is entitled to the sale proceeds, condemnation award, or insurance proceeds, ***but only*** to the extent that the, *e.g.*, sale proceeds can be traced and are on hand at the testator's death. [*See* N.Y. Est. Powers & Trusts Law §3-4.6] Under this type of statute, the gift is adeemed to the extent that the sale proceeds have been expended by the guardian for the ward's care. The courts of several states have reached this result without the aid of a statute. [*See, e.g.,* **Walsh v. Gillespie**, 154 N.E.2d 906 (Mass. 1959); 84 A.L.R.4th 462]

EXAM TIP	**gilbert**

Remember the common statutory exceptions to the ademption doctrine:

- If the property is, *e.g.,* lost or destroyed, the beneficiary receives the ***insurance proceeds*** paid after the testator's death.

- If the property is taken by eminent domain, the beneficiary receives the ***condemnation award*** paid after the testator's death.

- If the property is subject to an ***executory or installment contract***, the beneficiary receives all of the testator's rights under the contract.

- If a specific gift of securities is affected by, *e.g., **merger or consolidation***, the beneficiary is entitled to the additional securities owned by the testator.

- If a guardian or conservator (or someone acting under a durable power of attorney) sells specifically bequeathed property or receives insurance proceeds or a condemnation award for the property, the beneficiary is entitled to a ***general pecuniary legacy*** equal to the sale price, insurance proceeds, or condemnation award.

---

5. Satisfaction of Legacies [§802]

If, after executing a will, the testator makes a gift to a person who is a legatee under the will, the gift may be held to have been in partial or total satisfaction of the legacy—***provided*** that the testator intended that result. (*See supra,* §§134 *et seq.*)

EXAM TIP	**gilbert**

In general, the doctrine of satisfaction of legacies applies only to ***general legacies***. It does not apply to specific devises and bequests. For example, Leo's will bequeaths "my 10-speed Schwinn bike" to Ben, and thereafter Leo gives the bicycle to Ben. This case does ***not*** involve the doctrine of satisfaction of legacies but, instead, results in ***ademption by extinction*** since the bicycle (a specific devise) will not be in Leo's estate at his death.

E. Stock Splits and Stock Dividends

1. Introduction [§803]

Suppose that a will makes a specific bequest to Ben of "my 100 shares of Telecom stock." After the will's execution but *before the testator's death*, the stock splits two-for-one; or, alternatively, the corporation declares and pays a 10% stock dividend. Is Ben entitled to the additional shares produced by the stock split or stock dividend?

2. Stock Splits [§804]

It is generally held that the specific beneficiary is entitled to the additional shares of stock produced by a stock split. [*See, e.g.*, **Rosenfeld v. Frank**, 546 A.2d 236 (Conn. 1988); **Bostwick v. Hurstel**, 304 N.E.2d 186 (Mass. 1973); **Shriners Hospital for Crippled Children v. Coltrane**, 465 So. 2d 1073 (Miss. 1985); *In re* **Rees's Estate**, 311 P.2d 438 (Or. 1957)] Thus, if the Telecom stock splits two-for-one, Ben is entitled to all 200 shares of Telecom stock.

a. Rationale

The 200 shares of stock on hand after the stock split represent the same proportionate share of corporate ownership as the 100 shares before the split.

b. What constitutes a specific bequest of stock [§805]

Suppose that the will did not make a gift of "*my* 100 shares of Telecom stock" but instead made a gift of "100 shares of Telecom stock" (*i.e.*, without the possessive pronoun "my"). As has been pointed out, if the issue is ademption, many courts have held that this is a general legacy of the *value* of 100 shares of Telecom stock. Thus, the beneficiary is entitled to the date-of-death value of 100 shares even though the testator owns no Telecom stock at his death. (*See supra*, §785.) If, however, the testator does not sell the Telecom stock, and it splits two-for-one, many courts hold that the bequest of "100 shares of Telecom stock" is a *specific bequest*, meaning that the beneficiary is entitled to the additional 100 shares produced by the split. [*See, e.g.*, **Bostwick v. Hurstel**, *supra*; **Egavian v. Egavian**, 232 A.2d 789 (R.I. 1967); **O'Neill v. Alford**, 485 S.W.2d 935 (Tex. 1972); **Watson v. Santalucia**, 427 S.E.2d 466 (W. Va. 1993)] Thus, a bequest of stock can be classified as a *specific bequest* for one purpose *and as a general legacy* for another purpose.

3. Stock Dividends [§806]

If the will makes a bequest of "my 100 shares of Telecom stock," and thereafter Telecom declares and pays a 10% stock dividend, by majority rule the beneficiary is *not entitled* to the additional 10 shares of stock produced by the dividend.

a. Rationale

Stock dividends are paid out of the earned surplus of the corporation just the same as cash dividends. They should be treated as *income* on the original capital, rather than as part of the original capital. Thus, stock dividends paid during the testator's lifetime should be *treated the same as cash dividends*, and of course the beneficiary is not entitled to cash dividends paid to the testator during her lifetime. [*See, e.g.,* **Hicks v. Kerr,** 104 A. 426 (Md. 1918)]

EXAM TIP **gilbert**

Although in ademption cases the word "my" was important, note that "my" is *irrelevant in terms of stock splits and stock dividends*. Rather, the thing to focus on is that *stock dividends* are treated like *cash dividends* (as income), and just as a will beneficiary can't claim cash dividends paid during the testator's life, he cannot claim the stock dividends either. In a *stock split*, the shares themselves are split and the specific beneficiary gets all the shares—the original shares and the additional ones due to the split.

---

b. Minority view [§807]

Some courts take the position that the value of the original shares is diminished as much by the issuance of a stock dividend as a stock split. Hence, the new shares should go to the legatee of the specific gift whether there is a stock split or stock dividend. By statute in an increasing number of states, a specific bequest of securities includes additional securities produced by a stock dividend, as well as those produced by a stock split. [*See, e.g.,* UPC §2-605(a)(1); Mass. Gen. Laws ch. 191, §1A]

4. Distinguish—Post-Death Stock Splits and Stock Dividends [§808]

The rules above apply to stock splits and stock dividends occurring during the testator's lifetime. If a stock split or stock dividend takes place *after the testator's death*, the beneficiary is entitled to the stock produced by the split or dividend.

a. Rationale

The beneficiary owned the stock from the moment of the testator's death, subject to the executor's right of possession for purposes of administration. Thus, it was the beneficiary's own stock that produced the split or the dividend.

5. Cash Dividends [§809]

A specific beneficiary of securities is entitled to any cash dividends *declared and paid after the testator's death*, because the beneficiary owned the securities from the moment of death. However, the beneficiary is *not entitled* to any cash dividends *declared during the testator's lifetime*, even though the dividends are not paid until after the testator's death. For this purpose, it is the date the dividend is declared by the corporation, and not the date of its payment, that controls.

6. Statutory Solutions [§810]

Under the UPC and by statute in several non-UPC states, the specific beneficiary of corporate securities is entitled to additional or other securities of the same entity owned by the testator by reason of action initiated by the entity (*i.e.,* stock splits *and* stock dividends). However, this rule does *not* apply to any additional shares acquired by the testator's exercise of a stock option. [*See, e.g.,* Md. Est. & Trusts Code §4-405; Va. Code §64.1-62.3(1)] Under the revised UPC, the beneficiary is also entitled to additional shares acquired under a dividend reinvestment program. [*See* UPC §2-605(a)(3)]

IS THE SPECIFIC BENEFICIARY ENTITLED TO ADDITIONAL SHARES PRODUCED BY STOCK SPLITS, STOCK DIVIDENDS, AND CASH DIVIDENDS?		**gilbert**
	OCCURS BEFORE TESTATOR'S DEATH	**OCCURS AFTER TESTATOR'S DEATH**
STOCK SPLIT	Beneficiary is *entitled to additional shares*.	Beneficiary is *entitled to additional shares*.
STOCK DIVIDEND	Under majority law, the beneficiary is *not entitled* to additional shares.	Beneficiary is *entitled* to additional shares.
CASH DIVIDEND	Beneficiary is *not entitled* to the dividends *declared before the testator's death* even if paid after the testator's death.	Beneficiary is *entitled* to the dividends if *declared and paid* after the testator's death

F. Interest on General Legacies

1. Legacies Not Paid Within One Year [§811]

At common law, a beneficiary was entitled to interest on a general legacy *that was not paid within one year after the testator's death*. The interest is not retroactive to the testator's date of death but instead begins accruing in the second year. A number of states have enacted statutes embodying this rule. [*See, e.g.,* Mass. Gen. Laws ch. 197, §20—4%; Va. Code §64.1-68] Under the UPC, the entitlement to interest commences one year after the *appointment of a personal representative*, not one year after death. [UPC §3-904]

G. Exoneration of Liens

1. Majority Rule [§812]

At common law and in many states today, if specifically devised property is, at the testator's death, subject to a lien securing a note on which the testator was personally liable, the *beneficiary is entitled to have the lien exonerated* (absent a contrary provision in the will). That is, the beneficiary is entitled to demand payment of the debt out of the *residuary estate*, so that the property passes free of any encumbrance or lien. *Rationale:* The testator's personal estate was benefited because of the debt, and would have been smaller had the debt been discharged. Thus, the debt should be paid out of the general assets of the residuary estate. [*See, e.g.,* **Martin v. Johnson**, 512 A.2d 1017 (D.C. 1986); **Goldstein v. Ansell**, 258 A.2d 93 (Conn. 1969)]

---

e.g. **Example:** Phil's will devises land to Mary. At Phil's death, the land is encumbered by a mortgage that secures a $20,000 note on which Phil was personally liable. Under the exoneration of liens doctrine, the mortgage must be exonerated (*i.e.,* the debt must be paid out of the residuary estate) if the secured debt was a *personal obligation* of the decedent. [*See* **Currie v. Scott**, 187 S.W.2d 551 (Tex. 1945)]

---

a. Critique

This doctrine has been criticized on the ground that it is far more likely that the testator intended to give the beneficiary only what the testator owned at death—title subject to the lien. This position has particular force if the property was subject to the lien at the time the will was executed.

b. Distinguish—testator not personally liable [§813]

The exoneration of liens doctrine applies *only if* the decedent was *personally liable* on the debt involved. If the specifically devised property was subject to a lien but the testator signed a nonrecourse note (or if the testator took title under a "subject to" rather than an "assumption" transaction), such that the testator was not personally liable in the event of a deficiency on foreclosure, there is no exoneration. The beneficiary takes the property subject to the mortgage lien. [*See, e.g., In re* **Estate of Karrels**, 435 N.W.2d 739 (Wis. 1988)]

2. Minority Rule [§814]

Under the UPC and by statute in a growing number of states, liens on specifically devised property are *not* exonerated unless the will directs exoneration. A specific devise passes *subject to* any security interest existing at the time of death without right of exoneration, and regardless of a general direction in the will to pay all debts. [*See, e.g.,* UPC §2-607; Ill. Comp. Stat. ch. 755, §5/20-19] Under these statutes, a "just debts" clause (*e.g.,* "I direct that all of my just debts be paid as soon as practicable after my death") is a mere general direction to pay debts, and is not considered a direction that liens on specifically devised property be exonerated.

a. Rationale

This result is more likely to comport with the testator's probable intent because the beneficiary takes precisely what the testator owned—*i.e.,* title subject to a lien.

Chapter Eleven:
Will Contests and
Related Matters

CONTENTS

Chapter Approach

A will "contest" poses the issue of whether the document offered for probate is a valid will. While the contestant may contend that the will should be denied probate because it was **not validly executed** (*see supra*, §§345 *et seq.*) or that the will, although validly executed, was **revoked** by the testator (*see supra*, §§493 *et seq.*), when courts speak of will contests, they are referring to situations in which a will is challenged on the ground that the testator **lacked testamentary capacity** at the time the will was signed (*see infra*, §§826 *et seq.*), or **lacked testamentary intent** that the proffered document was to serve as the testator's will (*see infra*, §§847 *et seq.*), or that the will, or a particular gift in the will, was the product of **undue influence** (*see infra*, §§850 *et seq.*). The will also may be contested on the ground that the will or a gift therein was procured as the result of a **fraud** perpetrated upon the testator (*see infra*, §§868 *et seq.*), or that the document was executed (or a gift in the will was made) as the result of a **mistake** (*see infra*, §§886 *et seq.*).

Questions pertaining to will contests are fairly easy to identify. You will often see strange and eccentric behavior by an elderly testator, or overreaching and overbearing conduct by a beneficiary with respect to a testator who was susceptible to influence. Your approach to this type of question should be as follows:

1. **Determine whether the contestant has standing** to challenge the will. Generally, only an heir or legatee under an earlier will has standing. Look for an economic interest that would be adversely affected by the will's admission to probate.

2. **Determine whether the contestant has grounds to challenge** the will:

    a. Did the testator have **testamentary capacity at the time the will was signed**? Keep in mind that the standard for testamentary capacity is an easy one to meet, and remember that courts prefer to distribute property according to the testator's written wishes rather than by intestate succession. Remember also that the fact that the testator was, *e.g.*, very old and in poor health, had a serious drinking problem, had memory lapses, was heavily sedated with medicine, was eccentric, dressed oddly, or took Valium is insufficient to establish lack of testamentary capacity.

    b. Did the testator lack **testamentary intent** to make a will? Do the facts show that the document signed by the testator was intended by him to be his will? When this issue is raised on an exam, there are usually suspicious circumstances surrounding the will's execution.

    c. Did someone **unduly influence** the testator—*i.e.*, mentally coerce the testator into signing a will that reflects the intent, not of the testator, but of the coercer?

Keep in mind that the mere opportunity to influence, or the fact that the testator's condition made him susceptible to influence, are not enough to show that influence was exerted. But watch out for a person in a *confidential relationship* who was *active in procuring the will*, as this may give rise to a *presumption* of undue influence.

d.   Was the testator a victim of *fraud* as to the will or a gift in the will? Was the testator *willfully deceived*? Did the testator *execute or revoke a will in reliance* on the fraudulent act or misrepresentation?

e.   Was the will or a gift therein the result of a *mistake*? (Note, however, that for most mistakes, the courts do not grant relief.) Keep in mind that the courts are reluctant to change the clear language of a will. However, you need to be able to distinguish a mistake from a *latent or patent ambiguity*. As for ambiguity, you need to know the difference between the two types, and the types of evidence the courts will admit in an effort to cure the ambiguity.

3.   *If the will in your question has a no-contest (*in terrorem*) clause,* note that the majority of jurisdictions hold that such a clause does not trigger a forfeiture if the contest was brought in *good faith* and with *probable cause.* In any case, challenges to the jurisdiction of the court or a suit to construe the will are *not will contests.*

4.   *Finally, if a will cannot be set aside on the basis of undue influence or fraud,* consider an action in *tort* for *wrongful interference with an expected inheritance,* which is recognized in a growing number of jurisdictions.

A.   Standing to Contest Will

1.   Who May Contest Will [§815]

In most jurisdictions, a party who contests a will is called a "contestant." However, in a few jurisdictions the person is called a "caveator." A person has standing to contest a will only if she is an *interested party.* To be an interested party, the person must have a *direct economic interest* in the estate that would be adversely affected by the will's admission to probate. [*See, e.g.,* **Logan v. Thomason,** 202 S.W.2d 212 (Tex. 1947); N.Y. Surr. Ct. Proc. Act §1410] "Obviously the burden is upon every person appearing to oppose the probate of a will to allege, and, if required, to prove, that he has some interest in the estate of the testator which will be affected by such will if admitted to probate. In the absence of such interest a contestant is a mere meddlesome intruder." [**Abrams v. Ross's Estate,** 250 S.W. 1019 (Tex. 1923)]

a.   Intestate heir or legatee under earlier will [§816]
By majority rule, the only persons who are "interested" for purposes of challenging a will are the testator's intestate heirs [*See In re* **Powers's Estate,** 106

N.W.2d 833 (Mich. 1961)] and legatees under an earlier will whose gifts are reduced or eliminated by the will [*See, e.g.,* **Sheldone v. Marino,** 501 N.E.2d 504 (Mass. 1986); **Earles v. Earles,** 428 S.W.2d 104 (Tex. 1968); 39 A.L.R.3d 321]. *Note:* An heir who takes *more* under the will than by intestacy has *no standing* to contest the will, nor does a legatee under an earlier will who takes the *same or a greater interest* under the will being offered for probate.

(1) Objection to named executor [§817]

In a few states, a legatee named in the will has standing to object to the appointment of the person named in the will as executor, even though the amount of his legacy will not be affected by the appointment. [*See* N.Y. Surr. Ct. Proc. Act §709]

(2) Necessary parties must receive notice [§818]

In most states, *all heirs and all legatees* named in the will are necessary parties to a will contest and must be given notice of the proceedings. [*See* Mo. Rev. Stat. §473.083] Merely naming the executor in his representative capacity as defendant is insufficient; the will legatees also must be given notice. [*See* **Jennings v. Srp,** 521 S.W.2d 326 (Tex. 1975)]

b. Distinguish—persons without standing to contest will

(1) Creditors [§819]

Creditors of the decedent are *not* "interested" for purposes of having standing to contest a will because they can assert their claim against the estate whether or not the will is admitted to probate. [*See, e.g.,* **Montgomery v. Foster,** 8 So. 349 (Ala. 1890); **Hooks v. Brown,** 53 S.E. 583 (Ga. 1906)] Also, most courts hold that judgment creditors of an intestate heir have no interest in the *decedent's* estate, and thus cannot contest the will so as to procure property for the heir. [*See* **Lee v. Keech,** 133 A. 835 (Md. 1926); *but see* **In re Estate of Harootenian,** 38 Cal. 2d 242 (1951)—minority view that judgment creditor of an intestate heir has standing to contest the decedent's will]

(2) Executor named in earlier will [§820]

By majority rule, an executor or testamentary trustee named in an earlier will has *no standing* to contest a later will. *Rationale:* The only financial interest would be in the commissions to which the fiduciary would be entitled if the appointment were not revoked by the later will. This is not an interest in the decedent's *estate.* [*See, e.g.,* **Freeman v. De Hart,** 303 S.W.2d 217 (Mo. 1957); **State ex rel. Hill v. District Court,** 242 P.2d 850 (Mont. 1952); N.Y. Surr. Ct. Proc. Act §1410; 94 A.L.R.2d 1409]

(3) Legatee who accepted benefits [§821]

A legatee who *accepts benefits* (*e.g.,* partial distributions) under a will is *estopped* from later joining in a contest of the will. [*See* **Trevino v. Turcotte**, 564 S.W.2d 682 (Tex. 1978)]

2. Time for Contest [§822]

The will may be contested either at the time it is offered for probate or thereafter within the statutory period. The statutory time period in which a will contest may be filed after the will has been admitted to probate varies from state to state. [*See, e.g.,* Mo. Rev. Stat. §473.083—six months; Tex. Prob. Code §93—two years]

a. Comment

How can a will be contested after it has been admitted to probate? Wasn't the will's validity the central issue at the initial probate proceeding? It must be remembered that in most cases the will is offered for probate just a few weeks after the testator's death. At that point, the parties who might contest the will may not have had time to determine whether they have grounds to challenge the will, or if they think they do, whether they want to undergo the trauma and expense of a will contest. Most states' procedures recognize this by allowing initial probate of the will upon formal or informal proof that the will was properly signed and witnessed, and then giving the contestants a period of time in which to challenge the will on various grounds.

b. Uniform Probate Code [§823]

Under the UPC, a will contest is made in a *formal testacy proceeding.* (*See infra,* §981.) The formal testacy proceeding must be initiated within *three years* after the decedent's death or, if the will was probated in an informal probate proceeding (*see infra,* §981), within *12 months* after the informal proceeding is completed. [UPC §3-108(a)(3)]

3. Burden of Proof [§824]

In most jurisdictions, the burden is on the *contestant* to establish the grounds for the will contest (*e.g.,* lack of testamentary intent or capacity, undue influence, etc.). [UPC §3-407]

4. Attorney's Fees for Defense of Will [§825]

The executor named in a will has a duty to defend the will. As long as the attempt to probate the will was made in good faith, attorney's fees and other litigation expenses incurred by the executor are allowed as a charge against the estate *even if the will is denied probate.* [*See* **Huff v. Huff**, 124 S.W.2d 327 (Tex. 1939)] *Rationale:* Competent attorneys should be encouraged to represent a party who is seeking to defend what may be the valid last will of the decedent.

SUMMARY OF PROCEDURAL ASPECTS FOR WILL CONTESTS	**gilbert**
WHO CAN FILE CONTEST?	*Intestate heirs* who would receive less under the will than under intestacy and *legatees under an earlier will* who receive a lesser amount under the new will.
WHO *CANNOT* FILE CONTEST?	*Creditors*, *executors* named in earlier wills, and *legatees who accepted benefits* from the will.
WHEN MUST CONTEST BE FILED?	When the will is *admitted to probate* or later, within the *statutory period*. Under the UPC, the will must be contested in a formal testacy proceeding within *three years* after the decedent's death or within *12 months* after completion of an informal probate proceeding.
WHO HAS BURDEN OF PROOF?	The will *contestant* must establish the grounds for challenging the will.

B. Grounds for Will Contest

1. Testamentary Capacity

a. Legal test [§826]

While statutes in a few states lay out the test for capacity [*see, e.g.,* Cal. Prob. Code §6100.5; Ga. Code §53-4-11], statutes in most states merely specify that a testator must be of sound mind, leaving elaboration of the statutory test to judicial development. [*See* UPC §2-501] The test for determining whether the testator had sufficient capacity for executing a will consists of four issues [*See, e.g.,* **Santry v. France,** 97 N.E.2d 533 (Mass. 1951); **Tieken v. Midwestern State University,** 912 S.W.2d 878 (Tex. 1995)]:

(1) Did testator understand the nature of the act he was doing? [§827]

Did the testator have sufficient capacity to know that he was signing his will? The testator must have *actual knowledge* of the nature of the act he is undertaking; *i.e.,* he must actually know that he is executing his will. Mere capacity to understand is not sufficient.

(2) Did testator know the natural objects of his bounty? [§828]

The testator must have the capacity to *understand* (not necessarily have actual knowledge of) the relationship between himself and those persons who ought to be in his mind at the time of making his will (*e.g.,* did the testator have sufficient capacity to comprehend that he was married and had three children?).

(3) Did testator know the nature and value of his property? [§829]

The testator must have sufficient capacity to understand the *nature, extent, and approximate value* of his property. However, he does not need to know the *exact* value of his property. [*In re* **Estate of Persha**, 649 N.W.2d 661 (Wis. 2002)]

(4) Did testator understand the disposition he was making? [§830]

The testator must have the capacity to interrelate the factors above and form an *orderly scheme of disposition*.

TEST FOR TESTATOR'S CAPACITY TO MAKE A WILL — gilbert

THE FOUR QUESTIONS:	LOOK FOR FACTS SHOWING:
• *Did T understand the nature of the act he was doing?*	**Actual knowledge** that he is executing his will (*e.g.,* he knows what a will is and that he is signing a will and not some other paper).
• *Did T know the natural objects of his bounty?*	Ability to **understand his relationship** to others who likely would be remembered in his will, *e.g.,* spouse, children, other relatives. (*But note:* He doesn't have to leave them anything.)
• *Did T know the nature and value of his property?*	Ability to **understand** the **nature, extent, and approximate value** of what he owned (*e.g.,* he understands he owns a house and that it is a valuable bequest, but he doesn't have to know its fair market value).
• *Did T understand the disposition he was making?*	Ability to interrelate the above factors and make a **rational plan disposing of his estate** (even if it is not the plan his heirs would like).

---

b. Comparison with other legal tests [§831]

The mental capacity required for making a will involves a different, and much lower, legal standard than the capacity to, *e.g.,* make a contract. [*See* **In re Coddington's Will**, 112 N.Y.S.2d 4 (1952)]

Example: Herbert had been adjudicated incapacitated, and a guardian had been appointed to manage his affairs. Herbert executed both his will and a deed purporting to convey real property on the same day. The deed was set aside since, because of the adjudication of incapacity, Herbert lacked legal capacity to convey title to property. However, probate of Herbert's will was upheld upon a finding that the four-point test for capacity, *supra*, had been satisfied. [**Lee v. Lee**, 337 So. 2d 713 (Miss. 1976)]

c. Insane delusion [§832]

A person may have sufficient mental capacity to make a will generally, and yet suffer from an insane delusion that interferes with his ability to formulate a rational plan of disposition. A finding of insane delusion may cause a particular will (or a gift therein) to fail on the ground of testamentary incapacity.

(1) Definition [§833]

An insane delusion occurs "where one persistently believes supposed facts which have no real existence except in his perverted imagination, and against all evidence and probability, and conducts himself, however logically, upon the assumption of their existence." [*In re* **Hargrove's Will,** 262 A.D. 202 (1941)] In other words, it is a belief in *facts that do not exist* and that no rational person would believe existed. [*See* **Ingersoll v. Gourley,** 139 P. 207 (Wash. 1914)]

Example: Groundless beliefs about family members (*e.g.,* that the testator's child was sired by another man [**McGrail v. Rhoades,** 323 S.W.2d 815 (Mo. 1959)]) have been held to be insane delusions.

Example: A will was held to be the product of an insane delusion where the evidence supported a finding that the testator, at the time he made his will, was suffering under the warrantless delusion that his frail 75-year-old wife of many years was cheating on him by using knotted bedsheets to haul male callers to her bedroom on the second floor. [*In re* **Honigman's Will,** 8 N.Y.2d 244 (1960)]

---

(2) Test [§834]

A belief can be very illogical, yet not amount to an insane delusion. "Persons do not always reason logically or correctly from facts, and that may be because of their prejudices, or of the perversity or peculiar construction of their minds. Wills, however, do not depend for their validity upon the testator's ability to reason logically, or upon his freedom from prejudice." [*In re* **Hargrove's Will,** *supra*] The controlling question is whether there are *any facts* from which the testator *could* have reasoned, regardless how improperly and regardless of whether the average person would have reached the same conclusion.

(3) Effect of insane delusion [§835]

To set aside a will on the ground of insane delusion, it is not enough to show that the testator had delusions. It must appear that the delusion had some *effect on the testator's disposition of his property—i.e.,* that his will, or some portion thereof, was formulated in reliance on the irrational belief. [*See, e.g., In re* **Heaton's Will,** 224 N.Y. 22 (1918)] An insane delusion may invalidate the entire will, or it may affect only a particular gift therein, if it can be shown that the delusion runs only to that particular gift or to the beneficiary thereof. [*See, e.g., In re* **Perkins's Estate,** 195 Cal. 699 (1925)]

(a) Comment

"A man may believe himself to be the supreme ruler of the universe and nevertheless make a perfectly sensible disposition of his property, and the courts will sustain it when it appears that his mania did not dictate its provisions." [**Gulf Oil Corp. v. Walker,** 288 S.W.2d 173 (Tex. 1956)]

EXAM TIP	gilbert

Remember that *only the provisions resulting from the insane delusion are invalid*. The remainder of the will is admitted to probate. For example, Testator is survived by Son and Daughter. Testator's will devises half of his estate to Son, and the other half "to Neighbor because Daughter is plotting to poison me in my sleep." Daughter is actually 10 years old and has no ill will towards Testator. The provision in favor of Neighbor is invalid because it is a product of Testator's insane delusion. However, the provision for Son was not affected by the delusion. Thus, the estate is distributed one-half to Son per the terms of the will, and the remaining half passes through intestacy to Son and Daughter.

---

d. Burden of proof as to testamentary capacity [§836]

The UPC and most courts recognize a *rebuttable presumption of capacity,* the effect of which is to place the burden on those contesting the will to show that the testator lacked the requisite mental capacity. [*See, e.g.,* **Shevlin v. Jackson,** 124 N.E.2d 895 (Ill. 1955); UPC §3-407]

(1) Adjudication of incompetency [§837]

A proceeding to appoint a guardian or committee to handle an incompetent person's property involves a determination of whether the person has the capacity to enter into contracts. Such a determination involves a higher standard than the four-point test for testamentary capacity (*see supra,* §§826-830). Therefore, an adjudication of incompetency is *evidence* of testamentary incapacity, but will not support a directed verdict of testamentary incapacity. [*See* **Gibbs v. Gibbs,** *supra,* §359] "One may be capable of making a will yet incapable of disposing of his property by contract or of managing his estate." [**Gilmer v. Brown,** 44 S.E.2d 16 (Va. 1947)]

---

e.g. **Example:** Seven months before Daisy Hughes signed his will at age 93, a guardian was appointed in legal proceedings on ground that because of his age, health, and deteriorating mental condition, he was no longer capable of handling his own affairs. On this ground, the trial judge gave an instructed verdict that Daisy lacked testamentary capacity. The appellate court reversed, holding that a determination of whether to appoint a guardian to handle Daisy's affairs is based on a different test than the four-point test for testamentary capacity; and that even if Daisy had mental problems, a jury could find that he signed his will during a *lucid interval.* [**Duke v. Falk,** 463 S.W.2d 245 (Tex. 1971)]

(a) Minority rule [§838]

In a few states, an adjudication of incompetency raises a *rebuttable presumption* that the testator lacked sufficient capacity to make a will, and clear and convincing evidence is needed to rebut the presumption. [*See, e.g.,* **Hugenel v. Estate of Keller,** *supra,* §359]

e. Evidentiary matters

(1) In general [§839]

In all cases, the controlling test is the four-point test for capacity (*see supra,* §§826-830). The fact that the testator was very old, physically frail, in poor health, had memory lapses, and had a drinking problem did not mean that she lacked the requisite mental capacity or was unable to comprehend the nature of her act. [*See, e.g.,* **Lewis v. McCullough,** 413 S.W.2d 499 (Mo. 1967); **Palmer v. Palmer,** 500 N.E.2d 1354 (Mass. 1986)] The fact that the testator was scheduled to have life-threatening surgery the day after executing a will was not sufficient to indicate that she was not of sound mind. [*See* **Wimberly v. Jones,** 526 N.E.2d 1070 (Mass. 1988)] A testator's belief that she frequently communicated with the spirits of her deceased husband and her nephew, and her signing her husband's name on a letter that she believed was from her husband did not require granting a jury issue as to capacity in view of the testator's belief in spiritualism. [*See* **Donovan v. Sullivan,** 4 N.E.2d 1004 (Mass. 1936)]

(2) Capacity must exist at time of execution [§840]

Evidence as to the testator's capacity or lack thereof must relate to the date on which the will is signed, or shortly before or thereafter. The more distant in time a particular fact may be, the less probative it is on the central issue: Did the testator have capacity *at the time the will was executed*?

EXAM TIP | **gilbert**

Remember that the key time is *when the will was executed*. Facts in an exam question about mental confusion before and after the will's signing, or about the testator's extreme frailty or advanced age when he signed the will, should prompt you to mention the *issue* of capacity, but to decide that issue, you must *consider the four questions of capacity* (see *supra,* §§826-830) as you examine the facts relating to the *time of execution*.

---

(3) Testimony of subscribing witnesses [§841]

The testimony of the subscribing witnesses and others present at the will's execution is given considerable weight and, unless overcome by other persuasive evidence, settles the issue in favor of testamentary capacity. [*See* **Gilmer v. Brown,** *supra*]

(4) Medical testimony [§842]

Testimony derived from medical records by a physician-expert who did not treat the decedent or consult with any doctor who performed such treatment is "the weakest and most unreliable" type of evidence. [*In re* **Estate of Van Patten,** 215 A.D.2d 947 (1995); *and see* **Wright v. Wolters,** 579 S.W.2d 14 (Tex. 1979)] "[A] physician's opinion regarding mental capacity generally, or the mental capacity necessary to make a will, is, in the eye of the law, no better than that of any other person. . . . The science of medicine has made notable contributions to present-day civilization. It has traveled a long distance from the time when powdered owls' feathers and birds' nest soup were prescribed as an unfailing remedy for human ailments, but it is known to all intelligent men that perfection has not yet been reached. It is still a progressing science. That its learned followers may err in judgment, or even be lacking in veracity, is the statement of a truth too obvious to be denied. Unless the science itself and the personnel of its followers have reached a degree of perfection that approximates infallibility, certainly a court ought not to be compelled to accept their conclusions as against abundant testimony of an opposite character from credible sources." [*In re* **Finkelstein's Estate,** 61 S.W.2d 590 (Tex. 1933)]

(a) Psychiatric treatment [§843]

The fact that the testator was undergoing psychiatric treatment and had attempted suicide does *not* give rise to an inference of lack of testamentary capacity. [*See, e.g.,* **In re Hatzistefanous's Estate,** 77 Misc. 2d 594 (1974)]

(5) Witness cannot testify as to testator's legal capacity [§844]

A lay witness may testify as to *actions and statements* of a testator within his observation. However, neither a lay witness nor an expert witness may be asked whether the testator had legal capacity to make a will. [*See, e.g.,* **In re Estate of Vickery,** 167 A.D.2d 828 (1990)] *Rationale:* This "involves a legal definition and a legal test," and the witness's definition or understanding of capacity to perform the act in a legal manner may differ from the legal standard. [**Carr v. Radkey,** 393 S.W.2d 806 (Tex. 1965)] For the same reason, a witness cannot be asked whether the testator was suffering from an insane delusion. "[A] doctor's concept of what constitutes an insane delusion may be quite different from the legal concept." [**Lindley v. Lindley,** 384 S.W.2d 676 (Tex. 1964)]

(6) Distinguish—witness may testify as to testator's *mental* condition [§845]

A witness can testify as to the testator's *mental condition.* Competent evidence about the testator's mental condition and ability, or lack of it, which does not involve legal tests, legal definitions, or pure questions of law is admissible. A witness may be asked, assuming he knows or is a properly qualified expert, whether the testator knew or had the capacity to know the objects of her bounty, the nature of the transactions in which she was engaged, the nature and extent of her estate, and similar questions. [**Carr v. Radkey,** *supra*]

ESTABLISHING TESTAMENTARY CAPACITY THROUGH WITNESS TESTIMONY	**gilbert**
WITNESS MAY TESTIFY TO FACTS, *E.G.*:	**WITNESS MAY NOT TESTIFY TO LEGAL CONCLUSIONS, *E.G.*:**
• Testator's ***actions and statements, mental condition and ability***. • Whether testator knew or had the ***capacity to know the objects of his bounty,*** etc. (see *supra,* §§826-830).	• Whether testator had the ***legal capacity*** to make a will. • Whether testator was suffering from an ***insane delusion***.

f. Lucid and sensible holographic will is evidence of testamentary capacity [§846]

In jurisdictions that recognize holographic wills (*see supra,* §§457 *et seq.*), it is generally held that "a rational and sensible holographic will" prepared by a testator is evidence of the fact that the will was written during a lucid interval. [*See* **Carr v. Radkey,** *supra*]

2. Testamentary Intent [§847]

To be admitted to probate, it must be shown that the proffered document was written and executed with testamentary intent. (*See supra,* §§346 *et seq.*)

a. Presumption that testator knew contents of will [§848]

In the ordinary case, no issue is raised as to whether the testator knew the contents of the will. The will was prepared at the testator's direction, and it is presumed that he knew and understood its contents. This presumption arises even if the testator was blind or illiterate, or if the testator could not read or understand the English language, as long as it is shown that the attorney explained the will to the testator and was satisfied that he understood its contents. [*See, e.g.,* **Pepe v. Caputo,** 97 N.E.2d 260 (Ill. 1951); *In re* **Liquori's Will,** 142 N.Y.S.2d 220 (1955); **Jedlicka v. Wilkins,** 459 S.W.2d 956 (Tex. 1970)]

b. Proof required if suspicious circumstances [§849]

If, however, the will was prepared and executed under suspicious circumstances, the court may require an affirmative showing that the testator knew and understood its contents.

 Example: Hugh, unable to read or write, and gravely ill at the house of one of the legatees, signed (with an X) a will that disinherited his only child, who was in the same house at the same time and did not know that her father was executing a will. Neither beneficiary was related to Hugh, and there was no showing that he ever gave anyone instructions to write a will or requested that one be prepared. Since there was no evidence that Hugh knew the contents of the document he had signed, the will was denied probate. [**Kelly v. Settegast,** 2 S.W. 870 (Tex. 1887); *see also* **Bailey v. Clark,** 561 N.E.2d 367 (Ill. 1990)]

3. Undue Influence [§850]

A will or a gift therein may be set aside if it was the result of undue influence. Influence is not undue unless the free will of the testator was destroyed and the result is an instrument that reflects the will, not of the testator, but of the party exerting the influence. [*See, e.g.,* **In re Dunson's Estate,** 141 So. 2d 601 (Fla. 1962); **Rothermel v. Duncan,** 369 S.W.2d 917 (Tex. 1963)] However, mere solicitation of a will does *not* constitute undue influence. [48 A.L.R.3d 961] Importuning, persuasion, and even harassment may influence the testator, but do not constitute undue influence. It is not improper to advise, persuade, etc., as long as the testator "remains a free agent," and "the will is his and not that of another." [**Ginter v. Ginter,** 101 P. 634 (Kan. 1909)]

a. Legal test [§851]

The test of whether a testator has been subjected to undue influence is a subjective one, measured at the time of execution of the will. The *burden of proof* is always on the person contesting the will, who must establish that:

(i) Undue influence *was actually exerted* on the testator.

(ii) The effect of the influence was to *overpower the mind and will* of the testator.

(iii) The influence produced a will or a gift in the will that expresses the intent, not of the testator, but of the one exerting the influence, and that *would not have been made but for the influence.*

[*See* **Rothermel v. Duncan,** *supra*]

EXAM TIP　　　　　　　　　　　　　　　　　　　　　　**gilbert**

For exam purposes, remember that there must be more than mere pleading, begging, nagging, cajoling, or even threatening to constitute undue influence. The *free will of the testator must be destroyed* and the resulting dispositions must reflect the *intent and desire of the party exerting the influence*.

---

b. Circumstantial evidence [§852]

Undue influence is usually difficult to prove. Since it is rarely witnessed, it normally can be established only by circumstantial evidence. However, the evidence must be *substantial* and of probative force; it "cannot be based upon bare suggestion, innuendo, or suspicion." [**Core v. Core's Administrators,** 124

S.E. 453 (Va. 1924)] The mere existence of a motive, the opportunity, or even the ability to exert undue influence is not sufficient. There must be *affirmative evidence* that undue influence actually was exerted. [*See* **Kar v. Hogan,** 251 N.W.2d 77 (Mich. 1976)] The following four factors are said to be indicia of undue influence; *i.e.,* while *no one of them individually is sufficient,* the combination of all four may support a finding of undue influence. [*See* **In re Hull's Estate,** 63 Cal. App. 2d 135 (1944)]

(1) Susceptibility [§853]

The testator's weakened physical or mental condition may have left him susceptible to undue influence or domination by others.

(2) Opportunity [§854]

The person alleged to have committed the undue influence had the opportunity to exercise it. However, the mere fact that the opportunity existed does not, by itself, show that the person acted upon it. [*See* **Flynn v. Prindeville,** 98 N.E.2d 267 (Mass. 1951)]

(3) Activity [§855]

There was some activity, such as procuring the will or arranging for its preparation, or isolating the testator from his family or from independent legal advice, on the part of the party exerting the influence. [*See* 13 A.L.R.3d 381]

(4) Unnatural disposition [§856]

The disposition made in the will was "unnatural" in that one child was heavily favored over the others, property was bequeathed to an unrelated party to the exclusion of the testator's immediate family, etc. [*See* **In re Fiumara's Estate,** 47 N.Y.2d 845 (1979)]

Example: The only evidence of undue influence was that John was 92 years old and suffering from arteriosclerosis when he executed a will that gave $4,000 to each of three daughters and devised his residuary estate to his housekeeper of 25 years. A directed verdict admitting the will to probate was affirmed on appeal. Showing that John was in weak physical condition and became more and more dependent on the housekeeper in his later years merely showed the *motive and opportunity* for exercising undue influence, but did not show that influence had *actually been exerted.* There was no proof from which an inference of undue influence could reasonably be drawn, and the issue was properly removed from the jury. [*In re* **Colbeck's Will,** 45 A.D.2d 796 (1974)]

---

c. Undue influence as to part of will [§857]

If only one gift in the will was the product of undue influence, the remaining parts of the will are *valid,* as long as giving effect to the remaining portions does not defeat the overall testamentary plan. [*See* **Williams v. Crickman,** 405

N.E.2d 799 (Ill. 1980); 64 A.L.R.3d 261] If, however, the effect of upholding the unchallenged provisions, while rejecting the tainted gifts, would defeat the testator's presumed wishes for the disposal of his property, the entire will is set aside. [*See* **In re Klages's Estate,** 209 N.W.2d 110 (Iowa 1973)]

Example: Prior to his death, John revoked his will and executed a new one with substantially the same provisions as the first but decreasing his legacies to his daughter Dorothy and her children and deleting the clause creating a trust in favor of Dorothy. In both wills, John devised the residue of his estate to his two sons, Karl and Ralph. Dorothy brought a will contest against specific portions of the second will (*e.g.*, the residuary clause) claiming that Karl and Ralph unduly influenced their father's will. Although the will contest was successful, the result was to invalidate the *entire will*, rather than only the challenged provisions. *Rationale*: To set aside the clause devising the residuary estate would cause that portion of the estate to pass to Dorothy, Karl, and Ralph through intestacy and it was evident from his earlier will that John did not want Dorothy to receive such a large portion of his estate. Thus, the entire will is set aside and John's first will is admitted to probate. [*In re* **Klages's Estate,** *supra*]

---

d. Confidential relationship

(1) Effect of confidential relationship

(a) Majority rule [§858]

By majority rule, the mere existence of a confidential relationship between the testator and a will beneficiary (*e.g.*, attorney-client, doctor-patient, priest-penitent) does ***not, by itself,*** give rise to a presumption of undue influence unless the beneficiary played an active part in ***procuring*** the will. [*See* **In re Arnold's Estate,** 16 Cal. 2d 573 (1940)] However, some courts have indicated that the quantum of evidence necessary to prove undue influence is less where there is a confidential relationship. [*See* **McQueen v. Wilson,** 31 So. 94 (Ala. 1901)]

(b) Intermediate rule—presumption [§859]

A number of courts recognize a *rebuttable presumption* of undue influence where all three of the following factors appear. Once these elements are present, the burden *shifts to the proponent* of the will to prove that it was not induced by her undue influence. [*See* **Rhoades v. Chambers,** 759 S.W.2d 398 (Mo. 1988)]

1) *A confidential relationship existed* between the testator and the beneficiary at *the time the will was executed.*

2) *The beneficiary played some active part in drawing the will,* *e.g.*, by counseling the testator in regard thereto, arranging for an attorney to prepare the will, or engaging in other significant

activity in connection with the will's preparation and execution. [*See* 13 A.L.R.3d 381] A beneficiary who participates in preparation of a will and occupies a confidential relationship to the testator has a duty to see that the testator receives independent, disinterested advice. [*See In re* **Swenson's Estate**, 617 P.2d 305 (Or. 1980)]

3) *The disposition under the will is "unnatural,"* in that the beneficiary in question receives far more than the testator might normally be expected to leave to that person.

(c) **Minority rule—inference [§860]**

In some jurisdictions, the factors above give rise to only an *inference* of undue influence, such as to support a submission of the issue to the jury; the burden of proof does not shift. However, unless the will proponent produces sufficient rebuttal evidence, the inference is sufficient to satisfy the contestant's burden of proof. [*See In re* **Estate of Mikeska**, 362 N.W.2d 906 (Mich. 1985)]

DOES THE EXISTENCE OF A CONFIDENTIAL RELATIONSHIP BETWEEN THE TESTATOR AND BENEFICIARY AUTOMATICALLY POINT TO UNDUE INFLUENCE? **gilbert**	
MAJORITY RULE	There is a *presumption* of undue influence where there is a confidential relationship *only if* the beneficiary *actively participated in procuring the will*.
INTERMEDIATE RULE	There is a *rebuttable presumption* of undue influence if: (i) The confidential relationship existed *when the will was executed*, (ii) The beneficiary *actively participated in procuring the will*, and (iii) The disposition to that beneficiary is *unnatural*. The burden then shifts to the beneficiary to prove that there was no undue influence.
MINORITY RULE	There is an *inference* of undue influence if: (i) The confidential relationship existed *when the will was executed*, (ii) The beneficiary *actively participated in procuring the will*, and (iii) The disposition to that beneficiary is *unnatural*. The inference will stand *unless* the beneficiary offers proof that there was no undue influence.

(2) Gift to spouse [§861]

No presumption of undue influence arises from the confidential relationship that normally exists between a husband and wife. The fact that one spouse handled the couple's finances, wrote all checks to pay the bills, and prepared their joint income tax returns reflects a normal division of marital chores, and does not demonstrate undue control over the other spouse's financial affairs. [*See* **In re Estate of Glogovsek,** 618 N.E.2d 1231 (Ill. 1993)] A husband or wife may properly influence the making of a will, as long as the influence is not exercised in an improper manner or by improper means. [*See* **Snell v. Seek,** 250 S.W.2d 336 (Mo. 1952)]

---

e.g. **Example:** The will contestant's evidence showed that Inga knew the contents of her husband's (Marvin's) will, that the will was drafted by Inga's attorney and signed at his office immediately after the wedding ceremony, that her cousin drove them to the attorney's office for that purpose, that although Marvin had never met Inga's daughter, his will left half of his estate to her if Inga predeceased him, and that a confidential relationship existed because Marvin and Inga were engaged at the time the will was drafted. This evidence was insufficient to establish undue influence. The most that could be said of the evidence was that Inga married Marvin for his money. "A wife who urges and solicits her husband to make a will in her favor does not, by that fact, exercise an undue influence over its execution. Nor, to prove the issue, is it enough that the beneficiary of the will . . . dominated other aspects of the testator's life in ways adverse to the contestant. . . . Nor even does the fact that the wife 'procured the scrivener and was present when the will was executed . . . support an inference of undue influence.' Also, 'the fact that a husband bequeaths all of his property to his wife to the exclusion of his children by a former marriage is not an unnatural disposition,' and does not support the inference of undue influence." [**Morse v. Volz,** 808 S.W.2d 424 (Mo. 1991)]

---

cf. **Compare:** Raymond and Virginia married after the death of Raymond's first wife. During the months that followed their marriage, Virginia isolated Raymond from his children and told him they were after his money. Raymond eventually suffered a heart attack and required major surgery. Although Raymond already had a validly executed will that devised his property to his children, Virginia bought and prepared a fill-in-the-blank will for Raymond on the day before his surgery. Floyd, a witness to the will's execution, stated that Raymond wanted to devise his property to his children, and that Virginia had told him she had made such bequests in the will. However, she devised all of the property to herself. Virginia filed the will the day after Raymond's death and did not notify his children that their father passed away. This was a clear case of undue influence because the will prepared by Virginia did not reflect

Raymond's desires but instead was the product of Virginia's own undue influence over Raymond. [*In re* **Estate of Riley,** 824 S.W.2d 305 (Tex. 1992)]

---

(3) Illicit relationship [§862]

The mere existence of an illicit relationship does not give rise to a presumption or inference of undue influence, but existence of the relationship is a *factor* to be considered along with other factors in determining whether undue influence was exerted. [*See, e.g.,* **Reed v. Shipp,** 308 So. 2d 705 (Ala. 1975)] The modern view is that an illicit relationship is *not "confidential"* within the meaning of the rule that gives rise to a presumption or inference of undue influence when a confidential relationship plus other factors exist. [*See In re* **Spaulding's Estate,** 83 Cal. App. 2d 15 (1947)]

(a) Comment

While the above statement of the rule is found in modern cases as well as older decisions, the actual decisions in cases involving a will in favor of a mistress, paramour, or companion of the same gender as the testator tend to reflect the prevailing attitudes of society toward such relationships. Thus, more recent cases tend to reflect a less judgmental attitude toward sexual activities outside the marriage relationship, whereas older decisions reflect an inclination to find that the illicit activities tainted the will.

(4) Gift to testator's attorney [§863]

It is generally held that the mere existence of an attorney-client relationship, without more, does not give rise to a presumption that a testamentary gift to the attorney was the product of undue influence. In particular, if there has been an ongoing and long-term attorney-client relationship, and there is no evidence disclosing any pressure or urging by the attorney to make a will in the attorney's favor, the gift should not be set aside. [*See* **Swaringen v. Swanstrom,** 175 P.2d 692 (Idaho 1946)]

Where the testator devises a portion of his estate to his attorney, did the attorney-beneficiary *pressure the testator* into making the gift?

YES → *Presumption of undue influence* arises.

NO ↓

Was the will *prepared by the attorney-beneficiary*?

YES → *Presumption of undue influence* arises.

NO ↓

Was the will prepared *by independent counsel*, (*i.e.,* not by the attorney-beneficiary or his partner)?

NO → *Presumption of undue influence* arises.

YES ↓

No presumption of undue influence arises.

(a) Presumption of undue influence where attorney prepared the will [§864]

If, however, the attorney prepared the will in his favor and supervised its execution, a number of courts have held that a presumption or inference of undue influence arises. [*See* **Carter v. Williams,** 431 S.E.2d 297 (Va. 1993)—substantial gift to attorney's wife] This is especially so if other suspicious circumstances exist (*e.g.,* large bequest in relation to size of estate; testator, although he had capacity, was in a weakened mental or physical condition; attorney's arrangement for particular persons to serve as attesting witnesses). [*See, e.g.,* **In re Heim's Will,** 40 A.2d 651 (N.J. 1945); 19 A.L.R.3d 575] The presumption of undue influence, once it arises, can be overcome only by the clearest and most satisfactory evidence. [*See* **In re Witt's Estate,** 198 Cal. 407 (1926)]

(b) Compare—independent legal advice [§865]

If the will was prepared by another attorney on the basis of independent legal advice, no presumption of undue influence arises. [*See* **Frye v. Norton,** 135 S.E.2d 603 (W. Va. 1964)] However, preparation of the will by the attorney-beneficiary's partner based on the attorney-beneficiary's instructions is not the independent and impartial advice necessary to sustain a transaction between the fiduciary and his principal. [*See* **In re Lobb's Will,** 145 P.2d 808 (Or. 1944)]

(c) New York view [§866]

The New York courts go even further, and require the attorney "to explain the circumstances and to show in the first instance that the gift was freely and willingly made." [**In re Putnam's Will,** 257 N.Y. 140 (1931)] A hearing is held at which the bequest is subject to "*Putnam* scrutiny"—even if the will is not contested and no objection to the gift is filed.

(d) Texas view [§867]

By statute in Texas, a testamentary gift to the attorney who prepared the will, his spouse, or his employee is *void* unless the attorney, spouse, or employee was related to the testator. [Tex. Prob. Code §58B]

4. Fraud

a. In general [§868]

A will or testamentary gift that is made as the result of fraud is invalid. To establish fraud, it must be shown that the testator was *willfully deceived* as to the character or content of an instrument, or as to extrinsic facts that induced the will or a gift therein. If only part of a will is affected by fraud, only that part is invalid, and the remaining parts of the will may be admitted to probate. [*See* Mo. Rev. Stat. §473.081]

(1) Definition [§869]
Fraud consists of:

(i)   *False statements* of *material facts,*

(ii) *Known to be false* by the party making the statements,

(iii) Made with the *intention of deceiving* the testator,

(iv) Who is *actually deceived*, and

(v)   That *cause the testator to act* in reliance on the false statements.

[*See, e.g.,* **Glazewski v. Coronet Insurance Co.,** 483 N.E.2d 1263 (Ill. 1985); *In re* **Roblin's Estate,** 311 P.2d 459 (Or. 1957)]

(a) Deceit incidentally related to will [§870]
Although generally the fraud must be intended to influence the execution or content of a will, deceit directed at some other objective may have incidentally influenced the will as well. For example, a fraudulently induced marriage may not have been intended to procure a will, but a court may find that a will resulting from that marriage is a fruit of the original fraud and must fail. [*See In re* **Carson's Estate,** 184 Cal. 437 (1920)]

(2) Causation [§871]
Fraud invalidates a testamentary act only if the testator was in fact *deceived* and *acted in reliance* on the misrepresentations. There is no basis for challenging a will on grounds of fraud if the same will would have been made regardless of the alleged misrepresentations. [*See In re* **Roblin's Estate,** *supra*]

(3) Compared to other grounds

(a) Mistake [§872]
Fraud requires that the person know the statements he made are false. *Innocent* misrepresentation does not constitute fraud, although relief may be available on the ground of mistake. (*See infra,* §§886 *et seq.*)

(b) Undue influence [§873]
Fraud is distinguishable from undue influence in that in undue influence, *the testator knows what she is doing* but her act is impelled by the influence of another person; the will is not her own. (*See supra,* §§850 *et seq.*) An element of *coercion* is present, whereas fraud involves *deception*. (*See infra,* §§877 *et seq.*)

(c) Duress [§874]

Fraud is also distinguishable from duress in that duress involves the element of a *threat to physically harm the testator.* Again, fraud merely involves deception. (*See infra,* §§877 *et seq.*)

APPROACH TO EXAM QUESTIONS RAISING ISSUES OF FRAUD   **gilbert**

ANALYZE AN EXAM QUESTION DEALING WITH FRAUD IN THE FOLLOWING MANNER:

☑ Were *false statements of material fact* made by a party affected by the will's provisions?

☑ Did the party making those statements *know that they were false*?

☑ Did the party make the false statements with the *purpose of deceiving the testator*?

☑ Was the *testator deceived* by the false statements?

☑ Did the testator act in *reliance* on the false statements (*i.e.,* did she draft or change her will based on the false statements)?

---

b. Fraud in the execution [§875]

Fraud in the execution (sometimes called fraud in factum) includes cases where the testator was tricked into signing a document not knowing it was a will, or where, by sleight of hand, one "will" was *substituted* for another. Proof of this type of fraud establishes that there was *no testamentary intent* as to the instrument signed.

(e.g.) Example: Lucy signs an instrument upon Ricky's representation that it merely gives Ricky a power of attorney to pay Lucy's bills while Lucy is in the hospital. In fact, the instrument contains provisions devising all of Lucy's property to Ricky.

(e.g.) Example: Yolanda, an elderly widow, has a daughter (Tina) and three sons. Tina's husband, an attorney, prepares a will for Yolanda and tells her that the will leaves her estate to the four children in equal shares. Yolanda signs the will without reading it. In fact, the will leaves the bulk of Yolanda's estate to Tina. [*See, e.g.,* **Mitchell v. Mitchell,** 41 S.W.2d 792 (Mo. 1931)]

---

c. Fraud in the inducement [§876]

In this type of fraud, the testator has the requisite testamentary intent, but is *fraudulently induced* into making the will or a particular gift therein.

(e.g.) Example: Tony marries Carmella after representing that he is single, when in fact Tony is already married. Shortly after the marriage, Carmella executes a will making a substantial gift to Tony; Carmella dies a year later. If the testamentary gift "was in fact the fruit of the fraud," the gift can be set aside.

EXAM TIP   **gilbert**

To keep these two types of fraud straight, remember this:

- Fraud in the execution *directly affects the will*—the testator is deceived into executing a will. Testamentary intent is missing because the testator did not know that the document she executed was a will. Since there was no testamentary intent, *the entire will is invalid*.

- Fraud in the inducement *indirectly affects the will*, but that fraud causes the testator to execute a will in favor of the person perpetrating the fraud or some other beneficiary. Here, testamentary intent is present because the testator knew that she was making a will and understood the dispositions she was making; however, *any dispositions resulting from the fraud are invalid*.

---

(1) Misrepresentation must be sole inducement [§877]

It must be shown that the misrepresentation was the *sole inducement* for the testator's making the gift. If there were other inducing reasons for the testator to make the gift (*e.g.,* love and affection for the intended beneficiary), the gift will *not* be set aside. Thus, if in the above example, Tony and Carmella had lived together happily for 20 years, it would be difficult to say that the bequest to Tony was founded on Carmella's supposed legal relationship with him, and not primarily on their long and intimate relation. [*See, e.g., In re* **Carson's Estate**, *supra*, §870—dictum]

(2) Knowledge of true facts [§878]

There is no fraudulent inducement if the testator knew the true facts. [*In re* **Donnelly's Will**, 26 N.W. 23 (Iowa 1885)—testator knew that her "husband" had another wife]

(3) Fraud perpetrated by someone other than beneficiary [§879]

If fraud has been perpetrated on the testator, it is generally held to be immaterial that the beneficiary was innocent.

Example: If someone falsely tells the testator that Jason is the testator's long-lost son, and Jason has nothing to do with the deception, a testamentary gift to Jason still would be set aside. The fraud vitiates any testamentary intent to bestow benefits on Jason.

(a) Distinguish—gifts not a product of deceit [§880]

Even if the testator has been fraudulently induced to make a will, the gifts that are *not a product of the fraud* are valid. [*See, e.g., In re* **Carson's Estate,** *supra*] Thus, in the example above, if the will also gave property to Justine, the testator's daughter, the fraud pertaining to "long-lost son" Jason would *not* affect the gift to Justine.

d. Fraudulent prevention of will [§881]

Less frequently encountered are cases in which a testator is fraudulently dissuaded from making a will or a testamentary gift. For example, Lois tells her family that she is going to draw a will and leave all her property to a friend, Clark. To prevent this, Lois's daughter tells her that Clark has just died (which the daughter knows is not true). Believing Clark to be dead, Lois decides not to draw any will at all and let her property pass by intestate succession. Clark learns about the misrepresentation after Lois's death. What relief is available?

(1) No legal remedy available [§882]

It is universally held that *extrinsic evidence is not admissible,* in probate proceedings, to establish that the testator intended to make a gift to an allegedly omitted beneficiary (*e.g.,* Clark, above). Regardless of the strength of the evidence, the court will not write a will on behalf of the decedent, or identify supposed will beneficiaries on the basis of oral testimony. All testamentary gifts must be contained in a will executed by the decedent; and in the absence of such a writing, the laws of intestate succession must apply.

Example: Daughter alleged that Testator asked Attorney to prepare a will that included a gift to Daughter. Acting in collusion with Testator's husband, Attorney purposely omitted the gift but pretended that the gift was made when reading the will aloud to Testator. The court did not allow reformation of the will. If evidence of Daughter's allegations were admitted, the result would be that Testator's property would be disposed of, not according to the directions given in her will, but on the basis of oral testimony. Although steadfast adherence to the rule requiring that the testator's wishes be reduced to writing may work a hardship in a particular instance, the policy is "one which the Legislatures and the courts have deemed to produce the best results in the long run." [**Dye v. Parker,** 194 P. 640 (Kan. 1921)]

(2) Constructive trust may be imposed [§883]

Despite the fact that there is no *legal* remedy, many courts have imposed constructive trusts for the benefit of the persons who were intended to be beneficiaries, if proof of the fraud is established by the higher evidentiary standard of "clear and convincing evidence." (*See* Trusts Summary.)

(3) Tort liability may be imposed [§884]

Moreover, modern authorities recognize that the intended beneficiary

(Daughter, in the above example) may have a cause of action against the perpetrator of the fraud (Attorney, in the above example) for tort liability for wrongful interference with an expectancy. (*See infra,* §§936 *et seq.*)

e. Revocation prevented by fraud [§885]

Suppose that a will beneficiary pretends to revoke the testator's will by destruction at the testator's request and in her presence. In fact, the beneficiary destroys another document, thereby tricking the testator into believing that the will has been revoked. Even though it is clear that the testator would have revoked the will but for the fraud, the will is nonetheless *admitted to probate* since it was not validly revoked. However, upon proof of the beneficiary's deception by clear and convincing evidence, a court no doubt would impose a *constructive trust* in favor of the testator's heirs or the persons she wished to benefit by revoking the will. [*See* **Brazil v. Silva**, 181 Cal. 490 (1919)]

5. Mistake

a. In general [§886]

Where it is claimed that there was a mistake concerning a will, the admissibility of extrinsic evidence to show the mistake and the type of relief available, if any, depends upon the type of mistake claimed. When the alleged mistake relates to *execution* of the document offered for probate, the courts are more likely to accept parol testimony, and grant relief if the mistake is established, than if the alleged mistake relates to the *motive* for making the will or the *contents* of the will. This is because an alleged mistake in execution relates to testamentary intent, an issue on which the courts generally admit parol testimony in appropriate cases. (*See supra,* §§350-354.) But if the alleged mistake relates to the testator's reasons for making the will or the contents of an instrument that clearly was executed with testamentary intent, the courts are understandably reluctant to disturb the words contained in the will signed by the testator.

(1) Distinguish—mistake as to revocation [§887]

Mistake as a justification for refusing to give effect to a will or some part thereof must be distinguished from mistake as a ground for ignoring a revocation. Relief is much more freely given in the revocation situation, because revocation of a will requires both an act of revocation and the intent to revoke. Since extrinsic evidence is admissible on the issue of intent to revoke, evidence is also admissible to show that the intent to revoke was based on a mistake. (*See supra,* §§584 *et seq.*, on dependent relative revocation.)

b. Mistake in execution of will

(1) Mistake as to nature of instrument [§888]

Extrinsic evidence is *always admissible* to show that the testator was *unaware of the nature of the instrument* he signed (*e.g.*, he believed it to be a power of attorney). Such a mistake relates to the issue of whether the testator had the requisite testamentary intent, without which the will would be invalid. Therefore, if the testator was mistaken as to the nature or effect of the instrument when he signed it, *testamentary intent is lacking*, and probate is denied. [*See* **Hildreth v. Marshall,** 27 A. 465 (N.J. 1893)]

(2) Wrong will signed [§889]

Situations in which the wrong will is signed occur most often with "mirror" wills—*i.e.*, wills containing reciprocal provisions (usually prepared for a married couple). Even though the nature of the mistake is obvious, some courts deny relief.

Example: By mistake Hellen signs the will prepared for Vasil, and Vasil signs the will prepared for Hellen. Thus the will signed by Hellen reads: "I, Vasil, leave all my property to my wife, Hellen." The mistake is not discovered until after Hellen dies. In this situation, some courts have denied relief on the ground that Hellen lacked testamentary intent because she did not intend to execute the document she actually signed. [*In re* **Pavlinko's Estate,** 148 A.2d 528 (Pa. 1959)]

(a) Contrary view [§890]

Other courts have granted relief since the existence and nature of the mistake are so obvious. "[I]t would indeed be ironic if not perverse to state that because what has occurred is so obvious, and what was intended so clear, we must act to nullify rather than sustain this testamentary scheme . . . . There is absolutely no danger of fraud, and the refusal to read these wills together would serve merely to unnecessarily expand formalism, without any corresponding benefit." [*In re* **Snide,** 52 N.Y.2d 193 (1981)]

c. Mistake in the inducement [§891]

If the alleged mistake involves the reasons that led the testator to make the will (or the reasons for making or not making a particular gift therein), and the mistake was not fraudulently induced, *no relief* is granted. *Rationale:* Oral evidence as to the testator's purposes, or his reasons for making or not making a disposition, "would open the door wide to fraud" since "the testator is dead, and therefore cannot give his version of the matter." [**Bowerman v. Burris,** 197 S.W. 490 (Tenn. 1917)] Moreover, if the evidence could be at all effective, two points would have to be established: (i) that the testator was laboring under *mistake as to the fact;* and (ii) that if the truth had been known *he would have made a different disposition;* and both of these points involve the intent of a person who is no longer available to testify.

(1) Mistake as to relationship or status of beneficiary [§892]

Mistakes relating to the relationship or status of a beneficiary have no effect on the will; it is given effect as written.

Example: Lance's will leaves Blackacre to Brandon under the mistaken belief that Brandon was his nephew. The mistake was entirely Lance's; neither Brandon nor anyone else misled Lance. In such a case, the courts will enforce the will as written, including the mistakenly induced gift.

Example: Frankie's will makes small bequests to two of her children, Cora and Clifton, and devises her residuary estate to her other two children, Dor and Milton. Testimony is offered tending to show that Frankie mistakenly believed that her husband's will left his entire estate to Cora and Clifton, and that her will was motivated by a desire to equalize distribution of their property among the four children. The evidence is not admissible. There being no evidence of fraud, "courts have no right to vary or modify the terms of a will or to reform it even on grounds of mistake." [**Carpenter v. Tinney**, 420 S.W.2d 241 (Tex. 1967)]

---

(2) Limited exception—mistake appears on face of will [§893]

Some courts have recognized an exception (more often in dictum than in result) when the mistake *appears on the face of the will, and* the disposition the testator *would have made* but for the mistake *can at least be inferred* from the instrument. *Rationale:* Since the will discloses that a mistake has been made, it is apparent that giving effect to the will would frustrate the testator's true intent. Also, oral testimony and all of its attendant problems need not be relied upon either to establish the mistake or to show how the testator intended to dispose of his property if the mistake had not been made. [*See In re* **Tousey's Will**, 34 Misc. 363 (1901)—dictum]

Example: Tyrone's will reads: "Since my only son, William, was killed in action in Vietnam, I leave everything to the American Red Cross." If William is alive, the will may be set aside.

(a) Comment

Cases in which such relief is granted are few and far between, because it is rare for the mistake *and* the alternate disposition to appear on the face of the instrument. Moreover, even though the will appears to state an erroneous reason for not making a gift to a particular beneficiary, it may be that the testator was not mistaken at all but, instead, chose this more genteel means of explaining a disinheritance rather than disclosing the true reasons.

d. Mistake as to contents of will [§894]

Suppose it is contended that a provision was mistakenly omitted from the will, or that a provision contained in the will is not what the testator intended. Is parol testimony admissible to show the existence of the mistake and what the testator intended to provide had the mistake not been made? In general, the answer is a firm *no,* for two reasons: First, this *was* the will that the testator signed, and there is a strong presumption that the testator read the will and knew and understood all of its contents, including each provision thereof. [*See* **Downey v. Lawley,** 36 N.E.2d 344 (Ill. 1941)] This is true even if the testator did not understand English, as long as the will was explained to him and he indicated approval of its terms. [*See In re* **Knutson's Estate,** 174 N.W. 617 (Minn. 1919)—will explained to testator in Norwegian] Second, the courts are understandably reluctant to allow property to pass, not pursuant to the terms of the duly executed will, but on the basis of oral testimony. A proceeding to correct a mistake in a will cannot be allowed or sustained. As one court said, "Admit this doctrine, and you may as well repeal the statute requiring wills to be in writing . . . . Witnesses will then make wills and not testators." [**Goode v. Goode,** 22 Mo. 518 (1856)]

(1) Mistaken omission [§895]

Mistakes of omission *cannot be corrected.* Thus if the testator actually intended to make a gift to a particular beneficiary, but the instrument as drafted does not contain the gift, there is generally *no relief* available. [*See* 90 A.L.R.2d 924] *Rationale:* Correction would require the addition of a new provision, and the court cannot reform a decedent's will. A testamentary gift can only be made by a writing contained in a duly executed will.

Example: Although there may be overwhelming, uncontradicted evidence that Donny intended to make a gift of $1,000 to his sister Marie, if through mistake the will does not include such a gift, evidence is not admissible to show the mistake. Therefore, even if Marie could get the attorney's secretary to show her steno pad and testify that she omitted the clause by mistake, Marie has no claim against Donny's estate.

(a) Attorney liability [§896]

Suppose that in preparing a will pursuant to the testator's instructions, the attorney omits a clause that makes a gift to a beneficiary. If the jurisdiction has rejected privity of contract as a defense to such actions (*see supra*, §454), the attorney is liable to the intended beneficiary for the amount the beneficiary would have received under the will had the clause not been negligently omitted. [*See, e.g.,* **Needham v. Hamilton**, 459 A.2d 1060 (D.C. 1983)]

(b) Uniform Probate Code [§897]

Under the UPC and by statute in several non-UPC states, evidence is admissible to show the omission of the testator's *child* from a will because the testator mistakenly believed *that the child was dead*. [*See* UPC §2-302(c); Mo. Rev. Stat. §474.240]

EXAM TIP   **gilbert**

To understand the different rules for mistake in the execution and mistake in the inducement or contents, you need to understand the rationale behind a court's refusal to allow extrinsic evidence in cases of mistaken inducement or mistaken contents—*i.e.,* there is the potential of generating too much *fraud*. Furthermore, the courts prefer to dispose of property according to the testator's expressed intent in his will (as opposed to oral testimony of one having an interest in the property). But remember: Extrinsic evidence is allowed in cases of *mistaken execution* because the issue is *testamentary intent*, without which a will is *invalid*.

---

(2) Mistake as to meaning of terms of will—in general [§898]

It is sometimes contended that the testator "didn't mean" what he wrote in his will; *i.e.,* that he made a mistake in describing a beneficiary or the property that was to be the subject of the gift, or that he was mistaken as to the meaning or legal effect of the terms of the instrument. To what extent, if any, is parol evidence admissible when such a mistake is alleged?

(a) "Plain meaning" rule [§899]

Unless the language of the will is ambiguous (*see infra,* §§904 *et seq.*), the traditional and majority rule is that the will's terms must be construed according to their "plain meaning." Hence, parol evidence (even the testator's own statements as to what was intended) is *not admissible* to contradict or alter the ordinary meaning of the will's provisions. If no ambiguity exists, it is the testator's apparent intent that controls—not his supposed actual intent.

1) Rationale

"[I]t is against sound public policy to permit a pure mistake to defeat the duly solemnized and completely competent testamentary act. It is more important that the probate of the wills of dead people be effectively shielded from the attacks of a multitude of fictitious mistakes than that it be purged of wills containing a few real ones. The latter a testator may, by due care, avoid in his lifetime. Against the former he would be helpless." [*In re* **Gluckman's Will,** 101 A. 295 (N.J. 1917)]

(b) Mistake in description of beneficiary or property [§900]

A mistake in describing a beneficiary or item of property has *no effect on the will.* Thus, if the will makes a bequest "to my cousin, William Smith," and if such a cousin exists, evidence, no matter how compelling, is *not admissible* to show that "he meant me, his cousin *Thomas* Smith." Declarations of the testator—even those made to the attorney who drafted the will—are not admissible to show that the legatee named in the will was designated by mistake. [*See* **In re Smith's Will,** 254 N.Y. 283 (1930)] Similarly, if the will makes a bequest of "200 shares of Acme stock," evidence that a mistake was made (*e.g.,* that the testator had given written instructions to make a gift of 300 shares, but the attorney's secretary hit the wrong typewriter key) is not admissible.

---

e.g. **Example:** Lydia's will makes a bequest "to my nephew, William Root." Lydia has a blood nephew, William Root, and a nephew by marriage, William Root. Since, according to the law, only a nephew by blood is a "nephew," evidence is not admissible to show which William Root was intended; the blood nephew takes the bequest. [*See, e.g.,* **Estate of Carroll,** 764 S.W.2d 736 (Mo. 1989)]

---

e.g. **Example:** A Scotsman who had spent all his life in Scotland bequeathed 500 pounds to "The National Society for the Prevention of Cruelty to Children." These words correspond to the official name of a London society which did no work in Scotland and of which the testator had never heard. Near his home was a branch office of "The Scottish National Society for the Prevention of Cruelty to Children," whose activities he knew. The court held the London society should get the money, for the words used had a single plain meaning. [**National Society v. Scottish National Society,** (1915) A.C. 207]

---

cf. **Compare:** If, however, there were no organization with the exact name (*e.g.,* no "The National Society for the Prevention of Cruelty to Children"), there would be a *latent ambiguity,* and parol evidence would be admissible to cure the ambiguity. (*See infra,* §905.)

(c) Mistake as to meaning or legal effect [§901]

According to the prevailing view, if the testator knew and approved the contents of the will, it is immaterial that he mistook the legal effect of the language used. It is what the testator has said, not what he allegedly meant but failed to say, that controls. [*See* **Leonard v. Stanton**, 36 A.2d 271 (N.H. 1944)] The attorney-drafter's mistake as to the legal effect of the language used is regarded as the testator's mistake and is binding on him. [*See* **Hoover v. Roberts**, 58 P.2d 83 (Kan. 1936)]

Example: If the will gives a beneficiary a life estate, evidence is not admissible to show that the testator intended to give the beneficiary, and thought he had given her, a larger estate. [*In re* **Gluckman's Will**, *supra*]

Example: Where the gift of a remainder interest was contingent on the life tenant's dying "intestate," the gift is not effective if the life tenant left a will, even though there was clear evidence that the drafter of the will thought that "intestate" meant "without issue." [**Hoover v. Roberts**, *supra*]

(d) Modern trend [§902]

There is a modern trend to depart from the "plain meaning" rule, and *admit extrinsic evidence* to show that the testator meant something other than would be indicated by the words' ordinary meaning. Under this approach, the court admits evidence to determine whether there is an ambiguity that does not appear from the language of the will. If in light of such evidence the will's provisions are susceptible to two or more meanings, the court resolves the ambiguity on the basis of extrinsic evidence under the procedures described in §910, *infra*. If, on the other hand, the court concludes that in light of all such evidence there is no ambiguity—that the provisions are susceptible of only one meaning—the will is enforced in accordance with that meaning.

1) Rationale

To determine initially whether the terms of a will are clear, definite, and free from ambiguity, the court must examine the instrument "in the light of the circumstances surrounding its execution so as to ascertain what the parties meant by the words used. Only then can it be determined whether the seemingly clear language of the instrument is in fact ambiguous." "Failure to enter upon such an inquiry is failure to recognize that the . . . 'plain meaning' is simply the meaning of people

gilbert

DISTINGUISHING TYPES OF MISTAKE

	DEFINITION	EXAMPLE	IS EXTRINSIC EVIDENCE ADMISSIBLE TO CURE MISTAKE?	IS WILL ADMITTED TO PROBATE?
MISTAKE IN EXECUTION	The testator is mistaken in the **type of instrument** he executed or he signed the wrong will.	The testator thought he was executing a deed.	Yes	No; the will was not made with testatmentary intent.
MISTAKE IN INDUCEMENT	The testator has executed the will or made a particular disposition based on **mistaken facts or reasons**.	The testator devised his entire estate to his neighbor because he believed his parents were dead.	No	Yes, unless the mistake appears on the face of the will and an alternate disposition can be inferred.
MISTAKE IN CONTENTS	The testator made mistakes in the **substantive or dispositive provisions** of the will.	A provision was inadvertently left out of the will or the testator misdescribed a beneficiary.	No Exceptions: • A **child was omitted** because the testator thought he was dead. • The mistake is of a **minor or formal** nature (e.g., misspelling of testator's name). Modern trend allows extrinsic evidence to show ambiguity.	Yes

who did not write the document." [*In re* **Estate of Russell,** 69 Cal. 2d 200 (1968)]

---

e.g. **Example:** George's will devises property to "Robert J. Krause, now of 4708 North 46th Street, Milwaukee, Wisconsin." Under the minority view, extrinsic evidence is admissible to show that a Robert J. Krause lives at that address, but that George did not know him; that Robert **W.** Krause, who lived in the same general area in Milwaukee, was George's longtime friend and employee; that George had mentioned to others that he had made a gift in his will to "Bob Krause"; that George's will left most of his estate to relatives and other employees; and that an earlier will had made a similar gift to "Robert Krause" (without the middle initial and street address). Noting that there would have been an ambiguity and extrinsic evidence would have been admissible if the will had made a gift to "Robert Krause," the court concluded that "details of identification, particularly such matters as middle initials, street addresses, and the like, which are highly susceptible to mistake, particularly in metropolitan areas, should not be accorded such sanctity as to frustrate an otherwise clearly demonstrable intent . . . when the proof establishes to the highest degree of certainty that a mistake was, in fact, made." [*In re* **Gibbs's Estate,** 111 N.W.2d 413 (Wis. 1961)]

---

(3) Mistake in recital of facts of execution [§903]

The courts have consistently allowed correction of mistakes of a ***minor or purely formal nature*** that do not relate to the identity of a beneficiary or the description of property. Examples are the misspelling of the testator's name [**Succession of Crouzeilles,** 31 So. 64 (La. 1901)] or insertion of the attorney's name instead of the testator's name in the attestation clause [**Gage v. Hooper,** 169 A. 925 (Md. 1934)].

6. Ambiguity [§904]

Parol evidence may be admissible to resolve uncertainties or ambiguities in the will. In such a case, there is no "plain meaning" that can be given to the words used by the testator. The court, in the process of interpreting the will, may admit and rely on extrinsic evidence to resolve the ambiguity. Here there is no concern as to changing the meaning of language or adding words that the testator did not use. Rather, the concern is to ***find the testator's meaning*** as to the words she did use. The older decisions, however, draw distinctions according to the type of ambiguity involved.

a. Latent ambiguity [§905]

A latent ambiguity exists when the language of the will, although ***clear on its*** *face* in describing a beneficiary or property, is susceptible to *more than one meaning when applied to the extrinsic facts* to which it refers. [*See **In re Frost's Will**,* 89 N.W.2d 216 (Wis. 1958)] There are two classes of latent ambiguity. One type is where *two or more persons or things meet the description* in the will (*e.g.,* the will makes a bequest "to my cousin, Mary Smith," and testator has two cousins named Mary Smith; or the will devises "the farm that I own in Marion County," and testator owns two farms in Marion County). The other type is where *no person or thing exactly* matches the description in the will, but two or more persons or things meet the description *imperfectly* (*e.g.,* the will makes a bequest "to my nephew, John Paul Jones," and testator has a nephew named John Phillips Jones and another nephew named James Paul Jones, but no nephew named John Paul Jones). In these cases, the description of the beneficiary or the gift is imperfect, and uncertainty arises in attempting to determine exactly what the testator intended to give or to whom she intended to give it. It is universally held that *extrinsic evidence is admissible* to resolve a latent ambiguity of either type. If, however, the extrinsic evidence does not resolve the ambiguity, the gift fails, and the property passes under the will's residuary clause or by intestacy.

(1) Rationale

Reliance on extrinsic evidence to cure the ambiguity does not have the effect of "rewriting" the will or contradicting its terms. The evidence is merely being received to aid the court in giving meaning to the terms that the testator actually employed. [*See, e.g.,* **Farrell v. Sullivan**, 144 A. 155 (R.I. 1929)] In a sense, it is always necessary to admit extrinsic evidence to identify the beneficiary (does the testator have a cousin Mary Smith; and if so, who is she?) or the subject of the gift (what farmland did the testator own in Marion County?). If this inquiry shows that there is an ambiguity, the ambiguity can be removed by further extrinsic evidence. [*See, e.g.,* **Clymer v. Mayo**, *supra*, §514] "It is settled doctrine that as a latent ambiguity is only disclosed by extrinsic evidence, it may be removed by extrinsic evidence." [**Patch v. White**, 117 U.S. 210 (1886)]

Example: Frances's will bequeaths property to "Edward Bergner." It turns out that there are two Edward Bergners who might be the intended beneficiaries: a brother Edward G. Bergner and a nephew Edward C. Bergner. The imperfect description may be cured by extrinsic evidence as to which Edward Bergner Frances intended to benefit. [**Nicholl v. Bergner**, 63 N.E.2d 828 (Ohio 1945)]

Example: Newton's will makes a bequest "to my grandson, William N. Bond." Newton had two grandsons: Boyd C. Bond (the son of William N. Bond) and William H. Bond (the son of John C. Bond). Extrinsic evidence, including the drafting attorney's testimony as to Newton's declarations, is admissible to cure the ambiguity. [**Bond v. Riley,** 296 S.W. 401 (Mo. 1927)]

> **e.g.** **Example:** A devise of "my Lot #6, Square #403," which the testator did not own, could be shown by extrinsic evidence to have been intended to pass Lot #3 in Square #406, which the testator did own. [**Patch v. White,** *supra*]

b. **Partially inaccurate description—*"falsa demonstratio non nocet"* [§906]**
If the description is partially accurate and partially inaccurate, it is generally held that the gift may be saved by *striking out the inaccurate part*—if the remaining language is unambiguous; or, if ambiguous, the ambiguity can be cured by extrinsic evidence. This doctrine is sometimes referred to as *"falsa demonstratio non nocet"* (a mere erroneous description does not vitiate).

> **e.g.** **Example:** Andy bequeathed property to "my sister Annie Neary." Andy had one sister named Annie Flynn and another named Bridget Neary. The court struck out the surname "Neary," leaving the bequest to "my sister Annie," on the basis of extrinsic evidence showing that this was Andy's probable intent.

> **e.g.** **Example:** Catherine left property to "my niece Mary, living in New York." Catherine had a niece named Mary living in Ireland, and a niece named Annie living in New York. Extrinsic evidence showed that Catherine had a much closer relationship with Annie than with Mary. The court therefore struck the given name "Mary," which left the description unambiguous ("to my niece living in New York"). [***In re* Donnellan's Estate,** 164 Cal. 14 (1912)]

> **e.g.** **Example:** Grace's gift of "our former home at Ravenna, Mason County, Illinois, being lot 12, block 2, Max Meyer's addition" was upheld by striking "Ravenna" and "Max" upon a showing that (i) the will was prepared by an attorney in another state; (ii) there was no town named Ravenna in Illinois; (iii) the only Meyer's addition in Mason County, Illinois, was Marguerita Meyer's addition in the town of Havana; and (iv) Grace owned lot 12, block 2 in Marguerita Meyer's addition. [**Armstrong v. Armstrong,** 158 N.E. 356 (Ill. 1927)]

> **cf.** **Compare:** Suppose, however, that the testator devises property to "my cousin Henry," and she has a cousin Henry and a cousin Cecil. Here there is no ambiguity and no inaccurate description. Cecil cannot introduce evidence to show that the testator made a *mistake* and intended him to take; the plain meaning rule applies.

c. **Patent ambiguity [§907]**

A patent ambiguity exists where the uncertainty *appears on the face of the will.* (For example, Sophia's will bequeaths "the sum of twenty-five dollars ($25,000) to my brother Bob.") The courts are divided as to the admissibility of parol evidence to resolve this type of ambiguity.

(1) Traditional view [§908]

The traditional view is that parol evidence is *not* admissible to clarify or explain away a patent ambiguity. [*See, e.g.,* **Jacobsen v. Farnham,** 53 N.W.2d 917 (Neb. 1952)] Unlike the situation involving a latent ambiguity, where extrinsic evidence establishes the ambiguity, in the case of a patent ambiguity resort to extrinsic evidence is not necessary to show the ambiguity. And since extrinsic evidence is not admissible to *show* the ambiguity, it is not admissible to *cure* the ambiguity. In other words, once you get your foot in the door (extrinsic evidence establishes that there is a latent ambiguity), you can open the door; but if you cannot get your foot in the door, the door is closed. [*See* **Pickering v. Pickering,** 50 N.H. 349 (1870)] Thus, the gift to Bob above fails since the will does not identify which amount Sophia intended to give him.

(2) Modern trend [§909]

A growing number of courts reject the distinction between patent and latent ambiguities, and *admit extrinsic evidence* on the testator's intent in *any* case of ambiguity. [*See* **In re Estate of Brown,** 922 S.W.2d 605 (Tex. 1996)] *Rationale:* It is the court's duty to give meaning to the testator's will if it is possible to do so. Parol evidence is not being received for the purpose of "rewriting" the will, but to interpret that which has been written. [*See, e.g.,* **Payne v. Todd,** 43 P.2d 1004 (Ariz. 1935); **Weir v. Leafgreen,** 186 N.E.2d 293 (Ill. 1962)]

(a) Note

In several states, it is provided by statute that ambiguities or misdescriptions in the will can be resolved by extrinsic evidence. These statutes apply whether the ambiguity is latent or patent. [*See, e.g.,* Ga. Code §53-4-56]

d. **Type of extrinsic evidence admissible [§910]**

When extrinsic evidence is admissible, courts generally receive any competent evidence that may bear on the *testator's actual or probable intent.* Thus, *facts and circumstances evidence,* such as the circumstances surrounding execution of the will; the testator's relationship with the various beneficiaries; her age, health, and understanding at the time of execution; and her knowledge and comprehension of the language used is always admissible.

	DEFINITION	EXAMPLE
TYPES OF AMBIGUITIES THAT CAN ARISE IN A WILL — gilbert		
LATENT AMBIGUITY	The language of the will is *clear* but gives rise to *multiple meanings* when applied to the facts. For example, more than one person or thing meets the description in the will or no person or thing meets the description but more than one meets the description imperfectly.	"I devise my house to my daughter." The testator owns two homes and spends six months in each every year. The language of the will is clear but raises confusion when applied to the facts. *Note*: If extrinsic evidence does not resolve which house the testator meant, the gift *fails*.
PATENT AMBIGUITY	The language of the will is *not clear* and the ambiguity is *apparent* from the language in the will.	The testator's will devises "all my personal property to my mother" and "the remainder of my property both real and personal to the March of Dimes." It is unclear whether the testator wanted her personal property to descend to her mother or the March of Dimes.

EXAM TIP — gilbert

Don't confuse an ambiguity with a mistake on an exam because different rules apply regarding the admissibility of extrinsic evidence. An ambiguity is an *inconsistency in the will* that cannot be resolved by reading the plain meaning of the will. The ambiguity can be inconsistent when *applied to the facts* (latent ambiguity) (*e.g.*, the testator devises his property at 411 Willow Lane, but the property owned by the testator is actually located at 114 Willow Lane) or it can appear on the *face of the will* (patent ambiguity) (*e.g.*, "I devise five dollars ($500) to my sister."). Although courts traditionally did not allow extrinsic evidence to cure an ambiguity, a growing number of states now allow extrinsic evidence because it does not change the testator's intent or the nature of the dispositions made. However, a mistake does not involve an inconsistency, but instead involves an inaccurate or incorrect depiction of the testator's true intent. The plain meaning rule is usually applied and extrinsic evidence is admissible to cure mistakes only in *very limited circumstances* (see *supra*, §899).

(1) Time at which intent ascertained [§911]

The extrinsic evidence must reflect on the testator's intent at the time the will was *executed*. [*See, e.g.*, **Lydick v. Tate**, 44 N.E.2d 583 (Ill. 1942)]

(a) Comment

Although a will is said to "speak as of the date of the decedent's death," this relates to the effect and operation of the instrument—*not* to its construction. If the will is unclear or ambiguous, and thus requires interpretation, it must be construed according to the circumstances existing at the *time of its execution*.

> **e.g.** **Example:** A bequest to "my housekeeper" is interpreted as referring to the testator's housekeeper at the time she executed the will, not at the time of her death.

(2) Admissibility of testator's declarations [§912]

The courts are in disagreement as to the admissibility of the testator's declarations regarding what she intended when she executed the will.

(a) Majority rule—not admissible [§913]

By majority rule, a testator's alleged declarations to third parties are *not admissible*. [*See* **Breckheimer v. Kraft**, 273 N.E.2d 468 (Ill. 1971)]

(b) Modern trend—admissible [§914]

The modern and better view is that these declarations are admissible to cure *latent* ambiguities [*See, e.g.,* **Evans v. Volunteers of America**, 280 S.W.2d 1 (Mo. 1955); **Baker v. Linsly**, 379 S.E.2d 327 (Va. 1989)], but not patent ambiguities [*See, e.g.,* **Breckner v. Prestwood**, 600 S.W.2d 52 (Mo. 1980)].

(c) Limited admissions [§915]

Some courts admit declarations made by the testator prior to or at the time of executing the will, but reject so-called fugitive declarations (those made afterwards). Other courts admit only indirect assertions of the testator's state of mind as opposed to direct statements as to what she intended.

> **e.g.** **Example:** Nick's statement to Cyrus that "Nancy is my favorite niece" would be admissible to show that Nick had intended to benefit the niece in the will; but the statement that "my will makes a bequest to my favorite niece Nancy" would not. The difference is that the first statement is a form of "facts and circumstances" evidence, whereas the second statement is too direct and, if admitted, would result in placing too great a reliance on oral testimony in interpreting the will. [*See, e.g.,* **Scheridan v. Scheridan**, 207 S.E.2d 691 (Ga. 1974)]

e. Rules of construction where no evidence of testator's intent [§916]

If the meaning of the will is uncertain, and reference to the surrounding circumstances fails to disclose sufficient evidence of the testator's probable intent, the courts generally indulge in certain legal presumptions or rules of construction.

(1) Construe as a whole [§917]

A will is to be construed as a whole, and conflicting provisions are to be *harmonized* if possible. Also, every provision of the will should be given effect if it is possible to do so. [*See, e.g.,* **Wiglesworth v. Smith,** 224 S.W.2d 177 (Ky. 1949)] To overcome inconsistencies, the courts use the following rules:

(a) *Specific provisions control over general provisions.* [*See, e.g.,* **Reid v. Voorhees,** 74 N.E. 804 (Ill. 1905)]

(b) *Later provisions control over former provisions* (and later codicils over earlier codicils or wills). [*See, e.g.,* ***In re* Smith's Estate,** 75 So. 2d 686 (Fla. 1954); **Osburn v. Rochester Trust & Safe Deposit Co.,** 209 N.Y. 54 (1913)]

(c) *Provisions in the testator's own handwriting control over typed or printed provisions.* (This assumes, of course, that the handwritten portions were on the will when it was signed and witnessed. *See supra,* §396.)

(2) Construe to avoid intestacy [§918]

If two constructions are equally possible, courts choose the one that *avoids intestacy* in whole or in part. The courts presume from the very fact that the testator made a will that she intended to avoid intestacy and to have *all* of her property pass under the will. [*See, e.g.,* **Holmes v. Welch,** 49 N.E.2d 461 (Mass. 1943); **Wiechert v. Wiechert,** 294 S.W. 721 (Mo. 1927)]

(3) Construe in favor of kin [§919]

If two interpretations are possible, and the testator's blood relatives would take under one interpretation but not under the other, courts generally construe the will in favor of the relatives and against "strangers."

(4) Meaning of words [§920]

Words in the will are to be given their *ordinary meaning.*

---

e.g. **Example:** A gift of "cash" ordinarily does not include stocks and bonds; likewise, a gift of "land" would not convey a leasehold. [***In re* Chamberlain's Estate,** 46 Cal. App. 2d 16 (1941)]

(a) Distinguish—will drafted by nonlawyer [§921]

Keep in mind that the fundamental rule of construction is to discern the testator's probable intent. Hence, contrary results have been reached, particularly when dealing with holographic wills drawn by laypersons. If the will was drawn by an illiterate or poorly educated testator, courts occasionally have been willing to give words a meaning other than their usual meaning.

DEFECTIVE EXECUTION	One or more of the ***requirements for execution is missing*** (*e.g.*, signature missing; witnesses did not sign in testator's presence). (*See supra*, §§367 *et seq.*)
VALID REVOCATION	The will has been validly revoked by ***subsequent instrument, physical act, or operation of law***. (*See supra*, §§498 *et seq.*)
LACK OF TESTAMENTARY CAPACITY	At the time of execution, the testator was ***under the age of 18*** or ***lacked the mental capacity*** required. To have capacity, the testator must understand the nature of her act, the natural objects of her bounty, the nature of her property, and the disposition she is making. The will must not be the result of an insane delusion.
LACK OF TESTAMENTARY INTENT	The testator must have known and understood the ***contents of the will*** and ***intended to make the dispositions*** therein.
UNDUE INFLUENCE	Influence was exerted on the testator that ***overpowered her mind and free will***, resulting in a testamentary disposition that would not have been executed but for the influence.
FRAUD	The testator was ***intentionally deceived*** as to the will itself or the facts surrounding its execution. Fraud involves false statements of material fact knowingly made by another with the intent of deceiving the testator and which do in fact deceive the testator and prompt her to act in reliance on those statements. There are two types of fraud: (i) a misrepresentation made as to the ***nature or contents*** of the instrument, *i.e.,* fraud in the execution; or (ii) a misrepresentation of ***fact*** that induces the testator into making a will or gift, *i.e.,* fraud in the inducement.
MISTAKE	The testator is (i) mistaken as to the ***nature*** of the instrument (*e.g.,* thought it was a power of attorney); (ii) she executes the will or devises a gift based on ***mistaken reasons;*** or (iii) there is a mistake contained in the ***contents*** of the will. Remember that a mistake does not involve fraud and that it is treated differently from an ambiguity.

> **e.g. Example:** Where an illiterate testator drafted his own will leaving the "balance of my money" to his mother, it was held that "money" passed the balance of the testator's property, both real and personal. [*See In re* **Estate of Miller**, 48 Cal. 165 (1874)]

> **e.g. Example:** An illiterate testator drafted his own will, leaving his estate to his "children." The court admitted evidence showing that the testator's children were dead when he executed his will, and that he had meant to name his grandchildren. [*In re* **Estate of Schedel**, 73 Cal. 594 (1887)]

(b) Technical terms [§922]

Technical terms used in the will (*e.g.,* "per stirpes") are to be construed in their technical sense—at least where the will has been drafted by an attorney. [*See, e.g.,* **Lombardi v. Blois**, 230 Cal. App. 2d 191 (1964)]

(c) Personal effects [§923]

Frequently, problems are encountered with gifts of "personal property," "personal effects," or "belongings" in a will. Generally, these phrases are construed **narrowly** and are held to encompass only items of tangible personal property intimately associated with the person (*e.g.,* clothing, jewelry, furs, perhaps automobiles, etc.). [*See* 94 A.L.R.2d 1106] Again, however, if there is any evidence of the testator's probable intent, the latter controls.

C. No-Contest Clause

1. Effect of No-Contest Clause [§924]

A no-contest clause (sometimes called an *in terrorem* clause) is a will clause that provides that any person who contests the will shall *forfeit all interests* he otherwise would have received under that will. There is a split of authority as to the validity and effect of no-contest clauses.

a. Majority rule [§925]

In most states and under the UPC, a beneficiary who unsuccessfully contests the will does *not* forfeit the legacy *if* the court finds that the beneficiary challenged the will *in good faith* and on the basis of *probable cause*. [*See, e.g.,* **In re Seymour's Estate**, 600 P.2d 274 (N.M. 1979); UPC §3-905; 23 A.L.R.4th 369] However, the forfeiture provision is given effect if the court finds that the beneficiary had no reasonable basis for contesting the will, but filed the contest in order to squeeze a settlement out of the estate.

(1) Rationale

Giving effect to the forfeiture provision in all cases in which the contest was unsuccessful might discourage a person who had a legitimate basis for challenging the will from doing so. Such clauses should not be given effect so as to discourage meritorious litigation. "If fraud, coercion and undue influence . . . can be covered up and made secure by the insertion of a forfeiture condition into a will . . . we may . . . be putting another weapon into the hands of the racketeer." [**Barry v. American Security & Trust Co.,** 135 F.2d 470 (D.C. Cir. 1943)—dissenting opinion]

b. Minority rule [§926]

A minority of states give *full effect* to no-contest clauses even if the losing contestant had probable cause for challenging the will. [*See, e.g.,* **Barry v. American Security & Trust Co.,** *supra;* **Rudd v. Searles,** 160 N.E. 882 (Mass. 1928); **Commerce Trust Co. v. Weed,** 318 S.W.2d 289 (Mo. 1958); **Dainton v. Watson,** 658 P.2d 79 (Wyo. 1983)]

(1) Rationale

In will contests based on lack of testamentary capacity, and to some extent in contests based on undue influence grounds, the testator's character, habits, and personal traits are put in issue. A testator should be allowed to protect her reputation as well as her dispositive plan from post-death attack.

(2) New York view [§927]

By statute in New York, a no-contest clause is given effect despite the presence of probable cause for bringing the contest. However, the following *exceptions* are recognized by the statute: (i) a contest on the ground that the will was *forged* or was *revoked* by a later will, if the contest was based on *probable cause*; (ii) objection to the *jurisdiction* of the court (*e.g.,* a challenge to probate of a will on the ground that the testator was a domiciliary of another state); (iii) a contest brought on *behalf of an infant or incompetent*; or (iv) an action to *construe* the will's terms. [N.Y. Est. Powers & Trusts Law §3-3.5]

c. Florida view—clause unenforceable [§928]

Reflecting a policy that no heir should be discouraged from bringing a will contest that may have merit, a Florida statute provides that no-contest clauses are *unenforceable in all cases.* [Fla. Prob. Code §732.517]

d. Effect of clause if will denied probate [§929]

What is the effect of a no-contest clause if the will contest is successful? The answer, of course, is that if the will is denied probate, the no-contest clause is tossed out along with the will.

NO-CONTEST CLAUSES	gilbert
EFFECT OF CLAUSE	**Majority rule:** The clause is **not given effect if** the beneficiary challenged the will in **good faith** and with **probable cause**. **Minority rule:** The clause is given **full effect** regardless of whether or not the beneficiary had probable cause to challenge the will.
ACTIONS THAT DO NOT TRIGGER CLAUSE	• **Suit to construe** will's terms. • **Objection to jurisdiction** of court • **Challenge to appointment of executor or to accounting** • **Offering later will** • **Withdrawal of will contest** without pursuing matter.

2. Actions that Do Not Constitute a Contest [§930]

A challenge to the will based on lack of testamentary capacity or undue influence clearly triggers a no-contest clause. But what about other actions brought by a beneficiary? While the answer to this question turns in part on the language of the no-contest clause, it is generally held that the following actions do *not result in a forfeiture.*

a. Construction suit [§931]

An action brought to *construe the will* does not challenge the will's basic validity, but is simply asking: What did the testator mean? What interests were created? [*See* 49 A.L.R.2d 198] This includes an action to establish that a provision in the will violates the Rule Against Perpetuities. [*See In re* **Harrison's Estate**, 22 Cal. App. 2d 28 (1937)]

b. Objection to jurisdiction of court [§932]

A challenge to the will's probate on *jurisdictional grounds* (*i.e.,* that the decedent was domiciled in another state) does not challenge the will's validity, but merely seeks to have the will probated in the proper state. [*See* **Maguire v. Bliss,** 22 N.E.2d 615 (Mass. 1939)]

c. Challenge to appointment of, or accounting by, executor [§933]

A challenge to the *appointment of an executor* or to an *accounting made by the executor* is not a challenge to the will. Enforcement of a forfeiture on such grounds would be against public policy, as it would tend to prevent challenge of the executor's actions on behalf of the estate. [*See* **Wojtalewicz's Estate v. Woitel,** 418 N.E.2d 418 (Ill. 1981)]

d. Offering subsequent wills for probate [§934]

Offering a *subsequent will for probate* that the proponent believes to be genuine does not trigger a no-contest clause in an earlier will even if the subsequent will is denied probate. *Rationale:* The proponent had a duty to offer the subsequent will for probate, so that the court could rule on its validity. [*See In re* **Estate of Westfahl,** 674 P.2d 21 (Okla. 1983)]

e. Will contest filed but subsequently withdrawn [§935]

It is generally held that a no-contest clause is not triggered if a party files a will contest but subsequently *withdraws the contest without pursuing the matter.* [*See In re* **Estate of Stiehler,** 133 Misc. 2d 253 (1986)]

D. Tort Liability for Wrongful Interference with Expected Inheritance

1. In General [§936]

Even if an heir or intended beneficiary is not able to set aside a will or testamentary gift on the ground of fraud, duress, or undue influence, he may be able to obtain a tort recovery for wrongful interference with his expected inheritance. [*See, e.g.,* **King v. Acker,** 725 S.W.2d 750 (Tex. 1987); Restatement (Second) of Torts §774B] Although an heir apparent or a beneficiary named in a living person's will has only an "expectancy," in recent years courts have recognized a cause of action for wrongful interference with that expectancy, drawing an analogy to tort cases dealing with wrongful interference with a contractual or business relation. [*See* **Davison v. Feuerherd,** 391 So. 2d 799 (Fla. 1980)]

Example: Ted and his second wife Delia raised Ted's daughter Elizabeth from childhood. When Ted died, he left his entire estate to Delia, who then established a revocable trust that would make gifts to Elizabeth and others on Delia's death. Elizabeth alleged that Delia (80 years old, in poor health, and under the defendants' care and constant supervision) decided to amend the trust so as to name Elizabeth as sole beneficiary; that Delia instructed her attorney to prepare the amendment; and that the defendants, upon learning of this, falsely persuaded Delia that Elizabeth did not love her, was not concerned about her, and was not worthy of receiving her estate. They told Delia that they were the only ones who cared for her, that they should be rewarded by being left her estate, and that they would withdraw the care and comfort upon which she had become dependent if she did not amend the trust to leave the estate to them. The court held that Elizabeth's complaint stated a cause of action for tortious interference with an expected testamentary gift. [**Davison v. Feuerherd,** *supra*]

2. Proof Required [§937]

To recover, the plaintiff has the burden of proof to establish:

(i)   The *existence* of her expectancy;

(ii) That the defendants *intentionally interfered* with her expectancy;

(iii) The interference involved *conduct tortious in itself,* such as fraud, duress, or undue influence;

(iv) That there is a reasonable certainty that the devise to the plaintiff *would have been made but for* another's interference; and

(v)   Damages.

[*See, e.g.,* **Nemeth v. Banhalmi,** 425 N.E.2d 1187 (Ill. 1981)—facts similar to **Davison v. Feuerherd,** *supra*—plaintiff was primary beneficiary under two earlier wills]

a.   No relief available in probate proceedings [§938]

Some courts impose an additional requirement that the plaintiff must have attempted to pursue a remedy in probate proceedings, or else must show that no remedy is available in probate proceedings. [*See, e.g.,* **McGregor v. McGregor,** 101 F. Supp. 848 (D. Colo. 1951), *aff'd,* 201 F.2d 528 (10th Cir. 1951)—no attempt to probate alleged lost will]

3.   Distinguish—Tort Recovery for Suppression of Will [§939]

To be distinguished from the "expectancy" cases are cases in which the plaintiff alleges that the defendant *wrongfully suppressed a will* in the plaintiff's favor. Courts have always recognized a cause of action on this ground, since the gravamen of the complaint is that the plaintiff *had* a property interest given to him by the decedent's will, and that the defendant wrongfully interfered with that property interest.

Example: Wife destroyed Husband's will (allegedly containing a legacy to Beneficiary) because she was dissatisfied with its provisions. Two years later, Wife sought probate of the will as a lost will. Although the will was admitted to probate under the rules governing probate of lost wills (*see supra,* §§567 *et seq.),* there was insufficient evidence to establish Beneficiary's legacy in the probate proceedings. Beneficiary then sued for a tort recovery and won, the court holding that the decision of the probate court regarding Beneficiary's legacy was *not* res judicata. The probate court merely decided that the preliminary proof required by statute to enable the court to pass upon the legacy had not been furnished. "The issue here, whether as a matter of fact the will contained a legacy to plaintiff, never reached the stage of decision . . . ." Thus, in this *tort* case, Beneficiary could prove his legacy, and that Wife intentionally interfered with it. [**Creek v. Laski,** 227 N.W. 817 (Mich. 1929)]

Chapter Twelve: Probate and Estate Administration

CONTENTS

Chapter Approach

This chapter will give you a general understanding of the estate administration process. Most of this information is not likely to be tested in great detail on a law school exam (although you may see a question on abatement, the nonclaim statute applicable to creditors' claims, or the powers and duties of an executor). Nevertheless, a careful reading of this chapter will be important to a general understanding of exam questions. For example, you won't be thrown by unfamiliar terminology such as "ancillary administration," "formal" versus "informal" probate, or "guardian ad litem."

A. Overview of Estate Administration Process

1. Terminology [§940]

"Probate" refers to the judicial proceeding in which an instrument is established as the duly executed last will of the decedent (or, if there is no will, the proceeding in which the decedent's heirs are judicially determined). After the will is admitted to probate (or the heirs are determined) and a personal representative is appointed (*executor* if named in the will; *administrator* if appointed by the court), the administration of the decedent's estate begins. Estate administration is the process whereby the decedent's assets are marshalled, creditors' claims are paid, the tax authorities are satisfied, and the remaining assets are distributed according to the decedent's will or the intestacy statutes. Technically, a decedent's will is *probated,* and the decedent's estate is *administered*; however, the term "probate" is commonly used to refer to all steps in the process of estate administration ("probate administration" or "the probate process").

2. Steps in the Process [§941]

While the procedures vary in detail from state to state, the following steps are involved in administering a decedent's estate in all jurisdictions.

a. Opening the estate—probate [§942]

The first step in the estate administration process is to "open" the probate proceeding. The decedent's last will is offered for probate, and its due execution is proven. (*See infra*, §§987 *et seq.*) Or, if the decedent left no will, the decedent's intestate heirs are judicially determined. At the same proceeding, the decedent's personal representative (executor or administrator) is appointed by the court and is issued *letters testamentary* or *letters of administration* evidencing the authority to act on behalf of the estate. Only a duly appointed personal representative has the authority to act on behalf of the estate, *e.g.,* by giving a binding

Opening of the estate
- Duly executed will is admitted or intestate heirs are determined
- Personal representative is appointed

Collection of decedent's probate assets
- Personal representative takes possession and control of probate assets (nonprobate assets pass outside probate)
- Personal representative has right to sell assets if necessary to satisfy claims (although title vests immediately in will beneficiary or heir)

Protection of surviving family members
- If appropriate, a family allowance is paid, homestead rights are fixed, and an exempt personal property set-aside is made

Payment of creditors
- Notice to creditors is given by publication; personal notice is given to known or readily ascertainable creditors
- Creditors' claims are paid or disallowed

Payment of taxes
- Estate's and/or decedent's personal tax returns are filed by personal representative
- Taxes paid from estate assets

Distribution of assets
- After funeral and administration expenses, creditors' claims, and taxes are paid, assets remaining are distributed to will beneficiaries or heirs
- Personal representative is discharged

receipt and release upon collection of a bank account in the decedent's name. [*See* **Brobst v. Brobst**, 155 N.W. 734 (Mich. 1916)]

b. Collecting the decedent's assets [§943]

The personal representative is under a duty to take possession and control of the decedent's assets. Although title to a decedent's real and personal property *vests immediately* in the decedent's legatees, devisees, or heirs, the personal representative has the right to possess the assets for purposes of satisfying creditors' claims and winding up the decedent's affairs. [*See* UPC §3-709; Tex. Prob. Code §37]

(1) No hiatus in title [§944]

There is no hiatus or gap in the ownership of or title to any of the decedent's assets. The assets are owned by the decedent up to the moment of death, and immediately after death the assets are owned by the legatees, heirs, or devisees. It may take some time before the identity of the owners is determined (*e.g.,* if the decedent's will is contested), but once that ownership is determined, title *relates back* to the moment of death.

(2) Personal representative's right of possession [§945]

The personal representative is entitled to take possession of the decedent's assets, selling them if necessary to satisfy claims against the estate. Thus, in estates that are likely to be in administration for a fairly long period, it is customary to have securities that were in the decedent's name re-registered in the personal representative's name, so that income from the assets will be collected by the representative. However, in many instances (and particularly for assets such as tangible personal property) the personal representative does not assert this right of possession and, instead, leaves the assets in the physical possession of the surviving family members.

(a) Minority view [§946]

A substantial minority of states follow the common law rule that title to (and the right to possession of) *real property* vests immediately in the heirs or legatees, and the personal representative does not have the right to possession of the decedent's real property. Even in these states, however, the personal representative can sell the real property, if necessary, for the payment of claims against the estate.

(3) Nonprobate assets [§947]

Only assets owned by the decedent at death and passing by will or intestate succession are subject to the personal representative's possession for purposes of administration. Nonprobate assets, such as property passing by right of survivorship (*e.g.,* joint tenancies) or pursuant to a contract (*e.g.*, life insurance proceeds), are not subject to the rules and procedures governing estate administration. (*See supra*, §§13-17.)

c. Family allowance, homestead, and exempt personal property set-aside [§948]
Upon petition by the appropriate surviving family members, and upon approval by the court, the personal representative pays a family allowance, fixes any homestead right granted by the state (or pays the allowance in lieu of homestead), and makes a set-aside of any exempt personal property. (*See supra*, §§295 *et seq.*)

d. Creditors' claims [§949]
The personal representative gives *notice by publication* of the estate administration and gives *personal notice* to secured creditors and known or readily ascertainable creditors. The personal representative also pays or disallows creditors' claims. (*See infra*, §§1055 *et seq.*)

e. Taxes [§950]
The personal representative is responsible for filing all tax returns on behalf of the decedent or the decedent's estate, and is personally liable to see that all taxes are paid. Actual payment of the tax is, however, from estate assets.

(1) Decedent's final income tax return [§951]
Invariably, the personal representative has to file at least one income tax return even if the estate is too small to require the filing of a state or federal estate tax return. The personal representative must file an income tax return that reports income for the decedent's final taxable year.

---

e.g. Example: Xavier, who was a calendar year taxpayer, dies on May 19, and in due course Elle is appointed executor of Xavier's estate. On April 15 of the following year, Elle must file Xavier's final income tax return, which will report Xavier's income from January 1 to his death on May 19. (*See* Income Tax I Summary.)

---

(2) Income from estate assets [§952]
If the estate includes income-producing assets, all of the income from those assets will be received by the personal representative during the period the estate is in administration. The personal representative must select a taxable year (either a fiscal year or a calendar year) for the estate. If the estate has more than $600 of income in any taxable year, the personal representative must file a fiduciary income tax return (Form 1041) reporting the income.

(3) Death taxes [§953]
Depending on the size of the estate, the personal representative may be

required to file a state inheritance tax return and a federal estate tax return. (*See* Estate and Gift Tax Summary.)

f. Distribution [§954]

After the payment of funeral expenses, expenses of administration, valid claims against the estate, and any taxes that may be due, the personal representative distributes the assets remaining on hand to the will beneficiaries or intestate heirs. In most jurisdictions, this final distribution is made after a hearing at which the probate court enters a decree of distribution and discharges the personal representative from any further duties and all liabilities.

3. Court Supervised vs. Unsupervised Administration

a. Majority rule—supervised administration [§955]

In many jurisdictions, except for very small estates (*see infra,* §§1099-1100) all steps in the probate administration process are subject to the court's supervision and control. These states have one-size-fits-all procedures, which apply to all estates regardless of their size or complexity (or lack thereof). Before the personal representative can take any required action on behalf of the estate (*e.g.,* payment or disallowance of creditors' claims, sale of an asset to pay claims or expenses, distribution to a beneficiary or heir, etc.), ***court approval must be obtained*** at a hearing after notice is given to all interested parties. Although a number of jurisdictions permit a testator to provide in the will that some acts can be taken without court approval (*e.g.,* sale of real or personal property), except for purely ministerial acts, virtually every action taken on behalf of the estate involves court supervision. The personal representative is seen as a representative of the court in winding up the decedent's affairs. As a result, the administration of even a fairly modest estate can be expensive and time consuming.

(1) Need for supervision [§956]

An independent administration or an unsupervised administration under the UPC (*see infra,* §§957-961) has the advantage of simplifying the administration of estates. Nevertheless, a number of states have declined to adopt similar procedures on the ground that such advantages do not outweigh the opportunities for abuse by dishonest or incompetent representatives that might arise from insufficient judicial policing. *Comment:* This means that all estates must be subjected to time consuming and expensive procedures out of a concern that problems and disputes may be encountered in a handful of estates.

b. Minority rule—independent (unsupervised) administration [§957]

Several jurisdictions have enacted statutes allowing estates to be administered independent of court supervision. [*See, e.g.,* Wash. Rev. Code §11.68.011; D.C. Code §20-401; Ill. Comp. Stat. ch. 755, §5/28-1; Ind. Code §29-1-7.5-1; Mo. Rev. Stat. §473.780] Although these statutes vary greatly in detail, they are patterned on the Texas procedure. In Texas, a testator may designate an "independent executor," and may provide in the will that no action shall be taken in the probate court in regard to the estate other than the admission of the will to probate and the filing of an inventory, appraisement, and list of claims of the estate. After the will has been admitted and the independent executor has been appointed, the executor proceeds to administer the estate entirely on her own, *without* the many routine court appearances required in a supervised administration. [Tex. Prob. Code §145]

(1) Effect [§958]

Recognizing that most probate administrations are harmonious, nonlitigious affairs in which the surviving family members desire to wind up the decedent's estate with a minimum of formality and expense, an independent or unsupervised administration allows the personal representative to administer and distribute the estate *without court supervision.* Thus, notices and hearings attendant to a court supervised administration can be dispensed with. (*See infra*, §§1025 *et seq.* for a detailed discussion of the personal representative's duties.)

(2) California statute [§959]

The California independent administration procedure [Cal. Prob. Code §§10400 *et seq.*] is not widely used because the independent executor must give notice to interested parties with respect to numerous transactions, a time consuming and somewhat costly procedure. In California, revocable inter vivos trusts are widely used to avoid the complications and expense of a probate administration.

c. Uniform Probate Code [§960]

The UPC provides for both "unsupervised administration" and "supervised administration."

(1) Unsupervised administration [§961]

Under the UPC, all administrations are *unsupervised* unless a supervised administration is requested by the personal representative or any interested party (*e.g.,* beneficiary, heir, creditor). [UPC §3-502] Under an unsupervised administration, the personal representative administers and distributes the estate without court supervision [UPC §3-704], meaning that the notices and hearings attendant to a court supervised administration can be dispensed with. (*See infra*, §§1025 *et seq.* for a detailed discussion of the personal representative's duties.)

(2) Supervised administration [§962]

Under the UPC's supervised administration provisions, court approval must be obtained before a distribution of the estate may be made. [UPC §3-504] However, a personal representative may still exercise many other administration powers (*e.g.,* pay claims or the family allowance, sell property, etc.) without court approval. [UPC §3-504] The court considers the request for supervision and, if granted, supervises the distribution. Moreover, in appropriate cases the court may direct a supervised administration proceeding even though the will directs that the administration is to be unsupervised. [UPC §3-502]

d. Informal administration procedures [§963]

In the case of a very modest estate, no formal administration or court involvement may be needed to wind up the decedent's affairs. Many jurisdictions encourage informal family settlements (*see infra,* §1095), and a number of states have simplified administration procedures for handling small estates (*see infra,* §§1099-1100).

SUPERVISED VS. UNSUPERVISED ADMINISTRATION		gilbert
	SUPERVISED (MAJORITY RULE)	**UNSUPERVISED (MINORITY RULE)**
COURT APPROVAL AFTER NOTICE AND HEARING	Required for virtually all actions	Required to open estate and possibly to close
BENEFITS	Protection against dishonest or incompetent personal representative	Simplifies administration of estate; less expensive
DETRIMENTS	Expensive and time consuming	Less protection

4. Jurisdiction and Venue [§964]

Primary probate jurisdiction is in the state of the decedent's *domicile at the time of death*.

a. Court [§965]

In most states, the court having jurisdiction over probate matters and estate administrations is called a *probate court*. In some states, the court is called an orphan's court (Pennsylvania), and in others a surrogate's court (New York). Typically, these courts also have jurisdiction over guardianship and conservatorship administrations of the estates of minors and incapacitated persons.

b. In rem jurisdiction [§966]

A probate proceeding is *in rem; i.e.,* it *conclusively determines* as against *all persons* the title and ownership of the decedent's property that is subject to the court's jurisdiction.

c. Venue

(1) Resident [§967]

Under statutes found in nearly all states, venue for probate and estate administration lies in the *county of the decedent's domicile* at the time of death. [UPC §3-201]

(2) Nonresident [§968]

Where a nonresident left property located in the state, venue is proper in any county where the decedent *owned property,* or where *any debtor* of the decedent resides. [*See* Fla. Prob. Code §733.101]

d. Real property in another state—ancillary administration [§969]

Under the situs rule, a court in one state cannot adjudicate ownership and transfer of title to *real property* located in another state. (*See* Conflict of Laws Summary.) If the decedent owned real property located in another state, *ancillary* probate and administration proceedings are required in the other state in order to clear title to property. [UPC §4-101] The ancillary administrator takes *possession of the property* within his jurisdiction, satisfies the *claims of creditors* within that state, and then *distributes the surplus,* if any, to the principal executor or administrator.

e. Choice of law rules [§970]

As a general rule, all questions as to the validity or construction of a will are settled in the place of *primary administration* (domicile), and once determined are accepted as binding in the ancillary proceedings. [UPC §3-202] However, because of the situs rule, determinations made by the court handling the primary administration may not always be recognized as conclusive on questions regarding title to real property in another state. (*See* Conflict of Laws Summary.)

EXAM TIP **gilbert**

When ancillary administration is being tested on an exam, you will see a fact pattern in which the testator was domiciled in one state but owned *real* property in another state. Don't be confused by facts that state that the testator owned *personal* property in another state—this does not give rise to ancillary administration. In writing an answer to an ancillary administration question, analyze the administration procedures of each state separately and remember that the ancillary administrator is responsible only for the real property located in the other state, not for the property located in the state of the decedent's domicile.

B. Proof of Wills in Probate

1. Duty to Produce Will [§971]

By statute in many states, a person who has possession of a decedent's will must present the will to the probate court within a specified period. Failure to produce the will ("will suppression") results in *civil liability* to the beneficiaries harmed thereby, and in some states results in criminal liability. [*See, e.g.,* Ark. Code §28-40-105; Conn. Gen. Stat. §45a-282; D.C. Code §18-111; Wash. Rev. Code §11.20.010]

2. Who May Offer Will for Probate [§972]

A will may be offered for probate by *any person interested in the estate*: the named executor, a beneficiary named in the will, an intestate heir of the decedent, or even a creditor having a claim against the estate.

3. Time Within Which Will Must Be Probated [§973]

In most states, a will must be offered for probate within a specified number of years after the decedent's death or the decedent is deemed to have died intestate. [*See, e.g.,* Ind. Code §29-1-7-15.1—three years]

a. Uniform Probate Code [§974]

Under the UPC, a will must be offered for probate within *three years* after the decedent's death. If no will is probated within the three-year period, the presumption that the decedent died intestate becomes conclusive. [UPC §3-108]

b. Minority rule [§975]

In several states, there is no time limit on when a will must be offered for probate. [*See In re* **Estate of Schafroth**, 598 N.E.2d 479 (Ill. 1992)] In other states, while there is no time limit, there may be legal consequences if the will is not offered for probate within a prescribed period. [*See* Pa. Cons. Stat. tit. 20, §3133—bona fide purchaser of real property protected if will not probated within one year; Tex. Prob. Code §73—proponent must show she was "not in default" in failing to file for probate within four years after testator's death; Va. Code §64.1-95—if will not probated within one year, persons who purchase real property from the decedent's heirs are protected as bona fide purchasers]

EXAM TIP   **gilbert**

Be sure to address the following issues in an exam question that focuses on whether a decedent's will was properly probated:

- Did the person in *possession of the decedent's will* offer it for probate?

- Does the person offering the will for probate have the *authority* to do so—*i.e.,* does she have an interest in the decedent's estate?

- Was the will offered for probate within the statutorily prescribed *time period*?

If any of these elements is not satisfied (*e.g.,* the will is offered for probate *after* the three-year period prescribed by state statute has expired), the decedent's will is *denied probate* and his estate is distributed according to the intestacy statutes. Additionally, remember that if the person who failed to probate the will is the person who had possession of the will, she is subject to civil, and possibly criminal, liability.

---

4. **Informal vs. Formal Procedure for Admitting Will [§976]**

Although the term "probate" typically refers to the entire estate administration process (*see supra*, §940), in the following discussion it simply refers to the process required to prove whether a decedent's will is valid.

a. **Common law [§977]**

At common law, the procedure for admission of the will could take one of two forms:

(1) **Probate in common form [§978]**

Probate in common form was an *ex parte proceeding* in which no notice to interested parties was required. The will proponent offered the will for probate, the attesting witnesses testified as to due execution, and the will was admitted to probate. Unless the will was contested within a prescribed period of time, the order admitting the will to probate became final. Common form probate was frequently used, as most probates are harmonious and uncontested.

(2) **Probate in solemn form [§979]**

Under a probate in solemn form, *notice* was required to be given to all interested parties, who could challenge the will at the probate proceeding.

b. **Uniform Probate Code [§980]**

The UPC authorizes the two forms recognized at common law, but gives them different names.

(1) **Informal probate [§981]**

An informal probate is an *ex parte* proceeding held before a *registrar,* rather than the court, under which *no notice* is given to interested parties. [UPC §3-301] This procedure is used when there is no likelihood that the will is going to be contested. However, after a will has been admitted to probate in the informal proceeding, a contestant can initiate formal testacy proceedings within three years after the decedent's death.

(a) **Limitations [§982]**

The informal probate procedure may *not* be used if the decedent left a series of testamentary instruments, the latest of which does not expressly revoke the earlier. [UPC §3-304] Also, an informal proceeding may not be used if a will contest is filed. [UPC §3-401]

(2) **Formal testacy proceeding [§983]**

A formal testacy proceeding is, as the name suggests, a formal adjudication in which it is determined whether the decedent left a valid will. Such a proceeding may be brought by any interested party (i) to obtain a *formal adjudication* that a will should be admitted to probate, (ii) to *set aside or prevent informal probate* of a will, or (iii) to obtain an order that the decedent *died intestate*. The proceeding is held before the *court* after *notice* to interested parties. Personal notice is given to known interested parties (*e.g.*, heirs, devisees named in the will), and notice by publication is given to unknown heirs. [UPC §§3-401 - 3-414]

c. Majority rule [§984]

In most states, probate is a formal, adjudicative proceeding in which notice must be given to all interested parties. However, several states, mainly on the east coast, continue the common form/solemn form probate of the common law, and several non-UPC states have adopted the UPC's informal probate/formal testacy procedures. [*See* W. Va. Code §41-5-5]

5. Burden of Proof [§985]

At the time the will is offered for probate, the *will proponent* has the burden of proving that the will was duly executed. [*See* **Lee v. Lee**, 424 S.W.2d 609 (Tex. 1968)] If the challenge to the will's execution is made after the will is initially admitted to probate, the burden of proof *shifts to the contestants*. [*See* **Curtis v. Curtis**, 481 F.2d 549 (D.C. Cir. 1973)]

a. Proof of execution cannot be waived [§986]

The requirement of formal proof of due execution cannot be waived by the admission of opposing parties or by consent of all concerned parties. Even if all interested parties want the instrument to be admitted to probate, if the probate court finds that it was not properly executed, or if there is no evidence of due execution, probate must be denied. An instrument that has not been properly executed *is not a will*. [*See* **Hopkins v. Hopkins**, *supra*, §367]

6. Proof of Due Execution

a. Testimony of attesting witnesses [§987]

In most states, *both* attesting witnesses must testify in open court as to the facts surrounding execution of the will. That testimony must show that the requirements of due execution were complied with. [*See, e.g.,* Ill. Comp. Stat. ch. 755, §5/6-4; Mo. Rev. Stat. §473.053.1] In several states, the testimony can be taken by the court clerk rather than in open court if probate is unopposed. Some states are much more liberal, and require the testimony of only one attesting witness. [*See* Tex. Prob. Code §84]

(1) Absent or unavailable witness [§988]

If one attesting witness is dead, incompetent, or cannot be located, it is usually provided that her testimony can be dispensed with and the will can be admitted to probate on the testimony of the other attesting witness. If a witness resides outside the county (some jurisdictions) or outside the state (other jurisdictions), it is usually provided that the absent witness's testimony can be taken by deposition or interrogatory. If all the attesting witnesses are dead, incompetent, or otherwise unable to testify, proof of the handwriting of the testator and of at least one of the attesting witnesses is required in most states.

b. Attestation clause [§989]

A well-drafted will invariably contains an attestation clause appearing beneath the testator's signature line and above the signature lines for the attesting witnesses. The attestation clause recites the facts of due execution. (*See supra*, §440.)

(1) Prima facie evidence [§990]

An attestation clause is prima facie evidence of the facts recited therein. Accordingly, when a will contains an attestation clause, it can be admitted to probate even though the attesting witnesses' memories fail them and they have no recollection of the circumstances surrounding the will's execution. [*See In re* **Katz's Will**, 277 N.Y. 470 (1938)] The will can even be admitted if the witnesses' testimony is hostile to the will's probate. [*See* **Jones v. Whiteley**, 533 S.W.2d 881 (Tex. 1976)]

Example: A will was admitted to probate even though one attesting witness testified that he had not signed in the testator's presence, and that in fact the testator's signature on the will was forged. (There was other credible evidence of due execution.) [**Jones v. Whiteley**, *supra*]

---

(2) Not a substitute for attesting witnesses' testimony [§991]

Unlike in the case of a self-proving affidavit, a will cannot be admitted to probate on the strength of an attestation clause alone. The attestation clause can be used to corroborate evidence of due execution (*e.g.*, testimony of the attesting witnesses or proof of testator's and witnesses' signatures), but it is ***not a substitute*** for such evidence. (*See supra*, §446.)

c. Self-proved will [§992]

Where a self-proving affidavit was executed at the time the will was executed (or thereafter), the will is *admissible* to probate on the strength of the recitals in the affidavit. (*See supra*, §445.) The procedures described above apply only if the will was not self-proved.

7. Whether Will Was Validly Executed Is a Question of Fact [§993]

If the fact finder determines, on the basis of testimony by a handwriting expert, that the testator's signature was forged, the will is not entitled to probate even though disinterested, credible attesting witnesses testify that they saw the testator sign the will. [*See In re* **Estate of Sylvestri**, 44 N.Y.2d 260 (1978)—jury believed testimony of expert witness that the testator's signature was forged, and not testimony of three attorneys who testified that they saw the testator sign the will] If there was evidence to support the jury finding, that finding will not be disturbed on appeal. While the probate judge ordinarily rules on the validity of a will, many states provide for trial by jury upon the motion of any party. [*See* N.Y. Surr. Ct. Proc. Act §502(1)]

PROVING DUE EXECUTION OF A WILL — gilbert

A WILL'S PROPONENTS CAN PROVE THAT THE WILL WAS DULY EXECUTED BY ANY OF THE FOLLOWING METHODS:

TESTIMONY OF ATTESTING WITNESSES	Witnesses testify in *open court or before a court clerk regarding the facts surrounding the will's execution*. If one of the witnesses is unavailable (*e.g.*, dead), her testimony is dispensed with. However, if she merely resides in another county or state, most jurisdictions allow her testimony to be obtained by deposition or interrogatory. If both witnesses are, *e.g.*, dead, the handwriting of the testator and at least one witness must be proven.
ATTESTATION CLAUSE	A properly drafted attestation clause can be used *in conjunction with* the testimony of the attesting witnesses to prove the facts surrounding the will's execution.
SELF-PROVING AFFIDAVIT	Due execution can be established by the *information contained in a will's self-proving affidavit*. The testimony of the attesting witnesses is not necessary.

---

8. Will Written in Foreign Language [§994]

A will written in a foreign language may be admitted to probate under the same procedures that apply to an ordinary will, except that the will must be accompanied by an English translation. [*See* Fla. Prob. Code §733.204]

9. Lost Wills [§995]

All states have procedures whereby a will that has been lost or accidentally destroyed can be admitted to probate. Because questions concerning alleged lost wills arise most frequently in the context of the issue of revocation, this topic is discussed *supra,* at §§567 *et seq.*

10. Ante-Mortem Probate [§996]

Three states (Arkansas, North Dakota, Ohio) allow proof of the validity of a will *during the testator's lifetime* as a means of winning a will contest while the testator is still alive. [*See* Ark. Code §28-40-201; Ohio Rev. Code §2107.081; *and see* Aloysius A. Leopold & Gerry W. Beyer, *Ante-Mortem Probate: A Viable Alternative*, 43 Ark. L. Rev. 131 (1990); Mary Louise Fellows, *The Case Against Living Probate*, 78 Mich. L. Rev. 1066 (1980)] Absent such a statute, a court does not have jurisdiction, under the Declaratory Judgment Act or otherwise, to determine the validity of the will of a living person. [*See* **Cowan v. Cowan,** 254 S.W.2d 862 (Tex. 1952)]

C. Appointment and Qualification of Personal Representative

1. Terminology

a. Executor [§997]

An executor is a person *named in the will* to serve as personal representative. The executor's appointment is evidenced by the court's issuance of *letters testamentary,* which show the executor's authority to act on behalf of the estate.

b. Administrator [§998]

An administrator is a personal representative *appointed by the court* to administer an *intestate estate.* The administrator's appointment is evidenced by *letters of administration.*

c. Uniform Probate Code [§999]

The UPC uses one term, *personal representative,* in lieu of the more specialized terms such as executor and administrator. [UPC §1-201(35)]

d. Administrator c.t.a. [§1000]

If the decedent left a will but the will does not name an executor, or the named executor fails to act for some reason, the person appointed to administer the estate is titled an *administrator with will annexed,* or administrator c.t.a. (standing for *cum testamento annexo*).

e. Special or temporary administrator [§1001]

If it is necessary to obtain the *immediate* appointment of a personal representative prior to the formal appointment of a permanent executor or administrator, a special administrator may be appointed. [*See, e.g.,* UPC §§3-614 - 3-618; Ala. Code §43-2-47; Ark. Code §28-48-103] This might occur where there is a will contest, meaning that appointment of the executor named in the will is in doubt during the pendency of the contest, or where there is a dispute over priority of appointment as administrator between various next of kin. In some jurisdictions, the person holding this position is called a temporary administrator. [*See* Ga. Code §53-6-30]

f. Successor personal representative [§1002]

If an executor or administrator properly begins to serve but ceases to act for some reason, a successor executor or administrator is appointed by the court.

g. Guardian

(1) Guardian of the person [§1003]

A guardian of the *person* of a minor child is charged with the *custody and care* of the child and is responsible for the child's upbringing. A child's parents are, of course, the child's *natural guardians.* In many states, the surviving parent may designate a guardian of the person for his children in the will. [*See* Tex. Prob. Code §676] The nomination is not binding on the court, but is given considerable weight.

(a) If no designation of guardian by parents [§1004]

If minor children are orphaned and no guardian is designated in either parent's will, or if the parents left no will, the guardian is selected from a statutory list that, in most states, gives preference to grandparents, uncles and aunts, and other kin, in that order. (Of course, the statutes do not indicate which grandparents, maternal or paternal, or which uncle or aunt, is to be selected.) One of the primary reasons parents of minor children should have wills is to take advantage of the opportunity to designate who will be responsible for raising their children if the children are orphaned.

(2) Guardian of the estate [§1005]

If a minor inherits property and no provision has been made for the property's management (*e.g.*, by a settlement in trust), it may be necessary to appoint a guardian of the minor's *estate.* This situation would be encountered if the child were orphaned, but it also could arise if either or both parents are living if, *e.g.*, the child is given a substantial bequest by an uncle's will. In most states, a personal representative *cannot make a distribution to a minor;* only a duly appointed guardian of the child's estate can give the personal representative a binding receipt and release for the distribution. Although a parent is guardian of the child's person, he has *no authority* to handle the child's estate. In many states, guardianship laws are cumbersome and restrictive. Typically, the guardian must give *bond* (with annual premiums), must make *annual accountings,* can invest only in savings accounts and government bonds, and cannot expend anything other than income for the child's benefit *without court approval.*

(a) Distributions of small amounts of property [§1006]

Many jurisdictions have statutes that permit distribution of small amounts of tangible or intangible personal property from an estate or trust to the parents of a minor beneficiary or heir. [*See, e.g.*, Fla. Guard. Code §744.301—up to $15,000; Md. Est. & Trusts Code §13-501—up to $5,000]

(b) Distributions to custodian under Uniform Transfers to Minors Act [§1007]

In states that have enacted the Uniform Transfers to Minors Act ("UTMA"), and in several states that have amended their version of the Uniform Gifts to Minors Act ("UGMA"), distributions may be made from an estate or trust to a custodian for the minor heir or beneficiary under the UTMA (or UGMA). [*See, e.g.,* N.Y. Est. Powers & Trusts Law §7-6.22; Tex. Prop. Code §141.006] *Rationale:* A custodianship provides *flexible management and administration powers* without court involvement and expenses attendant to a guardianship administration.

(3) Guardian ad litem [§1008]

A guardian ad litem is a person appointed by the court to *represent the interest of a minor or incapacitated heir or beneficiary,* when no guardian of the estate has been appointed and the party's interests are not otherwise represented. The court may appoint a guardian ad litem even though a guardian has been appointed, if the court feels that the representation may be inadequate. An example of this latter situation would be where the guardian has an interest that is adverse to that of the ward. A guardian ad litem also may be appointed to represent the interests of unborn, unascertained, or unlocatable persons. [*See* Fla. Prob. Code §731.303]

TYPES OF GUARDIANS	gilbert
GUARDIAN OF THE PERSON	Responsible for the **custody and care of a minor child**. May be nominated by the parent's will or, if no guardian is designated, selected from a statutory list.
GUARDIAN OF THE ESTATE	Responsible for **managing a minor's estate**. Must give bond, make annual accountings, can invest only in savings accounts and government bonds, and may spend income only for the child's benefit (unless a court approves otherwise).
GUARDIAN AD LITEM	Responsible for representing the interests of a **minor or incapacitated heir or beneficiary**. Appointed by the court.

2. Qualification of Personal Representative [§1009]

To be eligible for appointment as a personal representative, a person must have the *capacity to contract.* Thus, minors and incompetent adults are ineligible to serve. Several states also provide for disqualification from appointment for drunkenness, conviction of a felony, etc. [*See, e.g.,* Fla. Prob. Code §733.302]

a. Conflict of interest [§1010]

The mere fact that the person seeking appointment has a claim against the estate or some interest adverse to that of the estate does not by itself disqualify the person from appointment. [*See, e.g.,* **Boyles v. Gresham**, 263 S.W.2d 935 (Tex. 1954); 18 A.L.R.2d 633]

> **e.g.** **Example:** "[W]hen the testator executed his will . . . he was aware of his nominee's position with the corporation, and of his own disputes with the corporation. He named him nevertheless. Testator's knowledge of a possible conflict of interest militates against denying appointment to his choice." [*In re Foss's Will*, 282 A.D. 509 (1953)]

b. Nonresidents [§1011]

In most jurisdictions, there is no impediment to naming a nonresident of the state as personal representative. The nonresident must, however, appoint a *resident agent for service of process*. In a few states, nonresident individuals are disqualified from acting as personal representatives. [Pa. Stat. Ann. tit. 20, §3157] Even more frequently, foreign corporations are disqualified. Finally, some states permit the appointment of a nonresident personal representative only if the person (i) is a relative of the decedent, or (ii) resides in a state that permits nonresidents to be appointed (a reciprocity rule). [*See* Ohio Rev. Code §2109.21]

EXAM TIP   **gilbert**

To determine whether an individual is qualified to serve as a personal representative, remember the following:

- The person must have **capacity to contract**.

- **Minors** and **incompetents** cannot serve.

- **Conflicts of interest** do not by themselves make a person ineligible.

- **Nonresidents** are eligible to serve in most states.

---

3. Priority for Appointment [§1012]

In all states, statutes fix the order of priority for appointment as a personal representative of an estate. The UPC provisions are representative. The UPC's priority is: (i) the person named in the will as executor; (ii) the surviving spouse (if a beneficiary under the will); (iii) any other will beneficiary; (iv) the surviving spouse (even if not a will beneficiary, or if there is no will); (v) any other heir; and (vi) if 45 days have elapsed since the decedent's death, any creditor. [UPC §3-203]

a. Executor named in the will [§1013]

Note that the person named in the will *must* be appointed as personal representative *unless* disqualified by statute or court-developed rule. [*See* Wis. Stat. §856.21] Objection by other family members that the named person is untrustworthy or irresponsible, has shown hostility to the principal will beneficiaries, is indebted to the estate, etc., are invariably rejected by the courts. *Rationale:* It "has ever been the policy of the law . . . that every citizen making a will has the right to select according to his own judgment the person or persons whom he would have execute it." [*In re* Svacina's Estate, 1 N.W.2d 780 (Wis. 1942)]

4. Bond [§1014]

In most states, the personal representative must give a fiduciary bond (typically, for double the value of personal property in the estate) *unless* bond is waived by the will.

a. Distinguish—Uniform Probate Code [§1015]

Under the UPC, bond is *not required in informal probate proceedings* unless the will expressly requires that the executor give bond. In formal testacy proceedings, the court can dispense with the necessity of a bond even if there is no will provision waiving bond. [UPC §3-603] In either type of proceeding, however, any person with an interest in the estate, including a creditor, may demand that the personal representative give bond. [UPC §3-605]

5. Compensation [§1016]

The personal representative is entitled to compensation for performance of his services. In many states, a *statutory rate* of compensation (based on the size of the estate) applies, absent a contrary will provision. [*See, e.g.,* Cal. Prob. Code §§10800 - 10803; N.Y. Surr. Ct. Proc. Act §2307]

a. Will provision [§1017]

If the will specifies the amount or rate of compensation for the personal representative, and the personal representative accepts the appointment, the will provision is *binding*. The personal representative cannot thereafter attempt to claim the higher fees authorized by statute. Acceptance of the appointment constitutes an acceptance of the decedent's offer of compensation, and the personal representative is bound by the contract. If, however, the personal representative performs *extraordinary services* beyond those ordinarily involved in an estate administration, the court may award additional compensation for such services. [*See* 19 A.L.R.3d 520]

b. Uniform Probate Code [§1018]

Under the UPC, a personal representative is entitled to *reasonable compensation* for his services. If a will provides for compensation of the personal representative and there is no contract with the decedent regarding compensation, the personal representative may renounce the provision before qualifying as personal representative and be entitled to reasonable compensation rather than the amount stated in the will. [UPC §3-719]

c. Reasonable compensation [§1019]

As noted above, the UPC provides for reasonable compensation of personal representatives. Also, a common practice in will drafting is to provide that the personal representative shall be entitled to "reasonable compensation" in lieu of the mode of compensation provided by statute. In implementing such a provision, the standard practice is to look to rates of compensation that prevail in the community, including fiduciary fees charged by banks and trust companies for serving as personal representative. In some jurisdictions, the local court promulgates a fee schedule to be used as a guideline in determining reasonable compensation. However, such guidelines may be challenged as providing excessive compensation. [*See In re* **Estate of Rolfe,** 615 A.2d 625 (N.H. 1992)]

d. Waiver of compensation [§1020]

If the will names the surviving spouse or some other family member as executor, it is quite common for the executor to waive the right to compensation and serve as personal representative at no cost to the estate. There may be tax advantages in doing so, as compensation received by the personal representative is taxable as ordinary income under the federal income tax. If no compensation is paid to the executor, the estate will not be entitled to a deduction for this item under the federal estate tax or state succession tax. However, under current tax laws, very few estates pay estate or succession taxes. (*See* Estate and Gift Tax Summary.) In such a case, loss of an estate tax deduction for this item would be of only theoretical concern.

Example: Svetlana dies leaving a will that bequeaths her entire estate to her son Vladimir and names him as executor. Under state law, Vladimir would be entitled to receive $8,000 in compensation for his services. He should waive the right to compensation. Since he will receive Svetlana's entire estate under her will, the only effect of accepting the compensation will be to increase his taxable income by $8,000.

Compare: If, however, Svetlana's estate will have to pay a federal estate tax or state succession tax, whether Vladimir should waive or accept the compensation (thereby entitling the estate to an $8,000 deduction at the cost of Vladimir's having taxable income) should be determined by comparing the estate's marginal estate tax bracket to Vladimir's marginal income tax bracket.

6. Termination of Appointment [§1021]

Certain events result in termination of a personal representative's appointment and authority. These include: death or disability, resignation, judicial determination of misconduct, judicial ruling that a prior determination of testacy was incorrect, entry of an order closing the estate, or passage of one year after a closing statement is filed. [UPC §§3-608 - 3-612]

a. Resignation [§1022]

Once appointed, the personal representative *cannot* merely resign. She is charged with the fiduciary duties and responsibilities set forth below until the court that appointed her has *accepted* her resignation. This usually requires an accounting that shows all receipts and disbursements, and a transfer of the estate's assets to the successor personal representative.

b. Removal [§1023]

The personal representative may be removed (and letters of appointment revoked) whenever she is shown to have been guilty of *misconduct* in administration, or to be lacking in any of the *qualities* required for a personal representative. [*See, e.g.,* UPC §3-611; *In re* **Estate of Frey,** 693 A.2d 1349 (Pa. 1997)] Failure to perform any of the duties required of the personal representative, or acting in adverse interest or hostility to the estate or the beneficiaries, constitutes grounds for removal. [*See In re* **Palm's Estate,** 68 Cal. App. 2d 204 (1945)] However, "the removal of a personal representative chosen by the testator is a drastic action which should be undertaken only when the estate . . . is endangered," and mere animosity between the executor and other beneficiaries does not constitute grounds for removal. [*In re* **Beichner's Estate,** 247 A.2d 779 (Pa. 1968)]

D. Duties and Liabilities of Personal Representative

1. Qualification [§1024]

Before letters testamentary or letters of administration are issued, the personal representative has a duty to file with the court a statement accepting the appointment. [UPC §3-601] In most states, the personal representative must give a *fiduciary bond* (*see supra,* §§1014-1015).

2. Powers and Duties [§1025]

Unlike a trust, which may continue for the lifetime of one or more beneficiaries, an estate administration is usually of short duration. Accordingly, the personal representative's powers and duties are limited to those required to manage and preserve the decedent's assets during the period of administration.

a. Marshalling assets [§1026]

The personal representative's initial duty is to *take possession or control* of the assets belonging to the decedent. The representative must do everything required to obtain possession of and care for all such assets. In carrying out this responsibility, the representative is granted the same powers that an absolute owner would have [*See* UPC §§3-709, 3-715], and is empowered to maintain an action to recover possession of property or to determine title to it [*See* Fla. Prob. Code §733.607].

(1) Exception—tangible property [§1027]

Any real or tangible personal property may be left with, or surrendered to, the person presumptively entitled to it (*i.e.,* will beneficiary or heir) unless possession of such property by the personal representative is necessary for purposes of administering the estate.

(2) Only probate assets [§1028]

The estate assets that are subject to the personal representative's management and control do *not* include nonprobate assets, such as property that passes by right of survivorship (*e.g.,* joint tenancy) or by the terms of a contract (*e.g.,* insurance proceeds), or property held in a trust, even if the decedent held a power of revocation or power of appointment. (*See supra,* §§13-17.)

(3) Duty not to commingle assets [§1029]

The personal representative may not commingle estate assets with his own, either in making investments or otherwise. Accordingly, the representative should open a separate bank account in the name of the estate.

b. Inventory [§1030]

The personal representative must file an inventory of the estate property, listing it with *reasonable detail* and including for each listed item its *estimated fair market value* as of the date of the decedent's death. [*See* Fla. Prob. Code §733.604] Several states require that one or more appraisers must be appointed to value estate assets, while in other states the appointment of an appraiser is optional. In most states, however, appointment of an appraiser is at the court's option. [*See* Tex. Prob. Code §248]

c. Accounting [§1031]

In most states, the personal representative must render periodic accountings to the probate court, typically within *12 months* after appointment and successive annual accountings thereafter. The personal representative cannot be discharged until his *final accounting* has been approved by the probate court.

d. Care and preservation of assets [§1032]

The personal representative must exercise *reasonable care* in preserving the assets of the estate. Basically, he must manage the estate with the degree of care that a prudent person would exercise in managing his own affairs, with an eye towards preservation of the property. This includes a duty to *insure property* for which a prudent person would obtain casualty insurance, the duty to *prevent property from being taken or damaged* by the acts of others, and the duty to *pay taxes* thereon.

e. Investments [§1033]

The representative's primary duty is to *preserve* the estate—not to invest it and make it productive. Consequently, in most states, the representative has no inherent power to invest funds belonging to the estate. However, monies belonging to the estate should be deposited in a bank account in the estate's name. [*See* Cal. Prob. Code §9700] Also, a duty to invest may be implied from the circumstances, particularly if the administration will remain open for an extended period of time. And, of course, if the will authorizes or directs the executor to invest, he may do so.

(1) Exception [§1034]

Under the duty to preserve the estate, the representative may be under a duty to sell assets or change investments if necessary to avoid loss or unreasonable risk of loss to the estate.

f. Carrying on decedent's business [§1035]

In most states, the personal representative ordinarily has *no duty or authority* to carry on a business owned by the decedent. If he does so without authorization or prior court approval (*see* below), he is *personally liable* for any losses and, of course, is personally accountable for the profits. [*See, e.g.,* **In re Kurkowski's Estate**, 409 A.2d 357 (Pa. 1979); 58 A.L.R.2d 365]

(1) Authority may be conferred [§1036]

Authority to continue the operation of the decedent's business may be conferred by the will, or by express consent of all beneficiaries, heirs, and other persons interested in the estate. Upon petition, the court may authorize the representative to continue the decedent's business.

(2) Minority rule [§1037]

Under the UPC and in several non-UPC states, the personal representative may continue any unincorporated business or venture in which the decedent was engaged at the time of death for a period of *four months.* Also, the representative may continue the business throughout the period of administration, if the business is incorporated by the representative and no interested party objects. [UPC §3-715(24), (25)] In addition, the representative may consent to the reorganization, merger, or consolidation of any corporation or other business enterprise. [UPC §3-715(19)]

g. Sale or mortgaging of estate assets [§1038]

In most jurisdictions, the representative has the power to sell property of the estate *only when authorized by the will or court order.* A sale of estate assets generally will be authorized by the court when necessary to pay debts of the estate, to provide funds for the payment of bequests, or to prevent loss to the estate (*e.g.,* the assets are declining in value). Also, if the decedent was bound by a specifically enforceable contract to convey or transfer real or personal property, the court may authorize the representative to make the conveyance or transfer pursuant to the contract.

(1) Borrowing [§1039]

The representative may be authorized to borrow on the credit of the estate and to give a mortgage on estate assets if necessary to pay estate debts or expenses of administration.

(2) Will provision [§1040]

If the decedent's will confers a specific power to sell or mortgage real property or a general power to sell any asset of the estate, the personal representative may sell, mortgage, or lease real property without court order for cash or credit, with or without security. Such actions need not be justified by a showing of necessity. [*See* Fla. Prob. Code §733.613]

(3) Uniform Probate Code [§1041]

Under the UPC, a personal representative need not obtain specific authorization to sell or mortgage assets, since this power is granted by the UPC. [UPC §3-715(23)] The representative is prohibited from selling, etc., only when express restraints have been imposed upon him under the will or by court order.

h. Leases [§1042]

If *authorized by the will or court order,* the personal representative may execute a lease of any asset belonging to the estate. [*See* Ala. Code §43-2-440] Typically, the statutes provide that the lease may extend beyond the expected period of estate administration [*See* Minn. Stat. §524.3-715(9)], but some statutes place a limit on the term of such leases [*See* Miss. Code §91-7-225— 15 years].

(1) Uniform Probate Code [§1043]

The UPC permits leasing of assets without court authorization, unless the representative has been *specifically restrained* from doing so. [UPC §3-715(23)]

3. Fiduciary Duties [§1044]

A personal representative is subject to the fiduciary duties and standards of conduct that apply to fiduciaries generally.

a. Standard of care, skill, and prudence [§1045]

A personal representative is held to the *general standard of care* that applies to trustees. [*See* Fla. Prob. Code §733.602] Therefore, he must observe those standards in dealing with estate assets that would be observed by a prudent trustee dealing with the property of another. If the representative has *special skills* or is named personal representative on the basis of representations of special skills or expertise, he is under a duty to use those skills. [*See, e.g.,* Fla. Prob. Code §737.302; *and see* Trusts Summary]

b. Duty of loyalty—no self-dealing [§1046]

The personal representative owes a duty of *undivided loyalty* to the estate that he represents. In general, a personal representative cannot "wear two hats" (his fiduciary "hat," representing the estate; and his personal "hat," representing his individual interest) in any transaction with respect to the estate.

Thus, a personal representative cannot sell assets to the estate nor buy assets from the estate. Also, the personal representative cannot borrow estate funds for his personal use, no matter how well-secured the loan may be, and no matter how fair the rate of interest may be. (*See* Trusts Summary.)

EXAM TIP   **gilbert**

Remember that a personal representative's duties of care and loyalty are to be exercised *in conjunction with* his other duties. In other words, you need to determine whether *each act* of the personal representative is carried out with due care and loyalty. For example, if your exam question presents facts where a personal representative sells or mortgages estate assets, you must not only assess whether he had authority to do so (*e.g.*, check to see if authority is provided in the will or by court order), but also whether he acted reasonably in doing so (*e.g.*, was the asset sold for a reasonable price?).

---

(1) Rationale

The theory underlying the self-dealing rules is *not* (or at least not necessarily) that the personal representative might act dishonestly or might use the fiduciary office to personal advantage. Rather, it is that the personal representative is not in a position to make a completely objective, impartial judgment if his personal interest is affected by the transaction. Should this loan be made? Should this particular asset be sold (or purchased); and if so, on what terms? The personal representative's judgment as to the wisdom of a particular course of action may be tainted, no matter how slightly, if his own personal interest is involved.

(2) Exceptions [§1047]

It is generally held that a personal representative may be allowed to buy or sell an estate asset from or to himself if he had entered into a *buy-sell agreement* with the testator during the testator's lifetime, or *if authorized by the court* upon a finding that the action is in the estate's best interests. Also, the *testator may waive* the self-dealing rules by an express provision to that effect in the will (*e.g.*, if the will gives the executor an option to purchase a particular asset in the estate).

(3) Uniform Probate Code [§1048]

Under the UPC, a sale of estate assets to the personal representative, his spouse, agent, attorney, or a corporation or trust in which he has a substantial interest, or a transaction that is affected by a substantial conflict of interest on the representative's part, is *voidable* unless (i) the will or a contract expressly authorizes the transaction, or (ii) the transaction is approved by the court after notice is given to interested persons. [UPC §3-713]

4. Liabilities [§1049]

As is true of any fiduciary, a personal representative is liable for any losses resulting from actions taken in bad faith, mismanagement, or breach of a fiduciary duty (including the duty not to self-deal). [*See* UPC §3-712]

a. Torts [§1050]

At common law and in most states today, an executor or administrator is *personally liable* for any torts committed by him or his agents in the course of administration of the estate. He is, however, entitled to *reimbursement* from the estate for any such liability, *provided* that (i) he was not personally at fault, and (ii) there was no breach of duty of care by him in incurring the liability (*e.g.*, the tort was committed by an agent or employee selected with reasonable care).

(1) Comment

For this reason, a personal representative should always take out liability insurance and charge the cost to the estate as an administration expense.

(2) Uniform Probate Code [§1051]

Under the UPC, a personal representative is individually liable for torts committed in the course of administration of the estate only if he was personally at fault. [UPC §3-808(b)]

b. Contracts [§1052]

By majority rule, the personal representative is *personally liable* on any contracts entered into on behalf of the estate unless the contract relieves him from liability. However, he is entitled to be *reimbursed* from the estate for any such obligation, *provided* the contract (i) was within his powers, and (ii) was entered into in the course of proper administration of the estate. Of course, if the estate is insolvent, the loss will fall upon the representative personally.

(1) Rationale

The personal representative is in a better position than the contracting party to know whether the estate's assets are sufficient to cover the obligation.

(2) Provisions that relieve personal representative of liability [§1053]

Signing a contract as "Sam Jones, Executor" does not eliminate personal liability but merely reflects the representative capacity. However, signing a contract "Mary Jones's Estate, by Sam Jones, Executor" reflects that the *contract is with the estate,* not the executor, and eliminates personal liability.

(3) Minority rule [§1054]

In several states, a personal representative is *not* personally liable on the estate's contracts unless (i) he fails to reveal his representative capacity, or (ii) the contract provides for personal liability. [*See, e.g.,* UPC §3-808(a);

N.Y. Est. Powers & Trusts Law §11-4.7; Fla. Prob. Code §733.619—exception for contracts for attorney's fees]

GENERAL DUTIES AND LIABILITIES OF PERSONAL REPRESENTATIVE — gilbert

DUTIES

- Give **notice** of estate administration to creditors of the estate (*see infra*, §1055).

- **Marshalling assets** (personal representative takes possession or control of the decedent's probate assets; commingling is not permitted).

- File **inventory;** each asset must be listed with reasonable detail along with its fair market value.

- Provide **accounting** of estate assets within 12 months after appointment and annually thereafter.

- **Preserve assets** with reasonable care; must also pay taxes on the assets.

- Administer estate pursuant to general standard of **care, skill, and prudence**; personal representative is under a duty to use any special skills.

- Exercise **loyalty** and not act with personal interest when administering the decedent's estate.

LIABILITIES

- Responsible for losses arising from **bad faith, mismanagement, or breach of fiduciary duty**.

- Liable for any **torts committed by him or his agent**. Can obtain reimbursement if he (i) was not personally at fault, and (ii) acted with reasonable care. Under the UPC, the personal representative is liable only if he was personally at fault.

- Liable for any **contracts entered into on behalf of the estate** unless the contract insulates him from liability. Can seek reimbursement if (i) estate is solvent, (ii) he had power to enter into the contract, and (iii) contract was entered into in course of proper administration of estate. Under minority law, the personal representative is liable only if (i) he failed to reveal his representative capacity, or (ii) the contract makes him liable.

E. Creditors' Claims

1. Notice to Creditors [§1055]

One of the personal representative's first duties is to give notice to creditors of the estate advising of the pendency of the administration and when and where claims must be filed. Within a time prescribed by statute, the representative must give *notice by publication* in a newspaper of general circulation.

2. Unsecured Claims

a. Nonclaim statutes [§1056]

Most states have nonclaim statutes (sometimes called bar statutes), under which a creditor must file its claim within a prescribed period of time. [*See, e.g.,* Fla. Prob. Code §733.702—three months; Mo. Rev. Stat. §473.360—six months] If not timely filed, the claim is *barred* even if the statute of limitations otherwise applicable to the claim has not run. The purpose of the short nonclaim period is to facilitate the winding up of decedents' estates so that estates can be distributed to the heirs or beneficiaries free of any concern about creditors' claims.

(1) Minority rule [§1057]

In several states, a creditor who does not file claims within the time prescribed by the nonclaim statute is *not* barred. The only consequence is that the creditor *loses priority* and is not paid until after all creditors who made timely filings have been paid. [*See* N.Y. Surr. Ct. Proc. Act §1802] In these states, failure to file a claim within the time prescribed by the nonclaim statute has significance *only if* the estate is partially insolvent.

b. Due process requirements [§1058]

Historically, only notice by publication was required to be given to general (*i.e.,* unsecured) creditors. In **Tulsa Professional Collection Services, Inc. v. Pope,** 485 U.S. 478 (1988), the Supreme Court held that an Oklahoma nonclaim statute requiring only notice by publication was unconstitutional as applied to known and reasonably ascertainable creditors. The Court ruled that, under the Due Process Clause, such creditors were entitled to *personal notice* before their claims could be barred by a nonclaim statute. The state action needed to invoke the Fourteenth Amendment was found in the probate court's involvement in the process. The probate court was directly involved in that only a personal representative appointed by a court could publish the notice that would start the nonclaim period. Although the *Pope* decision directly applied only to the Oklahoma statute, the effect of the decision was to invalidate, as to known or ascertainable creditors, all nonclaim statutes that relied on notice by publication only. The states responded in one of several ways:

(1) Majority rule—personal notice to known and ascertainable creditors [§1059]

Most states with nonclaim statutes have added the requirement that personal notice must be given to creditors who are known to, or whose identities are reasonably ascertainable by, the personal representative. Under the representative Illinois statute, if a creditor does not file its claim within the later of (i) six months after the first publication of the notice of administration, or (ii) three months after receiving personal notice, the claim is barred. [*See* Ill. Comp. Stat. ch. 755, §5/18-3] Under these statutes, personal notice does not have to be given to creditors with contingent or conjectural claims. Such claims are barred after expiration of the time period prescribed in the statute providing for notice by publication. [*See* **U.S. Trust Co. v. Haig**, 694 So. 2d 769 (Fla. 1997)]

(2) UPC—short statute of limitations [§1060]

The revised UPC adopts a *one-year* statute of limitations that applies to *all claims* against a decedent's estate, whether due or to become due, absolute or contingent, liquidated or unliquidated, whether founded on contract, tort, or any other legal basis. The one-year statute of limitations applies whether or not there is a formal estate administration proceeding, and thus applies even if there is no publication of a notice of administration. [UPC §3-803(a)]

(a) Comment

This approach is based on dictum in the Supreme Court's decision in the *Pope* case, to the effect that a self-executing statute of limitations that applies in all cases, and that is not triggered by any court proceeding, does not involve state action and is constitutionally permissible.

(b) Permissive personal notice [§1061]

The revised UPC also provides that a personal representative may give *personal notice* to known or reasonably ascertainable creditors, in which case the creditor's claim is barred *unless* presented within *the later of* (i) four months after the first publication of notice of administration, or (ii) 60 days after delivery of the personal notice. [UPC §3-801] Several non-UPC states have enacted similar provisions. [*See* Tex. Prob. Code §294(d)]

> **EXAM TIP**   gilbert
>
> Remember the following limitations periods for barring creditors' claims under the UPC: The claims of creditors who are not known to or reasonably ascertainable by the personal representative are barred *four months* after the first publication of the notice of administration. If known or ascertainable creditors are given personal notice, their claims are barred on the date that is the *later* of (i) *four months* after the first publication of the notice of administration, or (ii) *60 days* after delivery of the personal notice. In all other cases, all creditors' claims are barred *one year* after the decedent's death.

(3) Exception for claims covered by liability insurance [§1062]

The above statutes invariably provide that the time limit within which creditors' claims must be filed does not apply to claims to the extent that they are covered by liability insurance. [UPC §3-803(d)] These provisions reflect that the purpose of a state's nonclaim statute or short statute of limitations is to give protection to decedents' estates, not insurance companies.

3. Secured Claims [§1063]

Secured creditors must be given *personal notice* of the estate administration, typically by registered or certified mail. Upon receiving such notice, the secured creditor has two options:

a. Immediate payment of claim [§1064]

The creditor can *present its claim for full payment* (typically within four or six months after receipt of notice), even though the note secured by the lien has not matured and is not in default (*e.g.,* 12 years to go on a 30-year mortgage note). *Rationale*: The decedent was personally liable on the obligation secured by the lien. Inability to present the claim and collect from the decedent's estate would deny the creditor the opportunity to realize on the decedent's personal liability.

(1) Priority [§1065]

The secured creditor's claim for payment has priority (typically, as against all claims except funeral expenses) to the extent of the value of the security interest. In satisfying the claim, the personal representative may (i) pay the claim out of the general assets of the estate, or (ii) cause the property to be sold and apply the net sale proceeds against the claim.

(2) Deficiency [§1066]

If the property is sold and the net sale proceeds are insufficient to pay the claim in full, the secured creditor is entitled to collect the balance from the general assets of the estate. However, as to such deficiency, the creditor is relegated to the same priority as general creditors. Thus, if the estate is insolvent, as to the deficiency the secured creditor will collect, *e.g.,* 30 cents on the dollar along with the general creditors.

b. Reliance on lien [§1067]

Alternatively, the secured creditor can *waive the opportunity to be paid from the estate* and, instead, rely solely on its security interest in satisfaction of the obligation. (Under most statutes, if the creditor does not present its claim for payment with the prescribed period, it is automatically relegated to lien-only status.) The creditor might elect this option if the market value of the property exceeds the note balance by a healthy margin (*e.g.,* property worth $200,000; balance on secured note is $40,000) and the interest rate on the note is at or above market levels. Even though the person who succeeds to ownership of the property is not personally liable on the note, the creditor need not be concerned about nonpayment, as it can foreclose on the lien if payments on the note are not timely made.

(1) Personal representative's election to pay obligation [§1068]

It is generally provided that even if the secured creditor opts for lien-only status, the personal representative can elect to pay off the note without any prepayment penalty. This might be done if, for example, the property were specifically devised and the jurisdiction applies the common law "exoneration of liens" doctrine, requiring that the lien be exonerated by payment from the residuary estate. (*See supra*, §§812-814.)

4. Priority of Claims [§1069]

In all states, statutes fix the order in which claims against the estate are to be paid. Typically, it is provided that claims are to be paid in the following order:

(i) *Administration expenses;*

(ii) *Funeral expenses* and expenses of last illness (up to a stated dollar amount);

(iii) *Family allowance;*

(iv) *Debts given preference under federal law* (tax claims, etc.);

(v) *Secured claims* (up to value of security interest);

(vi) *Judgments* entered against the decedent during his lifetime; and

(vii) *All other claims.*

[*See, e.g.,* Cal. Prob. Code §11420; Fla. Prob. Code §733.707]

F. Abatement

1. Introduction [§1070]

Abatement problems arise in cases in which, after all creditors' claims have been paid, there are insufficient assets remaining to satisfy all of the gifts made by the will. The testator can specify in her will the source of funds from which claims against the estate are to be paid, and the order in which testamentary gifts are to be abated. If the testator has not done so, the rules set out below apply:

2. Classification of Testamentary Gifts [§1071]

The classes of gifts that can be made by a will are specific, demonstrative, general, and residuary. (*See supra,* §§767-771.)

3. Common Law Abatement (Minority View) [§1072]

At common law and in a handful of states today, all gifts of personal property, of whatever class, abate before dispositions of real property. [*See* **Edmunds's Administrator v. Scott**, 78 Va. 720 (1884)] The historical reason for this rule was that title to land passed directly to the heirs or devisees. The personal representative had the power to sell such real property *only* if the personal estate was insufficient to satisfy all claims against the estate.

a. Order of abatement [§1073]

In states following the common law, the order of abatement is:

(1) *Personal property* passing by *intestacy* (if there is a partial intestacy for some reason), if any.

(2) Next, personal property in the *residuary estate*.

(3) Next, *general* legacies, which abate pro rata.

(4) Next, *demonstrative* legacies.

(5) Then, *specific bequests* of personal property, which abate pro rata.

(6) Finally, *real property* but only after *all* personal property has been exhausted. Real property dispositions abate in the same order: any real property passing by intestacy, then real property in the residuary estate, and last to be abated are specific devises of real property.

b. Qualification [§1074]

A few jurisdictions nominally apply the common law rule (*i.e.,* that all gifts of personal property abate before any gifts of real property), but temper the rule if the court finds that the testator intended to charge the general and specific bequests on any real property in the residuary estate. Such an intent is found whenever the will contains a residuary clause that "blends" (*i.e.,* makes no distinction between) real and personal property, such as: "I give all of my residuary estate, both real and personal property . . . ." In such cases, the residuary estate must be exhausted (even as to real property in the residuary estate) before any other bequests are exhausted.

4. Modern Law (Majority View) [§1075]

In most states today, the distinction between real property and personal property has been abolished, at least insofar as abatement *between* categories of gifts are concerned. Thus, the order of abatement is:

(i) *Real or personal property* passing by partial *intestacy* is first exhausted.

(ii) Next, the *residuary estate* (both real and personal property) is abated.

(iii) Next, *general* legacies, which abate pro rata.

(iv) Finally, *specific* devises and bequests can be reached.

[UPC §3-902]

a. Abatement within categories [§1076]

In a handful of states, no distinction is made as to real and personal property *between* categories, but the distinction continues to be drawn *within* categories. Thus, personal property passing by partial intestacy abates before intestate real property; and personal property within the residuary estate abates before real property in the residuary estate. [*See* Tex. Prob. Code §322B]

b. Demonstrative legacies [§1077]

Demonstrative legacies are treated in the same category as specific gifts—at least to the extent that the property from which the gift was to be satisfied is in the estate at death. However, demonstrative legacies are classified the same as general legacies, and abate pro rata with general legacies, to the extent that the fund or property from which payment was directed is *insufficient* to satisfy the demonstrative legacy.

c. Variations [§1078]

There are numerous local variations in the operation of the above rules. In some jurisdictions, if gifts of the same class are made both to blood relatives and to others who are not related to the testator, the gifts to the nonrelatives abate first. [*See* Cal. Prob. Code §21402] In some states, gifts to the testator's surviving spouse do not abate until other gifts of the same category are exhausted. [*See* Fla. Prob. Code §733.805]

EXAM TIP **gilbert**

Remember that the abatement order under both the common law and modern views will take effect only if there is *no contrary instruction regarding abatement in the decedent's will*. Thus, if a decedent's will is probated in a state that still follows the common law view, and the will specifically directs that all real property should be used before any other property to satisfy claims in the event that there are insufficient assets to satisfy all bequests, *the will governs*.

G. Source of Payment of Death Taxes

1. State Inheritance Taxes [§1079]

An inheritance tax is considered a tax on the right to inherit. In states that have inheritance taxes, the tax rates and exemptions turn on the amount given to the beneficiary and the beneficiary's relationship to the decedent. Unless the testator specifies otherwise in the will, the burden of the tax is on the *recipient* of the gift. Thus, if the testator's will makes a bequest of $25,000 to Ben, and if an inheritance tax is payable by reason of this bequest, the burden of the tax is on Ben and must be paid out of Ben's legacy (absent a contrary will provision).

a. Estate taxes [§1080]

Until the 1970s, a majority of states had inheritance taxes as their primary succession tax. The remaining states had estate taxes which (as with the federal estate tax) are tied to the value of assets passing at death rather than the amount passing to each beneficiary as heir. Today, however, nearly all states have estate taxes, most of which do nothing more than absorb the "credit for state death taxes" allowed against the federal estate tax under Internal Revenue Code section 2011. (*See* Estate and Gift Tax Summary.) In such states, the source of payment of the state tax is the same as for the federal estate tax, discussed below.

2. Federal Estate Tax

a. Majority rule [§1081]

A majority of states follow common law principles in holding that federal (and state) estate taxes, as with other debts of the estate, are payable out of the *residuary* estate (absent a contrary will provision). This applies to all assets that generate estate tax, *including nonprobate assets* such as joint tenancy property passing by right of survivorship and revocable transfers.

(1) Exception [§1082]

The burden-on-the-residue rule is subject to exceptions created by federal statute. To the extent that the federal estate tax is attributable to life insurance proceeds, property over which the decedent held a general power of appointment, or property for which a marital deduction QTIP election was made, such proceeds or properties bear their pro rata share of the federal estate tax, subject to the following qualifications [I.R.C. §§2206, 2207]:

(a) Contrary will provision [§1083]

The testator can specify an alternative source of payment for the federal estate tax by a will provision to that effect.

(b) Marital deduction [§1084]

If the life insurance proceeds or general power of appointment disposition qualifies for the federal estate tax marital deduction, the federal statutes provide that such dispositions are relieved of any burden of the estate tax. (For the rationale for this exception, *see infra*, §1087.)

b. Apportionment statutes [§1085]

A substantial number of states have enacted apportionment statutes under which the estate tax is ratably apportioned *among all beneficiaries* of the estate—testamentary beneficiaries and beneficiaries of nonprobate dispositions, subject to the following qualifications [UPC §3-916; Cal. Prob. Code §20110]:

(1) Contrary will provision [§1086]

A testator can provide in the will that the apportionment rule shall not apply to her estate by expressly providing that the estate tax shall be paid from a specific source (*e.g.,* the residuary estate).

(2) Marital or charitable deduction [§1087]

A common feature of these statutes is that dispositions qualifying for the federal estate tax (or state succession tax) marital or charitable deduction are not subject to pro rata apportionment. *Rationale:* An estate tax deduction is available only for the net amount passing to the spouse or charity (*i.e.,* after all charges, including taxes). If these gifts were reduced by the taxes attributed to them, the deductions would be reduced and higher taxes would have to be paid.

H. Entitlement to Income During Period of Administration

1. Introduction [§1088]

The administration of an estate often takes a substantial period of time, and the classification of testamentary gifts determines the rights of the respective beneficiaries to earnings, interest, and profits on the estate assets.

2. Specific Gifts [§1089]

A specific devise or bequest carries with it the right to *all earnings,* profits, or other accessions produced by the particular property *after* the testator's death. [*See* Fla. Prob. Code §738.05] Thus, a devisee of real property is entitled to rent that becomes due on the property after the testator's death. On the other hand, the devisee is *not* entitled to rents that became due during the *testator's lifetime,* even though such rents are not paid until after the testator's death—the rental income is a general asset of the estate.

a. Bond interest and cash dividends [§1090]

The specific legatee of a bond is entitled to interest accruing on the bond *after* the testator's death. Likewise, dividends declared *after* the testator's death pass to the specific legatee. Dividends declared to stockholders of record during the testator's lifetime, although paid to the executor after the testator's death, do *not* pass to the legatee of specifically bequeathed stock. (For this purpose, it is the date the dividend is declared, not the date of its payment, that controls.)

b. Stock dividends and stock splits [§1091]

If the will makes a specific gift of stock, the beneficiary is entitled to stock dividends and stock splits declared *after* the testator's death. *Rationale:* The specific beneficiary owned the stock from the date of the testator's death, subject to the executor's possession for purposes of administration. [*See* **In re Marks's Estate,** 255 A.2d 512 (Pa. 1969)]

3. General Legacies [§1092]

In most states, a general legatee ("I bequeath $10,000 to my nephew Ned") is *not* entitled to interest on the legacy if it is paid within *one year* after the testator's death. If not so paid, the general legatee is entitled to interest at the legal rate, beginning one year after the testator's death (unless the will provides otherwise). [*See* Cal. Prob. Code §§12001 - 12003] The legal rate of interest varies, but in many states it is 6%. Under the UPC, interest on a general legacy begins to run one year after appointment of a personal representative (unless the will indicates a contrary intent). [UPC §3-904]

4. Residuary Gifts [§1093]

The residuary beneficiaries own all testamentary assets not specifically devised or bequeathed, after payment of all claims and satisfaction of all legacies. Thus, all earnings and profits not used to pay interest on general legacies, and not belonging to the recipients of specific gifts, are added to and become a part of the residuary estate.

WHAT IS A BENEFICIARY ENTITLED TO?	gilbert
SPECIFIC GIFTS	Beneficiary is entitled to *all earnings, profits, and accessions* to the property that *accrue after* the testator's death. He is also entitled to any *bond interest* that *accrues after* the testator's death and to any *cash dividends, stock dividends, and stock splits* that are *declared after* the testator's death.
GENERAL LEGACIES	Beneficiary is entitled to any *interest* on the legacy, beginning one year after the testator's death (or after the appointment of the personal representative, under the UPC), if the legacy is not paid within *one year after the testator's death*.
RESIDUARY GIFTS	Beneficiary is entitled to *all remaining assets* in the estate, including all earnings, profits, dividends, stock splits, etc., earned or declared *before* the testator's death.

I. Informal Administration Procedures

1. Introduction [§1094]

A major purpose of the estate administration process is to *clear title* to assets in the decedent's name, and to cause the appropriate records to reflect the *new ownership* of the persons who have succeeded to the decedent's property. In many instances, however, the decedent's estate is a modest one, consisting primarily of tangible personal property. In this situation, the decedent's successors may not need a court order or formal administration proceeding to deal with the decedent's assets or wind up his affairs. Insofar as the title-clearing function of probate is concerned, it is only when the decedent owned assets whose legal title is evidenced by a document (a deed to realty, a stock certificate, a certificate of title to an automobile) that a court proceeding may be required to establish the ownership rights of the decedent's successors. Recognizing that a formal administration proceeding is not necessary for modest-sized estates, all jurisdictions authorize one or more of the following simplified administration procedures.

EXAM TIP — **gilbert**

Remember that *nonprobate* assets are not part of a decedent's estate. (*See supra*, §§13-17.) Therefore, when figuring out whether probate is required, be sure to look for assets held in *joint tenancy with a right of survivorship* (usually bank accounts or real property) and for *life insurance policies, trusts,* and other contractual arrangements. Explain in your answer that these assets will pass outside of probate. Then see what is left in the estate to determine whether an informal administration procedure will suffice.

---

2. Informal Family Settlements [§1095]

If the decedent's estate is a small one (meaning that the authority of "letters of administration" is not needed to collect the assets), creditors' claims can be satisfied informally, and the decedent's family can reach an amicable agreement as to the proper distribution of the assets, there is no need to subject the surviving family members to the expenses and delays of a formal estate administration. They can wind up the decedent's affairs informally. [*See* **Heinz v. Vawter**, 266 N.W. 486 (Iowa 1936)] Statutes in several states recognize this principle by providing that there must be an affirmative showing that an estate administration is needed before letters of administration will be issued by the probate court. [*See* Tex. Prob. Code §§88(d), 178(b)] Moreover, empirical studies have shown that many small estates are handled informally even in the absence of statutory authority. [Robert A. Stein, *Probate Administration Study: Some Emerging Conclusions,* 9 Real Prop., Prob. & Trust J. 596 (1974)]

---

e.g. Example: Terrence dies survived by his wife, Rita, and several adult children. Terrence and Rita lived in an apartment (meaning that title to real property is not involved). Aside from the couple's checking account, a joint savings account (which passed to Rita by right of survivorship), and a life insurance policy that names Rita as beneficiary, Terrence's "estate" consists of the furniture and furnishings in the apartment and his personal effects. In this situation, it may occur to Rita and the children that there is no need to have a formal administration of Terrence's estate—and they are right. Rita can pay the funeral bill and the expenses of Terrence's last illness out of the savings account; and she can pay the gas bill and the monthly rent out of the checking account just as she did last month. If Rita decides to sell the color TV set, she is not going to have to furnish evidence of her title for such items. In this situation, *possession* is ten-tenths (not just nine-tenths) of the law. Terrence's successors, whether claiming under a will that is not probated or claiming as heirs, do not need any probate court involvement to wind up his affairs. (If Terrence died intestate, and a portion of the estate passed to his adult children, the children are not likely to assert any claim to his property as against their mother. The children's greatest concern is likely to be not their rights as heirs, but that they may be called upon to support their widowed mother who has been left such a modest estate.)

a. Comment

The rights of the surviving family members are further supported by the rule that title to a decedent's assets passes immediately and automatically to his legatees or heirs, subject to the personal representative's right of possession for purposes of administration. The effect of this provision is to legitimate the legatees' or heirs' simply taking possession of the decedent's property.

3. Affidavit Procedures [§1096]

Suppose, in the example, above that Rita and the children are able to handle Terrence's estate informally except for two items: the certificate of title to the family car, which is in Terrence's name (Rita now wants to sell the car); and a $2,000 bank account, which stands in Terrence's name with no survivorship provisions. Even here it may not be necessary to take out formal estate administration proceedings. Instead a *notarized affidavit* may suffice.

a. Bank accounts [§1097]

As a general rule, a bank cannot safely pay over an account in a decedent's name to anyone other than the decedent's duly authorized personal representative; only the representative can give the bank a binding "receipt and release" that will protect the bank against claims of others (*e.g.*, the decedent's creditors). [*See* **Brobst v. Brobst**, *supra*, §942] However, statutes in a number of states permit collection of small bank accounts by a notarized affidavit signed by the decedent's heirs. The bank is protected if it pays over the account pursuant to the affidavit. [*See, e.g.,* Miss. Code §81-5-63—$12,500 per bank; N.Y. Surr. Ct. Proc. Act §1310—not to exceed $15,000 in the aggregate]

b. Automobile certificates of title [§1098]

Similarly, a number of states permit the transfer of an automobile certificate of title to the decedent's heirs upon an affidavit signed by the heirs. [*See, e.g.,* D.C. Code §20-357; Iowa Code §321.47; Tex. Trans. Code §501.074]

4. Administration of Small Estates [§1099]

Nearly all states authorize simplified administration procedures for small estates. The appropriate family member files a verified petition stating that the value of the decedent's estate is less than a certain amount prescribed by the statute. The probate judge (in some states) or court clerk (in other states) then issues an affidavit that serves the same function as letters testamentary or letters of administration (*see supra,* §1096). Acting under the authority of the affidavit, the family member proceeds to collect accounts receivable or bank accounts standing in the decedent's name, reregister securities now in the decedent's name, or take whatever other actions are necessary to wind up the decedent's affairs.

a. **What constitutes small estate [§1100]**

The size of estate that qualifies for this streamlined procedure varies from jurisdiction to jurisdiction. [*See, e.g.,* D.C. Code §20-351—$40,000; Fla. Prob. Code §735.201—$75,000; N.Y. Surr. Ct. Proc. Act §1301—$20,000; Tex. Prob. Code §137—$50,000]

EXAM TIP   **gilbert**

Although it would appear that in states with only a $20,000 limit, only truly modest estates (*e.g.,* the estate of someone who qualified for the food stamp program) can qualify for a small estate administration. However, remember that "estate" means only the ***probate*** or testamentary estate; it does not include nonprobate assets. Second, in several states the amount of the qualifying estate is determined ***after*** deducting the family allowance, exempt personal property set-aside, and the homestead. [*See, e.g.,* Tex. Prob. Code §§137 - 144] Thus, if title to the decedent's $200,000 family home was held in a joint tenancy or tenancy by the entirety (or if it qualifies as a homestead), if the decedent's bank accounts and certificates of deposit had right of survivorship provisions, and if the decedent's principal wealth consisted of life insurance policies and employee death benefits under qualified retirement plans, it might even be possible for a millionaire's estate to qualify for a "small estate" administration.

---

5. **Probate of Will as Muniment of Title [§1101]**

Suppose, in the example above (*see supra,* §1095), that the family lived in a house, not an apartment, and that title to the family home is in Terrence's name. Except for the house, the estate can be handled informally under the procedures described above. In most states, it would be necessary to have a formal estate administration, so that the land title records would include a probate decree showing that all creditors' claims were satisfied and that Terrence's successors are now the owners of the property. Absent such a decree, the surviving family members could not sell or otherwise deal with the real property. The last deed in the chain of title would show Terrence as record owner, and getting his signature on the next deed out is going to be rather difficult.

a. **Muniment of title [§1102]**

In a few states, even in this situation it would ***not*** be necessary to have a formal estate administration. Upon a finding that there are no unpaid debts of the decedent (other than the mortgage on the homestead), the will is simply admitted to probate (*i.e.,* its due execution is proven as in the ordinary case). The will (which names the devisees, and thus the new owners) and the order admitting it to probate become part of the county records and constitute a "muniment of title"—*i.e., **a link in the chain of title*** that has the same effect as a deed. The executor named in the decedent's will does not petition to be appointed as executor, because letters testamentary are not needed to wind up the decedent's affairs. No other steps usually involved in an estate administration are required. [*See* Tex. Prob. Code §89A] If land is located in more than one county, a certified copy of the will and the order admitting it to probate are filed of record in the second county and constitute a muniment of title in that county as well. Since title insurance companies and title examiners will accept deeds signed by the parties named in the will, this procedure is effective to clear title to the decedent's lands (as well as to other assets, title to which is held in the decedent's name).

b. Statutory proceeding to determine heirship [§1103]

Several states have a similar procedure that can be used if the decedent left *no will.* Upon a hearing, the court enters a decree declaring that the decedent died intestate, that he was survived by the indicated family members, and that their respective intestate shares are as set forth in the order. The court decree becomes a part of the county records, and serves as a link in the chain of title. [*See* Tex. Prob. Code §48]

INFORMAL ADMINISTRATION PROCEDURES	gilbert
FAMILY SETTLEMENTS	The decedent's *family comes to an agreement* regarding the disposition of the decedent's assets, without court involvement.
AFFIDAVIT PROCEDURES	Bank accounts can be paid to, and automobile certificates of title can be transferred to, the decedent's heirs pursuant to a *notarized affidavit signed by the heirs*.
SIMPLIFIED ADMINISTRATION FOR SMALL ESTATES	A family member obtains an *affidavit by the court* upon filing a verified petition stating that the decedent's estate is worth less than the specified statutory limit for small estate administration. That family member then has authority to administer the decedent's estate.
MUNIMENT OF TITLE	To pass title to real property without going through a formal estate administration, the decedent's probated will *and* the court order admitting the will to probate form a muniment of title—together they establish a *link in the decedent's chain of title* to real property.

Appendix:
Representative Intestacy
Statutes

CONTENTS

A. Revised Uniform Probate Code

1. Introduction

Of the 18 states listed as having adopted the Uniform Probate Code [8 Uniform Laws Annotated Master Edition 1 (2002 Supp.)], eight have enacted all or virtually all of the revised UPC's intestate distribution provisions: Alaska, Arizona, Colorado, Hawaii, Minnesota (with variations), Montana, New Mexico, and North Dakota.

2. Intestate Share of Surviving Spouse

Under UPC section 2-102, a surviving spouse inherits the decedent's *entire estate only if* (i) all of the decedent's surviving descendants are also descendants of the surviving spouse and the surviving spouse has no other descendants who survived the decedent, or (ii) the decedent was not survived by descendants or either parent.

a. Survived by descendants

If an intestate decedent was survived by descendants, the amount of the surviving spouse's intestate share depends on whether either the decedent or the surviving spouse had descendants who were not descendants of the other spouse.

(1) Neither spouse has descendants from earlier marriage

If all of the decedent's surviving descendants are also descendants of the surviving spouse and the spouse does not have other descendants who survived the decedent (*e.g.*, a one-marriage situation), the surviving spouse inherits the *entire estate*.

(2) Surviving spouse has descendants from earlier marriage

If all of the decedent's surviving descendants are also descendants of the surviving spouse, but the spouse has other descendants who survived the decedent, the surviving spouse inherits the *first $150,000 plus one-half of any balance* of the estate. The remaining one-half of the balance (if any) passes to the decedent's descendants.

(3) Decedent had descendants from earlier marriage

If one or more of the decedent's descendants are not descendants of the surviving spouse, the spouse takes the *first $100,000 plus one-half of any balance* of the decedent's estate. The remaining one-half of the balance (if any) passes to the decedent's descendants.

b. Not survived by descendants

(1) Survived by parent

If the decedent was not survived by descendants but was survived by one or both of her parents, the surviving spouse inherits the *first $200,000* *plus three-fourths of any balance* of the estate. The remaining one-fourth of the balance (if any) passes to the decedent's parents or surviving parent.

(2) Not survived by parent

If the decedent was not survived by descendants or by either parent, the surviving spouse inherits the *entire estate*.

3. Share of Heirs Other than Surviving Spouse

Under UPC section 2-103, any part of the estate not passing to the surviving spouse, or the entire estate if the decedent was not survived by a spouse, passes as follows:

a. Survived by descendants

Under the UPC, inheritance by descendants is *per capita at each generation.* [UPC §2-106] Under this pattern of distribution, the estate is divided into shares at the first generational level at which there are living takers. Each living person at that level takes a share, but the shares of deceased persons at that level are combined and then divided equally among the takers at the next generational level. As a result, persons in the same degree of kinship to the decedent always take equal shares. (*See supra,* §38.)

Example: Widow dies intestate survived by her son A; by three granddaughters P, Q, and R (children of her deceased son B); and by two grandsons X and Y (children of her deceased daughter C).

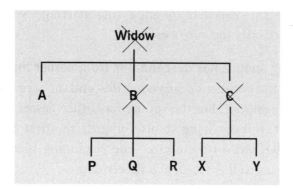

The distribution is per capita at each generation. A takes one-third. The remaining two-thirds is divided per capita at the grandchild level. The five grandchildren take two-fifteenths each.

---

b. Not survived by descendants

If the decedent was not survived by descendants but was survived by one or both parents, the share of the estate that does not pass to the surviving spouse, or the entire estate if the decedent was not survived by a spouse, passes by intestacy to the parents (one-half each) or surviving parent (all).

(1) When parent disqualified to take as heir

Under the revised UPC, a parent cannot inherit from or through a child *unless* the parent has openly treated the child as his own and has not refused to support the child. [UPC §2-114(c)]

c. Not survived by descendants or parents

If the decedent was not survived by a spouse, descendants, or parents, the estate is inherited by the decedent's brothers, sisters, and the descendants of deceased brothers and sisters, who take per capita at each generation.

(1) No distinction between whole bloods and half bloods

Half bloods are brothers and sisters who have only one common parent. The distinction made at common law between kindred of the whole blood and those of the half blood (*see supra*, §99) was abolished by the UPC. [UPC §2-107] Thus, if A dies intestate survived by her half sister B and her whole brother C as her nearest kin, B and C each inherit one-half of A's estate.

d. Not survived by descendants, parents, or descendants of parents

If the decedent was not survived by a spouse, descendants, parents, or descendants of parents, one-half of the estate passes to maternal grandparents or their descendants, and one-half passes to paternal grandparents or their descendants. As to each half, the grandparents or the surviving grandparent take first. If there is no surviving grandparent, the descendants of the grandparents (*e.g.*, uncles, aunts, and their descendants) take per capita at each generation. If there is no surviving grandparent or descendants of a grandparent on either the paternal or the maternal side, the entire estate passes to the relatives on the other side.

4. No Inheritance Beyond Descendants of Grandparent

If the decedent was not survived by a spouse, descendants, parents or their descendants, or by grandparents or their descendants, the estate *escheats* to the state. [UPC §2-105]

5. 120-Hour Survival Required

Any individual who fails to survive the decedent by 120 hours is deemed to have predeceased the decedent for purposes of intestate succession, homestead allowance, and exempt property. [UPC §2-104]

a. Where no proof of survival by 120 hours

If it is not established by *clear and convincing evidence* that an individual who otherwise would be an heir survived the decedent by 120 hours, it is deemed that the individual failed to survive for the required period.

b. Where result would be escheat

The 120-hour survival rule does not apply if the result would be an escheat.

Thus, if the decedent's only living relative was an uncle who died 48 hours after the decedent, the estate passes by intestacy to the uncle (and then to the uncle's devisees or heirs). If, however, the uncle left two children (the decedent's first cousins) who survived the decedent by more than 120 hours, the uncle is deemed not to have survived the decedent, and the estate would pass by inheritance to the two cousins.

6. Community Property States

a. Separate property

Under the UPC's rules for community property states, the surviving spouse's share of the decedent's separate property is determined under the rules described above.

b. Community property

The one-half of community property that belongs to the decedent passes to the surviving spouse. The other one-half does not pass by inheritance; the surviving spouse already owns it. The bottom line, though, is that the surviving spouse ends up with the entire community estate. [UPC §2-102A]

B. Original Uniform Probate Code

1. Terminology

The original UPC uses the term "issue" throughout, whereas the revised UPC uses the term "descendants." "Issue" and "descendants" are synonymous.

2. Intestate Share of Surviving Spouse

Under original UPC section 2-102, any part of the estate not passing to the surviving spouse, or the entire estate if the decedent was not survived by a spouse, passes as follows:

a. Survived by issue, all of whom are issue of surviving spouse

If the decedent was survived by issue, all of whom are also issue of the surviving spouse (*e.g.*, a one-marriage situation), the surviving spouse takes the *first $50,000 plus one-half of any balance* of the estate. The remaining one-half of the balance (if any) passes to the issue.

b. Survived by issue, some of whom are not issue of surviving spouse

If the decedent was survived by issue from an earlier marriage, the first-$50,000 rule does not apply. The surviving spouse takes *one-half* of the estate, and the remaining one-half passes to the decedent's issue.

c. Survived by parents but not survived by issue

If the decedent was not survived by issue but was survived by one or both parents, the surviving spouse takes the *first $50,000 plus one-half of any balance* of the estate. The remaining one-half of the balance (if any) passes to the parents or surviving parent.

d. Not survived by issue or parents

If the decedent was not survived by issue or parents, the surviving spouse inherits the *entire estate*.

3. Share of Heirs Other than Surviving Spouse

a. Survived by issue

That part of the estate not passing to the surviving spouse, or the entire estate if the decedent was not survived by a spouse, passes to the decedent's issue, who take *per capita with representation*. (*See supra*, §37.)

(1) Note

Under the revised UPC, the distribution scheme among descendants is per capita *at each generation*. (*See supra*, §38.)

b. Not survived by issue

If the decedent was not survived by issue but was survived by one or both parents, the share of the estate that does not pass to the surviving spouse, or all of the estate if the decedent was not survived by a spouse, passes by intestacy to the parents (one-half each) or surviving parent (all).

c. Not survived by issue or parents

If the decedent was not survived by a spouse, issue, or parents, the estate is inherited by the decedent's brothers, sisters, and the issue of deceased brothers and sisters, who take per capita with representation.

(1) No distinction between whole bloods and half bloods

Half bloods are brothers and sisters who have only one common parent. The UPC abolished the distinction made at common law between kindred of the whole blood and those of the half blood (*see supra*, §99). [Original UPC §2-107] Thus, if A dies intestate survived by her half sister B and her whole brother C as her nearest kin, B and C each inherit one-half of A's estate.

d. Not survived by issue, parents, or the issue of parents

As under the revised UPC, if the decedent was not survived by a spouse, issue, parents, or the issue of parents, one-half of the estate passes to maternal grandparents or their issue, and one-half passes to paternal grandparents or their issue. As to each half, the grandparents or the surviving grandparent take first. If there is no surviving grandparent, the issue of the grandparents (*e.g.,* uncles, aunts, and their issue) take per capita with representation. If there is no surviving grandparent or issue of a grandparent on either the paternal or the maternal side, the entire estate passes to the relatives on the other side.

4. **No Inheritance Beyond Issue of Grandparent**

If the decedent was not survived by spouse, issue, parents or their issue, or by grandparents or their issue, the estate *escheats* to the state.

5. **120-Hour Survival Required**

Any person who fails to survive the decedent by 120 hours is deemed to have pre-deceased the decedent for purposes of intestate succession, homestead allowance, and exempt property. [Original UPC §2-104]

a. **Where no proof of survival by 120 hours**

If the time of death of the decedent or of the person who otherwise would be an heir cannot be determined, and it cannot be established that the person survived the decedent by 120 hours, it is deemed that the person failed to survive for the required period.

(1) **Comment**

The original UPC does not lay out the standard of evidence needed to establish whether a person survived the decedent by 120 hours. Under the revised UPC, there must be clear and convincing evidence of such survival. (*See supra*, §120.)

b. **Where result would be escheat**

As under the revised UPC, the 120-hour survival rule does **not apply** if the result would be an escheat.

6. **Community Property States**

a. **Separate property**

Under the original UPC's rules for community property states, the surviving spouse's share of the decedent's separate property is determined under the rules (including the "first-$50,000" rule) described above.

b. **Community property**

Under original UPC section 2-102A, the one-half of community property that belongs to the decedent passes to the surviving spouse. The other one-half does not pass by inheritance; the surviving spouse already owns it. The bottom line, though, is that the surviving spouse ends up with the entire community estate.

C. California Probate Code

1. **Introduction**

The California intestate succession rules are set out in the California Probate Code sections 6400 *et seq.*

2. Community Property

The decedent's one-half of the community property passes by intestacy to the surviving spouse (who already owns the other one-half). Thus, the surviving spouse succeeds to ownership of the entire community estate, regardless of whether the decedent was survived by issue. [Cal. Prob. Code §6401(a)]

3. Quasi-Community Property

Quasi-community property is treated the same as true community property for intestate succession purposes. If the decedent (the "acquiring spouse") left a will, the will can dispose of only one-half of the quasi-community property. The other one-half passes to the surviving spouse. If the decedent left no will, the quasi-community property passes to the surviving spouse. [Cal. Prob. Code §6401(b)]

a. What constitutes quasi-community property

Quasi-community property is property acquired by a spouse while domiciled in another jurisdiction that would have been classified as community property had it been acquired under the same circumstances while domiciled in California. It also includes property acquired in exchange for real and personal property that would have been classified as quasi-community property. (*See supra*, §§65-68.)

b. Note

The above result occurs only if the acquiring spouse predeceases the nonacquiring spouse. If the nonacquiring spouse predeceases, she has no power of testamentary disposition over the quasi-community property of the acquiring spouse. If the nonacquiring spouse dies intestate, the acquiring spouse does not "inherit" the quasi-community property; he continues to own it as before. (*See supra*, §66.)

4. Separate Property—Intestate Share of Surviving Spouse

Inheritance of separate property owned by a married person is governed by California Probate Code section 6401(c).

a. Survived by one child or issue of one deceased child

If the decedent was survived by one child or by the issue of one deceased child, the surviving spouse inherits *one-half* of the decedent's separate property. The other one-half passes to the child (or to the issue of that deceased child).

b. Survived by two or more children or their issue

If the decedent was survived by (i) two or more children, (ii) one child and the issue of one or more deceased children, or (iii) the issue of two or more deceased children, the surviving spouse inherits *one-third* of the decedent's separate property. The other two-thirds passes to the children and the issue of any deceased children, who take per capita at each generation.

c. **Not survived by issue**

If the decedent was not survived by issue but was survived by parents or the issue of parents, the surviving spouse inherits *one-half* of the decedent's separate property. The other one-half passes to the parents or surviving parent. If neither parent survives, that one-half is inherited by the decedent's brothers and sisters or their issue, who take per capita at each generation.

d. **Not survived by issue, parents, or issue of parents**

If the decedent was not survived by issue, parents, or the issue of parents, the surviving spouse inherits the decedent's *entire estate*.

5. **Share of Heirs Other than Surviving Spouse**

The intestate shares of heirs other than the surviving spouse are governed by California Probate Code section 6402.

a. **Survived by issue**

The share of the decedent's separate property that does not pass to the surviving spouse, or the entire estate if the decedent was not survived by a spouse, passes to the decedent's issue, who take *per capita at each generation.* [Cal. Prob. Code §§240, 6402] Under this pattern of distribution, the estate is divided into shares at the first generational level at which there are living takers. Each living person at that level takes a share, but the shares of deceased persons at that level are combined and then divided equally among the takers at the next generational level. As a result, persons in the same degree of kinship to the decedent always take equal shares. (*See supra*, §38.)

---

e.g. **Example:** Widow dies intestate survived by son A; by three granddaughters P, Q, and R (children of her deceased son B); and by two grandsons X and Y (children of her deceased daughter C).

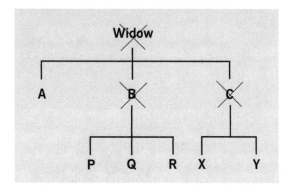

The distribution is per capita at each generation. A takes one-third. The remaining two-thirds is divided per capita at the grandchild level. P, Q, R, X, and Y each take two-fifteenths.

---

b. **Not survived by issue but survived by kindred of predeceased spouse**

California applies some unusual rules to property that is traceable to the decedent's marriage to a predeceased spouse. [Cal. Prob. Code §6402.5]

(1) When rules apply
The following rules apply if:

(a) The decedent was not survived by a spouse or issue, *and*

(b) The predeceased spouse died *not more than 15 years before the decedent* (as to *real property* attributable to the predeceased spouse) or *not more than five years before the decedent* (as to *personal property* attributable to the predeceased spouse), *and*

(c) The decedent was survived by the issue, parents, or issue of parents of *the predeceased spouse.*

(2) Property to which rules apply

(a) Former community property
These rules apply to (i) the decedent's one-half of the community property (and quasi-community property) in existence at the death of the predeceased spouse, and (ii) one-half of the community property (and quasi-community property) in existence at the death of the predeceased spouse that was given to the decedent by the predeceased spouse by gift or will or which vested in the decedent by right of survivorship.

(b) Former separate property
These rules also apply to any separate property of the predeceased spouse that passed to the decedent by gift, will, inheritance, or right of survivorship.

(3) Devolution
The former community property and former separate property passes to the predeceased spouse's issue who survived the decedent, taking *per capita at each generation.* If there are no surviving issue of the predeceased spouse, the property passes to the predeceased spouse's parents or surviving parent or, if neither parent is living, to the predeceased spouse's brothers and sisters and their issue, taking per capita at each generation.

c. Not survived by spouse or issue
If the decedent was not survived by a spouse or by issue, property not subject to the "predeceased spouse" rules (*supra*) passes to the decedent's *parents* (one-half each) *or surviving parent* (all).

d. Not survived by parents
If the decedent was not survived by either parent, the decedent's estate is inherited by his *brothers and sisters and their issue,* who take *per capita at each generation.*

(1) No distinction between whole bloods and half bloods

Half bloods are brothers and sisters who have only one common parent. The distinction made at common law between kindred of the whole blood and those of the half blood (*see supra*, §99) has been abolished in California. [Cal. Prob. Code §6406] Thus, if A dies intestate survived by her half sister B and her whole brother C as her nearest kin, B and C each inherit one-half of A's estate.

e. Not survived by parents or the issue of parents

If the decedent was not survived by any immediate family, the estate passes to the decedent's *grandparents or surviving grandparent or* (if no grandparent survived the decedent) to *the issue of grandparents*, who take *per capita at each generation.*

f. Not survived by grandparents or the issue of grandparents

If the decedent was not survived by grandparents or the issue of grandparents, the estate passes to the *issue of a predeceased spouse*, who take *per capita at each generation.*

(1) Note

Unlike the rules governing distribution of the former community property and former separate property of a predeceased spouse, *supra*, inheritance by the issue of a predeceased spouse does not involve any tracing of the source of the decedent's property.

g. Next of kin

If none of the above persons survived the decedent, the estate passes to the decedent's nearest kin in equal degree. If there are two or more collateral kindred in equal degree who claim through different ancestors, those who claim through the nearest ancestor are preferred to those claiming through a more remote ancestor.

h. Kindred of predeceased spouse

If the decedent had no next of kin and there is no issue of any predeceased spouse of the decedent, the estate passes to the parents or surviving parent of a predeceased spouse or, if none, to the issue of the predeceased spouse's parents.

i. Escheat

If the decedent has no known kindred, the estate *escheats* to the state of California. [Cal. Prob. Code §6800]

6. 120-Hour Survival Required

California adopts the UPC rule requiring that a person must survive the decedent by 120 hours in order to take as an intestate heir. As under the revised UPC, proof that a person survived the decedent by 120 hours must be established by *clear and convincing evidence.* [Cal. Prob. Code §6403; *and see supra*, §120]

D. Florida Probate Code

1. Introduction

The Florida intestate succession rules are set forth in Florida Probate Code sections 732.101 *et seq.*

2. Intestate Share of Surviving Spouse

a. Survived by descendants, all of whom are descendants of surviving spouse

If all of the decedent's descendants are also descendants of the surviving spouse, the surviving spouse takes the *first $60,000 plus one-half of the balance* of the estate. The remaining one-half of the balance (if any) passes to the descendants. [Fla. Prob. Code §732.102]

b. Survived by descendants, some of whom are not descendants of surviving spouse

If the decedent was survived by descendants, some of whom are not descendants of the surviving spouse, the spouse inherits *one-half* of the estate. The other one-half passes to the descendants.

---

e.g. **Example:** Ken dies intestate. He is survived by his wife Diane, his son Alton (child by his first marriage), and daughter Brianne (child by his marriage to Diane). Because Ken was survived by a descendant from another marriage (Alton), the first-$60,000 rule does not apply. Diane inherits one-half of Ken's estate. The remaining one-half passes to Ken's lineal descendants, Alton and Brianne (one-fourth each).

---

c. Not survived by descendants

If the decedent was not survived by lineal descendants, the surviving spouse inherits the *entire estate*.

3. Share of Heirs Other than Surviving Spouse

a. Survived by descendants

That part of the estate not passing to the surviving spouse, or the entire intestate estate if there is no surviving spouse, passes to the decedent's lineal descendants.

(1) Descendants take per stirpes

"Descent shall be per stirpes, whether to lineal descendants or to collateral heirs." [Fla. Prob. Code §732.104] Under this mode of distribution, sometimes called *"classic per stirpes"* (*see supra*, §36), the stirpital shares are divided at the first generational level, regardless of whether there are any living takers at that level.

Example: Widow dies intestate, survived by four grandchildren as her nearest kin: P (the daughter of Widow's deceased son A), and Q, R, and S (the sons of Widow's deceased daughter B).

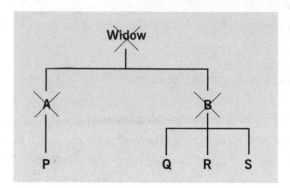

Most states apply a rule of distribution known as "per capita with representation" (*see supra*, §37), under which the four grandchildren would take equal shares because they are in the same degree of kinship to the decedent. In Florida, however, the grandchildren take by representation the share their parents would have taken had they survived to be heirs. P takes one-half (the share A would have received). Q, R, and S take one-sixth each (B's one-half share divided by three).

b.   Not survived by spouse or descendants

If the decedent was not survived by a spouse or lineal descendants, the estate passes to the decedent's *parents* (one-half each) or surviving parent (all).

c.   Not survived by spouse, descendants, or parents

If the decedent was not survived by a spouse, descendants, or parents, the estate passes to the descendants of parents (brothers, sisters, and the descendants of deceased brothers and sisters), who take *per stirpes*.

(1)   Half bloods inherit half as much as whole bloods

Half bloods are brothers and sisters who have only one common parent. In Florida, as is true in a number of states, half bloods inherit half as much as whole bloods *unless* all of the decedent's heirs are of the half blood, in which case they take equal shares. (*See supra*, §103.) [Fla. Prob. Code §732.105] Thus, if A dies intestate survived by her half sister B and her whole sister C as her nearest kin, B inherits one-third and C inherits two-thirds of A's estate. But if B and C were both half sisters, they each would take one-half.

d.   Not survived by descendants, parents, or descendants of parents

If the decedent was not survived by a spouse, descendants, parents, or descendants of parents, one-half of the estate passes to maternal grandparents or their descendants, and one-half passes to paternal grandparents or their descendants. As to each half, the grandparents or the surviving grandparent take first. If there is no surviving grandparent, the descendants of the grand-parents (*e.g.,* uncles, aunts, and their descendants) take per stirpes. If there is no surviving grandparent or descendants of a grandparent on either the paternal or the maternal side, the entire estate passes to the kindred on the other side.

4. **No Inheritance Beyond Grandparents or Descendants of Grandparents**
Florida has adopted the UPC's "laughing heir" rule, which cuts off inheritance by persons related to the decedent beyond the grandparent or descendant of grandparent level. If the decedent was not survived by a spouse or by grandparents or their descendants, the estate *escheats* to the state of Florida.

   a. **Exception for kindred of last deceased spouse**
   The Florida Probate Code carves out an exception to the "laughing heir" rule. Instead of an escheat, the estate "shall go to the kindred of the last deceased spouse of the decedent as if the deceased spouse had survived the decedent and then died intestate entitled to the estate." [Fla. Prob. Code §732.103(5)] While this provision will avoid an escheat in many cases, there nonetheless would be an escheat if (i) the decedent had never married, or (ii) there are no living grandparents or descendants of grandparents of the last deceased spouse.

5. **Uniform Simultaneous Death Act**
The Florida legislature did not adopt the UPC rule that a person must survive the decedent by 120 hours in order to take as an heir. Instead, the controlling law is the Uniform Simultaneous Death Act. [Fla. Prob. Code §732.601] Under the Act, if the title to property or the devolution thereof depends upon priority of death and there is no sufficient evidence that the parties have died otherwise than simultaneously, the property of each person shall be disposed of as if he had survived the other person. (*See supra,* §§105-114.) If, however, there is any evidence that the heir survived the decedent, even for a brief interval, the heir takes an intestate share.

E. Illinois Probate Act

1. **Introduction**
The statutes governing descent and distribution are contained in the Illinois Probate Act, Illinois Compiled Statutes chapter 755, sections 5/2-1 *et seq.*

2. **Intestate Share of Surviving Spouse**

   a. **Survived by descendants**
   If the decedent was survived by a spouse and by one or more descendants, the spouse inherits *one-half* of the estate. The remaining one-half passes to the descendants.

b. Not survived by descendants

If the decedent was survived by a spouse but not by descendants, the spouse inherits the *entire estate.*

3. Share of Heirs Other than Surviving Spouse

a. Survived by descendants

That part of the estate not passing to the surviving spouse, or the entire estate if the decedent was not survived by a spouse, passes to the decedent's descendants.

(1) Per stirpes distribution

In Illinois, inheritance by descendants is by *classic per stirpes,* under which the stirpital shares are always determined at the child level even if none of the decedent's children survived the decedent. (*See supra,* §36.)

---

e.g. **Example:** Widow dies intestate, survived by four grandchildren as her nearest kin: P (the daughter of Widow's deceased son A), and Q, R, and S (the sons of Widow's deceased daughter B).

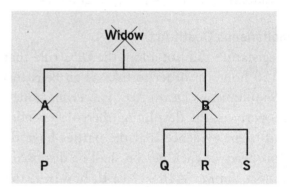

Most states apply a rule of distribution known as "per capita with representation" (*see supra,* §37), under which the four grandchildren would take equal shares because they are in the same degree of kinship to Widow. In Illinois, however, the grandchildren take per stirpes the share their parents would have taken had they survived to be heirs. P takes A's one-half. Q, R, and S take one-sixth each (B's one-half share divided by three).

---

b. Not survived by spouse or descendants

If the decedent was not survived by a spouse or descendants, the estate passes to the decedent's parents, brothers, and sisters in equal portions. Descendants of deceased brothers and sisters take per stirpes.

(1) Comment

The Illinois distributive plan is unusual in treating parents on the same basis as brothers and sisters. In most states, if the decedent was not survived by a spouse or descendants, the entire estate would pass to the parents or to the surviving parent. In other states, the estate passes to the parents if both survive. If only one parent survives, one-half passes to the surviving parent and the other one-half passes to the decedent's brothers and sisters or their descendants. (*See supra*, §§47-48.)

(2) Only one parent survives

In Illinois, if only one parent survives, that parent takes a double portion.

---

e.g. **Example:** Paula dies intestate, unmarried, and without descendants. She is survived by her mother Mary, her sisters Ann and Rose, and her nephews Pete, Antonio, and Rob (children of her deceased brother Luke). Since Paula's father did not survive, Mary takes a double portion (two-fifths). Ann and Rose each take one-fifth. Luke's three children take one-fifteenth shares (Luke's one-fifth share divided by three).

---

(3) When parent disqualified to take as heir

A parent who, for one year or more before the death of a minor or dependent child, willfully neglected or willfully deserted the child, or failed to perform her duty of support, is not entitled to receive any property, benefit, or other interest by reason of the child's death, whether as intestate heir, will beneficiary, or beneficiary of a nonprobate transfer. [Ill. Comp. Stat. ch. 755, §5/2-6.5]

c. Not survived by spouse, descendants, parents, or descendants of parents

If the decedent was not survived by a spouse, descendants, parents, or the descendants of parents, one-half of the estate passes to the decedent's maternal grandparents or surviving grandparent or, if neither is living, to their descendants, per stirpes. The other one-half passes to the paternal grandparents or their descendants in the same manner. If there is no surviving maternal grandparent or descendant thereof, the entire estate passes to the paternal grandparents or their descendants (and vice versa).

(1) Comment

Unlike the rule with respect to parents, grandparents are the preferred takers as against their descendants. Descendants of grandparents inherit only if both grandparents predeceased the decedent.

d. Not survived by grandparents or their descendants

If the decedent was not survived by a spouse, grandparents, or the descendants of grandparents, one-half of the estate passes to the decedent's maternal great-grandparents or the surviving great-grandparent or, if neither is living, to their descendants per stirpes. The other one-half passes to the paternal great-grandparents or their descendants in the same manner. If there are no surviving great-grandparents or their descendants on one side, the entire estate passes to the great-grandparents or their descendants on the other side.

e. Not survived by great-grandparents or their descendants

If the decedent left no kindred nearer in relationship than great-grandparents or the descendants of great-grandparents, the estate passes "in equal parts to the nearest kindred of the decedent in equal degree (computing by the rules of the civil law) and without representation." [Ill. Comp. Stat. ch. 755, §5/2-1]

f. Escheat

If the decedent has no known kindred, the estate *escheats*. Real property escheats to the county in which it is located. Personal property escheats to the county of which the decedent was a resident.

4. Uniform Simultaneous Death Act

Illinois has not enacted the UPC rule that a person must survive the decedent by 120 hours in order to take as an heir. Instead, the governing law is the Uniform Simultaneous Death Act. [Ill. Comp. Stat. ch. 755, §5/3-1] Under the Act, if the title to property or the devolution thereof depends upon priority of death and there is no sufficient evidence that the parties have died otherwise than simultaneously, the property of each person shall be disposed of as if she had survived the other person. (*See supra*, §§105-114.) If, however, there is any evidence that the heir survived the decedent, even for a brief interval, the heir takes an intestate share.

F. New York Estates, Powers and Trusts Law

1. Introduction

In New York, the term "distributee" is used in lieu of "heir." "Distributee" is defined as "a person entitled to take or share in the property of a decedent under the statutes governing intestate distribution." [N.Y. Est. Powers & Trusts Law §1-2.5] The statutes governing descent and distribution are set out in New York Estates, Powers & Trusts Law sections 4-1.1 *et seq.*

2. Intestate Share of Surviving Spouse

a. Survived by issue

If the decedent was survived by a spouse and one or more children or their issue, the surviving spouse inherits the *first $50,000 plus one-half of any balance* of the estate. The other one-half of the balance, if any, passes to the decedent's children and the issue of deceased children.

b. Not survived by issue

If the decedent was survived by a spouse but not by issue, the surviving spouse inherits the *entire estate*.

c. When spouse disqualified from being a distributee

Under New York Estates, Powers & Trusts Law section 5-1.2, a spouse is disqualified from taking as a distributee if:

(1) A final decree of *divorce or annulment* terminated the marriage before the decedent's death;

(2) A final decree of *separation* had been rendered *against the surviving spouse* (a one-way street rule);

(3) The surviving spouse obtained a *divorce in another jurisdiction,* not recognized as a valid divorce in New York;

(4) The marriage was *bigamous or incestuous*;

(5) The spouse *abandoned* the decedent, and the abandonment continued until the decedent's death; or

(6) The spouse *failed or refused to support* the deceased spouse.

3. Share of Heirs Other than Surviving Spouse

a. Survived by issue

The part of the estate not passing to the surviving spouse, or the entire estate if the decedent was not survived by a spouse, passes to the decedent's issue, who take *per capita at each generation.* Under this pattern of distribution, the estate is divided into shares at the first generational level at which there are living takers. Each living person at that level takes a share, but the shares of deceased persons at that level are combined and then divided equally among the takers at the next generational level. As a result, persons in the same degree of kinship to the decedent always take equal shares. (*See supra,* §38.)

e.g. **Example:** Widow dies intestate survived by son A; by three grandsons P, Q, and R (children of her deceased son B); and by X and Y (children of her deceased daughter C).

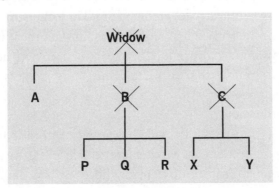

The distribution is per capita at each generation. A takes one-third. The remaining two-thirds is divided per capita at the grandchild level. The five grandchildren take two-fifteenths each.

---

b.   Not survived by spouse or issue

If the decedent was not survived by a spouse or issue but was survived by one or both parents, the estate passes to the parents equally if both survive, or all to the surviving parent if only one survives.

(1)   When parent disqualified to be a distributee

A parent cannot inherit from her child if she failed or refused to support the child or abandoned the child when the child was under the age of 21, whether the child died before or after age 21. If the parent is disqualified, the child's estate is distributed as though the parent predeceased the child. A biological parent is not disqualified from inheriting if she placed the child with an agency based on the agency's fraudulent promise, not kept, to arrange for the child's adoption. [N.Y. Est. Powers & Trusts Law §4-1.4]

c.   Not survived by spouse, issue, or parent

If the decedent was not survived by a spouse, issue, or parent, the estate passes to the decedent's brothers and sisters (and the issue of deceased brothers and sisters), who take per capita at each generation.

(1)   No distinction between whole bloods and half bloods

Half bloods are brothers and sisters who have only one common parent. The distinction made at common law between relatives of the whole blood and those of the half blood (*see supra*, §99) has been abolished. Thus, if A dies intestate survived by her half sister B and her whole brother C as her nearest kin, B and C each inherit one-half of A's estate. [N.Y. Est. Powers & Trusts Law §4-1.1(b)]

d.   Not survived by spouse, issue, parent, or issue of parent

If the decedent was not survived by a spouse, issue, parent, or the issue of a parent, one-half of the estate passes to the maternal grandparents or surviving grandparent or, if neither is living, to the maternal grandparents' issue, who take per capita at each generation. The other one-half passes to the paternal grandparents or their issue in the same manner. If the decedent was not survived by maternal grandparents or their issue, the entire estate passes to the paternal grandparents or their issue (and vice versa).

(1)   Limitation

For purposes of this rule, "issue of grandparents" is limited to issue at the decedent's own generational level (*i.e.*, the grandchildren of the decedent's grandparents, who are the decedent's first cousins). If and only if no such issue exist, the statute allows the next level of issue, the great-grandchildren of the decedent's grandparents (decedent's first cousins once removed), to take in the same manner as the grandchildren. In New York, first cousins once removed are the last in line to inherit. [N.Y. Est. Powers & Trusts Law §4-1.1(a)(6), (7)]

4. No Inheritance Beyond Great-Grandchildren of Grandparent

If the decedent was not survived by any of the foregoing persons—if his nearest kin are descendants of his great-grandparents, or his grandparents' great-great-grandchildren—his estate *escheats* to the state of New York.

5. Uniform Simultaneous Death Act

New York has not enacted the UPC rule that a person must survive the decedent by 120 hours in order to take as an heir. Instead, the governing law is the Uniform Simultaneous Death Act. [N.Y. Est. Powers & Trusts Law §2-1.6] Under the Act, if the title to property or the devolution thereof depends upon priority of death and there is no sufficient evidence that the parties have died otherwise than simultaneously, the property of each person shall be disposed of as if he had survived the other person. (*See supra*, §§105-114.) If, however, there is any evidence that the heir survived the decedent, even for a brief interval, the heir takes an intestate share.

G. Texas Probate Code

1. Community Property

Inheritance of community property is governed by Texas Probate Code section 45.

a. Survived by descendants from earlier marriage

If the decedent was survived by descendants, some of whom are not descendants of the surviving spouse, the *decedent's one-half community interest* passes by intestate succession to his *descendants*.

---

e.g. Example: Ned dies intestate survived by his wife Selma and by two children: Ashley (from an earlier marriage) and Jackie (from his marriage to Selma). Ned's one-half community interest passes by intestacy to Ashley and Jackie. Selma takes her one-half community—not by inheritance, but because death has dissolved the community entity and has compelled a division of the community estate. End result: Selma owns one-half of the property (her one-half community interest) as a tenant in common with Ashley and Jackie (who own one-fourth each by inheritance through Ned).

---

b. Survived by descendants, all of whom are spouse's descendants

If the decedent is survived by descendants, all of whom are descendants of the surviving spouse, the decedent's one-half community interest passes by intestacy to the spouse.

---

e.g. **Example:** Jane dies intestate survived by her husband Mitch and three children, all of whom are from Jane's marriage to Mitch. Mitch inherits Jane's one-half community interest. The other one-half community share does not pass by intestacy; Mitch already owns it. As a result, Mitch succeeds to the entire community estate.

---

c. Not survived by descendants

If the decedent is not survived by children or more remote descendants, the surviving spouse succeeds to the entire community estate. *Parents and collateral kin never inherit community property* unless the spouses die within 120 hours of each other, leaving no descendants. (*See* below.)

2. Separate Property—Intestate Share of Surviving Spouse

Inheritance of separate property owned by a married person is governed by Texas Probate Code section 38(b).

a. Survived by descendants

Unlike the situation with respect to inheritance of community property, for separate property it does not matter whether the decedent's descendants are from the marriage to his surviving spouse or from an earlier marriage.

(1) Separate personal property

If the decedent was survived by a spouse and descendants, *one-third* of the decedent's separate personal property passes to the surviving spouse. The other two-thirds passes to the descendants, who take per capita with representation. (*See supra*, §37).

(2) Separate real property

The surviving spouse inherits a *life estate in an undivided one-third* of the descendant's separate real property. The remaining estate passes to the decedent's descendants.

---

e.g. **Example:** Doug dies intestate owning separate personal property and separate real property. He is survived by his wife Pam and by three children: Drew, Ellie, and Tina. Pam inherits one-third of Doug's separate personal property, and the remaining two-thirds passes to Doug's children (two-ninths each). Pam inherits a life estate in an undivided one-third of Doug's separate real property, and the remainder passes to Doug's children. (Stated another way, all of the separate real property passes to the descendants, subject to a one-third life estate in the surviving spouse.)

---

b.   Not survived by descendants

(1)   Separate personal property
If the decedent was not survived by descendants, *all* of the decedent's separate personal property is inherited by the surviving spouse.

(2)   Separate real property
If the decedent was not survived by descendants, the surviving spouse inherits *one-half* of the decedent's separate real property, and the remaining one-half passes to the decedent's parents and descendants of parents under the rules set out below. The surviving spouse inherits all of the decedent's separate real property *only* if the decedent was not survived by descendants, parents, or the descendants of parents.

3.   Not Survived by Spouse
Inheritance of the estate of a single person is governed by Texas Probate Code section 38(a).

a.   Survived by descendants
If the decedent was survived by all of his children, they take equal shares. If the decedent was survived by children and/or the descendants of deceased children, the distribution is per capita with representation. (*See supra*, §37.)

b.   Not survived by descendants

(1)   Survived by parents
If both parents survive the decedent, each parent inherits one-half of the estate. If only one parent survives, that parent inherits one-half of the estate, and the other one-half passes to the decedent's brothers and sisters and their descendants, who take per capita with representation.

(2)   Not survived by parents
If neither parent survives the decedent, the entire estate passes to the decedent's brothers and sisters and their descendants, taking per capita with representation.

(3)   Half bloods inherit half as much as whole bloods
Half bloods are brothers and sisters who have only one common parent. In Texas, as is true in a number of states, half bloods inherit half as much as whole bloods unless all of the decedent's heirs are of the half blood, in which case they take equal shares. (*See supra*, §103.) [Tex. Prob. Code §41(b)] Thus, if A dies intestate survived by her half sister B and her whole sister C as her nearest kin, B inherits one-third and C inherits two-thirds of A's estate. But if B and C were both half sisters, they each would take one-half.

c. Not survived by parents or descendants of parents

If the decedent was not survived by parents or the descendants of parents, the estate is divided into two "moieties" or halves, one for maternal kin and the other for paternal kin. As to each half, if both paternal (or maternal) grandparents survive, each takes one-half of that one-half, or one-fourth of the total estate. If only one grandparent survives, she takes one-fourth and the other one-fourth passes to descendants of the grandparents, taking per capita with representation. If neither maternal (or paternal) grandparent survives the decedent, that one-half share passes to the descendants of grandparents.

d. No "laughing heir" statute

If there are no grandparents on the maternal (or paternal) side, that one-half passes to the maternal (or paternal) great-grandparents and their descendants on that side, or to great-great-grandparents and their descendants, "and so on without end" until a living relative is found on the maternal (or paternal) side. Unlike the UPC, Texas has no limit on the degree of relationship that qualifies one to take as an heir.

4. 120-Hour Survival Required

Texas adopts the 120-hour rule of the UPC, including the presumption of nonsurvival by 120 hours if there is no evidence of survival, and also including the exception if the result would be an escheat. [Tex. Prob. Code §47; *and see supra*, §§115-120]

a. Application to community property

If a husband and wife die within 120 hours of each other, one-half of the community property passes under the husband's will or by intestacy as though he survived his wife, and the other one-half passes under the wife's will or by intestacy as though she survived her husband. [Tex. Prob. Code §47(d)]

Review Questions
and Answers

Review Questions

1. Barney, a New York resident, dies intestate. Barney owned real and personal property in New York, and also owned a farm, a herd of cows, and two tractors in Iowa. In distributing Barney's estate, does the New York intestacy statute apply to all of Barney's assets?

    a. Suppose that Barney and his sister Bonnie also owned land in Ohio as joint tenants with right of survivorship. Is intestate distribution of the Ohio land governed by New York law or Ohio law?

2. Luis dies without a will. He is survived by his wife Sylvia, his children Audrey and Ben, and his mother Maria. Does Maria take an intestate share of Luis's estate?

    a. Luis left an estate of personal property worth $100,000 and real property worth $200,000. If Luis was a resident of a state that has enacted the UPC, what intestate distribution should be made?

    b. Suppose, instead, that Luis was a resident of a community property state, and that the $300,000 in assets were community property. What intestate distribution should be made?

3. Sarah, a widow, dies intestate. She is survived by her son Al, two grandchildren (Billy and Bob) by her deceased daughter Betty, and one grandchild (Curtis) by her deceased son Charley.

    a. Do the three grandchildren (Billy, Bob, and Curtis) take equal shares of Sarah's estate under majority law?

    b. Suppose, instead, that Al also predeceased Sarah, leaving no issue, meaning that Billy, Bob, and Curtis were Sarah's nearest kin. Do the three grandchildren take equal shares of Sarah's estate under majority law?

4. After living in Tennessee for many years, Jack and Jill move to a community property state, bringing with them 2,000 shares of Old Grandad Inc. common stock that Jack acquired from his earnings at a distillery. Jack dies intestate survived by Jill and the couple's two children, Peter and Piper. Does Jill take the 2,000 shares of Old Grandad stock by inheritance?

    a. Suppose, instead, that Jill dies intestate survived by Jack, Peter, and Piper. Do the 2,000 shares of Old Grandad stock pass by inheritance through Jill's estate?

5. Martha has a child (Cliff) out of wedlock. Cliff is placed for adoption and is adopted by Henry and Winnie. Some years later, Martha dies; then Martha's mother Gertrude dies intestate. Does Cliff have inheritance rights in his natural grandmother's estate? _____

    a. Suppose, instead, that Henry dies; then Henry's father George dies intestate. Does Cliff have inheritance rights in his adoptive grandfather's estate? _____

6. Herb has a child (Art) by his first marriage. Thereafter, Herb marries Winnie and they have two children (Bonita and Carla). Winnie does not adopt Art. If Winnie dies intestate, does Art have inheritance rights as a half blood? _____

    a. Herb and Winnie die; then Carla dies intestate, survived by her siblings Art and Bonita. Does Art take one-half of Carla's estate? _____

7. Donald and Rachel, who are both married but have no children, are both killed instantly when their car strikes a concrete abutment. Rachel's nearest kin are her mother and father. Donald (who had a modest estate) left a will bequeathing "all my property" to his brother Ronnie; Rachel (who owned assets worth $500,000) died intestate. Ronnie contends that all or a substantial portion of Rachel's estate passed by intestacy to Donald, and then under Donald's will to him. Is he right? _____

    a. Suppose, instead, that although Rachel was pronounced dead at the scene of the accident, Donald died at a local hospital two hours later. Does Ronnie end up with ownership of a share of Rachel's estate? _____

8. Pauline gives land worth $70,000 to her son Roderick on his 25th birthday. Two years later, Pauline dies intestate survived by Roderick and two other children. She leaves an estate valued at $300,000. Is Roderick entitled to one-third of Pauline's estate notwithstanding the lifetime gift to him? _____

9. Tony's will makes several bequests, including a bequest of $50,000 to his daughter Eileen. Two years before his death, Tony gives $20,000 to Eileen. Is Eileen entitled to the entire $50,000 bequest? _____

10. Glenda dies intestate survived by four children and several grandchildren. Five months after Glenda's death, one of her children (Denise, who has two children) disclaims in writing one-half of her interest in Glenda's estate. Is Denise's disclaimer effective? _____

    a. At the time Denise filed her disclaimer, Acme Finance had a $125,000 judgment against her. Can Acme reach the share of Glenda's estate that Denise purported to disclaim? _____

11. Rambo is charged with murdering his father. In plea bargaining, Rambo pleads guilty to the lesser charge of voluntary manslaughter. Is Rambo entitled to inherit from his father's estate? _____

a. Suppose, instead, that the case goes to trial, and Rambo is acquitted of both murder and the lesser charge of manslaughter. Is Rambo entitled to inherit from his father's estate? _____

12. Lucian, a resident of a common law state, dies leaving a will that bequeaths $22 to his wife Tammy ("$1 for each miserable year I spent with her"), and the remainder of his estate "to my faithful and efficient secretary, Lola LaTour, in consideration for her thoughtful and many services." Lucian left an estate valued at $200,000. Tammy has retained you to represent her. She wants to know: Is she entitled to more than $22 from Lucian's estate? _____

a. In addition to leaving a $200,000 estate, three years before his death Lucian gave his brother Morris securities worth $100,000. Do Tammy's rights extend to the securities given to Morris? _____

b. Suppose, instead, that Lucian had transferred the securities to a revocable trust that named Morris as trustee to pay the income to Lucian for life, and on Lucian's death to distribute the principal to Morris free of the trust. Do Tammy's rights extend to the securities settled in the revocable trust? _____

13. Jose and Juanita own Blackacre as community property. Jose, thinking that Blackacre (worth $100,000) was his because he had purchased it out of his salary, dies leaving a will that states: "I own Blackacre as my separate property. I devise the fee simple title therein to my brother Bernie. I give all the remainder of my [$200,000] estate to my wife if she survives me; otherwise to my brother Bernie." Juanita contends that since Blackacre was community property, she owns one-half of it, and that she also takes Jose's residuary estate under his will. Is she right? _____

14. Mona and Frank live in a community property state. Without Frank's knowledge, Mona gives securities worth $20,000 to Marcie, her daughter by a former marriage. Can Frank set the gift aside? _____

15. Ferd and Ann, who were married and lived in California for many years, move to a common law state, bringing with them securities worth $200,000. The securities were community property even though the stock certificates were registered in Ferd's name as owner. Ferd dies three years later, leaving a will that bequeaths "all my property" to his sister. Does Ann have any rights in the securities, given that Ferd is listed as their owner? _____

16. Hank is married to Wanda, and they have one child (Chauncey) at the time Hank executes his will bequeathing "all my property to my wife Wanda if she survives me, otherwise to my mother Mabel." Thereafter, Hank and Wanda adopt a child (Andrew); then Wanda dies. Hank dies without having revoked or modified his will. He is survived by Mabel, Chauncey, and Andrew.

a. Does Chauncey have any rights in Hank's estate? _____

b. Does Andrew have any rights in Hank's estate? _____

c. Suppose the same facts, except that Wanda also survived Hank. Does Andrew have any rights in Hank's estate? _____

d. Suppose that (i) shortly after Andrew's adoption, Hank took out a $10,000 life insurance policy that named Andrew as beneficiary, and (ii) Wanda predeceased Hank. Does Andrew have any rights in Hank's estate? _____

17. Ruth, an elderly widow, is an ardent fan of television evangelist Brother Billie Bob Boon and his Pass the Plate ("PTP") Club. She executes a will that bequeaths two-thirds of her $500,000 estate to the PTP Club, and the remaining one-third to her daughter Desiree. Ruth dies 20 days after executing the will. The will was not the product of undue influence and, despite Ruth's conviction that Brother Billie Bob was "a messenger of the Lord" with healing powers, the PTP gift was not the product of an insane delusion. Desiree contends that the testamentary gift to the PTP Club is invalid. Is there any basis for her claim? _____

18. Is each of the following an accurate statement of the law?

a. An instrument that makes no disposition of property cannot be admitted to probate as a will. _____

b. The right to make a will is both a natural and a constitutional right; and while the legislature may fix reasonable limits on the power of testation, it can neither withhold the right altogether nor place excessive restrictions thereon. _____

c. In many jurisdictions, a will is valid if it complies with the law in effect at the time of execution *or* death. _____

d. In determining whether the testator had testamentary intent, an objective test is applied. The requirement of testamentary intent is judged by a "reasonable person" standard—*i.e.*, whether such a person would consider the instrument and words used to be testamentary in nature. _____

e. If an instrument signed by Caroline in the presence of attesting witnesses begins by declaring, "I, Caroline, declare this instrument to be my Last Will," there is a conclusive presumption that the instrument was written and signed with testamentary intent. _____

19. Tommy, who is 17 years old, executes a will bequeathing all of his property to his mother. Tommy dies 10 years later; he never married and he is survived by his mother. Is Tommy's will admissible to probate? _____

20. Larry executes a will that bequeaths his rare book collection to State College. Thereafter, Larry sends a typewritten, signed letter to his friend Moe, stating that "I have decided to give my rare books to you rather than to State College. You can have them when I die." Is Moe entitled to the rare books on Larry's death? _____

21. Ted Smith, whose nickname is T.S., types out his will. In the presence of two neighbors (who sign as attesting witnesses), Ted signs the will with his initials, "T.S." Is the will admissible to probate on Ted's death? _____

22. Wendy executes what purports to be her last will and testament. The document contains three bequests, followed by Wendy's signature, two more bequests, a date, and the attestation and signatures of subscribing witnesses. On Wendy's death, is the will admissible to probate? _____

    a. Suppose instead that the material following Wendy's signature consisted of a statement that "this is the sum and substance of my dispositions," followed by the attestation clause and witness signatures. On Wendy's death, is the will admissible to probate? _____

    b. If it is shown that the two bequests following Wendy's signature were added *after* the will was signed and witnessed, can they be given effect? _____

    c. Is the will invalid if Wendy failed to declare to the witnesses (by words or conduct) that the instrument was her will? _____

23. Shari asks Percy and Yolanda to "witness my will." However, Percy and Yolanda sign the will before Shari signs. Is the will admissible to probate? _____

24. Smith asks Bill and Marion to witness his will, which he signs in their presence in his dining room. Smith then goes into his kitchen for a glass of water, whereupon Bill and Marion sign the document. Is the will admissible to probate? _____

    a. Would the will be admissible to probate if Smith had passed out in the kitchen when the witnesses were signing the will? _____

25. Fred's will devises his residuary estate to his friend Barney as trustee of a trust for the benefit of Fred's wife Wilma. Barney signs the will as one of the two attesting witnesses. Is Barney disqualified from receiving compensation or from serving as trustee by reason of his witnessing the will? _____

    a. Suppose the same facts, except that the will provides: "The trustee shall pay the trust income to my wife Wilma for life, and on her death the trustee shall distribute the trust principal to Barney free of the trust." Again, Barney signs the will as one of the two attesting witnesses. Is the will admissible to probate? _____

    b. Suppose again that Barney is given the trust remainder by the will, but he was *not* one of the two witnesses to the will. Two years after the will is executed, Fred executes a codicil that (i) bequeaths $10,000 to his nephew

Rocko and (ii) reaffirms and republishes his will. Barney is one of the two attesting witnesses to the codicil. Does the interested witness statute apply to the gift to Barney?

26. Agnes dies leaving a typed will that was dated and signed by her and also signed by Seth and Trevor immediately below the will's attestation clause, which recites that "each of the undersigned witnesses signed in the testator's presence and in the presence of each other." Seth testifies that Agnes's brother brought the will to him for signing and that he did not sign the will in Agnes's presence. Is the will admissible to probate?

   a. Suppose the same facts, except that (i) the will was handwritten by Agnes, and (ii) the court finds that Seth did not sign in Agnes's presence. Is the will admissible to probate?

27. After Tom's death a signed and dated instrument that bequeaths all of his real and personal property is found in his safe deposit box. The document is entirely in Tom's handwriting except for the third paragraph, which is partially hand-written and partially typed: "I bequeath **Riveracre**, my ranch in Fayette County, to my good friend Huck." "Riveracre" is typed. If the state permits holographic wills, is the document admissible to probate?

   a. Suppose the document was not dated. Is it admissible to probate?

28. Tess, who moved away from home at an early age, writes her sister Trudy a three-page letter that describes Tess's activities and the weather, asks about Trudy's family, and states how lonely she is. At the top of page three of the letter, Tess writes: "The only thing that comforts me is that after I am gone you and your children will get everything I own, and our good-for-nothing brother Bob won't get a dime." The letter is signed by Tess and dated. After Tess's death, Trudy offers the letter for probate. Should it be admitted to probate as a holographic will?

29. Parker is involved in a serious auto crash and finds himself bleeding profusely. He tells the three ambulance attendants that he wants his $500 camera to go to his niece Lili, and asks them to witness the request as his will. The attendants note the request in their written report of the accident filed the next day. Parker recovers from his injuries and dies of a heart attack five months later. May Lili offer the written accident report for probate?

   a. Suppose, instead, that Parker's oral bequest was of his five-acre ranch, not a camera. May Lili offer the written accident report for probate?

30. Ruth executes a will that provides, "I am about to swim the English Channel. If anything happens to me, I want all of my property to go to my sister Sarah." Ruth swims the channel in record time, but dies in an automobile accident five years later. The will is found in a desk drawer in Ruth's living room. Does Sarah take Ruth's estate under the will?

31. Toby executes a will leaving all his property to his neighbors Rhonda and Seth in equal shares. Thereafter, Toby marries Macy. Then Toby dies without having revoked or modified his will; he is survived by Macy, Rhonda, and Seth. Is Toby's will revoked by operation of law?

    a. Suppose the same facts, except that Toby and Macy also gave birth to a child Annette. Is Toby's will revoked by operation of law?

32. Stanley executes a will leaving his estate to his wife Vera if she survives him, otherwise to Tim. The will names Vera as executor and Tim as alternate executor. Several years later, Vera divorces Stanley, who thereafter dies without remarrying or changing his will. Stanley is survived by Vera and Tim. Does Vera take Stanley's estate under the will, and is Vera entitled to appointment as executor of Stanley's estate?

    a. Suppose the same facts, except that one year after the divorce Stanley and Vera reconcile and remarry. Does Vera take Stanley's estate under the will, and is Vera entitled to appointment as executor of Stanley's estate?

33. Ted executes a will that bequeaths $10,000 to Ann, $5,000 to Betty, and his residuary estate to Carolyn. A year later, Ted executes another will that bequeaths $5,000 to David and his residuary estate to Elsie. The second will makes no mention of the earlier will. Should both wills be admitted to probate?

34. Tashi decides to revoke his will by burning it. He places the will in his fireplace with numerous other papers and sets them afire. Unbeknownst to Tashi, only the upper corner of the will is burned; all of the provisions of the will still can be read. Has the will been revoked?

    a. Suppose, instead, that Tashi wanted to burn his old bank statements in the fireplace, but accidentally included the will in the pile of papers. The will was completely consumed by the flames. Has the will been revoked?

35. Mei writes to her attorney, "I hereby instruct you to destroy and negate my present will." The letter is entirely in Mei's handwriting and is signed and dated by her. The jurisdiction recognizes holographic wills.

    a. The attorney does not destroy the will. Is Mei's letter sufficient to constitute a revocation?

    b. If the attorney does destroy the will pursuant to Mei's instructions, has the will been revoked?

36. Andy Albertson's will bequeaths $15,000 to Ben, $5,000 to Celia, and his residuary estate to Della. Thereafter, Andy crosses out the $15,000 bequest to Ben and writes in the margin, "Cancelled. A.A." Is this an effective revocation of the gift to Ben?

37. Beulah's will is executed in duplicate: *i.e.,* **two copies** are signed and witnessed. The bond paper copy is left with the attorney for safekeeping; Beulah takes the signed photocopy home with her and places it in her desk. After Beulah's death, the executed photocopy cannot be found, but the bond paper copy is found in the attorney's possession. Should it be admitted to probate? _____

    a.   Suppose the same facts, except that after Beulah's death, the copy left with the attorney cannot be found, but the photocopy is found in Beulah's desk. Should the photocopy be admitted to probate? _____

38. Phil executes a will leaving his estate to Robert and Steve in equal shares. Some years later, Phil executes a new will in which he "hereby revoke[s] all earlier wills and codicils." The second will leaves Phil's estate to Robert. Shortly before his death, Phil destroys the second will with the intent to revive and restore his first will. Is the first will entitled to probate? _____

39. After Zoe's death, three sheets of paper in her handwriting are discovered inside a family Bible. The pages are unnumbered and consist of separate, unnumbered paragraphs devising Zoe's property to various persons. The first sheet was written with a ball point pen, the second with a pencil, and the third with a blue felt tip pen. The third page concludes with Zoe's signature, the signatures of two witnesses, and the date. Can the three pages be admitted as Zoe's will? _____

40. Randy executes a will that contains this provision: "I give my ranch in Collin County and several items of personal property that are important to me to the persons named in a list that I plan to prepare in the future and attach to my will." Thereafter, Randy types, dates, and signs a list that says, "Pursuant to the provisions of my will, I give my ranch in Collin County to my brother Danny, my golf clubs to my cousin Lanny, my Mercedes to my friend Manny, and $5,000 to my niece Nanny." After Randy's death, the list is found stapled to his will.

    a.   Is the gift of the ranch valid? _____

    b.   Is the gift of the golf clubs valid? _____

    c.   Is the gift of the Mercedes valid? _____

    d.   Is the $5,000 bequest valid? _____

41. Hershel transfers stocks and bonds worth $200,000 to his friend Tom as trustee: To pay the trust income to Hershel for life, then to Sarah for life, and on the death of the survivor of Hershel and Sarah to pay the trust principal to Nellie. Hershel reserves the power to revoke or modify the trust. Thereafter, Hershel executes a will that states, "I bequeath my residuary estate to my friend Tom, as trustee, such residuary estate to be added to the trust which I established during my lifetime." Shortly before his death, Hershel amends the trust by a written instrument that is signed by him but not witnessed. Under the amendment, on the

death of Hershel and Sarah, the trust principal is to be paid to Nellie and Noah in equal shares. Is the testamentary gift valid? _____

42. Gertie executes a will that devises her estate to her husband Hobart and her son Sean in equal shares, and that names Hobart as executor. Thereafter, Gertie and Hobart adopt a child: Cassidy. Two years later, Gertie executes a codicil to the will that names her brother Bill as executor in place of Hobart. Gertie dies; she is survived by Hobart, Sean, Cassidy, and Bill. Is Cassidy entitled to a share of Gertie's estate as a pretermitted child? _____

43. Xavier's will bequeaths his farm to Guillaume. Thereafter, Xavier tells Guillaume that he is thinking about bequeathing the farm to Terry, whereupon Guillaume offers to manage and improve the property and split the income with Xavier if he will agree not to revoke the bequest. Xavier orally assents. Despite Guillaume's extensive improvements to the farm, Xavier executes a codicil revoking the bequest and leaving the farm to Terry. Can Guillaume enforce the agreement? _____

44. Alicia and Brad execute a joint will wherein each leaves all of his or her property to the other for life, and on the death of the survivor, all of their property is to go to Stella and Dean in equal shares. Some time later, Brad executes a codicil that leaves all of his property to Dean. Do either Alicia or Stella have any right to enforce the original bequest? _____

   a. Would the result be different if the bequests were made "in consideration of the agreement by the other not to revoke"? _____

45. Hector's will bequeaths 1,000 shares of AT&T stock to his granddaughter Betty and devises his residuary estate to Martha. Betty predeceases Hector, leaving a child (Cuthbert) who survives Hector. Betty leaves a will that devises all of her property to her husband Bob. Does Cuthbert take the AT&T stock? _____

   a. Suppose the same facts, except that Betty survived Hector but died two days later. Does Cuthbert take the AT&T stock? _____

   b. Suppose that the bequest of the AT&T stock was "to Betty if she survives me." Does Cuthbert take the AT&T stock? _____

46. Donald's will bequeaths his residuary estate "in equal shares to my son Dewey, my friend Hughy, and my cousin Louie."

   a. Hughy predeceases Donald, leaving a child (Herkie) who survives Donald, as do Dewey and Louie. Does Herkie take a one-third share of Donald's residuary estate? _____

   b. Suppose instead that Dewey predeceases Donald, leaving a child (Duckie) who survives Donald, as do Hughy and Louie. Does Duckie take a one-third share of Donald's residuary estate? _____

47. Bert's will devises Greenacre "in equal shares to the children of my brother Vern." At the time the will is executed, Vern has three children: Alan and Bruce (both of whom were born to Vern's wife Molly), and Charlie (who was born out of wedlock; Vern's secretary was the mother). Thereafter, Vern adopts a child (Donna), and Alan dies survived by his daughter Alice. Then Bert dies, and his will is admitted to probate. Two years after Bert's death, Vern and Molly have another child, Elsie.

   a.   Does Alice take a share of Greenacre?   _____

   b.   Does Donna take a share of Greenacre?   _____

   c.   Does Charlie take a share of Greenacre?   _____

   d.   Does Elsie take a share of Greenacre?   _____

48. Herma's will contains the following bequests: "(A) I bequeath my Rembrandt painting to Patricia. (B) I bequeath my 200 shares of Ibix common stock to Ralph. (C) I bequeath 100 shares of Kytek common stock to Stanley. (D) I give, devise, and bequeath the rest, residue, and remainder of my estate to Tammy."

   a.   Herma is killed in a house fire in which the Rembrandt is also destroyed. After her death, her executor collects $100,000 in insurance proceeds to compensate for the loss of the Rembrandt. Is Patricia entitled to the $100,000?   _____

   b.   Suppose instead that the Rembrandt was destroyed two months before Herma's death and the insurance proceeds were collected by Herma shortly before her death. Is Patricia entitled to the $100,000?   _____

   c.   Before her death, Herma sold all of her Ibix stock and invested the sale proceeds in Series E Bonds. Is Ralph entitled to the Series E bonds?   _____

   d.   Suppose instead that Ibix Corporation was acquired by Goliath Corporation in a merger. As a result of the merger, Herma received 100 shares of Goliath stock in exchange for her 200 shares of Ibix stock. Is Ralph entitled to the Goliath stock?   _____

   e.   Also before her death, Herma sold all of her Kytek stock and invested the sale proceeds in Butane common stock. Does ademption apply to the gift to Stanley?   _____

49. Zack owns 100 shares of NuGrowth common stock. He executes a will that provides: "I bequeath 100 shares of NuGrowth common stock to Tess." Thereafter, NuGrowth declares a two-for-one stock split, and two years later NuGrowth declares a 10% stock dividend. As a result, Zack owns 220 shares of NuGrowth stock at his death.

a. Is Tess entitled to the additional 100 shares of NuGrowth stock produced by the stock split? _____

b. Is Tess entitled to the additional 20 shares of NuGrowth stock produced by the stock dividend? _____

c. Suppose instead that NuGrowth declared the stock dividend two months *after* Zack's death. Is Tess entitled to the additional 20 shares of NuGrowth stock produced by the stock dividend? _____

50. Trudy executes a will that devises her summer cabin to Astrid. Thereafter, Trudy borrows $10,000 and gives the lender a mortgage on the cabin as security for the loan. When Trudy dies, the loan has not been repaid. Astrid has taken the position that the executor must pay off the loan out of the residuary estate so that title to the summer cabin will pass to her free of the mortgage lien. Is Astrid correct? _____

51. Rupert's will bequeaths $20,000 to his son Alex, $20,000 to his son Ben, and his residuary estate [$500,000] "to my beloved daughter Daphne." The will further provides: "Anyone who contests this will, or any part thereof, shall forfeit his legacy and shall take nothing hereunder." Alex's wife Agnes is outraged by the will, and feels strongly that the will was the product of Daphne's undue influence. Can Agnes contest the will? _____

a. Suppose that Alex contests the will on the ground of undue influence, but the court finds no such influence. Are Alex's rights under the will thereby forfeited? _____

52. Wilbur's will makes modest bequests to each of his children and bequeaths his residuary estate to ESP Incorporated "because they have enabled me to talk to my dear, departed wife Ethel." Wilbur's children contest the will on the grounds of testamentary incapacity and insane delusion. Should they prevail? _____

a. Would the result be different if Wilbur had been adjudicated incapacitated several months prior to his executing the will? _____

53. Hortense's will makes a bequest of $50,000 to I. M. Slick, the attorney who prepared the will, and devises her residuary estate to her sister Sue. Sue contends that the gift to Slick was the product of undue influence. Should she prevail? _____

54. Michael executes a will that bequeaths $500,000 to Elise. After his death, several of Michael's heirs move to set aside the gift on the ground that Elise tricked Michael into making the bequest by falsely representing that she would use the funds to start a religious order. If the heirs can prove that Elise made such a false representation, is this enough to invalidate the gift? _____

a. Suppose instead that Michael made the bequest believing that Elise would start a religious order, even though Elise made no representation to that effect. Should the gift be invalidated?

55. Jafar executes a will that bequeaths "$5,000 to my niece Bahar" and devises the remainder of his estate to Ketty. After Jafar's death, Ketty challenges the gift to Bahar. She offers evidence that Jafar made the gift to Bahar because of a mistaken belief that she was Jafar's niece when in fact they were unrelated. Is the evidence admissible?

a. Bahar offers evidence that the amount of the bequest was intended to be $50,000, not $5,000, and that the attorney's stenographer made a mistake in incorrectly typing $5,000. Is the evidence admissible?

56. Brewster, a professor of history, bequeaths $50,000 "to my college." Brewster received a B.A. degree from Adams College, a Ph.D. from Baker College, and taught for 12 years at Clarendon College. Is extrinsic evidence admissible to show that Brewster intended the bequest for Adams College?

57. Professor Mens Rea summarizes his lecture on administration of estates by noting, "The informal probate procedure of the UPC has the advantage of safeguarding against possible abuse by the personal representative of the estate, but it does not really simplify the standard procedure." Is he correct?

58. Hans dies leaving a handwritten will that is signed by one witness. The state does not recognize holographic wills. Despite the lack of two witnesses, all of Hans's family members who would be heirs if there were no will petition the court to have the will probated and waive all rights they may have as heirs. Should the will be admitted to probate?

59. Babette's will, which contains an attestation clause, is signed by Sasha and Gina as attesting witnesses but is not self-proved. When the will is offered for probate, Sasha testifies that he has no recollection of signing the will at all, let alone in Babette's presence; Gina testifies that Babette's brother brought the will to Gina's house for her signature and Babette was not present. In light of this testimony, should the court deny probate of the will?

60. Antonio's will names his son Lino as the executor of his estate. When Antonio dies, Lino is 16 years of age but highly intelligent (he is a sophomore in college) and quite familiar with the nature and responsibilities of an executor. Is Lino qualified for appointment as executor?

61. Greta is appointed executor of Heinrich's estate. Greta decides that the sale of certain real property (not specifically bequeathed by the will) is necessary to pay creditors' claims. The will does not give the executor an express power of sale. Must Greta obtain a court order to sell the real property?

a. Greta retains a broker to sell the real property. Subsequently, the purchaser (Petra) sues Greta for false representations by the broker concerning the condition of the property. Can Greta be held liable to Petra?

b. If Petra obtains a judgment against Greta, is Greta entitled to reimbursement from Heinrich's estate?

62. Sven dies on March 11, leaving a will that names his friend Lars as executor. The will is probated two weeks later, and on March 28, Lars properly publishes notice to creditors, advising that all claims not presented within 90 days after publication of the notice will be barred. Seven months later, Niels presents a claim for $5,000 based on a promissory note signed by Sven. Niels points out that he, Lars, and Sven were all good friends, that Niels had loaned Sven the $5,000 to meet a pressing personal obligation (and that Lars knew of the loan), and that Lars knew that Sven would have wanted the loan paid off before any assets of the estate were distributed. Should Lars pay the $5,000 to Niels?

63. Ramona's will bequeaths $10,000 to her daughter Maria, $20,000 to her son Miguel, and her Corona stock (worth $6,000) to her neighbor Zapata. After administration, Ramona's estate has assets (including the Corona stock) worth $27,000.

a. Will Zapata's gift be paid in full?

b. Should Maria and Miguel receive the same amount under the will?

64. Nigel's will bequeaths $100,000 to his nephew Reginald. Nigel dies on February 15. After considerable dispute among the heirs and beneficiaries, a representative for the estate is appointed by the court on December 10. The representative distributes $100,000 to Reginald in satisfaction of the bequest on September 15 of the following year. Is Reginald entitled to interest on the bequest?

65. Isadore dies leaving a will that bequeaths his estate to his daughter Rebecca and his son Malachi in equal shares. Isadore's modest estate consisted of a nine-year-old sedan, the furniture and furnishings in his apartment, $1,500 in cash, a $5,000 savings account, and a $50,000 life insurance policy that names Rebecca and Malachi as co-beneficiaries. Will it be necessary to probate Isadore's will and take out a formal administration of his estate?

Answers to Review Questions

1. **NO**   The New York intestacy laws apply to the New York assets and to all of Barney's personal property wherever located, including the cows and tractors in Iowa. However, under the situs rule, disposition of the Iowa farmland is governed by the Iowa intestate succession statute. [§10]

   a. **NEITHER**   The joint tenancy estate was a nonprobate asset and thus not subject to intestate succession laws. Title to the land passes to Bonnie by right of survivorship. [§15]

2. **NO**   In all states, a parent never inherits if the decedent was survived by a spouse *and* descendants. [§34]

   a. **DEPENDS**   The answer depends on (i) whether the state follows the original or revised UPC, and (ii) whether Luis's children are also Sylvia's children. Under the original UPC, Sylvia takes $50,000 plus one-half of any balance (for a total of $175,000) if Audrey and Ben are her children. Audrey and Ben share the remainder, receiving $62,500 each. If Audrey and Ben are not her children (*e.g.*, they are Luis's children from a previous marriage), she takes one-half of the estate—$150,000. Audrey and Ben share the remainder, receiving $75,000 each. Under the revised UPC, Sylvia receives the entire estate if Audrey and Ben are her only children. If Audrey and Ben are her children but she also has children from a previous marriage, she receives $150,000 plus one-half of the balance of the estate (for a total of $225,000) and Ben and Audrey share the remaining $75,000. If Sylvia is not the mother of either Ben or Audrey, she receives $100,000 plus one-half of the balance of the estate (for a total of $200,000), and Ben and Audrey share the remaining $100,000, receiving $50,000 each. [§§25-28, *and see* **Appendix**]

   b. **SPLIT OF AUTHORITY**   In California and states that have enacted the original UPC, Sylvia would succeed to the entire community estate. In Texas and under the revised UPC, Sylvia receives the entire community estate only if Ben and Audrey are her children. If Sylvia is not the mother of either Ben or Audrey, she continues to own her one-half community share, but Luis's one-half community share would pass by intestacy to Audrey and Ben. [§§62-64; *and see* **Appendix**]

3.a. **NO**   Under the majority rule and the original UPC, descendants of deceased children take per capita with representation—*i.e.*, the shares are determined at the first generational level with living takers. Each living person at that level takes a share, and the share of each deceased person is divided among her descendants. Since Al is the only living child, he takes one-third of Sarah's estate. Billy and Bob share Betty's one-third share (receiving one-sixth each), and Curtis receives Charley's one-third share. [§37]

b. **YES**　Under the majority rule and the original UPC, descendants of deceased children take per capita with representation—*i.e.*, the shares are determined at the first generational level with living takers, who receive equal shares. Since the grandchild level is the first generational level with living takers, they take equal shares of one-third each. [§37]

4. **SPLIT OF AUTHORITY**　If Jack and Jill moved to California, Idaho, Washington, or Wisconsin, the stock would be classified as quasi-community property, and Jill would inherit the stock. If, however, the move was to one of the community property states that does not have a quasi-community property statute (*e.g.*, Texas), the stock would be Jack's separate property and would pass under the intestate succession rules applicable to separate property. [§§65-68]

a. **NO**　Even in states with quasi-community property statutes, if the nonacquiring spouse predeceases, she has no interest in the quasi-community property to pass by will or inheritance. [§67]

5. **NO**　In nearly all states, a child who is adopted by a new family has no inheritance rights from his natural parents or the natural parents' kin. [§77]

a. **YES**　All states have discarded the common law "stranger to the adoption" rule. With respect to the adopting family, an adopted child has the same inheritance rights as a natural child and can inherit from the adopting parents' kin. [§75]

6. **NO**　The half blood doctrine applies only to inheritance among collateral kin (*i.e.*, brothers and sisters). Art, a stepchild, has no inheritance rights in Winnie's estate unless he can invoke the equitable doctrine of "adoption by estoppel" based on an unperformed agreement to adopt. [§§93-94, 98]

a. **SPLIT OF AUTHORITY**　Under the UPC and in most states, Art would take one-half of Carla's estate. However, in some states, half bloods take half as much as whole bloods, meaning that Art would inherit one-third and Bonita would inherit two-thirds of Carla's estate. In still other states, Art would take nothing, and Bonita would inherit Carla's entire estate. [§§98-103]

7. **PROBABLY NOT**　If the Uniform Simultaneous Death Act ("USDA") applies, and because there is no sufficient evidence that the parties died otherwise than simultaneously, Rachel's estate will pass as though she survived Donald, and Rachel's parents will inherit her estate. If the state has enacted the UPC's 120-hour rule, Donald could not take as an heir because he failed to survive Rachel by 120 hours. [§§104-107, 110, 115-116]

a. **POSSIBLY**　Here there is sufficient evidence that Donald survived Rachel, and the USDA does not apply. In states that have enacted the USDA, Donald would have inherited all or a substantial share of Rachel's estate [*see* §30], and that share would pass under Donald's will to Ronnie. But again, if the state has enacted the UPC's 120-hour rule, Donald could not take as an heir because he failed to survive Rachel by 120 hours, and Rachel's parents would inherit her estate. [§§110, 115-116]

8. **YES**   At common law (and in a few states today), the lifetime gift to Roderick would be treated as presumptively being an advancement, and thus would be taken into account in making the intestate distribution. However, most states either have reversed the common law presumption (*i.e.,* a lifetime gift to an heir is presumptively *not* an advancement) or require that the intent to make an advancement must be evidenced by, *e.g.,* a writing signed by the donor *or* the donee. Absent evidence of intent that the gift was to be an advancement, or absent a writing, the lifetime gift to Roderick would be disregarded in distributing Pauline's estate. [§§121-128]

9. **SPLIT OF AUTHORITY**   Under the common law and in most states, a lifetime gift to a general legatee in a previously executed will is presumptively intended to have been in partial satisfaction of the legacy. Eileen would have to overcome this presumption by proof of Tony's intent; otherwise she would receive only $30,000 under the will. However, statutes in a number of states require that such a lifetime gift is to be treated as in partial satisfaction of the legacy *only if* shown by a writing signed by the donor *or* the donee. In still other states, a lifetime gift is in satisfaction of a legacy if the will provides that legacies are to be reduced by lifetime gifts. [§§134-36, 138-142]

10. **YES**   While at common law an heir could not disclaim an intestate share, nearly all states now have statutes permitting heirs (as well as will beneficiaries) to disclaim their interest in a decedent's estate. Partial disclaimers are expressly permitted. Under the federal (and most state) disclaimer statute, the disclaimer must be in writing, irrevocable, and filed within nine months after the decedent's death. Since Denise disclaimed her interest by a writing five months after Glenda's death, she takes one-half of her one-fourth share (total of one-eighth) of Glenda's estate; the other one-eighth (the disclaimed portion) passes to Denise's children as though Denise had predeceased Glenda. [§§145-146, 149]

a. **SPLIT OF AUTHORITY**   In most states, a disclaimer is effective as against the creditors of the disclaiming party. However, in several states, a disclaimer cannot be used to defeat creditor's claims—*i.e.,* the creditors can reach the property as though the disclaimer had not been made. [§§161-162]

11. **DEPENDS**   Under the UPC, a person who is convicted of feloniously and intentionally killing the decedent forfeits his interest in the decedent's estate. In the absence of a conviction, the court can determine that the killing was felonious and intentional by a preponderance of the evidence. In non-UPC states, the statutes vary widely: Some states hold that the beneficiary's interest is forfeited only if there is a conviction; others hold that in the absence of a conviction, the

court can determine that the killing was felonious and intentional by a preponderance of the evidence. Here, there was no conviction, but in states following the UPC or preponderance of the evidence rule, the court can use Rambo's guilty plea to voluntary manslaughter to establish a felonious and intentional killing. [§§165-173]

a. **DEPENDS**

Rambo will be entitled to inherit in the states that require a conviction before the interest can be forfeited. However, in states following the UPC or preponderance of the evidence rule, the court could find in the civil action (where the evidentiary test is "a preponderance of the evidence," not "beyond a reasonable doubt") that Rambo wrongfully brought about his father's death even if he was acquitted of the murder/manslaughter charges. If so, his interest would be forfeited. [§§168-173]

12. **YES**

All but one of the common law states give a surviving spouse a right of election to take a statutory share (usually one-third or one-half) of the deceased spouse's estate. Tammy is entitled to receive the elective share amount upon filing a notice of election within a prescribed period of time. [§§195, 200, 226] In addition, and depending on the particular state's laws, Tammy may be entitled to homestead rights, an exempt personal property set-aside, and a family allowance over and above the amount of her elective share. [§§295, 305, 309]

a. **PROBABLY NOT**

Under the common law, nonprobate transfers are not subject to the elective share. However, most courts today apply one of three tests to determine whether the surviving spouse can challenge a nonprobate transfer. Depending on the jurisdiction, Tammy can receive a share of the securities if: (i) Lucian retained any control over the securities ("illusory transfer" doctrine); (ii) Lucian transferred the securities with the intent to defeat Tammy's elective share right; or (iii) after considering all the factors surrounding the transfer (*e.g.*, whether it was revocable), the court determines that Tammy should receive a share ("balancing" approach). [§§240-243]

b. **SPLIT OF AUTHORITY**

Absent a statute dealing with the question, the courts are divided on whether property in a revocable trust is subject to the surviving spouse's elective share right. Under the UPC and in several non-UPC states, the surviving spouse's elective share applies to the augmented estate, which includes revocable transfers. In a minority of states, however, the elective share applies only to the probate estate, and does not include nonprobate dispositions such as revocable trusts. [§244]

13. **NO**

Jose's will put Juanita to an election. She can elect against the will and claim her one-half interest in Blackacre to which she is entitled under the community property laws. But if she does so, she must relinquish the testamentary gift of the residuary estate. If Juanita elects to take Jose's residuary estate under the will, she must allow the will to pass title to her one-half interest in Blackacre to Bernie. [§§260-265]

14. **DEPENDS**   First, it is unclear whether the securities were separate or community property. If they were Mona's separate property, Mona was completely free to give them to Marcie. (Remember, though, that all assets are presumptively community property unless they are affirmatively shown to be separate property.) But what if the securities were community property? In several states, neither spouse can make gifts of community property without the other spouse's written consent. In these states, Frank could elect to set the gift aside as to his one-half share after Mona's death. However, in most states, Frank can set aside the gift only if he can prove that the transfer was in fraud of his community rights. [§§267-274]

15. **YES**   Ann owns an undivided one-half interest in the securities even though they are registered in Ferd's name. Her ownership interest was not lost upon the move to the common law state and her ownership rights will be recognized under the theory of resulting trust or constructive trust. If the state has enacted the Uniform Disposition of Community Property Rights at Death Act, upon Ferd's death Ann owns one-half of the securities and the other half passes under Ferd's will. [§§275-277]

16.a. **SPLIT OF AUTHORITY**   Aside from Louisiana (with its forced heirship rules), in most states the pretermitted child statute applies only to children born or adopted *after the will's execution.* Thus, Chauncey would not receive an intestate share because he was born before the will was executed. However, in a minority of states children alive when the will is executed are pretermitted unless the will mentions them or there is other evidence of an intent that they were not to share in the estate. In these states, Chauncey would be entitled to his intestate share of Hank's estate because Hank's will does not indicate a contrary intent. [§§279-282]

b. **YES**   All pretermitted child statutes apply to after-adopted as well as afterborn children. Thus, Andrew is entitled to an intestate share of Hank's estate. [§§279, 290]

c. **DEPENDS**   In non-UPC states, Andrew is entitled to inherit as a pretermitted child because he was adopted after the will's execution. However, in UPC states, Andrew is not pretermitted because Hank's will bequeathed substantially all of his estate to his spouse (Wanda) *and* she was also Andrew's parent. [§§279, 289]

d. **PROBABLY NOT**   In most states and under the UPC, Andrew is not protected by the pretermitted child statute because he was provided for by lifetime settlement. The life insurance proceeds would qualify as a lifetime settlement. [§§288-289]

17. **NO**   Although Desiree is unhappy with the gift, there is no apparent basis to challenge it. There was no undue influence or incompetency on Ruth's part, and

mortmain statutes, which restrict testamentary gifts to charities, are unconstitutional. Desiree has no basis for her claim. [§§315-317]

18.a. **NO** An instrument that does not dispose of property may still be a will even if it does nothing more than name an executor, revoke an earlier will, or exercise a power of appointment. [§§330-332]

b. **NO** Except in Wisconsin, the right to make a will is *not* regarded as a natural right. The power of testation is entirely subject to legislative control and could be withheld altogether. [§§337-338]

c. **YES** Under both the UPC and the common law, a will is valid if it satisfies the law in effect either at the time of the testator's death or the time of the will's execution. [§§339-340]

d. **NO** It is the testator's *subjective* intent that governs: She must have actually intended that the document in question constitute her will. [§346]

e. **NO** The overwhelming majority view is that such facts give rise to a presumption that the instrument was written with testamentary intent, but the presumption is *rebuttable*. [§349]

19. **NO** In all but a handful of states, a testator must be 18 years of age or older to have capacity to make a will. (An exception is sometimes made for persons who are married or in the armed forces.) Capacity is determined at the time the will is executed. [§§358, 363]

20. **NO** The letter is not admissible to probate as a will since it was not executed with the required formalities; *i.e.*, it was not witnessed by attesting witnesses. [§367]

21. **YES** Signing with a nickname or initials is a valid signature. [§385]

22. **SPLIT OF AUTHORITY** In a majority of states, the testator can sign anywhere on the will—there is no subscription requirement. Thus, all provisions in the will are valid, even if they appear after the testator's signature, as long as they were present when the will was executed. However, a few states require that the testator's signature be at the end of the will. Thus, in these states, the two bequests following Wendy's signature will be disregarded. [§§388-396]

a. **YES** Even in states with the "signature at the end" requirement, the will is still admissible to probate. However, provisions following the testator's signature are disregarded unless doing so would subvert the testator's general testamentary plan (in which case the will would be void). Wendy's will is admissible and the clause following her signature is simply disregarded; her general testamentary plan is not affected. [§§393-395]

b. **NO**

Only words that were present when the will was executed can be given effect. Moreover, these facts do not invoke the "signature at the end" rule, because the two bequests were not part of the duly executed will. [§396]

c. **SPLIT OF AUTHORITY**

Most states and the UPC do *not* require "publication" of a will; thus, in these states, Wendy's will would be admissible to probate. In states that impose a publication requirement, the will would not be admitted to probate. [§§408-409]

23. **YES**

In nearly all states, the order of signing is immaterial as long as all of the parties sign as part of a single, contemporaneous transaction. Nor does it matter whether the testator's signature is below those of the attesting witnesses. [§§400-402]

24. **DEPENDS**

Most state statutes require that the witnesses sign in the testator's presence. There are two tests to determine whether the witness was in the testator's presence. In states that apply the "conscious presence" test, the will is admissible because Smith was conscious of where Bill and Marion were and what they were doing. In states that apply the "line of sight" test, the will is admissible if Bill and Marion signed within Smith's uninterrupted range of vision (*i.e.*, his view was not obstructed by a wall), otherwise it is not admissible. [§§403-405]

a. **DEPENDS**

If Smith was unconscious when the witnesses signed, the attestation would not meet either the conscious presence or line of sight test, and probate would be denied in most states. However, the will would be valid under the UPC because witnesses do not have to sign in the testator's presence. Further, under the revised UPC, the witnesses can sign the will a reasonable time after the testator signed. [§§403-406]

25. **NO**

In most states, a person designated in the will as trustee or executor is not a beneficiary within the meaning of the interested witness statute. Although Barney will be paid for serving as trustee, this is compensation and not a gift. [§422]

a. **YES**

Even though Barney is an "interested witness" within the meaning of the statute, this does not affect the validity of the will (assuming that it was otherwise validly executed). However, under most statutes, the gift to Barney of the remainder interest would be purged (void) because Barney was not a supernumerary witness and because Barney (a friend) would not be an heir if Fred had died intestate. [§§418-422, 429-431]

b. **NO**

The gift to Barney is not invalidated when he witnessed a codicil that did not make (or increase) a gift to him. The codicil actually operates against Barney's interest, since the $10,000 bequest will reduce the size of the trust in which Barney is given an interest. [§434]

26.	**DEPENDS**	In view of the recitals in the attestation clause, the court (or jury) could find that the will was validly executed (*i.e.*, that Seth signed in Agnes's presence) even in the face of Seth's hostile testimony. [§§440-443]
a.	**DEPENDS**	In states that recognize holographic wills, the will would be admissible to probate upon proof that it was entirely in Agnes's handwriting. Seth's signature would not be needed because holographic wills do not need to be witnessed. However, in states that (i) do not give effect to holographic wills and (ii) require the witnesses to sign in the testator's presence, the will would be denied probate. [§§403, 457]
27.	**YES**	Even though a holographic will (or at least its material provisions) must be entirely in the testator's handwriting, "Riveracre" can be disregarded as surplusage because it is not necessary to complete the will or its meaning. The instrument still makes a gift of Riveracre, in Tom's handwriting, with the provision "my ranch in Fayette County." [§§458-460]
a.	**PROBABLY**	In most states, a holographic will does not have to be dated to be valid. However, a few states require that a holographic will must be dated. [§§468-469]
28.	**PROBABLY NOT**	Although the letter makes "testamentary noises," the likely finding of a court is that the letter was not written with testamentary intent; *i.e.*, the letter itself was not intended to serve as Tess's will. It is more likely that Tess's statement in the letter referred to a will that she had already made or was thinking about making. [§§470-472]
29.	**PROBABLY**	While some states permit oral wills for dispositions of personal property, the will must be uttered during the person's last sickness or in contemplation of death. Parker's oral will was properly executed during a life-threatening accident. Lili may be able to offer it for probate unless it was automatically revoked (oral wills expire after a statutorily prescribed time period). [§§474-480]
a.	**NO**	In nearly all states that allow oral wills, such wills can dispose of personal property only. [§476]
30.	**PROBABLY**	The court must determine whether Ruth's statement was intended to operate as a condition to the will's taking effect or merely the motivation for making a will. The court will probably find that the language of the will ("if anything happens to me") merely expressed Ruth's motive for making the will. Ruth's intent that the will is not conditional is supported by the fact that she kept it for five years after it was executed. Thus, the will is likely to be admitted to probate. [§§481-486]
31.	**SPLIT OF AUTHORITY**	In about half of the states, Toby's marriage would have no effect on his previously executed will. In other states and under the UPC, Toby's marriage partially

revokes his previously executed will to provide Macy with an intestate share of the estate (with certain restrictions). Very few states follow the common law rule that marriage following execution of a will revokes the will in its entirety. In any case, if Toby was domiciled in a common law state, Macy could exercise her option to file for an elective share of the estate. [§§499-508]

a.	**SPLIT OF AUTHORITY**	In a few states, marriage followed by birth of issue revokes a previously executed will. In most states, however, the will would not be revoked, but Macy would have rights as a pretermitted spouse (as set out in the preceding answer), and Annette would have rights as a pretermitted child. [§§279, 502]
32.	**NO (as to both questions)**	In nearly all states today and under the UPC, divorce revokes all testamentary gifts and administrative appointments in favor of the ex-spouse, and the will is read as though the former spouse predeceased the testator. Thus, Stanley's estate would pass to Tim, and Tim would be appointed executor. [§§512-513]
a.	**YES**	In states with "divorce revokes" statutes and under the UPC, it is usually provided that if the couple remarries, the revoked provisions are revived. [§516]
33.	**YES**	There is only a partial inconsistency between the two wills, and there is an implied revocation of the first will only to the extent of the inconsistent provisions. The second will is read as a codicil to the first will and where provisions of the two documents are wholly inconsistent with each other, the subsequent instrument controls. Thus, Ann takes $10,000, Betty takes $5,000, David takes $5,000, and Elsie takes the residuary estate. The gift to Carolyn in the first will is revoked by the inconsistency in the second will. [§§532-533]
34.	**DEPENDS**	In most states, revocation by physical act requires that a material part of the will must have been physically acted upon. Merely singeing the corners is insufficient. Under the revised UPC, however, the revocatory act would be effective even if the burning did not touch any of the words on the will. [§§538, 541]
a.	**NO**	The physical act of destruction must be accompanied by a present intent to revoke the will, and here there was no such intent. Since the will was destroyed, it will be necessary to satisfy the "proof of lost wills" statute in order to gain its admission to probate. [§§546, 567-576]
35.a.	**NO**	The letter cannot effect a revocation by subsequent instrument because the letter did not itself reflect a present intent to revoke the will. A mere instruction to another to revoke the testator's will is insufficient. [§529]
b.	**NO**	Revocation by physical act by another person must be at the testator's direction *and in the testator's presence*. Since the will was physically destroyed, it

would be necessary to satisfy the "proof of lost wills" statute in order to admit it to probate. [§§547, 567-576]

36.	**SPLIT OF AUTHORITY**	Most states allow partial revocations by physical act; in these jurisdictions the revocation would be effective. However, a minority of states do not recognize partial revocations by physical act; in these jurisdictions, Ben would take the bequest notwithstanding Andy's attempted revocation. [§§548-552]
37.	**PROBABLY NOT**	If wills are executed in duplicate, both copies must be accounted for before either can be probated. If the copy last seen in the testator's possession cannot be found after diligent search, there is a presumption that the testator destroyed it by physical act with the intent to revoke it. Unless the presumption of revocation can be overcome by proof that it was not revoked (*e.g.*, that it was accidentally destroyed), the will cannot be probated. [§§558-559, 562-564]
a.	**YES**	No presumption of revocation arises when one copy of the duplicate will is found with the testator but the one in the possession of a third person cannot be located. Since the copy in Beulah's possession was found after her death, it is admitted to probate even if the copy last in her attorney's possession cannot be found. The fact that the instrument offered for probate is not the bond paper copy does not matter. [§559]
38.	**SPLIT OF AUTHORITY**	Under the UPC and in a few states, the first will is revived upon proof that this was the testator's intent. However, the majority rule is that revocation of a second will does ***not***, by itself, revive or restore an earlier will. To be valid, the earlier will must be revived by reexecution or republication by codicil. In these states, since the second will was revoked based on a mistake of law as to the validity of the first will, it is possible that the *second* will could be probated under the doctrine of dependent relative revocation. [§§579-583, 596]
39.	**NO**	The will cannot be admitted to probate because there is no proof that it was an integrated document. A presumption of integration arises when, *e.g.*, pages are physically connected or there is a sequence in numbering of consecutive pages. Here, there is no evidence that the pages were physically connected and the fact that they were written with different instruments and there is no sense of continuity brings into dispute whether all pages were present when the will was executed. [§§598-602]
40.a.	**NO**	The typewritten list cannot be incorporated by reference because it was not in existence at the time the will was executed. Also, the typewritten list had no independent significance; its only purpose was testamentary (*i.e.*, to dispose of property at death). Also, it would not be a valid gift under the UPC because the UPC only permits lists disposing of tangible personal property, not real property. [§§605, 621]

b.	**SPLIT OF AUTHORITY**	The gift of the golf clubs would be valid in states that have enacted the UPC provision giving effect to a list that disposes of *tangible personal property*. In states without such a rule, the gift would be invalid for the reasons given above. [§§616-617]
c.	**DEPENDS**	Under the original UPC, the gift of the Mercedes is valid only if it was Randy's personal automobile and was not used in her trade or business—the original UPC does not allow gifts of tangible personal property used in a trade or business to be devised by such lists. However, the gift would be valid under the revised UPC because it permits the disposition of *any* tangible personal property. [§§616-617]
d.	**NO**	Same answer as in a., above. The UPC rule applies to *tangible* personal property and does not apply to intangible property such as cash or securities. [§618]
41.	**YES**	This is a pour-over gift, valid in all states under the Uniform Testamentary Additions to Trusts Act or its equivalent. The gift is valid even though (as here) the trust is later amended by an unwitnessed instrument. However, in a few states execution of the trust would have to have been acknowledged before a notary public in order to receive a valid pour-over gift. [§§625-631]
42.	**SPLIT OF AUTHORITY**	Under the doctrine of republication by codicil, the will is deemed to have been executed on the date of the last codicil thereto, meaning that Cassidy is treated as having been adopted *before* the will's execution. In states whose pretermitted child statutes protect only afterborn and after-adopted children, Cassidy has no rights. However, in states that give protection to children alive when the will was executed, Cassidy would take a share as a pretermitted child. [§§279-282, 637, 640]
43.	**NO**	Generally, the contract between Xavier and Guillaume must have been evidenced by a writing to be enforceable. In states without statutes on the issue, oral contracts regarding wills are valid if they satisfy the Statute of Frauds. Here, the contract must have been in writing because *real property is involved* (though Guillaume's part performance may be enough to take it out of the Statute of Frauds in this instance). In states that do have statutes, and under the UPC, all contracts to make a gift by will must be in some kind of signed writing (*e.g.*, will or contract). The states vary in their requirements as to the writing. [§§646-650]
44.	**NO**	In a majority of states, the mere execution of a joint will is insufficient to prove that it was contractual. Thus, Brad could revoke the will and it would not be admissible to probate on his death but it is still the valid will of Alicia. [§§659-661, 670]
a.	**DEPENDS**	Generally, Brad can revoke the will if he gives Alicia notice of the revocation. In this instance, if Brad revoked the will without notifying Alicia and died

shortly thereafter, neither Alicia nor Stella have a remedy because Alicia is still free to change her will. However, if Brad revokes the will after Alicia's death, the joint will is not admissible to probate but Stella can seek to have a constructive trust imposed on the property. [§§672-674]

45.	**YES**	In all states, if the predeceasing beneficiary was a descendant of the testator and left a surviving descendant, that descendant is entitled to take as a substitute taker under the anti-lapse statute if he survives the testator. Since Betty is Hector's descendant and left a child, Cuthbert, who survives Hector, Cuthbert is entitled to the stock as a substitute taker. [§§695-704]
a.	**DEPENDS**	The anti-lapse statute applies only if Betty predeceased Hector. If the jurisdiction has enacted the UPC's 120-hour rule, Betty would be treated as having predeceased Hector since she failed to survive him by 120 hours. Thus, Cuthbert takes the bequest under the anti-lapse statute as explained above. In states that have adopted the USDA, Betty would have taken the AT&T stock under the will since she survived Hector; the stock would then pass to Bob under Betty's will and Cuthbert takes nothing. [§§686-688]
b.	**PROBABLY NOT**	In nearly all states, the anti-lapse statute does not apply if the testamentary gift was contingent on the beneficiary's surviving the testator. Since Betty failed to meet the condition of the gift, the gift fails according to its terms and the stock would pass to Martha under the residuary clause. However, under the revised UPC and in a small minority of states the anti-lapse statute applies because the will does not make an alternate gift in the event of Betty's nonsurvival. In these states, Cuthbert takes the stock. [§§707-709]
46.a.	**NO**	The anti-lapse statutes found in most states would not apply because Hughy was not related to Donald. Thus, Herkie is not entitled to share in the estate. Since the anti-lapse statute does not apply, some states apply the "no residue of a residue" rule, under which the one-third share that lapsed would "fall out of the will" and pass by intestacy—to Dewey. Dewey would take two-thirds and Louie would take one-third of the residuary estate. However, the revised UPC and a majority of states apply the "surviving residuary beneficiaries" rule, under which Dewey and Louie would each take one-half of the residuary estate. [§§717-719]
b.	**YES**	The anti-lapse statute applies in all states because Dewey is a descendant of the testator and left descendants who survived the testator. Duckie takes Dewey's one-third share of the residuary estate under the anti-lapse statute. Neither the "no residue of a residue" rule nor the "surviving residuary beneficiaries" rule applies if the anti-lapse statute applies. [§§695, 717-719]
47.a.	**DEPENDS**	Alice takes Alan's share only if the state's anti-lapse statute is broad enough to include descendants of the testator's parents or grandparents (or, in a few states, any beneficiary). If the anti-lapse statute is so narrow that it only operates in favor of the testator's descendants, then Alice will not take a share.

Rather, the class gift rule applies and Greenacre passes in equal shares to Vern's surviving children. [§§695-704, 751]

b. **YES**   In nearly all states and under the UPC, a gift to someone's children includes adopted children. Thus, Donna is entitled to a share of Greenacre. [§727]

c. **PROBABLY**   In most states today, a gift to someone's "children" presumptively includes nonmarital children. However, under the original UPC, such a gift presumptively includes nonmarital children of the *mother*, but nonmarital children of the father are not included unless the father openly acknowledged the child as his own. And under the revised UPC, nonmarital children are included only if they lived as regular members of the household of that parent while a minor. In this instance, Charlie is probably entitled to a share in a non-UPC state. If the state adopted the original or revised UPC, Charlie can take a share if Vern openly treated him as his own child, or if he lived with Vern as a minor, respectively. [§§735-739]

d. **NO**   Under the "rule of convenience," the class closed on Bert's death. Only Vern's children who were alive (or in gestation) when Bert died share in the gift. [§§758-759]

48.a. **SPLIT OF AUTHORITY**   In most states, Patricia does not take. Since the Rembrandt was specifically bequeathed and was not in the estate at Herma's death, ademption applies and the gift fails. Patricia is not entitled to the $100,000 because the will bequeathed a painting, not insurance proceeds; the $100,000 becomes a part of the residuary estate which passes to Tammy. However, under the UPC and by statute in several states, Patricia would be entitled to the casualty insurance proceeds paid after the testator's death. [§§772-773, 781, 794]

b. **NO**   All statutes that allow a beneficiary to take casualty insurance proceeds apply only to the extent that the proceeds are paid *after* the testator's death. Patricia would not be entitled to any proceeds paid before Herma's death. [§§794, 797]

c. **NO**   This was a specific bequest ("*my* 200 shares"). Ademption applies and the gift fails since Herma did not own any Ibix stock at her death. Ralph is not entitled to the Series E bonds because the will gave him Ibix stock, not bonds. [§§773, 785]

d. **YES**   Under the UPC and in most states, where new stock is acquired as the result of a merger, the change is one of form and not of substance, and thus ademption does not apply. Ralph is entitled to the Goliath stock. [§790]

e. **NO**   Since the bequest was of "100 shares" and not "*my* 100 shares" of Kytek stock, most courts would classify this gift as a general legacy for ademption purposes. Since ademption does not apply to general legacies, Stanley is entitled to the date-of-death value of 100 shares of Kytek stock. [§785]

49.a.	**YES**	By majority rule, under the UPC, and by statute in several states, a specific bequest of stock carries with it any additional stock produced by a stock split during the testator's lifetime. For purposes of the stock split rule, this gift would be classified as a specific bequest even though the gift was not of "*my* 100 shares" of stock. [§§804-805, 810]
b.	**SPLIT OF AUTHORITY**	Most courts have ruled that, unlike stock produced by a stock split, a specific bequest of stock does *not* include stock dividends declared during the testator's lifetime. Under the UPC and by statute in several states, however, stock dividends are treated the same as stock splits. [§§806-807, 810]
c.	**YES**	Tess owned the stock from the moment of Zack's death, and thus the stock dividend was declared on *her* shares of stock. [§§808, 1091]
50.	**SPLIT OF AUTHORITY**	A majority of states hold that Astrid is entitled to have the lien exonerated since the testator was personally liable on the note secured by the mortgage. However, the UPC and a growing number of states have discarded the "exoneration of liens" doctrine. In these states, the lien is not exonerated unless the will directs exoneration. [§§812-814]
51.	**NO**	Alex has a direct interest in the estate (and would be benefitted if the will were set aside), but his wife does not. Agnes is not an interested party because she is neither an heir nor a legatee named in an earlier will. [§§815-816]
a.	**DEPENDS**	Under the UPC and in most states, Alex would not forfeit the legacy even though he lost the will contest *if* the court finds that the contest was brought in good faith and with probable cause. However, a minority of jurisdictions would enforce the clause and hold that Alex had forfeited his legacy even if he had probable cause for challenging the will. [§§925-926]
52.	**DEPENDS**	Wilbur seems to have had the capacity to know the natural objects of his bounty. Further facts would have to be developed to determine whether he had sufficient capacity to understand the nature of the act he was doing, know the nature and value of his property, and understand the disposition he was making. And while most persons might conclude that Wilbur's belief that he had communicated with a dead person is, at best, illogical, a jury might find that such a belief is not so irrational as to constitute an insane delusion. [§§826-835]
a.	**POSSIBLY**	Although the adjudication would be admissible as evidence of incapacity, it is *not* conclusive. Determination of whether a person should be adjudicated incompetent involves a different (and more stringent) legal test than determination of capacity to make a will. [§837]
53.	**DEPENDS**	In many states, if an attorney prepares a will in his favor and supervises its execution, a presumption or inference of undue influence arises, especially if

other suspicious circumstances exist. More facts would have to be developed, *e.g.*, whether there was a long and ongoing attorney-client relationship, circumstances surrounding the will's preparation and execution, etc. [§§863-864]

54. **DEPENDS** Although Michael's heirs can show that Elise fraudulently induced him to make the will, it must also be shown that the misrepresentation was the *sole* reason for the bequest. If Michael had other inducing reasons (affection, esteem, etc.), the gift would not be set aside. [§§876-878]

   a. **NO** The gift could not be set aside for mistake even though the mistake involves Michael's reason for making the will. Some courts hold that the gift can be set aside if the mistake appears on the face of the will and an inference can be made as to how the testator would have disposed of the property absent the mistake. However, Michael's mistake does not appear on the face of the will. [§§891-893]

55. **NO** Absent a showing of fraud, parol evidence of mistake as to the inducement for a bequest is not admissible. [§§886, 891-893]

   a. **NO** Unless there is an ambiguity, extrinsic evidence is never admissible to cure a mistake as to the contents of the will. Bahar cannot offer extrinsic evidence to show that Jafar actually intended to bequeath a large amount of money. The will's plain meaning is given effect. [§§894-900]

56. **YES** There is a latent ambiguity in the description of the beneficiary, and extrinsic evidence is admissible to cure the ambiguity. [§905]

57. **NO** The opposite is more nearly correct. While the UPC informal probate procedures have distinct advantages in simplicity, it is arguable that they may provide a greater opportunity for abuse because of lenient notice requirements and lack of court supervision of the personal representative. [§§960-962]

58. **NO** Since the instrument was not properly executed, it cannot be probated because it is *not* a valid will. The requirement of formal proof of due execution cannot be waived. [§986]

59. **NOT NECESSARILY** The attestation clause is prima facie evidence of the facts recited therein (*i.e.*, that Sasha and Gina signed in the testator's presence). The trier of fact could find that the will was validly executed notwithstanding Sasha's poor memory and Gina's hostile testimony. [§990]

60. **NO** In addition to good moral character, etc., a personal representative must have *contractual* capacity—which thereby excludes minors. [§1009]

61. **SPLIT OF AUTHORITY** Under the UPC and in several states, a personal representative is given the power to sell or mortgage estate assets by statute, and she need not obtain court authorization. However, many states require court authorization unless the will grants a power of sale. [§§1038-1041]

a.	**SPLIT OF AUTHORITY**	In most states, a personal representative is personally liable to third persons for acts committed by her *or her agents* in administering the estate. In these states, Greta is liable but can seek reimbursement from the estate if she was not personally at fault and did not breach her duty of care. However, under the UPC, Greta is liable for an agent's acts only if she was at fault. [§§1050-1051]
b.	**DEPENDS**	Since Greta was not personally at fault, she is entitled to reimbursement *provided* she exercised reasonable care in hiring and instructing the broker regarding the sale. (Under the UPC, Greta is not liable because she was not personally at fault.) [§§1050-1051]
62.	**YES**	Notice by publication is insufficient as to known or reasonably ascertainable creditors. Lars had a duty to provide Niels with personal notice of the estate administration (because he was a known creditor) before his claim can be barred. [§§1058-1059]
63.a.	**YES**	In nearly all states, general legacies abate before specific bequests are abated. Thus, Zapata's gift is satisfied first. [§§1073, 1075]
b.	**NO**	General legacies abate pro rata. After distributing the stock to Zapata, there will be $21,000 on hand. Miguel should receive $14,000 and Maria $7,000. [§§1073, 1075]
64.	**SPLIT OF AUTHORITY**	In most states, a general legatee is entitled to interest at the legal rate commencing one year after the testator's death (February 15). In these states, Reginald would be entitled to seven months' interest on the $100,000. Under the UPC, however, interest would not commence until one year after appointment of the personal representative (*i.e.*, the following December 10). [§1092]
65.	**PROBABLY NOT**	It is likely that Isadore's children can wind up Isadore's estate informally. In many states, transfer of title to the car and collection of the bank account can be handled by a statutory affidavit procedure. Even if this is not the case, the estate may qualify for a small estate administration under special statutory procedures. In determining whether the estate qualifies for small estate administration, the life insurance would not be counted because it is a nonprobate asset. [§§1094-1100]

Exam Questions
and Answers

QUESTION I

Marisa, a widow, died three months ago. Marisa's duly executed will, dated June 1, 2003, contained the following provisions:

1. I bequeath my Lincoln Continental and my 500 shares of Rand Corporation stock to my daughter Sophia.

2. I bequeath 300 shares of Safeco Corporation stock to my son Marco.

3. I bequeath $50,000 to my son Domenic.

4. I give, devise, and bequeath all the remainder of my estate to my children, Sophia, Marco, and Domenic, in equal shares.

All three of Marisa's children survived her. However, Domenic died 30 days after Marisa (and before her will had been admitted to probate), leaving his wife Claudine as sole beneficiary under his will. Domenic also left two children who were not mentioned in his will. An investigation shows that one year after Marisa executed her will, she gave 300 shares of Safeco stock to Marco and traded in her Lincoln Continental for a new Cadillac. In 2003, the Rand stock split two-for-one, and early this year Rand Corporation merged into Amtex Corporation. The day after Marisa's death a new stock certificate arrived for 1,000 shares of Amtex stock registered in her name.

After all debts, taxes, and administrative expenses have been paid, there remains the following property for distribution: a Cadillac, 600 shares of Safeco stock, 1,000 shares of Amtex stock, and a $125,000 savings certificate registered in Marisa's name.

What are the rights of Marisa's three children or their heirs in the assets of Marisa's estate? Explain fully.

QUESTION II

Tony Testator suffered from multiple sclerosis and had great difficulty writing, although he was mentally competent. In 2003, under no mental or physical coercion, and using an old stationer's will form as a rough guide, Tony dictated to Sandy Oaks, the practical nurse who was caring for him, the following instrument, which was typed by Sandy on one side of a single sheet of paper. When Sandy finished typing, the instrument was as set out below. (The handwritten portions were added as hereinafter stated.)

I, Tony Testator, do make this, my Last Will and Testament.

After my just debts are paid, I devise all the rest and residue of my estate to my nephew, Arnold Smith, and I name Arnold as my executor, to serve without bond.

_____

Subscribed and sealed by the above-named testator, *Tony Testator*, as and for his Last Will and Testament in the presence of us, who were all present at the same time, and who in the testator's presence, and in the presence of each other, have subscribed our names as witnesses.

By Sandy Oaks
July 1, 2003

Witnesses:

Arnold Smith

Arnold Smith

Tony then called in Arnold Smith and Roger Jones and said to them: "Gentlemen, I would like you to witness my will." Tony managed, with some difficulty, to pick up a pen and to place it at the left side of the space where his handwritten name appears in the attestation clause. He started to write, but it was apparent that he had little control over his movements. Sandy, without more, firmly superimposed her hand over Tony's and guided it, the effect being a legible signature. Sandy then wrote "By Sandy Oaks" and "July 1, 2003." Arnold wrote his name and then Roger signed, inadvertently writing Arnold's name below Arnold's signature instead of his own. Tony then said "thanks" to Arnold and Roger, and they departed.

Tony died last month, survived by his nephews Arnold and Benny, his nearest kin. Disappointed that he did not share in Tony's estate, Benny has retained counsel to contest the will or otherwise assert any rights he might have in Tony's estate. Arnold has retained you to protect his right to Tony's entire residuary estate. Discuss with him the legal issues that the case presents and your conclusion as to the ultimate distribution of the estate assets.

QUESTION III

Luther married Esmeralda in 1978, and in 1980, a child, Ruby, was born of the marriage. Luther and Esmeralda were divorced in 1993, and in 1996 Luther married Beatrice.

In 1997, Luther duly executed a will in which, after making cash bequests of $5,000 to each of three brothers and two sisters (totaling approximately 5% of his net estate), he left the residue of his estate as follows: "One-half thereof to my wife Beatrice and the remaining one-half to my child Ruby." In 1998, Luther adopted Randolph, Beatrice's child by a previous marriage. In 2002, Ruby died survived by two minor children, Carter and Credence.

On January 20, 2003, Luther consulted his attorney and told her to prepare a new will, revoking all prior wills, and disposing of his estate as follows: $10,000 to each of the brothers and sisters named in the 1997 will, one-half of the residue to his wife Beatrice, and the remaining one-half in equal shares to his adopted son Randolph and his two grandchildren, Carter and Credence. While Luther was in the office, the attorney had her secretary type a memorandum correctly setting forth Luther's requests. After reading over the memorandum, Luther signed it and the attorney gave him a xerographic copy of the signed memo.

Luther died of a heart attack on January 24, 2003. The 1997 will was found in his desk with the word "Cancelled" written diagonally across the face of the will. Luther's initials and "1/21/03" appeared just under the word "Cancelled," all writing being in Luther's hand. The memo concerning the new will was found with the 1997 will.

Luther was survived by Beatrice, Randolph, Carter, Credence, and the brothers and sisters named in the 1997 will. Who is entitled to share in Luther's estate and in what shares? Discuss all issues raised by these facts.

QUESTION IV

Flavia, a 78-year-old widow, suffered from the infirmities of advanced age. On July 1, she entered a nursing home. Eduardo, a practical nurse and former neighbor of Flavia, frequently visited Flavia in the nursing home. He would often feed her and provide other minor assistance. On December 15, Eduardo suggested to Flavia that she should have a new will because the tax laws were recently changed (which was true). On December 20, Counsel, an attorney, came to the nursing home at Eduardo's request. Counsel prepared and supervised the execution of a new will which devised the bulk of Flavia's estate to Eduardo. Counsel then asked Flavia to give him the old will "because it is now obsolete." Flavia acceded to this request and handed the document to Counsel. After returning to his office, Counsel wrote "Void" across each page of the old will and placed it in the file with the new will. Under the old will, Flavia's entire estate was devised to her grandson Javier.

Flavia died on April 15 of the following year, while still in the nursing home. An investigation shows that her grandson Javier, her sole heir, never visited Flavia or called the nursing home to inquire about his grandmother's condition, even though he lived in the same city. Javier consults you as to the legal status of each of the two wills and the possibility of his inheriting Flavia's estate. What advice would you give to Javier? Discuss the controlling legal issues.

QUESTION V

Estelle, who was single, duly executed a will in 2000 which provided as follows:

1. I bequeath 50 shares of General Bank stock to my sister Margot.

2. I devise my home to my sister Solange.

3. I give, devise, and bequeath the rest of my estate to my brothers Jean, Michel, and Andre.

4. I intentionally make no provision for my sister Francine.

In 2001, Estelle sold her home to Antoine for $50,000. The sale was pursuant to an installment contract under which Antoine paid $5,000 down and agreed to pay Estelle $500 per month until the balance (with interest) was paid in full. A deed to the home was placed in escrow, to be delivered to Antoine upon full payment of the contract price. The note was secured by a vendor's lien on the property. At the time of sale, Estelle told Antoine that if she died before the price was paid in full, he was to pay the balance to her brothers.

In 2002, General Bank paid a 100% stock dividend, pursuant to which Estelle received an additional 50 shares of stock. Also in 2002, Estelle's brothers Jean and Michel died. Jean was survived by a widow and two adopted children. Michel, who never married, had no children.

Estelle died in 2003. Her estate contained 100 shares of General Bank stock; the note and vendor's lien from Antoine (with an unpaid balance of $35,000 when Estelle died); and other assets worth $100,000. Estelle was survived by her sisters Margot, Solange, and Francine, her brother Andre, and the widow and two adopted children of her brother Jean. How should her estate be distributed? Explain fully.

QUESTION VI

Sonny died leaving a purported last will and testament dated August 1, 2001. The will was in Sonny's handwriting and his signature was affixed at the bottom. To the left of Sonny's signature were the signatures of Cybil (his housekeeper), Trent (his uncle and only living blood relative), and Marty (his neighbor).

Sonny's will left his $10,000 savings account (which was registered jointly in Cybil's and his name) to Cybil, his stamp collection and automobile to Marty, and his residuary estate to Trent.

In 2003, Sonny became seriously ill. Just before the ambulance arrived to take him to the hospital, he called Cybil and Marty to his bedside and gave his savings passbook to Cybil and his stamp collection to Marty, saying, "I won't be coming back so you can have these now."

Sonny died two days later. Not counting the savings account and the stamp collection, his estate included the following assets: $75,000 in stocks and bonds; a checking account with a $12,000 balance; and a Mercedes automobile purchased in 2003. Sonny had traded in his Volkswagen as a downpayment for the Mercedes.

Should the purported will be admitted to probate and who should receive each of the assets mentioned? Discuss your reasoning and conclusions.

QUESTION VII

Martha died two months ago, leaving as her sole heirs four children: Andy, Bob, Carol, and David. Martha had executed a will with all appropriate formalities in 2000; the will was witnessed by two neighbors. Although Martha asked the neighbors to "witness my will," neither neighbor knew the contents of the will, which had been prepared by Martha's lawyer. The will contained the following provisions:

1. I devise Blackacre to my son Andy.

2. I bequeath $8,000 and all of the paintings in the master bedroom of my home to my daughter Carol.

3. I bequeath $10,000 to my college.

4. I bequeath $25,000 to my son David with the hope and expectation that he use a portion of this money to provide educational assistance to and/or custodial care for his son Dwayne.

5. I give my residuary estate to my good friend Mary.

6. I have not forgotten my son Bob. However, it is my intention that he shall not, under any circumstances, share in my estate.

Other pertinent facts are as follows: Martha, a retired college professor, earned an undergraduate degree from Central State College, a master's degree in education from Mega University, and taught for 15 years at Elysian College. Her grandson Dwayne was injured in a car accident in 1999, from which he suffered brain damage. In November 2001, Martha mortgaged Blackacre, and the unpaid balance on the mortgage note was $15,000 at her death. Mary died in March 2003, leaving her mother as her sole heir. When Martha was confined to her bed shortly before her death, she had a number of valuable paintings moved from other parts of her house to her master bedroom so that she might enjoy them; this more than doubled the value of paintings in the room.

What distribution should be made of Martha's estate? Explain fully.

QUESTION VIII

In 1995, Lorenzo, then a widower, entered into a written agreement wherein he agreed to devise Blackacre, an undeveloped tract of land then worth $150,000, to his son Silvio if Silvio would assist him in his business for a period of 10 years or until Lorenzo's earlier death. Lorenzo also had a daughter Anna. In 1997, Lorenzo duly executed a will that contained the following provisions:

1. I bequeath legacies of $25,000 to each of my children, Silvio and Anna.

2. I recognize my obligation to my son Silvio in assisting me in my business, and I therefore bequeath to him the additional sum of $150,000.

3. I devise Blackacre to my son Silvio for life, with remainder over to my daughter Anna.

Anna was named residuary beneficiary and executor. At the date of execution of the will, Blackacre had not appreciated in value.

In 2003, Lorenzo married Priscilla, a wealthy widow. They died in an automobile accident on their wedding trip. Lorenzo was killed instantly; Priscilla died a week later without ever regaining consciousness. She died intestate leaving an only child, Karla. Priscilla knew nothing of the agreement with Silvio. Silvio, Anna, and Karla, all of whom are adults, survive.

Anna has offered Lorenzo's 1997 will for probate. Because of the development of a "theme park" in the vicinity, Blackacre had recently skyrocketed in value, and of Lorenzo's total assets (before estate taxes but after payment of all other claims, charges, and expenses) of $1 million, it represents $750,000 thereof. Silvio has fully performed the agreed services.

Silvio has retained you to advise him as to his rights under the agreement and the will, and as to his best course of action. Discuss the distribution of the assets, considering the rights of Silvio, Anna, and Karla, and setting forth your reasoning for conclusions reached. (Assume that all documents were validly executed according to law. Also, disregard the impact of possible estate taxes on your conclusions.)

QUESTION IX

Margaret, age 73, lived with her daughter Amelia ever since her husband died 10 years ago. Amelia has taken care of Margaret's financial affairs and in the last few years Margaret's declining health has required Amelia to be a nurse as well as financial advisor. Margaret has been very thankful for Amelia's help and has often told her friends that she planned to take care of Amelia in her will.

One day while taking a walk, Margaret fell and broke her hip. She was rushed to the hospital and was told she would have to have surgery. Amelia told her mother that it was time to make her will and that she had arranged for a lawyer to come to the hospital. Margaret said that if that was what Amelia thought was best, she would tell the lawyer what to write and she would sign it.

Attorney visited with Amelia and Margaret the next day, and Margaret told him to draft her will so that she could execute it before her surgery. Attorney went back to his office and drafted a will in accordance with Margaret's instructions, as follows:

1. I bequeath $25,000 to my good friend, Ann.

2. I give my son John one-fifth of my property, both real and personal, wheresoever situated.

3. I give all the rest, residue, and remainder of my property, both real and personal, to my beloved daughter Amelia.

Attorney returned to the hospital and found Margaret about to go into surgery. She said she was too tired to read her will but asked Attorney if he had done what she told him. He said he had, and she executed her will in the presence of Amelia and two nurses. The nurses signed as witnesses to the will.

Margaret recovered from surgery and returned home. John wrote his mother and said he was gay. Margaret was so upset that she had Attorney draft a codicil to her will revoking the second provision. Margaret duly executed the codicil.

Two years later, John returned home to see Margaret and attend Ann's funeral. He and Margaret had a long talk, and Margaret decided it was time to make peace with her son. She took the codicil out of her desk, tore it up, and threw it in a wastebasket.

Margaret died two days later, leaving an estate valued at $200,000 after all debts and expenses. She was survived by John and Amelia, her only children.

John comes to see you and wants his mother's will set aside because of the actions of his sister Amelia at the time the will was prepared. Should John prevail, and if so, how will the estate be distributed? If the will stands, how will the estate be distributed? State the reasons for the conclusions that you reach.

QUESTION X

Tim Brown went to a program at his church, sponsored by the local bar association, on estate planning and the need for the average citizen to have a will. After the meeting, Tim decided he needed a will. Concluding that he did not own enough property to warrant paying a lawyer to draft his will, Tim wrote the following handwritten statements on a yellow legal pad:

I, Tim Brown, being of sound mind, leave my estate as follows:

1. I give my good friend Herb Hanson all of my fishing equipment and my 25-foot boat.

2. I give my church, First Baptist Church of Smithville, the sum of $10,000.

3. All the rest of my property I give to my sister Jane Brown.

After writing the will, Tim took it over to his preacher's house and asked the preacher and his wife if they would witness the will. They said that they would be happy to, and the preacher thanked Tim for the generous gift to the church. The preacher and his wife signed at the bottom of the page, and then Tim signed the will just above their signatures. Tim took the will home and placed it in his desk drawer.

About a year later, after a dispute with members of his church, Tim left the First Baptist Church and joined the Glory Baptist Church of Smithville. After he joined the Glory Baptist Church, Tim crossed out the words "First Baptist Church" and wrote in "Glory Baptist Church" in the second provision of his will. He then initialed the change in the margin and put the will back into his desk.

Tim died four weeks ago and his will has been offered for probate by his sister Jane. Jane has notified First Baptist Church and Glory Baptist Church about the will. Discuss the issues as to the validity of the will, and who will take the $10,000 under the second provision.

ANSWER TO QUESTION I

Sophia: Sophia takes the 1,000 shares of Amtek stock and one-third of the residuary estate. Marisa's will made a specific bequest of "my 500 shares" of Rand stock. Since a specific devisee of stock is entitled to any additional shares produced by a stock split declared after the will is executed, Sophia would have been entitled to all 1,000 shares of Rand stock. But then Rand Corporation was merged into Amtex Corporation. At common law and in a few states, this would result in ademption of the bequest of Rand stock. However, the UPC and most states hold that since this was a change of form and not of substance, the specific devisee of stock gets the equivalent shares in the new corporation that are produced by a merger, consolidation, reorganization, or similar action.

Sophia has no claim to Marisa's Cadillac. A specific bequest of an item that is not in the testator's estate at her death is adeemed; *i.e.*, it fails. Since the Lincoln Continental was not in Marisa's estate at her death, the bequest to Sophia is adeemed. The Cadillac falls into the residuary estate.

Marco: Marco takes one-third of the residuary estate. Whether Marco is entitled to the 300 shares of Safeco stock devised under the will depends on whether Marisa's lifetime gift of the 300 shares of Safeco stock to Marco constituted a satisfaction of that legacy. Under the common law, a gift to a child of the testator is presumed to be in partial or total satisfaction of any testamentary gift to that child. Thus, Marisa's lifetime gift to her son Marco would be in total satisfaction of the devise of the 300 shares of Safeco stock. However, under the UPC and in some states, the lifetime gift will be in satisfaction of the testamentary gift only if accompanied by a writing by either the testator (that the gift be in satisfaction of the legacy) or the donee (acknowledging that the gift was in satisfaction). The UPC and some states require that the testator's writing be contemporaneous with the lifetime gift, while other states hold that the writing can be made at any time. In this case, there was no writing by either Marisa or Marco indicating that the lifetime gift of stock was to be in satisfaction of the testamentary gift. Thus, Marisa's lifetime gift of the stock would not be in satisfaction of the testamentary gift—Marco would be entitled to an additional 300 shares of Safeco stock in addition to one-third of the residuary estate.

Domenic: Domenic inherited $50,000 plus one-third of the residuary estate under Marisa's will. The gifts to Domenic did not lapse because he did not predecease Marisa—he died 30 days after her. Since Domenic owned this portion of Marisa's estate as of her death, the property passed under his will to Claudine on his death. The fact that Marisa's will was not probated and the property had not been distributed before his death is irrelevant—his rights under Marisa's will relate back to her death.

Domenic's two children might share his estate with Claudine if they are pretermitted heirs. Under the UPC and in most states, a child is pretermitted only if he was born after the will's execution. Thus, if Domenic's children were born after he had executed his will, they will be entitled a portion of the estate. However, in a minority of states, the pretersmitted child statute applies also to children born before the will was executed. In those states, Domenic's children would be pretermitted regardless of when they were born.

In conclusion, Sophia receives 1,000 shares of Amtex stock and one-third of the residuary estate. Marco receives 300 shares of Safeco stock (if the lifetime gift of Safeco stock is not in satisfaction of the gift in the will) and one-third of the residuary estate. Claudine receives $50,000 and one-third of the residuary estate. Domenic's heirs will receive an intestate share of his estate if they are pretermitted. The residuary estate comprises the Cadillac, either 300 or 600 shares of Safeco stock (depending on whether the satisfaction of legacies doctrine applies to Marco's lifetime gift), and $75,000 from the savings certificate.

ANSWER TO QUESTION II

This question raises two issues: First, was Tony's will validly executed? Second, does Arnold lose his bequest because he is an interested witness?

Validity of will: The following requirements for valid execution must be met under the most stringent will execution statutes: (i) the will must have been signed by the testator, (ii) the testator's signature must appear at the end of the will, (iii) the testator must have signed the will in the presence of two witnesses, (iv) the testator must have declared to the witnesses that the instrument is his will, and (v) the witnesses must have signed the will in the presence of the testator and each other. All of these requirements have been satisfied in this case.

First, Tony's signature is valid despite the fact that Sandy had to guide his hand. It is generally held that the signature requirement is satisfied if the testator's hand is guided by another, provided that the testator desired and intended to sign the will. In this instance, Tony clearly intended to sign the will but his attempt was not successful because he suffered from multiple sclerosis and was incapable of signing by himself. The fact that Sandy assisted him does not destroy the validity of his signature.

Second, Tony's signature appears at the end of the will. The fact that he did not sign on the designated signature line does not alter the fact that Tony did impress his signature.

Finally, Tony signed the will in the presence of three witnesses—Sandy, Roger, and Arnold—after stating that the instrument was his will. Sandy, Roger, and Arnold then proceeded to attest the will in the presence of Tony and each other.

Benny may argue that Roger's signature is invalid because he inadvertently signed Arnold's name instead of his own. However, the signature requirement is liberally construed. Generally, any mark (whether that of the testator or a witness) will constitute a valid signature if intended to be a signature. Roger signed the will of his own volition and intended that the signing of Arnold's name, though inadvertent, be his signature. Furthermore, the will only needs the signature of two witness; thus, the signatures of Sandy and Arnold would be enough even if Roger's signature was invalid.

Tony's will has been validly executed as all of the necessary requirements have been satisfied.

Interested witness: Arnold will receive his full share under the will despite the jurisdiction's view regarding interested witnesses. Generally, an interested witness is one who is both a beneficiary under the will and an attesting witness to the will. It is universally held that attestation by an interested witness does not affect the validity of the will, although it may eliminate any gifts to that witness under the will.

Under the UPC and in a minority of states, the interested witness rule has been abolished—the witness is entitled to any bequests made to him in the will. In those states, Arnold would be entitled to Tony's entire estate despite the fact that he signed as a witness. However, a majority of the states have enacted purging statutes that void any gift in favor of a witness-beneficiary. However, an exception to the operation of the purging statute exists if the witness-beneficiary was a supernumerary witness (*i.e.*, an extra witness). Here, there were three witnesses to the will when only two were required. Thus, Arnold was a supernumerary witness and his signature was not necessary for the will to be valid. Thus, his gift will not be void.

Note: Should the court determine that Roger's signature is not valid, Arnold's signature will be necessary to the validity of the will and the supernumerary exception will not apply. However, a second exception to the purging statute exists if the witness-beneficiary would have been an heir of the decedent, in which case he takes the lesser of (i) his intestate share or (ii) the bequest in the will. Since Arnold and Benny were Tony's nearest kin, they would have taken if Tony had died intestate (one-half each). Thus, if Roger's signature was invalid Arnold would only receive the lesser of (i) his intestate share (one-half of the estate) or (ii) the bequest under the will (entire estate).

ANSWER TO QUESTION III

Luther's 1997 will was revoked by physical act in 2003 and the new will was never validly executed. As a result, Luther's estate passes by intestate succession to his spouse (Beatrice) and his heirs (Randolph, Carter, and Credence).

This question raises several issues: Was the 1997 will validly revoked? Can the 2003 memo be probated as Luther's will? Does the doctrine of dependent relative revocation ("DRR") apply to the revocation of the 1997 will? Does Randolph take as an heir? Do Carter and Credence succeed to any share Ruby may have been entitled to had she survived?

Revocation of 1997 will: The 1997 will was validly revoked and therefore cannot be probated. A testator can revoke a will by physical act if the act is accompanied by a present intent to revoke. If the revocation is by writing the word "Cancelled" on the will, the cancellation must touch the words of the will. (Under the revised UPC, there is no requirement that it touch the words of the will.) Here, Luther wrote the word "Cancelled" diagonally across the face of the will. It can be assumed from the facts that the revocation was made by Luther and that he made it with an intent to revoke the will because he signed and dated the will below the word "Cancelled." Thus, the 1997 will was properly revoked.

Probate of 2003 memo: The memo cannot be probated as Luther's will because it was not executed with testamentary intent and, alternatively, because it was not properly witnessed. To have testamentary intent, Luther must have intended that the memo constitute his will at the time he executed it. Here, it is clear from the facts that Luther did not intend for the memo to be his will. Instead, the memo merely reflected the provisions that were to be included in his new will, which was to be executed in the future. Even if the court were persuaded that the memo was executed with testamentary intent, it cannot be probated because it was not properly witnessed. Most jurisdictions require that a will be attested by two witnesses. Luther's memo had no attesting witnesses; it was signed only by himself. Additionally, the memo cannot serve as a holographic instrument because its material provisions are not in Luther's handwriting. Thus, the memo cannot be probated as Luther's will.

Applicability of DRR to 1997 will: DRR will not operate to disregard the revocation of the 1997 will. Generally, DRR will apply to disregard a revocation if it was premised on a mistake of law or fact as to the validity of another disposition which turns out to be ineffective. Luther did not revoke the 1997 will while relying on the validity of another instrument. As stated above, the memo was not executed with testamentary intent; thus, Luther could not have been relying on its validity when he revoked the 1997 will. DRR will not save the 1997 will. Luther's estate will pass under the intestate succession statutes because he died without a valid will.

Randolph: Randolph will inherit as if he was Luther's natural child. An adopted child has the same inheritance rights as a natural child of the decedent. Thus, Randolph will inherit a portion of Luther's estate under intestate succession.

Carter and Credence: Carter and Credence will share the portion that Ruby would have inherited had she survived. The portion of the estate that does not pass to the surviving spouse will pass to the decedent's children and the descendants of deceased children. The states apply one of three patterns of distribution to determine the intestate shares of children and descendants of deceased children: classic per stirpes, per capita with representation, and per capita at each generation. The distribution scheme employed by a majority of the states is per capita with representation—the division of shares is made at the first generational level with living takers. Since Luther left one surviving child (Randolph), the division will be made at that level; therefore, one-half of the remainder goes to Randolph and the other half passes to Ruby's children, Carter and Credence (one-fourth each), by representation. (*Note:* The outcome would be the same in this case regardless of which pattern of distribution is applied.)

ANSWER TO QUESTION IV

Javier needs to establish that either (i) Flavia lacked testamentary capacity at the time the second will was executed, or (ii) the second will was the product of Eduardo's undue influence over Flavia. If Javier can prove either, he will inherit Flavia's entire estate under the first will because it was not properly revoked.

Testamentary capacity: Under the UPC and in most states, a testator is presumed to have testamentary capacity. To rebut this presumption, Javier must establish that Flavia did not have sufficient capacity to: (i) understand the nature of her act, (ii) know the natural objects of her bounty, (iii) know the nature and value of her property, and (iv) understand the disposition she was making. Javier will be unsuccessful in establishing lack of testamentary capacity because it is tested at the time of the will's execution, and there is nothing in the facts indicating that Flavia did not have testamentary capacity at that time. The fact that she is in a nursing home and suffering from the infirmities of old age, by itself, is insufficient.

Undue influence: Javier will probably be successful in proving undue influence. Undue influence occurs when the free will of the testator is destroyed and the resulting will reflects the desires of the person exerting the influence. In most states, a presumption of undue influences arises when (i) a confidential relationship existed between the testator and the beneficiary; (ii) the beneficiary played an active part in procuring the will; and (iii) the disposition in favor of the beneficiary is unnatural (*e.g.*, favors an unrelated party over relatives). Here, Javier can establish that a confidential relationship existed between Flavia and Eduardo because of the nurse-patient relationship that had developed and because of the heavy reliance Flavia placed on Eduardo for care and companionship. Eduardo played an active part in procuring Flavia's will by suggesting that Flavia change her will and by hiring Counsel to prepare the will. Finally, the will makes an unnatural disposition by favoring Eduardo over Flavia's grandson, Javier. Furthermore, Flavia's weakened physical condition made her susceptible to the undue influence. These facts will give rise to a presumption of undue influence and the burden will then shift to Eduardo to rebut the presumption. (In a few states, these facts will merely raise an inference of undue influence and the burden of proof will not shift to Eduardo.) Eduardo will have a difficult time disproving that he exerted undue influence over Flavia. Since Flavia's entire will is the product of Eduardo's undue influence, it is void.

Revocation of first will: Counsel did not properly revoke Flavia's first will. When a testator's will is physically revoked by a third party, it must be done in the testator's presence and at her direction. In this instance, Counsel waited until he returned to his office to write "Void" across the face of the will. The attempted revocation is ineffective because it was not done in Flavia's presence; thus, that will is still valid and Javier takes Flavia's entire estate under its provisions. *Note:* The will is not revoked by the subsequent testamentary instrument because the subsequent instrument was the product of Eduardo's influence, as discussed above.

ANSWER TO QUESTION V

General Bank stock: Margot receives 50 shares of General Bank stock as devised under the will and might also receive the 50 shares produced by the stock dividend depending on the jurisdiction. In a majority of states, a beneficiary is not entitled to additional shares produced by a stock dividend before the testator's death. Here, the stock dividend occurred the year before Estelle's death. Under the majority view, Margot will not receive the 50 shares produced by the stock dividend (she would have been entitled to the additional shares if the dividend had occurred *after* Estelle's death). However, under the UPC and in a minority of states, the beneficiary of the stock is entitled to additional shares produced by a stock dividend, regardless of whether the dividend occurs before or after the testator's death. Under this view, Margot is entitled to the additional 50 shares of stock, leaving her with all 100 shares of stock in Estelle's estate.

Home: Solange will not receive the home because the gift adeemed when it was sold to Antoine. However, she might be entitled to the balance of the purchase price owed by Antoine. When a testator makes a specific devise of property in her will and that property is no longer in the testator's estate at her death (*e.g.*, because it was sold or destroyed), the gift adeems; *i.e.*, it fails and the devisee receives nothing. Here, Estelle entered into a contract to sell her home to Antoine. Although the contract has not been fully performed (Antoine still owes a balance of $35,000 on the purchase price), the doctrine of equitable conversion applied once the contract became enforceable. Under the doctrine of equitable conversion, the seller (Estelle) becomes the owner of a personal property right and the purchaser (Antoine) becomes the owner of the real property. (*See* Property Summary.) Thus, Estelle owned only a contract right on her death; she no longer was the owner of the home. Since the home was no longer in her estate on her death, the gift adeems and Solange has no rights in the home.

Although Solange has no rights in the home, she might still be able to receive the balance of the purchase price owed by Antoine. Under the UPC and in several states, the effects of ademption are softened in the case of an executory contract: The devisee is entitled to the remaining contract payments if the specifically devised property is subject to an executory contract at the testator's death. Here, the contract was still executory on Estelle's death as Antoine still owed $35,000; thus, Solange is entitled to the remaining payments on the balance. *Note:* She is not entitled to any payments made before Estelle's death. Estelle's oral instruction to Antoine to pay the balance of the purchase price to her brothers is ineffective because it was neither a part of her will or any codicil to the will, nor was it a part of the contract because the instruction was not written, thus violating the Statute of Frauds.

Residuary estate: Andre receives one-half of the residuary estate and Jean's children share the remaining half (one-fourth each). The first step is to determine what happens when there is a lapse in the residuary estate. Under majority law, if the residuary estate is devised to more than one beneficiary and the devise to one of those beneficiaries fails for any reason (*e.g.*, he predeceases the testator), that share will pass to the other residuary beneficiaries unless the anti-lapse statute applies. Since there were three residuary beneficiaries and two predeceased Estelle, it must be determined whether either gift is saved by the anti-lapse statute or whether it passes to the remaining residuary beneficiary (Andre).

Jean's share lapsed because he failed to survive Estelle. However, his one-third interest might be saved by the anti-lapse statute if he is within the specified degree of relationship to the testator and left surviving descendants. The facts already point out that Jean left two surviving children, so it must be determined whether he is in the specified degree of relationship to Estelle. Under the most narrow anti-lapse statute, the beneficiary must have been a descendant of the testator. Here, Jean was Estelle's brother and not her descendant; thus, the gift to him will lapse under that type of anti-lapse statute. However, under the UPC and in a majority of states, the anti-lapse statutes require that the beneficiary must have been a descendant of either the testator's parents or grandparents. Jean's gift will be saved under either of these anti-lapse statutes because he was Estelle's brother. Therefore, his two children will succeed to his share of the residuary estate.

Michel's share also lapsed because he failed to survive Estelle but his share will not be saved by the anti-lapse statute because he did not leave any descendants. His one-third share will instead pass to the surviving residuary beneficiaries—Andre and Jean's two children. Thus, Andre will receive one-half of the residuary estate and Jean's two children will receive one-fourth each.

ANSWER TO QUESTION VI

Admission of will to probate: The will should be admitted probate because it was validly executed. If the jurisdiction recognizes holographic wills, the will must be entirely in the testator's handwriting and signed by him. Here, Sonny's will was in his handwriting and affixed with his signature. The will would be valid and admissible to probate in such a jurisdiction.

However, if the jurisdiction does not recognize holographic wills, several elements must be proved under the most stringent will execution statute: (i) the will must have been signed by the testator, (ii) the testator's signature must appear at the end of the will, (iii) the testator must have signed the will in the presence of at least two witnesses, (iv) the testator must have declared to the witnesses that the instrument is his will, and (v) the witnesses must have signed the will in the presence of the testator and each other. Here, the will was signed by Sonny and three witnesses and the signatures appear at the end. The fact that it was not typed is irrelevant and the attestation by interested witnesses does not destroy its validity. The facts do not indicate whether the witnesses and Sonny signed the will in each others' presence. Thus, the presence element will have to be established by the testimony of two of the attesting witnesses since there is no attestation clause. It appears from the facts that all three witnesses are present in the jurisdiction; thus, due execution should be easy to prove.

Savings account: The savings account belongs to Cybil either by Sonny's lifetime gift or pursuant to the terms of the will. Cybil owns the savings account by lifetime gift if the delivery of the passbook was a valid transfer of ownership. (*See* Property Summary.) If so, then the specifically devised savings account is no longer in Sonny's estate at his death (*i.e.*, because he gave it away) and the gift to Cybil adeems; *i.e.*, it fails. She takes the savings account pursuant to the lifetime gift and takes nothing under the will. However, if the delivery of the passbook was not a valid transfer of ownership, then the lifetime gift never occurred and the savings account is still in Sonny's estate. However, Cybil is entitled to it under the terms of the will.

Stamp collection: The stamp collection passes to Marty by Sonny's lifetime gift because the physical transfer of the stamp collection was an effective inter vivos gift. The gift of the stamp collection to Marty under the will adeems because it is no longer in the estate.

Automobile: Marty is an interested witness but he will receive Sonny's Mercedes even if the jurisdiction has enacted a purging statute. An interested witness is one who is both a witness and a beneficiary under a will. Although the fact that a beneficiary was an attesting witness does not affect the validity of the will, the gift in favor of the witness-beneficiary might fail. Under the UPC and in a minority of states, the interested witness rule has been abolished—the witness is entitled to any bequests made to him in the will. In those jurisdictions, Marty would be entitled to the Mercedes even though he signed the will as a witness. However, a majority of the states have enacted purging statutes that eliminate any gift in favor of a witness-beneficiary. However, an exception to the operation of the purging statute applies if the witness-beneficiary was a supernumerary witness (*i.e.*, an extra witness). Here, there were three witnesses to the will when only two were needed. Marty was a supernumerary witness and his signature was not necessary for the will to be valid. Thus, his gift is not purged. The fact that Sonny owned a Volkswagon when he executed a will and died owning a Mercedes is irrelevant. Under the doctrine of "acts of independent significance," a testator can refer to extrinsic acts in his will for the purpose of designating the property that is the subject of the gift. Sonny made a bequest of "my automobile," not "my Volkswagon." The gift to Marty is valid even if Sonny bought a new car each year until his death as long as the act of buying a new car was independent of its effect on the will. Here, it is unlikely that Sonny traded in his Volkswagon for a Mercedes with the intent to change the bequest to Marty. It is more likely that he merely wanted a new automobile. Thus, Marty is entitled to the Mercedes.

Residuary estate: The residuary estate (comprising the stocks, bonds, and checking account) belongs to Trent despite the fact that he was an interested witness under the will. As discussed above, Trent will inherit the residuary estate if the jurisdiction follows the UPC or minority view regarding gifts to interested witnesses. However, Trent is entitled to the residuary estate even if the jurisdiction has enacted a purging statute under either exception to the statute's operation. The first exception, discussed above, applies because Trent was one of three witnesses to the will, making him a supernumerary witness. But if that exception did not apply for some reason, Trent would still take the residuary estate under the "whichever is least" exception to the purging statute. Under this exception, a witness-beneficiary who would have been an heir if the testator had died intestate takes the lesser of (i) his intestate share or (ii) the bequest in the will. Since Trent was Sonny's only living relative, he would stand to inherit Sonny's entire estate if Sonny had died without a will. Thus, under the "whichever is least" exception, Trent will take the residuary estate under the will because it is less than his intestate share.

ANSWER TO QUESTION VII

Martha's will was validly executed despite the fact that the witnesses did not know the contents of the will. Although some states require that the witnesses know that the instrument they are witnessing is a will, there is no requirement that they must know the provisions of the will. Since Martha's will is valid, her estate will be distributed as follows:

Andy: Andy will receive Blackacre. The $15,000 mortgage might be paid out of the residuary estate depending on the jurisdiction. In a majority of states, a lien on specifically devised property can be exonerated, *i.e.*, paid out of the residuary estate. Under this view, Andy can demand that the mortgage be paid out of Martha's residuary estate and he will take Blackacre free of the mortgage. However, under the UPC and in a minority of states, a lien on specifically devised property is not exonerated unless the will directs exoneration. In those jurisdictions, Andy would take Blackacre subject to the mortgage because Martha's will does not direct that the lien be exonerated.

Carol: Carol receives $8,000 and the paintings in the master bedroom. Under the doctrine of "acts of independent significance," a testator can refer to extrinsic acts in her will for the purpose of designating the property that is the subject of the gift provided the acts have independent significance from the will. Martha devised the paintings in the master bedroom to Carol. The fact that she later rearranged the paintings in her home is irrelevant, even if the effect was to increase the value of the paintings in the master bedroom, because her act was not related to the devise in her will. Instead, the facts clearly indicate that she rearranged the paintings "so that she might enjoy them"; she did not do so to increase the gift to Carol. Thus, Carol is entitled to $8,000 and the paintings in the master bedroom.

College: The devise to college gives rise to a latent ambiguity. A latent ambiguity is one that is susceptible to more than one meaning when applied to the facts. Extrinsic evidence is admissible to cure the ambiguity, and if it cannot be cured the gift fails and falls into the residuary estate. Here, the $10,000 legacy to "my college" is a latent ambiguity because there are three colleges that could be the potential beneficiary of the gift: Central State College, Mega University, and Elysian College. Extrinsic evidence will be admitted to help resolve which college Martha meant. For example, her statements to the attorney who drafted the will are admissible to discern her intent. If it cannot be determined which college Martha was referring to in her will, the gift will fail and the $10,000 will fall into the residuary estate.

David: David receives $25,000 free of the request that he use it to provide for his son Dwayne. Although Martha made the legacy in the "hope and expectation" that he use the money to provide for Dwayne, the words are merely precatory and have no legal effect. David can do whatever he wants with the money.

Mary: Mary receives nothing under the will because she predeceased Martha; thus her gift lapsed, *i.e.*, failed. Under the UPC and in a large majority of states, the anti-lapse statute will not save the gift in favor of Mary's mother because Mary was not related to Martha and she failed to leave surviving descendants. Therefore, the residuary estate will pass under intestate succession to Martha's four children: Andy, Carol, David, and Bob, receiving one-fourth each. *Note:* Under majority law, the fact that Bob was disinherited under the will does not preclude him from taking a one-fourth interest under intestate succession.

Bob: Bob receives one-fourth of the residuary estate under intestate succession (*see* above) but is not entitled to anything under the will because he was expressly disinherited.

ANSWER TO QUESTION VIII

Validity of the contract: Whether Silvio can enforce his right to Blackacre under the contract with Lorenzo depends on state law. Under the UPC and in many states, the contract would be enforceable even though not referred to in the will, because it was evidenced by a writing signed by the parties. Since Silvio's agreement with his father amounted to a contract for the sale of land, the Statute of Frauds applies; however, it appears that the written contract satisfied the Statute of Frauds. In a minority of states, a contract relating to making a gift by will can be established only by provisions in the will stating that a contract does exist and setting forth the contract's material terms. In these states, Silvio could not enforce the contract because it is not mentioned in Lorenzo's will and would be limited in his recovery to quantum meruit for the reasonable value of his services (unless the testamentary gift in paragraph 2 satisfies Silvio's claim; *see* discussion below).

Assuming, however, that an enforceable contract did exist, Lorenzo breached the contract. The agreement was for Silvio to receive fee simple title to Blackacre, not for him to get a cash sum equal to Blackacre's 1995 value plus a life estate in the property. Anna may argue that the breach occurred in 1997 when Lorenzo executed the will, and thus the statute of limitations has run on Silvio's remedy for breach of the contract, but she would lose this argument. The breach did not occur until Lorenzo died without having made the agreed-upon gift in his will. The proper remedy in this situation is to admit the will to probate and then impose a constructive trust in favor of Silvio.

Silvio's and Anna's legacies: Silvio and Anna will receive the $25,000 legacies under the will. But is Silvio also entitled to the $150,000 legacy? Silvio will argue that the cash bequest was entirely separate from the agreement regarding Blackacre, and that he should get both. Anna will argue that the language of the devise ("recognizing my obligation to my son") shows that Lorenzo intended the $150,000 gift to be in lieu of an outright devise of Blackacre, thus putting Silvio to an election: He can take the $150,000 plus a life estate in Blackacre under the will, or he can take a fee interest in Blackacre under the contract; he cannot take both. Anna's argument should prevail. The language describing the $150,000 gift stated that it was related to Lorenzo's obligation for Silvio's helping in his business; this is the same consideration that supported the agreement for Lorenzo to devise Blackacre to Silvio. Furthermore, to give Silvio both $150,000 and Blackacre (now worth $750,000) would give him over 90% of the estate. Lorenzo clearly intended for Anna to have something of value (remainder interest in Blackacre plus the residuary estate). Therefore, the better solution is for Silvio to take Blackacre under a constructive trust and let the $150,000 fall into the residuary estate—subject to Priscilla's (and now her daughter Karla's) claims.

Karla's interest: Although Lorenzo and Priscilla were both fatally injured in the same automobile accident, Priscilla survived Lorenzo by a week. Therefore, neither the Uniform Simultaneous Death Act nor the UPC's 120-hour rule applies.

Karla will inherit a portion of Lorenzo's estate only if Priscilla is considered a pretermitted spouse. Only half of the states have pretermitted spouse statutes, and in a majority of these states the statute operates to partially revoke the testator's will to provide for an intestate share to the subsequent spouse. Here, Priscilla would have rights as a pretermitted spouse because she married Lorenzo after he executed his will. Additionally, she was not mentioned in the will, the omission was not intentional because it was made before their marriage, and there is no evidence that Lorenzo executed the will in contemplation of marriage. As a pretermitted spouse, Priscilla is entitled to an intestate share of the estate. Since Priscilla died intestate, her share of Lorenzo's estate passes to her daughter Karla. In calculating Priscilla's intestate share, Blackacre would not be included if Silvio is successful in establishing a constructive trust because property subject to a valid contract to devise is not part of the estate—the testator had no dispositive rights over it at the time of his death. Further, under the UPC, any property devised to the testator's children is not included in making up the spouse's intestate share.

ANSWER TO QUESTION IX

John has two possible grounds for challenging Margaret's will: (i) Amelia exercised undue influence upon Margaret, and (ii) Margaret lacked testamentary capacity at the time the will was executed. However, John is not likely to prevail on either ground.

Undue influence: Undue influence occurs when the free will of the testator is destroyed and the resulting will reflects the desires of the person exerting the influence. In most states, a presumption of undue influences arises when (i) a confidential relationship existed between the testator and the beneficiary, (ii) the beneficiary played an active part in procuring the will, and (iii) the disposition in favor of the beneficiary is unnatural (*e.g.*, favors an unrelated party over relatives). Although Margaret was in a confidential relationship with, and very dependent upon, Amelia, there is no indication that Amelia exercised undue influence over her mother. She recommended that Margaret make a will and she arranged for the lawyer, but it does not appear that Amelia influenced the terms of the will. Although Amelia was present during Margaret's interview with the attorney, the directions concerning the will's terms came from Margaret, not Amelia. The terms of the will were consistent with Margaret's past comments to friends that "she planned to take care of Amelia in her will." It was natural for Margaret to leave more to the child who lived with her and who took care of her. The mere existence of the opportunity to exert influence and the testator's susceptibility to influence due to illness and advanced age are not, by themselves, sufficient to establish that undue influence was exerted. John must show that Margaret's free will was destroyed, and the facts as presented do not warrant such a finding. In fact, they probably do not even warrant submission to a jury.

Testamentary capacity: To establish that Margaret did not have testamentary capacity, John must prove that she did not have the capacity to: (i) understand the nature of her act, (ii) know the natural objects of her bounty, (iii) know the nature and value of her property, and (iv) understand the disposition she was making. The fact that Margaret was in a hospital and had a broken hip does not indicate a lack of testamentary capacity. There is no indication that her mind was unclear from pain or drugs. She knew the nature and extent of her property, the natural objects of her bounty, and understood the disposition she was making. It is also clear that she understood the nature of the act that she was doing, *i.e.*, making a will. Also, Margaret lived several years past the execution of the will. Her mind was clear; she remembered the terms of the will; and she had further contact with Attorney concerning the codicil. Obviously, if the will had not reflected her testamentary intent, she would have changed it. Furthermore, it was not necessary for Margaret to have read the will before executing it. She had dictated the terms herself and Attorney had correctly assured her that these terms were all included in the will. She knew what she was signing and the execution was valid.

Thus, John's grounds for contesting the will are very weak. It is highly unlikely that he could meet his burden of proof for establishing undue influence or lack of testamentary capacity. But if John were to prevail and the will were set aside, the estate would be distributed as though Margaret died intestate. John and Amelia would each inherit one-half of the estate.

If John is unsuccessful in contesting the will, Margaret's estate will be distributed as follows:

Ann: Ann and her heirs receive nothing because Ann predeceased Margaret. The $25,000 legacy to Ann lapsed and falls into the residuary estate. Under the UPC and in a large majority of states, the anti-lapse statute will not save the gift in favor of Ann's heirs because Ann was not related to Margaret.

John: John will take one-fifth of the $200,000 estate, or $40,000, under the terms of the will. Under majority law, the destruction of a codicil revokes only the codicil and not the prior will. The will is read as though the codicil had never been executed. Here, Margaret properly revoked her codicil and her will is read as it was originally written. Thus, John takes under the terms of the original will.

Amelia: Amelia takes the residuary estate, or $160,000.

ANSWER TO QUESTION X

Validity of will: Tim's will was validly executed and is admissible to probate. Tim's will can be probated as a holographic will if such wills valid in the jurisdiction. To be valid, the material provisions of a holographic will must be in the handwriting of the testator and the will must be signed by him. Here, it is clear that the will is entirely in Tim's handwriting and he affixed his signature at the end. Thus, the will is a valid holographic will.

If the jurisdiction does not recognize holographic wills, the will can still be probated because it was validly executed (it does not matter that it was handwritten). The following requirements must be satisfied under the most stringent will execution statute: (i) the will must have been signed by the testator, (ii) the testator's signature must appear at the end of the will, (iii) the testator must have signed the will in the presence of at least two witnesses, (iv) the testator must have declared to the witnesses that the instrument is his will, and (v) the witnesses must have signed the will in the presence of the testator and each other. Here, Tim's will was signed by him at the end in the presence of two witnesses (the preacher and his wife), who also signed the will in Tim's presence and in the presence of each other. Additionally, Tim informed the witnesses that the instrument was his will. The fact that the witnesses signed before Tim does not affect the validity of the will because the signatures were part of one continuous transaction. Nor does it matter that the witnesses belong the First Baptist Church, the beneficiary of the second provision in the will, because in order for a witness to be "interested," he must receive a direct bequest in the will. Here, the preacher and his wife are indirectly benefited by the bequest to the church; thus, they are not interested witnesses (but even if they were, the validity of the will would not be destroyed). Therefore, Tim's will is validly executed.

$10,000 legacy: The $10,000 legacy passes to Glory Baptist Church if the jurisdiction recognizes holographic wills. There is no requirement that a holographic will be written at one time—it can be written in spurts. Interlineations and crossouts on a holographic will are given full effect as long as the evidentiary test is met: The will must be in the testator's handwriting and signed by him. As discussed above, the will, and the interlineation in favor of Glory Baptist Church, were entirely in Tim's handwriting. Tim signed the will and he initialed the change in favor of Glory Baptist Church. Therefore, Glory Baptist Church receives the $10,000 legacy in a jurisdiction that recognizes holographic wills.

However, the attempted gift to Glory Baptist Church is ineffective if the jurisdiction does not recognize holographic wills. Words added to a will after it has been executed are not given effect because they are unattested; *i.e.*, they were not executed with the requisite testamentary formalities. Only the words that are part of the will at the time it is executed have testamentary effect. Thus, Glory Baptist Church does not take the $10,000 legacy.

But does First Baptist Church take the $10,000 legacy in such a jurisdiction? First Baptist Church will take the $10,000 only if the jurisdiction does not recognize partial revocations by physical act. In the few states that do not recognize partial revocations by physical act, First Baptist Church will take the bequest notwithstanding the attempted revocation. In these states, Tim's striking the words "First Baptist Church" would be without legal effect and the original gift to First Baptist Church is effective. However, partial revocations by physical act are valid in a majority of states and First Baptist Church would take nothing—the $10,000 legacy would lapse and fall into the residuary estate. First Baptist Church could attempt to save the gift by invoking the doctrine of Dependent Relative Revocation ("DRR") to disregard the prior revocation. DRR operates to disregard a revocation if it was based on a mistake as to the validity of another disposition and only if disregarding the revocation comes closer to effectuating the testator's intent than would an intestate distribution. Here, Tim did act under a mistake as to the validity of another disposition; *i.e.*, he mistakenly thought that he could make a new gift to Glory Baptist Church by his interlineation. However, it is clear that Tim's intent to revoke the gift to First Baptist Church was independent of his intent to make a gift to Glory Baptist Church. To disregard the revocation would be contrary to Tim's intent, for Tim made it clear that he did not want First Baptist Church to take under his will. Thus, First Baptist Church will not receive the $10,000 under a jurisdiction that recognizes partial revocations by physical act.

Table of Cases

Palmer v. Riggs - §326

Palmer's Will, *In re* - §548

Parker's Estate, *In re* - §330

Parsons's Trust, *In re* - §736

Pascal's Estate, *In re* - §483

Pascucci v. Alsop - §502

Patch v. Squires - §242

Patch v. White - §905

Patecky v. Friend - §215

Patrick v. Patrick - §550

Pavlinko's Estate, *In re* - §889

Payne v. Payne - §538

Payne v. Todd - §909

Peck v. Drennan - §672

People v. - *see name of party*

Pepe v. Caputo - §848

Pepper v. Peacher - §518

Perkins's Estate, *In re* - §835

Perry v. Boyce - §94

Perry, *In re* Estate of - §563

Persha, *In re* Estate of - §829

Peters v. Peters - §358

Petty's Estate, *In re* - §451

Phelps v. La Moille Lodge - §§605, 606

Phinizee v. Alexander - §559

Pickering v. Pickering - §908

Plemmons v. Pemberton - §671

Politowicz's Estate, *In re* - §441

Poss v. Kuhlmann - §472

Potter v. Richardson - §388

Pounds v. Litaker - §465

Powers v. Wilkinson - §737

Powers's Estate, *In re* - §816

Price v. Huntsman - §355

Pritchett v. Henry - §165

Proctor v. Handke - §671

Proley's Estate, *In re* - §391

Puckett's Estate, *In re* - §601

Pulvermacher's Will, *In re* - §409

Putnam v. Neubrand - §586

Putnam's Will, *In re* - §866

Pye's Estate, *In re* - §430

Q

Quintana v. Ordono - §276

R

Ranney, *In re* Will of - §438

Rape v. Lyerly - §§646, 657

Rau v. Rau - §67

Reagan v. Bailey - §415

Reardon's Will, *In re* - §358

Reed v. Shipp - §862

Reed's Estate, *In re* - §463

Rees's Estate, *In re* - §804

Rehwinkel, *In re* Estate of - §707

Reid v. Voorhees - §917

Remmele v. Kinstler - §122

Reynolds's Estate, *In re* - §574

Rhoades v. Chambers - §859

Rice, *In re* - §586

Riley, *In re* Estate of - §861

Roberts v. Conley - §680

Roberts v. Fisher - §558

Roberts' Estate, *In re* - §634

Robinson v. Lee - §780

Roblin's Estate, *In re* - §§869, 871

Rogers v. Helmes - §430

Rogers v. Mutch - §765

Rogers v. Russell - §673

Rolfe, *In re* Estate of - §1019

Rosenbloom v. Kokofsky - §431

Rosenfeld v. Frank - §804

Rossi v. Rossi - §709

Rothermel v. Duncan - §§850, 851

Roysten v. Watts - §707

Rubenstein v. Mueller - §214

Rubinstein's Estate, *In re* - §788

Rudd v. Searles - §926

Russell, Estate of - §787

Russell, *In re* Estate of - §902

S

Salvation Army v. Pryor's Estate - §673

Sample's Estate, *In re* - §452

Santry v. France - §826

Sargavak's Estate, *In re* - §§349, 350, 351

Schafroth, *In re* Estate of - §975

Schedel, *In re* Estate of - §921

Scheridan v. Scheridan - §915

Schroeder v. Danielson - §728

Schultheis, *In re* Estate of - §352

Scott v. Gastright - §609

Scott's Will, *In re* - §324

Seaman's Will, *In re* - §§319, 320

Second Bank-State Street Trust Co. v. Pinion - §626

Security Trust Co., *In re* - §786

Selby v. Fidelity Trust Co. - §135

Seymour's Estate, *In re* - §925

Shamberger v. Dessel - §769

Shapira v. Union National Bank - §320

Sharp's Estate, *In re* - §353

Shaw, *In re* Estate of - §540

Sheaffer v. Sheaffer - §96

Sheehan's Will, *In re* - §386

Sheldone v. Marino - §816

Shepherd's Estate, *In re* - §673

Shevlin v. Jackson - §836

White v. White - **§792**
Whitlow v. Weaver - **§441**
Whittington v. Whittington - **§243**
Whyte's Will, *In re* - **§603**
Wiechert v. Wiechert - **§918**
Wiglesworth v. Smith - **§917**
Wilkes v. Wilkes - **§742**
Will of - *see* name of party
Williams v. Crickman - **§857**
Willis v. Barrow - **§§768, 788**
Wimberly v. Jones - **§839**
Windsor v. Leonard - **§243**
Winter's Will, *In re* - **§393**
Witt's Estate, *In re* - **§864**
Wojtalewicz's Estate v. Woitel - **§933**

Wolf v. Rich - **§682**
Wolfe v. Wolfe - **§348**
Wolfe's Estate, *In re* (1973) - **§792**
Wolfe's Estate, *In re* (1957) - **§264**
Woodson v. Woodson - **§587**
Wright v. Wolters - **§842**

Y

Young, *In re* Will of - **§773**

Z

Zschernig v. Miller - **§184**

Index

ATTORNEY LIABILITY FOR DEFECTIVE EXECUTION

omissions, §896

privity of contract, §§454-456

    majority view—no defense, §§454-455

       statute of limitations, §455

    minority view—defense, §456

subsequent marriage of testator, §510

C

CAPACITY TO MAKE A WILL

See also Will Contests

age, §363

aliens, §364

at time of execution, §358

capacity for other acts compared, §359

felons, §365

testamentary capacity, §§360-362

    four-point test, §360

    statutory modifications, §361

    will contests, §362

CHARITABLE GIFTS

common law mortmain rules, §315

modern law—no restrictions, §316

unconstitutional restrictions, §317

CLASS GIFTS

anti-lapse statute, §§752-754

class designations, §§724-749

    adult adoption, §§729-733

    children, §§724-728

       adopted, §§726-728, 741

       by all marriages, §725

       grandchildren excluded, §724

       nonmarital, §§735-739

    cousins, §749

    descendants or issue, §§740-743

       adopted and nonmarital, §741

    family terms, §§746-747

    friends, §747

    heirs, §745

    nieces and nephews, §749

    siblings, §748

class gift rule, §§750-754

closing the class, §§758-766

    outright gift to class, §§759-761

       child in gestation, §760

       no class members, §761

    per capita gifts, §§763-766

    postponed gifts, §762

    rule of convenience, §758

contrary will provision, §§723, 766

death of class member, §§751-757

    before will execution, §§755-757

    in testator's lifetime, §§751-754

in general, §723

CLASSIFICATION OF TESTAMENTARY GIFTS

demonstrative legacy, §769

general legacy, §770

rationale for, §767

residuary estate, §771

specific devise or bequest, §768

CODICILS

conditional, §§488-489

defined, §633

destruction, effect of, §§553-554

effect of, §§636-643

    republication of valid will, §§637-641

       incorporation by reference, §639

       interested witness, §638

       limitation, §641

       pretermitted child or spouse, §§294, 509, 640

    revival of revoked will, §643

    validation of prior invalid will, §642

formalities, §634

holographic, §634

oral, §§480, 531

purging statutes, effect on, §§432-436

revocation of will, §496. *See also* Revocation of Wills

separate document unnecessary, §635

COMMUNITY PROPERTY

See also Elective Share; Intestate Succession

disposal of entire interest attempt, §260

election wills, §§260-266

    accidental election wills, §§264-265

       joint tenancy, §265

    common law states, §266

    election against the will, §262

    election to take under will, §263

lifetime gifts to third party, §§267-274

    fraudulent transfer, §§269-272

    nontestamentary transfers, §273

property taken to common law state, §§275-277

    Uniform Disposition of Community Property Rights at Death Act, §277

CONDITIONAL WILLS

absolute will, §484

    factors, §§484-486

avoidance of intestacy, §485

condition vs. motive, §§483-486

conditional codicils, §§488-489

extrinsic evidence, §487

in general, §481

must appear on face of will, §482

preservation of will, §486

CONTRACT NOT TO MAKE A WILL

consideration, §680

in general, §680

remedies, §684

Statute of Frauds, §§681-683

inheritance from mother, **§83**

NUNCUPATIVE WILLS

See Oral Wills

O

ORAL WILLS

automatic revocation, **§479**

dollar limit, **§477**

formalities, **§478**

in general, **§474**

limited use, **§474**

oral codicil, **§480**

personal property only, **§476**

PQ

PER CAPITA DISTRIBUTION

See also Intestate Succession

at each generation, **§§38, 42, 46**

class gifts, **§§763-766**. *See also* Class Gifts

with representation, **§§37, 41, 45**

PER STIRPES DISTRIBUTION

See also Intestate Succession

class gifts, **§742**

classic per stirpes, **§§36, 40, 44**

PERSONAL REPRESENTATIVE

bond, **§§1014-1015**

compensation, **§§1016-1020**

 waiver, **§1020**

duties, **§§1024-1048**

 accounting, **§1031**

 care and preservation of assets, **§1032**

 carrying on decedent's business, **§§1035-1037**

 inventory, **§1030**

 investments, **§§1033-1034**

 leasing assets, **§§1042-1043**

 loyalty, **§§1046-1048**

 marshalling assets, **§§1026-1029**

  no commingling, **§1029**

 sale or mortgage of assets, **§§1038-1041**

 standard of care, **§1045**

liabilities of, **§§1049-1054**

 contracts, **§§1052-1054**

 torts, **§§1050-1051**

priority for appointment, **§§1012-1013**

qualifications, **§§1009-1011**

 conflict of interest, **§1010**

 nonresidents, **§1011**

removal of, **§1023**

resignation, **§1022**

terminology, **§§997-1008**

 administrator, **§998**

 administrator c.t.a., **§§1000-1002**

 executor, **§997**

 guardian ad litem, **§1008**

 guardian of the estate, **§§1005-1007**

  Uniform Transfers to Minors Act, **§1007**

 guardian of the person, **§§1003-1004**

PLAIN MEANING RULE

See Will Contests

POSTHUMOUS CHILDREN, §§89-91

POUR-OVER GIFT TO INTER VIVOS TRUST

defined, **§625**

purpose, **§625**

Uniform Testamentary Additions to Trust Act, **§§627-632**

 added requirements, **§631**

 effect of trust amendment, **§§626-627**

 existence of trust, **§§628-630**

 unfunded trust, **§632**

validity of, **§626**

PRETERMITTED CHILDREN

amount of share, **§§290-293**

 abatement, **§291**

 intestate share, **§290**

 pro rata abatement, **§292**

 revised UPC, **§293**

forced heirship in Louisiana, **§278**

intentional omission, **§§285-287**

lifetime settlement for child, **§288**

republication by codicil—effect, **§294**

UPC, **§289**

who is protected, **§§279-283**

 children alive when will executed, **§282**

 children born after will executed, **§279**

 grandchildren, **§283**

 mistaken belief that child is dead, **§280**

PROBATE ESTATE, §12

See also Estate Administration

PROBATE, PROOF OF WILLS IN

See also Estate Administration

ante-mortem probate, **§996**

burden of proof, **§§985-986**

common law, **§§977-979**

 common form, **§978**

 solemn form, **§979**

duty to produce will, **§971**

foreign language will, **§994**

formal testacy proceeding, **§§983-984**

informal probate, **§§981-982**

lost will, **§§567-576, 995**

 cause of nonproduction, **§§569-571**

  fraudulent destruction, **§571**

  presumption, **§570**

 contents of will, **§§572-574**

  standard of proof, **§573**

 inadvertent loss or destruction, **§567**

 proof of due execution, **§568**

revocation of prior will proved, **§576**
time limitation, **§§973-975**
valid execution issue, **§§987-993**
   attestation clause, **§§989-991**
   attesting witness's testimony, **§§987-988**
      absent or unavailable witness, **§988**
   question of fact, **§993**
   self-proved will, **§992**
who may offer will, **§972**

PURGING STATUTES
See Witnesses

R

RECIPROCAL WILLS
See Joint Wills

RESIDUARY ESTATE
See also Classification of Testamentary Gifts
death taxes from, **§§1081-1084**
defined, **§771**
lapse in, **§§717-719**

RESTRICTIONS ON POWER OF TESTATION
See also Elective Share; Family, Protection of; Pretermit-
        ted Children
exempt personal property, **§§305-308**
family allowance, **§§309-314**
homestead allowance, **§§295-304**
pretermitted children, **§§278-294**
public policy, **§§318-324**
   crime or tort, encouragement of, **§323**
   destruction of property, **§324**
   divorce, encouragement of, **§321**
   partial restraint on marriage, **§320**
   termination on remarriage valid, **§319**
   total restraint on marriage, **§319**

REVISED UNIFORM PROBATE CODE (UPC), §§1-6
See also individual topics

REVIVAL OF REVOKED WILLS
common law, **§578**
in general, **§577**
majority rule, **§§579-582**
   reexecution, **§§579, 581**
   republication by codicil, **§§579, 582**
UPC, **§583**

REVOCATION OF WILLS
See also Revival of Revoked Wills
all wills revocable, **§493**
dependent relative revocation, **§§584-597**. *See also*
        Dependent Relative Revocation
methods, **§§494-566**
   operation of law, **§§495, 499-524**
      birth or adoption of children, **§524**
      divorce, **§§511-523**
         legal separation, **§523**

nonprobate transfers, effect on, **§§518-522**
only testator's divorce relevant, **§517**
remarriage, **§516**
spouse's provisions revoked, **§513**
spouse's kin unaffected, **§514**
   revised UPC distinguished, **§515**
intent presumed, **§498**
marriage, **§§499-510**
   attorney's negligent drafting, **§510**
   common law, **§499**
   pretermitted spouse statutes, **§§503-509**
      entire will revoked, **§508**
      partial revocation—intestate share, **§504**
      republication by codicil—effect, **§509**
      revised UPC, **§§506-507**
        nonprobate transfers to spouse, **§507**
   states without statute—no effect on will,
      §§501-502
      minority—birth after marriage revokes, **§502**
   Wills Act of 1837, **§499**
physical act, **§§497, 536-566**
   act of another, **§547**
   act on copy of will, **§§543-545**
      constructive trust, **§544**
   act on testator's signature, **§542**
   effect of revocation on another instrument, **§§553-**
      559
      codicil destroyed, **§§553-554**
      duplicate wills, **§§556-559**
        destruction of duplicate, **§558**
        testator's duplicate missing, **§559**
      will destroyed—effect on codicil, **§555**
   partial revocation, **§§548-552**
      extrinsic evidence to show intent, **§549**
      increased gift limitation, **§550**
      minority rule—no partial revocation, **§552**
   present intent to revoke, **§§536, 546**
   presumptions, **§§560-566**
      continuity, **§561**
      missing or mutilated will, **§§562-565**
        adverse party's access to, **§565**
        extrinsic evidence, **§564**
        presumed revoked, **§563**
        will in third party's possession, **§566**
      when no presumption arises, **§566**
   types of, **§§538-542**
      burning, **§538**
      obliterating or canceling, **§540**
      tearing, **§539**
subsequent testamentary instrument, **§§496, 525-**
      535
   express revocation, **§§526-531**
      explicit language, **§528**
      holographic instrument as, **§530**
      oral will as, **§531**
      present intent to revoke, **§529**

NOTES

NOTES

NOTES

NOTES

NOTES

NOTES